# Origin and Evolution of Tropical Rain Forests

Frontispiece   Tropical lowland evergreen rain forest, Brunei (Courtesy of A. McRobb, Media Resources, Royal Botanic Gardens, Kew.)

# Origin and Evolution of Tropical Rain Forests

Robert J. Morley

**JOHN WILEY & SONS, LTD**
Chichester • New York • Weinheim • Brisbane • Singapore • Toronto

*Other Wiley Editorial Offices*

John Wiley & Sons, Inc., 605 Third Avenue,
New York, NY 10158-0012, USA

WILEY-VCH Verlag GmbH, Pappelallee 3,
D-69469 Weinheim, Germany

Jacaranda Wiley Ltd, 33 Park Road, Milton,
Queensland 4064, Australia

John Wiley & Sons (Asia) Pte Ltd, 2 Clementi Loop #02-01,
Jin Xing Distripark, Singapore 129809

John Wiley & Sons (Canada) Ltd, 22 Worcester Road,
Rexdale, Ontario M9W 1L1, Canada

*Library of Congress Cataloging-in-Publication Data*

Morley, Robert J.
    Origin and evolution of tropical rain forests / Robert J. Morley.
        p.   cm.
    Includes bibliographical references (p.    ) and index.
    ISBN 0-471-98326-8
    1. Rain forests History.   2. Forests and forestry—Tropics
History.   I. Title.
SD247.M67   1999
577.34—dc21
                                                        99–299654
                                                        CIP

*British Library Cataloguing in Publication Data*

A catalogue record for this book is available from the British Library

ISBN 978-0-471-98626-2

Typeset in 10/12pt Times by Mayhew Typesetting, Rhayader, Powys

This book is printed on acid-free paper responsibly manufactured from sustainable forestry,
in which at least two trees are planted for each one used for paper production.

**To Santi**
without whose encouragement
this book would not have been written

# Contents

# Preface

There is no need for a time machine in order to travel back through time – all you need is a good microscope, some patience, a little imagination, and some carefully chosen rock samples to explore exotic palm-lined rivers of South America before the Amazon ever existed, or to drift through the mangrove swamps which lined the coasts of Europe before the ice caps developed over the northern continents.

The diversity of animal and plant life within tropical rain forests, where every second tree may be a different species, is awe-inspiring compared to the temperate forests of Europe, where every second tree is likely to be an oak or pine. Because of the immense diversity of these forests, and their constituent fauna, their intrinsic value is much greater than the forests of temperate lands. They contain an immensely greater gene pool, necessary to safeguard a long future for plant and animal life on this planet.

This book attempts to determine the antiquity of these forests, and emphasise that their immense diversity is due not to a long, unchanging history, with stable climatic conditions over millions of years, but to the ability of opportunistic plants to survive through periods of climate change and geological upheaval, to expand their distributions when changing climates permit, to retreat to favourable refuges when climates were unfavourable and to disperse to other land areas when land bridges became temporarily available within their range of climatic tolerance, taking advantage of animal vectors to maximise their likelihood of range extension and survival.

Tropical rain forests are wholly dominated by flowering plants. They also contain a high concentration of more primitive angiosperms, especially in the Far East, and biogeographical distributions of these have long been used to suggest that angiosperms evolved in rain forests in that area. Recent palaeobotanical studies, however, suggest that an origin in Western Gondwanaland (Africa and South America) is more probable, but fail to provide reasons to explain the present-day distributions of the most primitive angiosperm groups. Clearly, a knowledge of vegetational history within the tropical Far East is necessary in order to resolve the issue. Two serious obstacles have up until now prevented such reconstructions: firstly, previous palaeobotanical data from that area were inadequate and had very poor age control, and, secondly, a sufficiently clear understanding of the tectonic history of this geologically complex area has only become available in the last 10 years. I have spent many years using palynology as a stratigraphic tool for the petroleum industry, largely across the Far East, and from this, coupled with fieldwork undertaken during a training programme in Jakarta, sufficient palynological data became available to begin to reconstruct a more confident vegetational history for the SE Asian region, covering the whole of the Tertiary period. Since much of the story is based on data proprietory to the petroleum companies, and would be difficult to present in international journals, it seemed appropriate to publish an overview of the resulting story in book form, at the same time placing the story for the Far East in a global perspective.

The book follows a number of themes; the development of moist megathermal forests is traced on each of the Earth's tectonic plates.

More emphasis is placed on structure and physiognomy of such forests, especially during their initial phases of development, and also on the occurrence through time of taxa which have present-day representatives. An attempt is made to explain disjunct distribution patterns within rain forest taxa by considering the setting of each plate through time, and identifying times at which plates may have been in contact, or closely juxtaposed, and interplate plant dispersals may have occurred. Evidence for such dispersals is then brought to attention mainly by reference to the palynological record. Emphasis is also placed on the distribution of rain forests in relation to changing global climates, and, in particular, to their survival during the coolest periods of the Quaternary ice age. Finally, the present-day destruction of rain forests by humans is placed in a geological perspective, and suggestions are made as to their future, at least on a human time scale.

The preparation of this book has required a multidisciplinary approach, using state of the art knowledge of rain forest ecology and biogeography, Tertiary and Cretaceous palynology and palaeobotany, as well as high resolution stratigraphy and plate tectonics, and has been achieved only with the help of many friends and colleagues over the years, who I hope are acknowledged below. To help the non-specialist reader, jargon is kept to a minimum (although inevitably creeps in). Reference to palaeobotanical and palynological names is avoided as far as possible, except where nearest living relatives are unknown, and the first mention of each generic name in each chapter is followed by a reference to the family, with the more familiar traditional names, such as Gramineae and Palmae, being used in preference to Poaceae and Arecaceae etc. A list of the palaeobotanical and palynological names for the taxa mentioned is given in an appendix, arranged according to the classification of Takhtajan (1969), and the first mention of each geological epoch in each chapter is followed by its age in millions of years (Ma) by using the scheme presented in Figure 3.6.

I am certain that the 'story' presented here has many deficiencies and errors, but I am convinced that it is appropriate to present it now, as our rain forests are being exterminated across the globe. I hope that it will bring to attention the loss, on a geological scale, to both the human race and the planet, if these forests are destroyed to such an extent that a significant loss of biodiversity occurs.

Many people and organisations, both knowingly and unknowingly, have helped bring this book to fruition. These include, in particular, the many petroleum exploration companies with whom I have worked as a consultant over the years, especially Atlantic Richfield (ARCO), LASMO and UNOCAL in the Far East, and BP/STATOIL and Chevron Nigeria Ltd and Shell Petroleum Development Company in Nigeria. The development of the SE Asian story has particularly benefited from a long association with LEMIGAS in Jakarta, especially since my inclusion within the Indonesian RUT research cooperation programme (Riset Unggulan Terpadu). I am also grateful to Robert Hall, Director of the University of London SE Asia Geology Group, for allocating funds to help with the preparation of the figures, for continued support, and also for encouraging me to learn to use computer graphics programs. I also thank Alan Smith (University of Cambridge) for providing me with the 'ATLAS' computer programme with which each of the palaeocontinental connections discussed in the book were initially tested.

Among the many individuals who have helped in providing literature and unpublished data, or whose association has led to new ideas, who I would like to thank are: Chris Atkinson (ARCO British, UK); Chris Bates (Robertson, Jakarta, Indonesia); Diane Cameron (London University SE Asia Research Group, Royal Holloway, University of London, UK); Ian Carter (LASMO, Jakarta, Indonesia); Margaret Collinson (Royal Holloway, University of London, UK); Lydie Dupont (University of Bremen, Germany); John Flenley (Massey University, Palmerston North, New Zealand);

Phil Gibbard (University of Cambridge, UK); Richard Haack (Chevron, Nigeria); Neville Haile (Oxford-Brookes University, UK); Joesril Hainim (PT Eksindo Pratama, Jakarta, Indonesia); Madeline Harley (Royal Botanic Gardens, Kew, UK); Nur Hassim (LEMIGAS, Jakarta, UK); Henry Hoogheimstra (Hugo de Vries Laboratorium, Amsterdam, Netherlands); Jaizan Hardi Jais (Petronas, Malaysia); Peter Kershaw (Monash University, Australia); Eko Budi Lelono (Royal Holloway, University of London, UK); Mike McPhail (Australian National University, Canberra, Australia); Andrew McRobb (Royal Botanic Gardens, Kew, UK); Mudjito (Director, LEMIGAS, Jakarta, Indonesia); Dick Murphy (Walton on Thames, UK); Lucila Nugrahaningsih (LEMIGAS, Jakarta, Indonesia); Freedom Ogbe (Geo-Group, Benin City, Nigeria); Netty Polhaupessy (GRDC, Bandung, Indonesia); Imogen Poole (University of Swansea); Wartono Rahardjo (Gaja Mada University, Jogjakarta, Indonesia); Rashel Rosen (Excalibur Interpretation Company, Houston, USA), Mike Simmonds (University of Aberdeen, UK); Steve Sinclair (ARCO, Rio de Janiero, Brazil); Charles Turner (Open University, Milton Keynes, UK); O.K. Ulu (Chevron, Nigeria); Paul Ventris (BP/Statoil Alliance, Stavanger, Norway); Manas Watanasak (Mahidol University, Bangkok, Thailand); Eileen Williams (UNOCAL, Houston, USA); Geoff Wilkinson (Premier Oil); Moyra Wilson (London University SE Asia Research Group, Royal Holloway, UK); and Pierre Zippi (ARCO Plano, USA).

The late Jan Muller (Rijksherbarium, Leiden, Netherlands) and G. Thanikaimoni (Institute de Pondicherry, India), also deserve mention, since they helped formulate some of my early ideas as to what Tertiary palynology is all about.

I am particularly grateful to Tim Whitmore of the Department of Geography, University of Cambridge, Tony Barber, Emeritus Reader in Geology, Royal Holloway University, and Peter Ashton of the Arnold Arboretum, Harvard University, who have unselfishly read the entire text, and whose innumerable suggestions have allowed great improvements, clarifications and corrections compared to the initial draft. Tim Whitmore's comments on some very early chapter sketches were particularly helpful in establishing the layout and direction of this book.

Finally, I want to thank my wife Santi, who initially encouraged me to write this book, and who has given continuous support for more than three years during the course of preparing the text. She also prepared the drawings of pollen grains and spores for Chapters 5–10.

Robert J. Morley, April 1999
*PALYNOVA*, Littleport, Cambs
email: pollenpower@dial.pipex.com

Honorary fellow, Geology Department, Royal Holloway, University of London

# CHAPTER 1

# Introduction

Tropical rain forests (Frontispiece; Figure 1.1) display a biodiversity unparalleled by that of any other vegetation type; their extreme botanical variety has attracted the attention of eminent naturalists for over three centuries. Their floristic diversity perplexes anyone who has spent the time to examine them. Most studies of rain forest biogeography or evolution, whether on a local, regional or global scale, relate essentially to the spatial distribution of taxa, or may involve temporal factors on a relatively short time scale. It was emphasised over 50 years ago by Wulff (1943) that biogeographical conclusions can only find confirmation when it is possible to base them on a foundation of historical geology. The records of wood, leaves, fruit and flowers provide mere fleeting glimpses of past floras, and are often considered wholly inadequate at providing a firm foundation with respect to evolutionary studies of flowering plants. Palynology, however, is rapidly providing a database with which it is possible to test many biogeographical ideas, and a fragmentary picture of rain forest history is now emerging for the last 40 000 years from which some generalisations can be made. Data for the Late Quaternary were reviewed by Flenley (1979a), who concluded that many previous views emphasising the *unchanging* and *stable* nature of rain forest were misconceptions. He demonstrated that the distribution of equatorial rain forest formations, and their species make-up, has changed with changing global climates during the last 30 000 years. It is now clear, however, that many of the characteristic features of tropical rain forests relate to much longer time scales. The high species-richness of

rain forest floras clearly reflects evolution over periods of time much longer than that covered by the studies of Quaternary palynologists. This book attempts to address such questions on a longer geological time scale, by reviewing palaeobotanical data within a plate tectonic and palaeoclimatic framework over the last 100 million years, roughly coinciding with the time of the radiation and diversification of the angiosperms.

Despite Flenley's demonstration of the dynamic character of tropical rain forests, a commonly quoted reason as to why some tropical rain forests are extremely rich in species is a long and stable climatic history, without episodes of extinction, in an equable climate. Does the fossil record on a geological time scale support this proposition? What is meant by 'long and stable history'? Is there evidence for major extinctions within rain forest floras from the fossil record? Comparison of the number of taxa within the British and Malay Peninsula floras provide food for thought on this issue as the age of the British flora is known. The flora of the Malay Peninsula has been estimated to contain 7900 species in about 1400 genera (Whitmore, 1973), compared to about 1750 species and 620 genera in Great Britain, an area double the size of the Malay Peninsula. The British flora has established itself by dispersal from unglaciated refuges and from Europe in only 14 000 years, since the melting of the ice cap at the end of the last glaciation, and would be much richer were it not for the English Channel. Certainly, the Malay Peninsula flora is older than 14 000 years, since the area was not glaciated, but how much older – 10 times older, 100

Figure 1.1    Inside tropical lowland evergreen rain forest, Brunei. Note absence of branching, lack of ground cover, liane to left of picture, and fan palm *Licuala* sp. to right. (Courtesy of A. McRobb, Media Resources, Royal Botanic Gardens, Kew.)

times or 1000 times, i.e. 140 000 years, 1 400 000 years or 14 000 000 years? Popular literature from the Malay Peninsula leads us to believe that the lofty Malaysian rain forests are 100 million years old, or more than 7000 times older than the British flora. Such a time scale seems hardly consistent with the suggestion that tropical rain forests are regions of active plant speciation, as many authorities currently suggest! Could the persistent rain forest climate have allowed the continuing evolution of species without extinction episodes induced by climatic change? Hopefully the fossil record will help us to place the evolution of such floras into a realistic time scale.

Other fundamental problems of tropical rain forest biogeography and ecology may now be addressed by reference to the fossil record. Prior to plate tectonics becoming universally accepted by earth scientists, plant geographers proposed land bridges and submerged continents to explain disjunctions between rain forest floras, especially to account for the presence in each of the three tropical land areas of megathermal families, which cannot exist outside the frost-free tropics. Can these disjunct groups be explained if tropical land masses were previously closer together, or are there other explanations for these distributions, bearing in mind that, in the 1960s, such biogeographical patterns were considered as providing strong evidence against the theory of continental drift (van Steenis, 1962a).

Two additional problems concern the Neogene history of African and Malesian (the region encompassing the Malay Peninsula and the islands of Indonesia, Philippines and the E Pacific) rain forests. Firstly, the African rain forest flora exhibits very low species-richness, compared to those in South America and SE Asia. What is the historical reason for this? Secondly, can the fossil record help to explain the origin of the rain forest flora in E Malesia; this flora is dominantly of Asian origin (Good, 1962; van Balgooy, 1987), although the geological substrate is Gondwanan, or explain why Wallace's Line, so clearly reflected by mammals,

birds and other groups of animals, is more subtly reflected by plant distributions?

Finally, the history of rain forests is inexorably linked with the history of angiosperms, which form their dominant plant group. The supposition is that since angiosperms are so successful in rain forests, they must have evolved there. Many of the supposedly most primitive angiosperm taxa occur in today's tropical rain forests, especially those within SE Asia, some Pacific islands and NE Australia, and this has led many eminent botanists to propose that angiosperms evolved in a rain forest environment, 'somewhere between Assam and Fiji' (Takhtajan, 1969). Is there any geological evidence to suggest that the rain forests formed the 'cradle of the angiosperms', or does evidence point to a different origin?

Can the fossil record help to answer any of these questions? In the past, numerous protagonists of botanical evolutionary theory have virtually dismissed the fossil record as providing such limited information as to be useless, but recent discoveries, and improved methodologies, are clearly changing this attitude (Crane et al., 1995). Also, how does the current phase of rain forest destruction rank when viewed on a long geological time scale? Answers to some of these questions can be found if the fossil record is placed into a firm temporal framework. Several recent developments in geology and palaeobotany now permit interpretations of rain forest history on a geological time scale in a manner which would not have been possible only a few years ago. These developments may be summarised as follows.

Firstly, the understanding of past continental positions in the low latitudes is now well understood as a result of developments in plate tectonics. The former positions through time of Africa and Europe with respect to the Americas are now well established (Smith et al., 1973; Smith and Briden, 1979), but from the point of view of rain forest history, it is the timing of former *land connections* between the different plates which is important, and many of these are now becoming clarified. The breakup of

Gondwanaland, and the timing of the separation of Madagascar and India, and India's subsequent collision with Asia, are also now reasonably well delineated, but the complex intermingling of the Asian, Pacific and Australian plates in the Indo-Pacific area is only now becoming unravelled; in the mid-1980s quite contradictory reconstructions were proposed within this area, which includes the zone of intermingling of the Eurasian and Gondwanan flora and fauna, and is also considered by many to be the cradle of the angiosperms (Takhtajan, 1969; Thorne, 1976). One of these reconstructions (Audley Charles, 1987) was based heavily on the assumption that Eurasian and Gondwanan floras were in contact in the eastern Tethys area during the time of initial radiation of the angiosperms! Now there is a reasonably firm framework for plate assembly within this critical area, interpretations of vegetation histories which make sense with respect to both the fossil record and with biogeographic distributions need no longer be excessively speculative.

Secondly, rain forests also require a dryland environment in which to grow, with the exception of a very few which can grow with their roots in salt water. This may seem an obvious statement, but numerous reconstructions occur in the literature which propose former vegetation in areas which were previously submerged beneath the sea. Reconstructing former palaeogeographies is a very complex and time-consuming task, but the publication of global palaeocoastlines at approximately 5 Ma intervals by Smith et al. (1994) for the Mesozoic and Tertiary provides the basis for the explanation of many biogeographical distributions and a firm foundation for global reconstructions. The coastline reconstructions by Smith et al. (1994) were based on the study of over 2000 publications, and required many man-years of work, taking over 10 years to complete. For much of the SE Asian region, however, where the last time of emergence is important in the consideration of island floras, reference here is made to local literature and to the more recent reconstructions of Hall (1998a).

The distribution of tropical rain forest, as the name suggests, is essentially controlled by climate, and, from a geological viewpoint, 'tropical' climates are those which *today,* are characteristic of tropical latitudes. There are many examples in the fossil record which indicate that vegetation of a 'tropical' aspect, from both a floristic and physiognomic point of view, previously grew well outside the tropics, even taking into account former plate positions. Tropical rain forests are generally defined to be limited by a mean monthly temperature minimum of 18° C and a short dry period with less than 100 mm of rainfall per month. However, today, the tropics more or less coincide with the distribution of frost-free lowland climates (Figure 1.2). This raises the question as to what *are* the main climatic controls on tropical rain forest. Clearly, a frost-free environment and an abundance of rainfall are of primary importance, but the 'tropics' are strictly defined on their insolation regime. To what extent did different insolation patterns at temperate latitudes also have a significant control? It is considered here that the insolation regime is secondary to the absence of frosts and to the lack of a dry season, and that, from a geological context, the term 'megathermal moist forest' might be more appropriate!

The third development relates to our understanding of past climates. There are many geological criteria which permit the reconstruction of former rain forest climates even in the absence of any palaeobotanical records. Utilising the former distributions of climatically sensitive lithologies, to some degree augmented by palaeobotanical and geochemical evidence, and following the principles of climatic modelling as propounded by Parrish et al. (1982), global maps illustrating reconstructions of former tropical palaeoclimates for six 'time slices' during the last 90 Ma have been constructed as a concluding theme for this volume (Chapter 13). These maps provide a 'window through time' showing areas within which tropical-rain-forest-like vegetation could have prospered, and help to form a more factual

5

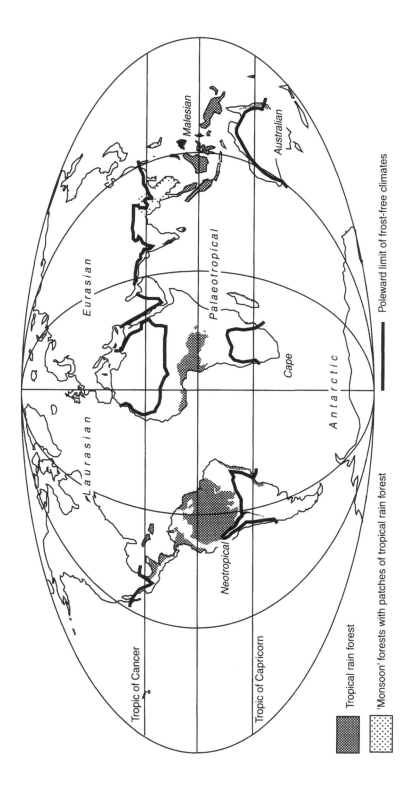

Figure 1.2   Global distribution of tropical rain forests (after Richards, 1996), in relation to frost-free climates (Pettersen, 1958). Floristic regions mentioned in the text are shown in italics. This and all subsequent world maps use Mollweides equal area projection.

basis for beginning to explain many of the distributional curiosities among tropical plants which are frequently brought to our attention by biogeographers.

Palynological studies of the Late Quaternary clearly demonstrate that tropical climates have changed as frequently as in temperate latitudes, with 'interglacial' periods with high sea levels being wetter and warmer, and 'glacial' periods with low sea levels being cooler and drier (Flenley, 1979a). Studies from low latitudes which extend into the older Quaternary suggest that this pattern was repeated with successive glacial/interglacial cycles, but the rarity of suitable 'Quaternary style' deposits in the Tertiary precludes following this approach further back in time, except in very rare instances (e.g. Hoogheimstra, 1984; Hoogheimstra and Ran, 1994).

The fourth development, taking place over the last 20 years, has been the emergence of sequence stratigraphy, which has brought a revolution to the manner in which geologists view the process of sedimentation, especially in marine environments. Sequence stratigraphy emphasises the importance of sea level fluctuations as a major factor controlling sediment accumulation. Sequence stratigraphic theory argues that sediments largely accumulate in 'packages' of genetically associated sediments, depending on whether sea levels are falling, at stillstand or rising relative to a particular depositional setting and that within the younger Tertiary, glacio-eustatic factors controlling global sea levels would have been paramount in determining many of the sea level fluctuations proposed. There remains hot debate, however, about the 'global' nature of sea level fluctuations during earlier 'greenhouse' phases (time periods without polar ice accumulations) as opposed to 'icehouse' phases (periods with polar ice caps). The comparison of the microfossil content of sediment packages of Tertiary age which accumulated during periods of lowered sea level (lowstand packages) with those from sediments deposited during high sea levels (highstand packages) allows judgements

to be reached with respect to the character of vegetation during 'glacial' and 'interglacial' intervals at many different times through the younger Tertiary, and provides a wholly new perspective to the reconstruction of Tertiary vegetation. In my opinion, the examination of microfossil assemblages in a sequence stratigraphic context has permitted an understanding of the complex changes seen in Tertiary low latitude microfossil assemblages in a manner which can bring order, where previously there seemed to be chaos. Without the confidence of interpretation brought about through the unifying concept of sequence stratigraphy, this book would not have been attempted. Sequence stratigraphy also permits establishment of the timing of marked global sea level lowstands. It was during these periods that most intercontinental plant dispersals took place.

The last two developments are concerned more with the interpretation of palaeobotanical, as opposed to geological data. The fifth development concerns the manner in which criteria which reflect the former existence of rain forests might be gleaned from the macro-, and megafossil record. In addition to the predominance of entire leaves and drip tips (Flenley, 1979a), it is now understood that many additional features of leaf form have an adaptive significance in a rain forest environment, such as leaf texture and thickness, leaf size and leaf arrangement. Diaspore (disseminule) size, some features of wood anatomy, abundance of epiphytes, floristic diversity and botanical affinity are some of the additional criteria which have left a mark in the fossil record, and can be used to piece together the distribution of former rain forests. The value of each of these criteria in evaluating rain forest climates is reviewed by Upchurch and Wolfe (1987).

Finally, the sixth development concerns the Tertiary and Cretaceous palynological record, on which many of the interpretations of rain forest history presented in this book are based. Although there are many reconstructions of past vegetation based on palynological data from Europe, North America and Australia, very little attention has been paid to the interpretation of past vegetation from tropical areas using the same source. The mine of detailed palynological information within the archives of petroleum companies is often brought to attention, but, with a few exceptions, biogeographers and ecologists would probably be disappointed with such data, which are usually generated only to solve stratigraphic problems, and would need very careful examination in order to give up hidden secrets with respect to the history of rain forests. The availability of such archives encouraged me to venture into the petroleum industry in the mid-1970s, but I was disappointed with what I discovered. Many of the unpublished reports on tropical regions did little more than demonstrate that sediments actually did contain palynomorphs. Subsequently I applied some of the basic techniques of Quaternary palynologists to the study of Tertiary and, later, Mesozoic sediments (often against strong opposition)[1] in order to develop such a database.

Today, such methods have become widely applied in the typically conservative petroleum industry, with the result that glimpses of the former distributions of tropical rain forests are emerging as a result of studies in W, C and N Africa, and through much of the Far East. I have had only limited opportunities to study the palynological record from South America. It must be remembered, however, that the purpose of palynological studies within the petroleum industry is to determine stratigraphy and sedimentation histories, and that if information on vegetation history is forthcoming at the same time, this must be regarded as fortuitous. This must be borne in mind when data quality is less than would be desired to clearly answer particular questions regarding tropical rain forest history.

## NOTE

1　'Quaternary' methods in Tertiary biostratigraphy were initially introduced by Shell palynologists (Kuyl et al, 1955), who clearly laid out the appropriate methodology, and were able to demonstrate the first cross-facies correlation using palynology. This methodology was subsequently abandoned by most stratigraphic palynologists in favour of placing emphasis solely on the presence of age-restricted palynomorphs for correlation studies.

# CHAPTER 2

# Present-day Tropical Rain Forests

Tropical rain forests can be found today in each of the three land areas which occur within the tropical zone (Richards, 1952, 1996; Longman and Jenik, 1974; Flenley, 1979a; Whitmore, 1998) and, prior to the destructive effects of humans during the past century, as a result of which much of the rain forest has now been destroyed, occupied about one-third of the tropical land surface (Ewel, 1980; Mabberley, 1992). Neotropical rain forests, those of the Americas, are the most extensive, where about half the global total are found, followed by SE Asia, with about a third, and Africa with a fifth. They are found chiefly over much, but not all of the areas astride the equator between 5°N and S. These areas are affected either throughout, or during most of the year, by convection-enhanced weather disturbances of the intertropical low pressure area sandwiched between the northern and southern subtropical high pressure belts (Walsh, in Richards, 1996). Rain forests also occur along eastern coastlines which lie within the path of moist trade winds, where orographic uplift creates winter moisture, mainly by means of dew formation (P.S. Ashton, personal communication) in addition to summer convectional rain, and results in everwet climates well north and south of the equator.

In the Americas, rain forests are centred in three main areas (Figure 1.2; Map Chapter 6). They are most extensive in the Amazon and Orinoco catchments, mainly within 5° of the equator. A second centre stretches west of the Andes from Equador, western Colombia, through Panama, into eastern Central America, reaching into Mexico. The third centre occurs in a narrow strip from about 5°S along the Brazilian coast, extending just beyond the tropics.

African rain forests are divided into two main blocks (Figure 1.2; Map Chapter 7), the largest being centred on the Congo catchment, and continuing along the coast of the Gulf of Guinea to Sierra Leone, but with a gap in the vicinity of Togo (the Dahomey Gap) and with outliers in E Africa. The second block stretches along the east coast of Madagascar.

In SE Asia (Figure 1.2; Map Chapter 9), rain forests are widely distributed from Myanmar to the Pacific islands, with centres of species diversity in Sundaland (Malay Peninsula, Sumatra, Borneo and Java), and in the region of New Guinea (van Steenis, 1957). Within continental Asia, they extend patchily through Thailand into Indochina and S China and NE India, where rain forests occur further from the equator than anywhere else (Whitmore, 1998). The S Chinese rain forests close to the latitudinal ecotone have been used as an analogue for the tropical aspect rain forests which were widespread at mid-latitudes during the earlier Tertiary by Wolfe (1977, 1978). He termed these forests, which will be discussed later in this chapter, 'paratropical' rain forests (closed, multistoreyed, tropical aspect rain forests currently occurring outside the tropics). Rain forest outliers also occur in the Western Ghats of India (Map Chapter 8), in Sri Lanka, the Andamans, many Pacific islands and Queensland in Australia (Map, Chapter 10).

Tropical rain forests are evergreen to partly evergreen, and occur in areas typically receiving more than 2000 mm of rain annually, with not

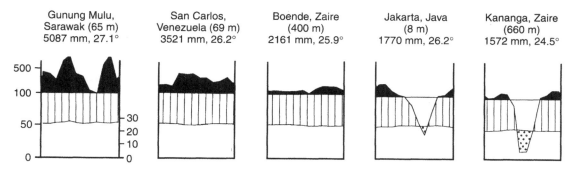

Figure 2.1   Climate diagrams for typical tropical rain forest localities, grading from superwet (Gunung Mulu, Sarawak, San Carlos, Venezuela); tropical wet (Boende, Zaire); tropical wet, seasonal (Jakarta, Java) and tropical wet–dry (Kananga, Zaire). Monthly rainfall (mm) to left, with annual total at top; monthly temperature (°C) to right, with annual average at top. Dry periods dotted, rainy periods with vertical lines (or where rainfall exceeds 100 mm per month, shown in black at 1/10 scale) (after Walsh, 1996, in Richards, 1996).

more than four consecutive months with less than 100 mm of precipitation in two years out of three, with the coldest mean monthly temperatures not falling below 18°C, with small annual temperature variations (Figure 2.1) and essentially frost-free. Wolfe (1979) found the 18°C coldest month isotherm unrealistic for defining the limits of tropical rain forests in E Asia, and proposed that the 25°C mean annual isotherm was more meaningful, a definition which has since been widely used by palaeobotanists for reconstructing Tertiary vegetation, although Walsh (in Richards, 1996) points out that a mean annual isotherm of 24°C, which was proposed by Holdridge (1947), would exclude some lowland tropical rain forests in the trade wind zones. Rain forests can be characterised on the basis of physiognomy and structure into different formations, determined by different habitats and climate, which are listed in Table 2.1.

Tropical rain forests grade into other vegetation types along three ecotones, controlled by global climate and local topography. To the north and south of the Amazon/Orinoco and Congo catchment blocks, moving toward the subtropical high pressure zones, semi-evergreen rain forests give way to semi-deciduous and deciduous forests, which in turn merge into savanna and desert. Along those eastern continental margins which receive high rainfall from moist, onshore trade winds, tropical rain

forests may merge via para- (sub)tropical rain forests into warm temperate rain forests, which in turn may grade into cool temperate rain forests with increasing latitude. The third ecotone relates to increasing altitude within the tropical zone, where lowland rain forests grade into montane rain forests, and subsequently, above the tree line, to tropicalpine grassland. Since information on the former distribution of tropical rain forests may be forthcoming from changes in the distribution of bounding vegetation types, brief outlines of the main features of each of these ecotones are given below.

In this chapter, the discussion is firstly of primary forests occurring in well-drained (and hence erosional) settings, then edaphic vegetation of poorly drained, depositional situations, and, finally, the vegetation of the three rain forest ecotones. Throughout, emphasis is placed on features and formations which are likely to be reflected in the fossil record, or which are pertinent with respect to rain forest evolution. Thus emphasis is placed on coastal formations, and vegetation of swamps and rivers, since fossils are most likely to be derived from these sources. Strong emphasis is given to montane forests, since many mountain plants are wind pollinated, and their pollen may be preserved in freshwater and marine sediments, often in substantial quantities. Emphasis is also given firstly to Far Eastern and African examples,

Table 2.1   Rain forest formation types considered in this book, from Whitmore (1998), with modifications and additions.

| Climate | Physiography and soils | | Rain forest formation |
|---|---|---|---|
| Short dry season | Lowlands, on zonal soils | | Seasonal evergreen rain forest* |
| | | | Semi-evergreen rain forest |
| Everwet | | | Lowland evergreen rain forest |
| | Lowlands, on podsols | | Heath forest |
| | Uplands, zonal soils | *c.* 1500 m–3000 m | Lower montane rain forest |
| | | *c.* 1000 m–1500 m | Upper montane rain forest |
| | Coastal sands | | Beach vegetation |
| | Brackish muds | | Mangrove forest |
| | Oligotrophic peats | | Peat swamp forest |
| | Permanently wet | | Freshwater swamp forest |
| Seasonally dry | Periodically wet | | Seasonal freshwater swamp forest |

* In Australia only

with which I have personal experience. For more comprehensive accounts of rain forests, the reader is referred to the standard texts of Schimper (1903), Richards (1952, 1996) and Whitmore (1975, 1998).

## 2.1   PRIMARY RAIN FORESTS

Since most primary rain forests occur away from depositional settings, their past representation based on the fossil record can be determined only by indirect means, from fossils which have been transported, by water or air currents, into adjacent freshwater or marine deposits. Obviously, tiny spores and pollen will stand more chance of being transported in this manner than larger parts. For this reason, the character of rain forest communities of well-drained soils has to be inferred from the occurrence of pollen types of taxa which are poorly represented in associated macrofossil assemblages and emphasis is therefore placed here on taxa which have a fossil *pollen* record.

### 2.1.1   Tropical Lowland Evergreen Rain Forests

The tropical lowland evergreen rain forest formation is the richest, and most luxuriant, of all plant communities, and occurs in areas which experience a wet tropical climate without pronounced dry seasons (Figure 2.1). It is this vegetation type with respect to which frequently exaggerated descriptions have been made by early explorers and writers, and it is often referred to as 'jungle', mainly through popular writings. These are also the forests which are currently being most extensively exploited for their rich timber resources.

Tropical lowland evergreen rain forest is physiognomically similar in all the three continental areas where it occurs, although floristically there are hardly any similarities except at the family level, thus providing us with one of the classic examples of convergent evolution. It is typically dense and evergreen, with trees reaching 50–70 m, especially in SE Asia, and is often devoid of ground flora (Figure 2.2). The tree component is typically very diverse, gregarious

Figure 2.2   Profile diagram of multistoreyed rain forest, Riviere Sinnamary, French Guiana, showing outline of both trees and shrubs. Understorey trees with stippled outline; the emergent tree with a dashed outline is outside the plot and is 42 m tall (from Oldeman, 1974), modified from Richards (1996). Reproduced by permission of ORSTOM.

Figure 2.3    Leaves of *Ficus* sp with pronounced drip tips, Bogor Indonesia.

Figure 2.4    Peltate, palmately veined leaf of *Macaranga diepenhorstii*, near Kuala Lumpur, Malaysia.

dominants generally being uncommon. Tropical rain forest is popularly regarded as being multilayered, with tree crowns forming distinct strata. In practice, such layers are rarely well defined; for instance, in Equador, no clear vertical discontinuity of structure could be discerned at any level and strata could be delimited only arbitrarily (Grubb et al., 1963). Tree crowns are rarely clearly stratified in tropical rain forest because they are composed of a very large number of tree species, each maturing at different heights and reacting differently to light and other factors (Richards, 1996).

Boles are usually straight (Figure 1.1), and buttresses are common. Cauliflory and ramiflory are frequent. Leaves and leaflets are generally coriaceous, and of mesophyll size, with pinnate leaves being common. Leaf margins are

typically entire, frequently with drip tips (Figure 2.3). Lianes are common and often bear cordate, palmately veined leaves (Figure 2.4). Epiphytes are also common and diverse.

All other rain forest formations differ from tropical lowland rain forest in having lower species diversities, fewer life forms, and simpler structure.

### Floristic characterisation

The singular most distinctive feature of tropical lowland evergreen rain forest is its very high species diversity. In the richest examples, every second tree may comprise a different species. There are very few instances where the total number of species within an area of such forest have been determined, since different synusiae

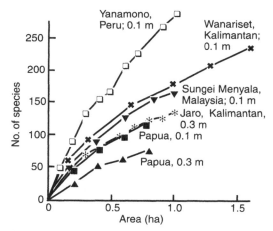

Figure 2.5 Species area curves from tropical lowland evergreen rain forests; the Yanamono forest is the second richest yet found, with every second tree on the hectare plot being a different species (from Whitmore, 1998). Reproduced by permission of Oxford University Press.

(ecological units based on life forms) occur at different scales and require separate sampling strategies. A complete enumeration of all synusiae on a 0.1 ha plot from Costa Rica revealed the presence of 233 species in 2171 specimens, of which 144 were free standing, 41 were climbers and 61 were epiphytes (Whitmore et al., 1986). More typically, diversities of trees only are recorded; the richest communities occur on the eastern flanks of the Andes, in Peru and Equador, where around 300 tree species may be found on a single 1 ha plot (Gentry, 1988a; Valencia et al., 1994). Very high diversities have also been recorded from SE Asian localities (Figure 2.5), whereas diversities of African forests are all much lower (Richards, 1973); for instance, the palm flora of the tiny island of Singapore is richer than that of the whole of the African continent.

A consequence of such high diversities within tropical lowland rain forests is that representatives of many families and genera tend to occur together. In a few families, many closely related species may occur in the same plot, and exhibit sympatry (have the same geographical distribution). This is exemplified by the tree family Dipterocarpaceae in the SE Asian region, where, for instance, Borneo has 287 species in nine genera, the majority of which occur within lowland evergreen rain forests. Similarly, in the Americas, Lecythidaceae has 199 species in 11 genera (Mori, 1989).

The generic and specific make-up of tropical lowland evergreen rain forest exhibits great variation within each of the three centres of rain forest development. However, at the family level, the composition of trees within lowland forests is remarkably similar, with Leguminosae, Annonaceae, Moraceae, Rubiaceae, Euphorbiaceae, Sapindaceae, Apocynaceae, Burseraceae and Guttiferae being represented by considerable diversity in each region (Figure 2.6), the most important regional difference being the substitution of Dipterocarpaceae for Leguminosae as the most species-rich woody family in SE Asian forests (Gentry, 1988b), where it is overwhelmingly dominant in terms of biomass (Figure 2.7). Other important differences are the widespread representation of Bignoniaceae (as woody climbers) and Palmae (as canopy elements) in South American rain forests, the common representation of Sterculiaceae, Dichapetalaceae and Olacaceae in Africa, and the high diversity of Myrtaceae in SE Asia (Gentry, 1988b). Conifers are characteristic of lowland evergreen rain forests only in the eastern tropics.

Plant geographers have attempted to explain these remarkable floristic affinities between the rain forest blocks in terms of former land bridges, or they have been used in the absence of fossil evidence as justification for an ancient origin for certain exclusively tropical angiosperm groups. This most important group of pantropical angiosperm families has been termed *megathermal* by van Steenis (1962a), in that they are limited, or almost so, by the action of frosts to the present-day tropical zone (Figure 2.8a,b), and/or by their mode of reproduction to areas of permanently moist climate, many being unable to germinate outside the protection of the rain forest canopy (Table 2.2).

Van Steenis (1962a) also listed 54 additional families which he considered *almost tropical*

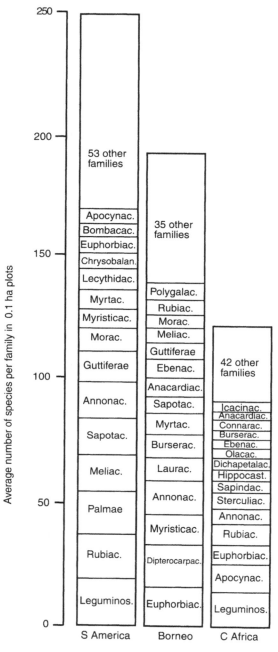

Figure 2.6 Comparison of average numbers of tree species per family for 0.1 ha samples from rain forest plots from South America (two sites in Choco, Colombia), Borneo (two sites) and C Africa (five sites). (Modified from Gentry, 1988b). Reproduced by permission of Annals of the Missouri Botanical Garden.

*or can be considered tropical* pro majore parte *with subtropical or a few temperate outliers.* The families from this list which have a good (principally pollen) fossil record are brought to attention in Table 2.3.

The controversy regarding these families stems from the fact that many have representatives equally spread within each of the three continental regions, and that many have diaspore dispersal mechanisms which prohibit trans-oceanic dispersal. Some of these families, such as Myristicaceae, bear seeds which can only germinate under the protection of the rain forest itself. Others have heavy seeds which are unlikely to be dispersed far from the parent tree. Obtaining an explanation for the origin of this group of families has been one of the fundamental problems of tropical plant geography. Clearly, the fossil record of representatives from these groups of families will be implemental in determining the history of tropical rain forests.

### 2.1.2 Semi-evergreen Rain Forests

Tropical semi-evergreen rain forests are probably the most extensive of all tropical rain forest formations, occupying the eastern part of the Amazon Basin, and the Caribbean; also virtually all of the African rain forests are semi-evergreen. They occur in areas where there is a regular annual period of moisture stress, due either to rainfall seasonality or soil conditions, except in the Congo where dry periods occur irregularly through the year. In SE Asia, semi-evergreen rain forests are of very limited extent compared to evergreen rain forests, occurring marginally to them in Myanmar, Thailand, Indochina, India and the Andamans, and, presumably, would have formerly occurred in much of Java (Whitmore, 1975).

Semi-evergreen rain forest is a closed, high, rain forest and has much in common with evergreen rain forests. The principal differences are that deciduous trees are more common in the upper canopy, comprising up to one-third of all the taller trees; diversity remains high, but less

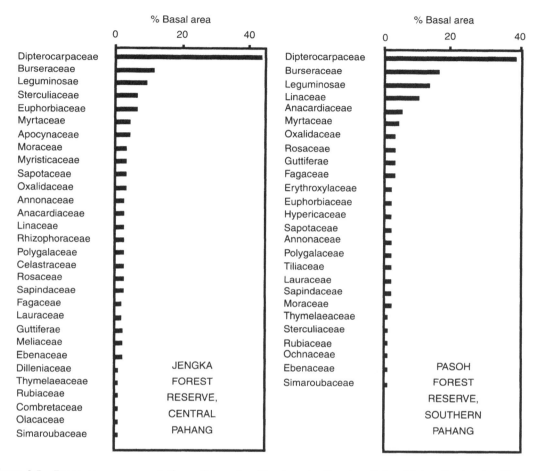

Figure 2.7 Percentage representation of tree families in rain forests of the Malay Peninsula. Data are presented in terms of basal area, which is the cross-sectional area of tree boles at breast height, based on girth measurements. Data for Jengka from Poore (1968), and Pasoh from unpublished data by P.S. Ashton (compilation from Morley, 1976).

than in evergreen forests; bark tends to be thicker, and rougher; and cauliflory and ramiflory are rarer. Buttresses continue to be frequent and occur in both evergreen and deciduous species; big woody climbers are abundant, and bamboos common, especially in disturbed forest. Epiphytes are common to frequent. Apart from its deciduous tendency, the most characteristic feature of semi-evergreen rain forests is the tendency to gregarious species occurrence, and hence to definite tree-crown stratification not seen in evergreen rain forests (Whitmore, 1998).

In W Africa, drier forests tend to be dominated by members of the families Sterculiaceae, Ulmaceae and Moraceae, whereas in SE Asia, *Lagerstroemia* (Lythraceae), *Terminalia* (Combretaceae), *Pterocarpus* (Leguminosae) and *Tetrameles* (Datiscaceae) are important.

The climate of the Queensland rain forests is similar to that of semi-evergreen rain forests of other regions, but since the deciduous condition is poorly developed in Australasian trees, these forests are evergreen, and are better termed evergreen seasonal rain forests (P.S. Ashton, personal communication). They are dominated by members of Lauraceae, and contain abundant

(a) Myristicaceae

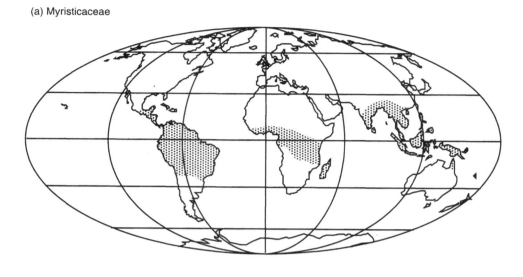

(b) Sapotaceae

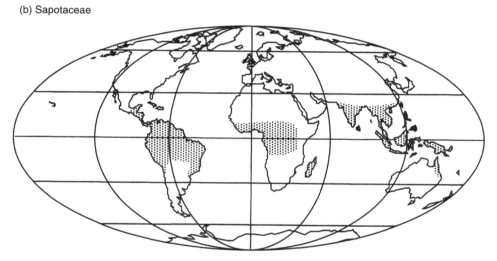

Figure 2.8   Global distribution of (a) Myristicaceae and (b) Sapotaceae (from Heywood, 1978). Reproduced by permission of Andromeda Oxford Ltd.

representatives of families not widely seen in rain forests elsewhere, such as Elaeocarpaceae, Monimiaceae, Myrtaceae and Proteaceae.

### 2.1.3   Heath Forests

On siliceous soils which are commonly coarsely textured and free draining, closed-canopy, ever-green forests are replaced by heath forest, widely termed *kerangas* in SE Asia, and this is strikingly different in flora, structure and physiognomy (Figures 2.9; 2.10; 2.11). In heath forest, the storey formed by large saplings and small poles predominates, forming a dense forest which is difficult to penetrate. The canopy is low, uniform and very dense, with no trace of layering. Single emergents may occur, but these usually

Table 2.2   Megathermal pantropical plant families, according to van Steenis (1957, 1962a).

| | | | |
|---|---|---|---|
| Annonaceae* | Dichapetalaceae | Hippocrataceae* | Opiliaceae |
| Bombacaceae** | Dilleniaceae* | Lecythidaceae** | Pandanaceae** |
| Burseraceae* | Dipterocarpaceae*± | Malphigiaceae** | Rhizophoraceae** |
| Cannaceae | Erythroxylaceae | Marantaceae | Taccaceae |
| Cochlospermaceae | Flagellariaceae* | Musaceae* | Triuridaceae |
| Combretaceae* | Guttiferae** | Myristicaceae* | Zingiberaceae* |
| Connaraceae | Hernandiaceae | Ochnaceae | |

**Families with good fossil record
* Families with some fossil record
  Families without significant fossil record unmarked
± Not in van Steenis list since records in South America were found in last 20 years

Table 2.3   Megathermal, pantropical families *pro majore parte*, of van Steenis (1957, 1962a) which have a fossil pollen record.

| | | | |
|---|---|---|---|
| Acanthaceae | Euphorbiaceae | Moraceae | Sapotaceae |
| Anacardiaceae | Icacinaceae | Myrsinaceae | Sterculiaceae |
| Apocynaceae | Lauraceae | Myrtaceae | Theaceae |
| Caesalpinoidae | Loranthaceae | Olacaceae | Tiliaceae |
| Chloranthaceae | Melastomataceae | Palmae | |
| Cucurbitaceae | Meliaceae | Rubiaceae | |
| Cunoniaceae | Mimosoidae | Sapindaceae | |

Figure 2.9   Heath forest (*kerangas*), with *Casuarina nobilis*, in Berakas Forest Park, Brunei.

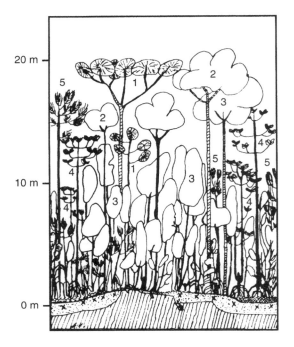

Figure 2.10   Profile through heath forest (*kerangas*), Merurong Plateau, Sarawak (Brunig, 1968). (1) *Dacrydium elatum*; (2) *Shorea coriacea*; (3) *Parastemon urophyllus*; (4) *Ploiarium alternifolium*; (5) *Casuarina nobilis*.

indicate extreme site conditions. Brown and red colours prevail in the upper part of the canopy, and generally leaf sizes are smaller and leaves more sclerophyllous than in evergreen rain forest. Bryophytes frequently occur, and buttresses are smaller. Big woody climbers, including rattans, are rare. Epiphytes, myrmecophytes and insectivorous plants are common.

Brunig (1974) provided a comprehensive account of the heath forests of Sarawak. He noted that the most well-represented families are Myrtaceae, Dipterocarpaceae, Sapotaceae and Euphorbiaceae. Other important families are Guttiferae, Casuarinaceae, Podocarpaceae (especially *Dacrydium*) and Anacardiaceae. These eight families constitute 77% of the basal area of plots studied by Brunig. The flora of heath forests in Sarawak, with 948 tree species, is poorer than adjacent evergreen rain forests, but richer than peat swamp forests, to which their floras are closely similar (Section 2.4.1).

In SE Asia, heath forests are widespread on Tertiary terraces in Borneo (Whitmore, 1984), and are also represented to a lesser degree in other coastal areas in Indochina and Thailand, Banka in Sumatra, and the Malay Peninsula. The Bornean localities often include areas of peat accumulation, especially in areas of

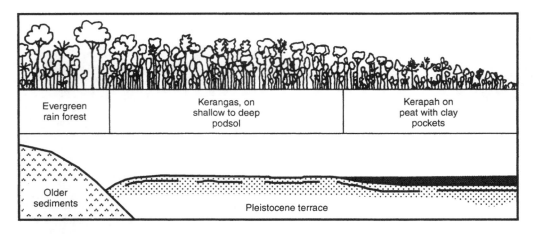

Figure 2.11   Schematic transect through *kerangas* forests in Borneo; from lowland evergreen rain forest on sandy loam, through a sequence of *kerangas* forest types on podsolic soils to *kerapah* on peat (Brunig, 1990). Reproduced by permission of Elsevier Science.

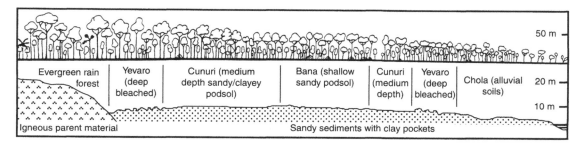

Figure 2.12  Schematic transect through heath forest in Amazonia; from lowland evergreen rain forest on 'terra firma', through *yevaro* forest (*Eperua* spp. dominant) through *cunuri* (*Micrandra* spp. dominant), and through *bana* to *chola* (Brunig, 1990). Reproduced by permission of Elsevier Science.

impeded drainage, where an iron or humic pan has developed, and these bear distinctive peat swamp forests termed *kerapah* (described below). Heath forests are rare in Africa, being restricted to coastal sands around the Gulf of Guinea. They are most extensively represented, however, in the upper reaches of the Rio Negro and Orinoco in South America (Whitmore, 1998). They were first described by Davis and Richards (1933–34) from Guyana where they are dominated by the genus *Eperua* (Leguminosae) with common *Duguetia* (Annonaceae), *Catostemma* (Bombacaceae) and *Ecclinusa* (Sapotaceae) (Figure 2.12).

Since heath forests occur on predominantly erosional sites, it might be anticipated that they will be poorly represented by fossils. This is probably not the case; because of their typically coastal distribution (at least in SE Asia), their pollen is often transported to marine environments. Sands and associated coals, possibly representing *kerapah* peats, are sometimes found in the sedimentary record, where perhaps they become 'trapped' as a result of fluctuating sea levels, or are preserved since their organic soil surfaces are highly resistant to erosion (P.S. Ashton, personal communication).

## 2.2  COASTAL VEGETATION

The coastal location of mangroves and beach vegetation ensures the widespread preservation of their fossils in paralic (coastal plain) and marine sediments, despite, in the case of beach vegetation, their often very limited extent. Remains of mangroves are frequently seen in paralic sediments, and, in certain deltaic settings, mangrove pollen may comprise over 95% of pollen incorporated into coastal and shallow marine sediments.

### 2.2.1  Mangroves

Mangroves (Figure 2.13) are composed of trees and shrubs remarkably adapted to tidal land through their ability to live in poorly oxygenated muds and to tolerate inundation by salt water through physiological mechanisms. They often possess special breathing roots (Figure 2.14). They are characteristic of depositional, especially muddy, coastlines in the vicinity of freshwater outflows throughout the tropics, where they may form a belt which in favourable circumstances may reach many kilometres in width (Figure 2.15). Compared to other tropical forests, mangrove floras are of low diversity. The component species of mangroves come from several unrelated families, but with Rhizophoraceae dominant (Table 2.4), and their joint tendency toward xerophylly, sclerophylly and vivipary form a further remarkable example of evolutionary convergence. Mangroves are of particular importance from the geological viewpoint because, as they occur along depositional

Figure 2.13    Mangrove swamp with *Rhizophora* spp., Brunei Bay.

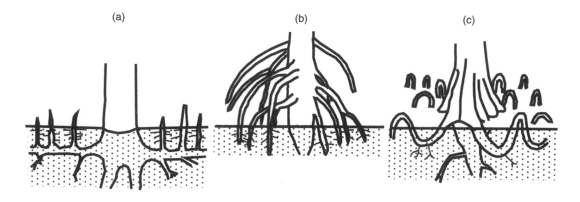

Figure 2.14    Schematic indication of types of roots in mangroves: (a) spike roots as found in *Avicennia* and *Sonneratia*; (b) stilt roots as found in *Rhizophora*, and (c) knee roots, as found in some *Bruguiera* spp.

Figure 2.15 Satellite photo of mangrove belt in the eastern Niger Delta. Mangrove swamps, consisting mostly of *Rhizophora* spp., have a medium tone, areas of open, lightly disturbed vegetation are pale, and areas of heavily disturbed ground dark. From a colour-enhanced image, courtesy of Shell Nigeria.

Table 2.4 The main species of mangroves in South America, Africa and the eastern tropics, with an indication (*) as to the occurrence of their pollen in the fossil record. Note that pollen of genera of Rhizophoraceae (marked '+') is very similar to that of *Rhizophora*; pollen of *Lumnitzera* (marked **) is similar to many other Combretaceae, and also Melastomataceae. The position of the asterisk indicates whether pollen determination is at the generic or specific level.

| South America | West/East Africa | Eastern tropics |
|---|---|---|
| **Mangroves**<br>Avicennia* bicolor<br>A.* germinans<br>Pelliciera rhizophorae*<br>Rhizophora* mangle<br>R.* x harrisonii<br>R.* racemosa<br><br>**Backmangroves**<br>Acrostichum* aureum<br>Conocarpus erectus<br>Laguncularia racemosa<br>Pterocarpus officinalis | **West Africa**<br><br>**Mangroves**<br>Avicennia* germinans<br>Rhizophora* mangle<br>R.* racemosa<br>R.* x harrisonii<br><br>**Backmangroves**<br>Acrostichum* aureum<br>Conocarpus erectus<br>Laguncularia racemosa<br><br>**East Africa**<br><br>**Mangroves**<br>Avicennia* marina<br>Bruguiera+ gymnorrhiza<br>Rhizophora* mucronata<br>Sonneratia alba*<br><br>**Backmangroves**<br>Acrostichum* aureum<br>Ceriops+ tagal<br>Heritiera littoralis<br>Pemphis* acidula<br>Xylocarpus granatum | **Mangroves**<br>Avicennia* alba<br>A.* eucalyptifolia<br>A.* intermedia<br>A.* marina<br>A.* officinalis<br>Bruguiera+ cylindrica<br>B.+ exaristata<br>B.+ gymnorrhiza<br>B.+ hainsii<br>B.+ parviflora<br>B.+ sexangula<br>Ceriops+ decandra<br>C.+ tagal<br>Kandelia+ candel<br>Lumnitzera** littorea<br>L.** racemosa<br>Rhizophora* apiculata<br>R.* mangle<br>R.* mucronata<br>R.* racemosa<br>R.* stylosa<br>Sonneratia alba*<br>S. apetala*<br>S. griffithii*<br>S. ovata*<br><br>**Backmangroves**<br>Acanthus ebracteatus*<br>A. ilicifolius*<br>Acrostichum* aureum<br>A.* speciosum<br>Aegialitis* annulata<br>A.* rotundifolia<br>Aegiceras corniculatum<br>Brownlowia* argentata<br>Camptostemon* philippinense<br>C.* schultzii<br>Cerbera odallum<br>C. manghas<br>Derris uliginosa<br>Excoecaria* agallocha<br>Ficus* retusa<br>Heritiera* littoralis<br>Hibiscus* tiliaceus<br>Intsia* bijuga<br>Nypa fruticans*<br>Oncosperma* filamentosa<br>Osbornia octodonta<br>Scyphiphora hydrophyllacea<br>Sonneratia caseolaris*<br>Thespesia populnea*<br>Xylocarpus granatum<br>X. mekongensis |

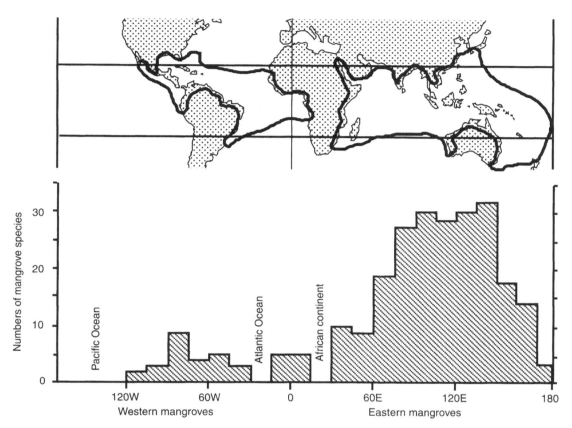

Figure 2.16   Generalised distribution of mangroves. Above: approximate limits for all species: eastern and western groups do not overlap. Below: histogram showing approximate numbers of species per 15° of longitude. Note concentration of species in eastern tropics (from Tomlinson, 1986). Reproduced by permission of Cambridge University Press.

coastlines, their fossils, especially of pollen and roots, are frequently recorded and are valuable sedimentological indicators. The fossil record of their constituent genera is particularly complete. Especially noteworthy are *Sonneratia* (Sonneratiaceae), in which all of the constituent species can be differentiated on their pollen (Muller, 1969), and have an extensive fossil record (Section 9.10).

Mangroves reach outside the tropics as far as 32°N and 35°S, but they attain their most prolific development within the everwet tropics. They show their greatest species concentration within the aseasonal Eastern tropics (Figure 2.16; Table 2.4), and this has led to the sugges-

tion that they evolved in this area, a supposition which needs to be tested from fossil data.

In addition to obligate mangroves (those confined to brackish environments) growing along the coast, the Eastern tropics are rich in brackish-water forests, which are essentially composed of facultative halophytes (can grow under either brackish or fresh conditions), and can tolerate only low salinities. Backmangrove communities are well developed throughout SE Asia, but are poorly developed in the Americas, and are virtually absent from Africa. In SE Asia, the backmangrove community includes the palm *Nypa* (Figure 5.20), which in some instances lines tidal rivers but elsewhere, such as on the

Mahakam and Rajang Deltas in Borneo, may form consociations covering thousands of hectares. Well-developed mangroves may form a single-storeyed forest up to 30 m in height, and exhibit a striking zonation, reflecting the degree of marine inundation and hence salinity (eg Watson, 1928), which sometimes reflects a true succession. They can also occur far inland along rivers, where the effects of tides are still felt, and occasionally facultative mangroves occur far inland, presumably left behind a rapidly advancing coastline. Mangroves do not assist in the process of trapping sediment, as frequently supposed (Thom, 1967; Scholl, 1968).

Mangroves are also characteristic of carbonate substrates, as in Florida (Spackman et al., 1966) and Jamaica (Robinson, 1976, 1978), in which settings they may grow on peats, and on some coral reefs, but, surprisingly, despite their excellent facilities for dispersal, they are absent from islands in the eastern Pacific, to the east of the Marshall Islands and Samoa (Woodroffe and Grindrod, 1991).

The global representation of mangrove swamps relates closely to the behaviour of global sea levels (Woodroffe and Grindrod, 1991; Morley, 1996). They were generally of limited occurrence when sea levels were much lower than at present, below the levels of the continental shelves, but became much more extensive than today during former periods of rapid sea level rise, especially immediately following the times at which sea levels rose above the continental shelf break, such as during the early Holocene.

## 2.2.2 Beach Vegetation

The vegetation of tropical sandy beaches is distinctive, forming a narrow strip bordering coasts. Two main plant associations are found along beaches: herbaceous communities often dominated by grasses, directly bordering the sea on unstable sands above the effect of tides, and beach forest, where the substrate is more consolidated. Herbaceous communities are often dominated by creeping stoloniferous herbs,

including the grass *Spinifex littoreus* and *Ipomoea pes-caprae*, after which this vegetation is often termed the *Pes-caprae* Formation. Other typical taxa include *Ipomoea gracilis* and other Convolvulaceae, and the legumes *Canavallia obtusifolia* and *Vigna marina*. Many of the constituents of the *Pes-caprae* Formation are pantropical in their distribution, occurring along the tropical shores of the Indian and western Pacific Oceans, and also in the West Indies. This formation sometimes includes shrubs, such as *Scaevola frutescens* (Goodeniaceae), and, in the West Indies, *Tournefortia gnaphalodes* (Boraginaceae).

Beach forest occurs along the damper coasts throughout the tropics, but is best developed in the regions of the Indian and Pacific Oceans. It comprises a narrow strip of trees, perhaps a few tens of metres wide (Figure 2.17), which in some areas, such as in the Solomons and New Guinea, where undisturbed, may reach a height approaching that of inland forests (Richards, 1952) and may be rich in lianes. As with the *Pes-caprae* Formation, its composition is very uniform throughout the eastern tropics, many species ranging to Africa and the Pacific, or are pantropical, and have seeds adapted for water dispersal. Locally, one species may become dominant, but usually there is a mixture of species. The most characteristic and constant species of the Indian and Pacific Oceans (comprising the Indo-Pacific strand flora) are *Barringtonia asiatica* (Lecythidaceae), *Calophyllum inophyllum* (Guttiferae), *Terminalia catappa* (Combretaceae), *Thespesia populnea* and *Hibiscus tiliaceus* (Malvaceae) and *Pandanus tectorius* (Pandanaceae), whereas, in the West Indies, *Coccoloba uvifera* (Polygonaceae), *Hippomane mancinella* (Euphorbiaceae) and *Chrysobalanus icaco* (Chrysobalanaceae) occupy the same niche. An example of single species dominance within this formation is the widespread occurrence of *Casuarina equisetifolia* (Casuarinaceae) in SE Asia (Figure 2.18), especially along accreting sandy coasts. On small coral islands, beach forest may form the principal forest type; there it is often dominated by *Pisonia grandis* (Nyctaginaceae).

Figure 2.17 Profile through beach forest, Jason's Bay, southern Malay Peninsula. c = *Casuarina equisetifolia*; e = *Eugenia grandis*; n = *Nypa fruticans*; p = *Pandanus* spp.; sc = *Sonneratia caseolaris*; d = dry climax forest; s = freshwater swamp forest species (Corner, 1978). Reproduced by permission of Gardens Bulletin Singapore, published by Singapore Botanic Gardens.

Figure 2.18 Beach forest, dominated by *Casuarina equisetifolia*, east coast of Peninsula Malaysia.

## 2.3 RIVERINE VEGETATION

The vegetation bordering the lower reaches of lowland rivers often exhibits a clear zonation, both with distance from the sea, and parallel to the river bank, relating on the one hand to brackish and tidal influence, and on the other to water depth and current action. Descriptions of such vegetation are rarely seen, but fortunately the particularly clear zonation which occurs along Malaysian rivers has been brought to attention by Corner (1940) and described in detail for the Sungei (river) Sedili Besar (Corner, 1978), and is summarised below. Longitudinal

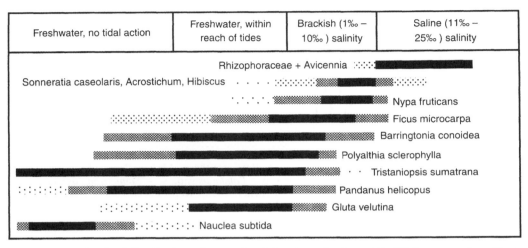

Figure 2.19   Longitudinal distribution of vegetation belts along the Sungei Sedili Besar, southern Peninsular Malaysia. Density of shading indicates frequency of occurrence, highest density suggests continuous occurrence. Transect length 35 km. (Modified from Corner, 1978). Reproduced by permission of Gardens Bulletin Singapore, published by Singapore Botanic Gardens.

zonations for rivers in Guyana are described by Fanshawe (1952), and Richards (1996) notes that similar zonations occur along African rivers.

In the same manner as mangrove swamps, the vegetation bordering lowland rivers is a major contributor to pollen and spore assemblages found in nearshore fluviomarine sediments, and, although riverine vegetation is of relatively limited extent, compared to vegetation of well-drained soils, its history is relatively clearly revealed by the fossil record.

### Longitudinal zonation of Sedili Besar, West Malaysia

The lower reaches of the Sungei Sedili Besar, southern Peninsular Malaysia, can be divided into four clear zones which relate on the one hand to salinity, and on the other to the effect of tides. These variables are reflected by vegetation belts (Figure 2.19), which are arranged longitudinally along the river, and also parallel to the river bank, grading either into freshwater swamp forest (Section 2.4), or into dryland rain forests in areas where soils are well drained. In the lower reaches of the river, where salinities exceed 10‰, mangrove swamps, mainly char-

acterised by the genera *Rhizophora*, *Bruguiera*, *Ceriops* and *Kandelia* (Rhizophoraceae), *Avicennia* (Verbenaceae) and *Sonneratia alba*, border the river, whereas as salinities fall below 10‰, these are replaced by backmangrove trees, such as *Sonneratia caseolaris*, and *Hibiscus tiliaceus*, the palm *Nypa fruticans* (Figure 2.20), and the fern *Acrostichum aureum* (Pteridaceae). Beyond the effect of brackish water, but still within the reach of tides, *Pandanus helicopus* forms a broad belt, extending to the limit of tidal influence, with a narrow zone of the low, pioneering shrub *Barringtonia conoidea* along the water's edge, and, behind, *Tristaniopsis sumatrana* (Myrtaceae) forming a distinct belt on levées (Figure 2.21). There is a distinctive zone behind the *Pandanus* belt which is dominated by *Polyalthia sclerophylla* (Annonaceae) and other trees with an impenetrable tangle of erect pneumatophores which is clearly replacing the *Pandanus*, and in places this in turn is being invaded by freshwater swamp forest.

The tidally influenced, but wholly freshwater zone of the Sedili River has analogues elsewhere in New Guinea, where stilt-rooted 'freshwater mangroves', dominated by *Myristica hollrungii*

Figure 2.20   Tidal creek, lined with *Nypa fruticans*, Temburong River, Brunei. Courtesy of A. McRobb, Media Resources, Royal Botanic Gardens, Kew.

(Myristicaceae) occupy the freshwater intertidal zone (Paijmans, 1987), and in freshwater channels around the mouth of the Amazon (the *furos*), where the giant aroid *Montrichardia arborescens* and *Machaerium lunatum* (Leguminosae) form a pioneering community on tidal but freshwater mudbanks. This community is subsequently shaded out by *Rhizophora racemosa*, growing under wholly freshwater conditions (Richards, 1996).

## 2.4   FRESHWATER WETLANDS

Since freshwater wetlands are essentially depositional, their floras are particularly well represented in the fossil record, both in the form of macrofossils, mainly preserved *in situ*, or close to their place of origin, and pollen and spores, deposited either close to their place of origin, or transported by rivers to the sea and preserved in marine sediments. The vegetation and ecology

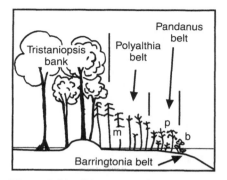 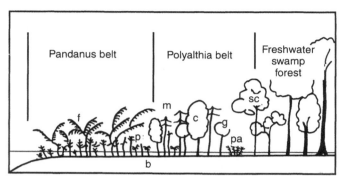

Figure 2.21  Diagrammatic transect at beginning of freshwater intertidal zone, Sungei Sedili Besar, S Peninsula Malaysia. b = *Barringtonia racemosa*; c = *Carapa moluccensis*; f = *Ficus microcarpa*; g = *Garcinia bancana*; m = *Polyalthia sclerophylla*; p = *Pandanus helicopus*; pa = *Pandanus affinis*; sc = *Sonneratia caseolaris* (Corner, 1978). Reproduced by permission of Gardens Bulletin Singapore, published by Singapore Botanic Gardens.

of tropical freshwater wetlands, however, remains relatively poorly understood compared to areas which are well drained, and most classifications of such vegetation, although perhaps appropriate within a single rain forest block, remain unsatisfactory when applied on a pantropical basis. Broadly following Whitmore (1998), wetland vegetation is discussed here under two headings: firstly, the forests of peat swamps, which are dependent primarily on rainfall, and are markedly oligotrophic; and, secondly, freshwater swamp forests, growing on muck or mineral substrates, which are principally fed by rivers, and may be either eutrophic or oligotrophic.

### 2.4.1  Peat Swamp Forests

Tropical peats form only in swamps with very low nutrient availability, and minimal seasonality of climate (Morley, 1981a), and are either wholly rainfall-maintained, or occur in areas where surface waters are oligotrophic, and soils podsolic, otherwise bearing heath forests. Suitable climates and topographic settings for tropical peat formation are mainly in SE Asia, although occurrences of peat swamps in South America are now becoming better known (Suszczinski, 1984; Whitmore, 1998). SE Asian peat swamps mostly occur as ombrotrophic,

blanket-bog-type mires, but rheotrophic, topogenous mires, in which topographic factors retard drainage, occur locally. On shallow peats, peat swamp forests are physiognomically similar to lowland rain forests, being floristically diverse, structurally complex, multistoreyed and mesophyllous, whereas on thick peats, dense, single-storeyed pole forests with sclerophyllous, notophyll-sized leaves are characteristic, and, in the most advanced stages, microphyll-leaved open woodland may occur. Ombrotrophic peat swamps occur in three settings (Morley, in press): along coasts behind accreting mangrove swamps or coastal beach ridges (termed basinal peats); in inland settings in areas of podsolic soils, where there is some degree of impediment to water movement, such as the presence of a well-developed humic pan (in SE Asia, termed *kerapah*, see above); and in watershed areas where peats drape the surface in the manner of temperate blanket bogs (watershed peats).

### *Basinal peat swamp forests*

Basinal peat swamps are widely represented in SE Asia, where they have been intensively studied in Sarawak and Brunei by Anderson (1963, 1964, 1983), and their main features are summarised below on the basis of his work. These swamps have formed since the stabilisation of global sea levels, some 6000 years ago (Anderson

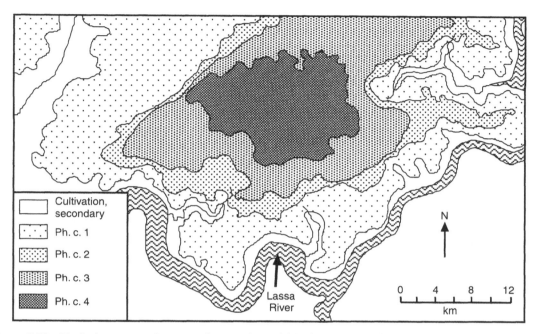

Figure 2.22   Typical pattern of concentric zonation of Phasic Communities in peat swamp forest, Lassa Forest Reserve, Rajang Delta, Sarawak. Phasic Community 1 (Ph. c.) = *Gonystylus – Dactylocladus – Neoscortechinia* association; Ph. c. 2 = *Shorea albida – Gonystylus – Parastemon* association; Ph. c. 3 = *Shorea albida* consociation; Ph. c. 4 = *Shorea albida – Litsea – Parastemon* association (Brunig, 1990). Reproduced by permission of Elsevier Science.

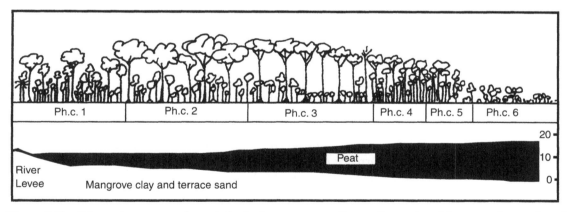

Figure 2.23   Schematic transect through basinal peat swamp forest, Sarawak, with a complete series of Phasic Communities from 1 to 6 (Brunig, 1990). Reproduced by permission of Elsevier Science.

and Muller, 1975). They are often domed, with the central parts being several metres above the surrounding terrain, with reduced nutrient availability and poorer drainage. The vegetation of peat swamps in Sarawak is divided into concentric zones, described by Anderson (1964) in terms of a catena of six Phasic Communities of decreasing stature and diversity (Figures 2.22, 2.23, Table 2.5). Palynological studies by Anderson and Muller (1975) show that

Table 2.5 Main characteristics of the six peat swamp Phasic Communities of Anderson (1963).

---

Phasic Community 1; structurally the most complex and species-rich mesophyll phase, 40–45 m high, principal taxa *Gonystylus bancanus*, *Dactylocladus stenostachys*, *Neoscortechinia kingii*, *Shorea* spp., *Campnosperma* and *Lophopetalum*

Phasic Community 2; characterised by tall emergents of *Shorea albida*, with common *Gonystylus bancanus* and *Stemonurus secundiflorus*; height typically 45–55 m; mesophyll

Phasic Community 3; *Shorea albida* consociation, reaching 50–60, sometimes 70 m; mesophyll/ notophyll; middle and lower storeys typically poorly developed

Phasic Community 4; characterised by small-boled leptophyll *Shorea albida* emergents, with *Litsea crassifolia*, *Parastemon spicatum* and others reaching 30–40 m; poorly developed understorey, shrub layer with many taxa characteristic of *kerangas*, *kerapah* and montane forest

Phasic Community 5; species-poor leptophyll pole forest with *Tristaniopsis* spp., *Parastemon spicatum*, *Palaquium cochlearifolium*, *Dactylocladus stenostachys* and *Combretocarpus rotundatus* dominant

Phasic Community 6; stunted open notophyll/ microphyll sclerophyllous forest to 12 m developing on deep peat; *Combretocarpus rotundatus*, *Dactylocladus stenostachys*, *Garcinia cuneifolia* and *Litsea crassifolia* abundant; myrmecophytes and insectivorous herbs/shrubs common, also with *Sphagnum* moss

---

the swamp catena represents a true temporal succession. The ecology of Sarawak swamps is complicated by the common occurrence of one species of dipterocarp, *Shorea albida* (Figure 2.24), which dominates the intermediate phasic communities. This species is missing in S Kalimantan, the Malay Peninsula and Sumatra, and here the catena is structurally and floristically more simple, with peat swamps being divided into two main types: mixed swamp forest over shallow peat, and pole, or padang (open) forest in the centre on deeper peats (Wyatt-Smith, 1959; Anderson, 1976; Morley, 1981a). The composition of the central padang forest is somewhat

variable; *Combretocarpus rotundatus* (Rhizophoraceae) and *Dactylocladus stenostachys* (Crypteroniaceae) dominate Phasic Community 6 in Sarawak (Anderson, 1964), whereas *Ploiarium alternifolium* (Theaceae) and *Tristaniopsis obovata* are dominant in some Sumatran swamps (Endert, 1920, Polak, 1933).

A total of 242 tree species have been recorded in Sarawak peat swamp forests. Many of the constituent taxa of the peripheral communities are shared with freshwater swamp forest and lowland forests of well-drained soils, whereas the inner communities, which occupy environments with lower nutrient availability and putative periodic water stress, share their species with heath forests, which they also resemble physiognomically. Altogether, 146 species have been recorded as common to peat swamp forest and heath forest (Brunig, 1974).

Peat swamps with concentrically zoned vegetation also occur in the superhumid climate of Pacific coastal Colombia (Christen, 1973; Brunig, 1990), These peat swamps are presumably analogous to the basinal peat swamp forests of SE Asia, and include phases of single-species dominance of *Iryanthera juruensis* (Myristicaceae) and *Campnosperma panamensis* (Anacardiaceae). Possible basinal-type peat swamps also occur in the West Indies (Beard, 1944), where they are dominated by *Amanoa caribbaea* (Euphorbiaceae), and also locally in the Niger Delta, where *Cleistopholis patens* (Annonaceae), *Syzygium guineense* (Myrtaceae) and *Ficus congoense* (Moraceae) are dominant (Clayton, 1958). In New Guinea, peats up to 2 m thick are reported to be extensive in more or less permanent swamps away from river courses (Paijmans, 1987), but few studies have been made of their vegetation.

There has been speculation as to why peats form in the lowland tropics, since it might be expected that high decomposer activity would preclude peat formation. It is suggested (Anderson, 1964) that the abundance of toxic sulphides in waterlogged brackish mangrove muds reduces bacterial activity permitting initiation of peat formation.

Figure 2.24 *Shorea albida*, basinal peat swamp forest, Phasic Community 2, Baram Delta, Brunei. Photo courtesy of Peter Ashton.

*Kerapah peat swamps*

A second type of peat swamp forest, termed *kerapah*, closely allied to *kerangas* (heath forest) is characteristic of more inland localities in Sarawak (Figure 2.11), developing in areas where gradients are minimal and soils lack nutrients, and where there is almost permanent waterlogging due to impeded drainage (Brunig, 1990; P.S. Ashton, personal communication). *Kerapah* forests are floristically much more diverse than peat swamp forests and show marked local and regional variation. *Casuarina nobilis* and *Dacrydium elatum* are common dominants. Advanced stages of *kerapah* closely resemble Phasic Communities 4 to 6 of peat swamps.

In S America, the *igapo* swamp forests of blackwater rivers (described in Section 2.4.2) closely resemble *kerapah* forests in terms of physiognomy (Brunig, 1990), although they develop only locally on peat (Bouillienne, 1930). *Kerapah*-type swamps have not been described from the African continent, but since heath forests are rare in Africa, such swamps would not be expected to occur.

*Watershed peat swamp forests*

Recent research in SE Kalimantan by Reilly et al. (1992) and Reilley and Page (1997) show that many peat swamps in that area, which are dominated by *Calophyllum* spp. and *Combretocarpus rotundatus*, occur on low-lying watersheds, and have not accumulated behind prograding mangrove swamps as previously assumed. Furthermore, the peats have been radiocarbon dated, and it is clear that accumulation began much earlier than for basinal peats, beginning in the earlier Holocene, and that accumulation terminated about 3000 years ago; the peats are thought to have accumulated at a time of much wetter climate than at present, during the phase of early Holocene sea level rise. These peat swamp forests are probably closely related to the *kerapah* forests described above.

## 2.4.2   Freshwater Swamp Forests

Freshwater swamp forests are rain forests which are permanently or temporarily submerged by river water, and generally occur behind the mangrove belt, where the rivers first enter the plains (van Steenis, 1957). They can be divided into swamps of eutrophic rivers, typified by the *varzea* swamps of the Amazon, and those of oligotrophic rivers, such as the *igapo* swamps of the Rio Negro.

*Swamps of eutrophic rivers*

The vegetation of eutrophic freshwater swamps is highly variable in character, depending on whether flooding is permanent or periodic, with swamping either annual, seasonal, or even daily, as in the case of the freshwater tidal swamps described in Section 2.3. Where flooding is brief, they may occur as floristically diverse, distinctly storeyed forests with large emergent trees, closely resembling lowland evergreen rain forest; however, with increasingly frequent inundation, they may consist of a low scrub, with scattered taller trees. In some areas, they are dominated by palms or, in the Old World, by pandans. Swamp forest trees are often characterised by stilt and knee roots, and, sometimes, sinuous plank buttresses, and climbers and epiphytes are abundant. Freshwater swamp forests are particularly widespread along the great rivers of the Amazon Basin and in New Guinea, but in SE Asia have mostly been destroyed and replaced with rice paddy.

*Eastern tropics*

The most comprehensive study of freshwater swamp forest in SE Asia is that of Corner (1978), who described the flora and composition of the swamps which previously occurred in Singapore and the southern part of the Malay Peninsula, along the Sedili River (Figure 2.21). Corner considered these forests more or less transitional with peat swamp forests, with

(a)

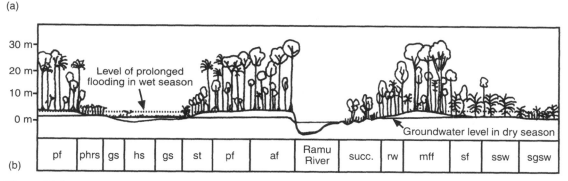

(b)

Figure 2.25 (a) *Metroxylon sagu* swamp, Irian Jaya (Courtesy of A. McRobb, Media Resources, Royal Botanic Gardens, Kew). (b) Transect across Ramu River, Papua New Guinea; af = well-drained forest on alluvium; gs = grass swamp; hs = herbaceous swamp; mff = mixed floodplain forest; pf = palm floodplain forest; phrs = *Phragmites* swamp; rw = rattan woodland; sf = sago (*Metroxylon*) forest; sgsw = sago grass swamp; ssw = sago swamp; st = swamp thicket; succ. = hydroseral successional stages. (From Richards, 1996, after Robbins, 1961). Reproduced by permission of Cambridge University Press.

which they shared many species, although they were of much higher diversity, with Dipterocarpaceae having the most species, followed by Moraceae, Leguminosae, Sapotaceae and Guttiferae, and with abundant palms, especially rattans, and pandans.

Physiognomically similar freshwater swamps in New Guinea, described by Paijmans (1987), are dominated by species of *Campnosperma*, *Nauclea*, *Neonauclea* (Rubiaceae), *Syzygium* and *Terminalia*, with the fern *Stenochlaena palustris* (Blechnaceae) as a very common bole climber. The sago palm (*Metroxylon sagu*) and pandans often form a dense second stratum, or, where flooding is more frequent, may occur as dominants (Figure 2.25a). The variety exhibited

by freshwater swamp vegetation in New Guinea is clearly shown by the vegetation of the Ramu River, in northern Papua (Figure 2.25b), characterised by arboreal and palm-dominated swamps, or herbaceous swamp, depending on the degree of flooding during the wet season (from Richards, 1996, after Robbins, 1961).

Extensive areas of freshwater swamp forest, maintained by periodic flooding, also remain in Indochina and Myanmar along the Mekong and Irawaddy Rivers, and also locally in Java, where the climate is more strongly seasonal. They are particularly well represented around the northern end of the Tonle Sap, in Cambodia (Figure 2.26), where they are characterised by the genera *Lagerstroemia* and *Barringtonia* (Schmid, 1974;

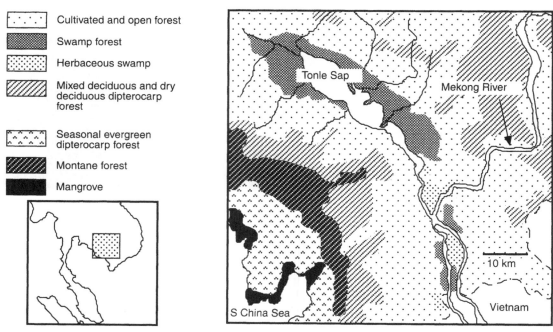

Figure 2.26   Distribution of seasonal freshwater swamp forest and herbaceous marsh around Tonle Sap, Cambodia (adapted from Dy Phon, 1981). Seasonal swamp characterised by *Barringtonia* spp. and *Lagerstroemia* spp.

Dy Phon, 1981). Grass-dominated swamps are widespread to the south of the Tonle Sap, and along the lower reaches of the Mekong. Seasonally inundated grassy swamps, and floating vegetation mats, also sometimes occur along river courses in Borneo, such as in the lakes of the Mahakam River, where they are thought to be a fire climax community (Beccari, 1904; van Steenis, 1957). Natural grasslands are thought to be of very limited extent in areas of everwet climate in SE Asia (Morley, 1981a).

Seasonal swamps are also widespread in New Guinea (Paijmans, 1987). Pure stands of *Melaleuca* spp. (Myrtaceae), without ground flora or epiphytes (possibly maintained by fire), are widespread in the Fly–Merauke river area and Lakekamu Tauri river area, whereas *Barringtonia acutangula* swamps occur in seasonally dry sites in the Fly, Merauke, Meervlakte and Sepik areas. *Livistona brassii* (Palmae) and grass swamps are typical of vast areas of the Fly and Strickland Rivers.

*South America*

The river systems of the South American ever-wet tropics differ from those of SE Asia in that many are subject to seasonal flooding unprecedented in the Far East, the bigger rivers of the Amazon Basin showing water level differences of up to 20 m between the wettest and driest seasons. The character of the extensive swamp vegetation which lines these rivers is primarily dependent on the nutrient levels of the river waters: silt-laden eutrophic, or whitewater rivers bear highly characteristic swamp forests and associated herbaceous swamps termed '*varzea*', whereas blackwater rivers, which are oligotrophic with strongly acid water, are characterised by '*igapo*' swamps (see below). Intermediate, clear water, circumneutral rivers also occur. The differences between these three river types depend on the geology of the substrate: whitewater rivers are mainly sourced in the easily eroded sedimentary rocks which form the Andes; clearwater rivers are sourced from ancient Precambrian shield areas, which have very hard rocks; whereas blackwater rivers rise within the Amazon Basin itself in areas of white podsolic soils.

The *varzea* swamps associated with whitewater rivers may be of an extremely heterogeneous nature, varying from low scrub to a high forest. Also their floras may be quite diverse, in their richer parts sometimes coming close to that of lowland rain forests. In general, however, the floras of such swamp forests remain poorly described. *Varzea* swamp forests are typically composed of huge emergents of *Ceiba pentandra* (Bombacaceae), with common *Symphonia globulifera* (Guttiferae), *Hevea* spp. (Euphorbiaceae), *Viriola surinamensis* (Myristicaceae) (a major timber tree) and many Leguminosae and palms. They exhibit an irregular profile, and fluctuate markedly in diversity, the better developed and more stable containing 70 to 130 species per hectare (Revilla, 1988), with 220 species being recorded in one 10 ha plot (Junk, 1989), whereas diversities of low-lying forests are much lower, pioneer vegetation consisting mainly of palms, such as *Mauritia flexuosa*,

*Euterpe oleracea*, *Raphia* spp. and others. The total flora of *varzea* forests probably exceeds 400 species but displays relatively little regional variation (Kubitszi, 1989). Herbaceous swamps are also associated with whitewater rivers, and may occur as grasslands, developed during the low water season on unstable alluvium, or as floating mats or meadows, characterised by grasses and sedges, the water lily *Victoria amazonica* (Nymphaeaceae) and *Eichornea crassipes* (Pontederiaceae). They may sometimes even bear small trees (Junk, 1970).

### Africa

In Nigeria, high freshwater swamp forest occurs widely behind the mangrove swamps of the Niger Delta (Keay, 1959), and is sometimes dominated by *Symphonia globulifera*, and sometimes *Mitragyna ciliata* with common *Nauclea gilettii* (Rubiaceae), *Cleistopholis patens*, *Uapaca paludosa* (Euphorbiaceae), *Spondianthus preussii* (Anacardiaceae) and the palm *Raphia farinifera* (Figures 2.27; 2.28). Fringing swamp and open areas are characterised by *Pandanus candollea*, the oil palm *Elaeis guineensis*, *Calamus deerata*

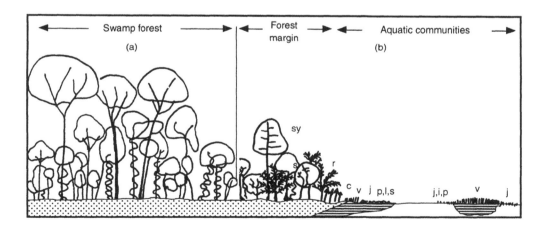

Figure 2.27 (a) Transect through high swamp forest, Afi River Forest Reserve, Niger Delta, with *Cleistopholis patens* (Annonaceae), *Uapaca guineensis* (Euphorbiaceae) and *Treculia* spp. (Moraceae); (b) Marginal swamp forest and aquatic communities, Lekki Lagoon, Nigeria. (c = *Cyrtosperma* (Araceae), i = *Ipomoea* (Convolvulaceae), j = *Jussiaea* (Onagraceae), l = *Lemna* (Lemnaceae), p = *Pistia* (Araceae), r = *Raphia farinifera* (Palmae), s = *Salvinia* (Salviniaceae), sy = *Symphonia globulifera* (Guttiferae) and v = *Vossia*. From Keay (1959).

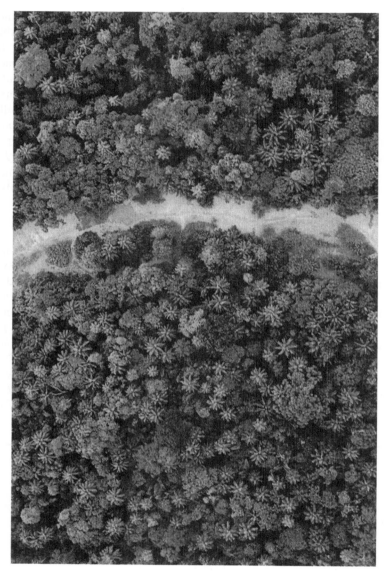

Figure 2.28    *Raphia*-dominated freshwater swamp forest, lining narrow freshwater creek, Niger Delta.
(Courtesy of Shell Nigeria.)

and other climbing palms, which in turn are bordered by grass and fern-dominated marshes.

Tall, multistoreyed seasonally flooded swamp forests, similar to *varzea* of the Amazon, are widespread in the Congo Basin, with *Oubanguia africana* (Scyphopetalaceae) and *Guibourtia demeusii* (Leguminosae) as dominants. Locally, as in the Amazon Basin, *Ceiba pentandra* is sometimes a conspicuous element. Swamps characterised by *Raphia* spp. are very widespread throughout W Africa and the central Congo Basin (Evrard, 1968). The palm *Phoenix reclinata* occupies this niche in E Africa (Thompson and Hamilton, 1983).

## Swamps of oligotrophic, blackwater rivers

Oligotrophic *igapo* swamp forests, which are maintained primarily by the influence of nutrient-poor, blackwater rivers, are widespread in the Amazon–Orinoco rain forest block, and along the Pacific coast of Colombia. They are also widely distributed in Africa, although their distribution there is less clearly delimited compared to South America.

Brunig (1990) describes *igapo* forests from the Rio Negro in Venezuela (Figure 2.12) as very similar in physiognomy to heath forests of Sarawak, and, as noted above, particularly to *kerapah* forests. *Igapo* swamp forests are less rich in species than *varzea* swamps because of low nutrient levels and water stress (Prance, 1979).

In the Congo Basin of Central Africa, oligotrophic swamp forests with *Entandrophragma palustre*, *Coelocaryon botryoides* (Myristicaceae) and *Lasiodiscus mannii* (Rhamnaceae) are widespread and closely resemble *igapo* (Evrard, 1968). In SE Asia, on the other hand, they are less well represented, the best example being the *Pandanus*-dominated swamps of Tasek Bera, in Pahang, Malaysia (Merton, 1962; Morley, 19981b, 1982a).

## 2.5 ECOTONAL VEGETATION

### 2.5.1 Paratropical Rain Forests and the Ecotone Associated with Increasing Latitude

The ecotone relating to increasing latitude is particularly difficult to characterise since it is poorly represented at the present time, and is differently represented in the two hemispheres. As noted in Section 2.1.2, deciduous taxa make an important contribution within the temperate zone of the northern hemisphere, but are virtually absent at southern latitudes. Seasonality gives rise to two different limits for species at their latitudinal boundaries: minimum temperatures determine winter survival, whereas minimum

heat requirements during the summer determine whether reproduction can take place and life cycles are completed (Hutchins, 1947; Ohsawa, 1990). With respect to lowland vegetation, the former determines the latitudinal limits of temperature-sensitive megathermal plants, whereas the latter determines the latitudinal forest limit.

The ecotone in S and E Asia is characterised by four latitudinal zones with contrasting life forms: evergreen mesophyll trees occupy the tropical zone, in which megaphyll taxa are dominant; evergreen notophyll trees characterise subtropical/warm temperate latitudes, in which a few megathermal taxa may be present; deciduous broadleaved trees dominate in the cool temperate zone; and evergreen, needle-leaved trees occur throughout the cold temperate zone (Ohsawa, 1993).

The character of the latitudinal ecotone of tropical rain forest in the northern hemisphere has been widely discussed by Wolfe (1977, 1979) and Ohsawa (1991, 1993). Wolfe, who envisaged that this ecotone includes forests which were the closest analogue to many Early Tertiary tropical aspect vegetation types, noted that the term 'subtropical' *sensu* Richards (1952) was inadequately defined, and 'extra-tropical' *sensu* Wang (1961) misleading, and introduced the term 'paratropical' (para meaning close) for evergreen rain forests delimited by the 20–25° mean annual temperature isotherms and occupying the coastal lowlands between 17 and 26°N. These forests are essentially free of frost, although temperatures as low as −1°C are recorded.

Paratropical forests do not comprise a formation separate from tropical lowland evergreen rain forests, but the term is a useful one for making reference to tropical rain forests close to the latitudinal ecotone. Compared to evergreen rain forests in the equatorial zone, paratropical rain forests are floristically less diverse, with fewer megathermal elements, but with more frost-tolerant species. Otherwise they contain most physiognomic elements of tropical rain forests. Many of the more frost-tolerant

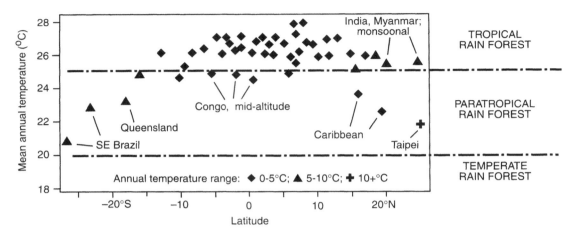

Figure 2.29   Relationship between temperature parameters used by Wolfe (1977, 1979) to delimit tropical and paratropical rain forests, and mean annual temperatures and temperature ranges for tropical lowland and subtropical marginal rain forest stations illustrated by Walsh, in Richards (1996). To avoid crowding, some tropical wet localities have been omitted.

species of the latitudinal ecotone have serrate-margined leaves, and the change in representation of leaf types from dominantly entire to partially serrate provides the most diagnostic feature of rain forests along the latitudinal ecotone, and has been shown to relate closely to mean annual temperature (Figure 4.2). This feature has been widely used by Wolfe (1977, 1979) and others to interpret palaeoclimates for fossil angiosperm floras.

The term 'paratropical' for tropical rain forests at their latitudinal limits, and its temperature limits based on mean annual temperatures, has been widely taken up by palaeobotanists, but not by ecologists. These isotherms do indeed delimit equatorial rain forests from latitudinally marginal sites (Figure 2.29) and deserve attention since mean annual temperatures can be estimated by a number of geological parameters (Chapter 4), but the somewhat arbitrary 18°C mean monthly temperature minimum currently used to delimit the latitudinal boundary of tropical rain forests (Chapter 1) has no geological proxy.

In Australian rain forests, there is also a clear leaf size change associated with this ecotone (Figure 2.30), where tropical rain forest, with

mesophyll-sized leaves, gives way to forests characterised by nanophyll and microphyll leaf sizes, respectively, in warm and cool temperate rain forests (Webb, 1968).

### 2.5.2   Ecotone Associated with Limiting Rainfall

Moving away from tropical rain forests along a gradient of increasing seasonality and decreasing rainfall, there is an overall decrease in diversity, structural complexity and occurrence of emergents, and reduction in stature, together with a decrease in representation of buttresses, cauliflory, lianes and epiphytes. There is an increase in deciduous species, initially among emergents, and subsequently within the canopy, and an increasing tendency toward single species dominance. Leaves change from predominantly mesophyll to microphyll and nanophyll, and sclerophylly tends to predominate. The ground flora becomes more prolific as the forest opens, and grasses become common as forest grades into savanna.

The trends outlined above are clearly seen within West Africa (Figure 2.31), moving

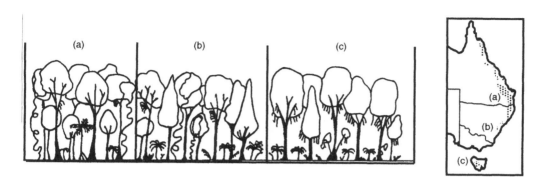

Figure 2.30   Schematic profile along latitudinal rain forest ecotone in eastern Australia (after Williams et al., 1984). (a) 'subtropical' rain forest, dominants *Argyrodendron* spp. (Euphorbiaceae), *Sloanea woollsii* (Tiliaceae), *Dysoxylum fraserianum* (Meliaceae), *Ficus* spp., *Acnema* sp. and *Syzygium* sp.; (b) warm temperate rain forest, dominants *Ceratopetalum apetalum* (Cunoniaceae), *Doryphora sassafrass* (Monimiaceae) and Lauraceae; (c) cool temperate rain forest, with *Nothofagus moorei* (Fagaceae) as sole dominant. Profiles reproduced by permission of Australian Journal of Botany.

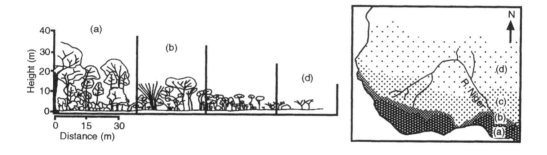

Figure 2.31   Schematic profile through rain forest to savanna, Nigeria, modified from Keay (1959). (a) high forest in rain forest zone, with well-developed structure. Emergents are *Erythrophleum ivoriense* and *Triplochiton scleroxylon*, upper storey with *Strombosia*, *Pausinistasia* and *Diospyros*, grasses are absent. (b) transition woodland at margin of forest outlier in forest–savanna mosaic; forest trees such as *Khaya grandifolia*, *Cola hispida* and *Malacantha alnifolia* occur with savanna species such as *Anogeissus leiocarpus*, *Combretum molle* and the bamboo *Oxtenanthera abyssinica*, field layer of savanna grasses and shrubs. (c) *Isoberlina doka* savanna woodland in Guinea savanna, *I. doka* dominant, with shrubs *Bridelia ferruginea* and *Gardenia eburescens*, field layer of savanna grasses. (d) *Acacia seyal* open savanna in Sudan savanna, trees are *Balanites aegyptica* and *Acacia seyal*, climber is *Capparis corymbosa*, field layer of burnt grasses.

inland, northward from the coast, where they have been described by Keay (1959), Richards (1952) and many others, and are similarly observed in South America (Ellenberg, 1959) and Indochina, where they are outlined by Dudley-Stamp (1925) for Myanmar, and Schmid (1974) for Vietnam and Webb (1968) and Adam (1992) for Australia. The forest/savanna boundary is usually abrupt and maintained by fire (Hopkins, 1974), occurring over a few hundred metres, approximately where rainfall drops below 1500mm or thereabouts.

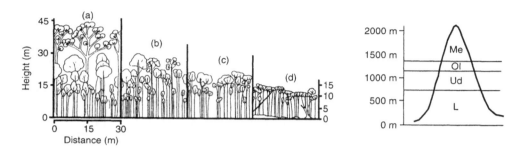

Figure 2.32    Altitudinal forest formation series in Malay Peninsula: (a) lowland evergreen rain forest, 150 m asl; (b) lower montane rain forest 'upper dipterocarp', 780 m; (c) lower montane rain forest, 'oak–laurel' 1500 m asl; (d) upper montane rain forest, 'montane ericaceous'. (From Robbins and Wyatt-Smith, 1964; Whitmore, 1998).

The rain forest ecotone associated with decreasing rainfall thus contrasts strongly with those associated with increasing latitude and altitude (see below).

### 2.5.3    Ecotone Associated with Increasing Altitude

The third ecotone of tropical rain forest relates to altitude. With increasing elevation, the vegetation of tropical mountains exhibits clear changes in structure and physiognomy (Figure 2.32), resembling lowland rain forests at lower altitudes, but grading to low scrub close to the tree line. The changes observed show many parallels with the latitudinal ecotone (Andrade Marin, 1945; van Steenis, 1972), especially with respect to leaf size, and the presence of buttresses, lianes and cauliflory. However, there are also some clear differences; because of the lack of seasons, the minimum temperature limits for tree survival on tropical mountains occur in the opposite order to those of the latitudinal gradient (Ohsawa, 1993), with the boundary limiting minimum heat requirements for tree growth occurring well below the level at which coldest month temperatures are too low for winter survival (Figure 2.33). The latitude at which the two limits coincide corresponds to

the boundary between the Palaeotropical and Holarctic floristic kingdoms (Ohsawa, 1990).

Although montane vegetation exhibits a more or less uniform reduction in tree species richness with altitude (Flenley, 1979a; Morley, 1982b), structure and physiognomy show sharp breaks, on which basis they are classified into lower, upper and subalpine rain forest formations (Figures 2.33; 2.34, Table 2.6), each clearly represented in each tropical continent.

Lower montane forest (Figure 2.35) is of slightly lower stature than lowland evergreen rain forest, is lacking in emergents, and is generally without big woody climbers, buttresses and cauliflory, although bole climbers and epiphytes are abundant. Upper montane forest, on the other hand, is sharply demarcated by a microphyll-dominated canopy of smaller, more slender trees with gnarled limbs and dense subcrowns (Whitmore, 1998), generally festooned with ferns and bryophytes. There is a further decrease in stature, and leaf size, in subalpine forests. The altitude at which formational boundaries occur is dependent primarily on soil type with respect to the lowland/lower montane transition, with more humus-rich soils occurring in the lower montane zone, whereas the lower/upper montane ecotone is dependent on a combination of climatic, topographic and edaphic factors, and may be markedly depressed on steep slopes and along ridges (P.S. Ashton,

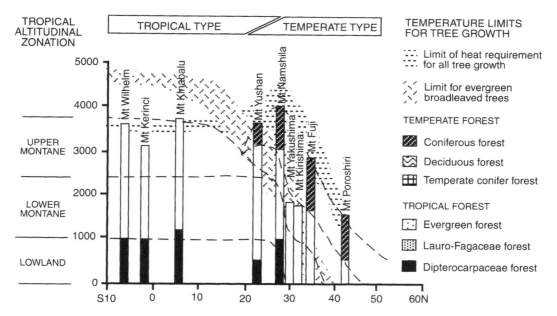

Figure 2.33 Altitudinal and latitudinal representation of forest zones in SE and E Asia (compiled from Ohsawa, 1990, Fig. 6, and 1993, Figs 2 and 4). The limit for evergreen broadleaved trees is the −1°C mean temperature for the coldest month, whereas the limit of heat requirement for all tree growth is the 15°C month temperature sum (the annual sum of mean monthly temperatures over 5°C). Reproduced by permission of Journal of Vegetation Science and Journal of Ecology.

personal communication). These boundaries also tend to be higher on very large mountains, since lapse rates tend to be less steep over large mountain masses (e.g. Hastenrath, 1985; Parrish and Barron, 1986). Tropical montane forests are mostly evergreen, although on East African mountains, where rainfall is seasonal, evergreen forests grade to montane woodlands and scrub (Hamilton, 1982).

At the same time as the physiognomy of montane forests changes, there is a corresponding floristic change, with the typical megatherm families diminishing and subtropical and temperate taxa increasing. These are termed mesothermal and microthermal taxa respectively. Typical families rich in (principally herbaceous) microtherm taxa are Gentianaceae, Labiatae, Liliaceae, Primulaceae, Ranunculaceae and Violaceae. There is also an increase in the representation of conifers in montane forests, typically of *Podocarpus* (Podocarpaceae) in the Andes and East African mountains,

but also with other southern conifers such as *Dacrydium*, *Phyllocladus* (Podocarpaceae) and *Libocedrus* (Cupressaceae) in the eastern tropics. In Indochina, northern conifers such as *Abies*, *Cunninghamia*, *Fokienia*, *Keeteleeria* and *Picea* intermingle with southern podocarps, and *Pinus* (Pinaceae) extends from here to its only southern hemisphere locality in Central Sumatra.

There is a greater tendency toward anemophily (wind pollination) in many montane forest trees compared to the lowlands, with wind pollination occurring in the conifers as well as oaks, Betulaceae, *Engelhardia* (Juglandaceae), *Myrica* (Myricaceae) and others. Pollen of these taxa is often transported great distances, principally by rivers; for instance, low frequencies of *Alnus* pollen occurs regularly in the sediments of the Orinoco Delta, 4000 km from their source (Muller, 1959). Montane pollen forms a significant component of assemblages from marine Tertiary sediments in each tropical

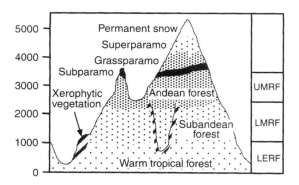

Figure 2.34 Altitudinal distribution of montane rain forest formations in the Colombian Andes. Lowland evergreen rain forest is characterised by *Byrsonima*, *Iriartea* and *Mauritia*; lower montane (Subandean) forest has *Acalypha*, *Alchornea* and *Cecropia* as main taxa; upper montane forest (Andean forest) consists mainly of *Podocarpus*, *Hedyosmum*, *Weinmannia*, *Quercus*, *Alnus*, *Vallea*, *Myrsine*, *Symplocos*, *Ilex*, *Juglans*, *Miconia*, *Myrica* and *Eugenia*; subparamo has Ericaceae, *Hypericum*, Compositae, *Polylepis* and *Acaena*, whereas grass paramo is rich in grasses and temperate herbs (Cleef and Hoogheimstra, 1984; Hoogheimstra and Ran, 1994). Reproduced by permission of Elsevier Science.

area. Making meaningful interpretations about the changing character of montane vegetation through time, based on pollen grains which have been transported such great distances, is a formidable palynological challenge.

## 2.6 ECOLOGY VERSUS PALAEOECOLOGY

Ecology is the study of the structure and function of nature. Ecological observations are made through the analysis of patterns within and between organisms and environment, and ecology is successful with respect to extant communities since there are numerous parameters which can be measured, and compared. With respect to fossil data, this is not always the case, as a single fossil resembling a 'tropical' plant may or may not provide evidence for the previous occurrence of tropical vegetation. However, a combination of biological and palaeoenvironmental factors may exhibit a pattern which

Table 2.6 Characters of structure and physiognomy used to define the principal montane rain forest formations (Whitmore, 1998). Reproduced by permission of Oxford University Press.

| Formation | Lowland evergreen rain forest | Lower montane rain forest | Upper montane rain forest |
|---|---|---|---|
| Canopy height | 25–45 m | 15–33 m | 1.5–18 m |
| Emergent trees | Characteristic to 60(80) m tall | Often absent, to 37 m tall | Usually absent, to 26 m tall |
| Pinnate leaves | Frequent | Rare | Very rare |
| Main leaf size class | Mesophyll | Mesophyll | Microphyll |
| Buttresses | Usually frequent and large | Uncommon, small | Usually absent |
| Cauliflory | Frequent | Rare | Absent |
| Big woody climbers | Abundant | Usually none | None |
| Bole climbers | Often abundant | Frequent to abundant | Very few |
| Vascular epiphytes | Frequent | Abundant | Frequent |
| Non-vascular epiphytes | Occasional | Occasional to abundant | Often abundant |

Figure 2.35 Lower montane forest, 1600–1700 m, Kerinci–Seblat National Park, Sumatra. Forests with variegated crowns in foreground are dominated by *Eugenia* (Myrtaceae), *Ficus* (Moraceae), *Quercus* and *Lithocarpus* (Fagaceae), *Schima* (Theaceae) and *Turpinia* (Staphyleaceae). More uniform toned forests in background with common *Podocarpus* (Podocarpaceae), *Schima* (Theaceae), *Symingtonia* (Hamamelidaceae) and *Weinmannia* (Cunoniaceae).

provides unequivocal evidence. The criteria which the ecologist uses to define tropical rain forest communities may not be preserved in the fossil record at all, due to taphonomy (factors relating to the differential preservation of fossils), in which case alternative indicators are sought which may be preserved as fossils. In the following two chapters, the fossil and lithological criteria which may throw some light on the former occurrence of tropical rain forests are reviewed.

# CHAPTER 3

# Geological Time Framework, Palaeoecological and Palaeoclimate Definitions

The past distribution of tropical vegetation has varied on several different time scales. On the one hand, long-term changes, possibly related to changes in the proportions of 'greenhouse' gases in the atmosphere, and the disposition of the Earth's lithospheric plates, have caused climate changes on a time scale of millions of years. During the time of evolution of tropical rain forests, at least since the Early Tertiary, the trend has been mostly one of stepwise global temperature decline, clearly indicated by the oxygen isotope record from deep sea cores (Figure 3.1). On the other hand, global climates have also changed on much shorter term time scales, as a result of cyclical changes in the level of insolation reaching the Earth, due to cyclical variations in the eccentricity, tilt and precession of the Earth's orbit around the Sun (Figure 3.2). These short-term climatic changes, although epitomised by glacial and interglacial climates of the Quaternary, have in fact occurred throughout geological time. The degree of change within these short-term cycles may be greater than the long-term ones, and, in order to make sense out of the seemingly chaotic fossil record, it is necessary to have a reasonably clear idea as to the scale of change to which a particular set of palaeofloral data should be compared.

## 3.1  SEQUENCE STRATIGRAPHY

Quaternary studies at low latitudes (presented in detail in Chapters 6–10) clearly show that

'interglacial', high sea level intervals experienced warm and wet climates, with the widespread occurrence of tropical rain forests, whereas 'glacial', low sea level intervals were cooler and drier, with the more restricted representation of rain forests (Flenley, 1979a). Also, periods of maximum sea level rise, such as the beginning of the Holocene or the beginning of the last interglacial, tended to be wettest, and at these times rain forests were most widespread (e.g. Morley, 1996; Dupont and Wienelt, 1996). For the Quaternary, the availability of radiocarbon dates, or attribution to oxygen isotope stages (Figure 3.3), provides the control necessary to place data into the perspective of late Quaternary climatic fluctuations, but misinterpretations are likely for older periods where such control is lacking. The sedimentary record, however, gives a clear indication of whether sea levels were high or low throughout geological time. The unifying concept of sequence stratigraphy, developed by Vail and his co-workers in the 1970s (Vail et al., 1977; Wilgus et al., 1988) has changed the way in which stratigraphers view the process of sedimentation by emphasising that eustacy is as important as sediment supply and subsidence in determining how and where sediments are deposited. They proposed that sediments were deposited in genetically associated packages which they termed systems tracts, depending on whether sea levels were low, rising, or high, and that falling sea levels resulted in periods of erosion, creating bounding unconformities (Figure

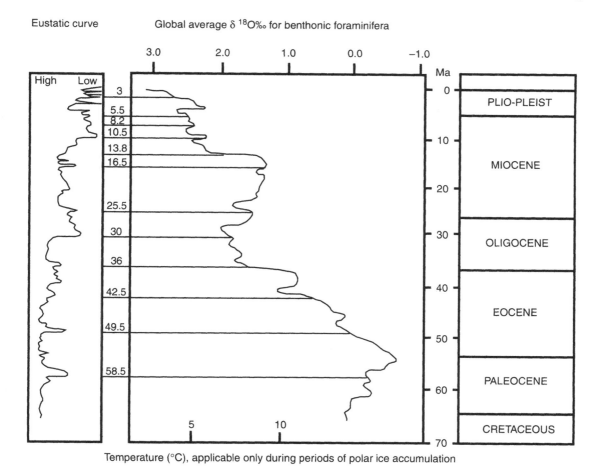

Figure 3.1   Generalised oxygen isotope curve for benthonic (bottom dwelling) foraminifera through the Cenozoic (from Miller et al., 1987). The ratio of $^{16}O$ to $^{18}O$ for benthonic foraminifera provides a proxy for high latitude surface marine temperatures (Hudson and Anderson, 1989), and therefore is a guide to global temperature trends. The precise correlation with temperature depends on the presence of polar ice. The temperature scale shown is applicable only for the late Neogene, when there were well-developed polar ice caps. The oxygen isotope curve is compared to the third-order eustatic sea level curve of Haq et al. (1988), based on sequence stratigraphy. There is a clear correlation between times of falling global temperatures, based on the oxygen isotope record, and periods of sea level fall, based on sequence stratigraphic data.

3.4). Sediment packages deposited during low sea level phases form the lowstand systems tract, are here termed 'lowstand' sediments, and are mainly deposited in a distal setting in a sedimentary basin, off the continental shelf. Sediments deposited during rising sea level phases form the transgressive systems tract, and are here termed 'transgressive' sediments,

whereas sediments deposited when sea levels are high form the highstand systems tract, and here are simply referred to as 'highstand' deposits. Transgressive, and highstand sediments are predominantly deposited on the continental shelf. Each tripartite group of systems tracts is termed a 'sequence', and is separated from others by bounding unconformities, created by

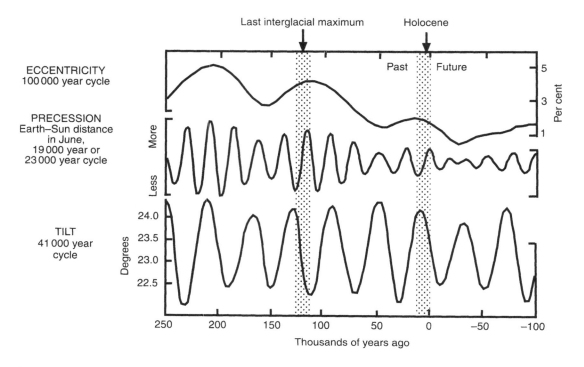

Figure 3.2   Changes in eccentricity, tilt and precession of the Earth over the last 250 000 years, and with a 100 000-year projection into the future. Planetary movements give rise to variations in the gravitational field, which in turn cause changes in the geometry of the Earth's orbit. These changes can be calculated for past and future times (Imbrie and Imbrie, 1979). Reproduced by permission of John Imbrie.

erosion which occurred during phases of falling sea levels.

Knowledge of the systems tract allows palaeobotanical data to be viewed in a context of sea level, and hence climate change, even when the precise stratigraphic position of a sediment package remains unknown. This is very important when constructing models of vegetation change on a global scale through the Tertiary. The availability of two sets of palaeobotanical data from the same general time interval, with one derived from a highstand depositional phase, and the other from a lowstand, would create confusion when viewed in isolation, but when placed into a systems tract context, their different assemblages would be easy to explain.

A further implication of the sequence stratigraphic model is that 'highstand' and 'low-stand' sediment packages are rarely juxtaposed (Figure 3.5) and also differ in their mode of sedimentation, and likelihood of preservation of plant fossils. Highstand sediments are mostly deposited in shallow water settings on continental shelves by normal fluvial and marine depositional processes. In deep marine settings, highstand sediments are represented by very thin, condensed pelagic muds, which, with the exception of low concentrations of palynomorphs, are void of terrestrially derived microfossils. Lowstand sediments, on the other hand, are generally absent from the continental shelves, and are mostly deposited by mass flow processes in deep marine settings. Clearly, plant fossils are most likely to be preserved in highstand settings, where they stand the best chance of being *in situ*. The plant fossil record is therefore strongly biased toward the high sea

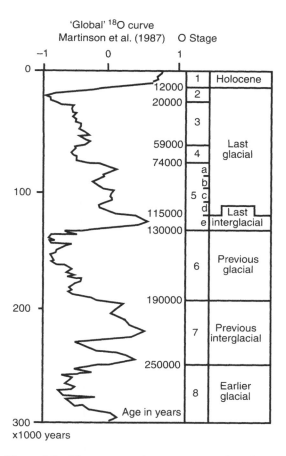

'Global' $^{18}$O curve
Martinson et al. (1987)    O Stage

Figure 3.3 The oxygen isotope curve based on planktonic (surface dwelling) foraminifera provides an index of the amount of ice locked up in the polar ice caps, and therefore reflects sea levels, and indirectly relates to sea surface temperature. Warm ('interglacial') and cool ('glacial') phases revealed by the curve have been referred to oxygen isotope 'stages' numbered sequentially back in time from the Holocene. These stages now extend back into the latest Miocene, with over 100 being defined, and in deep marine sedimentary successions which bear planktonic foraminifera, permit very precise age interpretations to be made.

level, 'interglacial'-type deposits which occupy only 30% of the sedimentary, and half of the time record, rather than those sediments deposited during periods of low sea level. It follows that when viewed outside a sequence stratigraphic framework, palaeobotanical data

are likely to reflect vegetation distributions during the warmest part of climatic cycles, and seriously to underestimate the nature of vegetation during the cooler part.

An understanding of the patterns of sea level fluctuations through time is also important from another viewpoint. Lowstand phases were the main periods for plant migration between continents. Many of the first appearances of pollen types from well-dated Neogene sequences can be demonstrated to appear immediately following major lowstands, suggesting that migration occurred during lowstand phases, with evolution of the parent plants occurring elsewhere. The sudden appearance of such taxa often provide good datums for palynological correlation, whether or not their association with a sea level lowstand phase is understood. In order to make judgements as to whether the pollen record supports the 'punctuated equilibrium' hypothesis of evolution (Eldredge and Gould, 1972) as opposed to gradual change, the positions of the first appearances of palynomorphs in the fossil record needs to be checked to see whether they coincide with sequence boundaries or transgressive surfaces, in which case, their appearance may simply relate to migration when sea levels were low!

## 3.2  TIME FRAMEWORK

It is a preconception of sequence stratigraphic theory that the sea level changes which were responsible for individual systems tracts and sequence boundaries were of global extent. Since the Eocene, this is highly probable, since most sea level changes over this time period were glacio-eustatic, and there is a strong correlation between sea level changes and phases of climatic deterioration (Figure 3.1). Whether this premise applies to Eocene and older sediments is still a matter of controversy (Hallam, 1992). The global eustatic curve established for the Tertiary and Cretaceous by Haq et al. (1988) is used here for discussion of sea level changes, and because of this the chronostratigraphic

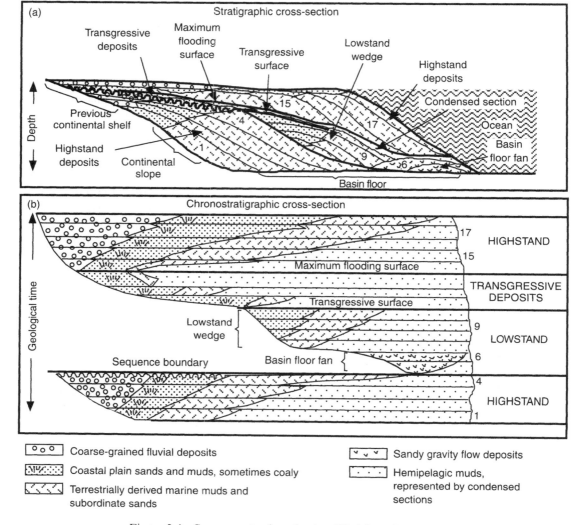

Figure 3.4   Sequence stratigraphy (modified from Haq, 1991).

(a) The pattern of sediment deposition along a typical continental margin during a single cycle of sea level change. Sediment packages are numbered 1–18, each representing a successively younger phase of sedimentation. Packages 1–4 accumulated during a phase of high sea level on the previous continental shelf; as sea levels fell, this package was eroded, and sediments dumped by gravity flow processes on the basin floor in a lowstand fan (sediment packages 5–6); as sea levels subsequently rose, sediments continued to accumulate off the former continental shelf until the shelf break was reached (sediment packages 7–10), following which time deposition on the former continental shelf resumed with the transgressive systems tract (sediment packages 11–13); when sea levels cease to rise, near the peak of the sea level cycle, progradation began, resulting in the formation of a delta (sediment packages 14–18).

   Mangrove swamps are most extensively distributed during the transgressive systems tract (Morley, 1996), and freshwater swamps most widespread during deposition of the highstand systems tract. Macrofossils will be preferentially preserved within these two systems tracts, occurrences of which will clearly be biased toward periods of high sea level and warmer climates.

   (b) The same diagram as (a) placed into a chronostratigraphic framework.

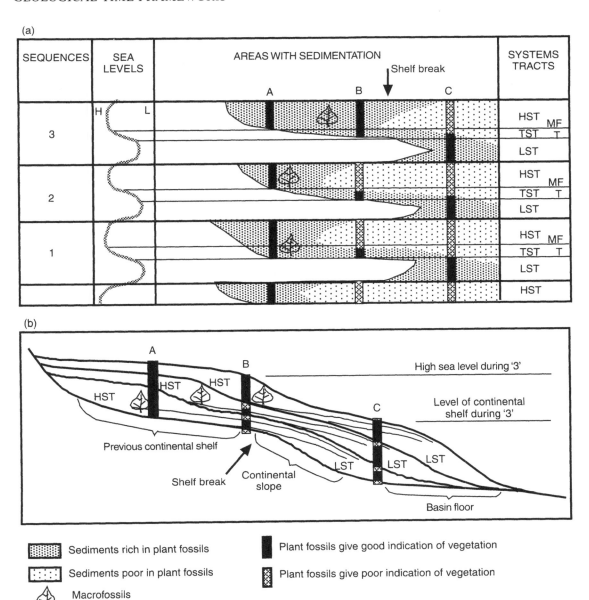

Figure 3.5 Differential representation of high sea level and low sea level sediments in continental margin and deep marine settings: (a) placed into a chronostratigraphic framework, (b) actual depositional setting. Since lowstand sediments are typically preserved off the continental shelf on the basin floor, and transgressive and highstand sediments mostly on the continental shelf, sedimentary profiles from different positions relative to the former shelf break will give conflicting information. Sedimentary profile A will sample only highstand, warm climate sediments, and in the field may appear as a continuous succession without obvious stratigraphic breaks, plant fossils providing the impression of continuously warm climates. Profile B samples a stacked succession of transgressive and highstand sediments, and will also give the impression of continuously warm climates. Profile C, on the other hand will sample cool climate lowstand intervals, with high sea level, warm climate episodes being represented by intervals which are poor in plant microfossils.

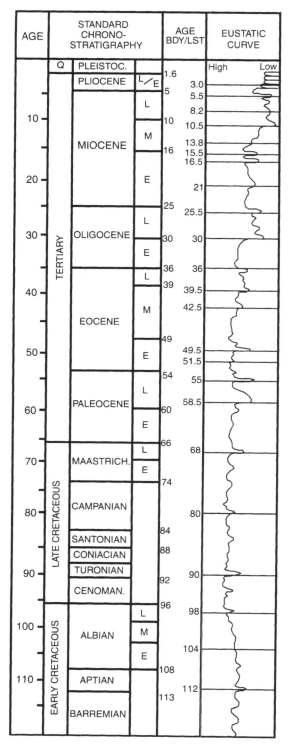

time scale of Haq et al. (1988) is also used (Figure 3.6). This time scale differs in detail from the more widely used scheme of Harland et al. (1990) and the more accurate scheme (for the Tertiary) of Berggren et al. (1995). Most precise references to absolute time have been made through cross-referencing palynological events against the planktonic foraminiferal zonation scheme of Blow (1979) and the low latitude nannofossil zonation scheme of Martini (1971), which have then been correlated with the absolute time scale by reference to Haq et al. (1988).

## 3.3  PALAEOECOLOGICAL AND PALAEOCLIMATE DEFINITIONS

In Chapters 5 to 11 of this book, evidence for the former distribution of tropical rain forest is considered by reference to the occurrence of fossils of megathermal plants, to the occurrence of plant associations indicative of tropical rain forest, and other evidence for rain forest climates. The distributions of tropical rain forests for six 'time slices' within the Tertiary are then mapped in Chapter 13.

Throughout, the definitions of forest formations of Wolfe (1971, 1979) summarised in Figure 3.7 are followed; reference to 'tropical rain forest' infers the presence of a multi-storeyed, closed-canopy forest (unless indicated otherwise), an everwet, or only slightly seasonal climate, and *mean* annual temperatures exceeding 25°C. When dealing with former occurrences of megathermal vegetation outside the tropical zone, reference to 'paratropical rain forest' infers the presence of a similar, although perhaps less complex rain forest, but with average

Figure 3.6  Time framework and global eustatic curve according to Haq et al. (1988). In the third main column, figures to the left (Bdy) are the ages, in Ma, of stage (for the Cretaceous) and epoch (for the Tertiary) boundaries; figures to the right (Lst) indicate the age in Ma of the main periods of sea level lowstand according to the eustatic curve.

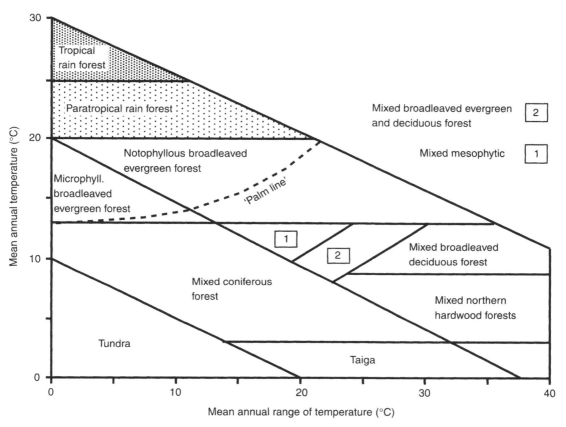

Figure 3.7   Plot of mean annual temperature versus mean annual range of temperature for different climatic and vegetation types, showing the temperature relationships between tropical rain forest, and paratropical rain forest (Wolfe, 1971, 1977, 1978, 1979). The 'palm line' *sensu* Wing and Greenwood (1993) provides an idea of the climatic limit of megathermal taxa.

annual temperatures within the range of 20 to 25°C. Many essentially megathermal taxa may occur outside these limits, where climates are moisture deficient, or highly equable. With respect to the latter, instances where low frequencies of megathermal taxa occur in associations which clearly suggest warm rain temperate forests, but highly equable climates, are discussed in the text, but excluded from the maps.

The detailed criteria by which the former distributions of rain forests and rain forest climates can be determined form the subject of Chapter 4.

# CHAPTER 4

# Geological Evidence for Rain Forests

This chapter summarises the features of fossils and sediments which could have a bearing on the former distribution of tropical rain forests. Evidence may be in the form of fossils of plant taxa which are found in present-day rain forests (although care must be exercised to ensure that such taxa are not *relict* to rain forests, previously occurring in other vegetation types) or in the form of physiognomic features which are restricted to closed-canopy, megathermal vegetation. Faunal evidence may also provide useful information; the most convincing evidence being from vertebrate body size variations within a population, and habit. Palaeobotanical records may be in the form of macrofossils (eg, wood, leaves and seeds) either *in situ*, or transported, and microfossils may include pollen, spores and cuticular fragments. A surprising new source of information is from geochemical fossils, such as the derivative compounds of resins which are produced by some plant taxa. In addition, the presence of temperature-sensitive marine microfossils (such as larger foraminifera), corals, palaeosols, climatically sensitive lithologies and isotope data provide evidence for the former occurrence of rain forest climates.

## 4.1 FLORA

Macrofossils and microfossils provide complementary evidence with respect to past vegetation types. Pollen and spores are particularly valuable for the establishment of regional vegetation patterns through time, since they are composed of resilient sporopollenin and are readily preserved as fossils; they are produced, and deposited, in very large numbers and they can be easily extracted from most argillaceous deposits, including deep, oceanic sediments. Pollen and spores are the most widely distributed of all fossil types, since they are deposited throughout both non-marine and marine depositional systems, and may be extracted equally well from 'high' and 'low' sea level sediment packages (Section 3.1). Because of their wide dispersal, they tend to provide a better picture of the 'regional' vegetation than plant macrofossils, except in small depositional basins such as the terrestrial sites typically studied within the Late Quaternary, where they may also show variations in the local vegetational succession. Good macrofossil assemblages are rare in the sedimentary record, since they are preserved only under ideal conditions of deposition and preservation. Because leaves tend to be damaged when transported, well-preserved assemblages invariably reflect very local vegetation types, and there is also a bias toward 'high' sea level, 'interglacial' sediment packages. However, where it does occur, a rich leaf flora provides unequivocal information about the physiognomy of former vegetation.

Integrated studies of both macrofossils and pollen from the same sedimentary successions provide the most convincing examples of vegetational reconstruction, an excellent example being the reconstruction of mid-Cretaceous vegetation in the eastern USA, which is described in some detail in Chapter 5.

There are two main approaches to the determination of former vegetation using plant fossils. The first is the nearest living relative approach, which assumes that the ecology of a Tertiary species was similar to that of its nearest extant relative; palynology relies almost exclusively on this approach. The second distinguishes morphological features of leaves, wood or fruit which today are restricted to, or characteristic of, a particular vegetation type. Both methods contribute valuable information, but the morphological approach is more useful in older sediments, when only a few of the plant taxa recorded can be referred to extant families.

### 4.1.1 Plant Macrofossils

#### *Leaves*

Although there are abundant leaf fossil determinations in the literature, a very high proportion have only limited reliability. Leaf physiognomy, however, can be correlated closely with vegetation types irrespective of botanical affinity, and therefore, emphasis is usually placed on form, rather than affinity. The main diagnostic features of leaf fossils, summarised by Upchurch and Wolfe (1987), are as follows.

#### *Leaf size*

Leaves are large in understoreys of humid, evergreen forest, and decrease in size with decreasing temperature and seasonality. Mesophyll and megaphyll size classes are characteristic of megathermal closed forests, although large leaf sizes may occur at high latitudes under conditions of low light levels and moderate temperatures (Wolfe, 1985), and are also characteristic of riparian and eutrophic swamps at both tropical and temperate latitudes (P.S. Ashton, personal communication).

#### *Leaf margin*

There is a close correlation between the ratio of entire- (Figure 4.1) to serrate-margined leaves

Figure 4.1 Entire-margined leaf, length 7.5 cm, Lower Bagshot Sands, Bournemouth, UK.

and mean annual temperature (Bailey and Sinnot, 1916; Wolfe, 1978). Serrate-margined leaves are virtually absent from tropical rain forest settings, and become progressively better represented in cooler (Figure 4.2), and more seasonal climates (Figure 4.3). Serrate margins also correlate with thin, deciduous leaves

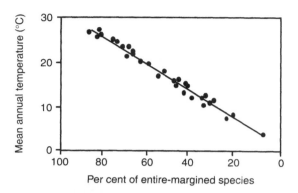

Figure 4.2  The percentage of species with entire-margined leaves increases in direct proportion to mean annual temperature (based on E Asian humid to mesic broadleaved forests (after Wolfe. 1978).

(Givnish, 1979). The ratio of entire to serrate leaves has evolved differently in the southern and northern hemispheres, with increased numbers of serrate-leaved taxa in the northern hemisphere. This is largely due to the rarity of the deciduous habit in the southern hemisphere.

*Leaf texture*

Thick, xeromorphic leaves typify evergreen, megathermal and mesothermal vegetation, and thin, hygromorphic leaves are typically deciduous, and predominate in microthermal climax and successional mesothermal vegetation.

*Drip tips*

Drip tips (Figure 2.3) are particularly characteristic of leaves in humid environments, especially in the understorey of multistratal forests

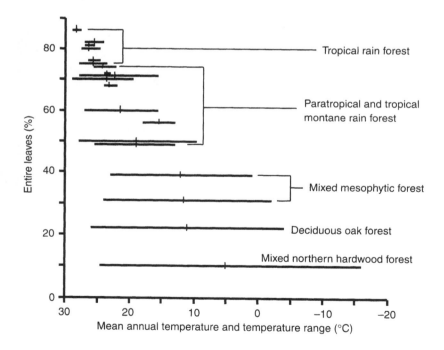

Figure 4.3  The relationship between the percentage of species with entire-margined leaves, and mean annual temperature and temperature range (from Flenley, 1979a). The horizontal lines give an indication of mean annual temperature range, but are plotted equally either side of the mean, and do not therefore indicate mean maxima and minima. Reproduced by permission of John Flenley.

(Richards, 1952). Drip tips have been shown to accelerate draining the moisture from the leaf surface (Whitmore, 1998). Deciduous leaves generally lack leaf tips, perhaps due to their shorter life span.

## Leaf shape

Narrow (stenophyllous) leaves characterise streamside plants (Richards, 1952; van Steenis, 1981), broad, cordate, typically palmately veined leaves occur on lianes, sprawling shrubs in successional vegetation and light-gap colonisers (Figure 2.4), whereas lobed leaves (Figure 4.4) are characteristic of successional or understorey plants (Givnish, 1979).

## Wood anatomy

Fossil woods can often be determined with confidence on the basis of anatomical features (Figure 4.5). Also, since annual variations in temperature or precipitation may result in the formation of growth rings, the absence, or presence of only weak rings may indicate growth in a climate without marked seasonality.

Figure 4.4   Lobed leaves, *Sterculia* sp. (Sterculiaceae), Bogor, Indonesia.

## Seeds

Seed size in living plants is correlated to some extent with the habit of the parent plant, and the mode of dispersal of the diaspore. As a general rule, seedlings arising from small seeds need to photosynthesise immediately in order to survive; hence taxa with small seeds tend to occur in open, light-rich areas. Seedlings arising from large seeds may grow to a substantial size supported jointly by seed storage tissues and photosynthesis and, as a result, large-seeded taxa commonly occur in closed, light-poor communities, where small-seeded seedlings would perish (Wing and Tiffney, 1987). Many large seeds are dispersed by frugivorous vertebrates. Fossil records of large seeds may therefore provide strong evidence for closed-canopy, multistoreyed forests. Curiously, how-

ever, small seeds are also characteristic of many shade-tolerant rain forest understorey shrubs and treelets (P.S. Ashton, personal communication).

Many seed fossils can be convincingly referred to megathermal families, but identification of seeds is a complex process requiring both a detailed knowledge of seeds of extant plants, and also an understanding of the process of diagenesis (the process of lithification) on seed preservation. Often, a single seed species may exhibit a great diversity of appearances in the fossil state. Collinson (1983) emphasises this point by considering the different possibilities of preservation in the hypothetical case of an orange. The fossil may be: a cast of all parts internal to the skin (i.e., with the outside looking like the inside of the skin);

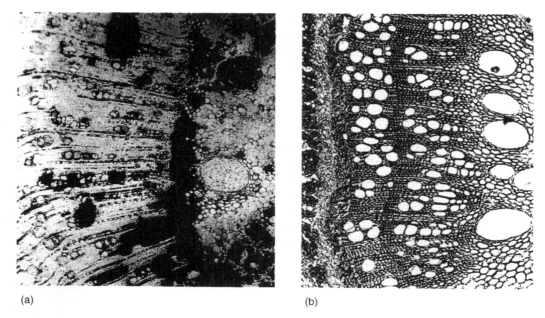

(a)                                                    (b)

Figure 4.5   (a) Polished transverse face of fossil twig *Anisopteroxylon ramunculiformis* (Dipterocarpaceae) from the Eocene London Clay showing the medullary canals, pith parenchyma cells and vessel distribution (× 38), compared to (b) transverse section of stem of recent SE Asian species *Anisoptera oblonga*, showing same features (× 120). Photos kindly provided by Imogen Poole.

the orange minus the skin, revealing the segments; individual segments; casts of the internal cavities (locules) which contain the seeds; the seeds themselves; and the internal casts of the seeds!

### 4.1.2   Plant Microfossils

#### *Pollen and spores*

Pollen and spores exhibit a great diversity of surface sculpture, structure and apertural arrangement. Morphological variation occurs at different taxonomic levels in different families. Some exhibit hardly any differentiation, such as Graminae and Myrtaceae (termed stenopalynous families by Erdtman, 1952) and, in some instances, related families have the same type, such as Melastomataceae and Combretaceae, or Chenopodiaceae and Amaranthaceae. At the other extreme, families may show considerable variation, such as Euphorbiaceae and Acanthaceae, and Erdtman termed these eurypalynous There are even some families in which most individual species can be differentiated, and two of these have an extensive fossil record. In Sonneratiaceae, all species can be differentiated (Muller, 1969) and are all recorded as fossils (Morley, 1991), and, in Alangiaceae, some species include several pollen types whereas, in other instances, pairs of related species possess the same type (Reitsma, 1969; Morley, 1982c). Most families fall somewhere between these extremes, however, and, as a general rule of thumb, the palynomorph diversity probably gives an idea of the *generic* diversity of a fossil flora, irrespective of age (cf. Germeraad et al., 1968).

One complication, in dealing with tropical rain forest floras, is that rain forests have acted as a refuge for a large number of primitive taxa, and many of these have very generalised pollen types which are virtually the same. This is especially the case with tricolpate pollen in the groups Dilleniidae and Rosidae. Such taxa will be virtually without a fossil pollen record.

There was initial reticence as to whether palynology could provide any information as to the history of tropical rain forest vegetation, owing to the prevalence there of zoophily over anemophily, absence of strong winds, and the high diversity of rain forest floras (Faegri, 1966). However, Flenley (1973), through the study of surface samples, showed that tropical vegetation types could readily be differentiated on the basis of their pollen production, and that differences with palynological studies from temperate latitudes were only of degree. Clearly, consideration needs to be given as to whether pollen was derived from wind- or insect-pollinated plants, but in instances where percentage contribution to vegetation is compared to percentage pollen production, many zoophilous taxa may clearly be significant pollen producers (Figure 4.6) and Muller's (1981) evaluation of the angiosperm fossil record clearly shows that although there is a more complete history for anemophilous plants, zoophilous taxa are represented by a substantial fossil pollen record. The likelihood of preservation of pollen also needs to be taken into account; for instance, members of the important family Lauraceae presently produce pollen which does not fossilise, although, curiously, some Early Tertiary pollen types are convincingly attributed to this family (Muller, 1981).

## Naming fossil pollen

Fossil pollen is generally formally described according to the rules of botanical nomenclature. However, this often results in some confusion, partly because the details of the code concerning the nomenclature of fossil pollen which can be confidently attributed to extant plant families has not yet been properly worked out, with the result that most names for fossil pollen from the younger Tertiary are technically invalid. Another problem is that there is no clear consensus concerning the delimitation of

either fossil pollen 'species' or 'genera'. Following the Code also preserves names which were initially somewhat ambitiously compared to representatives of extant families before the pollen morphology of those families was properly known; hence, the Indian Eocene pollen genus *Pellicieroipollenites* (named after the South American mangrove genus *Pelliciera*) is really an *Alangium*, *Compositoipollenites*, from the European Palaeogene, is a member of Icacinaceae, and *Dipterocarpacearumpollenites*, from Roumania, has nothing to do with dipterocarps, but is noteworthy in having the longest name of any fossil pollen genus!

Informal characterisation of fossil pollen is also widely used, generally by reference to an extant taxon (usually a genus) to which the pollen most closely compares, and in cases where the pollen type is similar to that of two or more extant taxa, the suffix 'type' is added. This approach has been severely criticised as 'backwards systematics' by Hughes (1976, 1994), encouraging the unrealistic extension of histories of extant taxa back through time. Such criticism is blind, since it is only through the study of modern pollen that the observer becomes aware of the true taxonomic value of pollen morphological variation, much of which is ignored in fossil material when viewed in isolation.

## Use of palynomorph names

In general, many Oligocene and younger pollen can be compared to that of extant taxa with confidence. However, caution needs to be exercised in comparing Eocene and older material since, although light microscope studies may reveal superficial similarity, examination with the scanning and transmission electron microscope may show hidden differences of sculpture and structure. In the text which follows, a standard format is maintained to permit pollen affinities to be presented in a manner which is informative to the non-stratigraphic palynologist, but not excessively cumbersome (Table 4.1). Reference is made to an extant taxon with

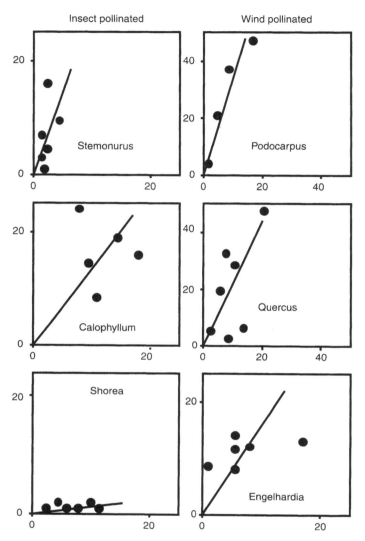

Figure 4.6  Comparison of percentage pollen production and percentage basal area of some characteristic wind- and insect-pollinated rain forest trees from Kalimantan peat swamp. Vertical axis shows percentage arboreal pollen, horizontal axis shows percentage basal area. Basal area is the cross-sectional area of tree boles at breast height based on girth measurements. Percentage basal area provides a good index of percentage contribution of tree species to vegetation. Percentage pollen production was determined from the analysis of the pollen content of the surface peat layer from directly beneath the enumerated stands (Morley, 1982b).
Reproduced by permission of *Journal of Biogeography*.

which a fossil pollen type compares if this is known, along with an indication of its family. In cases where a pollen type compares to two or more taxa, it is followed by the suffix 'type'. However, if the affinity of the pollen type is not clear (perhaps its parent plant is extinct), it is referred to a form-genus, again followed by an indication of its family, if known. A full list of the fossil form-taxa used within this account, together with their affinities, is given in the

Table 4.1 Types of names applied to fossil pollen.

| Name of pollen | Taxonomic status |
| --- | --- |
| *Sonneratia apetala* (Sonneratiaceae) | Only *Sonneratia apetala* |
| *Alangium kurzii* type (Alangiaceae) | In more than one species, i.e. in either *Alangium kurzii* or *A. rotundifolium* |
| *Alnus* (Betulaceae) | Only *Alnus* |
| *Shorea* type (Dipterocarpaceae) | In more than one genus, i.e. in *Shorea* or *Hopea* |
| Gramineae | Pollen referable only to family |
| *Palmaepollenites kutchensis* (Iguanurinae) | Extinct taxon, within Palmae, subtribe Iguanurinae |
| *Proxapertites operculatus* (Nypoidae) | Extinct taxon, within subfamily Nypoidae |
| *Cicatricosisporites dorogensis* (Schizaeaceae) | Extinct taxon, within family Schizaeaceae |
| *Meyeripollis nayarkotensis* (indet.) | Extinct taxon, family not known |

Appendix, classified according to the system of Takhtajan (1969). Taxa excluded from this list, but referred to in the text, remain undescribed as form-taxa, but fossils have been informally compared to pollen of extant plants.

## Palynological Indicators of Tropical Rain Forests

Two approaches are used with respect to the palynological characterisation of tropical rain forests. The first relates to the identification of fossil pollen with known megathermal taxa in the sense of van Steenis (1962a). The most important megathermal families which have a record of fossil pollen (Figure 4.7) include Annonaceae, Bombacaceae, Combretaceae, Dilleniaceae, Dipterocarpaceae, Guttiferae, Hippocrataceae, Lecythidaceae, Malphigiaceae, Myristicaceae, Pandanaceae and Rhizophoraceae, whereas within those families considered megathermal *pro majore parte* by van Steenis (1962a) and listed in Table 2.4, the most important members with a fossil pollen record are Euphorbiaceae, Icacinaceae, Leguminosae, Olacaceae, Palmae, Rubiaceae, Sapindaceae, Sapotaceae and Tiliaceae. Clearly, discretion needs to be exercised in attributing all members of these families to vegetation types from frost-free climates.

The second approach involves the examination of abundance changes of fossil pollen derived from moist tropical and other vegetation types through time by means of percentage pollen diagrams. Generally, pollen diagrams presented here use 'total freshwater pollen and spores' as the main sum, with mangrove pollen being presented using a sum of 'total pollen and spores' and presented adjacent to the main sum (Figure 4.8); this is necessary because mangrove pollen may be present in very high percentages (up to 95% in many Neogene samples) and, if included in the same sum as the other pollen, would swamp out any changes which might reflect changes in other vegetation types.

### Palynomorph assemblage diversity

Although high species richness levels form one of the most diagnostic features of present-day tropical rain forests, assessment of taxonomic diversity using palynology, either within low latitudes or elsewhere, has been attempted only rarely (Morley 1982b; Birks and Line, 1990). Palynomorph assemblage diversity is clearly affected by operator bias (some individuals differentiate more palynomorph types than others) and taphonomic criteria. Also palynomorph assemblages will clearly be derived from more than one plant community, and will reflect either $\alpha$ or $\gamma$ diversity, or both; also, most diversity indices assume that biological associations follow a logarithmic distribution, which need not be the case for all pollen data. In this review, three different diversity 'indices' are

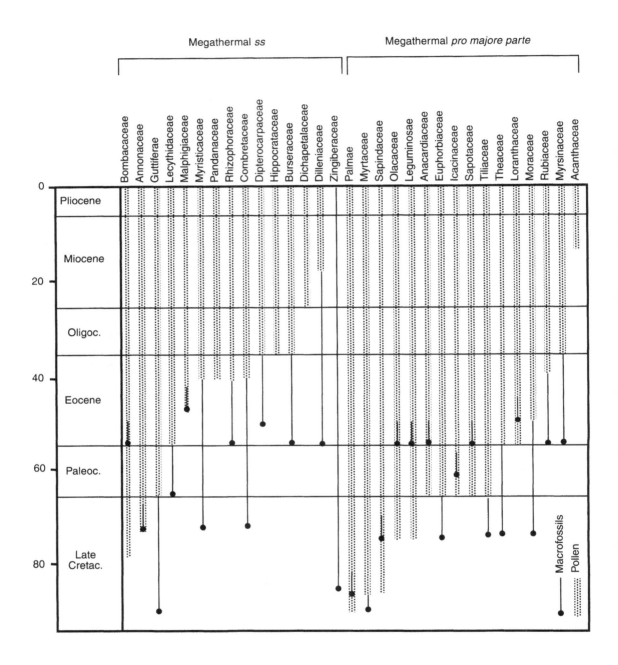

Figure 4.7   Geological record of pollen and macrofossils of megathermal, and megathermal *pro majore parte* angiosperm families according to Muller (1981) for pollen, and Collinson et al. (1993), updated with unpublished records.

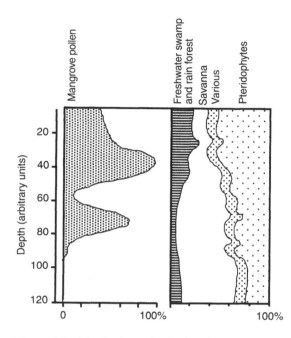

Figure 4.8 Idealised method showing percentage representation of pollen and spore groups within this book. The pollen sum is based on total pollen and spores from freshwater swamp and dryland sources; mangrove pollen abundances are presented independently in terms of total pollen and spores.

used. In instances where diversities of actual data are presented, with analyses being undertaken by the author, diversity data is simply presented in terms of 'number of pollen and spore types noted in the first count of 100, excluding mangrove pollen', both determined, and indeterminate forms being included in the calculations (e.g. Figures 7.13; 9.13). Two further approaches are used to illustrate diversity trends on a long geological time scale: firstly, following the approach of Fredriksen (1994a), which assumes that a taxon is present in every sample from its first geological appearance to its last, whether it was actually seen in the sample or not (e.g. Figure 11.1), and, secondly, from the number of taxa indicated to be present per epoch in regional compilations of pollen floras for the Cretaceous and Tertiary (e.g. Figures 5.15; 8.2).

### Cuticle

Cuticular fragments are common in palynological preparations, but are rarely determined by palynologists. An exception is the determination of burned grass cuticle, which is produced in large amounts by savanna fires (Morley and Richards, 1993). Abundance maxima of this cuticle from equatorial areas provide strong evidence for the *absence* of closed forests.

### 4.1.3  Geochemical Fossils

An important aspect of hydrocarbon source rock evaluation by oil companies involves characterisation of organic molecules in oils and possible source rocks using a GCMS analyser (gas chromatography–mass spectrometry) with a view to determine their origin. Such studies in the Far East have identified high levels of the geochemical biomarker bicadinine with fossil resins of the Dipterocarpaceae (van Aarssen et al., 1990, 1992), although elsewhere, some other taxa, such as *Mastixia* (Cornaceae), have proved to produce similar biomarkers (van Aarssen et al., 1994). Nevertheless, it is considered that the majority of records of bicadinene from SE Asian sediments are from Dipterocarpaceae, and provide the most comprehensive history of the family. It is likely that other biomarkers will eventually be linked with other angiosperm taxa in a similar manner.

## 4.2  TERRESTRIAL FAUNA

Vertebrate fossils can provide very strong evidence of vegetation types, through determination of dietary habit and method of locomotion. A dominance of tree-dwelling fruit eaters over terrestrial browsers or grazers clearly suggests a closed multistratal forest. Body weight 'cenograms' have also been widely used to infer former vegetation types (e.g. Figure 4.9).

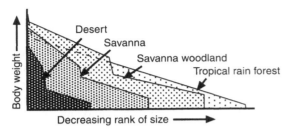

Figure 4.9  Faunal cenograms, differentiating vertebrate faunas of rain forest, savanna and desert. Species are ranked sequentially from heavy to light. Rain forest faunas are characterised by high diversity but small size; a gap in the medium-sized species indicates an open environment, such as savanna or desert. Rain forest example from Gabon, woodland savanna from Rwanda, open savanna from Congo and desert from Iran (from Prothero, 1994). Reproduced by permission of Columbia University Press.

## 4.3  LITHOLOGICAL INDICATORS OF RAIN FOREST CLIMATES

### Lignites and coals

Lignites and coals are the katagenic products of peats, which form only in areas where annual precipitation exceeds evaporation (Gore, 1983). Where there is no dry season, peats can develop in cold, warm temperate, or tropical rain forest climates. Cold temperate peats are produced largely of *Sphagnum* and herbs, and warm temperate from coniferous and angiosperm wood (e.g. from *Taxodium* and *Nyssa*). Peats of tropical rain forest climates are formed predominantly of wood and roots from tropical angiosperms. In much of the Amazon Basin and equatorial Africa, present-day climates are currently too seasonal to permit extensive ombrotrophic peat development; in the Far East, however, there is a close relationship between areas of peat formation and areas exhibiting negligible evidence for seasonality (Morley, 1981a). Where evidence for tropical temperatures is available from other sources, the presence of coals provides strong evidence for former tropical rain forest climates, but since peat formation is by no means ubiquitous within

the present day range of tropical rain forests, the absence of coals may not necessarily be taken as evidence for the *absence* of rain forest climates.

### Evaporites

Evaporites principally form in hot, arid areas (Perthuisot, 1980; Parrish and Barron, 1986), but warm temperatures are not essential for their formation since they may occur anywhere where net evaporation exceeds net moisture influx, and have even been reported from polar deserts. Subaqueous evaporites may be precipitated anywhere where net annual evaporation exceeds 100 mm, once a system has reached the permanently evaporitic stage (Schmalz, 1969). Most evaporites accumulate between latitudes 10° and 40°, corresponding to the limits of the subtropical high pressure belts, but under monsoonal climates, which were particularly well developed during the Permian and Triassic, also occurred near the equator (Robinson, 1973; Parrish et al., 1982; Parrish and Barron, 1986). Evaporite deposits are principally indicative of desert climates.

### Laterites and bauxites

Laterite is a diagenesis product which forms where the water-table fluctuates. It is rare in areas of everwet climate, but becomes common in climates which are seasonally, or absolutely drier, and most common in regions of monsoon climate, outside the rain forest zone proper (Whitmore, 1975). Bauxite, on the other hand, indicates extreme weathering of the host rock. Laterite and bauxite may have formed outside tropical latitudes (e.g. Miocene of Germany and Oregon, Late Eocene to Oligocene of Ireland, Pliocene of Australia) where formation took place on basalt substrates (Gill, 1964).

The major problem in using laterite and bauxite as palaeoclimatic indicators is that they are extremely difficult to date, since lateritisation can occur at any time after the formation of the host rock, and the development of bauxite is progressive over a long time period;

also, because of their mode of formation, they are unlikely to contain organic fossils, such as palynomorphs. In addition, since their iron content is periodically mobilised, they cannot be dated by palaeomagnetism (P.S. Ashton, personal communication).

### *Limestones*

Limestones are formed primarily in low latitudes in clear, shallow, tropical to subtropical seas where little terrigenously derived clastic material is introduced, although they may also form locally in cold waters, in which case they are composed wholly of shell debris. Since clastic influx into marine continental shelf environments will be greater in areas of higher rainfall, there is a tendency for limestones to form more prolifically along arid or seasonal climate continental margins. Their distribution is therefore useful in mapping the distribution of tropical seasonal and arid climates.

## 4.4  MARINE FAUNA

The present distributions of many marine faunal elements, such as foraminifera and corals, are strongly controlled by sea surface temperatures, and fossils of these groups are widely used for palaeotemperature estimations. Larger foraminifera are one of the best of such indicators, being currently more or less restricted to the tropical zone (Figure 4.10), and with fossil distributions which strongly suggest warmer Tertiary global climates (Adams et al., 1990).

## 4.5  ISOTOPE DATA

Oxygen isotopic analyses provide a widely used quantitative method for deriving marine palaeotemperatures for the Cenozoic. Of the two stable isotopes of oxygen, the lighter $^{16}O$ isotope evaporates more readily than the heavier $^{18}O$. During glacial episodes, a greater proportion of the lighter isotope is locked up in polar ice caps,

leaving the ocean depleted. Calcareous-shelled microorganisms develop their shells from the $CO_2$ obtained from the sea water, and thus the ratio of these oxygen isotopes in their shells reflects the composition of the sea water in which they lived. Within 'icehouse' phases of earth history, the ratio of these isotopes closely reflects global ice volume, indirectly reflecting global sea level change, and palaeotemperatures.

The interpretation of oxygen isotope ratios during 'greenhouse' phases, during which time there were virtually no polar ice caps, remains poorly understood. Isotope studies for the Late Paleocene/Early Eocene thermal maximum clearly demonstrate that sea surface temperatures at mid-latitudes were much higher than at present, and this is consistent with the extension of paratropical forests up to 15° poleward of their present limits (Chapter 10), but estimates at tropical latitudes are 4–7° C below present values (Shackleton and Boersma, 1983), suggesting reduced poleward temperature gradients and sluggish atmospheric circulation, but with the need for greater heat transport out of the tropics into the mid-latitudes. Such a scenario is, however, difficult to reconcile both from the point of view of energy balance models (Horrell, 1990), or faunal and floral data (Adams et al., 1990). The view taken here is that the global temperature gradient was more pronounced than that proposed from isotope data, and more likely followed computer-modelled temperature gradients for the mid-Cretaceous (Barron and Washington, 1985), and that equatorial temperatures were warmer than at present, in a similar manner to the mid-Cretaceous.

## 4.6  PALAEOCLIMATE MODELLING

Although global climates have changed dramatically through the period of evolution of tropical rain forests, from the mid-Cretaceous, at which time they were probably as warm as at any time during the Phanerozoic, to the glacial maxima of the Quaternary, some critical aspects of global climate have remained more

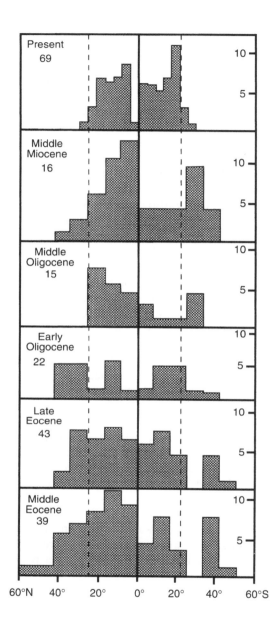

Figure 4.10   Latitudinal representation of larger foraminifera in present and Tertiary seas. The histograms are based on the maps of Adams et al. (1990) and show the average number of larger foraminiferal genera occurring within 5° (for the present) and 10° (for the Tertiary) latitudinal slices. The numbers to the left hand side indicate the number of faunal localities on which the histograms are based.

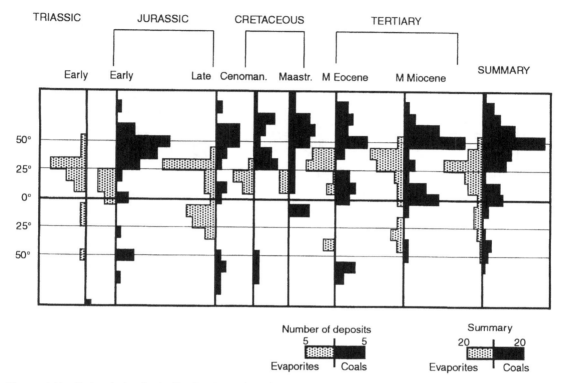

Figure 4.11   Palaeolatitudinal distribution of coals and evaporites in the Mesozoic and Cenozoic (from Parrish et al., 1982). Histograms show the number of known deposits of each lithotype from 10° palaeolatitudinal slices for each of the time periods indicated, and also a summary for the Triassic to Tertiary. Note the maxima of coal deposits at mid-latitudes, and, for the Tertiary, at equatorial latitudes. Evaporite deposits are concentrated at subtropical latitudes throughout the Tertiary, emphasising the presence of strong Hadley Cell circulation throughout this time period. Reproduced by permission of Elsevier Science.

or less unchanged. Most important with respect to the history of tropical rain forests are the global patterns of atmospheric circulation which create the Hadley Cells, which determine the presence of the subtropical high pressure zones. It is likely that these have remained in approximately the same place, between latitudes 10 and 40°N and S, throughout Late Mesozoic and Cenozoic time. This is clearly indicated by the geological record of evaporites, which, as noted within Section 4.3, mostly accumulate within the limits of the subtropical high pressure belts. After corrections have been made for movements of lithospheric plates, Late Mesozoic and Cenozoic evaporite accumulations are almost wholly restricted to these

latitudes (Parrish and Barron, 1986), whether global climates were close to their warmest, during the Middle Eocene, or in the process of cooling, during the Miocene (Figure 4.11).

By taking into account those aspects of global atmospheric circulation which have remained essentially unchanged through geological time together with direct evidence for palaeoclimates, such as palaeotemperature data, which have varied through time, and also taking into account evidence for past continental positions, it has been possible to model past climates sufficiently precisely to enable prediction of the locations through time of certain economically important lithologies, such as petroleum source rocks (e.g. Parrish and Barron, 1986; Scotsese

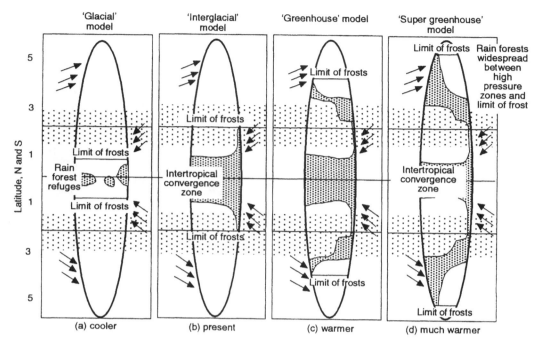

Figure 4.12   Idealised distributions for tropical rain forests on a uniform continent spanning both hemispheres for four global climatic scenarios. (a) 'Cooler' scenario, typified by Quaternary glacial maximum. Tropical rain forests are restricted to refuges in favoured localities within the equatorial zone; since low latitude sea level temperatures were lower, frosts would have occurred at sea level within the tropics; refuges along eastern coasts, which receive rainfall from moist trade winds would have been extremely restricted. (b) 'Interglacial' scenario, typified by present day. Increased precipitation in the equatorial zone results in the expansion of rain forests to 5°N and S, and with frosts limited to extratropical areas, rain forests would have developed along moist, eastern coastlines. (c) 'Greenhouse' scenario, typified by ice-free global climate. Rain forests occur extensively within the tropical zone, and along moist eastern coasts within the high pressure cells; with frost-free climates occurring well outside the subtropical high pressure zone, tropical aspect and paratropical rain forests expand into the lower mid-latitudes. (d) 'Super greenhouse' scenario, typified by Late Paleocene/Early Eocene thermal maximum. With frosts limited to high latitudes, tropical aspect and paratropical rain forests expand throughout the mid-latitudes, particularly along western coastlines, where moist westerlies result in high levels of precipitation.

and Summerhayes, 1986). Equally, palaeoclimatic modelling can help delimit likely areas of former tropical rain forest on a global basis, even in areas lacking a fossil record. Four tropical rain forest scenarios for contrasting global climate regimes are presented in Figure 4.12, for a hypothetical continent extending into both hemispheres. These models indicate the idealised distribution of present day rain forests (Figure 4.12b), as well as those for a cooler Earth, using the last glacial maximum as

representative (Figure 4.12a). Scenarios are also presented for warmer 'greenhouse' global climates (Figure 4.12c,d). The main factors which limit the occurrence of rain forests are the occurrence of frosts, and the presence of seasonal climates within the subtropical high pressure zones. Within these zones, tropical rain forests will occur only in areas where moist, onshore winds bring year-round rainfall. For further discussion, reference must be made to Chapters 5 and 13.

# CHAPTER 5

# Early Angiosperm History and the First Megathermal Rain Forests

## 5.1 BIOGEOGRAPHICAL VERSUS GEOLOGICAL EVIDENCE OF ANGIOSPERM ORIGINS

### 5.1.1 Angiosperm Ancestors

Since Darwin's (1859) reference to the origin of the angiosperms as an 'abominable mystery', the suggestions as to the place and time of their origin, and also the nature of their ancestors, have been nearly as numerous as hypotheses concerning the demise of the dinosaurs. The theories regarding angiosperm ancestry which have received most consideration are divided into those which consider entomophily as the original mode of pollination (the Euanthial theory of Arber and Parkin (1907), which argues that the complex *Magnolia* type flower is the more primitive), with derivation possibly from the hermaphroditic Bennettitales, and those proposing that anemophily is the more primitive, with derivation from unisexual gymnosperms, such as the Gnetales (the Pseudanthial theory of Wettstein (1907), with the catkin-producing Amentiferae as basic). Other noteworthy theories include those which require a polyphyletic origin for angiosperms, which has recently received renewed attention by Hughes (1994), and the Durian theory of Corner (1949), which is based on the comparative morphology of tropical rain forest trees.

Current views (Crane et al., 1995) suggest that angiosperms are one of the most strongly supported monophyletic groups in the plant kingdom, and that they shared a common origin with the Bennettitales and Gnetales (which, together with angiosperms, have been termed the 'Anthophytes' by Doyle and Donaghue (1986) to emphasise their shared possession of flower-like reproductive structures). Such an origin requires the initial evolution of angiosperms (though not their radiation) in the Late Triassic (235–206 Ma), and thus entails an 80 Ma gap in the angiosperm fossil record from then to the Early Cretaceous (145–96 Ma) (Figure 5.1). The possibility of the existence of angiosperms prior to the Cretaceous has been widely accepted (Doyle, 1969, 1978; Muller, 1970), since some primitive magnoliid pollen is indistinguishable from that of some gymnosperms, and pre-Cretaceous members of the angiosperm line might be indistinguishable from Bennettitales in most characters commonly preserved as fossils (Doyle and Donaghue, 1987). Also, the systematic diversity of Barremian (116.5–113 Ma) angiospermid pollen may be considerable (Hughes and McDougall, 1987), and such diversity is unlikely to have appeared suddenly. Furthermore, molecular evidence favours a pre-Cretaceous origin (Martin et al., 1989).

There are currently many claims of pre-Cretaceous angiosperm records, but none are presently accepted (Crane et al., 1995). The oldest known angiosperm fossils are flowers of possible lauralean affinity of Valanginian? (128–121 Ma) to Hauterivian (121–116.5 Ma) age from Portugal (Friis et al., 1994), and the pollen type *Clavatipollenites*, recognised as being produced by ancestral members of the family Chloranthaceae (Muller, 1981; Walker

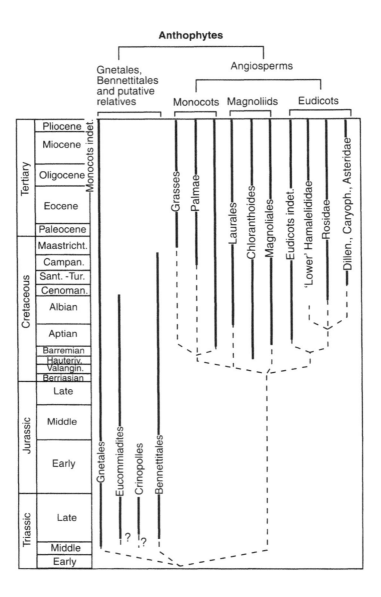

Figure 5.1  Simplified phylogenetic tree showing the relative stratigraphic ranges of selected angiosperm groups and putative close gymnosperm relatives. Bennettitales, Gnetales, the parent plants of crinopolles pollen and *Eucommiadites* combined with the angiosperms to form the anthophytes, emphasised by their shared possession of flower-like reproductive structures. Current hypotheses of angiosperm evolution recognise two large clades (monocotyledons, with monosulcate or monosulcate-derived pollen, and eudicots, with triaperturate, or triaperturate-derived pollen), embedded within a basal grade of magnoliid dicotyledons (Crane et al., 1995). Reproduced by permission of the authors and of *Nature*.

and Walker, 1984), widely recorded from the Barremian onwards. The earliest known flowers were clearly insect pollinated (Crepet and Friis, 1987), with small anthers producing little pollen, too small for effective wind dispersal. It is unlikely, however, that the *Magnolia* type flower was primitive; more likely it was markedly elaborated, and, likewise, the very simple flower of Chloranthaceae reduced, compared to the basic angiosperm condition (Crane et al., 1995).

### 5.1.2  A Tropical Origin for Angiosperms?

The occurrence of megathermal families, i.e. those wholly restricted to tropical latitudes (Section 2.1.1; Table 2.2), and of many families which are essentially tropical but with a few temperate-derived taxa (Section 2.1.1; Table 2.3), leads to the suggestion that many angiosperm groups actually evolved in the tropics. Thorne (1968, 1976) took this further by suggesting that most angiosperm families are basically tropical in their adaptations and their geographical distribution, and, because of this, the whole group evolved in the tropics. In his analysis of 316 angiosperm families, he demonstrated that 167 are exclusively or primarily tropical and only 43 are exclusively or largely temperate, but that each of the temperate families appears to be closely related to a 'tropical' cousin, which invariably exhibits features which are less specialised, and hence more primitive. Macrofossil evidence has led to the suggestion that the origin was in the equable mid-latitude uplands (Axlerod, 1959, 1970), but this suggestion has probably been based on a fossil record strongly biased toward the northern hemisphere, and has received little general support. An upland origin, however, would easily explain why it is difficult to find early angiosperm fossils! The palynological record, on the other hand, provides strong support for a tropical origin (Hickey and Doyle, 1977; Thomas and Spicer, 1986), especially with respect to the pattern of radiation of plants producing tri-

colpate pollen (Figure 5.2c), which show well-documented Aptian (113–108 Ma) occurrences in Central Africa and Brazil, with first appearances at successively younger times towards the poles (Figure 5.3). The pattern is not so clear for monosulcate pollen (Figure 5.2a), but this may be due to the difficulty of differentiation of Barremian and older earliest Cretaceous sediments in low latitude settings, the differentiation usually being made on the presence or absence of monosulcate angiosperm pollen!

### 5.1.3  Mesic or Arid?

Biogeographical reasoning has been used to suggest that angiosperms may have evolved in a primarily tropical montane, or summer-wet-temperate, mesic setting with a minimum of water stress. Thorne (1976) bases this argument on the diversity of supposedly primitive angiosperms, especially those relics with vesselless xylem or with primitive tracheid-like vessel elements, in present day tropical montane and subtropical forests. An alternative origin, in response to a stressful warm climate with distinct dry and wet seasons, has been proposed by Stebbins (1974). To what extent can an origin within an everwet *tropical rain forest* setting, or an environment with a markedly seasonal climate, be tested using the fossil and sedimentary record?

Support for Stebbins' proposal came from studies of the pollen record from Gabon, where angiosperm pollen exhibits a pronounced early development (Doyle, 1977) in a section characterised by the presence of evaporites, and the proliferation of ephedroid pollen (Doyle et al., 1982), suggesting an origin in a setting exhibiting marked water shortage. An origin in a stressful climate at tropical latitudes would also be consistent with the climatic reconstructions of Vakhrameev (1992), which show that from the Early Jurassic, through to the mid-Cretaceous, arid and semi-arid climates were the rule in tropical latitudes. Crane (1987), however, pointed out that the earliest angiosperms are

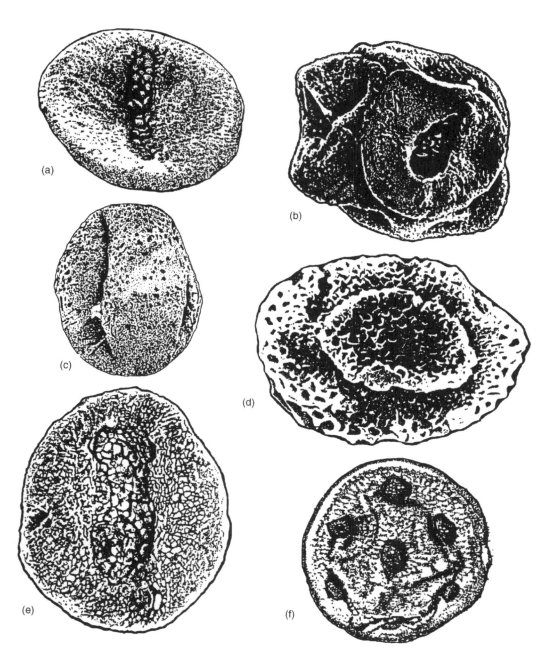

Figure 5.2   Earliest angiosperm pollen: (a) *Clavatipollenites* cf. *tenellis*[1] ×2000, Early Aptian Potomac Group, believed to be from ancestral Chloranthaceae, but also bearing similarities to some Myristicaceae according to Walker and Walker (1979); (b) *Walkeripollis gabonensis*[2] ×2000, Late Barremian to Early Aptian N'Ganzwe Formation, Gabon, considered ancestral to Winteraceae; (c) early tricolpate[3] ×3300, from Middle Albian Potomac Group, from fossil inflorescence referred to Hamamelididae; (d) *Afropollis operculatus*[2]

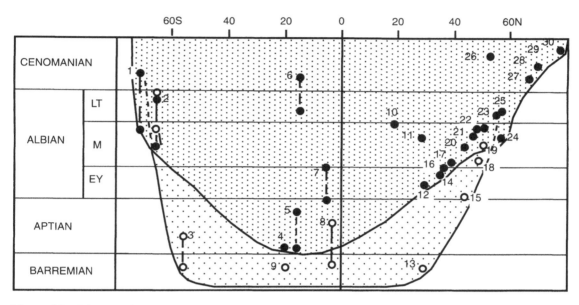

Figure 5.3   Diagram showing the palaeolatitudinal relationship of first occurrences of angiosperm pollen. Open circles and light shading, monosulcate grains, reflecting a 'grade' of early dicotyledons and monocotyledons; closed circles and dense shading, tricolpate grains, reflecting eudicots. Geographic areas: 1) New Zealand; 2) Australia; 3) Patagonia; 4) Congo; 5) Brazil; 6) Peru; 7) Ivory Coast; 8) Israel; 9) Gabon; 10) Portugal; 11) Oklahoma; 12) Potomac Group; 13) Maryland, Virginia and S England; 14) SW Siberia; 15) not known; 16) Denver Basin; 17) E England; 18) Saskatchewan; 19) E USA; 20) Wyoming; 21) W Central Siberia; 22) SE Alberta and SW Manitoba; 23) SE Siberia; 24) Central Canada; 25) Central Alberta; 26) Greenland; 27) Ellesmere Island and NE Siberia; 28) Yukon; 29) Kuk River, Alaska; 30) Umiat Region, Alaska (after Hickey and Doyle, 1977).

recorded simultaneously in England (Hughes and McDougall, 1987), Israel (Brenner, 1984), W Africa, Argentina and E North America (Hickey and Doyle, 1977), and that these regions include areas exhibiting both aridity and more equable climates. He emphasised that there is no clear palaeontological evidence to support the hypothesis that angiosperms originated and diversified in seasonally arid environments. Doyle and Donaghue (1987), however, continue to emphasise the early adap-

tation to arid and/or disturbed environments by comparison with their presumed sister groups, the Bennettitales and Gnetales, both of which suggest similar adaptations.

The suggestion of the initial radiation from an area of stressful climate would be consistent with an origin in Western Gondwanaland, where the angiosperm pollen record exhibits early diversity. However, an origin in a humid rain forest setting would imply an origin in the eastern tropics, as favoured by many

×2000, Late Barremian to Early Aptian N'Ganzwe Formation, Gabon, thought to be from an extinct line of Winteraceae; (e) *Tucanopollis crisopolensis*[1,4] ×2000, Late Barremian N'Ganzwe Formation, Gabon, thought to represent an extinct line of Chloranthaceae; (f) *Cretacaeiporites scabratus*[5] ×800, from Cenomanian of DSDP 364, offshore Angola, possibly ancestral to Caryophyllales. Sources: [1]Doyle and Hotton (1991); [2]Doyle et al. (1990); [3]Friis et al. (1987); [4]Regali (1989); [5]Morgan (1978); a–e from SEM, f from LM photomicrographs. Drawn by Harsanti Pribatini.

proponents of angiosperm evolution such as Thorne (1963), Takhtajan (1969) and Smith (1970), where there is a great proliferation of endemic primitive angiosperms, mostly growing in moist lowland and montane or insular rain forests, in SE Asia, some of the Pacific islands, such as New Caledonia and Fiji, and NE Australia. Many of these endemic taxa are characterised by primitive features such as the presence of vesselless xylem, thought to indicate the restriction of the earliest angiosperms to highly mesic sites (Thorne, 1976). Also, the overlap of family or subfamily pairs in SE Asia, with one exhibiting an essentially northern hemisphere distribution, and the other a southern one, has been used to imply their common origin in that area. Examples are Magnoliaceae (northern) and Winteraceae (southern), and the northern Fagoidae, but southern Nothofagoidae. However, recent evidence suggests that the critical family Winteraceae is relict, and that it formerly enjoyed a cosmopolitan distribution (Doyle et al., 1990). Also, fossil data suggest that members of the northern Fagoidae and southern Nothofagoidae came together well after their initial radiation, with *Nothofagus* dispersing into New Guinea only in the Middle Miocene (Morley, 1998). Such developments place continuing doubt on primitive angiosperm groups originating in SE Asia, and also on the use of modern distribution patterns to explain the place of origin of taxa which have had a long and chequered history.

Compared to both the E and W Atlantic coasts, the understanding of both the Early Cretaceous geological history and fossil pollen record of SE Asia is very poor, but recent improvements in knowledge of the region provide important contrasts, both with respect to the pollen record, and also to palaeoclimate, based on lithological data.

Sediments of Early Cretaceous age occur in three main areas: the Khorat and associated groups of Indochina (Buffetaut et al., 1993; Drumm et al., 1993; Mouret et al., 1993), the Tembeling Group of the Malay Peninsula (Gobbett and Hutchison, 1973), and the

Pedawan Formation of Borneo. Unfortunately, each of these sequences has been substantially buried or tectonised to some degree, and hence plant fossils are poorly preserved. Geological studies of the Khorat Group of Indochina suggest that deposition occurred in a dominantly fluviatile setting, often with strong periodic water stress, as suggested by the presence of mid-Cretaceous evaporites in Laos and Thailand (Mouret et al., 1993) and of braided streams and redbeds indicative of strongly seasonal climates. There is no evidence of coals, or other indicators of everwet climates, and palynomorph assemblages are dominated by *Classopollis* spp. (derived from the extinct gymnospermous family Cheirolepidaceae, which some authorities have suggested are adapted to xeric settings, e.g. Vakhrameev, 1981, 1991). They are also lacking in angiosperm pollen (Racey et al., 1994).

Palynological studies of the Tembeling Group in Malaysia, of sediments believed to be of Barremian age (Shamsuddin and Morley, 1995), reveal the presence of rare possible *Clavatipollenites* sp. in an assemblage dominated by *Classopollis* spp., whereas other earliest Cretaceous assemblages from the Malay Peninsula are void of angiosperm pollen (Ayob, unpublished). The current (still poor) data suggest that the initial appearance of angiosperm pollen in the SE Asian area does not predate that of Western Gondwanaland. The oldest tricolpate pollen recorded in the region is still that described by Muller (1968), from the Pedawan Formation of Sarawak. This sequence was originally dated as Cenomanian (96–92 Ma) by Muller, but the common occurrence of small *Classopollis* spp., and of abundant *Exesipollenites tumulus* (also produced by members of the gymnosperm family Cheirolepidaceae), together with *Vitreisporites pallidus* (a bisaccate gymnosperm pollen type), strongly suggests an older, probably Aptian (113–108 Ma) or Early Albian (108–104 Ma) age (Figure 5.4a), the abundance of *E. tumulus* and ephedroid pollen also arguing for a palaeoclimate with a strong degree of water stress.

The emerging Early Cretaceous palynological record from the eastern tropics appears to differ from that of Western Gondwanaland in its lower species richness, and currently provides no evidence to suggest an initial radiation from 'somewhere between Assam and Fiji', in a region without water stress. The low latitude prevalence of early angiosperm records from areas exhibiting stressful Early Cretaceous climates, paucity of lithologies such as coals (indicative of everwet climates) from the Early Cretaceous tropics, and prevalence in each tropical region of evaporites, supports the hypothesis of Stebbins (1974) that angiosperms initially developed in response to a warm, subhumid climate, with Western Gondwanaland being the likely centre of radiation. Reconstruction of Early Cretaceous plant communities (see below) suggests that angiosperms first became established as early successional weedy herbs or shrubs, colonising predominantly open environments and streamsides (Doyle and Hickey, 1976). It appears unlikely their origin was in Early Cretaceous rain forests, if such forests existed in tropical latitudes. With respect to the initial expansion of angiosperms into rain forests, the suggestion of Doyle et al. (1982) is noteworthy, that although it is likely that vessels in angiosperms developed as an adaptation to aridity, their availability may have been a pre-adaptation for the evolution of large, undissected leaves in the everwet tropics.

### 5.1.4  Origin on a Geographically Isolated 'Noah's Ark'

Judgement as to angiosperm origins in the Far East is compounded by the suggestion raised in Whitmore (1981) that angiosperms may have evolved on a 'shard' (terrane) of Gondwanaland, which had drifted to Laurasia during the late Mesozoic, favouring the comment by Darwin that angiosperms 'must have been largely developed in some isolated area, whence owing to geographical changes, they

at last succeeded in escaping, and spread quickly over the world' (in Takhtajan, 1987). The Sibumasu Terrane, which now occupies parts of Sumatra, West Malaysia, Myanmar and Tibet, was identified as such a 'Noah's Ark' by Audley-Charles (1987), who proposed rifting from Gondwanaland during the Jurassic, although he admitted that dating the time of rifting was conjectural, and could have been earlier in the Permian (290–245 Ma). More recent evidence (Metcalfe, 1988, 1996) suggests that the rifting of Sibumasu in fact began in the Late Permian (256–245 Ma), and that it became welded onto the E Asian continent in the Late Triassic as a result of the Indosinian Orogeny (Hutchison, 1989), from which time it has remained in approximately the same latitudinal position (Smith et al., 1994). If angiosperms evolved on the Sibumasu Terrane as it drifted from Gondwana, their initial appearance would not be inconsistent with the Late Triassic age proposed by Doyle and Donaghue (1987), but would not answer the sudden expansion of angiosperms in the Barremian, and Darwin's 'escape', as proposed by Takhtajan (1987). Other possible microcontinental fragments accreted onto Sundaland during the Cretaceous include the metamorphic basement of the East Java Sea, accreting during the mid-Cretaceous (Bransden and Matthews, 1992), and possibly material accreted onto S Sumatra (Metcalfe, 1996). Both were probably too old to have carried angiosperms.

## 5.2  CRETACEOUS ANGIOSPERM EXPANSION AND DIVERSIFICATION

Angiosperms passed through four main phases of diversification between their radiation in the Valanginian?/Hauterivian and the end of the Cretaceous (Muller, 1981). The first phase, up to the Early Cenomanian, witnessed their gradual diversification, as exemplified by the appearance of successively more diverse pollen and macrofossils, their gradual increased importance in terms of contribution to regional

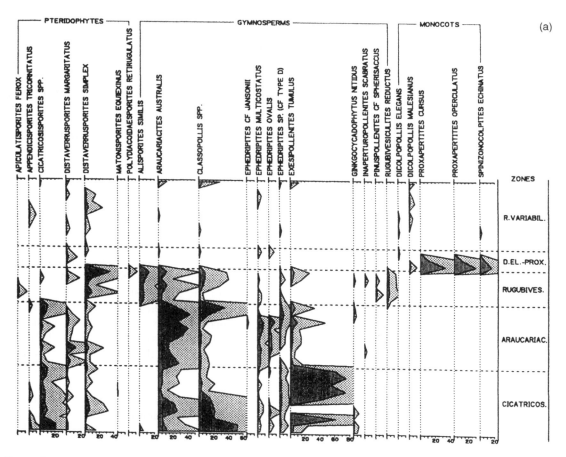

Figure 5.4 (a) and (b). Palynological data from Bungu-Penrissen area, Sarawak. Data from Muller (1968), presented in percentage format, with zones and ages reinterpreted according to Morley (1998). Zones: R. variabil. = *Retitriporites variabilis*; D.el. = *Dicolpopollis elegans*; Prox. = *Proxapertites*; Rugubives. = *Rugubivesiculites*; Araucariac. = *Araucariacites*; Cicatricos. = *Cicatricosisporites*. Taxonomy updated where appropriate. Stipple = ×5 exaggeration.

vegetation, as suggested by their successively greater percentage representation in both micro- and macrofloras, and a parallel appearance of novel foliar physiognomic types. By the Early Cenomanian, most of the physiognomic foliage types known today are recorded (Figure 5.5), their order of appearance through the Aptian and Albian paralleling an ecological succession, but taking place over 20 Ma (Upchurch and Wolfe, 1987). This first phase witnessed the Barremian appearance of early Magnoliidae and Liliopsida, indicated by the

presence of *Clavatipollenites* and *Liliacidites*, and of the clade of non-magnolioid dicotyledons (Crane, 1987), based on the Aptian appearance of tricolpate pollen. This initial angiosperm expansion coincided with a parallel decline of Gnetales and Cycadophytes, but conifers at this time were little affected.

The subsequent three phases, from the Late Cenomanian to the Maastrichtian, witnessed the ascendency of angiosperms over other groups and their migration to the polar regions; their pronounced floristic diversification, with

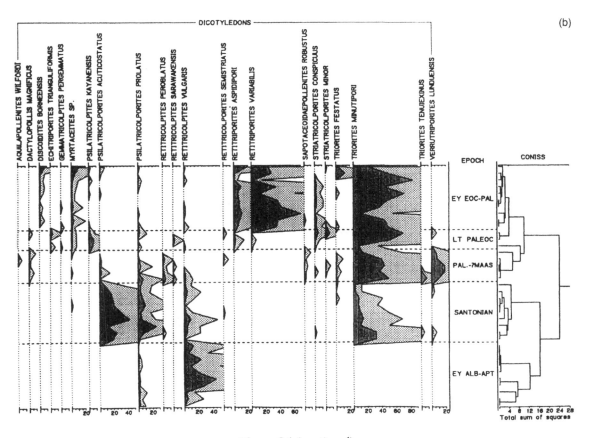

Figure 5.4 (*continued*)

the appearance of many modern angiosperm groups; and the development of a distinct latitudinal vegetational zonation. These phases were accompanied by relatively few new developments in foliar physiognomy (Wolfe and Upchurch, 1987).

The character of mid-Cretaceous vegetation is most clearly understood through integrated macrofossil and palynological studies (e.g. Lidgard and Crane, 1990). Widely dispersed palynomorphs tend to reflect regional vegetation, whereas leaves and fruit are generally more indicative of plants growing near the site of deposition. Unlike for the Tertiary, few direct vegetational inferences can be made for Cretaceous angiosperm pollen, since most Cretaceous morphotypes are unrepresented in

present day floras. Such integrated studies are few and far between; the best example of Early Cretaceous vegetational succession within which the angiosperms diversified, and eventually came to dominance, is from the Barremian Horsetown Group and Aptian/Albian Potomac Group from eastern USA (Hickey and Doyle, 1977; Crane, 1987; Upchurch and Wolfe, 1987), followed by the Dakota Formation and others within the later Cretaceous. Glimpses of the pattern of vegetational development in low latitude areas over the same period can then be gleaned from comparison of the more diverse low latitude palynofloras and very scattered macrofossil records, with the Cretaceous floristic and vegetational succession for North America.

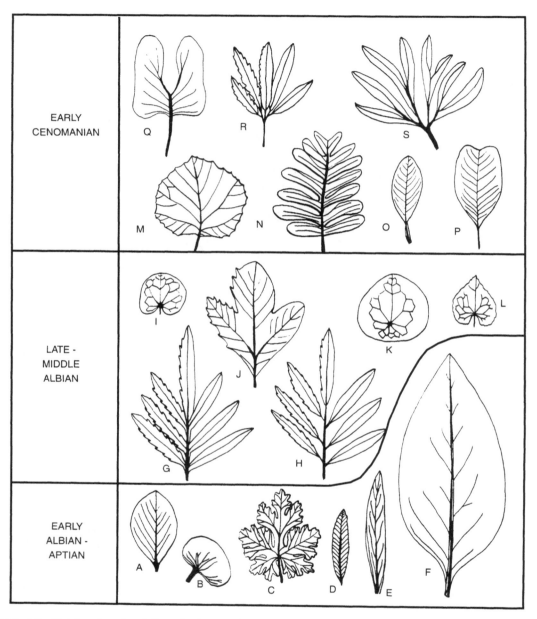

Figure 5.5  Origin of major foliar physiognomic types during the Aptian to Early Cenomanian of North America. A) microphyllous, not elongate; B) incipiently palmate, semi-aquatic or vine; C) bipinnitifid; D) stenophyllous, serrate; E) stenophyllous, entire margined; F) mesophyllous, unlobed; G) pinnatifid; H) pinnately compound; I) cordate, orbicular; J) lobed, palinactinodromous primary venation (platanoid); K) peltate, orbicular, aquatic; L) cordate, non-orbicular, serrate; M) unlobed, serrate, with highly branched basal secondary veins; N) pinnatifid, more than one secondary vein per lobe; O) simple, entire-margined, with winged petiole; P) simple, entire-margined, emarginate apex; Q) bilobed; R) palinactinodromously compound; S) 'dichotomously' compound (after Upchurch and Wolfe, 1987). Reproduced by permission of Cambridge University Press.

### 5.2.1 Cretaceous Vegetation in North America

#### Barremian to Early Albian

During the American Barremian to Early Albian, angiosperms were an unimportant early successional element of regional vegetation which was composed primarily of coniferous trees, gymnospermous shrubs and herbaceous lycopods. Angiosperms contributed only 1% to regional palynofloras, and formed a sporadic element in macrofloras from streamside facies (Hickey and Doyle, 1977). About 12 different angiosperm taxa have been recognised from the Potomac Group on the basis of megafossils, and most of these can be referred to Magnoliales, Chloranthaceae and Illiciales (Upchurch, 1984, a,b). Most leaves from this period are entire, pinnately veined microphylls (Figure 5.5), with the most diverse physiognomic group being elongate (stenophylls), suggesting streamside, rheophytic, plants (Richards, 1952; van Steenis, 1981). Incipient palmate leaves are also recorded, possibly belonging to lianes or vines, and larger pinnately veined leaves suggest understorey plants. Stems with attached leaves provide direct evidence for herbaceous angiosperms (Hickey and Doyle, 1977), but angiosperm woods have not been recorded from the Potomac Group. However, since fossil woods are absent, woody plants, if present, are likely to have been small, suggesting they belonged to early successional trees and shrubs. Upchurch and Wolfe (1987) suggest that mean annual temperatures for this period were of the order of 20°C, but estimates are uncertain since the vegetation was evolving rapidly. Water supply was probably in surplus, but the climate was not everwet.

#### Middle to Late Albian

Middle to Late Albian (104–96 Ma) floras contain much higher percentages of angiosperm pollen (up to 20%), and 40 to 50% of leaf floras (Crane, 1987), but sometimes locally produced angiosperm fossils dominate both palynomorph and macrofossil assemblages (Hickey and Doyle, 1977). This expansion corresponds to a marked reduction in importance of cycadophytes, other seed plants and pteridophytes, but conifers remain well represented (Figure 5.6). Angiosperm leaves are considerably more diverse than in the Early Albian; Doyle and Hickey (1976) estimated that 36 different kinds are represented, distributed within the Magnoliidae, Hamamelididae, Rosidae and monocotyledons. Angiosperm leaves are larger than previously, with serrate, pinnate-compound, pinnatifid and palmately lobed configurations being represented, in addition to the earlier types, and in the Late Albian platanoid leaves are also well developed. Deeply cordate, peltate or orbicular leaves with palmate venation are thought to represent scrambling herbs; entire leaves are less frequent than in older formations, and drip tips are rare (Upchurch and Wolfe, 1987). Crane (1987) suggests that in addition to increased systematic diversity, angiosperms had also attained considerable ecological amplitude by the end of the Early Cretaceous. The new physiognomic types were largely characteristic of early successional plants (Givnish, 1979), but, in addition, full aquatics and riparian trees may have been present at this time (Doyle and Hickey, 1976). Late Albian temperatures were probably similar to those for the Early Albian (Upchurch and Wolfe, 1987), and the reduction in abundance of entire leaves may indicate drier climates.

The earlier expansion and diversification of macrofloras, as opposed to microfloras, characteristic through much of the mid-Cretaceous, is particularly marked in the Middle to Late Albian, and has been explained in terms of the high palynomorph production of wind-dispersed ferns and gymnosperms, the possible preference of gymnosperms for areas of well-drained soils, where preservation of organic material is minimal (Retallack and Dilcher, 1981), and the early abundance and diversity of Laurales (Upchurch and Dilcher, 1984; Lidgard and Crane, 1990), whose pollen rarely is preserved in the geological record due to their

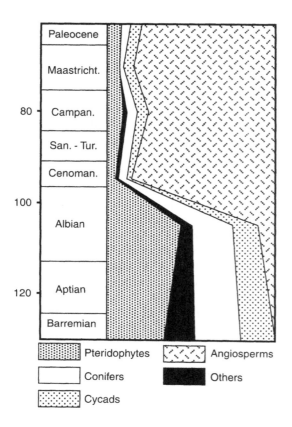

Figure 5.6   Changes in mean contribution of major plant groups to Jurassic, Cretaceous and Paleocene floras (after Crane, 1987). Scale in Ma. Reproduced by permission of Cambridge University Press.

dominantly cellulosic pollen walls. The latter may also explain the early abundance of pollen of Chloranthaceae in comparison with that of Magnoliales (Friis et al., 1987).

### Early Cenomanian

Within the Early Cenomanian (96–94 Ma), leaf assemblages increase further in diversity, with angiosperm pollen accounting for up to 40% of the regional palynofloras, and angiosperm macrofossils representing about 75% of leaf floras. Conifers are reduced to about half their Neocomian (145–113 Ma) levels (about 15%), but pteridophytes exhibit substantial reductions

(from 30 to 6%, and the change in representation of cycadophytes and other seed plants is even more dramatic, from 50% in the Neocomian to 3% (Crane, 1987). The diversity of angiosperm leaves far exceeds that known from Albian floras, with magnoliid taxa becoming particularly widespread and with increasingly organised venation. Entire-margined angiosperm leaves show a marked latitudinal gradient (Wolfe and Upchurch, 1987), with larger-leaved deciduous vegetation developing at higher latitudes, and thick-textured, smaller-leaved, entire-margined evergreen vegetation occurring at middle latitudes. The former reflect moist mesothermal forests, whereas the latter are thought to indicate megathermal, subhumid conditions (Upchurch and Wolfe, 1987).

There is one localised flora of a different physiognomy, from the Dakota Formation in Kansas. In addition to increased leaf size, this flora is characterised by high percentages of species with entire margins, drip tips and probable vine habit. Upchurch and Wolfe (1987) interpret this assemblage as indicating the occurrence of megathermal, closed-canopy multi-stratal forest, which developed during a shortlived wetter and warmer phase, possibly lasting less than 2 Ma, although they emphasise that the controls on the distribution of these assemblages remain unclear.

### Late Cenomanian to Maastrichtian

The Late Cenomanian (94–92 Ma) to Maastrichtian (74–66 Ma) represents a stable period in the history of North American angiospermous vegetation (Upchurch and Wolfe, 1987). Angiosperms rise to dominance in the palynological record, first at lower, then at higher latitudes. Many of the palynomorphs newly evolving during this time can be clearly related to extant groups at the ordinal level or below, with the Magnoliidae, Hamamelididae and Rosidae being best represented. Conifers and pteridophytes each account for about 10% of floras, whereas other groups are generally

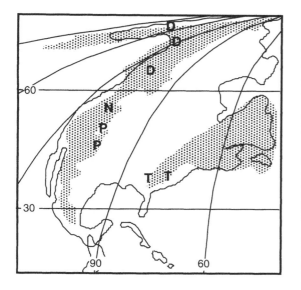

Figure 5.7 Generalised map of Late Cretaceous vegetation for North America, based on Late Maastrichtian macrofossil data; land areas shown stippled. T, tropical forest; P, paratropical forest; N, notophyllous broadleaved forest; D, polar broadleaved deciduous forest (Upchurch and Wolfe, 1987). Reproduced by permission of Cambridge University Press.

insignificant. Three latitudinal zones are represented, at low–middle, high–middle and high palaeolatitudes (Figure 5.7). Vegetation of tropical aspect occurs only in the first latitudinal zone, mesothermal notophyll and polar broadleaf deciduous forest characterising the other two zones, which will not be considered here.

Low–middle palaeolatitude floras belong to the Normapolles palynological province (Figure 5.8), which extends from E North America to Europe and W Asia. The Normapolles province is characterised by high diversities of triporate 'normapolles' pollen, which, at least in part, is derived from early Juglandales (Friis, 1983). In North America and W–C Europe, these floras have a very distinct physiognomy; proportions of thick-textured, entire-margined leaves usually exceed 70% indicating megathermal evergreen vegetation, with paratropical temperatures (mean annual temperature (20–25°C) for most localities of Late Cretaceous age considered by Upchurch and Wolfe (1987), with tropical temperatures in E North America during warmer

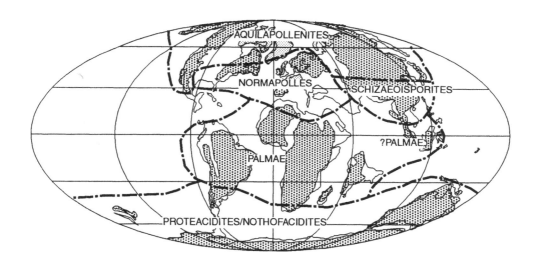

Figure 5.8 Late Cretaceous palynofloral provinces according to Herngreen et al. (1996), superimposed on Maastrichtian palaeogeographic reconstruction by Smith et al. (1994). Reproduced by permission of AASP Foundation.

intervals). Species with drip tips and probable vine habit are of low diversity, and seed size is small. Together, these features indicate open canopy conditions and perhaps a subhumid climate. New foliar physiognomic types are few, with the exception of the large monocots such as palms and gingers. Fossil wood assemblages indicate little seasonality of climate, since growth rings are generally absent, contrasting with modern subhumid climates, where seasonality is reflected by growth rings in deciduous taxa (P.S. Ashton, personal communication; Creber and Chaloner, 1985). The above pattern is characteristic of much of the lower latitude parts of the Normapolles palynological province. Upchurch and Wolfe (1987) suggest that the closest living analogue to this vegetation type may be the heath forests of tropical podsols (Section 2.3), where there is abundant rainfall all year round, although it cannot be considered as true tropical *rain* forest, since it was probably moisture deficient.

### 5.2.2   Cretaceous Low Palaeolatitude Vegetation in Africa and South America

The palynological record from the W and C African, and N South American Cretaceous has been intensively studied during the exploration for petroleum (e.g. Jardiné and Magloire, 1965; Muller, H., 1966; Regali et al., 1975; Muller, J.

et al., 1987) revealing very similar palynological successions, reflecting broadly comparable vegetational and climatic histories, which are particularly relevant to the early history of angiosperms and timing of the development of the first low latitude rain forests. Macrofossil studies from this area, however, are of very limited extent. The main palynomorph assemblage changes recorded for the region, clearly documented by Jardiné and Magloire (1965), are illustrated in Figure 5.9.

### *Barremian to Aptian*

The pattern of appearance of angiosperm pollen in both Central Africa and South America differs from that seen in the Potomac Group, in that many angiosperm pollen types, such as tricolpates, occur earlier, and exhibit greater morphological diversity, although the age of first appearance of monosulcate angiosperms is the same (Figure 5.10). However, dating the earliest angiosperm pollen occurrences, in the non-marine Cocobeach Group of Gabon and the Reconcavo Series of Brazil, is not easy, due to the absence of fossils other than non-marine palynomorphs, and an earlier appearance in this area should be given consideration.

There are many angiosperm pollen types which occur regularly in the Early Cretaceous of Africa and South America, but which are rare or absent in North America, and some of

Figure 5.9   Cretaceous palynological succession from Senegal, after Jardiné and Magloire (1965), data replotted and taxonomy updated. The Barremian to Middle Albian was characterised by gymnosperms producing *Classopollis* pollen (Cheirolepidaceae), Araucariaceae, Ephedraceae and subordinate pteridophytes with the low representation of ancestral eudicots (producing tricolpate pollen), probable Winteraceae (*Afropollis*) and angiosperms producing monosulcate pollen. The Late Albian vegetation also included Gnetales producing elaterospores, and early Caryophyllidae (producing periporate *Cretacaeiporites*), and possible ancestral Proteaceae became widespread in the Late Cenomanian (producing the triporate pollen type *Triorites africaensis*). A major change at the end of the Cenomanian resulted in the complete disappearance of Cheirolepidaceae, coinciding with the sudden expansion of eudicots and monosulcate pollen producers, many of which were probably ancestral Palmae, and the appearance of possible members of the order Illiciales (*Retitricolpites gigantoreticulatus*) in the Turonian. The remainder of the Late Cretaceous saw the disappearance of the group of elaterosporites-producing Gnetales, but the expansion of Proteaceae (*Proteacidites* spp. and *Echitiporites* spp.), Myrtaceae and Sapindaceae (producing *Syncolporites* sp. 148 and other syncolpate pollen), and in the Maastrichtian, the mangrove palm *Nypa* (*Spinizonocolpites baculatus*), and plants producing *Aquilapollenites* pollen. Note that the 'sequences' of Jardiné and Magloire equate with 'zones' and not to sequences in the sense of sequence stratigraphy as described in Chapter 2.

81

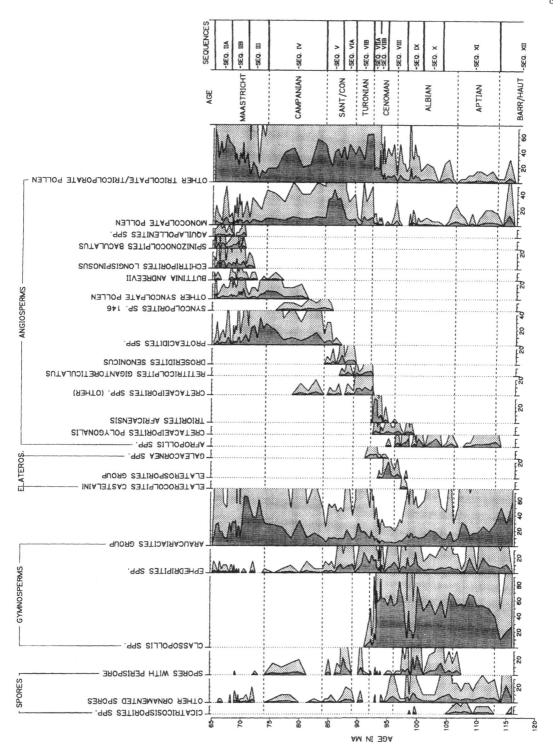

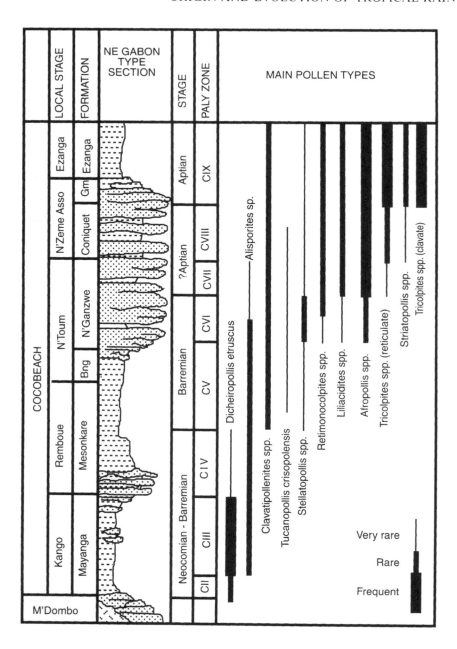

Figure 5.10 Palynological zonation for the Early Cretaceous of Gabon (Doyle et al., 1977). The first angiosperms to be reflected by the pollen record were members of Chloranthaceae, producing *Clavatipollenites* and *Tucanopollis crisopolensis* from the Barremian to Early Aptian; probable Winteraceae (*Afropollis*) appear in the latest Barremian, associated with the expansion of angiosperms producing monosulcate pollen (*Retimonocolpites* spp. and *Liliacidites* spp.), with diverse eudicots producing tricolpate pollen appearing during the course of the Aptian. (Note: *Dicheiropollis etruscus* is a gymnospermous pollen type of unknown affinity, whereas *Alisporites* spp. were produced by early podocarps.)

which can be attributed to modern families. The earliest is *Walkeripollis* (Figure 5.2b), interpreted by Doyle et al. (1990) as belonging to the primitive magnolioid family Winteraceae. *Afropollis* (Figure 5.2d), also appearing in the latest Barremian, is of similar morphology, and may also be related to this family, whereas *Tucanopollis crisopolensis* (Figure 5.2e) is considered by Regali (1989) as being a tectate relative of *Clavatipollenites*, and hence of the Chloranthaceae. Within the Late Albian/Early Cenomanian, *Cretacaeiporites* (Figure 5.2f) occurs commonly, together with the diorate (with two pores positioned on each colpus) pollen type *Hexaporotricolpites*. *Cretacaeiporites* might have been derived from early Caryophyllales (Boltenhagen, 1975), although such an affinity was not considered positive by Muller (1981), who, instead, compared this type, although not with confidence, to the primitive Australasian family Trimeniaceae. The diorate configuration, which includes *Hexaporotricolpites* and *Schizocolpus*, is strongly reminiscent of that of the primitive monotypic Mascarene genus *Didymeles* (Didymelaceae); fossil pollen with this configuration is restricted to Late Cretaceous and Early Tertiary of Africa, South America, and Australasia (Figure 5.11), suggesting that the parent plants of these pollen types were related, and that *Didymeles* is one surviving member of a once widespread family.

As with the Potomac Group, angiosperm pollen occurs in very low frequencies in the Barremian, but it may comprise over 10% of Early Aptian palynofloras from the Ivory Coast (Doyle et al., 1982). The most marked abundance increase occurs in the Late Albian, where up to 20% of palynomorphs may be angiospermous (Figure 5.9). Throughout the Early Cretaceous, increases of angiosperm pollen are generally associated with increases of *Ephedra*-like and elater-bearing pollen such as *Elaterosporites*, *Elateropollenites* and *Galeacornea*, the parent plants of which are generally thought to be associated with dry climates. The remaining assemblages are dominated by *Classopollis* and *Araucariacites*, consistent with Early Cretaceous

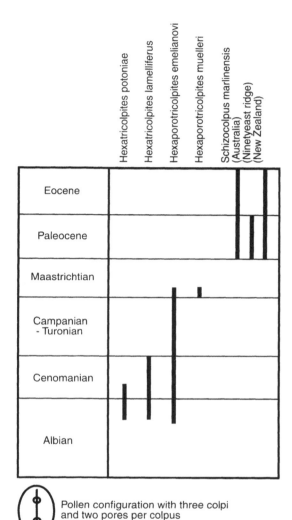

Pollen configuration with three colpi and two pores per colpus

Figure 5.11  Fossil records of diorate pollen, with the same apertural configuration as the primitive Mascarene family Didymelaceae. Muller (1981) thought that the *Hexaporotricolpites* bore no affinity to Didymelaceae since *H. emelianovi* has a different exine structure, but the variety of exine structure seen in this genus, the occurrence of *Schizocolpus marlinensis* in Australasia, which is very close to *Didymeles*, and the restriction of this morphological arrangement to the Late Cretaceous of Africa and South America, and the Early Tertiary of Australasia, suggests that the group is related, and that *Didymeles* is the only surviving member of a once widespread family.

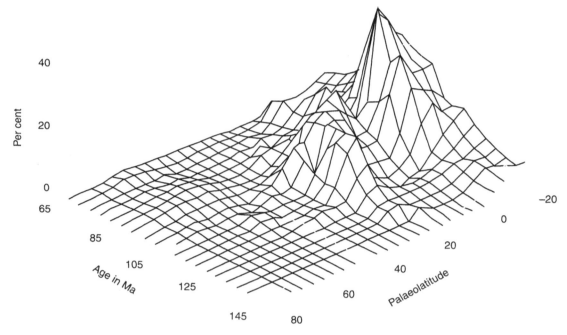

Figure 5.12    Temporal and latitudinal trends in the relative diversity of ephedroid pollen 'species' in Cretaceous palynofloras (from Crane and Lidgard, 1990). Reproduced by permission of Oxford University Press.

African fossil woods, which predominantly comprise Cheirolepidaceae (members of which produce *Classopollis* pollen) and Araucariaceae (Duperon-Laudoueneix, 1991).

Most lines of evidence suggest that Early Cretaceous low latitude climates were warmer than today, strongly moisture deficient (Hallam, 1985), and aseasonal, arid or semi-arid, rather than with seasonally distributed rainfall, since fossil woods mostly show few growth rings (Creber and Chaloner, 1985; Duperon-Laudoueneix, 1991). There is only weak evidence for climatic stratification during this period; ephedroid pollen diversity data, prepared by Crane and Lidgard (1990), show weak diversity maxima toward the subtropical highs at 15–20°N and 10°S (Figure 5.12), probably reflecting areas of drier climate, whereas Doyle et al. (1982) suggest a somewhat more humid climate in the vicinity of the Ivory Coast in the Aptian.

Early Cretaceous dryland vegetation was probably of low diversity, consisting chiefly of gymnospermous sclerophyllous woodland or scrub, probably with *Ephedripites*-producing plants forming a herb or shrub component. Angiosperms and pteridophytes, possibly also with Cheirolepidaceae, probably occupied more moist floodplains and river courses. The common occurrence of Barremian bisaccate podocarpoid pollen (e.g. *Alisporites* sp., Figure 5.10) from both Gabon and Brazil may be explained in terms of gymnospermous forests on high mountains on either side of the proto-Atlantic rift. Bisaccate pollen is virtually absent from low latitude Aptian and younger African and South American sediments, and remains so until the latest Tertiary (see Chapters 6 and 7), suggesting that the upland areas were subsequently reduced by erosion.

### Albian to Cenomanian, Elaterates province

The Albian and Cenomanian of low palaeolatitude Africa and South America are characterised by elater-bearing pollen, the geographical

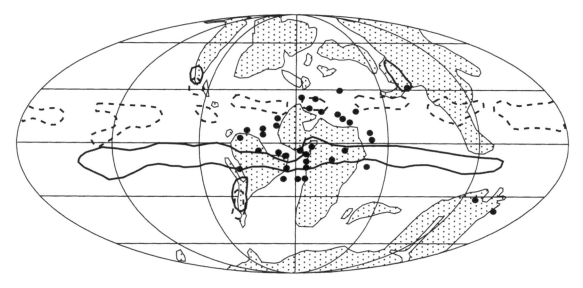

Figure 5.13   Geographic extension of Albian–Cenomanian Elaterates province (continental reconstruction after Smith et al., 1994); black dots indicate position of characteristic *Elaterosporites* province assemblages (after Herngreen and Duenas-Jimenez, 1990). Data is superimposed on mid-Cretaceous precipitation simulations based on ice-free polar seas of Barron and Washington (1982); contours indicate simulated precipitation maxima (more than 1.5 cm per day) for July (dashed) and January (solid).

distribution of which defined the ASA (Africa, South America) microfloral province of Herngreen (1974). The geographical delimitation of this group was subsequently found to extend well outside this area (Herngreen and Duenas-Jimenez, 1990) and the province was updated and renamed the 'Elaterates' province by Herngreen et al. (1996) to include the localities in Asia and Australasia (Figure 5.13).

The Elaterates province is also characterised by the common occurrence of ephedroid pollen, a remarkable abundance of angiosperm pollen, a scarcity of pteridophyte spores, and an absence of bisaccate and trisaccate gymnosperms, and is generally considered to reflect arid to semi-arid, warm climates (e.g. Herngreen and Duenas-Jimenez, 1990; Herngreen et al., 1996). Although this may in part be the case, considerable assemblage variation is recorded within the province which suggests a relationship between climate and vegetation at this time. Ephedroid pollen diversity maxima, presented by Crane and Lidgard (1990), show

marked diversity maxima in the vicinity of the subtropical highs (Figure 5.12), probably reflecting drier climates, whereas more humid climates were suggested for the region of the palaeoequator by Doyle et al. (1982).

The final separation of Africa from South America is purported to have taken place at the end of the Albian (Parrish, 1987), although evidence for floristic provincialism between the two land areas does not occur until the Turonian (92–89 Ma), and dispersals between the two regions are thought to continue into the Maastrichtian and beyond (Chapter 12).

The Late Cenomanian is characterised by very low frequencies of pteridophyte spores (cf. Jardiné and Magloire, 1965), and the proliferation of limestones (cf. Lawal and Moullade, 1986), suggesting a period of apparently dry climates. It also corresponds with the appearance of the first Gondwanan triporate pollen (*Triorites africaensis*), considered ancestral to the Proteaceae (Herngreen, 1974; Muller, 1981), and a major expansion of tricolp(or)ate pollen.

This was also the period during which gymnosperm pollen went through a major reduction in abundance.

Comparison of climatic inferences drawn from low latitude Cenomanian palynomorph data with mid-Cretaceous climatic models, produced either empirically (Parrish et al., 1982) or numerically (Barron and Washington, 1982), are in conflict, as recognised by Herngreen and Duenas-Jimenez (1990), in that climatic models propose often moist, seasonal low latitude climates, but fossil data infer uniformly drier climates, and minimal seasonality. Comparison of the distribution of the Elaterates province with 100 Ma July and January precipitation simulations by Barron and Washington (1982) shows a remarkably close correspondence (Figure 5.13), strongly suggesting that its distribution is mainly controlled by the movement of tropical precipitation belts. How can such an anomaly be reconciled with fossil data? A possibility is that mid-Cretaceous 'greenhouse' climates were somewhat warmer than at present, and that although moisture was freely available, higher temperatures would have resulted in an overall moisture deficiency, registered by plant fossils as indicating aseasonal aridity. Such a suggestion is supported by climatically modelled 'greenhouse' Cretaceous climates (Barron and Washington, 1985), which predicted substantially warmer low latitude climates (Figure 5.14) if $CO_2$ levels were quadrupled to accommodate ice-free polar climates.

Vegetation types within the Albian were probably initially similar to those of the Aptian. The marked reduction of conifers during this period, and expansion of angiosperms, suggest that angiosperms began to colonise dryland areas as well as more moist floodplains and river courses. Early angiosperms occupying dryland areas were probably herbaceous, in view of the rarity of mid-Cretaceous fossil angiosperm woods. There must have been very few locations which might have favoured the development of any vegetation which might be considered closed, multi-statal forests.

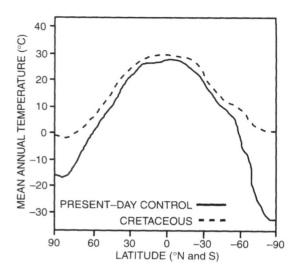

Figure 5.14  Mid-Cretaceous palaeotemperatures, based on a simulation in which atmospheric $CO_2$ is quadrupled (Barron and Washington, 1985).

The terminal Cenomanian was a period of marked extinction (Figure 5.9), particularly of plants producing *Classopollis*, ephedroid and elater-bearing pollen, many pteridophyte spores, and also the recently evolved *Triorites africaensis* (cf. Muller et al., 1987). Some of these extinctions may relate to the expansion of angiosperms, but the abruptness of the event, and its coincidence with the extinction of several 'mid-Cretaceous' angiosperm pollen types, suggests that other factors were involved which are currently not understood. Climatic change is unlikely, since Turonian climates were little different to those of the Late Cenomanian.

### Turonian to Santonian

The Turonian was marked by the initial expansion of existing groups, such as plants producing *Hexaporotricolpites* and *Cretacaeiporites* in Gabon, and *Cretacaeiporites* with subordinate *Hexaporotricolpites* in Nigeria (Lawal and Moullade, 1986) and Senegal (Jardiné and Magloire, 1965). Palynomorph diversities from the Turonian through to the

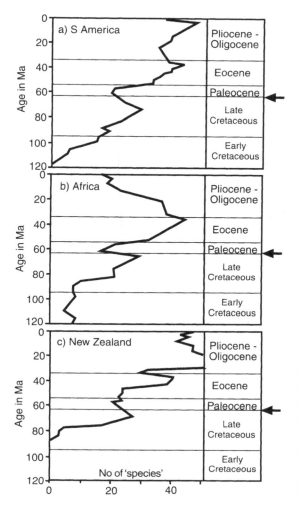

Figure 5.15 Numbers of stratigraphically useful angiosperm pollen types per epoch, for different areas: (a) South America (data from Muller et al., 1987); (b) West Africa. Note drop (arrowed) at K/T boundary (data from Salard-Chebaldaeff, 1990); (c) New Zealand (data from Couper, 1960).

continued to take place, probably during phases of low sea levels.

It is within the Turonian that monosulcate pollen, definitely attributable to Palmae, is first recorded in both areas (Figure 5.16), such as *Monocolpopollenites sphaeroidites* (e.g. Lawal and Moullade, 1986) for W Africa, unpublished records for South America. A number of pollen types show a Turonian appearance in one area, followed by a somewhat later appearance in the other, such as *Auriculiidites* and *Gunnera* (Gunneraceae), which are first recorded in the Turonian of Peru (Brenner, 1968), but are recorded respectively from the Coniacian (89–88 Ma) and Campanian (84–74 Ma) onward in W Africa (e.g. Boltenhagen, 1976), and *Droseridites senonicus* (a pollen type not necessarily related to *Drosera*, but exhibiting some similar morphological features), which first appears in the Turonian of Gabon (Boltenhagen, 1976), and subsequently in the Coniacian of South America (Muller et al., 1987). Examination of the global eustatic sea level curve of Haq et al. (1988), and regional curves for South America by Marcellari (1988) and Arabia by Harris et al. (1984), indicates the presence of a pronounced period of low sea level at the end of the Turonian (Figure 3.6), during which time it is suggested plants could have dispersed more freely between Africa and South America, possibly via the Walvis/Rio Grande and Sierra Leone Ridges. Several other pollen types appear virtually simultaneously in the latest Turonian or basal Coniacian in both continents, and also in India (see below), and their appearance may also relate to migration during this phase of lowered sea levels. These include syncolpate pollen attributable to *Cupanieidites* (and referable to Sapindaceae, Van der Ham, 1990) and porotrichotomosulcate pollen referable to *Constantinisporis*, *Victorisporis* and *Andreisporis*. The porotrichotomosulcate apertural configuration occurs today in the taxonomically isolated W African palm genus *Sclerosperma*, to which Belsky and Boltenhagen (1963) and Srivastava (1987/88) suggested a relationship, but this is considered unlikely;

Maastrichtian in widely separated areas exhibit virtually uniformly increasing trends (Figures 5.15a–c); because of this, the changes seen are thought to be due to competition and evolution, rather than to catastrophic outside influences. By this time, the African and South American continents were clearly separated, although dispersal between the two areas

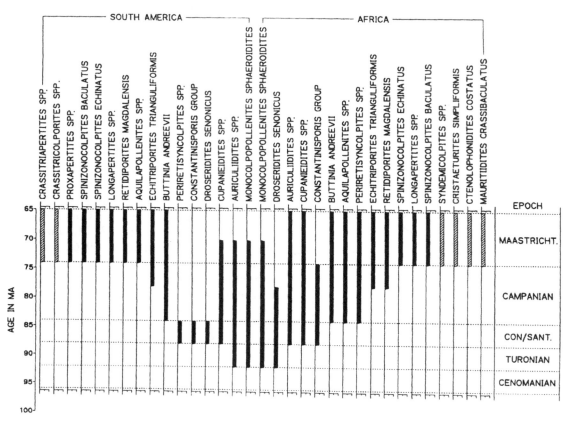

Figure 5.16   Times of appearance of some common and distinctive pollen taxa in the Turonian to Maastrichtian of Africa and South America, during the course of the opening of the S Atlantic. Black columns indicate taxa which occur on both continents, inferring intercontinent dispersal; shaded columns indicate taxa which are restricted to a single continent.

broadly comparable apertural configurations are also seen in some Myrtaceae and Sapindaceae (Harley, 1996a), and an affinity to one of these families is considered much more probable, since, as noted above, data suggest that they initially diversified from this region, the oldest record of pollen referable to Myrtaceae (*Myrtaceidites psilatus* and *M. lisamae*) and Sapindaceae (*Cupanieidites reticularis* and *C. acuminatus*) being from the latest Turonian or Coniacian of W Africa (Belsky et al., 1965; Boltenhagen, 1976).

Ephedroid pollen attains its maximum diversity in the Turonian (Crane and Lidgard, 1990), particularly in South America (De Lima,

1980), whereas pteridophyte spores display a global minimum at this time (Figure 5.17). Isotope data suggests that the highest global temperatures were reached during the Turonian, and a particularly hot, and moisture-deficient climate was likely. Surprisingly, there are no records of angiospermous fossil wood from the Turonian to Santonian (88–84 Ma) of Africa, recalling the paucity of wood fossils from sediments of the same age in North America. One possibility which might explain this is that angiosperm trees at this time were characterised by very soft woods (which were unlikely to fossilise, or might fossilise as broken fragments), with stout pachycaul trunks,

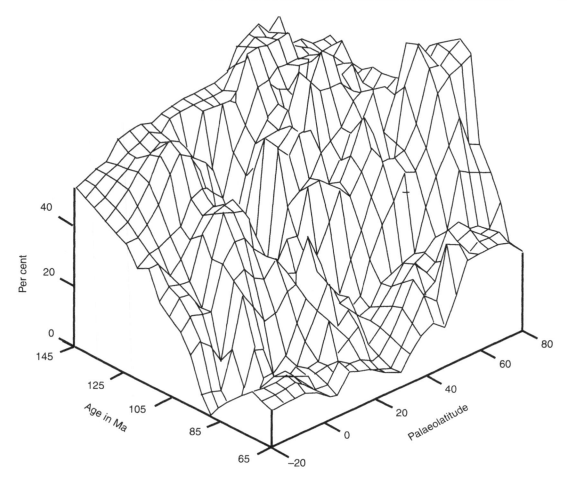

Figure 5.17   Temporal and latitudinal trends in the relative diversity of pteridophyte spore 'species' in Cretaceous palynofloras (from Crane and Lidgard, 1990). Reproduced by permission of Cambridge University Press.

adapted for water retention, as found in arboreal taxa from African and Australian arid climates. The openness of dryland vegetation at this time would suggest little need for tall trunks, since competition would have been for water retrieval and retention, not for light. Mabberley (1977) emphasises that the pachycaul habit (Figure 5.18) has been particularly successful in aseasonally dry (desert), and cold (tropicalpine) environments with diurnal temperature variations, but not beyond the tropics in seasonal climates. Thus pachycauly may have been advantageous over large areas of the

aseasonally subhumid mid-Cretaceous low latitudes. It is likely that pachycauly was widespread prior to the first major expansion of tropical rain forests, recalling Corner's (1949) speculation that a large proportion of the ancestors to modern rain forest trees were pachycauls.

Evidence for Turonian (and early Senonian[1]) latitudinal climatic stratification is provided again by the correlation of ephedroid pollen diversity maxima with subtropical highs, and also by regional abundance variations of echinate *Hexaporotricolpites* spp. (Figure 5.19)

Figure 5.18  Pachycaul *Espeletia* spp., in the paramo, high Andes of Colombia. Pachycauls are currently more or less restricted to aseasonal climates (Mabberley, 1977), and are now most characteristic of tropicalpine vegetation and tropical rain forests. Pachycauls were likely to have been much more widely distributed in the Late Cretaceous, when aseasonal climates were more widespread.

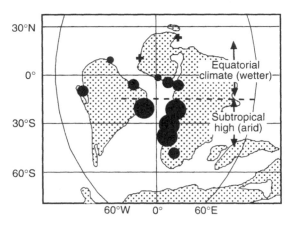

Figure 5.19  Geographical variations in abundance of *Hexaporotricolpites emelianovi* in the Late Cretaceous of W Africa and South America (from Jardiné et al., 1974). Circle size proportional to frequency of occurrence; small circles indicate rare or isolated specimens; crosses indicate absence. The data suggest a major climatic gradient at about 15°S.

(Jardiné et al., 1967, 1974). *Hexaporotricolpites* spp. show an inverse relationship to pteridophyte spore abundances, and a direct relationship with carbonate distribution, suggesting that their parent plants preferred drier climates. The distinctly increased abundances in the vicinity of the southern hemisphere subtropical high infers drier climates at palaeolatitudes of 10–20°S.

Within the Coniacian and Santonian, ephedroid pollen and cycads show reduced abundance, and pteridophyte spores became more common (e.g. Jardiné and Magloire, 1965; Lawal and Moullade, 1986), suggesting the development of more moist climates, with vegetation dominated by palms (which may have replaced cycads, that have the same growth form) and with Myrtaceae and Sapindaceae. A wetter climate is also suggested by the Coniacian appearance of pollen comparable to the moisture-loving *Ilex* (*Ilexpollenites chmurae*) in Gabon (Boltenhagen, 1976). The presence of climatically zoned vegetation is suggested from the distribution of the porotrichotomosulcate group of pollen, mentioned above, since it shows a distinctive increased representation in Gabon (Belsky and Boltenhagen, 1963), within the subtropical high pressure zone, rather than in areas to the north, where it occurs in low frequencies only, and thus follows the climatic lineament indicated by *Hexaporotricolpites* in the Cenomanian/Turonian. The common occurrence of the *Constantinisporis* group in S India at the same time (which would have been at an equivalent palaeolatitude) suggests that similar climatically dependent vegetation was present in the Indian subcontinent at this time.

It is tentatively suggested that the Coniacian to Santonian was a period during which the low latitude aseasonally subhumid mid-Cretaceous climates were beginning to be replaced by more moist, but probably seasonal, more zonal climates. It is unlikely that everwet climates had developed, since there are hardly any records of coals from the low latitudes at this time. True low latitude rain forests were apparently still undeveloped.

### Campanian to Maastrichtian, Palmae Province

The Campanian and Maastrichtian experienced a more rapid diversification of angiosperms than at any time previously, with a particularly rapid diversification of the Palmae. This phase of diversification coincided with the development of true everwet climates through most of the equatorial tropics, and the establishment of a more strongly zoned global climate, resulting in more clearly delineated global vegetation zones, as indicated by palynological provinces (Figure 5.8), and also by the concurrence of well-developed coals along the palaeoequator in Brazil, W Africa (Reyment, 1965; Salami, 1991), and Somalia (Schrank, 1994), coupled with floristic provincialism in South America (Romero, 1993), the equatorial expansion of schizaeaceous spores, and the proliferation of plants producing periporate pollen in the subtropical high pressure zones (Crane and Lidgard, 1990). This period also saw the development of groups ultimately to become important rain forest components; wood, pollen and macrofossil records of Bombacaceae, Caesalpinioidae, Celastraceae, Combretaceae, Ctenolophonaceae, Euphorbiaceae, Icacinaceae, Malvaceae, Meliaceae, Moraceae, Myristicaceae, Olacaceae, Proteaceae, Rutaceae and Theaceae date from this time (fossil woods reviewed by Duperon-Laudoueneix, 1991).

The appearance of a number of bizarre pollen types peculiar to each geographical area, such as *Triporotetradites gemmatus* and *Sindorapollis* (referable to the legumes ?*Dinizia* and *Sindora* respectively) and crassiaperturate pollen in South America (Herngreen, 1972), and *Cristaeturites*, *Cristaecolpites* and *Syndemicolpites* in Africa (Schrank, 1994), clearly suggests that African and South American floras were beginning to diverge as a result of their separation by the Atlantic. Continued dispersal between the two areas is suggested, however, by the more or less simultaneous appearance of several pollen types, such as *Buttinia*, *Mauritiidites* (*Mauritia*), *Longapertites* (possibly ancestral to *Eugeissona*) and the

Figure 5.20   The monotypic *Nypa fruticans* (Palmae), in mangrove, West Java, one of the few extant angiosperm genera (and perhaps species) which were already present in the latest Cretaceous.

nypoid taxa *Spinizonocolpites* and *Proxapertites* (Figure 5.16).

Evidence for the appearance of typical closed, multi-stratal forest synusiae is suggested from the presence of casts of large seeds and fruit, attributable to Annonaceae, Caesalpinioideae, Meliaceae and Sterculiaceae from Senegal (Monteillet and Lappartient, 1981), a large supply of endosperm in an enlarged seed allowing successful germination under a closed forest canopy. The presence of pollen of *Malmea* type (Annonaceae) in Colombia (Sole de Porta, 1971) and seeds or fruit from Nigeria (Chesters, 1955) attributable to Icacinaceae and Passifloraceae suggests the presence of climbers, and the presence of large-dimensioned wood

from Africa, suggests the appearance of tall canopy trees. Niklas et al. (1980) have proposed that the diversity peak of angiosperm fossils within the latest Cretaceous relates to evolutionary adaptations associated with the development of the forest canopy.

Palynological data from Nigeria (Salami, 1991) and Somalia (Schrank, 1994) provide an indication of the character of coastal and swamp vegetation. *Nypa* pollen indicates the presence of coastal mangrove communities (Figure 5.20), whereas freshwater swamp vegetation included a low, herbaceous, possibly floating, community dominated by ferns, hepatics, lycopods and the floating fern *Salvinia*, which gave way to a herbaceous and shrub community, with common palms, including mauritioid and (in Somalia) calamoid forms, and Restionaceae (Hochuli, 1979). Freshwater swamp forests included the arillate *Ctenolophon*, Annonaceae and possible Proteaceae, pollen of other angiosperms presumably being derived from nearby dryland rain forests. The restriction of normapolles pollen to Egypt and NE Africa, and calamoid pollen (*Dicolpopollis malesianus*) to Somalia (Schrank, 1994) suggests a dispersal barrier between E and W Africa, presumably due to semi-arid conditions in the continental interior; climbing palms (Calamoidae) dispersed from E Africa to Europe and E Asia at an early date, but remained absent from W Africa until the Late Tertiary.

### 5.2.3   Cretaceous Vegetation in the Eastern Tropics

#### Southeast Asia

The fossil record for Cretaceous angiosperms in SE Asia is very limited; only the tentative record of *Clavatipollenites* sp. from the Barremian of the Malay Peninsula, by Shamsuddin and Morley (1995), refers to Cretaceous angiosperms since Muller's (1968) study of the Cretaceous Pedawan and lower part of the Kayan

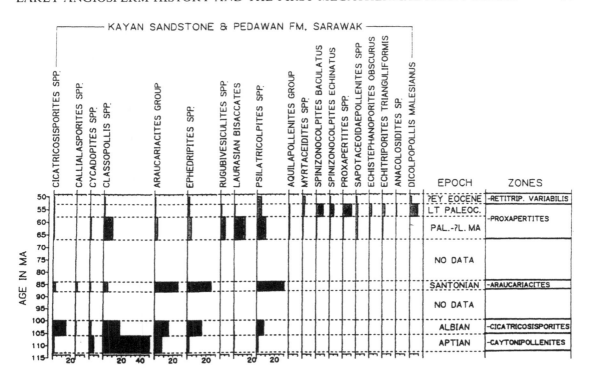

Figure 5.21   Ages for Sarawak palynological zones of Muller (1968), as reinterpreted by Morley (1998). The *Cicatricosisporites* and *Caytonipollenites* zones, previously referred to the Cenomanian, are believed to be Aptian to Early Albian; the *Araucariacites* zone, previously referred to the Turonian, is more likely of early Senonian (Santonian) age, although a Turonian age cannot be wholly ruled out; the *Rugubivesiculites* zone is thought to be Paleocene, but a Maastrichtian age cannot be fully ruled out, as all of the taxa which Muller used to suggest a Late Cretaceous age have now been recorded from the Paleocene of China by Song-Zhichen et al. (1981). Reproduced by permission of Backnuys Publishers.

(previously Plateau Sandstone) Formation of Sarawak. It was previously brought to attention (Section 5.1.3 and Morley, 1998) that the ages of the formations studied by Muller require some modifications (Figures 5.4, 5.21), and that the sections which he examined from the Pedawan formation are Aptian or Albian and Santonian for the *Araucariacites* zone (although a Turonian age for the latter cannot be wholly ruled out). The Kayan Formation, however, is now thought to be mainly of Paleocene (66–54 Ma) age, although it is possibly extends into the Maastrichtian. This classic study by Muller, generally considered to include a full Late Cretaceous pollen record, actually includes very little Late Cretaceous section. However, in order to make comparisons with Late Cretaceous successions elsewhere, some aspects of palynomorph assemblages from the Maastrichtian? to Paleocene Kayan Formation are considered here; because of the fragmented nature of the fossil record within the Far East, attribution to the Maastrichtian or Paleocene does not seriously affect arguments raised in this book.

With the ages of Muller's Sarawak zones reinterpreted, it is important in discussing the vegetational consequences of Far Eastern Cretaceous palynomorph assemblages to realise that there is more gap than record for SE Asia, and also that there will inevitably be taphonomic bias since so few localities have been studied, especially in the Late Cretaceous. The Early Cretaceous sections (Figure 5.4) contain similar, but reduced diversity angiosperm pollen to those of the same age from Western Gondwanaland, with gymnosperm pollen reflecting distinctly subhumid to semi-arid climates. The Santonian assemblage is also similar to those from Africa, but some groups are missing, such as *Hexaporotricolpites* spp., presumably as a result of geographical isolation. The *Elaterosporites* and *Afropollis* groups may be missing from the region because sediments of Late Albian to Turonian age have not yet been studied; Aptian records of *Afropollis zonatus* are known, however, from SW China (Morley, unpublished), thus there is no biogeographical reason why the parent plant of *Afropollis* should not also have occurred in SE Asia.

The character of Aptian/Albian vegetation is best indicated by palynomorph assemblages from the marine *Cicatricosisporites* zone, in which palynomorphs from different terrestrial plant communities are intermixed. The common occurrence of *Classopollis* spp. and *Ephedripites* spp. suggests xerophytic dryland vegetation with Cheirolepidaceae and Gnetales, whereas common pteridophyte spores and angiosperm pollen are more likely to have been derived from successional vegetation and low-lying coastal swamps. Rare bisaccate conifer pollen may reflect montane vegetation in the hinterland region. Much drier climates are likely for the Santonian, in view of the expansion of *Ephedripites* spp. and reduction in abundance of pteridophyte spores. There is no published data to indicate the character of late Senonian (84–66 Ma) vegetation, although recently discovered assemblages from the Sunda region suggest that Palmae were important in SE Asia at this time, as in other tropical regions.

The common occurrence of bisaccate conifer pollen of Laurasian affinity in the Maastrichtian? to Paleocene is a unique feature of SE Asian palynomorph assemblages, and is interpreted as indicating the presence of high mountains, presumably with a direct connection with the Asian mainland, in close proximity to depositional sites, allowing Asian montane conifer forests (and associated angiosperms?) to extend to equatorial latitudes. The climate at this time would have been much more moist, indicated by the reduced representation of *Ephedripites* spp. and expansion of pteridophyte spores, but not necessarily everwet, since lithologies lack any trace of coals. A considerable diversity of angiosperm pollen at this time could reflect early rain forest vegetation, in which Sapotaceae, *Ilex* and possibly early Ulmaceae (*Verrutriporites lunduensis*, in Muller, 1981), were conspicuous components. Freshwater swamp vegetation was composed of pteridophytes, whereas brackish water swamps with *Nypa* formed an early mangrove vegetation.

By the latest Cretaceous or earliest Tertiary, some of the geographic features which characterise SE Asia today were already in place, in particular, the presence of high mountains, on the equator, probably with direct connections to those of E Asia and terrestrial connections to North America via Beringia, directly prior to the time that widespread paratropical rain forests were to develop across the northern hemisphere. Also, moist climates were widespread. However, with respect to lowland floras, there is no evidence to suggest that any of the floristic features which particularly characterise the region today were in place.

### India and Australia

At the time of the initial radiation of angiosperms, the Indian and Australian Plates were located too far south to include a significant angiosperm element, or to bear vegetation of tropical aspect, the first records of angiosperm pollen occurring in the latest Barremian of Australia (Burger, 1991; Dettmann, 1994) and Aptian of India (Srivastava, 1983). The Indian Plate separated from Gondwanaland in the Aptian, and drifted rapidly northward during the mid-Cretaceous, during which time it bore a Gondwanan flora similar to that of Australia. By Cenomanian to Turonian times, it lay in

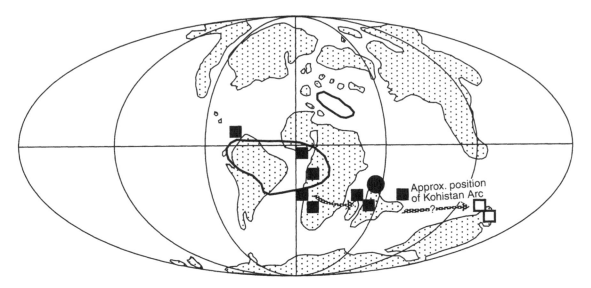

Figure 5.22 Mid-Cretaceous migration routes along the southern shore of Tethys. *Elateropollenites africaensis* (□) is recorded from the Turonian of Irian Jaya (Bates, unpublished) and Papua New Guinea (Lowe, unpublished), and has a Late Albian to Turonian centre of abundance in Africa and South America (marked by solid line); *Afropollis jardinus*, widespread throughout most of Africa and South America, exhibits an identical temporal distribution pattern in the Cenomanian of Pakistan (●) to that seen in W Africa (IEDS, 1995), demonstrating dispersal from Africa to the Indian Plate in the Cenomanian; *Constantinisporis, Victorisporis* and *Andreisporis* (■) are very well represented in the Turonian to Campanian of sub(palaeo)equatorial Africa, but appear in the Senonian of Madagascar (Chen, 1978) and India (Venkatachala, 1974; Nandi, 1991; Morley, unpublished), reflecting a Late Turonian or early Senonian dispersal route. Turonian palaeogeographic reconstruction by Smith et al. (1994).

close proximity to Madagascar (Figure 5.22), and at this time many plant taxa were able to disperse from Africa, via Madagascar and its associated islands, to India. One of the first of these was a winteraceous plant which produced *Afropollis* pollen (which became extinct in the mid-Cenomanian), since this pollen type shows the same temporal succession in the Cenomanian of Pakistan to that in W Africa (IEDS, 1995). This was succeeded in the Turonian, or early Senonian, as India drifted across the southern hemisphere high pressure zone, by the *Constantinisporis* group, discussed earlier for Africa, and recorded from Madagascar by Chen (1978), and widely from the Late Cretaceous of India (Venkatachala, 1974; Nandi, 1991). During this time, and immediately following, as India drifted into equatorial latitudes during the Campanian and early

Maastrichtian, many other taxonomic groups dispersed to the Indian Plate, including members of the Sapindaceae (Van der Ham, 1990), Palmae (including nypoid palms and the *Longapertites* group), Myrtaceae, *Ctenolophon* (Srivastava, 1987/88), and normapolles (Nandi, 1991). There is no evidence from the Indian palynological record to suggest that extinctions caused by changing climates, as the Indian Plate was rafted through different climatic zones, left India with a rather generalised flora, as suggested by Raven and Axelrod (1974). Dispersals from Africa became reduced during the later Maastrichtian, as India separated from Africa, and drifted across the equator toward the Asian Plate. During this time, prior to collision with Asia, the Indian Plate bore a flora with three distinct components: an ancient, autochtonous gondwanic component, carried

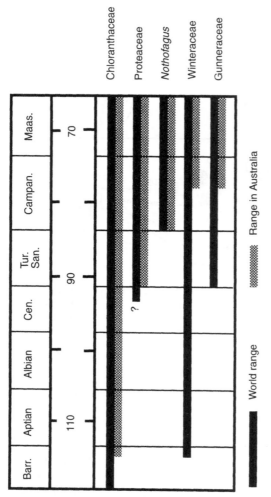

Figure 5.23   Time ranges of angiosperm taxa represented in the Cretaceous vegetation of Australia, which dispersed via South America and Antarctica (from Dettmann, 1994).

arillate seeds, suggest a rain forest habitat, strongly indicate that multistoreyed rain forests became well developed on the Indian Plate during the latest Cretaceous as it drifted across the lower palaeolatitudes.

Some lines of evidence suggest that the Cenomanian/Turonian dispersal path to India also reached Australia. The elater-bearing ephedroid pollen type *Elateropollenites africaensis* provides the best evidence for this dispersal route, being widespread throughout the Cenomanian and Turonian of Africa and South America, but appearing suddenly in the Turonian of Irian Jaya (Figure 5.22). It is possible that other, otherwise palaeotropical, angiosperms followed the same route, perhaps following the Kohistan Arc, with which the Indian Plate collided during its northward drift from Gondwanaland (Treloar et al., 1989; Treloar and Coward, 1991).

The appearance of angiosperms in Australia is mostly due to Late Cretaceous dispersal from South America, across the Antarctic continent, and to endemism within, and around, the southern continent (Dettmann, 1994, 1997). The earliest immigrant was the chloranthaceous *Ascarina*, which first appeared in the latest Barremian, well after its appearance to the north. Other early immigrants included Proteaceae in the Turonian, and *Gunnera* and Winteraceae (*Drimys* type) in the Campanian (Figure 5.23), the latter 30 Ma after the Aptian record of *Drimys* pollen from Israel by Walker et al. (1983). The palynological record does not support the suggestion of Raven and Axelrod (1974) that the region had acquired a significant angiosperm component prior to the 'medial' Cretaceous. The Late Cretaceous was also a period of pronounced angiosperm radiation within Australia and the Antarctic (Dettmann and Jarzen, 1990), with *Nothofagus* appearing and diversifying in the Santonian, and Proteaceae showing remarkable diversification in the Campanian. Surprisingly, *Ilex* has its centre of origin in this area, with its earliest appearance in the Turonian of Australia (Martin, 1977).

from Gondwana, and consisting principally of gymnosperms and pteridophytes, possibly with a few angiosperms; an allochthonous component from Africa, consisting of megathermal angiosperm elements; and a diverse endemic component which evolved as India drifted across many climatic zones.

The widespread representation of megathermal groups, especially of the Ctenolophonaceae, at this time, which by possession of large,

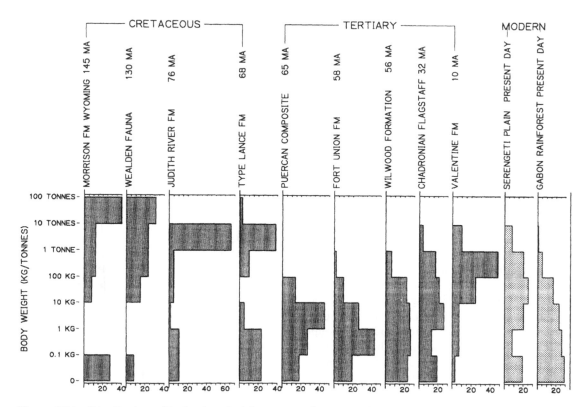

Figure 5.24   Distribution of body sizes (in kilograms and tonnes) of herbivorous tetrapod faunas during the last 160 Ma, from Wing and Tiffney (1987), compared to modern faunas from savanna and rain forest environments. Reproduced by permission of Cambridge University Press.

## 5.3   THE TERMINAL CRETACEOUS EVENT

### Cretaceous herbivores and diaspore vectors

Literature dealing with the effects of dinosaurs and meteorites on tropical rain forests is limited. Despite this, both were critical in determining the present character of tropical, and indeed all, vegetation. Prior to 66 Ma, Cretaceous forests lived side by side with dinosaurs. During most of the Cretaceous, up until the Campanian, herbivore dinosaurs were of huge size and generalist feeders (Figure 5.24) and would have caused major and repeated disruption of the vegetation (Wing and Tiffney, 1987). It cannot be discounted that the open

nature of much Cretaceous vegetation was due, in part, to the effects of herbivore pressure. Wing and Tiffney (1987) also suggest that because of the limited representation of small Cretaceous herbivores which might have been seed eaters, selective pressures for large angiosperm diaspores were weak. Small seeds imply limited amounts of endosperm, and consequently a light-rich habitat for growth. Without large seeds and animal vectors, widespread closed angiosperm forests simply did not exist. However, within the latest Cretaceous, Campanian to Maastrichtian, small, possibly frugivorous herbivores became more diverse, and paralleled a tendency toward increasing diaspore size, increasing tendency toward 'k'-selection (low reproductive rates), and the development of latest Cretaceous closed-canopy forests.

## Meteorite impact[2]

Palynomorph diversity graphs for Africa, South America and New Zealand (Figures 5.15a–c) clearly show that, by the end of the Cretaceous, angiosperm floras were quietly and successfully proliferating. One June morning (Wolfe, 1991) 66 Ma ago, all that came to an end. A giant meteorite fell out of the sky (Alvarez et al., 1980), landing maybe in Mexico in an area of carbonate rocks (Hildebrand et al., 1991). The resulting impact caused a cataclysmic explosion, which probably made Hiroshima look like a bursting puffball. Fallout from the explosion was distributed throughout the world, resulting in a layer of microscopic fragments of 'shocked' quartz (easily identified under the scanning electron microscope), distributed widely through the oceans. The vaporisation of the target rock on impact caused an order of magnitude increase in $CO_2$, and brought acid rain and increased warming (O'Keefe and Ahrens, 1989). Material from the bolide itself was also vaporised, and disseminated equally widely, leaving a tell-tale trace of the rare earth element Iridium along with the shocked quartz (Figure 5.25). The blast, and associated tsunamis, destroyed forests over a huge area, and the resulting dust cloud is thought to have affected global climates over several years by cutting out sunlight. The result was the destruction of both fauna and flora on a massive scale; 38% of marine animal genera became extinct (Raup and Sepkopski, 1984), including all pliosaurs, ammonites, mososaurs and ichthyosaurs, together with dinosaurs and pterodactyls on land. It has, however, been suggested that the event had little effect on tropical vegetation. In fact, the effect of this event on tropical vegetation is clearly indicated from the palynomorph diversity curves (Figure 5.15); whether from Venezuela, Central Africa or New Zealand, at the end of the Cretaceous, palynomorph diversities exhibit a dramatic decline, by up to

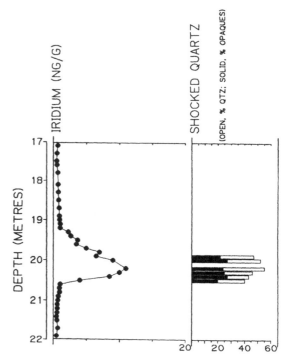

Figure 5.25  Iridium spike at the K/T boundary, from Lei Zhou et al. (1991). DSDP site 596, S Pacific, 9000 km from the supposed impact crater in Mexico.

40%. The effect of the terminal Cretaceous event on tropical vegetation was clearly quite dramatic, and many niches must have become available virtually overnight for the accelerated expansion and diversification of angiosperms, within the Early Tertiary.

## Post-impact vegetational succession

Palynological and foliar remains provide evidence for the mass-kill at the Cretaceous/Tertiary (K/T) boundary in North America (Tschudy et al., 1984; Upchurch and Wolfe, 1987; Wolfe, 1991), with an initial recolonisation of the landscape by ferns (Figure 5.26), followed by a vegetational recovery which physiognomically mimicked secondary succession seen in extant megathermal vegetation, but occurred over a longer time scale (Upchurch and

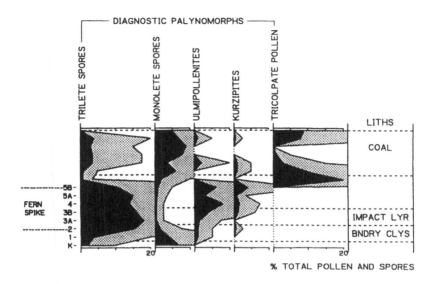

Figure 5.26   Palynomorph diagram across K/T boundary. The sample from bed 1 contains typically Cretaceous '*Proteacidites*' (probably nothing to do with Proteaceae; not shown); the highest relative abundance of ferns (fern spike) occurs in beds 2–3b; relative abundance of fern spores decreases as pollen of probable deciduous plants increase (*Kurzipites*, *Ulmipollenites*, *Tricolpites*). From Wolfe (1990). Stipple = ×5 exaggeration. Reproduced by permission of *Nature*.

Wolfe, 1987). The late successional forests which followed were characterised by increased leaf size (Figure 5.27), higher percentages of species with drip tips, and higher percentages of species with hairless foliage (Upchurch and Wolfe, 1987) and increased diaspore size (Figure 5.28). The first extensive closed-canopy multi-storeyed North American rain forests appeared following the disappearance of the dinosaurs, and their proliferation may be directly linked with the removal of large generalist herbivores and their replacement by small mammals, which developed, for their own selfish benefits, a great interest in seed dispersal!

## 5.4   THE FIRST MEGATHERMAL RAIN FORESTS?

In judging the earliest appearance of rain forests, there remain some lines of evidence from biogeography which still need to be taken into account, which suggest that closed-canopy rain forests may have been in existence as early as the mid-Cretaceous, prior to the main separation of the major tropical land masses. It has already been brought to attention that some members of the Magnoliales and Laurales were prominent at this time, especially the Winteraceae (Doyle et al., 1990) and Chloranthaceae. The nutmeg family Myristicaceae, which is an important megathermal rain forest tree family, is a member of this group and is recognised as of great antiquity; fossil wood, attributed to *Myristicoxylon*, has recently been recorded from the uppermost Cretaceous of Ethiopia (Duperon-Laudoueneix, 1991). However, Myristicaceae pollen is poorly known (Walker, 1976), and the family has a poor fossil pollen record, not having been observed prior to the Eocene, although Walker and Walker (1984) note close similarities to some Early Cretaceous pollen types. The family is characterised by dioecious flowers (i.e. male and female flowers occur on different trees), rendering it an unlikely prospect for dispersal across extensive water bodies, or through areas without

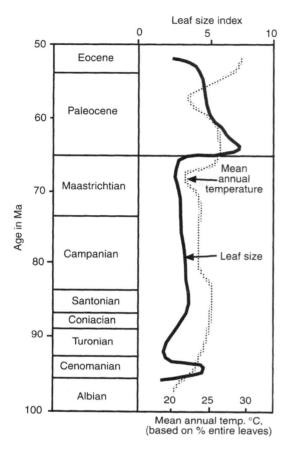

Figure 5.27 Percentage of entire-margined species, and average leaf size for low–middle palaeolatitudes of North America. Leaf-margin percentages are standardised for palaeolatitude, using inferred latitudinal temperature gradients (from Upchurch and Wolfe, 1987). Reproduced by permission of Cambridge University Press.

a dense rain forest cover. For these reasons, the Myristicaceae is considered one of the most important among modern megathermal families for suggesting patterns of distribution within the earliest phase of angiosperm development, and indirectly indicates the presence of closed-canopy forests, possibly initially within gallery forests along rivers, at an early stage of angiosperm development.

It is perhaps appropriate here to summarise briefly the fossil evidence for early rain forests.

The earliest claims of megathermal closed-canopy rain forests are from the Cenomanian Dakota Formation of North America, described by Upchurch and Wolfe (1987). They acknowledge that this occurrence is rather isolated, however, both in time and spatially. Other North American workers, e.g. Crane (1987) and Wing and Tiffney (1987), are more guarded in their interpretations, and suggest that there is little evidence for the development of closed-canopy rain forests until the earliest Tertiary, at least in North America, emphasising in particular that, at least with respect to North American floras, pre-Tertiary seeds were too small to germinate within a closed forest. Examination of the mid-Cretaceous palaeoclimate reconstruction of Barron and Washington (1985), based on $CO_2$ levels four times greater than today, indicate that the northern hemisphere mid-latitude climate would have been similar in its temperature regime to that of the present-day low latitudes, but that the palaeoequatorial region would have been much warmer (Figure 5.14). Barron and Washington's model suggests that the presence of closed-canopy rain forests in the Cenomanian of North America should be given serious consideration, and that similar settings may have occurred at the same palaeolatitudes in Eurasia, and also in the southern hemisphere, particularly in S South America, and in the regions of Madagascar and N Australia/New Guinea, especially since the earlier model of Barron and Washington (1982) suggests both moist summer and winter mid-Cretaceous climates in some mid-latitude settings (Figure 5.13). The initial radiation of megathermal taxa from middle- rather than low latitudes, and their later dispersal to the tropics, would help explain the disjunct distributions of numerous primitive angiosperm taxa with very limited means of dispersal. Also, the present-day rain forests of Madagascar, New Caledonia and E Australia are likely to be the remnants of such forests, evolving in a mid-latitude setting, but being preserved since the northern drift of these land masses kept pace with Tertiary climatic deterioration.

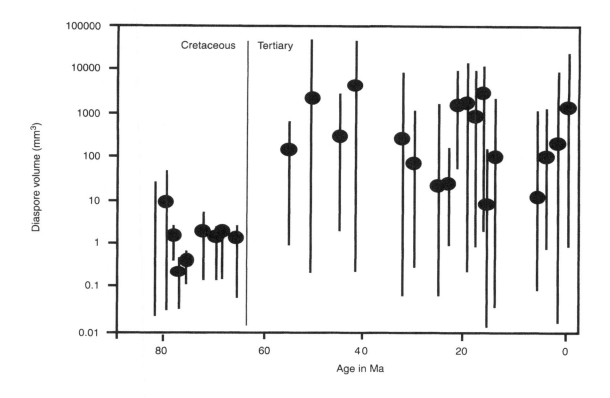

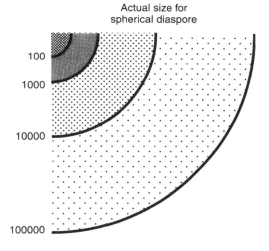

Actual size for
spherical diaspore

Figure 5.28  Distribution of angiosperm diaspore sizes in Tertiary floras from North America. Note the dominance of very small sizes in the Cretaceous, and great increase in size range in the Paleocene. Solid circles are means for assemblages, vertical bars are maxima and minima. From Wing and Tiffney (1987). Stippled quadrants (below) indicate diameter of seeds of different volumes (in mm³). Upper figure reproduced by permission of Cambridge University Press.

Conditions within the equatorial area during the mid-Cretaceous were too hot, or dry, for rain forest development. Everwet climates, however, became well developed in both the African and South American tropics during the Campanian and Maastrichtian, following global climatic deterioration at the end of the Cretaceous. Both palynological and macrofossil evidence from W Africa, Somalia and also from India suggest that closed-canopy rain forests were well established in those areas at that time.

Although rain forests clearly became established within the latest Cretaceous, it was the extinction of the dinosaurs that paved the way for the proliferation of mammals, and with the concurrent diversification of birds and insects, the stage was set at the beginning of the Tertiary for angiosperms to adapt along with their mammalian and avian vectors and diversify into what we understand today as *tropical rain forest*.

## 5.5 SUMMARY OF EARLY ANGIOSPERM EVOLUTION

Following their initial appearance between the Late Triassic? and earliest Cretaceous, until the widespread proliferation of rain forests in the Early Tertiary, angiosperm history can be divided into five phases, previously differentiated using pollen alone by Muller (1981), as follows:

### Phase I Valanginian?/Hauterivian to Late Albian/Early Cenomanian

Initial radiation of angiosperms with early Magnoliales, Laurales and Illiciales as small, successional 'r'-selected (opportunist) weeds and possibly woody shrubs along rivers in aseasonally subhumid low latitudes and, subsequently, of early successional vegetation throughout low and middle latitudes. Evolution of most dicotyledonous foliar types by Late Albian, evolution of late successional foliar types, and very localised occurrence of possible closed-canopy forests to the north (and possibly south) of the subtropical high pressure belts.

### Phase II Late Cenomanian

Ascendency of angiosperms over all other groups, migration to polar regions and development of latitudinal zonation, expansion of Amentiferae and general increase in species diversity.

### Phase III Turonian to Santonian

Aseasonal subhumid climates characterise lower and middle latitudes during the Turonian, with the widespread development of open sclerophyll vegetation, and rapid evolution of 'r'-selected taxa, but limited evolution of new foliar types, except in monocotyledons. Angiosperms of xeric environments may have included many taxa exhibiting the pachycaul habit. Widespread dispersals occurred in the Turonian during a phase of very low sea levels. The Coniacian and Santonian are thought to have witnessed the development of more zonal climates, with a tendency toward increasing seasonality. Families appearing in this phase with rain forest representatives include Aquifoliaceae and Palmae (in the Turonian), and Myrtaceae, Sapindaceae and Zingiberaceae (in the Coniacian/Santonian).

### Phase IV Campanian to Maastrichtian

More zonal climates became established culminating in the development of a wet equatorial zone. Small herbivores and large fruit show increased abundance suggesting parallel development, and, as a result, 'k'-selected angiosperms appeared for the first time. Closed-canopy rain forests became widespread within the equatorial moist climate zone. Rain forest families appearing during this phase, but not necessarily within equatorial localities, include Bombacaceae, Caesalpinioidae, Celastraceae, Ctenolophonaceae, Euphorbiaceae, Meliaceae, Olacaceae, Sterculiaceae, Symplocaceae and Ternstroemiaceae. The appearance of diverse families of modern aspect parallel with the development of low latitude everwet climates was no coincidence. It emphasises that, although angiosperms initially evolved to colonise warm subhumid environments not fully exploited by other plant groups, they were pre-adapted to rapid evolution within warm perhumid climates (Doyle et al., 1982). In fact, the perhumid equatorial climate was to become the setting in which angiosperms were to establish a floristic and physiognomic diversity unparalleled in other vegetation types.

Moist montane forests were already in place at this time in the region of the palaeoequator in the Far East, and were probably directly connected to those in E Asia, with terrestrial connections through Beringia to North America. At this time, however, both Africa and South America were separated from continents to the north by extensive seaways.

### Phase V Paleocene

Following the K/T boundary event, a shortlived basal Paleocene successional phase and the removal of giant herbivores allowing a major proliferation of 'k'-selection, there was wide-spread expansion of rain forests through much of the lower and middle latitudes. The consequence of this, of continued plate disassembly, and of climatic change on rain forest floras and vegetation in each continental region bearing Tertiary rain forests, is the subject of the next six chapters.

## NOTE

1 The Senonian sub-epoch includes the Coniacian to Maastrichtian stages (89–66 Ma).

2 It is not intended here to attempt to justify the impact explanation of the K/T boundary, except to emphasise that a major, catastrophic event, such as a meteorite impact, as opposed to climatic change or transgression, remains the only hypothesis which explains all the major anomalies (iridium spike, shocked quartz) and extinctions associated with this boundary.

# CHAPTER 6

# South and Middle America

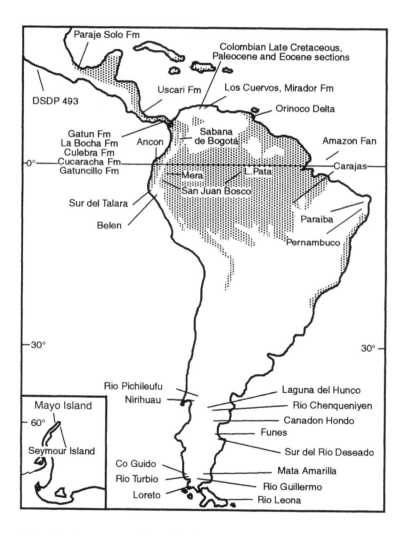

Map showing present-day rain forest distributions in the Neotropics
(after Richards, 1996), and locations mentioned in the text.

## 6.1   INTRODUCTION

Half of present-day rain forests occur in South and Middle America. They include the most species-rich forests anywhere recorded (Section 2.1), and the largest expanse of semi-evergreen rain forests. They are also noteworthy in having the highest number of genera of palms, with the greatest concentration of primitive members of this family, but surprisingly the representation of other primitive angiosperms is far less than that of the tropical Far East and NE Australia (Thorne, 1976), which led Takhtajan (1969, 1987) to suggest that angiosperms must have first evolved in that area. South American rain forests have also been the subject of discussion with respect to the maintenance of their high diversity during periods of 'glacial' low sea levels, especially in relation to the 'Pleistocene Refuge' hypothesis, which not only suggests a mechanism which enabled the maintenance of species-richness through the Pleistocene (1.6–0 Ma), but also encouraged speciation (e.g. Haffer, 1969, 1987). There has also been debate as to whether South American savannas are natural or of anthropogenic origin. This chapter tries to provide some explanations to the above anomalies and questions.

South America witnessed the 'birth' of tropical Cenozoic palynology (Hopping, 1967), which was initially used by oil companies purely as a tool for stratigraphic correlation in sediments lacking marine fossils (Kuyl et al., 1955). Although most of these studies remain unpublished, some of the conclusions reached, and botanical implications of the fossil pollen record, were summarised by Germeraad et al. (1968). Most of our knowledge of South American palynology, however, both with respect to the Tertiary, and the history of Quaternary vegetation, is due to the pioneering work of van der Hammen (e.g. 1954, 1957, 1961, 1963), initially in Colombia and subsequently, with many co-workers, at the Hugo de Vries Laboratorium in Amsterdam. Cenozoic plant macrofossil remains have been known from S South America and the region around the

Antarctic Peninsula for more than a century, but considerable controversy surrounds both taxonomic determinations and age of the sediments containing the fossils (Hill and Scriven, 1995). In this account, reference is made only to leaf-margin data, taxonomic determinations and climatic inferences accepted by Romero (1986, 1993).

## 6.2   TECTONIC SETTING

South America remained as a single tectonic plate, with most of its surface subaerially exposed, throughout the Tertiary. During this time, it drifted slowly westward, with the opening of the S Atlantic, its western margin overriding and subducting the oceanic crust of the Nazca (E Pacific) Plate. The compression and volcanism associated with this plate collision resulted in the formation of the Andean Cordillera along the entire western margin. Within the N Andes, the most pronounced phase of uplift took place during the Neogene (25–1.6 Ma), and was responsible for substantial changes in the pattern of flow of the major South American rivers, such as the Orinoco and Amazon (Hoorn et al., 1995). Some N–S movement of the South American Plate also occurred. During the earlier Tertiary, there was some movement to the south, but from the Oligocene (36–25 Ma) onward, drift has been essentially to the north.

Since the separation of the South American and Antarctic Plates in the mid-Cretaceous, there have been a number of times when there were probably direct land connections with both Antarctica, and the North American Plate, although details of both these connections have been widely debated (Parrish, 1987). Dalziel and Eliott (1973) suggested that a cordillera, through South Georgia and the Sandwich Isles, probably existed during the Late Cretaceous. The rectilinear Scotia Sea was probably already in place during the earlier (Dalziel and Elliott, 1973), or later (Barker et al., 1976; Craddock, 1982) Palaeogene (66–25 Ma), but faunal evidence

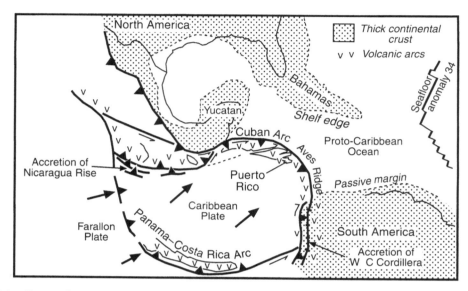

Figure 6.1   Campanian reconstruction of Middle America (Pitmann III et al., 1993). The Greater Antilles and Aves Ridge, created by subduction of the Proto-Caribbean Ocean by the Caribbean Plate, formed a land bridge between the Americas from the Late Cretaceous and Paleocene. The Caribbean Plate drifted eastward relative to the Americas in the mid-Tertiary, breaking this connection by the Eocene. During the Neogene, the Panama–Costa Rica Arc collided with North and South America, creating the Panama Isthmus. Reproduced by permission of Yale University Press.

suggests that land connections continued until the Early Eocene (Marshall, 1980). South America finally became separated from Antarctica during the Late Eocene (39–36 Ma), with the opening of Drake's Passage, resulting in the initiation of the circum-Antarctic current. The latter event is thought to have been responsible for initiating the late Cenozoic global cooling by cutting off oceanic heat exchange from the tropics to Antarctica (Kennett, 1977, 1980).

During the Early Cretaceous, the proto-Caribbean Ocean separated North and South America (Pindall et al., 1988; Pitmann III et al., 1993), but during the mid-Cretaceous subduction of the proto-Caribbean ocean crust below the northeast margin of the Caribbean Plate resulted in the formation of the Greater Antillean island arc. This formed a land bridge between both continents from the Campanian (84–74 Ma) to the Paleocene (66–54 Ma) (Figure 6.1), which was utilised by hadrosaur and ceratopian dinosaurs (Brett-Surman, 1979; Rage, 1988) and many other vertebrates

(Hallam, 1994). This land bridge was severed after the Paleocene, as the Antilles Arc moved to the northeast, after colliding with Yucatan, and subsequently with the Bahama Plateau in the mid-Tertiary. Subduction of the Pacific Farallon Plate by the southwest margin of the Caribbean Plate during the Late Cretaceous and earliest Tertiary resulted in the formation of the Panama–Costa Rica Arc, which by the end of the Eocene formed a continuous morphological feature, but was not yet emergent, and lay in the Pacific. During the mid-Tertiary, this arc shifted eastward, relative to the Americas, colliding with these continents during the Miocene (Pitmann III et al., 1993), and forming a continuous land bridge by the Pliocene, as indicated by the faunal migrations of the 'Great American Interchange'.

During the Eocene, volcanism also occurred extensively along the Lesser Antilles (Tomblin, 1975), and there is evidence of a subaerial weathering surface on the adjacent Aves Ridge, which led Parrish (1987) to suggest that there

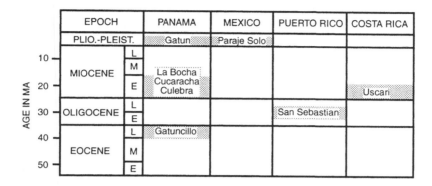

| | EPOCH | | PANAMA | MEXICO | PUERTO RICO | COSTA RICA |
|---|---|---|---|---|---|---|
| | PLIO.-PLEIST. | | Gatun | Paraje Solo | | |
| 10 | MIOCENE | L | | | | |
| | | M | La Bocha | | | |
| 20 | | E | Cucaracha Culebra | | | Uscari |
| 30 | OLIGOCENE | L | | | San Sebastian | |
| | | E | | | | |
| 40 | EOCENE | L | Gatuncillo | | | |
| | | M | | | | |
| 50 | | E | | | | |

(AGE IN MA)

Figure 6.2   Sedimentary formations from Central America examined by Graham.

may have been an Eocene land connection between North and South America, but the vertebrate fossil record provides little support for this suggestion (Hallam, 1994).

## 6.3   MEXICO AND CENTRAL AMERICA

The history of both the vegetation and continental connections in Middle America is critical when assessing N–S Palaeogene dispersals, and in understanding the environment within which vertebrate migrations took place during the late Neogene 'Great American Interchange'. Knowledge of Tertiary floras in the Caribbean is due largely to a long succession of studies by Alan Graham. Assessing Caribbean Tertiary vegetational history is hampered by difficulties in unravelling the plate tectonic history of the region (Section 6.2), and by the fragmentary nature of the record, which has come largely from short, often coal-bearing stratigraphic intervals, many from former volcanic islands, widely distributed in space, and often with poor time control (Figure 6.2). Nevertheless, the summation of his work provides some relatively clear images of the origins and history of rain forests in this region.

The oldest records are from the Panamanian Gatuncillo Formation, of Middle? to Late

Eocene age, which has yielded a diverse pollen and spore flora. Many of the pollen and spores recorded can be compared to modern taxa, and predominantly indicate low-lying, moist tropical communities with remarkable similarities to those growing in Panama at present, and primarily with North American-derived affinities rather than South American ones (Graham, 1985, 1987a). Mangrove swamps are indicated by the occurrence of pollen of *Rhizophora* (Rhizophoraceae) and *Pelliciera rhizophorae* (Pellicieriaceae), whereas the occurrence of Palmae, *Crudia* (Leguminosae), *Ilex* (Aquifoliaceae), *Coccoloba* (Polygalaceae), Combretaceae, Myrtaceae, *Faramea* (Rubiaceae) and *Mortiodendron* (Tiliaceae), together with ferns and lycopods, suggests the occurrence of moist to wet tropical forest communities, and without evidence for either dry or elevated vegetation.

The palynological record of three stratigraphically associated successions of Early Miocene age (25–16 Ma) from Panama (Culebra, Cucaracha and La Bocha Formations), and the Uscari Formation from Costa Rica, which comprise deposits that accumulated near to volcanic islands, reveal coastal mangrove fringes, and moist, tropical forests again with many similarities with present-day Caribbean vegetation, and with Middle and North American affinities (Graham, 1987b, 1988a,b, 1989b). Differences primarily reflect the character of lowland swamps and montane communities; the assemblages from Panama suggest widespread fern-dominated marshes with palms, such as *Attalea*, *Manicaria* and *Synecanthus*. Palms seem to have been absent from such swamps at the time of deposition of the Uscari Formation, where the presence of common *Podocarpus* (Podocarpaceae) and Ericaceae pollen, together with spores of the filmy fern *Hymenophyllum* (Hymenophyllaceae) suggest the presence of cloud forest above lowland rain forests.

Diverse palynomorph assemblages from the Pliocene (5–1.6 Ma) Paraje Solo Formation from S Mexico (Graham, 1976, 1979, 1987a, 1989a) suggest increased environmental diversification compared to older assemblages, reflecting greater topographic relief. As well as mangroves with *Rhizophora*, *Laguncularia* (Combretaceae) and possibly other species bordering coastlines, high evergreen lowland rain forest, and semi-evergreen forest at low altitudes, assemblages also suggest an altitudinal vegetation zonation, with evergreen oak and deciduous oak–*Liquidambar* (Hamamelidaceae) forest, succeeded by needle-leaved pine forests at higher altitudes. The needle-leaved forests also included *Alnus* (Betulaceae), and the conifers *Abies* and *Picea*. The latter genus is currently restricted to areas 1000 km to the north, in northern Mexico and beyond, and on the basis of this Graham (1989a) suggested that Pliocene climates were cooler than the present-day.

The Pliocene Gatun Formation from Panama (Graham, 1991a,b,c) yielded the richest microflora from any of the Caribbean localities, which in addition to moist rain forests, montane forests with *Podocarpus* and *Quercus*, and mangroves, demonstrates the presence of well-developed and extensive tropical dry forest and grasslands, and the possible development of wetter, Atlantic, and drier, Pacific, provinces.

An interesting, although little-used, palynological diagram was published by the late George Fournier from a DSDP (Deep Sea Drilling Project) site DSDP 493 offshore Mexico

(Fournier, 1981, 1982). This is presented in summarised form in Figure 6.3, after deciphering his codes, and transforming his data from a log to a linear scale. This diagram, accurately dated using nannofossils, provides a clear temporal framework within which the isolated Caribbean assemblages can be viewed, since the section provides a more or less continuous coverage from the Early Miocene, through to the Pleistocene, but with the Middle Miocene (16–10 Ma) missing. The presence of rain forests throughout the Early Miocene is suggested by the presence of pollen of Sapotaceae and Bombacaceae, with *Pinus* (Pinaceae) forming needle-leaved forests in areas of drier climate or at high elevations. The consistent occurrence of *Pinus* throughout the Neogene suggests the continuous representation of conifer forests, either at high altitudes, or in xeric conditions. The presence of Compositae pollen throughout probably suggests open vegetation. Following the Middle Miocene stratigraphic break, Sapotaceae show a marked increase in abundance, and *Quercus* make a sudden appearance, its southward dispersal reflecting Late Miocene (10–5 Ma) climatic deterioration. Gramineae pollen, together with *Ambrosia*, increases in abundance through the later Late Miocene and then shows a further increase in the Pliocene, coinciding with the appearance of *Artemisia* and an expansion of *Pinus*, while forest elements diminish in abundance. These changes reflect, on the one hand, the widespread development of drier climates, with the expansion of savanna, and, on the other, continued cooling, probably coinciding with the expansion ice caps in the northern hemisphere. The Pliocene appearance of *Alnus* pollen is noteworthy, and probably reflects climatic deterioration, contrasting with its appearance in South America, which postdated the closure of the Panamanian Isthmus.

The DSDP 493 core clearly shows the development of the savanna corridor which enabled the interchange of large mammals following the closure of the Isthmus of Panama. The cyclical fluctuations within most groups of taxa throughout the late Neogene probably relate to

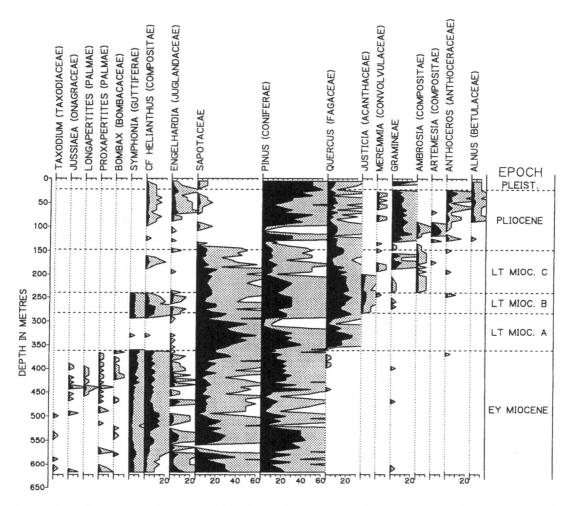

Figure 6.3   Pollen diagram from DSDP 493, from offshore the Mexican Pacific coast (data from Fournier, 1982). Independent dating is provided by nannofossils; stipple = ×5 exaggeration; subdivisions of Late Miocene are arbitrary, but compare to zones M1–M6, for the Late Miocene of W Africa (Figure 7.13).

fluctuating sea levels, and to global climate, and show parallels to the pattern seen in the late Neogene of W Africa (Chapter 7).

## 6.4   SOUTH AMERICA

### 6.4.1   Paleocene Vegetation

The effect of the terminal Cretaceous extinction event is shown by a marked reduction in floristic diversity, reflected by the reduction in the number of stratigraphically useful palynomorph types used within the latest Cretaceous and Paleocene of N South America (Figure 5.15a). The Paleocene flora which followed contained many modern elements, including representatives of 34 extant angiosperm families based on a combination of macrofossil and microfossil records (Romero, 1993).

During the Late Cretaceous, many South American plant taxa were shared with Africa, but by the Paleocene, with increasing separation of these land masses, transatlantic dispersals became less frequent. At this time, however, land connections remained both with Antarctica and North America and, especially at the time of warming global climates during the Late Paleocene, opportunities developed for dispersal into South America of taxa of both North American/Laurasian and southern hemisphere Antarctic/Australasian affinity, the former group mainly comprising taxa poorly represented in Africa, such as Bombacaceae (Figure 6.4a), *Symplocos* (Symplocaceae) and members of the family Tiliaceae. These groups are represented differently in equatorial and S South America, with the result that Paleocene floras fall into two distinct provinces: a northern one, characterised by diverse Palmae and dominated by megathermal taxa, and referred to the Palmae province following Herngreen and Chlonova (1981); and a southern province, which is characterised on the one hand by megathermal elements and on the other by southern hemisphere taxa, which Romero (1993) refers to his 'mixed' province (Figure 6.5).

The north coast of South America clearly experienced a very wet climate during the Paleocene, indicated by the widespread accumulation of peats, extending from Colombia (van der Kaas, 1983) to Guyana (Leidelmeyer, 1966), now heavily exploited for coal. Palynomorph assemblages from these coals are overwhelmingly dominated by palm pollen (Figure 6.6), mainly consisting of generalised, smooth forms which cannot be determined to a genus and *Proxapertites* spp., which is believed to be derived from a mangrove palm, allied to *Nypa* (e.g. Muller, 1979; Morley, in press), but also including *Mauritia* and *Longapertites* spp. (possibly ancestral to the SE Asian palm *Eugeissona*). In addition to Palmae, assemblages are characterised by pollen of megathermal taxa such as *Anacolosa* (Olacaceae), Annonaceae, Bombacaceae and *Ctenolophon* (Ctenolophonaceae). The presence of common *Proxapertites* spp. in these coals suggests that many formed under brackish conditions as well as freshwater ones. Coastal peats

are rare today in South America, but are known from the superwet Pacific coast of Colombia, where they are restricted to freshwater environments, as are the widespread peats of SE Asia (Section 2.4.1). Present-day mangrove peats are of very limited occurrence, being restricted to carbonate substrates (Section 2.2.1). Clearly, the palm-dominated freshwater to brackish-water peats of the South American Paleocene have no present-day analogue.

Elsewhere in equatorial South America, the climate may not have been so wet as along the northern coast; for instance, the regular occurrence of Gramineae pollen in the Paleocene of Brazil may reflect more open vegetation and seasonal climate.

At more southerly latitudes, in Romero's (1993) mixed floristic province, palm pollen is also particularly characteristic of the Early Paleocene (66–60 Ma), and is represented by no less than 12 different pollen types, with smooth, undifferentiated forms and *Longapertites* being the commonest (Archangelsky, 1973). However, *Nypa* did not reach to such high latitudes as in Australia (Chapter 10) and Europe (Chapter 11), its southernmost locality being at 10°S in Brazil (Romero, 1986). The mixed character of this flora is shown by the regular occurrence of pollen of *Casuarina* (Casuarinaceae), *Beauprea* (Proteaceae), *Nothofagus* (Fagaceae), the conifers *Podocarpus* and *Microcachrys*, and macrofossils of Cunoniaceae, Polygalaceae, other Proteaceae, Sapindaceae and *Peumus* (Monimiaceae), and also the common occurrence of pollen of southern hemisphere relics, such as Restionaceae and *Gunnera* (Gunneraceae). Romero and Hickey (1976) have also identified leaves of the Australian rain forest tree *Akania* (Akaniaceae, allied to Sapindaceae) from this region.

Leaf-margin analyses for southernmost South America, summarised by Romero (1986), indicate increasingly warm climatic conditions through the Paleocene, with the development of paratropical rain forests at 45°S by latest Paleocene times (Figure 6.7). The southernmost evidence for Paleocene megathermal elements is

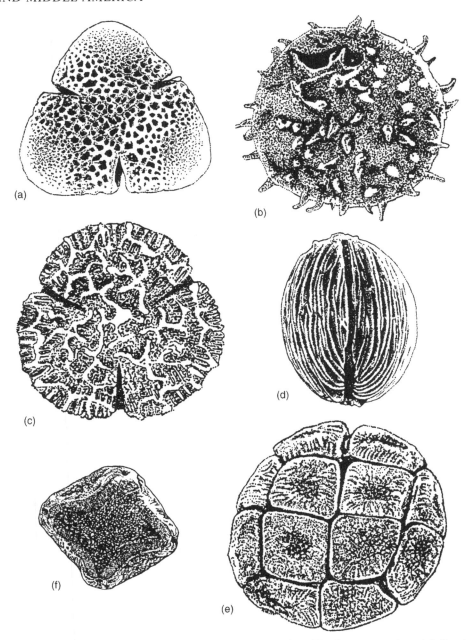

Figure 6.4   Pollen of selected taxa characteristic of South American Tertiary vegetation. (a) Bombacaceae
(*Bombax ceiba*[1] ×1200), have been important throughout the Tertiary; (b) *Mautiria*[2] (Palmae) ×2000,
important element throughout the Tertiary; (c) *Amanoa*[3] (Euphorbiaceae) ×1500, common swamp tree from
Eocene onward; (d) *Crudia*[4] (Leguminosae) ×1500, common genus from Eocene onward; (e) *Albizia*[5]
(Leguminosae) ×1000, Mimosoidae show a clear radiation from the Late Eocene onward; (f) *Alnus*[6]
(Betulaceae) ×1500, dispersed into South America following closure of the Panama Isthmus, and cooling late
Neogene climates.[1], Nilsson and Robyns (1986); [2], Harley (1996b); [3], Erdtman (1952); [4], Ferguson (1987); [5],
Ghazali (1993); [6], Moore et al. (1991). Drawn by Harsanti Pribatini.

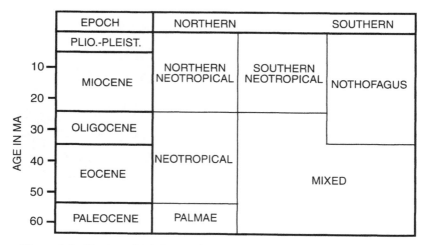

Figure 6.5   Tertiary floristic provinces within South America (Romero, 1993).
Reproduced by permission of E.J. Romero.

from Seymour Island, then at about 65°S, where Duzen (1907) described a fern-rich flora of 64 taxa containing a mixture of megathermal and microthermal species of which 42% of angiosperms had entire-margined leaves, and Cranwell (1959) recorded palm pollen, suggesting the presence of moist, warm temperate rain forests (subtropical according to Romero, 1986), with some megathermal elements. These assemblages indicate that, during the earliest Tertiary, some megathermal elements were able to survive as far south as Antarctica, perhaps in a climatic setting analogous to that of parts of New Zealand today, which has warm temperate rain forests rich in ferns, and with a sufficiently equable climate to support a few tropical species, such as the palm *Rhopalostylis*.

*Nothofagus* pollen and macrofossils show a noteworthy distribution within the S South American Paleocene, apparently in conflict with leaf-margin data, being rare in the Early Paleocene, but increasing in frequency by Late Paleocene times (Archangelsky, 1973; Romero, 1986). This distribution pattern is difficult to explain, and may reflect an incomplete fossil record, but may also relate to the presence of subhumid climates, indicated by macrofossils referred to taxa currently restricted to xeric localities, such as *Shinopsis* (Anacardiaceae), or

to the establishment of new ecological niches; a similar pattern exists in the Paleocene of Australia, and is also difficult to explain in ecological terms (Chapter 10).

### 6.4.2   Eocene Vegetation

The pattern of modernisation of the South American flora, already noted in the Paleocene, continued into the Eocene, with 45 angiosperm families being recognised from Eocene deposits by Romero (1993). This author considered that the degree of modernisation seen in equatorial South America was such, coupled with the reduced importance (although not reduced diversity) of Palmae, to justify attribution to a different floristic province, referring the northern part of South America to his Neotropical province (Figure 6.5). The overall character of S South American floras is not markedly different to that of the Paleocene, since they include a combination of megathermal and temperate southern hemisphere elements, and so the southern area remains in Romero's 'mixed' province.

The presence of coals and diverse palynomorph assemblages in many Eocene sediments from N South America (Muller et al., 1987) suggests that moist climates with diverse rain

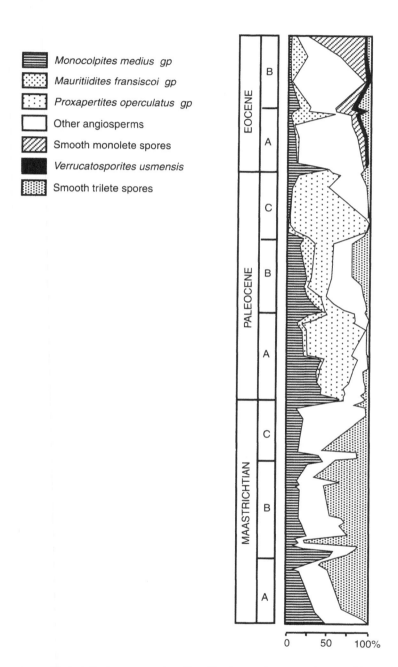

Figure 6.6   Summary of latest Cretaceous and earliest Tertiary palynomorph assemblages from the El Guajira region, Colombia (van der Hammen, 1964). Reproduced by permission of Springer-Verlag.

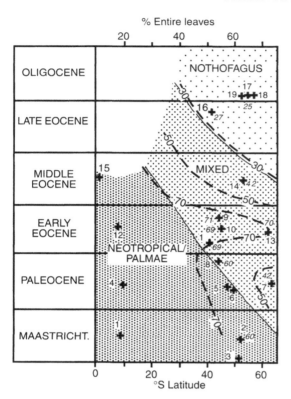

Figure 6.7   Vegetational provinces and leaf-margin data from S South America. Romanised numbers refer to locations below, italics refer to % entire leaves in selected floras. Dashed lines show trends in the percentage representation of entire leaves. Note that there is not a clear relationship between the representation of species with entire leaves and floristic provinces prior to the Middle Eocene. 1) Paraiba, Brazil; 2) Co Guido, Chile; 3) Mata Amarilla, Argentina; 4) Pernambuco, Brazil; 5) Funes, Argentina; 6) Sur del Rio Deseado, Argentina; 7) Seymour Is., Argentina; 8) Laguna del Hunco, Argentina; 9) Rio Chenqueniyen, Argentina; 10) Canadon Hondo, Argentina; 11) Rio Pichileufu, Argentina; 12) Sur del Talara, Belen, Peru; 13) Mayo Is. 25, Argentina; 14) Rio Turbio, Argentina; 15) Ancon, Equador; 16) Nirihuau, Argentina; 17) Loreto, Chile; 18) Rio Leona, Argentina; 19) Rio Guillermo, Argentina (modified from Romero, 1986).

forests persisted through most of the epoch. The beginning of the Eocene, however, was a period of major change; there were many extinctions at this time, and also many new appearances in the earliest Eocene, and Palmae became less well represented than during the Paleocene Palmae

province (e.g. Wymstra, 1971). This sudden change coincided with the Late Paleocene/Early Eocene thermal maximum of the mid-latitudes, and changes at this time were presumably in response to this climatic event, which is more fully discussed in Chapters 7 and 13.

Gonzalez (1967) made a particularly valuable palynological study of the Early and Middle Eocene (49–39 Ma) of Colombia, describing and recording abundance changes of all the palynomorphs observed in a suite of samples from the Los Curvos and Mirador Formations. Altogether, 148 different pollen types were recorded, which included a large number of different tricolpate pollen grains, most of which cannot be referred to modern families. Although his diagrams suggest that some of the plants which produced the commonest pollen types continued throughout the section studied, less dominant types showed distinctive periods of change, initially at the base of the Early Eocene, and subsequently at the base of the Middle Eocene. Palm pollen is particularly well represented through the profile, with common types, such as that of *Mauritia* (Figure 6.4b) and an indeterminate form (*Psilamonocolpites medius*) occurring throughout, and other types, several of which compare to *Iriartea*, showing a distinct succession. With the exception of palms, the early part of the Early Eocene contains very few pollen types which can be referred to extant taxa, but, in the later part, pollen of *Alchornea* and *Amanoa* (6.4c) (Euphorbiaceae), *Jussiaea* (Onagraceae) and *Merremia* (Convolvulaceae) were noted. More determinable forms occur in the Middle Eocene, and include pollen of Annonaceae, Gramineae, *Crudia* (Figure 6.4d), *Caryocar* (Caryocaraceae) and *Mirabilis* (Nyctaginaceae). He attempted to reconstruct coastal vegetation types by comparing patterns of change of certain palynomorph groups with Quaternary sections (Figure 6.8), and proposed that 'brevitricolpate' pollen was derived from a plant with a similar habitat to *Rhizophora*. He constructed a model of coastal vegetation change (Figure 6.9), and went on to interpret an ecological succession through the Early to Middle Eocene (Figure 6.10), with

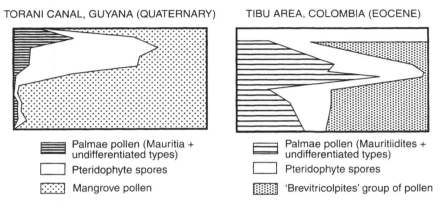

TORANI CANAL, GUYANA (QUATERNARY)          TIBU AREA, COLOMBIA (EOCENE)

≡ Palmae pollen (Mauritia + undifferentiated types)
☐ Pteridophyte spores
⋮⋮ Mangrove pollen

≡ Palmae pollen (Mauritiidites + undifferentiated types)
☐ Pteridophyte spores
▦ 'Brevitricolpites' group of pollen

Figure 6.8  Comparison of Early Eocene and Quaternary palynomorph assemblages from Colombia. Gonzalez (1967) noted a similarity between palynomorph successions seen in regressive Late Quaternary sections from Guyana, where *Rhizophora*-dominated assemblages are succeeded by fern spore-rich assemblages, which are in turn replaced by assemblages with palm pollen dominant, with the Early Eocene succession from the Los Cuervos Formation, from a succession initially with brevitricolpate pollen dominant, followed by fern spore-rich, and palm pollen-dominant assemblages. On the basis of this similarity, he proposed that the parent plants of brevitricolpate pollen were mangroves, analogous to *Rhizophora*. Reproduced by permission of Brill, Leiden.

widespread 'mangrove' swamps, grading to palm-dominated swamps in the Early Eocene. He suggested that the occurrence of Gramineae pollen in the Middle Eocene indicated savanna vegetation, but the very high number of different pollen types recorded in the Middle Eocene suggests diverse rain forests, and it is likely that grasses, with *Jussiaea* and Malvaceae, were present in open swamps rather than savanna.

Bombaceae pollen (Figure 6.4a) shows a distinct phase of diversification through the Early and Middle Eocene, which continued through the remainder of the Tertiary (Figure 6.11), indicating that South America has been a centre of diversification for this family for over 60 Ma.

It was during the Late Eocene that true mangroves with *Rhizophora* became established in N South America, presumably dispersing from Tethys (Chapter 9), together with another possible mangrove which produced the pollen type *Verrutricolporites rotundiporus*, which is thought to have been ancestral to the SE Asian mangrove genus *Sonneratia* (Sonneratiaceae) (Chapter 9). The Late Eocene was also a time of differentiation of many legumes, such as members of the *Acacia* and *Albizia* (Figure 6.4e)

groups, *Mimosa* and *Fillaeopsis* (Caccavari, 1996).

To the south of the southern hemisphere subtropical high pressure zone, megathermal forests reached their greatest extent during the Early Eocene. Several macrofossil floras with more than 100 described species each are recorded from Chile and Patagonia, which indicate that floristically diverse, closed megathermal forests were widespread at this time. The richest flora, described by Berry (1938), is from Rio Pichileufu in Patagonia, then at about 47°S, it consisted some 140 species, and included both moist tropical and temperate elements, as well as numerous species of probable lianes and several species which today prefer seasonally dry conditions, such as *Cupania* (Sapindaceae), and *Schinopsis* and *Schinus* (Anacardiaceae). Romero (1986) indicated that 69% of the species within this flora possessed entire-margined leaves, which, bearing in mind the different representation of entire-margined leaves in present-day southern and northern hemisphere temperate floras (Section 4.1.1), indicates a marginal position between paratropical and warm temperate rain forest, but with a seasonally dry

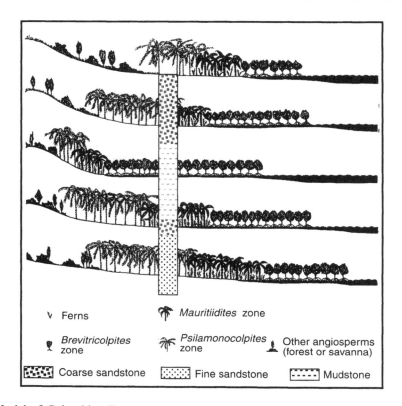

Figure 6.9   Model of Colombian Eocene coastal vegetation with changing sea levels (Gonzalez, 1967). As rising sea levels drown a coastal plain, mangrove swamps largely replace freshwater palm-dominated swamps, which then expand with subsequent falling sea levels. The model assumes some penecontemporaneous steepening of relief during the depositional cycle. Reproduced by permission of Brill, Leiden.

climate. A setting on the ecotone between para-tropical and warm temperate forests goes some way to explain the mixture of megathermal and microthermal elements. However, the widespread geographical extent of mixed floras (Romero, 1986) suggests that there were important differences with present-day vegetation; that in this high latitude setting the combination of equable, frost-free temperatures, coupled with seasonal variations in day length, provided a setting where megathermal and microthermal elements grew together; and that there is no real living analogue to these Early Tertiary South American forests. Similar patterns, discussed in more detail later, are seen in contemporaneous floras in Australia (Chapter 10), and the northern hemisphere (Chapter 11).

The southernmost evidence for Early Eocene megathermal vegetation is from King George Island, off the Antarctic Peninsula, at 65°S, where Orlando (1963) described a small flora with 70% entire-margined leaves, which includes members of Lauraceae and Monimiaceae, together with *Nothofagus*. Further indications of the occurrence of megathermal taxa in this area is provided by records of pollen of Palmae and Pedaliaceae (disputed by Truswell) by Cranwell (1959), from Seymour Island. It is clearly unrealistic to propose that megathermal rain forests occurred at such a high latitude during the Eocene thermal maximum, but the data strongly suggest that some megathermal taxa were able to survive at these southerly latitudes within otherwise warm temperate

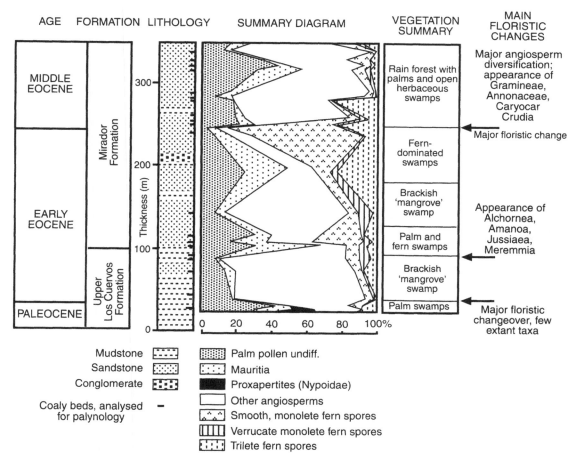

Figure 6.10  Ecological succession for the Early and Middle Eocene of Colombia (Gonzalez, 1967). Reproduced by permission of Brill, Leiden

forests. During the Late Cretaceous and earliest Tertiary, the Antarctic Plate drifted slowly toward the Pacific, so that by the Early Eocene much of the coastline from the Antarctic Peninsula to New Zealand would have been at a similar latitude, suggesting that the Antarctic coast may have provided a dispersal filter for megathermal plants between South America and Australasia at the time of the Late Paleocene/ Early Eocene thermal maximum. This issue will be discussed further in Chapters 10 and 12.

Within the Middle and Late Eocene, the representation of southern hemisphere elements, and especially of *Nothofagus*, continued to increase, but at this time paralleling a decrease

in the representation of entire-margined leaves, indicating an overall reduction in temperatures and the gradual withdrawal of paratropical forests to more northerly latitudes (Figure 6.7).

### 6.4.3 Oligo-Miocene Vegetation

Data from the South American Oligocene is limited for two reasons. Firstly, in many areas, it is represented by a period of weathering and erosion from the Late Eocene until the Early Miocene, during which time thick bauxites formed in the coastal basins of Guyana (Wymstra, 1971), and, secondly, it has received

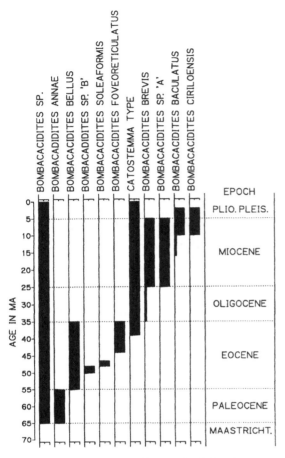

Figure 6.11 Palynological record of Bombacaceae through the South American Tertiary (data extracted from Muller et al., 1987).

scant attention in this region since for many years there was a disagreement as to the position of the Oligo-Miocene boundary.

The terminal Eocene global cooling event, which had a marked effect on the floras of other tropical regions, seems to have been less marked in South America. Although several extinctions are associated with the boundary on the basis of the palynological record (Muller et al., 1987), there was no major regional change to drier climates, as in the Far East (Chapter 9), and there were few extinctions within the Palmae, as was the case in W Africa (Chapter 7). The continuous occurrence of everwet climates,

presumably supporting rain forest vegetation, in at least part of equatorial South America, is shown by the occurrence of coal-bearing sediments throughout the Oligocene of western Venezuela (Liddle, 1928, in Gonzalez, 1967). However, the widespread occurrence of bauxites, sometimes with evaporites, sandwiched between the Middle Eocene and Early Miocene in Guyana and Suriname may indicate that an Oligocene dry phase occurred in some parts of equatorial South America.

It is believed that the high generic diversity of Palmae in South America, compared to other tropical areas, is explained largely by the limited number of extinctions of palms following the terminal Eocene cooling event.

The South American Oligocene is associated with few new immigrants; only the aquatic fern *Ceratopteris* shows a distinct representation, but it is also possible that this genus made its first appearance somewhat earlier, in the Late Eocene. However, there were new appearances in the Miocene. The presence of *Byrsonima* (Malphigiaceae) pollen in the Early Miocene reflects the appearance of woodland elements, and *Eperua* (Leguminosae) may reflect the development of heath forests. Pollen of *Trichanthera* (Acanthaceae) also appears in the earliest Miocene. Most new appearances during the remainder of the Miocene reflect the general diversification of herbs and shrubs of open habitats, such as Compositae and Acanthaceae (*Cuphea* and *Justicia* type). Two first appearances deserve further comment, since their appearance clearly reflects transatlantic dispersals. Spores comparable to the climbing fern *Lygodium scandens* (Schizaeaceae) show a shortlived occurrence during the Middle Miocene, and, more remarkably, the pollen record shows that the swamp forest tree *Symphonia* (Guttiferae) makes an appearance at the same time, and today *Symphonia globulifera*, the same species as occurs in the freshwater swamps of W Africa, is a major contributor to the seasonal *varzea* swamps of South American rivers.

Up until the Middle Miocene, South American rain forests would have formed a continuous belt from the Atlantic to Pacific coasts. With the Late Miocene uplift of the Andes, this belt was split into two: one centred on the Amazon Basin, formed at the same time as a result of the diversion of northward-flowing rivers to the east, and the second along the Pacific coast. This disjunction is clearly shown by the present-day distributions of vicariad taxa, such as the ivory palm genera *Ammandra*, *Palandra* and *Phytele-phas* (Uhl and Dransfield, 1987), which have no species in common on either side of the Andes (Figure 6.12). Similar patterns are shown by many other groups, such as *Couepia*, *Licania* and *Parinari* of the Chrysobalanaceae (Whitmore, 1998).

In S South America, the effect of cooling global temperatures is clearly reflected by the development of *Nothofagus*-dominated forests in the very south. Most of S South America was characterised by subhumid climates, as evidenced from both macrofossils and palynomorphs such as Chenopodiaceae and Ephedraceae. Romero (1993) suggested that his 'mixed' floristic province reflected the development of wooded savannas, which were later to give way to the savannas of Chaco and Patagonia. There is no fossil evidence for the re-establishment of megathermal rain forests in the Middle Miocene of S South America, as was the case in Africa (Chapter 7), Australia (Chapter 10) and the northern hemisphere (Chapter 11).

### 6.4.4 Plio-Pleistocene Climatic Change and the Uplift of the Andes

Evidence for rain forest history during the Pliocene and Pleistocene comes firstly from palynological studies from the coastal basins of Guyana, Suriname and Trinidad, which principally reflect the expansion and contraction of rain forests, mangroves and savanna along the ecotone associated with limiting rainfall. Such evidence also comes from the high plain of the Sabana de Bogotá in Colombia, where fluctuations of pollen from montane forests and paramo grasslands reflect vertical shifts of rain

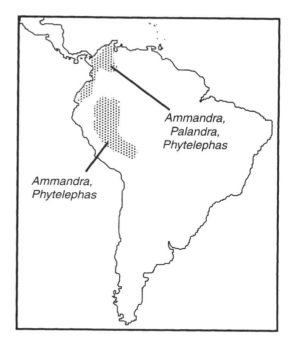

*Ammandra, Palandra, Phytelephas*

*Ammandra, Phytelephas*

Figure 6.12 Vicariant plant distributions in S America, relating to the late Neogene uplift of the Andes in N South America. Reproduced from Uhl, N.W. and Dransfield, J. *Genera Palmarum*, 1987 with permission of the authors.

forest in relation to the ecotone associated with increasing altitude.

### Coastal plains of northern South America

The Neogene sedimentary successions in the coastal basin of Guyana and Suriname have been studied palynologically by van der Hammen (1963), van der Hammen and Wymstra (1964) and Wymstra (1969, 1971), and reveal a history of vegetational change in relation to both climate and fluctuating sea levels along a coastline presently bordered by seasonally dry rain forest with savanna behind. Palynomorph assemblages reveal alternating phases of dominance by mangrove pollen, in which *Rhizophora* regularly exceeds 95% in frequency, and intervals with common pollen of Gramineae and savanna trees which are sometimes poor in mangrove pollen (Figure 6.13),

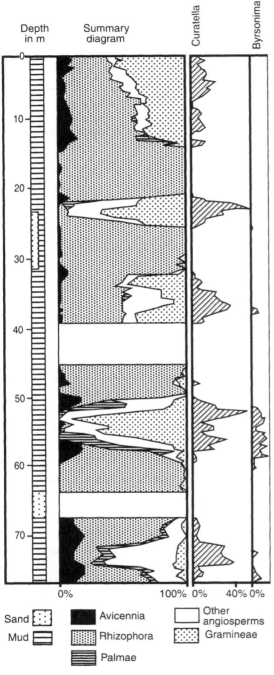

Figure 6.13 Palynological succession through the late Neogene and Quaternary from Guyana (Wymstra, 1971). Selected pollen spectra shown only, pollen sum total pollen and spores.

and have previously been interpreted as reflecting alternating phases of high and low sea levels (Wymstra, 1969; Flenley, 1979a), which is misleading since coastal successions such as this, accumulating predominantly on the continental shelf, need to be interpreted in terms of the sequence stratigraphic model illustrated by wells 'A' and 'B' in Figure 3.5. In this setting, the shoreline would fall below the continental shelf break during periods of low Pleistocene sea levels, resulting in long periods without deposition on the shelf; sediments preserved would principally comprise transgressive and high sea level deposits, only palaeosols being preserved during low sea level phases.

The intervals with abundant mangrove pollen contain higher frequencies than occur beneath present-day mangrove forests growing around the Orinoco Delta (Muller, 1959), and such high frequencies are most easily explained as indicating periods when mangroves were much more extensive than today, such as would have occurred during 'transgressive' periods, when sea levels were rising, typified by the early Holocene. Unfortunately, these intervals are virtually void of pollen from non-mangrove sources, and so provide very little information about the nature of freshwater swamp or dryland vegetation. We can only surmise that since periods of rising sea levels tended to be characterised by wetter climates at low latitudes (Morley, 1996), these periods would have corresponded with phases of maximum extension of tropical rain forest.

Intervals with intermediate frequencies of mangrove pollen are most likely to represent periods of minor sea level change, switches in sediment supply or of coastal progradation at times of high, stable sea level, whereas only those intervals void of mangrove pollen might reflect periods of low sea level. The coastal profiles from Guyana and Suriname thus provide a glimpse of late Neogene vegetation during high sea level phases, and of the development of mangrove swamps during phases of rising sea level. The four phases of sea level rise and highstand corresponding to the last 1 Ma

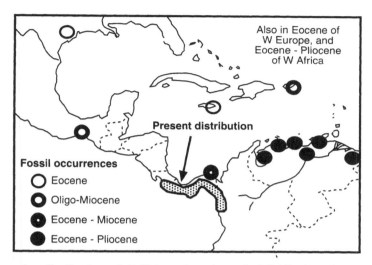

Figure 6.14   Present-day distribution of *Pelliciera rhizophorae* in Middle America (Wymstra, 1968), and fossil data (circles) from Wymstra (1968) Fuchs (1970) Graham (1977) and Frederiksen (1988). For localities in Europe and Africa, refer to Chapters 7 and 11.

(age determined on the basis of the occurrence of *Alnus* pollen (Figure 6.4f), see below) most probably equate to the four phases of major sea level change reflected in the sediments of the region of the Gulf of Mexico over the same time interval (Vail and Wornardt, 1990).

With this scenario in mind, the palynological succession provides a clear pattern of change since the Miocene, during which time rain forest elements were common and pollen of savanna elements rare or absent. During the Pliocene and Early Pleistocene, the presence of abundant pollen of *Byrsonima* and *Curatella* (Dilleniaceae), with low frequencies of Gramineae and *Ambrosia* (Compositae), suggests open woodland rather than grass-dominated savanna, following which a more open vegetation, with savanna trees, Chenopodiaceae and Melastomataceae was represented. It is only following the last three phases of sea level rise, perhaps representing the last 800 000 years, that grass-dominated savannas became widespread.

The pattern of climate change reflected by the expansion of savannas also coincided with major changes in the character of mangrove vegetation. *Pelliciera rhizophorae*, currently restricted to the Pacific coast of Colombia

(Figure 6.14), disappeared from this region at the same time as the parent plant of *Verrutricolporites rotundiporus* and the related *V. laevigatus*. Immediately following their extinction, *Avicennia* (Verbenaceae) pollen shows its first appearance, possibly taking advantage of the niche left following these extinctions.

### Sabana de Bogotá

The high plain of the Sabana de Bogotá (2250 m asl, Figure 6.15) within the Andean forest zone in the Eastern Cordillera of Colombia has been the setting for a most remarkable palynological study, initiated by Thomas van der Hammen in the early 1950s (van der Hammen and Gonzalez, 1960, 1964). This intensive study (Hoogheistra, 1984), provides an unrivalled highly detailed history of vegetation and climate for N South America which spans the whole of the Quaternary and most of the Pliocene.

The major phase of uplift of the Colombian Andes was in the Late Miocene and Early Pliocene (5–3.5 Ma), with the final upheaval taking place between 5 and 3 Ma, during which time an intermontane basin became established in the vicinity of present-day Bogotá. During

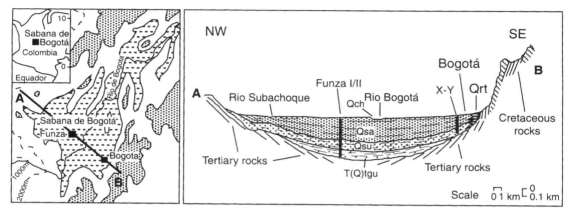

Figure 6.15   Location and stratigraphy of Sabana de Bogotá (2550 m). Borehole X–Y reached bedrock at 195 m, Funza II in the basin centre penetrated 586 m of lacustrine and fluvial deposits spanning 3.5 Ma. T(Q)tgu = Upper Tilata Formation; Qsu = Subachoque Formation; Qsa = Sabana Formation; Qrt = Rio Tunjuelito Formation; Qch = Chia Formation (Andriessen et al., 1993). Reproduced by permission of Elsevier Science.

the initial phase of basin formation, during the Late Miocene, coarse-grained sands and gravels, with some muds and organic-rich sediments, accumulated, now preserved around the basin margins, and these have yielded pollen of lowland rain forest taxa, such as the palms *Mauritia* and *Iriartea*, *Amanoa* (Euphorbiaceae) and Bombacaceae, testifying to the low elevation of the region at this time (Figure 6.16). By about 3.5 Ma, however, following the final upheaval of the N Andes, the present configuration of this region became established with the formation of a large lake-filled basin, which with continued subsidence, more or less in equilibrium with sediment accumulation, now contains a virtually continuous sedimentary succession for the Late Pliocene (3.5–1.6 Ma) and Pleistocene, nearly 600 m in thickness (Andriessen et al., 1993).

The palynological record from this succession (Figures 6.17a,b; 6.18) has revealed a very detailed picture of changing montane vegetation and climate within the Colombian Andes spanning 117 oxygen isotope stages, and covering 3.2 Ma, accurately correlated with the marine record (Andriessen et al., 1993). It reveals the successive immigration of the characteristic species which today contribute to the vegetation of the Andean forest and paramo, and also successive oscillations between arboreal pollen, reflecting periods of expansion of forest and paramo, and Andean forest, paralleling the climatic perturbations of the Quaternary. It also shows the gradual increase in taxon diversity, and the successive modification of composition of both forest and paramo.

The Andean climate went though four main phases during this period. Initially, from 3.2 to 2.7 Ma, the conditions were relatively warm, with the forest limit oscillating between 2800 and 3600 m, but at about 2.7 Ma there was a sudden period of cooling, perhaps by 4–5°C, coinciding with the build-up of ice in the northern hemisphere, after which time the forest limit oscillated from 2600 to 2800 m until about 2.2 Ma. The following time interval, from 2.2 to 1.0 Ma, was a long period of mainly cold climate, with the tree line dropping to 1900 m a number of times, and only rarely rising above 2500 m, following which the profile shows a succession of climatic oscillations, reflecting the major glacial–interglacial cycles of the Middle and Late Quaternary, with the tree line oscillating around 2880 m during warmer phases, but falling as low as 1800 m during glacial maxima. Hoogheimstra and Ran (1994) have analysed the cyclicity of the

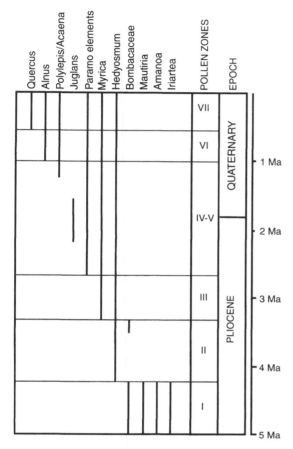

Figure 6.16 Immigration and extinction reflected by the Sabana de Bogotá pollen record (summarised from Hoogheimstra and Ran, 1994, and Hoogheimstra, 1995) Zones I–VII are biozones of van der Hammen et al. (1973). Reproduced by permission of Elsevier Science.

detailed pollen record for the last million years, and established that climatic cycles with a period of 100 000 years characterised the last 800 000 years (reflecting oscillations relating to the Earth's orbital eccentricity), and periodicities of 23 000 years (relating to precession) were present throughout the pollen record, testifying to the overwhelming effect of astronomical cycles in driving patterns of climatic change in the equatorial tropics.

The increase in diversification of the vegetation resulted, firstly, from the immigration of taxa into the area from surrounding regions, and, secondly, from the adaptation or evolution of taxa from the surrounding lowland forests. A third group consists of taxa of clearly North American affinity, able to disperse into South America as a result of the combined effect of the formation of the Isthmus of Panama, and reduced late Neogene low latitude temperatures. These taxa included *Myrica* (Myricaceae), at about 3.3 Ma, *Juglans* (Juglandaceae), and possibly *Plantago* (Plantaginaceae) and other paramo elements after 2.7 Ma, and, most notably, *Alnus* at 1.0 Ma and *Quercus* at 300 000 years, the latter two taxa both being major contributors to present-day northernmost Andean vegetation (Figure 6.16). Megathermal elements are also thought to have immigrated from North America during the late Neogene as suggested by the sudden appearance of *Hedyosmum* (Chloranthaceae) pollen at about 4 Ma in Sabana de Bogotá and within the Late Miocene of Guyana (Wymstra, 1971). It is possible that other 'amphi-Pacific' elements of the Andean and Subandean forests also dispersed into South America via the Isthmus of Panama, such as *Trigonobalanus*, *Saurauia* and *Meliosma*, especially since these taxa have a fossil record in the mid-Tertiary of Europe or North America (van der Hammen and Cleef, 1983). This will be discussed further in Chapters 7, 12 and 13.

During the warm phase from 3.2 Ma until 2.7 Ma, the Andean forests had no direct modern analogue, being relatively open and rich in *Podocarpus*, with *Hedyosmum* and *Weinmannia* (Cunoniaceae) at lower latitudes, *Miconia* (Melastomataceae) at higher elevations, and *Myrica* at the tree line. Notably, pollen assemblages exhibited seemingly irregular fluctuations of taxa such as *Dodonea* (Sapindaceae), *Eugenia* (Myrtaceae), *Ilex* and *Symplocos*, suggesting the intermittent development of azonal forests with pioneer qualities (Hoogheimstra and Ran, 1994), or possibly dry montane conditions in the case of *Dodonaea*. *Podocarpus* continued to be common until 2.2 Ma, during which time *Hedyosmum* and *Miconia* dominated Andean

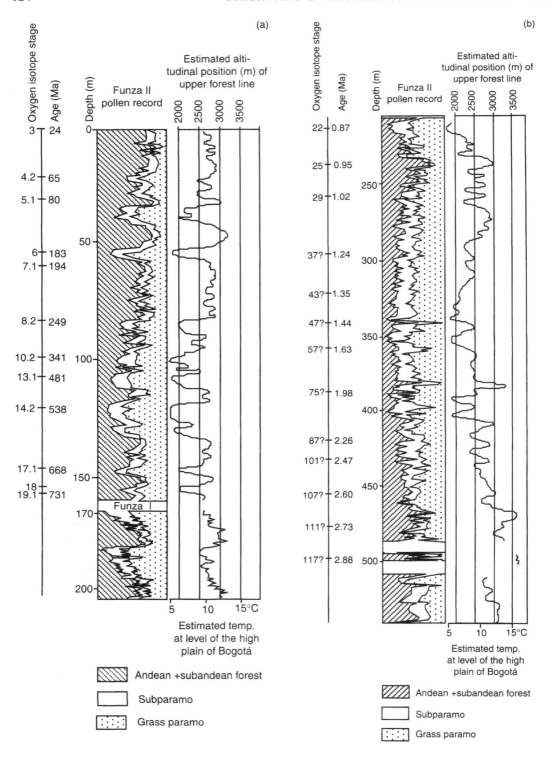

forests. After 2.2 Ma the forest became more closed with the disappearance of light-demanding elements such as *Borreria*, and dwarf forest elements, such as *Hypericum* (Guttiferae) and *Polylepis* (Rosaceae) became important above the tree line. After 1.4 Ma a *Hedyosmum* forest, possibly with contributions from *Eugenia*, *Myrsine* (Myrsinaceae) and Ericaceae, constituted a precursor of the present-day *Weinmannia* forest, and *Vallea* (Elaeocarpaceae) became an important element with *Miconia* at higher elevations and with *Polylepis* and *Myrica* contributing substantially near the tree line.

The immigration of *Alnus* after 1.0 Ma resulted in a major change to swamp vegetation, where it formed large areas of carr on wet flats around the lake, and also as an element of zonal forests, but Andean forests did not take on a wholly modern aspect until the immigraton of *Quercus* at about 350 000 years. Initially, *Quercus* forest occurred in local patches, over a wide altitudinal range. It was only after 180 000 years ago that *Quercus* formed zonal forests and the composition of the Andean forests changed dramatically, that the main characteristics of the present-day Andean forest types became established (Figure 2.34). After this time, *Quercus* forests and *Weinmannia–Hedyosmum* forests dominated the Andean forests,

---

Figure 6.17 (a and b) Summary of palynological succession from Funza II, Sabana de Bogotá; estimated altitudinal position of upper forest line, and interpreted mean annual temperature for the high plain of Bogotá covering the last 3 Ma with provisional correlation to $^{18}$O stratigraphy of Imbrie et al. (1984); from Hoogheimstra and Ran (1994). Section from 170 to 210 m (not recovered from Funza II) is from Funza I (Hoogheimstra, 1984). Reproduced by permission of Elsevier Science.

---

Figure 6.18 Correlation of palynomorph data from Funza I, Sabana de Bogotá, and the oxygen isotope record from a deep sea core (ODP site 677; Shackleton et al., 1990). The pollen record was minimally stretched and squeezed between 36 control points (indicated by arrows) in order to show a time-correlation with the $^{18}$O record (Hoogheimstra, 1995). Reproduced by permission of Elsevier Science.

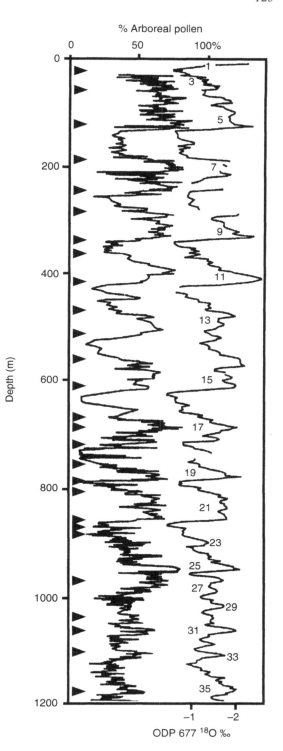

% Arboreal pollen

ODP 677 $^{18}$O ‰

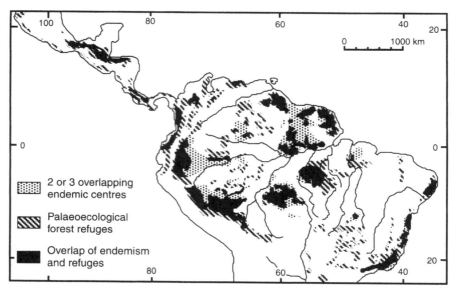

Figure 6.19   Pleistocene refugia in New World rain forests. The overlap of endemic centres with areas of palaeoecological forest refuges, deduced from palaeoclimate, geomorphology and soils, lends strength to the argument for Pleistocene refugia (from Whitmore and Prance, 1987). Reproduced by permission of Oxford University Press.

with *Alnus* carr on the high plain and *Polylepis* dwarf forest above the tree line.

Paramo vegetation showed a marked increase in representation and diversity after the climatic deterioration at 2.7 Ma, and, initially, Caryophyllaceae and *Valeriana* were dominant, together with *Aragoa* (Scrophulariaceae) and *Plantago*. After 2.2 Ma *Plantago* became abundant, possibly replacing grass paramo over wide areas. With the large altitudinal shifts of all montane vegetation belts in response to glacial–interglacial climatic cycles after 1.0 Ma, paramo took on a more modern aspect, with grasses, rosettes of the composite *Espeletia* (Figure 5.18) and numerous herbs, and, at times of cold climate, replaced Andean forests at the level of the Sabana de Bogotá.

## 6.4.5   Quaternary Refuges

The world's most species-rich plant communities occur in rain forests along the lower slopes of the Peruvian, Equadorian and Colombian Andes (Gentry, 1988a). South American rain forests exhibit marked regional variations in species-richness and degrees of endemism (Prance, 1987). Parallel variations are also seen in other groups of organisms, such as birds and butterflies, and these variations have been explained in terms of the 'Pleistocene Refuge' theory (Haffer, 1969, 1987), which contends that disjunct centres of lowland species endemism in diverse plant and animal groups often appear to correlate with mid-elevational hilltops (Figure 6.19). It has been proposed that these hilltops captured orographic rainfall, and supported isolated refugia throughout dry glacial periods (Haffer, 1987). The successive expansion and contraction of populations from and to these refugia is thought to have provided a 'species-pump' by isolating populations by areas of lowland aridity during glacial intervals, restricting gene flow between refugia and encouraging allopatric speciation.

Refugia have been proposed in four main areas (Figure 6.19). Firstly, in an arc along the lower flanks of the Andes, secondly, along the

Atlantic seaboard, and, thirdly, in hill areas of the Guyanan Shield. The fourth area of refugia, proposed for the central part of the Amazon Basin, has since been dismissed as an artefact based on overcollecting in areas of easy accessibility such as near airports (Nelson et al., 1990). The Pleistocene Refuge theory has been widely debated, but, until recently, there was little unequivocal historical data available either to support or refute it. Now a number of pollen profiles are available which provide an insight into Amazon climate and vegetation during the latter part of the last glacial period, and allow some of the predictions of the Pleistocene Refuge theory to be tested.

An extensive Late Quaternary pollen diagram from the South American lowland rain forest zone, from Carajas in NE Brazil, at 700–800m asl spanning 50 000 years (Absy et al., 1991), shows a sequence of forested and open savanna phases, with dry conditions occurring intermittently during the mid-glacial, at the last glacial maximum, during the late glacial and mid-Holocene (Figure 6.20). Van der Hammen and Absy (1994) suggested an overall precipitation reduction of 25–40% at the time of the last glacial maximum to explain available pollen data from the South American lowland rain forest zone, supporting the suggestion of aridity proposed by the Pleistocene Refuge theory.

However, there is very little unequivocal palaeoecological evidence for lowland aridity in the main Amazon catchment. The strongest evidence for Amazonian glacial climate and vegetation is from a 40 000-year profile from the central Amazonian lowlands (Colinvaux et al., 1996) and two 30 000 to 26 000-year-old montane sites from Equador by Bush et al. (1990).

The lowland site, Lake Para (Figure 6.21), suggests continued rain forest cover over the last 40 000 years, and that savannas were absent from the study area during the last glacial maximum. Glacial-age forests were comparable to modern forests in some respects, but also included taxa such as *Podocarpus* and *Hedyosmum*, suggesting that glacial-age rain forests consisted of a mixture of lowland and montane

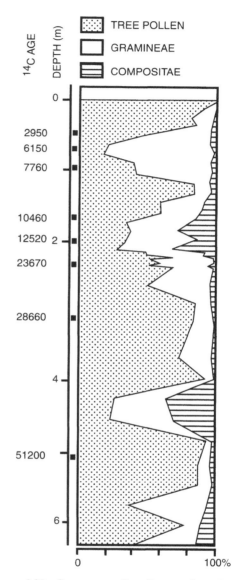

Figure 6.20   Summary pollen diagram from Carajas, NE Brazil, altitude 700–800 m asl (from Absy et al., 1991 in Hoogheimstra 1995). Reproduced by permission of Yale University Press.

elements, without a modern analogue. Similarly, the glacial-age lower montane sites Mera and San Juan Bosco from Equador (Bush et al., 1990) include pollen and wood which suggest that *Alnus, Drimys* (Winteraceae), *Hedyosmum, Podocarpus* and *Weinmannia* grew at 1100 m and

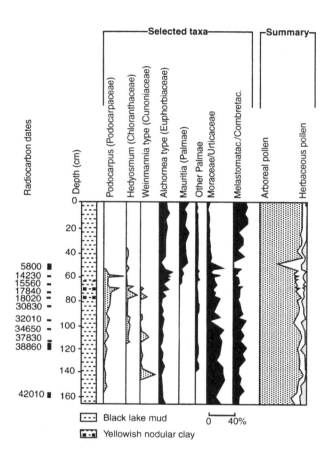

Figure 6.21    Summary pollen diagram from Lake Para (*c.* 300 m), Amazonia (Colinvaux et al., 1996). Selected pollen spectra only; pollen sum total pollen; stippled spectra exaggerated ×5. Reproduced by permission of *Science.*

900 m asl. The three Amazonian sites each suggest a substantial depression of temperatures, but the maintenance of moist conditions, since these taxa have their lowest localities at 1600 m in Venezuela (P.S. Ashton, personal communication). Pollen data from the two Equador sites suggest *Alnus* carr at 30 000 years, followed by assemblages which suggest a mixture of the montane elements noted above and lowland taxa, such as Marantaceae, Palmae, Proteaceae, *Apeiba* (Tiliaceae) and *Erythrina* (Leguminosae). Palynological studies of marine cores from

the Amazon Fan (Haberle and Piperno, 1996) also suggest cooler conditions, and the expansion of savanna, but not to the extent seen in comparable time-equivalent sections from off the W African coast (Chapter 7).

The temperature depression suggested from the three Amazonian sites is greater than that anticipated from the Pleistocene Refuge theory, and suggests that glacial-age cooling was as important in moulding Amazonian forests as reductions in precipitation, and that many species survived the glacial maxima by the formation of novel plant associations with both lowland and montane elements.

Bush (1994) also criticised the Pleistocene Refuge theory as a species-pump, suggesting that it was not only Quaternary climatic change which drove speciation in Amazonian forests, but that speciation has taken place over at least the last 25 Ma, with different forcing mechanisms (e.g. orogeny (Figure 6.12), the formation of giant rivers, inhibiting dispersal, and the sheer size of the basin). Bush (1994) also emphasised that most refugia are located around the periphery of the region, in ecotonal areas, and proposed that species-richness has been maintained by instability, rather than stability, as generally believed. This is considered improbable, since the highest diversities, on the lower flanks of the Andes, are most likely to have been maintained by the presence of moist conditions in these areas as a result of uninterrupted orographic rainfall throughout the Quaternary period irrespective of the global climatic scenario, coupled with the ease of migration on gentle hillslopes with changing temperature regimes. The world's most species-rich rain forests are thus probably due to stable, moist climates over a very long time period. With respect to refuges in other areas, their concentration in coastal positions suggests that rain forests may have found refuge on the now-submerged continental shelves, where temperatures would have been at their highest during glacial maxima.

Clearly, much more work is needed in order to understand how such high levels of species diversity have been maintained through the Quaternary in South American rain forests.

## 6.5 SUMMARY

### Middle America

The presence of a land connection with North America up until the Paleocene resulted in some floristic interchange until this time. Middle American floras were essentially North American-derived, until the closure of the Isthmus of Panama in the Pliocene. Dry savannas, which formed the corridor for the dispersal of fauna during the Great American Interchange, developed from the Late Miocene onward, and were particularly well developed during the Pliocene.

### South America

Following the terminal Cretaceous event which caused a substantial diversity reduction of South American species, very wet climates resulted in the widespread development of tropical rain forests in the South American continent. In S South America, Paleocene vegetation consisted of a mixture of megathermal and southern hemisphere taxa. Palms were particularly characteristic of Paleocene vegetation throughout the continent.

Wet tropical climates at low paleolatitudes enabled the development of diverse vegetation. Palms exhibited considerable diversity at this time, but were less prominent in terms of contributors to vegetation after the Paleocene. Rapid palynomorph assemblage changes at low palaeolatitudes at the time of the Late Paleocene/Early Eocene thermal maximum suggest rapid vegetational change, whereas in southern latitudes tropical and paratropical rain forests extended to 45°S.

The terminal Eocene event probably had a less deleterious effect on the diversity of South American vegetation than in other tropical regions, illustrated by the persistence of palms into the Oligocene in South America, such as *Mauritia*, which became extinct elsewhere. It is believed that the increased representation of primitive Palmae in South America, compared to other tropical areas, is explained largely by the limited number of extinctions following the terminal Eocene cooling event.

Subhumid wooded savannas became widespread in S South America from the Oligocene onward; there are no palaeobotanical data to indicate the presence of moist megathermal forests in S South America during the Neogene.

Grass-dominated vegetation became widespread in N South America during the Pliocene, initially, as open woodland; grass-dominated savannas appear to have expanded only during the last 1 Ma.

A detailed record of climate change in equatorial South America is provided by a continuous pollen record from the Sabana de Bogotá in Colombia covering the last 3.5 Ma. There was a sudden phase of cooling after 2.7 Ma, coinciding with the build-up of ice in the northern hemisphere, and, following a period of climatic oscillation, a long, cold period set in from 2.2 to 1.0 Ma. Climates oscillated on a 100 000 year cycle over the last million years, paralleling phases of glacial advance and retreat in polar regions.

During cooler phases of the Pleistocene, lower temperatures pushed lowland rain forests to the lowest altitudes, and at mid-elevations lower montane forest taxa grew together with lowland rain forest elements in plant associations which have no modern analogue, maintained by orographic rain. Elsewhere, the distribution of lowland rain forests was restricted by a combination of lower temperatures and reduced moisture. The desiccation associated with glacial maxima does not seem to have been so pronounced in South America as in Africa (Chapter 7), and these more moist conditions probably enabled the survival of very diverse rain forest communities through the most unfavourable periods of the Pleistocene.

# CHAPTER 7

# Africa

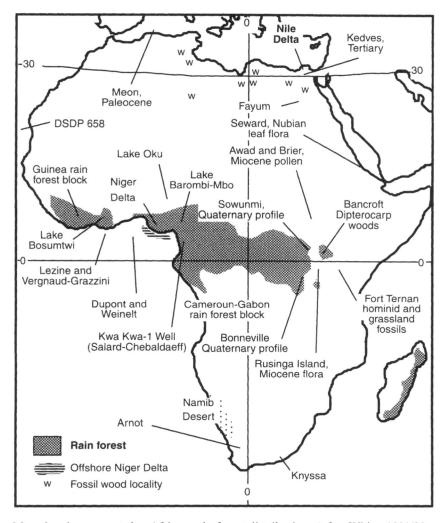

Map showing present-day African rain forest distributions (after White, 1981/83, and Richards, 1996), and locations mentioned in the text.

## 7.1  INTRODUCTION

The African rain forests have been described as
the 'odd man out' by Richards (1973) on account
of their much lower species-richness, and the
poor representation of important groups which
are well represented elsewhere. For instance, the
whole of continental Africa has fewer palms
than the tiny island of Singapore, Annonales and
orchids are poorly represented, there is only a
single species of bamboo, and forest under-
growth taxa, epiphytes and lianes are less conspicuous than in the rain forests of South
America, Madagascar and SE Asia. They are
also less extensive geographically and account
for only about one-fifth of the global rain forest
coverage (Figure 1.2, map). Africa is also the
cradle of mankind, and, for this reason, its
Neogene history receives much attention. This
chapter attempts to provide some reasons for the
low diversity of the modern flora, and also
presents a detailed history of the interaction of
rain forest and savanna in W and C Africa for
the last 10.5 million years, forming a backdrop
for the evolution of hominids, and based on an
extensive pollen record from the offshore Niger
Delta.

## 7.2  TECTONIC SETTING

The African lithospheric plate bears the largest
of the three tropical land masses. It has also been
the most geographically isolated, and stable
through much of its Tertiary history, and is
currently the most elevated (Figure 7.1).

At the beginning of the Tertiary, Africa was
separated from South America by a wide S
Atlantic Ocean, although a string of oceanic
islands (McDougal and Douglas, 1988) are
thought to have provided transatlantic step-
ping-stones (Axelrod and Raven, 1978). It
became separated from Australia/Antarctica in
the earliest Cretaceous, but remained in juxtaposition with the Malagasy/Mascarene and
Indian subcontinent well into the Senonian

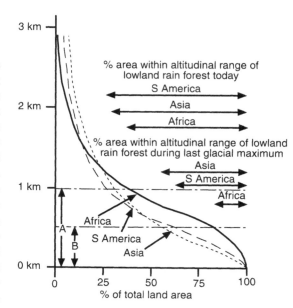

Figure 7.1  Normalised hypsographic curves for
Africa, South America and Asia, comparing their
relative elevations (Harrison et al., 1981). During the
Holocene, about 60% of the area of the African
continent lay within the altitudinal range of tropical
rain forest, compared to about 70% in South
America and Asia (delimited by 'A'). During the last
glacial maximum, with tropical rain forests possibly
depressed by 500 m (see Section 7.7), 40% of the area
above present sea level in Asia and 35% in South
America was within the altitudinal range of tropical
rain forest (delimited by 'B'), but in the more
elevated African continent only 15% of the land area
would have been within this altitudinal range. It is
clear that the limited representation of low altitude
terrain needs to be given as much consideration as
moisture reduction in explaining diversity loss in
African tropical rain forests.

(84–66 Ma). In the earliest Tertiary, Africa was
separated from Eurasia by the wide Tethyan
ocean; thus in the Late Paleocene (60–54 Ma),
when most other continents were intercon-
nected by land bridges and climates were
becoming globally equable, Africa was in an
isolated position, as evidenced by its diverse
Early Tertiary fauna preserved in the Eocene/
Oligocene of Fayum, Egypt (Andrews, 1906), in
which Eurasian mammals are virtually lacking
(Prothero, 1994).

The African Plate has slowly drifted north at a more or less constant rate through the Early Tertiary, and although the Iberian Peninsula came into close proximity to North Africa by the Late Eocene (39–36 Ma) (Smith et al., 1994), the main collision with Eurasia, resulting in the closure of Tethys, was in the Middle Miocene (16–10 Ma), at which time African and Eurasian faunas were able to intermingle, with proboscidans and giraffids moving north, and mustelids and perissodactyls (including horses) moving to the south (Van Couvering and Van Couvering, 1975). The possibility was also raised by Van Couvering and Van Couvering (1975) of mammalian interchange in the earlier Tertiary, on microplates which detached from Africa, and joined Europe, acting as 'Noah's Arks' (*sensu* McKenna, 1973); in this respect, the region of Tethys in the Early Tertiary may have borne some similarities to the Malay Archipelago today.

North and Central Africa were mostly of low relief in the earlier Tertiary, although upland areas may have been present in E Africa as a result of upwarping prior to the development of the African Rift Valley. It is noteworthy, however, that palynomorphs suggesting a montane origin, such as bisaccate pollen, are completely absent from the pollen record of W and C African basins until the latest Tertiary, suggesting that montane forests were poorly developed around westward-draining river catchments, since such pollen tends to be very well dispersed. Significant areas of S Africa were substantially elevated, however, throughout the Tertiary (Smith et al., 1994).

The present elevated configuration of the African land mass is the result of uplift which began in the mid-Tertiary, with flexure of the pre-Miocene surface into a number of warps and basins (Burke and Wilson, 1972), and the initiation of the E African Rift Valley (Baker et al., 1972), but has been most prominent since the Late Miocene (King, 1962), since which time the Eastern Plateau was raised by more than 1800 m, and the great rift valleys began to take on their present configuration, with the

growth of high volcanoes on their margins (Baker and Wohlenburg, 1971).

## 7.3 EFFECT OF THE LATE CRETACEOUS AND EARLY TERTIARY ISOLATION OF THE AFRICAN CONTINENT ON ITS FLORISTIC DIVERSITY

Since the African continent was somewhat isolated from other tropical land masses through the Late Cretaceous and Early Tertiary, the question needs to be asked as to whether this isolation affected the taxonomic diversity or make-up of its present flora? This can be examined by considering the history of those taxa which are present in other tropical regions, but are absent from Africa. The *amphi-Pacific* flora has been given great attention by van Steenis (1962a, 1963), who enumerated 290 supraspecific plant taxa which are present both in the Americas and the Far East, but are absent from Africa and Europe, of which 80 may be considered 'megathermal' taxa. He believed that the distribution of these megathermal taxa could be explained only in terms of a transpacific land bridge, the only one of his five land bridges which he considered necessary to explain the distribution of present-day floras, which cannot be readily accounted for by reference to past continental movements. Raven and Axelrod (1974), however, concluded that these elements were absent from Africa as a result of Neogene aridity.

Eleven of van Steenis' 80 megathermal amphi-Pacific taxa have a pre-Quaternary fossil pollen or macrofossil record (Table 7.1) with no records from Africa; several have been described from the North American and European Tertiary, such as *Engelhardia* (Juglandaceae), *Gordonia* (Theaceae), *Meliosma* (Sabiaceae), *Microtropis* (Celastraceae), *Saurauia* (Saurauiaceae), *Symplocos* (Symplocaceae) and *Trigonobalanus* (Fagaceae), whereas others reflect very ancient lineages, such as *Hedyosmum*

Table 7.1   Amphi-Pacific megathermal taxa of van Steenis (1962a, 1963) which have a fossil record.

**Northern hemisphere records**
1 *Cinamommum* type (Lauraceae)
  *Inaperturopollenites palaeogenicus*, Late Paleocene, France (Kedves, 1968; Gruas-Cavagnetto, 1978)
  *Inaperturopollenites spicatus*, Belgium, Late Paleocene (Roche, 1973)
2 *Gordonia* (Theaceae)
  *Gordonia axillaris* type
  *Tricolporopollenites srivastavai*, France, Early Eocene (Gruas-Cavagnetto, 1978; Ollivier-Pierre, 1979)
  *?Verrutricolporites irregularis*, *?V. theacoides*, *?V. magnotectatus*, France, Oligocene (Roche and
  Schuler, 1976; Ollivier-Pierre, 1979)
  *Gordonia lasianthus* type, Vermont, Oligocene (Traverse, 1955)
3 *Engelhardia* type (Juglandaceae)
  *Triatriopollenites engelhardtioides*, France, Late Paleocene (Gruas-Cavagnetto, 1978)
  *Momipites quietus* group Central Europe, middle Paleocene (Krutzsch, 1966, 1979)
  *Momipites* sect *coryloides* group, Carolina, Paleocene (Frederiksen and Christopher, 1978),
  Maastrichtian, Gulf Coast and Western Interior (Nichols, in Muller, 1981)
4 *Symplocos* (Symplocaceae)
  *Triporopollenites andersonii*, *T. scabroporatus*, California, Maastrichtian (Chmura, 1973)
  *Symplocospollenites* spp. SE USA, Paleocene, scarce, Eocene, common (Tschudy, 1973)
  *Porocolpopollenites vestibulum*, Central Europe, Early Eocene (Krutzsch, 1970), France, Late Eocene
  (Gruas-Cavagnetto, 1978)
  Many records in the Miocene according to Menke (1976)
5 *Microtropis* (Celastraceae)
  *Microtropis* type, France, Oligocene (Lobreau-Callen and Caratini, 1973), Pliocene (Suc, 1976)
6 *Trigonobalanus* (Fagaceae)
  *Trigonobalanus exacantha* (fruit/seeds) Europe (Gregor, 1978)
7 *Meliosma* (Sabiaceae)
  *Meliosma jenkinsi* (Collinson, 1983); *M. cantiensis* (leaves), Early Eocene, London Clay (Collinson,
  1983)
8 *Saurauia* (Actinidiaceae)
  *Saurauia* (seeds) from European Maastrichtian and Early Tertiary (Knobloch and Mai, 1986), and
  leaves from middle Eocene of North America (Taylor, 1990)

**Others**
1 *Hedyosmum* (Chloranthaceae)
  *Hedyosmum* type, Mexico, Late Miocene (Graham, 1976), Guyana, Late Miocene, Wymstra, 1971),
  Colombia, Late Miocene, van der Hammen et al. (1973). Note that Doyle (1969) compares some Early
  Cretaceous pollen with the genus *Hedyosmum*
2 *Weinmannia* (Cunoniaceae)
  *Weinmannia* type, New Zealand, Miocene, Pliocene (Couper, 1953), Oligocene (Mildenhall, 1980),
  Colombia, Pliocene (van der Hammen et al., 1973; Hoogheimstra, 1984)
3 *Spathiphyllum* (Araceae)
  *Spathiphyllum* type, Mexico, Late Miocene (Graham, 1976), Palau, E Pacific, Late Miocene (Leopold,
  1969)

(Chloranthaceae), or are taxa with southern hemisphere distributions, such as *Weinmannia* (Cunoniaceae). The fossil distributions of these taxa suggest that the amphi-Pacific tropical element is clearly explained in terms of relicts of northern temperate paratropical floras (surviving in the Tertiary refuges of the Americas and E Asia, but becoming extinct in Europe), or migrations from the Antarctic, but with the group absent from Africa because of Early Tertiary isolation, and not because of African Neogene aridity, as suggested by Raven and Axelrod (1974).

Although previous isolation may account for the absence of several characteristic families which are well developed in the other tropical regions, it is unlikely to account for the low floristic diversity of the African flora, since, given ideal warm and perhumid climatic conditions, very diverse floras have become established elsewhere within a much shorter time than that available to the African flora, as in the case of New Guinea (Chapter 9).

## 7.4 EARLIER TERTIARY (PALEOCENE TO EOCENE) VEGETATION

The terminal Cretaceous event must have resulted in many extinctions throughout Africa, especially among gymnosperms, as the number of palynomorph taxa described during stratigraphic palynological studies falls by nearly 50% at this time (Figure 5.15b), and it is not unreasonable to suggest that this figure may apply to the entire African flora. Examination of the occurrences of angiosperm taxa above and below the Cretaceous/Tertiary boundary, using the compilation of Salard-Chebaldaeff (1990), suggests that extinctions occurred more or less equally in both monocots and dicots, but the number of new evolutionary appearances in the Paleocene were few. The same data source suggests that from the Late Paleocene until the end of the Eocene, the W African flora diversified almost without interruption. Diversification occurred through the appearance, and radiation, of taxa indigenous to the African continent, and, to a lesser degree, by dispersals from other areas. Records are mainly from pollen, but also from wood and leaves.

### 7.4.1 Paleocene to Middle Eocene

The African continent lay further to the south during Paleocene (66–54 Ma) to Middle Eocene (49–39 Ma) times, its bulge straddling the equator. Reconstructing palaeoclimates and vegetation during this period is problematic, firstly because there are few macrofossil studies avail-

able to provide data on leaf physiognomy and, secondly, because most palynological studies concentrate on the presence of morphotypes only, and place little emphasis on assemblage variations, which might provide information about vegetation types.

Compared to the latest Cretaceous, the equatorial climate at this time is thought to have been less moist, and possibly seasonal, since coals, which are extensively present in the W African Maastrichtian (74–66 Ma), are absent from the Paleocene. Geomorphological evidence also points to seasonal climates, on the basis of the distribution of bauxites and ferruginous crusts of Eocene age across equatorial Africa (Guiraud and Maurin, 1991).

Palynological data indicates that mangroves were well developed in the Paleocene, and included the palm *Nypa* (Figure 7.2a), and the parent plant of *Proxapertites* pollen, to which it was allied. The pollen type *Echitriporites trianguliformis*, common in the Palaeogene, is also believed to have been produced by a mangrove taxon (Germeraad et al., 1968). In addition to palm pollen from mangroves, pollen of probable mauritioid (*Mauritiidites crassibaculatus*), lepidocaryoid (*Longapertites* spp., ancestral to *Eugeissona*), and other palms (e.g. *Palmaepollenites* spp., *Psilamonocolpites medius*) forms a major component of Paleocene palynomorph assemblages, and these are thought to be derived largely from freshwater swamp vegetation. Today, Palmae are particularly characteristic of freshwater swamps in both Africa and South America, and it is likely that they occupied this ecological setting throughout the Tertiary.

Suggestions regarding the character of other vegetation types at this time must be regarded with caution, since evidence is very fragmentary. It is possible that open vegetation is indicated by the presence of pollen of Gramineae, which occurs in modest frequencies in Nigeria (4%, Adegoke et al., 1978), although it is equally possible that the first Gramineae were dwellers of swamp vegetation. Several lines of evidence suggest closed, more ombrophilous forests in

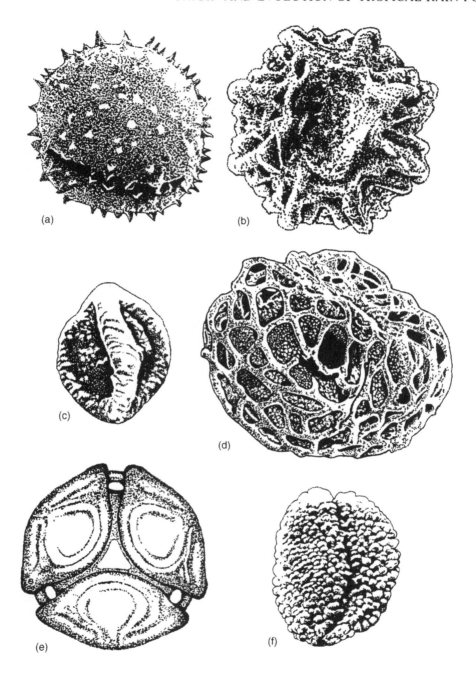

Figure 7.2  Pollen of taxa important in African Tertiary vegetation. (a) *Nypa*[1] (Palmae) ×1500, common mangrove element until end Eocene. (b) *Ctenolophon engleri*[2] (Ctenolophonaceae) ×1000, present throughout Tertiary. (c) *Verrutricolporites rotundiporus*[3] ×2000, which compares closely with pollen of ancestral Sonneratiaceae from SE Asia, was common through the Early and Middle Miocene. (d) *Praedapollis africanus*[3] ×700, a common palynomorph from Late Eocene to basal Miocene, compares closely with

widely scattered localities. Seward (1935) has described a mesophyll macroflora from the Early Paleocene of the the Red Sea, an area which has also yielded wood of megathermal rain forest trees, such as *Myristicoxylon princeps* (Myristicaceae) (Boureau et al., 1983). The rain forest family Ctenolophonaceae was particularly prominent in Cameroun at this time, since Salard-Chebaldaeff (1990) has Paleocene records of pollen closely comparable to both *Ctenolophon engleri* (Figure 7.2b) and *Ctenolophon parvifolius*. *Ctenolophon* pollen is, however, absent from the Paleocene of the nearby Niger Delta, despite its presence in the latest Cretaceous (Germeraad et al., 1968), and conditions there may have been less favourable for rain forests than during the latest Cretaceous. Pollen of other megathermal taxa recorded from equatorial palaeolatitudes at this time include that of the olacaceous tree *Anacolosa*, which appeared at the same time in South America, probably dispersing into both areas from the south (since its earliest records are from Australia, Dettman, 1994), and a species of Annonaceae (*Madanomadhiasulcites maximus*), recorded by Caratini et al. (1991) from Senegal.

Data therefore provide limited evidence for closed forest and possibly open woodland within the equatorial zone, and suggest that palm-dominated swamps were extensive in low-lying areas.

Limited evidence for Paleocene vegetation to the north of the equatorial belt is available from fossil woods from Algeria and pollen from Tunisia. Louvet (1968) recorded wood comparable to that of the rain forest emergent *Entandrophragma angolense*, together with wood of several Leguminosae, from the Paleocene of Algeria (in Boureau et al., 1983), but pollen analytical studies from N Africa suggest that Eurasian elements were also

widespread components of the vegetation (e.g. Meon, 1990). Floristic differences with the equatorial belt, shown by the absence of many characteristic low palaeolatitude pollen types in N Africa, suggest that the region of the Sahara formed a major biogeographical divide at this time, either comprising an upland area, centred on the regions of Tibesti and Hoggar (Axelrod and Raven, 1978), or characterised by arid climates. Floras in S Africa also differed from those of the equatorial zone, and included many southern hemisphere elements. In the Cape floral region, palynological studies at Arnot by Scholtz (1985) suggest the presence of open-canopied, dry, warm temperate forest with *Araucaria*, *Casuarina* and *Proteaceae*, and an understorey of Epacridaceae, Ericaceae, Restionaceae and *Gunnera* (Gunneraceae) but without *Nothofagus*. Within the earliest Tertiary, the S African flora thus showed a close relationship with the Australian region, emphasising the antiquity of the Cape Floristic Kingdom.

Evidence for African vegetation during the Late Paleocene/Early Eocene climatic maximum is meagre. Coetzee (1993) indicated that microfossil assemblages from the Paleocene/Eocene boundary point to a significant change in the lowland vegetation, and suggested the coexistence of a mosaic of dry and humid forest, with savanna woodland extending over most of the Congo Basin. This suggestion is to some extent supported by the data of Salard-Chebaldaeff (1990) from Cameroun, who showed that Gramineae pollen was common there together with forest elements. A change to drier, probably strongly xerophytic, vegetation in Egypt is likely on the basis of palynological studies by Kedves (1971), who showed that the earliest Eocene vegetation was dominated by Gramineae and cycads (Figure 7.3).

---

*Arapatiella*[4] (Leguminosae) from Brazil. (e) *Sarcolaena*[5] (Sarcolaenaceae) ×400, widespread in S Africa during the Miocene, now restricted to Madagascar. (f) *Racemonocolpites hians*[3] ×1500, which compares closely with the brackish-water palm *Oncosperma* from SE Asia, was common from the Oligocene to earliest Late Miocene. [1], Tomlinson (1986); [2], van der Ham (1980); [3], Legoux (1978); [4], Graham and Barker (1981); [5], Erdtman (1952). Drawn by Harsanti Pribatini.

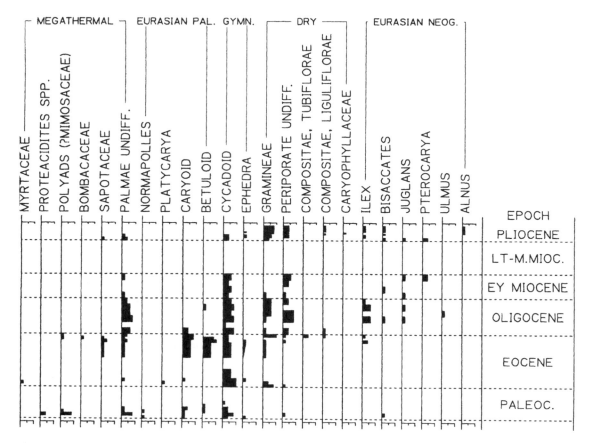

Figure 7.3 Summary of palynological analyses from the Tertiary of Egypt, data from Kedves (1971). Selected taxa only are shown, Histograms indicate the presence of rare, frequent, common and abundant pollen, and do not indicate percentage representation.

The most characteristic feature of the C African Early (54-49 Ma) and Middle Eocene is the sudden appearance of numerous bizarre pollen types, absent at higher latitudes and without analogues in modern floras, such as *Doualidites laevigatus*, *Auriculopollenites echinatus* and *Periretipollis spinosus*, the ecological significance of which is unclear.

Within the Early and Middle Eocene, some increase in diversification of rain forest taxa occurred, mainly through dispersals from elsewhere, with the appearance of *Crudia* (Leguminosae), *Amanoa* (Euphorbiaceae), *Bombax* (Bombacaceae) and additional Palmae, such as ?*Lepidocaryum* (*Echimonocolpites rarispinosus*).

The first two of these occurred simultaneously in Africa and South America, and were followed by *Bombax*, which has an earlier appearance in South America (Chapter 6). Further immigrations followed in the Middle Eocene with *Alchornea* (Euphorbiaceae) and *Merremia* (Convolvulaceae), which both appear more or less simultaneously across the tropics. Endemic taxa appearing at this time included *Pentaclethra macrophylla* (Leguminosae) and the freshwater swamp forest genus *Symphonia* (Guttiferae).

Fossil wood and seed determinations from N Africa, discussed by Boureau et al. (1983), suggest that mangroves were well developed there in coastal districts, with records of the palm *Nypa* from various localities, and of *Flacourtioxylon gifaense* (thought to be a rhizophoraceous wood by Louvet (1971)), *Palaeowetherella* from Egypt (Chandler, 1973) and *Sonneratioxylon aubrevillei* (Lythraceae or Sonneratiaceae) from Libya (the evolutionary significance of the latter taxon is discussed more fully in Chapter 9). In this region a coastal forested zone bordered by mangroves gave way to a more open, seasonal forest inland, with gallery forests along rivers (Boureau et al., 1983). Palynological studies from N Africa, however (Figure 7.3), continue to emphasise floristic differences from the equatorial region, through the presence of a significant Laurasian warm temperate element, which included *Platycarya* and trees which produced *Carya*-like pollen (Juglandaceae), in addition to myricoid and *Castanea*-like forms (Kedves, 1971, 1986). Although some pollen of tropical elements, such as the *Crudia* or *Isoberlinia* and *Acacia* (Leguminosae) were represented, the majority of those taxa characteristic of equatorial Africa were missing.

## 7.4.2  Late Eocene

A major change occurred in the equatorial African flora during the Late Eocene (39–36 Ma), with the disappearance of plants producing the bizarre pollen types characteristic of the earlier Eocene, and the sudden appearance of pollen of many extant taxa, particularly legumes, most of which occur in extant African rain forests. These included *Rauwolfia* (Apocynaceae), *Terminalia* (Combretaceae), *Pentadesma butryacea* (Guttiferae), *Acacia*, *Adenanthera*, *Brachystegia*, *Caesalpinia*, *Calpocalyx ngoumiensis*, *Parkia* and *Sindora* (Leguminosae), *Brachypteris* (Malphigiaceae) and *Pycnanthus* (Myristicaceae). The rain forest tree *Ctenolophon* reappeared in Nigeria, after an absence in the earlier Eocene (Germeraad et al., 1968) and Gramineae became less common in Cameroun

(Salard-Chebaldaeff, 1990). To the north, palynological analyses by Kedves (1971) show some significant changes in the vegetation of Egypt. Pollen of warm temperate taxa of caryoid and myricoid affinity and cycads continue to dominate in this region, as during the earlier Eocene, but pollen of tropical tree taxa are much more common than previously, and can be referred to Sapotaceae, Bombacaceae, Mimosaceae and Palmae (Figure 7.3).

Differences between N African and equatorial vegetation are also shown by mangroves, which were characterised by ancestral Sonneratiaceae in N Africa, but in W Africa continued to be characterised by Nypoidae (*Nypa* and the parent plant of *Proxapertites*).

Despite the marked floristic changes at this time, only a few taxa appear to have arrived from outside Africa. Possible immigrants comprise Sapotaceae, maybe dispersing from Europe, *Brachypteris*, from South America, and *Caesalpinia*, probably from India (see Muller, 1981), via S Asia (an earlier, Middle Eocene dispersal for *Caesalpinia* is more likely since it is already present in the Middle Eocene in South America). *Rauwolfia* and *Acacia* appeared widely across the tropics at this time, as did the fern *Stenochlaena palustris*, and a species of Schizaeaceous fern, producing the spore type *Cicatricosisporites dorogensis*.

### Early Tertiary climates

Data on the Paleocene and Eocene of Africa are sketchy, and probably open to different interpretations of detail. However, there is clear evidence for a latitudinal zonation of vegetation throughout this period, and that this zonation was least marked during the Late Eocene when global climates were cooling, and closed rain forests were extensive at equatorial latitudes. In contrast, it was best developed prior to this, during which time there is evidence for both open and closed vegetation at equatorial latitudes. The data are best explained in terms of a pronounced latitudinal temperature gradient throughout the Early Tertiary, and that during the Late Paleocene/Early Eocene thermal maximum, equatorial vegetation may have been more open than during the Early Paleocene or Late Eocene, as a result of increased temperatures, and perhaps monsoonal or aseasonal subhumid equatorial climates. Perhaps the bizarre pollen types characteristic of this time interval were produced by a vegetation without a present-day parallel, adapted to very hot climates.

## 7.5 MID-TERTIARY (OLIGOCENE TO MIDDLE MIOCENE) VEGETATION

The terminal Eocene event seems to have had a lesser effect on the fauna of the African continent than elsewhere. This is particularly well illustrated from the mammalian succession from Fayum in Egypt, which spans the Eocene/Oligocene boundary. Rasmussen et al. (1992) show no significant faunal change during the time of the Oligocene climatic deterioration. Prothero (1994) suggests that, due to the isolation of the African continent at this time, N Africa was a refuge from the 'big chill' which so severely affected temperate and polar latitudes. In contrast, there was a marked floristic change at the end of the Eocene. Particularly notable was the extinction of many Palmae (Figure 7.4), especially of the brackish-water Nypoidae (*Nypa*, *Proxapertites*), and also of the mauritioid palm *Mauritiidites crassibaculatus*; there was an overall diversity decrease (Figure 5.15b) suggesting that all vegetation types were affected by this event. For an explanation of this change it is necessary to compare the rich palynological record from equatorial Africa with the much more fragmentary record of pollen and macrofossils from N Africa.

A sudden sea level fall probably explains the disappearance of nypoid mangroves, since as sea levels fell below the Late Eocene shelf break, habitats for such taxa would have been drastically reduced, but, in the same manner as with the mammals at Fayum, there is little

evidence within the Early Oligocene (36–30 Ma) from plant fossils from equatorial regions for cooling or drying. Unpublished palynological data which has very recently become available from the Niger Delta (courtesy of Chevron Nigeria) suggests that the first evidence for drier climates is within the Late Oligocene (30–25 Ma) immediately following the 30 Ma mid-Oligocene sea level fall (Figure 3.6), where grass pollen maxima, suggesting the widespread expansion of grasses, coincide with periods of lower sea levels. The Late Oligocene phases of increased representation of grasses were not so pronounced as those of the late Neogene (Section 7.6), and it is most likely that grasses formed the understorey of open forests, rather than in vegetation of savanna aspect.

Oligocene (36–25 Ma) palynomorph assemblages from W Africa are also characterised by the evolutionary appearance of pollen of many, typically African, trees and climbers, many characteristic of rain forest, such as *Annona* (Annonaceae), *Landolphia* (Apocynaceae), *Taccazea* (Periplocaceae), *Campylostemon* and *Hippocratea* (Hippocrateaceae), *Petersianthus* (Lecythidaceae), *Adenanthera*, *Amblygonocarpus*, *Calpocalyx*, *Leucaena*, *Pseudoprosopis*, *Tetrapleura* and *Xylia* (Leguminosae), *Trichilia* (Meliaceae), *Polygala* (Polygalaceae), *Parinari* (Rosaceae) and *Macrosphyra* and *Mitragyna* (Rubiaceae), together with a number of taxa of coastal habitats, such as *Scaevola* (Goodeniaceae), and some taxa which subsequently became extinct in Africa, such as the austral *Sicyos* (Cucurbitaceae). *Sclerosperma* (Palmae) also has its earliest positive record at this time (refer to Section 5.2 for other opinions).

One possibility which might explain the limited evidence for a climatic explanation of the terminal Eocene event at equatorial latitudes is that in W Africa, where the Eocene/Oligocene boundary is generally associated with an unconformity, Early Oligocene sediments are often missing, with the result that the precise character of earliest Oligocene floristic changes remain unstudied. Prothero (1994) emphasises that the main extinction

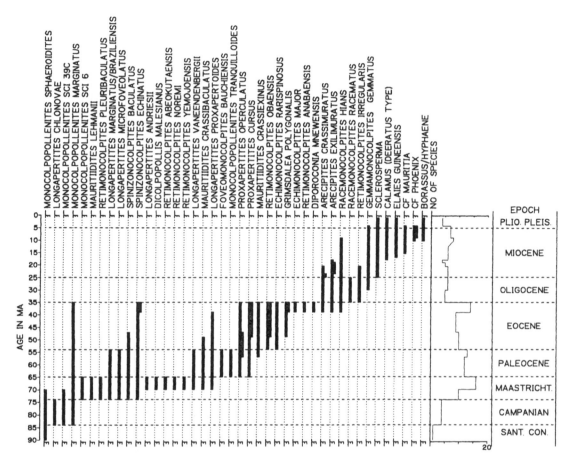

Figure 7.4   Fossil pollen tentatively attributable to Palmae from the Late Cretaceous to Quaternary in W Africa, compiled mainly from Salard-Chebaldaeff (1990), together with unpublished data. This is not intended to be a critical comprehensive list, but has been constructed to show the main trends in the stratigraphic distribution of Palmae pollen. Narrow vertical bars indicate the known stratigraphic range of each taxon, whereas wide bars reflect periods during which abundance maxima are stratigraphically important, and during which time parent plants were particularly common.

event at the end of the Eocene was associated with a shortlived massive cooling event at 33 Ma in the earliest Oligocene (36 Ma according to the time scale used here), and the likelihood is that, due to the Early Oligocene unconformity which is present in many African sedimentary successions, the precise character of this event in Africa is yet to be seen. Whatever the details of changes in the earliest Oligocene, the remainder of the Oligocene was clearly characterised by widespread rain forests

through much of the equatorial region, and grassland communities were clearly subordinate. In this respect, its flora reacted very differently to the terminal Eocene 'big chill' than to Late Neogene global cooling, which is discussed further below.

There is clear evidence for a significant drying at the terminal Eocene in Egypt. Kedves (1971) showed that, whereas Late Eocene palynomorph assemblages are characterised by Eurasian warm temperate and megathermal elements, these were replaced in the earliest Oligocene by plants producing periporate pollen (possibly Chenopodiaceae/Amaranthaceae) and Gramineae, with all of the megathermal elements, except Palmae, being absent (Figure 7.3). It is therefore most likely that in Africa the terminal Eocene 'big chill' resulted in the expansion of drier and cooler climates, and an associated widespread retraction of tropical forests toward the palaeoequator, but resulted in relatively few extinctions at equatorial latitudes.

The character of N African Oligocene vegetation is also revealed by wood and leaf fossils, particularly from Algeria, Libya and Egypt, reviewed by Boureau et al. (1983). They suggest that, in the Oligocene, N Africa was characterised by a mosaic of savanna, open forests and gallery forests, with continuous forest developing locally in low-lying coastal areas. Some of the wood fossils recovered from these areas can be closely matched with modern genera (and, in some instances, species): savanna is suggested by records of the wood *Combretoxylon bussoni* (suggesting the savanna tree *Anogeissus leiocarpus*), *C. primigenium* (suggesting savanna Combretaceae) and *Detarioxylon aegypticum* and the leaf fossils *Detariophyllum coquinense* (suggesting the savanna tree *Detarium microphyllum*) and *Pterocarpophyllum erinacoides* (which compares to *Pterocarpus erinaceus*); gallery forests by the wood *Harunganoxylon vismioides* (Hypericaceae); and dense forests from the meliaceous woods *Entandrophragmoxylon magnieri* and *E. candollei* (suggesting *Entandrophragma* spp.). Also noteworthy among the Oligo-Miocene fossil wood records from Libya and Egypt are *Xymaloxylon zeltenense* and *Atherospermoxylon aegypticum*, referable to the primitive, southern hemisphere family Monimiaceae, which is currently very poorly represented in continental Africa compared to other southern land masses, and its presence in the mid-Tertiary of N Africa confirms the view of Ashton and Gunatilleke (1987a) on the basis of present-day ranges, that Monimiaceae have become extinct over much of Africa.

Despite the Oligocene cooling trend, temperatures in N Africa were sufficiently warm to support mangroves, but, in the same manner as for the Eocene, these were characterised by ancestral Sonneratiaceae (on the basis of the pollen type *Florschuetzia trilobata* from the Oligocene of the Red Sea). Equatorial regions were characterised by *Pelliciera rhizophorae* and the mangrove fern *Acrostichum* (Pteridaceae) which together were wholly dominant (since *Nypa* was no more).

As noted above, most of the new taxa appearing in the Oligocene were endemic to Africa, but there were a few immigrants. Spores of the aquatic fern *Ceratopteris* are regularly recorded (Germeraad et al., 1968; Salard-Chebaldaeff, 1976), suggesting dispersal from India, which is thought to have been the centre of origin of this genus (Kar, 1982), although *Ceratopteris* spores are also recorded in low numbers in the latest Eocene (e.g. Kedves, 1986; Morley, unpublished), and hence the actual time of dispersal may have been slightly earlier. *Fillaeopsis* (Leguminosae), *Klaineanthus* (Euphorbiaceae), *Thespesia* (Malvaceae) and *Mirabilis* (Nyctaginaceae) probably dispersed from South America.

During the earliest Miocene, prior to Neogene uplift and volcanism when the continental divide was low, climates were moist over most of equatorial Africa, with rain forests extending more or less from coast to coast (Andrews and Van Couvering, 1975). This is suggested by mammalian fossils preserved in Early Miocene deposits east of the divide which chiefly indicate forest dwellers. Palynological studies from S Sudan indicate the presence of rain forest vegetation during the Oligo-Miocene (Awad and Brier, 1993; Awad, 1994), and a rich leaf flora of Early Miocene age described from Rusinga Island, Lake Victoria, by Chesters (1957), has been considered to represent lowland rain forest by Andrews and Van Couvering (1975). It was probable, however, that some sort of biogeographical barrier existed between east and west throughout the Tertiary, in order to account for the restriction of certain wood and leaf fossils to E and N Africa. In particular, fossil wood of the Asian genus *Dipterocarpus* has been positively identified from the Miocene of Kenya by Bancroft (1935), who demonstrated from the presence of multiseriate rays that the fossil wood *Dipterocarpoxylon africanum* should be unequivocally referred to the Asian Dipterocarpoidae. In addition, Chiarugi (1933) has described fossil *Dipterocarpus* wood from the Early Tertiary of Somalia, and Seward (1935) described leaves referable to *Dipterocarpophyllum*, from Nubian Early Tertiary deposits.

The trend of floristic diversification seen in the Oligocene became reduced in the Early Miocene. New appearances, according to Salard-Chebaldaeff (1979, 1981), were *Balanophora* (Balanophoraceae), *Rhodognaphalon* (Bombacaceae), *Hippocrataea myrianthe* (Hippocrataceae), *Iodes africana* (Icacinaceae), *Elaeis guineensis* (Palmae), *Gardenia pterocalyx* and *Morelia* (Rubiaceae) and *Butyrospermum* or *Manilkara* (Sapotaceae) and, in the latest Early Miocene, a schizeaeceous climbing fern with spores identical to those of *Lygodium scandens* (Hopping, 1967). Two new arrivals at the beginning of the Early Miocene which substantially modified coastal vegetation were *Rhizophora* (Rhizophoraceae), and the parent plants of the *Verrutricolporites* group of pollen (Lythraceae or Sonneratiaceae, see Section 9.8). Both of these taxa dispersed from South America. *Rhizophora* subsequently became the most important element of mangroves, and pure swamps of this genus must have been extremely widespread during phases of Neogene rising sea levels (Figure 7.5). The parent plants of *Verrutricolporites* spp. were possibly trees of freshwater swamps, but could have been mangroves, in view of their close relationship to the ancestors of the SE Asian mangrove genus *Sonneratia* (although Germeraad et al. (1968) previously suggested an affinity to *Crenea* (Lythraceae), which was disputed by Graham and Graham (1971)). As with *Sonneratia*, pollen evolution within this group was rapid (Figure 7.6), as brought to attention

by Legoux (1978), with pronounced phases of speciation after 21 Ma and 15 Ma. The group disappeared at the end of the Middle Miocene, probably due to coastal swamp habitat loss as a result of falling sea level and drier climates following the 10.5 Ma sea level fall.

The palynological record from both the Niger Delta and Cameroun suggests a gradual change in the character of vegetation during the course of the Miocene. The Niger Delta succession of Legoux (1978) shows a successive series of extinctions within the Early and Middle (16–10 Ma) Miocene, including taxa producing coarsely reticulate pollen of probable Leguminosae such as *Praedapollis africanus* (Figure 7.2d) and *Spirosyncolpites bruni*, also a number of palms producing reticulate pollen (Figure 7.7) and the *Anacolosa* (Olacaceae) pollen type. The pollen type *Praedapollis africanus* compares favourably with pollen of the Brazilian legume *Arapatiella* (see plate 4e in Graham and Barker, 1981), whereas *Anacolosa* type occurs today in *Anacolosa* (Madagascar and SE Asia) and the South American genera *Cathedra* and *Ptychopetalum*. At the end of the Middle Miocene, *Belskipollis elegans* (?possibly an ally of *Chrysophyllum*, Sapotaceae) also suddenly disappeared from the record. Within Cameroun, pollen of *Sicyos*, *Leucaena*, *Anacolosa* and *Cicatricosisporites dorogensis* (Schizaeaceae), are present in the Oligocene, but absent from the basal Miocene onwards. During the same period, Gramineae pollen, suggesting open grassy woodland or savanna, increases in representation during periods of low sea level from 21 Ma onward, with the first evidence of burning (from the presence of charred Gramineae cuticle) at about 15 Ma, at the end of the Early Miocene (Morley and Richards, 1993), and subsequently becomes successively more common during the Middle Miocene. Drier conditions are suggested over a wide area, with the expansion of open woodland and savanna at the expense of rain forests.

Rain forests in E Africa also became greatly reduced during this period and were replaced by open woodland and grassland. The character of

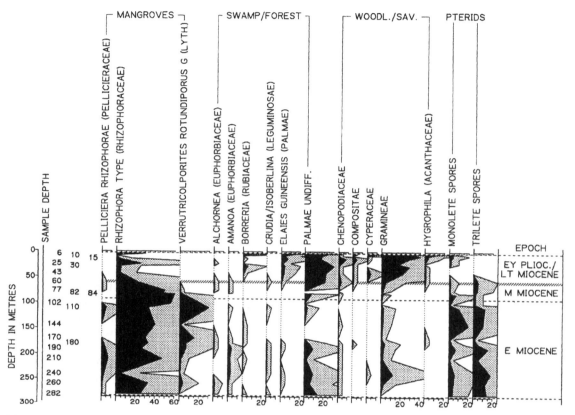

Figure 7.5 Summary pollen diagram reconstructed from pollen profile from Ziguinchor-3 well, Senegal, by Medus (1976). Main pollen sum is total freshwater pollen and spores, with mangrove pollen being presented in terms of total pollen and spores. Obvious contaminants and mud additives excluded. Stipple = ×5 exaggeration.

Middle Miocene grass-dominated vegetation and gallery forest in E Africa has been eloquently reconstructed by Retallack et al. (1990) and Retallack (1992a,b), through the study of plant fossils and palaeosols associated with the *Kenyapithecus* site, which is dated at about 14 Ma. Retallack interprets a mosaic of early successional woodland, grassy woodland and wooded grassland (Figure 7.8) and observed that Middle Miocene grassland ecosystems differed substantially from modern grasslands in that, although the subfamily Chloridoideae and supertribe Panicanae were common, there was no evidence for the supertribe Andropogonae, which is now dominant in seasonally

arid, overgrazed and burned African grasslands.

Although there was a major interchange of Eurasian and African mammals in the Middle Miocene, following the collision of the African and Asian plates, no such interchange is apparent from the record of plant fossils, at least, with respect to tropical taxa. This is probably due to the presence of a strong latitudinal vegetational zonation, restricting dispersal between higher and lower latitudes, from the terminal Eocene onwards. Only the appearance of the conifer *Juniperus* within the E African highlands can be considered a candidate for such dispersal, since its pollen was regularly

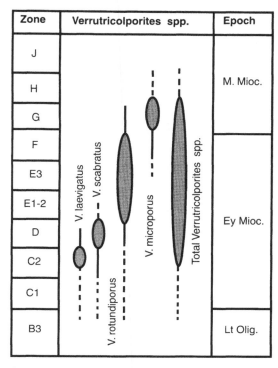

| Zone | Verrutricolporites spp. | Epoch |
|------|-------------------------|-------|
| J | | |
| H | | M. Mioc. |
| G | | |
| F | | |
| E3 | | |
| E1-2 | | Ey Mioc. |
| D | | |
| C2 | | |
| C1 | | |
| B3 | | Lt Olig. |

*V. laevigatus* · *V. scabratus* · *V. microporus* · Total Verrutricolporites spp. · *V. rotundiporus*

Figure 7.6 Stratigraphic distribution and generalised abundance trends of species of the form-genus *Verrutricolporites* (Lythraceae or Sonneratiaceae) in the Niger Delta from Legoux (1978). Compare to Figure 9.37.

recorded from the *Ramapithecus* site at Fort Ternan (Bonneville, 1984) together with pollen of *Podocarpus* (Figure 7.9). The dispersal of these taxa from the north and south respectively was made possible by the Miocene uplift within E Africa, and their joint occurrence at Fort Ternan may relate as much to this phase of uplift, as to dispersal following plate collision.

Palynological data from Egypt by Kedves (1971) shows first appearances of pollen of a few Laurasian taxa in the Early Miocene and Pliocene (Figure 7.2), such as *Pterocarya* and *Alnus*, possibly reflecting Neogene dispersal into Africa, but, as noted earlier, the palynological record indicates that many Eurasian elements were well established in the N African region through most of the Early Tertiary with

most Neogene appearances being due more to climatic deterioration than plant dispersal following plate collision.

There is little evidence for moist forests within N Africa during the Miocene, which from the pollen record of Kedves (1971) was characterised by woodland and savanna. However, in southern Africa, mesothermal to megathermal, paratropical vegetation extended as far south as the southern tip of Africa during periods of warmer climate and high sea levels (Coetzee, 1978). She recorded two periods, which she interpreted as within the Early Miocene, about 19 Ma, and Middle Miocene, 16–14 Ma, when palm-dominated vegetation was widespread at the Cape (Figure 7.10). These intervals are associated with the occurrence of pollen of the primitive angiosperms *Ascarina* (Chloranthaceae) and *Drimys* (Winteraceae) and of the endemic Madagascan rain forest tree family Sarcolaenaceae (Figure 7.2e) (Coetzee and Muller, 1984), suggesting that during warmer, moist periods, the Cape vegetation bore similarities to the present-day humid forests of Madagascar. Such forests were also probably widespread along the east coast of southern Africa, but not in the west, since the west coast probably experienced a very dry climate since the inception of the cold Benguela Current, which became established following the mid-Tertiary development of polar ice in the Antarctic (van Zinderen Bakker, 1975). During intervening times, moist temperate woodland, with the southern hemisphere gymnosperms *Podocarpus*, *Microcachrys* and *Widdringtonia*, as well as *Cupaniopsis* (Sapindaceae), *Myrica* (Myricaceae) and *Casuarina* (Casuarinaceae), were widespread (Coetzee and Praglowski, 1984). The common occurrence of *Casuarina* perhaps indicates drier, sclerophyllous vegetation. Subtropical evergreen forest patches with Cunoniaceae and Proteaceae survive today as refugia in gulleys in the mountains of the Cape region, and may be relics of the tropical aspect rain forests which were widespread during the Miocene (P.S. Ashton, personal communication).

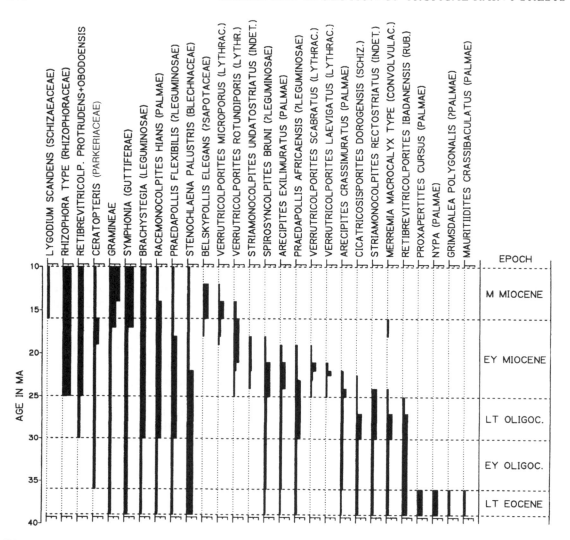

Figure 7.7   Stratigraphic ranges of pollen types described from the Niger Delta by Legoux (1978), with additions, and with ages modified according to Morley and Richards (1993).

## 7.6   LATE TERTIARY (LATE MIOCENE TO PLIOCENE) VEGETATION AND CLIMATIC CYCLICITY

The African Late Neogene is of particular interest since it includes the time of appearance and radiation of hominids, and also holds the explanation of the present-day depauperate nature of the African flora.

Continuous sedimentary successions from areas yielding hominid fossils have not been found, pollen data from hominid sites displaying at best an intermittent record (Bonnefille, 1984). The very thick sedimentary succession of the Niger Delta contains the most complete palynological record for the Late Neogene, and is also located in a very sensitive position for recording climatic change in W Africa, between the Dahomey Gap and the Cameroun–Gabon

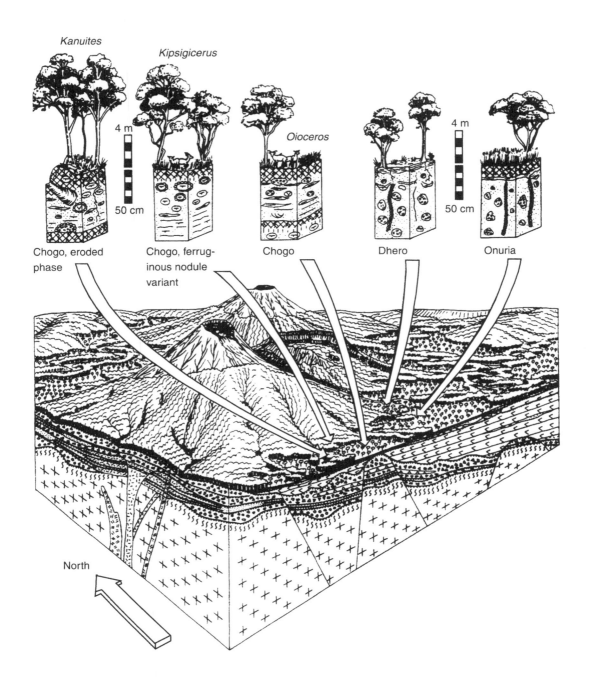

Figure 7.8   Interpreted palaeoenvironment, soils and vegetation of SW Kenya during Middle Miocene time, at about 14 Ma, based primarily on the analysis of palaeosols (Retallack, 1992a). Reproduced by permission of Academic Press.

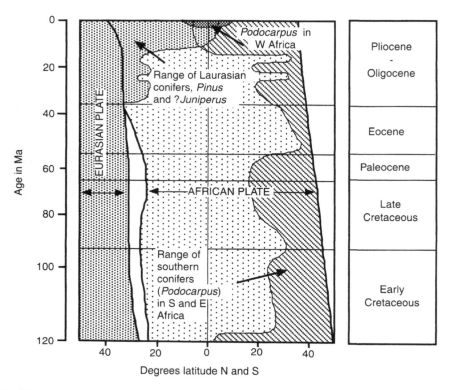

Figure 7.9  Tentative sketch showing schematic distribution of conifers along a north–south transect through the African continent for the Late Cretaceous and Tertiary.

rain forest block (Morley, 1986; Poumot, 1987; Morley and Richards, 1993). The most complete record is that of Morley and Rosen (1996), based on the detailed palynological study of 26 petroleum exploration wells, and provides a virtually continuous record of vegetational and climatic change for the last 10.5 Ma. Most of the analyses for the latter study were undertaken on fully marine, delta front and pro-delta sediments, which receive their pollen content from a very wide catchment, and reflect regional vegetational changes, within both the delta plain area and the river catchment itself.

The style of palynomorph assemblages from the Late Miocene onward differ from those from earlier sediments in that pollen of Gramineae forms a major component, often exceeding 60% of the pollen derived from freshwater environments (Figure 7.11). Gramineae pollen maxima

are thought to reflect periods of expansion of savanna, possibly across the Niger Delta, and a parallel reduction in range of rain forests. The savannas are believed to have been maintained by natural fires, since the grass pollen is generally accompanied by common charred Gramineae cuticle (Figure 7.12). The many fluctuations of pollen from savanna and rain forest (Figure 7.13) closely parallel sea level fluctuations identified by sequence stratigraphy (Vail and Wornardt, 1990; Morley and Rosen, 1996).

### 7.6.1  Late Miocene, Alternating Expansion and Contraction of Rain Forest and Savanna

A major phase of expansion of savannas is suggested on the basis of a distinctive abundance

| Zone | Vegetation | Climate | Epoch |
|------|-----------|---------|-------|
| M | Present Macchia | Present | Quaternary |
| Lviii | First strong development of Macchia | Colder, drier | Pliocene |
| Lvi | Forest; Coniferae, *Casuarina*, Sapindaceae | Cool, wet | Lt Miocene |
| Lv | Palmae | Subtropical to tropical | M Miocene |
| Liv | Restionaceae swamp | Temperate, locally wet | Ey Miocene |
| Liii | Forest; Coniferae, first Compositae | Cool, wet | Ey Miocene |
| Lii | Palmae | Subtropical to tropical | Ey Miocene |
| Li | Forest; Coniferae | Cool, wet | Lt Oligocene |

Figure 7.10 Characteristic palynomorph assemblages recorded from the Miocene of South Africa by Coetzee (1978). Reproduced by permission of Palaeoecology of Africa.

maximum of grass pollen and charred Gramineae cuticle (Figure 7.12), coinciding with the most pronounced of the Neogene sea level falls at about 10.5 Ma. The climatic change responsible for this sea level fall must have had a profound effect on the vegetation of the Niger Delta region, for the succeeding period of rising sea levels and moist climate, up to 7.5 Ma, was initially characterised by low diversity palynomorph assemblages (Figure 7.13), with abundant fern spores but relatively little pollen of typical rainforest or swamp forest taxa. Characteristic rain forest and freshwater swamp taxa, such as Sapotaceae, became common only after sea levels subsequently rose to their previous maximum levels, the climate became more moist, and mangrove swamps expanded. However, at this time the overall diversity of rain forest communities probably remained very low. Remarkably, a palm species producing the pollen type *Racemonocolpites hians* (Figure

7.2f), with pollen comparable to *Oncosperma*, from the Far East, became extinct at this time, following a sea level rise, and expansion of *Rhizophora* mangroves (Figures 7.13; 7.14).

Periods of expansion of savanna were more pronounced after 6.3 Ma, at which time trees such as *Brachystegia* and members of Sapotaceae became much less well represented although few total extinctions of rain forest taxa have been noted during the Late Miocene (10–5 Ma). Through the successive moist phases, rain forest/freshwater swamps exhibited very little change, although there was a general increase in diversity with time. Their main components were *Amanoa*, *Symphonia*, *Crudia/ Isoberlina* and Sapotaceae, together with an extinct group of Rubiaceae (*Retibrevitricolporites* spp.) and a probable palm (*Gemmamonocolpites* sp). The dry, savanna periods were each characterised by abundant Gramineae, and the presence of common charred Gramineae cuticle fragments within each of these indicates that the savannas were regularly subject to burning.

Dry or seasonal climate vegetation clearly increased in diversity during the Late Miocene. The dry phase at about 10 Ma coincided with the initial appearance of several acanthaceous taxa, indicated by regular pollen of the *Justicia* type, and also of *Isoglossa*, *Strobilanthes* and *Hygrophila*. *Phaecoceros* (Anthoceraceae) spores show a distinct increase in abundance after 7.0 Ma; some Anthoceraceae bear water-retaining swollen stems, and probably occurred in seasonal swamp vegetation on the delta plain. Cyperaceae became a widespread element of savanna or freshwater swamp after about 6.6 Ma.

### 7.6.2 Early Pliocene, Predominantly Moist Climates

The Early Pliocene (5–3.5 Ma) was characterised by moist climates, the expansion and diversification of rain forests, and the retraction of savanna (Figures 7.11; 7.13). This is in keeping with oxygen isotope data, with respect to which the

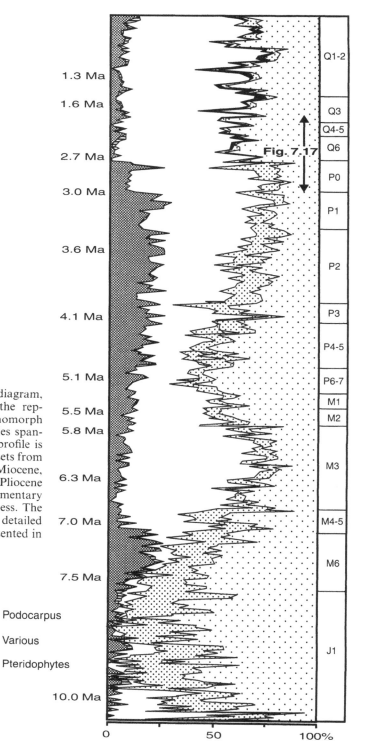

Figure 7.11 Summary palynological diagram, excluding mangrove pollen, showing the representation of major freshwater palynomorph groups in offshore Niger Delta boreholes spanning the last 10.5 Ma. The composite profile is constructed from four overlapping datasets from well sections which penetrated Late Miocene, latest Miocene to Early Pliocene, Late Pliocene and latest Pliocene to Quaternary sedimentary successions and totals 7000 m in thickness. The time interval represented by the very detailed study of Leroy and Dupont (1994), presented in Figure 7.17, is indicated.

Figure 7.12   Charred Gramineae cuticle, formed as a result of savanna fires are widespread in Neogene marine sediments from W Africa. Left: stomatal cell; centre: 'long' cells; right: 'dumbell' cells. All from Late Miocene (palynological zone M1) of Niger Delta, magnification ×700.

consistently warm and moist Early Pliocene has been termed the 'Golden Age' (Sarthein and Fenner, 1988). The rich palynomorph assemblages from this period indicate that, in addition to the Late Miocene rain forest taxa, Early Pliocene moist forests included common *Ctenolophon engleri*, *Klaineanthus* and *Uapaca* (Uapacaceae), *Iodes* (Icacinaceae), *Petersianthus*, *Pycnanthus*, *Elaies guineensis* and an additional extinct palm and *Pandanus* (Pandanaceae). There is a clear trend to increased palynomorph assemblage diversification with time, diversities achieving their maximum just prior to the end of the Early Pliocene, at about 3.5 Ma (Figure 7.13). The end Early Pliocene event had a wide effect across W Africa; offshore Senegal, a deep-sea core dated by reference to oxygen isotope stages, and studied for palynology by Leroy and Dupont (1994), indicates a change to a much drier climate after 3.48 Ma, prior to which time tropical forests extended to 20°N.

### 7.6.3   Late Pliocene, With Successively Drier and Cooler Climates

The Late Pliocene (3.5–1.6 Ma) saw much more pronounced climatic changes, with marked drying and cooling (Figures 7.13; 7.15). A drying phase at 3.2 Ma was followed by a much more pronounced period of desiccation at 3.0 Ma, both being accompanied by the marked expansion of grasses, reduced assemblage diversities and numerous regional extinctions.

The first phase of drying resulted in the extinction of a species of ?palm producing *Gemmamonocolpites* sp., and the parent plants of *Retibrevitricolporites obodoensis* and *R. protrudens*, whereas the more pronounced drying phase at 3.0 Ma, coinciding with a sea level fall equalling that of the latest Middle Miocene, resulted in the extinction of the parent plants of *Praedapollis flexibilis* (?Leguminosae), *Cinctiporipollis mulleri* (family unknown), and a further unidentified palm. At about 2.7 Ma, coinciding with the onset of glaciation in the northern hemisphere, a sudden change to a cooler climate is suggested by the appearance of *Podocarpus milanjianus* type pollen,[1] an event first brought to attention by Knaap (1972). This was the first gymnosperm to occur in W Africa since the end of the Cretaceous. Its initial appearance is reflected in two successive maxima (Figure 7.15), following which its abundance is reduced. Studies of the last glacial/interglacial cycle (Dupont and Weinelt, 1996; Maley, 1996) suggest that *Podocarpus* was common in W Africa at times when climates are cooler than at present, but still moist, at which time cloud forest was probably widespread (Maley, 1987, 1989, 1996), and it is thought that such conditions must have created a suitable pathway for the dispersal of *Podocarpus milanjianus* from upland areas in E Africa via Angola and Gabon (Figure 7.16). Opportunities for dispersal of this species may also have been assisted as a result of the Late Miocene – Early Pliocene uplift of the African Plateau (King, 1962).

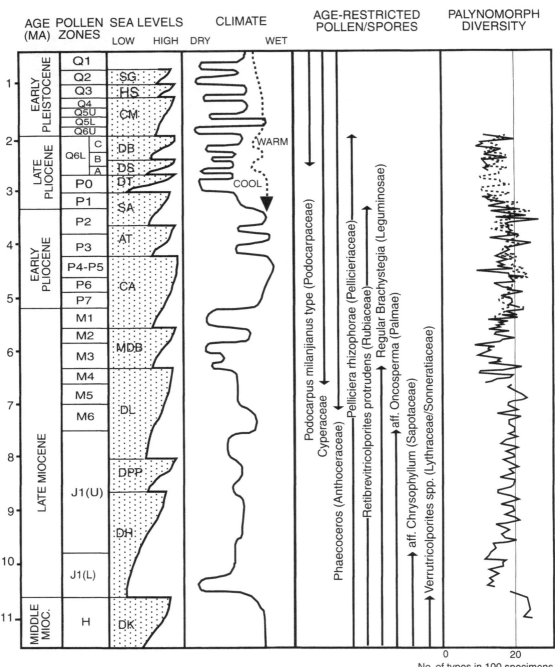

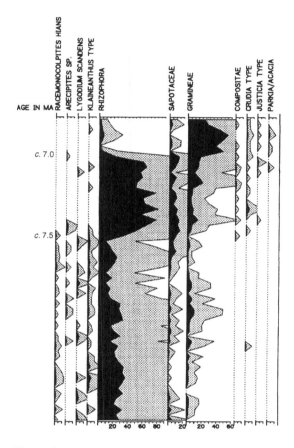

Figure 7.14 Summary palynological diagram for 1000 m interval from offshore Niger Delta well, covering time interval represented by zones J1 (upper) to M4 (6.5–9 Ma) showing extinction of *Racemonocolpites hians* (?*Oncosperma* pollen) as a result of the sudden expansion of *Rhizophora* mangroves following a sudden sea level rise. Stipple = ×5 exaggeration.

Aridification was a continent-wide feature of the Late Pliocene. Studies of ODP site 658 by Leroy and Dupont (1994) indicate an increase in trade wind activity between 3.3 and 2.5 Ma, with a marked phase of aridification after 3.2 Ma (isotope stage 130). Further aridification occurred around 2.7 Ma, with desert conditions developing after 2.6 Ma. Similarly, Bonnefille (1984) records a change to much drier conditions after 2.5 Ma for E Africa. Detailed studies of the Late Pliocene by Leroy and Dupont (1994) show that high frequency vegetation changes were driven by orbital forcing (Figure 7.17), and emphasise that the record of vegetational change revealed from the examination of petroleum exploration wells, although detailed, is highly generalised.

### 7.6.4 Reduced Diversity of Modern African Rain Forests

Based on the main times of Neogene extinction, the diversity of W African rain forests became reduced in two stages (Figure 7.18), firstly, during the latest Early and Middle Miocene, and, secondly, during the mid and late Pliocene. The first phase of extinction was gradual, taking place over several million years, and paralleled the phase of Miocene expansion of grasslands. The second phase was relatively sudden, and coincided with sudden drying and cooling events at 3.2, 3.0 and 1.8

Figure 7.13 Summary of palynological zonation for the offshore Niger Delta in relation to sea level change, together with an indication of palaeoclimate trends over the time interval 10.5 Ma to 0.5 Ma, the main extinctions and appearances over this time interval, and also miospore diversity trends. Sea level trends relate to the representation of stratigraphic sequences determined from the Niger Delta, which parallel those reported from the Gulf of Mexico over the same time period by Vail and Wornardt (1990), named after stratigraphically restricted nannofossils which characterise the maximum flood of each sequence (SG = small *Gephyrocapsa* spp.; HS = *Helicosphaera sellii*; CM = *Catinaster macintyrei*; DB = *Discoaster brouweri*; DS = *Discoaster surculus*; DT = *Discoaster tamalis*; SA = *Sphenolithus abies*; AT = *Amaurolithus tricorniculatus*; CA = *Ceratolithus acutus*; MDB = *Discoaster berggreni*; DL = *Discoaster loeblichi*; DPP = *Discoaster prepentaradiatus*; DH = *Discoaster hamatus*; DK = *Discoaster kugleri*). The climate curve essentially reflects abundance variations of Gramineae pollen and charred grass cuticle. Palynomorph diversity estimates are presented in terms of the number of miospore types recorded in the first count of 100 specimens, excluding mangrove pollen; solid and dashed lines are from different profiles.

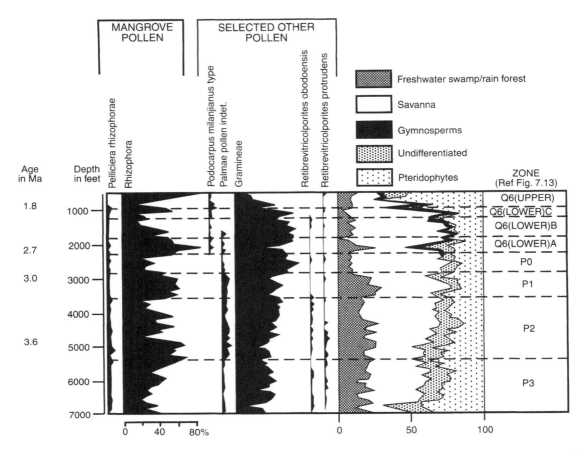

Figure 7.15  Summary palynological diagram for offshore Niger Delta well spanning the Late Pliocene and Early Pleistocene. Note the sudden expansion of Gramineae pollen at 3.0 Ma, and associated reduction in representation of palm pollen, and the sudden appearance of *Podocarpus milanjianus* type pollen after 2.7 Ma.

Ma. The second phase is clearly associated with the onset of glaciation in the northern hemisphere, but the reason for the first phase remains problematic. If this phase of extinction related wholly to global climatic deterioration, it is puzzling that the terminal Eocene cooling, which would have been of similar magnitude, had so little impact on equatorial vegetation, and, also, that similar climatic changes remain unrecorded in South America at this time. Two possible explanations are proposed: firstly, the final closure of Tethys may have altered climatic circulation patterns, resulting in more seasonal equatorial climates, and,

secondly, the general uplift of the African continent in the mid-Miocene may have resulted in fewer opportunities for lowland rain forest elements to disperse to suitable refuges (see Figure 7.1).

The reduced representation of Palmae relates to extinctions at the end of the Eocene, as well as to during the Neogene as a result of changing climates. By contrast, many other groups, which form the amphi-Pacific element of van Steenis (1962a), are absent as a result of the geographical isolation of the African Plate during the Early Tertiary, and not to changing climates.

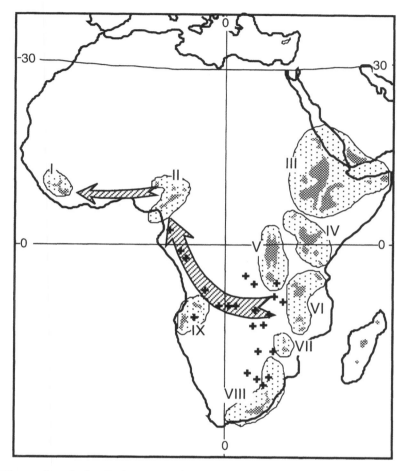

Figure 7.16 Dispersal path for *Podocarpus milanjianus* into W Africa. West African regional mountain systems as follows: I, West African; II, Cameroun-Jos; III, Ethiopian; IV, Imatonga–Kenya–Usambara; V, Ruwenzori–Kivu; VI, Uluguru–Mlanje; VII, Chimanimani; VIII, Drakensberg; IX, Angolan. The crosses show distant populations of Afromontane plant species outside the main centres (simplified), arrows show probable migration routes (from Maley et al., 1990, adapted from White, 1981). Reproduced by permission of Kluwer Academic Publishers.

## 7.7 QUATERNARY VEGETATIONAL HISTORY

Discontinuities in the geographical distributions of African birds (Moreau, 1963, 1966), and rain forest plant species (Hamilton, 1976; Brenan, 1978; White, 1979) are believed to reflect the restriction of rain forests to refugia during the driest and coolest periods of the Pleistocene (1.6–0 Ma), from which they subsequently spread during the Holocene (Mayr and O'Hara, 1986).

Four such refuges are now recognised (Figure 7.19), the Upper Guinea, in W Africa, Cameroun–Gabon, Eastern Zaire, and the Congo Basin (Maley, 1996). Early palynological studies from the E African highlands provided very little evidence to either support or refute such suggestions; they mainly showed that during the last glacial maximum, montane vegetation zones were depressed altitudinally by 1000 m or more.

Recent palynological data from low altitude sites and marine cores are now providing clear

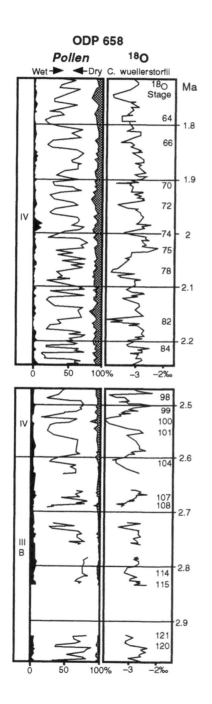

evidence for the retraction of rain forests during the time of the last glacial maximum and of the occurrence of refugia. Lake Bosumtwi in Ghana (Maley and Livingstone, 1983; Maley, 1989, 1991, 1996) and Lake Barombi Mbo in Cameroun (Brenac, 1988; Maley, 1996), are currently surrounded by closed forests, but pollen records show that the area surrounding Lake Bosumtwi was unforested during the time of the last glacial maximum, whereas Lake Barombi-Mbo, close to the Cameroun–Gabon refuge, was surrounded by open forest, with grassland at this time (Figure 7.20). Similarly, palynological studies of a deep marine core offshore the Dahomey Gap to the southwest of the Niger Delta indicate that during the period of the last glacial, savanna was much more extensive in the Niger Delta catchment than today (Figure 7.21), and also that rain forests formed a continuous belt from Cameroun to Guinea during the early Holocene (Dupont and Weinelt, 1996). Offshore cores from W Africa also show that during the last glacial maximum, the savanna belts substantially shifted to the south (Hoogheimstra and Agwu, 1988). On the other hand, palynological studies from a core offshore Ghana recorded the presence of rain forests on adjacent coasts throughout the last glacial maximum (Lezine and Vergnaud-Grazzini, 1993), and pollen analyses from Uganda (Sowunmi, 1991) and Burundi (Bonnefille and Riollet, 1988) provide evidence for forest continuity in areas proposed as forest refuges. There is thus unequivocable palynological evidence from equatorial Africa to support the Pleistocene refuge theory, unlike the situation in South America.

Figure 7.17 Summary pollen diagram and oxygen isotope data for the Pliocene, from ODP 658, offshore NW Africa (Leroy and Dupont, 1994). Pollen summaries from left to right: *Rhizophora* and tropical forest elements (left, black), Cyperaceae and Gramineae (left, open); Amaranthaceae–Chenopodiaceae (right, open) and *Artemesia*, *Ephedra* and 'Mediterranean' elements (right, hatched). Isotope stages after Tiedemann (1991). Reproduced by permission of Elsevier Science.

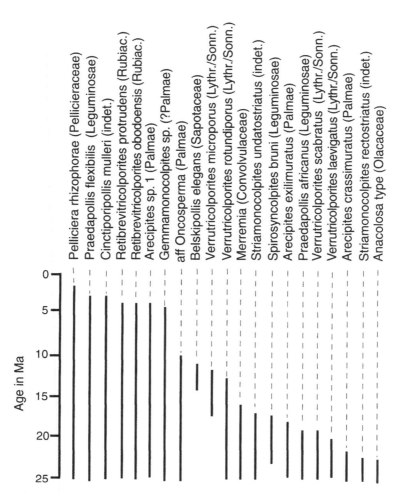

Figure 7.18   Times of extinction of W African pollen types during Neogene, data from Legoux (1978) and others (including unpublished) sources.

Studies from offshore cores are now beginning to show the nature of vegetation change in equatorial Africa during the last interglacial and beyond. The offshore Niger delta deep-sea core studied by Dupont and Weinelt (1996), showed that rain forest vegetation during the last interglacial (oxygen isotope stage 5e) was very similar to that of the Holocene, and that at that time, also, rain forests were probably continuous along the coastal region of the Gulf of Guinea. During stages 5d–a, however, although rain forests were still widespread, there was some expansion of woodland, but,

most notably, mountainous *Podocarpus* forest expanded in Cameroun and possibly Nigeria, as a result of some degree of lowering of temperatures, but without major changes in rainfall.

Palynologists working on the Quaternary of Africa have long sought a very long terrestrial profile, comparable to the Fuenza core from the Sabana de Bogotá in Colombia, penetrating the whole of the Quaternary. Failure to obtain such a section forced the search offshore, where ocean floor punch cores and DSDP/ODP (Deep Sea Drilling Project/Ocean Drilling Program) sections have yield well-dated long Quaternary

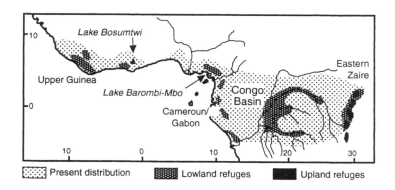

Figure 7.19    Rain forest refugia in equatorial Africa during the last glacial maximum (*c.* 18 000 BP), from Maley (1996). Reproduced by permission of the author and Royal Society of Edinbuurgh.

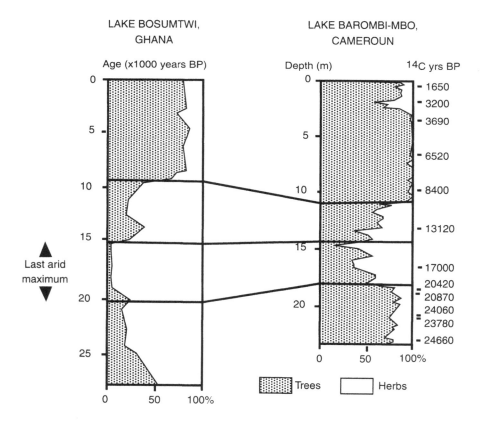

Figure 7.20    Summary pollen diagrams for Lake Bosumtwi, Ghana, and Lake Barombi-Mbo, Cameroun (Maley, 1996). Reproduced by permission of the author and Royal Society of Edinburgh.

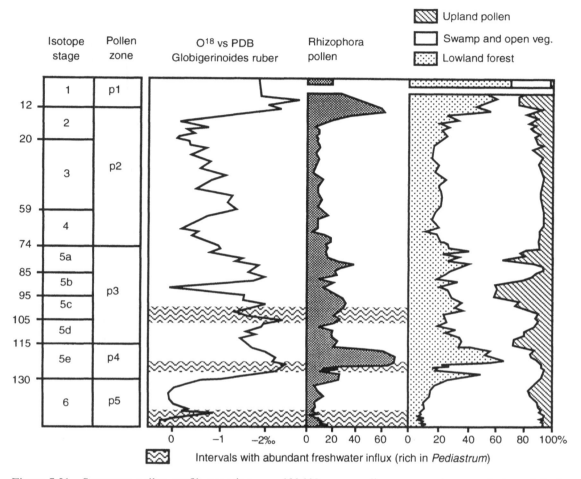

Figure 7.21   Summary pollen profile covering over 130 000 years, pollen zones and oxygen isotope data for core GIK 16856, offshore Niger Delta; pollen sum total freshwater pollen, PDB = arbitrary standard (Dupont and Weinelt, 1996). Reproduced by permission of the authors and Springer Verlag.

records, but lack the sensitivity of terrestrial sites to subtle climatic change. One such terrestrial section, otherwise overlooked, exists at Lake Oku, which lies in a tectonic depression at the southern end of the Benue Trough (7°N) in Nigeria (Medus et al., 1988). The sedimentary succession from this site is 150 m in thickness, and is characterised by rapid fluctuations of Gramineae and Cyperaceae pollen (Figure 7.22). The section is too old for radiocarbon dating and has been erroneously attributed a Miocene age, but the presence of *Podocarpus* pollen throughout this profile provides strong

evidence for a latest Pliocene to Pleistocene age. The occurrence of two *Podocarpus* maxima in the lower part of the profile, coupled with rapid fluctuations of Gramineae pollen, seen in the the upper 65 m of this section, compare very closely with the pattern of events seen in the latest Pliocene to Pleistocene of the Niger Delta, from 2.7 to *c.* 0.8 Ma (Figures 7.11; 7.13; 7.15). This profile, which lies in the Guinea Savanna belt, provides evidence for fluctuations of savanna grasslands, marshes, gallery forests and montane vegetation, and clearly demonstrates that rain forests failed to reach the which had become established by the latest Cretaceous.

Within the Paleocene and Eocene, the vegetation of W and C Africa exhibited continuous diversification. During the Late Paleocene/ Early Eocene thermal maximum, warmer climates may have occurred in the equatorial zone, following which time, during the Late Eocene, rain forests with many modern elements became very widespread. This was the period during which taxa that today characterise W African rain forests showed their most prolific appearance.

There are numerous dispersal events within the Early and Middle Eocene, especially from South America, but also from Eurasia and India.

The terminal Eocene cooling event resulted in the extinction of nypoid palms, and a general reduction in species diversity. Although no significant climatic change appears to have been associated with this event at equatorial latitudes, there is clear evidence for Early Oligocene aridification in the vicinity of the subtropical high pressure zones. The first evidence for cooler and drier climates at low latitudes is from Late Oligocene low sea level periods, immediately following the 30 Ma global sea level fall. These periods were characterised by the expansion of grasses.

The Oligocene was a period of continued diversification of the flora, but with relatively few new immigrants from outside. The rain forest flora subsequently diversified more gradually through the Early and Middle Miocene, with important dispersal events, particularly of mangrove and freshwater swamp species, in the earliest Miocene. Rain forests became very widespread in the Early and Middle Miocene, with megathermal, paratropical forests developed as far south as the Cape. However, numerous extinctions at equatorial latitudes heralded changes to drier and cooler climates, witnessed also by increased pollen of Gramineae in the fossil record.

There appears to be no record of Middle Miocene floristic interchange with Eurasia,

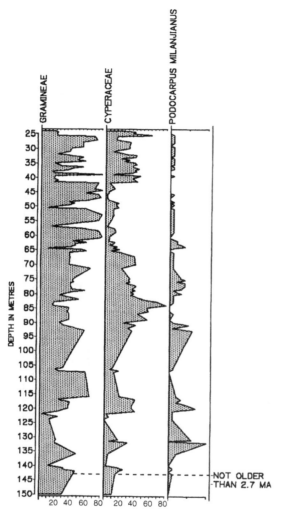

Figure 7.22 Summary of palynological data from Oku Lake, redrawn into a single profile, showing vegetational succession through most of the Quaternary and Late Pliocene, previously considered to be Miocene in age. Data from Medus et al. (1988).

southern end of the Benue Trough at any time over the last 2.7 Ma.

## 7.8 SUMMARY

The terminal Cretaceous event resulted in substantial extinctions within the rain forests comparable to that seen in mammals, This was probably due to the marked zonality of climate at this time, rendering dispersal unlikely. However, it is possible that temperate taxa were able to disperse along the highlands of E Africa, and Eurasian warm temperate plants were able to extend into N Africa.

Following global climate change at the end of the Middle Miocene, savanna successively expanded over much of the African tropics, at the expense of rain forests. At the same time, large areas of the continent underwent uplift. This resulted in more limited opportunities for dispersal of lowland rain forest taxa into refuges due to the restricted presence of suitable low altitude habitats, with the result that widespread extinctions within the rain forest flora occurred from the Late Miocene into the Pliocene.

Desert climates of the Sahara developed only since the Late Pliocene, although the Namib desert of South Africa may be much older, dating from the time of initiation of the cold Benguela Current. Periods of Late Pliocene drying occurred at 3.2 Ma and after 3.0 Ma with subsequent cooling at 2.7 Ma, coinciding with the expansion of ice sheets in the northern hemisphere. This cooling phase allowed the dispersal of the montane gymnosperm *Podocarpus milanjianus* into W Africa. During the Quaternary, rain forests expanded and contracted along with the glaciations of polar regions, as a result of orbital forcing. 'Interglacial' periods were probably characterised by a slightly greater rain forest distribution than today (as also was the early Holocene) during which time rain forests extended across the Dahomey Gap. During periods of intermediate global temperatures, rain forests remained extensive, but there were notable expansions of moist, montane forests with *Podocarpus*. During glacial maxima, rain forests withdrew to their Pleistocene refugia in Upper Guinea, Cameroun–Gabon, Eastern Zaire and the Congo Basin; at such times they probably occupied an area of about 10% of that of the Holocene.

## NOTE

1 Poumot (1987) shows gymnosperm pollen occurring commonly throughout the Late Miocene and Pliocene of the Niger Delta, and this has been interpreted by Maley (1996) as indicating the presence of *Podocarpus* in the Late Miocene. Poumot shows two gymnosperm maxima, one close to a foraminiferal event based on *Globorotalia miocenica*, and the second with a N15 foraminiferal assemblage. In over 30 petroleum well sections studied in detail by the author over the Pliocene and Late Miocene, only extremely rare *Podocarpus* specimens have been observed below the *Gr. miocenica* event. The Miocene gymnosperm event is therefore considered to be in error.

# CHAPTER 8

# India

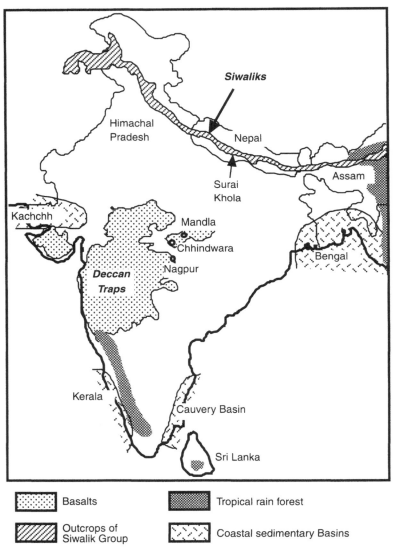

Map showing present-day Indian rain forest distributions (after Richards, 1996), outcrops of Siwalik sediments, the main coastal sedimentary basins and locations mentioned in the text.

## 8.1  INTRODUCTION

India provides a crucial key to understanding current biogeographical patterns in palaeotropical floras. Its vegetation has probably undergone more changes than that of any other tropical region since the Indian Plate began to drift away from Antarctica in the Aptian (Figure 8.1), and it provides the classic example of a 'Noah's Ark' (*sensu* McKenna, 1973), receiving diverse elements of the African Late Cretaceous flora, as it drifted close to the African Plate (Section 5.2.3) and rafting these into S and E Asia (Morley, 1998). The ravages of Neogene climatic change have resulted in the extinction of the majority of the lineages which formed its rich Early Tertiary rain forests, and so, with the exception of tiny refuges in Sri Lanka (Ashton and Gunatilleke, 1987a,b), very little evidence for this rich history is forthcoming from the examination of the present-day flora of the Indian subcontinent.

Deciphering the story for India poses special problems. The area has a prolific literature in Tertiary palynology and palaeobotany, which developed from the early work of Professor Birbal Sahni, but many early studies were carried out in isolation, with nomenclatural problems inevitably developing, and it is only in the last decade that such issues, in palynology at least, are becoming partially resolved (Thanikaimoni et al., 1983; Venkatachala et al., 1996). There are immense difficulties in obtaining accurate dates for many palynomorph or macrofossil-bearing deposits. Some, such as the Intertrappean beds, are dated by reference to radiometric dates from sandwiching basalts, and in some areas foraminifera provide independent dates, but the age of many very important palaeobotanical localities can be determined only by reference to their palynomorph content, with inevitable circular arguments developing, since the Indian palynofloral succession has few parallels elsewhere. A classic problem is presented by the 'Miocene' Neyveli Lignite (e.g. Ramanujam, 1966, 1982), which is clearly Eocene on the basis of its pollen content (Deb et al., 1973; Venkatachala, 1973;

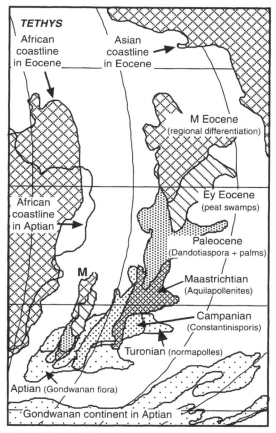

Figure 8.1   Position of Indian landmass and Madagascar during Aptian, Turonian, Campanian, Maastrichtian, Paleocene, Early and Middle Eocene, together with positions of Gondwanan continent at time of separation of Indian Plate, and Asia, at time of collision of Indian Plate with Asia. Also, position of African Plate during the Aptian and Middle Eocene. For each time period, palaeocoastlines are shown according to Smith et al. (1994). Land areas are given the same shading for the same time intervals. Some characteristic pollen types for each time interval are indicated.

Siddhanta, 1986). This coal has been variously considered as 'Miocene', 'Miocene to Eocene' and 'Eocene' by different authors, with a current critical review, accepted by the present author, suggesting an Early to Middle Eocene age (Saxena, 1992). Nevertheless, numerous review articles continue to accept a Miocene age for this critical locality (e.g. Guleria, 1992; Misra et al., 1996).

## 8.2  TECTONIC HISTORY

At the beginning of the Tertiary, the Indian Plate
had separated from Madagascar, and drifted
rapidly NNE, on a collision course with S Asia.
The actual time of collision is disputed, but has
been suggested to be either at about 45 Ma
(Dewey et al., 1989), or about 54 Ma (Patriat
and Achache, 1984). The time of initial collision
must not be confused with the time of establishment of a land connection, which would form
some time after the initial contact. Palynological
evidence favours the earlier time of collision,
firstly because depositional environments in the
Himalayan foothills region became too shallow
for marine fauna and flora after the Early
Eocene (Mathur, 1984; Rowley, 1996), and,
secondly, as brought to attention in Chapter 9,
many plant taxa dispersed from the Indian Plate
to SE Asia during the Middle Eocene, at which
time collision must have been complete.

There are numerous references to the presence of non-marine faunal elements of Eurasian affinity within the Deccan Intertrappean
beds, and these have been used to argue for an
earlier collision with Asia than suggested by
geophysical data (Sahni et al., 1982; Jaeger et
al., 1989; Sahni and Bajpai, 1991). Sahni et al.
(1982) and Sahni and Bajpai (1991) quote
palynological data to support an early collision,
using Indian occurrences of *Aquilapollenites*
(Baksi and Deb, 1976, 1981) and normapolles
(Nandi, 1984) as evidence, but, as explained in
Section 5.2.3, the typically Laurasian genus
*Aquilapollenites* has a low palaeolatitude sub-
group, present in South America and W Africa,
with different morphotypes to the Laurasian
group, and it is this group to which the Indian
*Aquilapollenites* relate. Also, normapolles in the
Indian Senonian are most easily explained in
terms of dispersal along the east coast of Africa,
and via Madagascar, for the group is well
documented from Late Cretaceous successions
in Egypt. The views of Thewissen (1990), who
suggests that it is premature to propose such
conclusions until comparable faunal data is
available from E Africa, are followed here.

## 8.3  PALAEOGENE VEGETATION

### 8.3.1  Paleocene

At the time of separation of the Indian Plate
from Gondwanaland, it bore a flora closely
similar to that of contemporaneous Australia,
with southern conifers and ferns (Figure 8.1). As
the Indian Plate drifted north, into the southern
hemisphere high pressure zone, and came into
contact with the African Plate, between the
Cenomanian and Campanian, its Gondwanan
flora was largely replaced by tropical African
and Tethyan angiosperms which were presumably already well adapted to seasonal tropical
and equatorial climates of the African Plate (see
Section 5.2.3). As it drifted unhindered into
moist, equatorial climatic zones during the
Maastrichtian/Paleocene, many new lineages
evolved, and by the close of the Cretaceous
India bore a rich, rapidly diversifying, megathermal angiosperm flora (Figure 8.2) and
Gondwanan gymnosperms were in decline
(Mehrota and Awasthi, 1995). The palynological record certainly does not support the
suggestion of Raven and Axelrod (1974) that
India was left with a rather generalised flora
prior to its collision with the Asian Plate.

The Paleocene (66–54 Ma) of the Indian
subcontinent was characterised by a great
abundance and diversity of palms, several
which remain extant. Coastal areas bore *Nypa*,
probably represented by several species, in view
of the morphological variation shown by pollen
(e.g. Frederiksen, 1994b), and also the nypoid
palm which produced *Proxapertites* pollen.
Other palms included rattans, many iguanuroid
forms (based on the diversity of the *Palmaepollenites* group (Harley and Morley, 1995)),
diverse palms which produced pollen type
*Longapertites* (Frederiksen, 1994b), thought to
have been ancestral to the SE Asian genus
*Eugeissona*, and numerous other palms which
produced spiny pollen, placed in the form-genus
*Couperipollis*, of which the identity is less
certain. A number of dicotyledonous families
were also represented for the first time, which

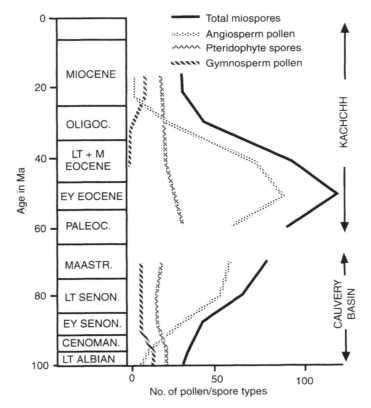

Figure 8.2   Number of pollen types recognised during each epoch, for the Cauvery Basin (from Venkatachala, 1974) and for Kachchh (from Kar, 1985).

now have widely distributed descendants, and included the SE Asian genus *Durio* (Bombacaceae), indicated by *Lakiapollis ovatus* (Thanikaimoni et al., 1983), and similar morphotypes but with different exine structure, such as *Lakiapollis matanomadhensis*, which suggest early diversification of Durioneae (Kar, 1985). Caesalpiniodae have some of their oldest representatives here, and include the *Caesalpinia* type (Muller, 1981) and striate pollen broadly comparable to *Bauhinia* or *Crudia*. The Paleocene has also yielded pollen referable to *Ctenolophon* (Ctenolophonaceae), *Ixonanthes* (Ixonanthaceae), the South American genus *Kielmeyera* (Guttiferae), *Mischocarpus* (Sapindaceae), *Anacolosa* (Olacaceae) and *Gonystylus* (Gonystylaceae), as well as Annonaceae, Polygalaceae, Restionaceae and numerous triporate

grains, which bear similarities to Proteaceae, particularly to *Grevillia*.

Paleocene palynomorph assemblages clearly suggest the presence of diverse, closed-canopy rain forests, in view of the occurrence of large-seeded tree genera such as *Durio*, *Ctenolophon* and *Gonystylus*, but the dominance of fern spores in the Early Paleocene, and palm pollen in later Paleocene assemblages (Kar, 1985), suggest that freshwater swamp vegetation, which was probably the source, consisted mainly of fern-dominated marshes and palm thickets.

### 8.3.2   Early to Middle Eocene, Superwet Vegetation During Climatic Optimum

In the Early Eocene (54–49 Ma), the Indian Plate straddled the equator, and extremely wet, equatorial climates resulted in the formation of often very thick peats in the coastal lowlands, now preserved as lignites and coals in the majority of areas in which sediments occur, within the northeast, in Kutch or Kachchh (Kar, 1985), the Lakadong Member of the Syalet Formation in Assam (Sah and Dutta, 1966) and the frequently misdated Neyveli Lignite in the south (see above). These coals are sometimes very thick, and may be analogous to the thick basinal or watershed peats which have built up during the course of the Holocene in SE Asia (Section 2.4; Anderson, 1983; Morley, in press). The Early Eocene bears the richest and most diverse palynomorph assemblages within the Indian Palaeogene (Figure 8.2), reflecting optimum conditions for angiosperm proliferation, and that, at this time, the entire subcontinent must have been completely clothed by dense, multistoreyed rain forests.

The Early Eocene coincides with the appearance of further palm genera, including *Arenga*, and increased diversification of Caesalpinoidae. *Durio* and *Alangium* (Alangiaceae) were particularly abundant, and included swamp forest trees, since their pollen is very common in lignites and associated fluvial sediments. Pollen spectra from lignites show few abundance fluctuations which parallel lithology changes (Kumar, 1996), making it difficult to interpret the detailed ecology of peat-forming and swamp vegetation. The Early Eocene is also characterised by the common representation of large, strongly ornamented pollen (Singh and Misra, 1991a,b), which bear few analogies to present-day floras and, although morphologically different, are reminiscent of Early to Middle Eocene palynomorphs in other equatorial areas, especially Central Africa (Chapter 7).

One pollen group which particularly characterises the Indian Palaeogene, and is best represented in the Early to Middle (49–39 Ma) Eocene, comprises stephanocolpate pollen, some members of which closely resemble pollen of the modern, disjunct genus *Ctenolophon*, which today has representatives in Central Africa (*Ctenolophon engleri*) and SE Asia (*C.*

*parvifolius*). As noted in Chapter 7, these species have quite different pollen, and both types are well represented in the Indian Eocene. Following Muller (1981), morphologically similar stephanocolpate pollen from the Indian Early Tertiary is also believed to be derived from Ctenolophonaceae, with the first records (*Retistephanocolpites septacolpites*) from the Late Cretaceous, reflecting the dispersal of *Ctenolophon* from Africa (Chapter 5). Subsequently, many morphotypes showing the same general pattern, but placed in such form-genera as *Ctenolophonidites*, *Retistephanocolpites*, *Pseudonothofagacidites*, *Stephanocolpites* and *Polycolpites*, become widespread (Ambwani et al., 1981; Srivastava, 1987/88), suggesting that the greatest diversification of Ctenolophonaceae occurred in the Early and Middle Eocene (Figure 8.3).

### 8.3.3  Late Eocene to Oligocene, Following the Collision with Asia

Warm, perhumid conditions, supporting diverse rain forest vegetation, was probably the rule across the Indian subcontinent through most of the Late Eocene (39–36 Ma) and Oligocene (36–25 Ma). During this time, however, the Indian flora appears to have undergone distinct changes, in that, firstly, overall palynomorph diversity tends to have decreased, and certain palynomorph groups characteristic of the earlier Palaeogene became much less well represented, and, secondly, clear regional differences become apparent.

Regional differentiation is shown by the widespread occurrence of pollen of the form-genus *Meyeripollis* (family indeterminate) in the Late Eocene and Oligocene of Assam (Figure 8.4), but its absence from W or S India. Two proposals are made to explain this distribution: firstly, since this pollen is also widespread in SE Asia, where it has the same age range, it may have originated in that area and dispersed westward only as far as Assam; secondly, its distribution in SE Asia suggests that its parent plant was a peat swamp tree (Chapter 9), which

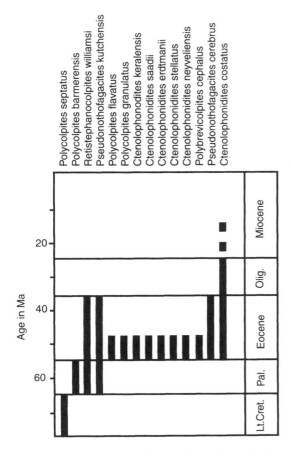

Figure 8.3 Schematic distribution through Late Cretaceous and Tertiary of pollen types tentatively referable to Ctenolophonaceae (from various sources).

shows a clear diversity reduction through the Eocene (Figure 8.3). It is unlikely that the reduction of this group was uniform across the Indian subcontinent; it first disappeared from the north, from Kachchh (Kar, 1985) and Assam (Baksi, 1962), but it persisted much later in the south, and has recently been clearly documented in the Oligocene of Kerala, by Rao (1995) and may have persisted into the Miocene before its final extinction.

In view of the Early Tertiary collision of the Indian Plate with Asia, a widespread immigration of Eurasian taxa might be expected, especially since, at this time, the SE Asian flora was being enriched by dispersals from the Indian Plate (Morley, 1998; Chapter 9). Surprisingly, few such immigrants can be proposed. A few taxa show a first appearance during the Late Eocene, and include *Adansonia* type (Bombacaceae), possibly reflecting dispersal from Africa, and the palm *Eugeissona* (*Quillonipollenites*), which is probably of Indian origin. More pollen types first appear in the Oligocene, and include *Acacia* (Leguminosae), *Bombax* (Bombacaceae), *Delonix* (Leguminosae), Chenopodiaceae/ Amaranthaceae, and the rubiaceous shrubs *Gardenia* and *Oligodon*; several of these taxa probably relate to the development of drier, or more seasonal climates.

The oldest record of Dipterocarpaceae from the Indian subcontinent is of pollen attributable to *Dipterocarpus* (determined by SEM) from the Oligocene Barail Group of Assam (Jan Muller, Subhendu Baksi, personal communication, 1974). However, biogeographical evidence suggests that dipterocarps have had a much longer history in India which has not yet been detected by the fossil record. The endemic genera *Stemonoporus* in Sri Lanka, *Vateria* in Sri Lanka and S India, and *Vateriopsis* in the Seychelles have large, heavy seeds with poor means of dispersal; their relict occurrences reflect a former continuous distribution (Ashton and Gunatilleke, 1987a), dating from before the separation of the Indian Plate from Madagascar.

One of the most widely used palynological events in low latitude mid-Tertiary stratigraphic

would be compatible with the widespread occurrence of coals in the Late Eocene and Oligocene Barails Group of Assam, its absence to the west resulting from climatic factors.

The reduced diversity of palynomorph assemblages through the mid-Tertiary is clearly illustrated in the diversity data of Kar (1985) from Kachchh (Figure 8.2), and suggests an equivalent reduction in species-richness of vegetation. Many taxa disappear gradually through the later Eocene, but, as in Africa, *Nypa* (surprisingly) and the parent plant of *Proxapertites* became extinct at the Eocene/Oligocene boundary. The *Ctenolophon* group of pollen types

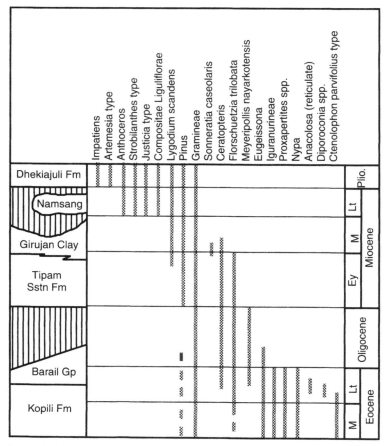

Figure 8.4  Stratigraphic distribution of key pollen and spore types through Eocene to Pliocene of Assam (Handique, 1993, based on analyses by Morley, unpublished). Reproduced by permission of Department of Geological Sciences, Chiang Mai University.

zonation is the first appearance of spores of the fern *Ceratopteris* (Parkeriaceae), which is usually taken to mark the base of the Oligocene (Germeraad et al., 1968). Records from India are widely reported in the Middle to Late Eocene, which prompted Kar (1982) to propose India as its place of origin, and then suggest complex dispersal paths to other continents. *Ceratopteris* spores have been noted as a minor element in the latest Eocene of N and W Africa (Kedves, 1971; Morley, unpublished), and similarly in Central and South America (Graham, 1985; Gonzalez, personal communication), and if this genus were to range into the Late Eocene in SE Asia, a major stratigraphic anomaly in

that area would be resolved (Chapter 9). *Ceratopteris* may have radiated from India, but it is more likely that it was already widely distributed by the Late Eocene, and its sudden pantropical expansion in the Oligocene related more to widespread disruption at that time as a result of global climate deterioration, and the sudden appearance across the tropics of niches which were particularly suited to *Ceratopteris*.

### 8.3.4  Deccan Traps

The Deccan intertrappean macroflora is one of the most thoroughly studied in the Indian

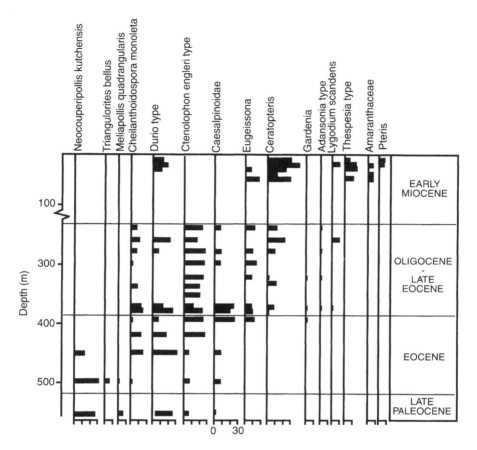

Figure 8.5   Distribution of selected pollen types recorded from the Tertiary of Kerala, SW India (adapted from Rao, 1995).

Palaeogene, and includes fossils of considerable biogeographic importance. However, controversy remains as to the age of formation of the Deccan basalts, with Alexander (1981) suggesting eruption over a span of 70 Ma, from the mid-Cretaceous to Oligocene, and others (Courtillot et al., 1988; Duncan and Pyle, 1988) suggesting rapid eruption at the Cretaceous/Tertiary boundary. If plant macrofossils preserved between basalt flows were as old as basal Tertiary, some would comprise the oldest records of their respective lineages. For this reason, the broader age range is assumed here, until ages of individual macrofossil localities are radiometrically tested.

Noteworthy macrofossil records are reviewed by Bande (1992) and are mainly from three localities in central Peninsular India (see map). Records from Chhindwara include fruit of *Nypa*, which suggests a major marine incursion, occurring with *Musocaulon* (*Musa*, Musaceae) and *Cyclanthodendron* (Cyclanthaceae) now restricted to South America. Fossil woods from this area are mostly referred to Indomalaysian families, and include *Barringtonioxylon*; as noted above, *Barringtonia* has an extensive palynological record in India, but the earliest records are in the Early Eocene.

Two further prolific localities at Nagpur and Mandla are rich in both palm and dicotyledon fossils. These include a fruit and petiole showing affinities to the African palm *Hyphaene*, and woods referred to *Livistona*, the Madagascan palm *Dypsis*, and many arboreal Indomalaysian genera including *Sonneratia* (see Chapter 9). *Eucalyptus* and other myrtaceous woods have also been described by Bande et al. (1986), which is surprising, in view of the paucity of eucalypt fossils in the Australian region (Hill, 1994b).

## 8.4 NEOGENE AND QUATERNARY RAIN FOREST HISTORY

Northern India provides the best evidence for Neogene rain forest history, with palynological records from Assam (Baksi, 1962, 1972; Sah and Dutta, 1966), Himachal Pradesh (Mathur, 1984) and Kachchh (Kar, 1985), but the most complete and convincing histories, mostly based on macrofossil records, have been obtained from the Siwaliks, a succession of alluvial fan deposits which bear fossils of the primate *Sivapithecus* (Pilbeam, 1982), and which formed by accumulation of alluvial detritus into a long, narrow foredeep, derived from the rising Himalayas to the north between the Middle Miocene (16–10 Ma) and Early Pleistocene. The Siwaliks are some 6000 m thick, and form a belt in the Himalayan foothill region some 25 km in width, and 2400 km long, stretching from Assam to Pakistan (see map). The group is unique for a non-marine succession in the completeness of its stratigraphic record, and the precision to which it has been dated by reference to magnetostratigraphy (Flynn et al., 1990).

Early Miocene (25–16 Ma) fluvial and coastal plain sediments have been studied mainly using palynology, with pollen and spore assemblages reflecting either local, edaphic communities, or the character of temperate vegetation growing in the rising Himalayas, since a large component of palynomorph assemblages is clearly transported (Figure 8.6). Information on regional vegetation, however, is often less convincing. Edaphic communities are indicated largely by the

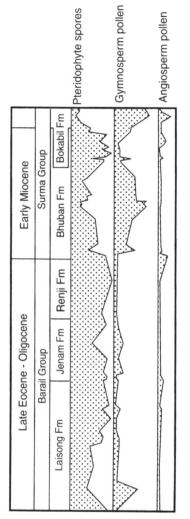

Figure 8.6  Distribution of Laurasian gymnosperm and other pollen through the Eocene to Early Miocene of Assam (Singh et al., 1986). Reproduced by permission of the *Palaeobotanist*.

presence of abundant spores, especially of the aquatic fern *Ceratopteris*, which is sometimes very common, and must either have covered shallow lakes, or formed wide floating mats, perhaps in oxbow lakes, or behind levees. Other common ferns and fern allies, probably also growing in swampy settings, were *Phaecoceros* (Anthoceraceae), *Stenochlaena* (Blechnaceae) and members of Schizaeaceae. Angiosperm pollen is often represented by striate tricolpate/ tricolporate forms, comparable to *Bauhinia* or *Crudia* (Leguminosae), often associated with pollen of *Barringtonia* and Gramineae, suggesting seasonal swamp vegetation as found in the Tonle Sap region of Cambodia, with savanna or open forest in hinterland regions. Such vegetation would also be consistent with the limited available macrofossil data (Awasthi, 1992), which consists of palms, 'small' dicotyledonous leaves, and probable grasses.

There was a major change in vegetation and climate with the beginning of Siwalik deposition in the Middle Miocene. The lower Siwaliks of Himachal Pradesh have yielded abundant leaf impressions, clearly indicating the presence of evergreen tropical rain forests of Malesian affinity, since they include the dipterocarps *Anisoptera*, *Dipterocarpus* (Figure 8.7), *Hopea* and *Shorea*, together with *Koompassia* (Leguminosae) and *Mangifera* (Anacardiaceae) and many others (summarised by Awasthi, 1992). The Lower Siwaliks are also characterised by a brackish-water incursion, possibly coinciding with one of the mid-Miocene sea level highs, since palynomorph assemblages from the Middle Miocene of the Jawalamukhi area in Himachal Pradesh yielded abundant sonneratioid and *Rhizophora* (Rhizophoraceae) pollen (Mathur, 1984). It is widely accepted that changes in physiography, resulting from the onset of the Himalayan uplift, altered atmospheric circulation patterns, resulting in a more moist, and warmer climate in the Himalayan foothill region, allowing the development of evergreen tropical forests, many elements of which are thought to have dispersed from SE Asia, via Myanmar. The allochthonous flora was also able to mix with the local one, with the result that the Middle Miocene was the time of maximum diversification of the Neogene flora in N India (Awasthi, 1992). However, it is unlikely that moist climatic conditions extended across the whole of the Indian Plate, or today we would expect to find Malesian relics in the rain forest outliers of Sri Lanka and the Western Ghats.

Figure 8.7 *Dipterocarpus* leaf from the Middle Miocene of the Siwaliks, N India (Lakhanpal and Guleria, 1986). Reproduced by permission of the *Palaeobotanist*.

Macrofossil remains from the Surai Khola region of Nepal (Figure 8.8) show that evergreen rain forests continued until late middle Siwalik time (probably until the end of the Miocene), but after that time they were gradually replaced by deciduous forests, which included *Flacourtia* (Flacourtiaceae), *Milletia* and *Bauhinia* and other legumes. By this time, rain forests with dipterocarps had totally disappeared from the western and central sectors of the Himalayan foothills, and were replaced by dry deciduous forest and grassland (Awasthi, 1992). Increased frequencies of Gramineae pollen within the upper part of the Middle and Upper Siwaliks suggest that savannas or savanna woodland also became widespread as the climate became drier (Mathur, 1984).

At the same time, palynomorph assemblages from the Siwaliks tend to be characterised by

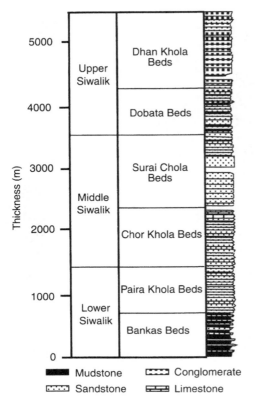

Figure 8.8 Lithological succession through the Surai Khola region of Nepal, which yields rich Middle Miocene and younger plant macrofossil remains of SE Asian affinity (Awasthi, 1992). Reproduced by permission of the *Palaeobotanist*.

common elements which are unrepresented as macrofossils, such as Laurasian gymnosperms and temperate angiosperms (Mathur, 1984), suggesting the development of widespread montane forests on the higher slopes of the Himalayas through most of the Neogene.

The late Neogene change to drier climates in the W Siwaliks, in Pakistan, is illustrated from carbon isotope studies, where $C_3/C_4$ analyses show a change from a $C_3$ (mainly forested) setting to $C_4$ grassland at about 7 Ma (Quade et al., 1989). Also, drier Pliocene (5–1.6 Ma) climates in Rajasthan, NW India are shown by the presence of fossil woods which indicate deciduous forests at that time (Guleria, 1992). Perhaps the most notable feature of these woods is that they

contain a distinct African element, in assemblages which are otherwise characteristic of Indian and SE Asian floras. The African element included the legumes *Baphia*, *Erythrophleum* and *Tetrapleuria*, together with *Entandrophragma* and *Khaya* (Meliaceae). The appearance of these taxa shortly after the formation of a land connection between the African and Indian plates is noteworthy, but it is remarkable that today such elements are missing from the Indian flora, presumably wiped out by Pleistocene (1.6–0 Ma) desertification (Guleria, 1992). It is also remarkable that there are so few relict occurrences of rain forest taxa which might reflect India's rich rain forest history. Only the genus *Hortonia* (Monimiaceae) is considered to be a Gondwanan endemic (P.S. Ashton, personal communication), although this genus could equally reflect Late Cretaceous dispersal from Africa, and there is only a single species of *Podocarpus* (Podocarpaceae).

## 8.5  SUMMARY

During the period of differentiation of angiosperms, the Indian flora has probably undergone more changes than any other, as a result of its drift from Gondwanaland. At the beginning of the Tertiary, its flora consisted of three components: remnants of the Gondwanan flora carried from the southern hemisphere, an allochthonous, tropical flora which dispersed into the Indian Plate as it drifted past Africa during the Late Cretaceous, and an endemic element, which developed as the Indian Plate drifted in isolation across the equatorial climatic zones in the Paleocene.

During the Early Eocene, the Indian Plate straddled the equator, and experienced a very hot, and wet, equatorial climate, and was clothed with floristically diverse, dense tropical rain forests. At this time, widespread peat swamps formed across the region.

Floristic diversity decreased during the later Eocene and Oligocene, possibly as a result of the establishment of a climatic gradient toward the northwest. Despite the collision of the Indian and Asian plates, there were apparently few plant dispersals into the subcontinent from Eurasia.

More seasonal, monsoonal, climates prevailed during the Early Miocene in N India, but a change to a more everwet climate in the Middle Miocene resulted in the widespread development of evergreen rain forests across the region. These forests bore close affinities with the flora of SE Asia.

A trend to more seasonal climates set in during the Late Miocene and Pliocene, with very dry conditions developing in the northwestern part of the subcontinent. This climatic change resulted in the disappearance of rain forests across much of India, and their eventual restriction to refuges in Sri Lanka and the Western Ghats.

# CHAPTER 9

# Southeast Asia and the Eastern Pacific

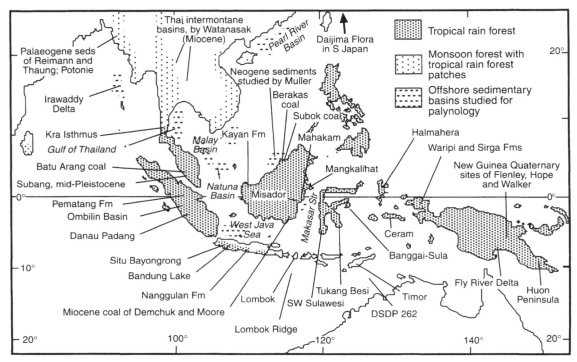

Map of SE Asia, showing the present-day distribution of tropical rain forests, and monsoon forests which include rain forest patches, and also the main localities mentioned in the text.

## 9.1 INTRODUCTION

Compared to its westerly counterparts, the SE Asian region experienced intensive tectonic activity throughout the Tertiary. Following Early Tertiary volcanism and the collision of India with Asia, which resulted in the extrusion of Indochina to the southeast (Tarponnier et al., 1982, 1986), the region was fractured along massive shear zones during the Late Eocene (39–36 Ma) and Early Oligocene (36–30 Ma), with

much of the Sunda region being broken into horst and graben, or half graben topography, and extensive regions undergoing subsidence. During the Neogene (25–1.6 Ma), the region was compressed from the south and east by the combined forces of the approaching Pacific and Australian plates (Rangin et al., 1990; Hall, 1995, 1996), which were drifting west and north respectively, entangling themselves along its eastern margin, resulting in the formation of the islands of E Indonesia. Such an active tectonic history has left a clear mark on the flora and vegetation of the region, in that, firstly, opportunities developed in the eastern tropics for the wholesale dispersal and intermixing of diverse tropical floras in a manner not seen elsewhere, and, secondly, the formation of major new land masses surrounded by wide seas allowed the rapid proliferation of endemic floras. Thirdly, the reduced competition experienced in insular settings, particularly in the E Pacific region, permitted the continued proliferation there of primitive plant groups which elsewhere were lost through competition or climatic change at an early stage in rain forest history.

This chequered history has resulted in distribution patterns within many plant families which, in the absence of a comprehensive foundation based on historical geology, have tested the minds of many of the greatest plant geographers and evolutionary theorists. Some theories, especially with respect to the origin of higher altitude mountain floras (van Steenis, 1934a,b, 1936, 1972) and monsoon forests (van Steenis, 1939, 1961; van Steenis and Schippers-Lammertse, 1965), have stood the test of time reasonably well, with geological data mainly providing rationalisation and a temporal framework. Other theories, especially those which have attempted to explain distribution patterns seen in lowland and lower montane floras, relationships with Australian floras, and angiosperm origins, require careful re-examination. This chapter attempts to clarify some of these issues.

## 9.2   PRE-TERTIARY PLATE TECTONIC AND CLIMATIC SETTING

Although the Late Cretaceous and earliest Tertiary tectonic history of the SE Asian region still remains poorly understood, sufficient is known to make important judgements with respect to plant geography. Since at least middle Cretaceous time, the Sunda Craton (the ancient core of SE Asia) remained approximately in its present latitudinal position (McElhinny et al., 1974; Haile, 1981), comprising a long, and sometimes narrow southeasterly extension to Asia, with its southern margin at about 5–10° S (Daly et al., 1987; Smith et al., 1994). It did not extend to over 20° south, as suggested by Audley-Charles (1987); it remained distantly separated from Gondwanaland by the wide ocean of eastern Tethys. The palaeotopography at this time was pronounced, with upland terrain dominating over lowland (Figure 9.1), providing extensive regions for montane floras, but relatively restricted areas for lowland ones. As discussed in Chapter 5, latest Cretaceous climates were probably moist, but only locally perhumid.

## 9.3   PALEOCENE TO EARLY EOCENE, PRIOR TO THE COLLISION OF INDIA WITH ASIA

### Tectonic setting and palaeogeography

During the earliest Tertiary, the Sunda Craton is believed to have formed a broad, mountainous, NNW–SSE orientated plateau, bounded to the west and south by subduction zones and with the Pacific and Philippine plates lying directly to the east (Figure 9.2). It was connected to Indochina and E Asia by a broad continuous mountain belt which extended to over 60°N. The southwestern arm of Sulawesi was attached to SE Kalimantan. The land area of the Sunda region at this time was probably greater than at any time subsequently. The Philippines and some islands of E Indonesia, such as Halmahera, comprised, firstly, a series of oceanic ridges, aligned to the east and southeast, and separated from the Sunda Craton by oceanic crust (Hall, 1998a), and may have been connected, via further oceanic ridges, to eastern Gondwana, and, secondly, continental fragments such as Palawan and Mindoro, which were attached to continental Asia, prior to the opening of the South China Sea. The northern margin of the Australian Plate, which was

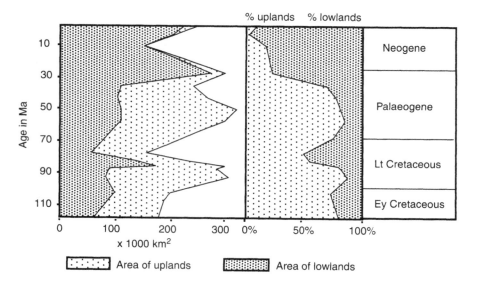

Figure 9.1   Areal and percentage presentation of upland and lowland topography through time in SE Asia. Source of data, palaeogeographic maps of Smith et al. (1994).

eventually to break into fragments which were to become part of SE Asia, at this time lay far to the south, separated by 2000 km of ocean, within, or to the south of, the arid subtropical high pressure zone, as evidenced by the presence of Early Eocene evaporitic sediments of the Waripi Formation, which are today exposed within the Bird's Neck area of Irian Jaya.

The Sunda region and Indochina experienced extensive volcanic activity at this time, activity ranging from N Thailand, through Sumatra to Java. The sedimentary record for the Paleocene (66–54 Ma) and Early Eocene (54–49 Ma) is very poor, and many of the sediments were probably deposited in basin floor settings off the present shelf margin. Those deposited to the south and west of the region may now be largely consumed by subduction along the boundary with the Indian Plate. Thick sediments accumulated offshore Myanmar at this time, and some palynological studies have been performed on these by Reimann and Thaung (1981). Palynological assemblages of this age have also been recently discovered from the East Java Sea and also from the Early Eocene Waripi Formation in

Irian Jaya (Morley, 1998). The most important palynological studies from this period, however, are from the Kayan Formation (previously Plateau Sandstone) of Sarawak by Muller (1968). Other Paleocene/Early Eocene dates recorded in the literature from outside East Java are considered to be misinterpretations based on palynology (e.g. Koesoemadinata and Matasak, 1981, Ombilin Basin Sumatra).

### Sunda region and Indochinese palynofloras

Palynomorph assemblages from the Kayan Sandstone are of low diversity compared to present-day assemblages from the Sunda region, and most have no modern analogue. However, some do exhibit close similarities with modern taxa, and by comparing abundance variations of these with pollen types of which the botanical affinity is uncertain, using correspondence analysis, a rough idea can be obtained of the diversity of major vegetation types (Figure 9.3) and of temporal changes (Figure 9.4). Pollen spectra for the mangrove palm *Nypa* (Figure 5.20) are closely related to

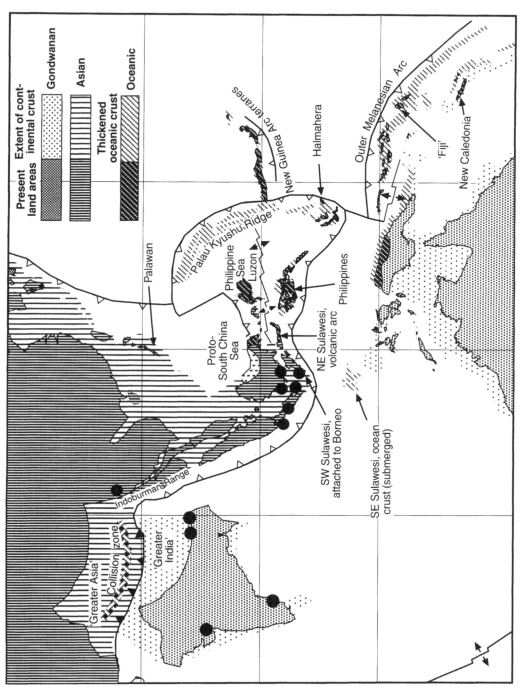

Figure 9.2  Latest Middle Eocene (40 Ma) plate tectonic setting and palaeogeography for SE Asia and the E Pacific (after Hall, 1996 and unpublished). Distribution of Middle and Late Eocene records of *Palmaepollenites kutchensis* (Palmae, subtribe Iguanurinae) shown by black circles, locations according to Harley and Morley (1995) and Morley (1998).

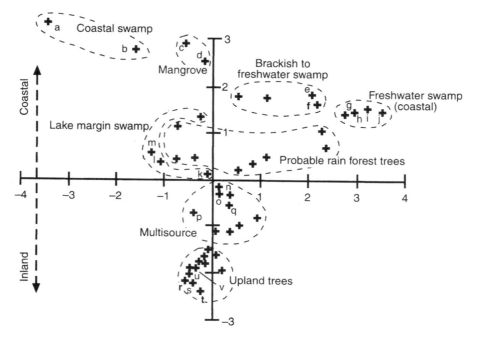

**Figure 9.3** Correspondence analysis of palynomorph assemblages from the Kayan Formation, Sarawak (raw data from Muller, 1968). 'y' axis relates primarily to distance of pollen source from coast, clearly shown by relative position of known mangrove, freshwater swamp and gymnosperm pollen: a, *Psilatricolporites kayanensis*; b, g, calamoid; c, d, *Proxapertites*; e, *Ilex*; f, *Nypa*; h, *Anacolosa*; i, *Spinizonocolpites baculatus*; j, Apocynaceae; k, Myrtaceae; l, *Retitriporites variabilis*; m, *Brownlowia* type; n, v, *Ephedra*; o, *Celtis*; p, Pteridioid; q, Sapotaceae; r, *Rugubivesiculites reductus*; s, *Pinus*; t, Taxodiaceae; u, *Classopollis*.

those for *Proxapertites* spp., which are also thought to have been derived from mangrove palms within the subfamily Nypoidae, as noted previously in Chapters 6 and 7. It is probable that *Nypa* was better represented in slightly brackish settings on the lower coastal plain, whereas the parent plants of *Proxapertites* spp. occupied more saline settings along the coastline, occurring together with the parent plants of *Psilatricolporites kayanensis* and *Echitriporites trianguliformis* which display the same distribution patterns as *Proxapertites* spp. Freshwater swamps probably bore palm thickets with rattans, and swamp forest with *Anacolosa* (Olacaceae), *Ilex* (Aquifoliaceae), Myrtaceae and Apocynaceae. Upland vegetation is suggested by the occurrence of diverse bisaccate conifers and *Ephedripites* spp. (Gnetaceae), the latter suggesting a subhumid

climate. Pollen types which correlate with none of these groups have been derived from dryland vegetation, or were multisourced.

Palynomorph assemblages from the Late Paleocene (60–54 Ma) to Early Eocene *Retitriporites variabilis* zone of the Kayan Sandstone (Figure 5.4) are very different to those of the Late Paleocene in their reduced diversity, and dominance of dicotyledonous pollen. These differences are not thought to reflect a major temporal change in regional vegetation, but instead provide a glimpse of freshwater swamp communities bordering a broad lake, since assemblages also contain abundant skeletons of the freshwater alga *Pediastrum*, and lack pollen types derived from plants clearly associated with brackish environments. The assemblages comprise a few, common to abundant pollen types, which were

179

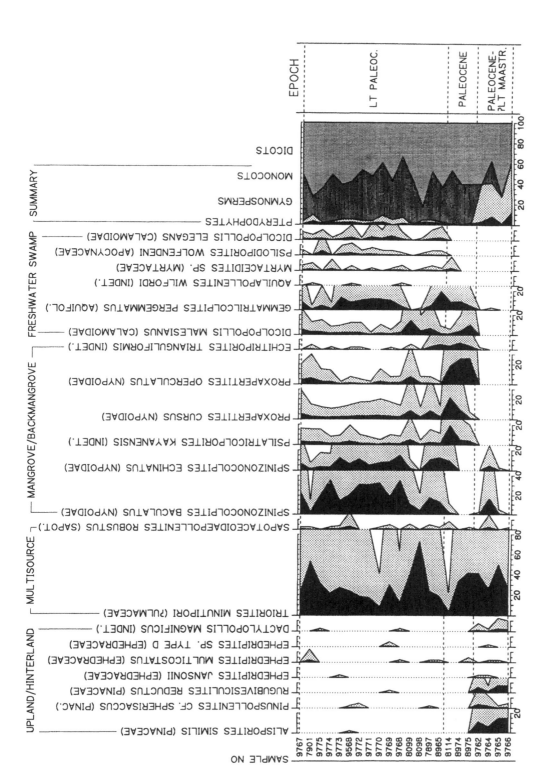

Figure 9.4  Paleocene palynomorph assemblages from the Kayan (previously Plateau Sandstone) Formation, Gunung Pueh, Sarawak. Constructed from raw data of Muller (1968). Pollen 'sum total pollen and spores'; selected taxa shown only; stipple = ×5 exaggeration.

most probably locally produced, and a few, very rare types, which were most probably derived from regional vegetation, or reworked from older deposits. The freshwater swamp vegetation bordering the lake must have been of considerable extent in order to overwhelm the regional pollen component. If the climate were perhumid, peats would have been expected to form, but the absence of coals suggests a seasonal climate. The most common components of this vegetation were plants producing *Retitriporites variabilis* and *Triorites minutipori*. The botanical affinity of the former is unknown, but Muller (1981) attributed the latter, with some degree of confidence, to *Celtis* (Ulmaceae). Other noteworthy features of this vegetation were the common occurrence of Myrtaceae, rattans and plants allied to *Brownlowia* (Tiliaceae), producing the pollen type *Discoidites borneensis*. In younger, Neogene deposits much of the pollen attributable to *Discoidites* is clearly derived from mangroves, where *Brownlowia argentata* occurs today, but this adaptation does not necessarily appear to have taken place in the Paleocene to Early Eocene. Initial adaptation to freshwater swamp settings was probably a prerequisite for subsequent adaptation to brackish substrates as discussed in Section 9.10 for other mangroves.

Paleocene to Early Eocene coal-bearing sediments from the East Java Sea and Myanmar (Figure 9.5) are characterised by very different assemblages to those of Sarawak (Reimann and Thaung, 1981), with abundant trichotomosulcate, probable palm pollen and spores derived from early Pteridaceae (*Distaverrusporites margaritatus*). Assemblages from both areas are of low diversity, and probably derived from freshwater swamp vegetation, with an everwet climate. This flora bears few affinities with the present-day rain forests of the region; trichotomosulcate reticulate palm pollen is principally known today from palms from South America, such as *Bactris*.

The abundance of palm pollen in earliest Tertiary SE Asian assemblages suggests that

the the Palmae province of Herngreen and Chlonova (1981) (Figure 5.8) extended across the tropics in the Paleocene, but, since the Paleocene and Early Eocene pollen assemblages from both everwet Myanmar swamps and those from moist, but seasonal climates from Sunda are very different from those reported from other tropical regions, it is likely that during this time the SE Asian region consisted of a distinct biogeographical subprovince, which was probably quite isolated from other tropical floras.

### Sahul region palynofloras

A glimpse at the Early Tertiary vegetation from the Sahul region is provided from a single suite of samples from the Waripi Formation, from the Bird's Neck region of Irian Jaya (Figure 9.6). The presence of *Nothofagus* (Fagaceae) pollen, together with Proteaceae and Myrtaceae, emphasises the wholly Australian affinity of this low diversity microflora, whereas the dominance of *Casuarina* (Casuarinaceae) (Figure 9.7e) suggests a predominance of sclerophyllous vegetation, which is in keeping with the indications of aridity forthcoming from the presence of evaporitic sediments (anhydrite) within the Waripi Formation.

Palynological data is therefore in keeping with modern plate tectonic reconstructions, which emphasise that the Sunda and Sahul regions were widely separated latitudinally at this time, and that there is no evidence for earliest Tertiary floristic affinities between the two areas.

### The Philippine Plate, and Pacific floras during the Early Palaeogene

Most historical accounts of the SE Asian flora consider only the intermingling of the Asian and Australasian floras, and overlook the Philippines and the Pacific as a significant primary floristic source. This is largely because the Philippines now form part of SE Asia, but in the Early Tertiary that was not the case. Current

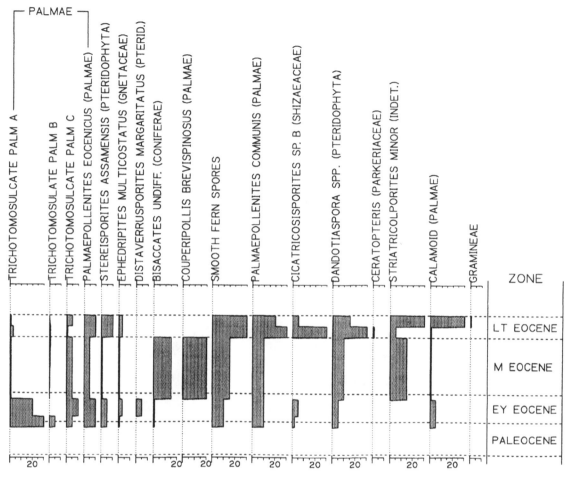

Figure 9.5  Palynological succession from the Paleocene and Eocene of Myanmar, reconstructed from Fig 3 of Reimann and Thaung (1981). Data presented in terms of percentage 'total pollen and spores'.

plate tectonic reconstructions of Rangin et al. (1990), Zonenshayn and Khain (1990) and Hall (1995, 1996) clearly suggest that during the Eocene (54–36 Ma) the Philippines in part formed island arc systems, then lying south of the equator, 2000 km east of Sundaland, which were associated with subduction zones relating to phases of sea-floor spreading and zones of collision in the S Pacific, and only in part comprised continental fragments of Asian origin (Figure 9.2). The Philippine and Pacific island arc systems, with the island of Fiji forming part of the Outer Melanesian Arc, would certainly have borne their own, possibly distinctive, flora at this time, and may also have provided a possible trackway for dispersal by island hopping between Sunda and New Caledonia, which in the earliest Tertiary lay far to the south, on the northern margin of disassembling Gondwana. However, at the present time, there is no fossil data to substantiate such floras, or any present-day biogeographic distributions which can *only* be explained with recourse to such a dispersal path.

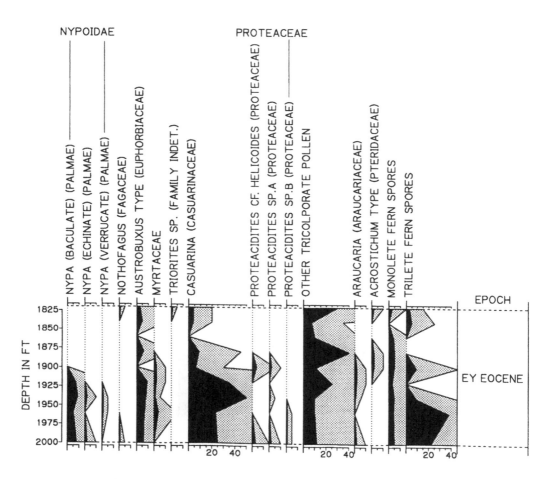

Figure 9.6  Early Eocene palynomorph assemblages from the Bird's Neck area of Irian Jaya, from a stratigraphic equivalent of the Waripi Formation; pollen sum 'total miospores', selected taxa shown only; stipple = ×5 exaggeration. Reproduced by permission of Bakhuys Publishers.

Figure 9.7  Some characteristic pollen types from the SE Asian Tertiary. (a) *Ctenolophon parvifolius* type[1] (Ctenolophonaceae) ×1000, first appears in the Middle Eocene, following dispersal from the Indian Plate; (b) *Burretokentia*[2] (Palmae) ×1000, now restricted to New Caledonia, compares closely with the fossil pollen type *Palmaepollenites kutchensis*, which also appears in SE Asia in the Middle Eocene following dispersal from India; (c) *Mischocarpus*[3] (Sapindaceae) ×2000, bears similarities with *Cupanieidites flaccidiformis*, which also first appears in the Middle Eocene; (d) *Meyeripollis naharkotensis*[4] (Family indet.) ×1200, ranging from the Late Eocene to Early Miocene from Assam to Sunda; (e) *Casuarina*[5] (Casuarinaceae) ×1300, dispersing to SE Asia from Australia at the end of the Oligocene; (f) *Phormium* (Phormiaceae) ×1000, dispersing from the Australian Plate during the Early Miocene; (g) *Stenochlaena milnei*[6] ×1200, crossing Wallace's Line in the Late Miocene; (h) *Sonneratia caseolaris*[7] (Sonneratiaceae) ×1500, evolved in SE Asia during the Early Miocene. [1], van der Ham (1980); [2], Harley and Morley (1995); [3], van der Ham (1980); [4], Muller, unpublished; [5], Coetzee and Praglowski (1984); [6], Erdtman (1972); [7], Muller (1981). Drawn by Harsanti Pribatini.

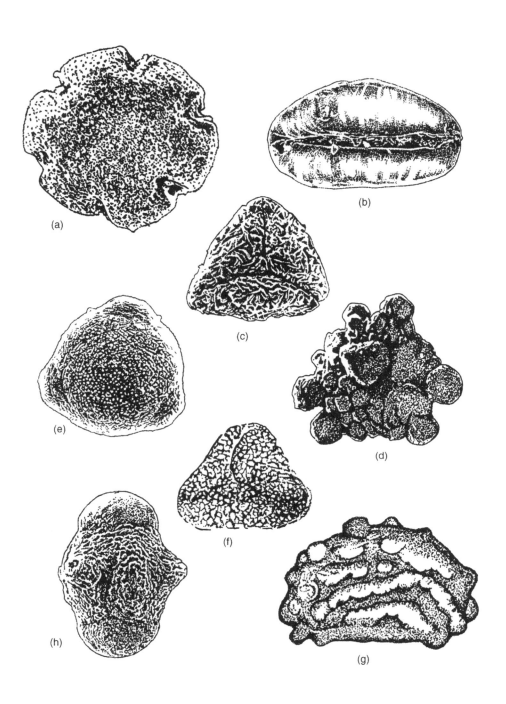

## 9.4  MIDDLE TO LATE EOCENE, PRIOR TO TECTONIC RESTRUCTURING: DISPERSAL FROM INDIA

### 9.4.1  Tectonic Setting and Palaeogeography

The general plate tectonic setting for Sundaland during the Middle Eocene (49–39 Ma) was similar to that for the Early Eocene. However, the Indian Plate was in the process of colliding with S Asia, and during the Late Eocene the profound effects of this collision on the geography of the region were already beginning to occur. Much of the region began to subside, reducing niches for montane vegetation, and increasing opportunities for lowland communities throughout the region (Figure 9.1). At the same time, rapid rifting and subsidence resulted in the initiation of the Malay, Natuna, Sarawak, Java Sea and Sumatran basins. The Makasar Straits began to open (Situmorang, 1982), leading to the isolation of the southwestern arm of Sulawesi from Kalimantan, and intermontane basins were initiated in Central Sumatra (Ombi-lin) and the Malay Peninsula (Batu Arang).

Very thick sediment packages accumulated in Myanmar and Kalimantan, although many of these were subsequently largely tectonised, or buried, and are not easily studied for palynology. Excellent palynomorph assemblages have, however, been recovered from the Middle and Late Eocene Nanggulan Formation in Central Java (Morley, 1982c; Takahashi, 1982; Barton, 1988; Harley and Morley, 1995; Morley et al., 1999) and SW Sulawesi (Morley, 1998), and the latest Eocene of the Mangkalihat Peninsula in Kalimantan (Morley, in press), which together with data from Myanmar (Potonie, 1960; Reimann and Thaung, 1981) provide the basis of current knowledge of Middle and Late Eocene vegetation of SE Asia.

The Middle and Late Eocene of Irian Jaya and most of the islands of E Indonesia were wholly characterised by carbonate deposition during this period (Simanjuntak and Barber, 1996) and, apart from ephemeral communities on coral islands, would have been essentially without vegetation. However, oceanic ridges in the Pacific region, such as the New Guinea arc terranes, the Philippines and Halmahera (Figure 9.2), probably continued to bear substantial floras, although, as for the older Tertiary, there is currently no palaeobotanical evidence for these.

### 9.4.2  Middle to Late Eocene Vegetation

Palynomorph assemblages from the Middle Eocene of Nanggulan in Central Java and the Ngimbang Formation to the east of Java contrast strongly with the earlier Tertiary assemblages from Sarawak, Myanmar and the East Java Sea and provide a glimpse as to how SE Asian floras and vegetation changed between the Paleocene/Early Eocene and Middle Eocene times. The Javanese Middle Eocene assemblages are of high diversity, reflecting a rich and diverse vegetation, with a dominance of pollen of dicotyledons, but also a good representation of monocots, especially palms, and initially without gymnosperms (except very rare *Ephedra*). Pteridophytes were well represented in terms of taxa, but the percentage representation of their spores is generally low, suggesting that ferns were not major contributors to regional vegetation. These assemblages, coupled with the presence of coaly lithologies, suggest a luxuriant, diverse vegetation and a moist, warm climate (Katz, 1991; Harley and Morley, 1995). The presence of pollen of many taxa which are today characteristic of rain forests, such as *Durio* (Bombacaceae), *Ctenolophon parvifolius* (Ctenolophonaceae) (Figure 9.7a) and *Ixonanthes* (Linaceae), and of epiphytes, such as Loranthaceae, suggest that the dryland vegetation consisted of tall, dense, closed-canopy rain forests of modern aspect.

Many of the novel pollen types recorded from the Javanese Middle Eocene (Figure 9.8) have also been recorded from much older, Paleocene and Early Eocene sediments in India (Chapter 8). Their sudden appearance in the Javanese

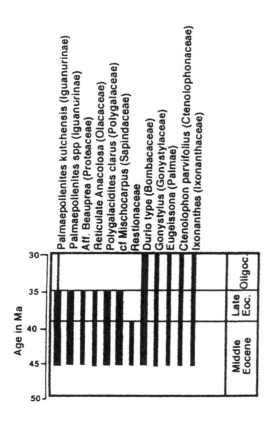

Figure 9.8 Ranges of taxa recorded within the Eocene of Java with either Gondwanan affinities, or recorded from the Early Eocene or Paleocene of India.

Middle Eocene reflects a major dispersal event following the collision of the Indian and Asian plates, at which time both regions experienced everwet climates, indicated by the widespread presence of coals in sediments of this age in India (Section 8.3.2) and also from the Middle Eocene of Java, SE Kalimantan and SW Sulawesi (Morley, in press), and thus an everwet corridor was established between the two regions at this time. It is likely that the Indian flora was the more aggressive, since the invasion of taxa from the Indian Plate is thought to have resulted in the extinction of many Paleocene and Early Eocene plant taxa, for, whereas those Kayan Sandstone taxa with modern affinities,

such as *Nypa,* Calamoidae, *Barringtonia* (Lecythidaceae) and Sapotaceae, remain, most of the other palynomorph taxa from the Kayan Formation are absent. Also, few taxa of SE Asian origin dispersed to India at this time (Chapter 8). Middle Eocene immigrants from the Indian subcontinent appear in two phases, an earlier phase, probably during the earlier part of the Middle Eocene, and a later phase, close to the Middle/Late Eocene boundary.

Taxa appearing within the first phase of immigration include southern hemisphere elements such as *Anacolosa* with reticulate pollen, aff. *Beauprea* (aff. *Beaupreadites matsuokae,* Proteaceae) and Polygalaceae (*Polygalacidites clarus*), and rain forest elements, such as *Alangium* (Alangiaceae), *Durio,* ancestral *Eugeissona* (*Longapertites* spp., Palmae), *Ctenolophon parvifolius* and *Gonystylus* (Gonystylaceae). The Palmae subtribe Iguanurinae (*Palmaepollenites kutchensis,* Figure 9.7b) also appears within this first phase. This subtribe was widely represented across the Indian subcontinent and the Sunda region in the Early Tertiary (Harley and Morley, 1995). The distribution of fossil occurrences of *Palmaepollenites kutchensis* clearly emphasises the range within which Indian and Sunda Middle Eocene floras exhibit close similarities (Figure 9.2), and suggests that the Indian–Sundanian region could be considered to have comprised a single floristic region at this time. Other taxa suggest wider, including Tethyan, affinities, such as *Diporoconia* (Palmae, cf. Frederiksen et al., 1985), the schizaeaceous fern *Cicatricososporites eocenicus,* and Restionaceae. Taxa originating on the Indian Plate include *Durio, Ixonanthes, Gonystylus,* a Sapindaceous taxon, possibly *Mischocarpus* (Figure 9.7c) (*Cupanieidites flaccidiformis*) and some which cannot be compared to modern families (Figure 9.8), and, clearly, many of these taxa are now more or less restricted to the Malesian region, disappearing from India following drying during the Late Neogene (Section 8.4).

The second wave of immigration (Figures 9.8; 9.9) included the southern gymnosperm *Podocarpus* (the *polystachyus* type). *Podocarpus*

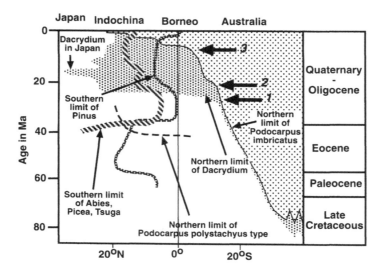

Figure 9.9   Latitudinal distribution through time of gymnosperm pollen in the Far East. The diagram shows a transect from Japan to Australia, with northern and southern limits of southern and northern conifers through time. The gradual northern expansion of *Podocarpus imbricatus* reflects the northern drift of the Australian Plate: 1) Time of collision of Australian and Asian/Philippine plates; 2) dispersal of *P. imbricatus* into New Guinea following widespread uplift; 3) Uplift in Eastern Indonesia following shift in movement along Sorong Fault, allowing *P. imbricatus* (later followed by *Phyllocladus*) to disperse into Sunda. The parent plant of the *Podocarpus polystachyus* type is thought to have dispersed from the Indian Plate.

pollen (*Podocarpus Polystachyus* type) is first observed at about the Middle/Late Eocene boundary.

The character of some Middle Eocene swamp vegetation types can be envisaged from Figure 9.10. This shows a palynological analysis of a coal seam from the Nanggulan Formation (Morley, in press), with an initial abundance of *Acrostichum*-like spores (Pteridaceae), followed by common pollen of *Nypa*, with *Proxapertites* spp. reflecting a brackish-water mangrove swamp, which in turn is succeeded by the common occurrence of Iguanurinae, and, to a lesser extent, Calamineae (Palmae), and ancestral *Lagerstroemia* (Lythraceae). This coal has also yielded common pollen of Polygalaceae (Takahashi, 1982). Pollen assemblages from the Nanggulan coals exhibit much lower diversities compared to those from adjacent fluviomarine shales into which pollen from inland plant communities would have been washed (Morley, unpublished), suggesting that the vegetation

of upland areas at this time was particularly diverse.

*Nypa* pollen within this section is restricted to the echinate *Spinizonocolpites echinatus*, the plant producing the baculate type being extinct by this time. It exhibits considerable morphological variation (Barton, 1988), suggesting the possibility that more than one species of *Nypa* may have been present. Variation is less, however, than that observed by Frederiksen (1994b) from the Late Paleocene of Pakistan. *Brownlowia* type pollen may well have been sourced by mangrove plants at this time. No specimens firmly attributable to the Rhizophoraceae have been recorded in SE Asia prior to the Late Eocene (Morley, in press).

The Sundanese Middle Eocene flora extended eastward as far as the southwest arm of Sulawesi, which at that time was connected directly to SE Kalimantan (Morley, 1998). This flora is thought to have remained on Sulawesi long after the Late Eocene formation of the

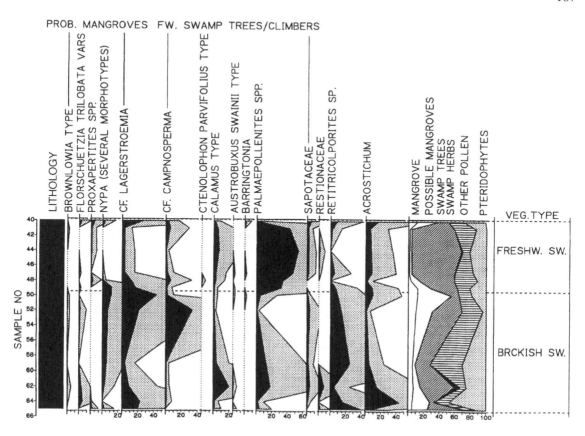

Figure 9.10 Palynological succession through a 50 cm thick Middle Eocene coal from Nanggulan Formation, Java. Selected taxa shown only; pollen sum 'total pollen and spores'; stipple = ×5 exaggeration; raw data from Barton (1988) and Morley (unpublished); (from Morley, in press).

Makasar Straits, and the formation of Wallace's Line, and subsequently provided the source of Laurasian plant taxa for the islands of East Malesia (Section 9.8).

The immigration of Indian Plate plant taxa to Myanmar is less clear from the work of Reimann and Thaung (1981) than from studies from Java, but the appearance of *Couperipollis varispinosus* (Palmae) and *Alangium* in Myanmar in the Middle Eocene probably reflects the same dispersal event (Figure 9.5). Evidence fully consistent with the establishment of a Middle Eocene dispersal corridor through Myanmar is forthcoming from geochemical analysis of potential petroleum source rocks

(Curiale et al., 1994) which are characterised by the common occurrence of the geochemical biomarker bicadinane, which van Aarssen et al. (1990, 1992) demonstrated to be derived from resins of Dipterocarpaceae (Section 4.1.3). Ashton (1982) and Ashton and Gunatilleke (1987a) proposed that dipterocarps were also rafted from Africa via the Indian Plate on the basis of biogeographical data, a suggestion which would be fully supported from geochemical fossil and palynological data from SE Asia. The history of Dipterocarpaceae will be discussed more fully in Sections 9.6 and 13.6.

Evidence for Late Eocene vegetation in SE Asia is very limited, mainly because much of the region was undergoing subsidence at this time and suitable localities for palynomorph preservation are few. Potonie (1960) studied the palynology of a coal of Late Eocene age, from Myanmar, and the assemblages recorded indicated a low diversity vegetation dominated by Calamoidae with *Pandanus* (Pandanaceae). The richest Late Eocene assemblages recorded are from coals from the Mangkalihat Peninsula in Kalimantan (Figure 9.11). Coals from this region yield excellent palynomorph assemblages, which are characterised by pollen of *Nypa*, Calamoidae, Iguanurinae, *Alangium*, *Durio* and Sapotaceae, in addition to sonneratioid pollen (*Florschuetzia trilobata* vars), and many indeterminate pollen taxa. A particularly characteristic pollen type from this locality is *Meyeripollis naharkotensis* (Figure 9.7d), also characteristic of the latest Eocene to Oligocene of E India and Assam (Baksi, 1962, 1972; Handique, 1993), and although its affinity is unknown, its stratigraphic association with coals, both in India and Sunda, suggests that the plant producing this pollen type was also characteristic of peat swamps. *Meyeripollis* has also been recorded elsewhere from the Late Eocene in Kalimantan and Java, and the mid-Tertiary of the Philippines (Bates, personal communication), and since the pollen type remains urecorded west of Assam, this taxon may well have originated on the Sunda Plate, and dispersed westward only as far as Assam.

## 9.5   THE TERMINAL EOCENE EVENT

The effect of the terminal Eocene cooling event on SE Asian vegetation cannot anywhere be examined directly, because an effect of the tectonic activity on sedimentation at that time is that palynomorph-bearing Eocene and Oligocene (36–25 Ma) sediments are rarely juxtaposed. As with the low palaeolatitudes to the west, the effect of this climatic global event must have been profound, although since Eocene palynofloras are still in the process of being

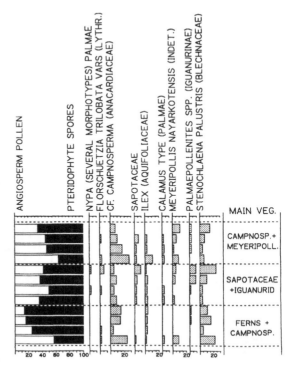

Figure 9.11   Palynomorph assemblages from Late Eocene coals from the Mangkalihat Peninsula, Kalimantan. Pollen sum 'total pollen and spores' (Morley, in press).

evaluated, are difficult to quantify. Palynomorphs which are clearly absent from the Oligocene include *Proxapertites cursus*, *P. operculatus*, *Diporoconia*, *Calystegiapollis* (Convolvulaceae), *Monoporites punctatus* (Restionaceae), reticulate *Anacolosidites* spp. and aff. *Beaupreadites matsuoki* (aff. *Beauprea*), whereas Iguanurinae pollen shows a marked reduction in abundance and diversity. It is noteworthy that *Nypa* survived the terminal Eocene event in SE Asia, whereas elsewhere it became extinct. On a more general note, although it is difficult to attribute many Eocene pollen types to extant taxa, a relatively high proportion of Oligocene forms may be thus attributed, emphasising the extent of extinction at this boundary, and, coupled with this, it is much easier to interpret palynomorph assemblages in terms of plant communities from the Oligocene onward, compared to the older Palaeogene.

The main climatic effect of the terminal Eocene event in Sundaland was a marked reduction in moisture availability (Katz, 1991; Harley and Morley, 1995), resulting in the lack of peat formation, reflected by the absence of coals except locally in Central Sumatra (although some of these may be misdated, see below). Distinctly dry climates characterised the Oligocene in Vietnam (Dzanh, 1994), whereas at 20°N, in the vicinity of the Pearl River Basin, *Taxodium* swamps with rattans (recalling the Oligocene in Turkey (Ediger et al., 1990) and England (Chandler, 1957)), were followed by coniferous forest with common Loranthaceae suggesting moist, warm temperate rather than tropical climates. An important effect of tectonics would have been a pronounced reduction in the representation of elevated terrain (Figure 9.1) coupled with the breakup of much of the Eocene landscape into horst and graben topography, although elevated mountain belts would have continued as a prominent feature of SE Asian palaeogeography up until the present.

## 9.6  OLIGOCENE TO PLIOCENE

Whereas for the Paleocene and Eocene, the number of localities yielding palynofloras can be virtually counted on one hand, for the Oligocene to Pliocene (5–1.6 Ma) many localities have been examined through the oil-bearing basins of the region. There are also numerous localties for fossil wood, in Sumatra, Java and Kalimantan, but stratigraphic control for these is often poor (Bande and Prakash, 1986). The account which follows is based mainly on unpublished palynological data from many localities, in addition to the pioneering work of Muller (1963, 1964, 1966, 1972).

### *Tectonic setting*

During the Early Oligocene the pattern of rifting and subsidence, which began in the Late Eocene,

continued with the opening of pull-apart basins in the regions of the South China Sea, Sumatra and the West Java Sea. Uplift was mainly restricted to the Indoburman Ranges and the Andaman/Nicobar Ridge. At the same time the subsiding southwest arm of Sulawesi continued to separate from Kalimantan. Later, new ocean floor was created in the E South China Sea, with the further eastward extrusion of S China, and clockwise rotation of Kalimantan. The pull-apart basins assumed N–S lineaments in the case of the Sumatran, West Java Sea and Gulf of Thailand rifts, NW–SE lineaments for the Malay Basin, and WSW–ENE lineaments for the Natuna Sea and Vietnamese rifts. To the north of about 5° palaeolatitude, these rifts are thought to have been bounded by substantially elevated terrain, whereas to the south of this line elevations were probably less pronounced. Most of the rifts contained large, often deep, fresh-water lakes, which gradually filled with often organic-rich muds (which following 'cooking' by subsequent burial, produced most of the hydrocarbons of SE Asia), or with fluvial sands, during periods of low lake levels. By the beginning of the Early Miocene (25–16 Ma), most of these rifts were filled, but subsidence continued over a wider area, further reducing the land area and, coupled with a sudden sea level rise at the beginning of the Miocene, a huge part of the Sunda region, from Vietnam to Natuna, became submerged by a very shallow, brackish-water sea. Further widespread transgressions occurred during the latest Early Miocene and earliest Middle Miocene, at which time the land area for SE Asia was at its minimum for the Tertiary (Figure 9.1). Following Middle Miocene (16–10 Ma) tectonism, further widespread transgressions occurred during the Late Miocene (10–5 Ma) and the Early Pliocene (5–3.5 Ma).

In the Oligocene, the Philippines and other island arc systems associated with Pacific Plate boundaries continued to form oceanic ridges, well separated from Sundaland by oceanic crust, but rapidly drifting westward, rather than to the north. The Palawan microplate, on the other hand, was drifting rapidly southward as the South China Sea opened, to collide with Borneo at about 20 Ma (Hall, 1996). The northern margin of the Australian continent initially lay to the south, also without connection to Sunda, and largely submerged by shallow seas, resulting in thick accumulations of limestone in the region of the Sahul Shelf. First indications of collision between the Philippine and Australian plates are in the latest Oligocene (Hall, 1995, 1996), and uplift and erosion at this time probably resulted in the formation of the clastic Sirga Formation in W Irian Jaya. However, the Makasar Straits continued to deepen, forming a major barrier to dispersal across the region in the area of Wallace's Line. Most of the islands to the east of SW Sulawesi were as yet either unformed or submerged, limestones being virtually the only sediments accumulating (Simandjuntuk and Barber, 1996) until the collision with the Sunda Plate was well under way.

By Middle Miocene times, the Australian Plate was in full collision with the Sunda Plate, resulting in the formation of the Banda Arc in Indonesia (Hall, 1996). The mountains of New Guinea were rapidly uplifted, first in the region of Papua New Guinea, and later in Irian Jaya, and many of the islands of Eastern Indonesia were raised above sea level (Simandjuntuk and Barber, 1996). Increased subduction of the Indian Plate along the length of Sumatra resulted in a substantial phase of uplift along the Barisan Mountains (Cameron et al., 1980; Kirby et al., 1993), followed slightly later by the creation of the Meratus mountains in SE Kalimantan. The Javanese volcanic arc became widely exposed in the Pliocene, and, at the same time, the Kinabalu batholith in Sabah underwent substantial uplift as surrounding mountain chains were undergoing rapid erosion.

## Vegetation

From the Oligocene onward, the SE Asian flora experienced continued diversification, as indicated by palynomorph assemblage diversity data from the Mahakam Delta (Figures 9.12; 9.13). This does not mean that the region experienced a uniformly moist and unchanging climate during that time. On the contrary, as will be brought to attention later, it is likely that the present-day species-richness of the flora relates to the rapidity of geological and environmental change, coupled with the *dominance* of moist, but with episodically dry, climates. The trend toward increased palynomorph assemblage diversity with time is made more pronounced by the greater predominance of drier, more seasonal, monsoonal climates, supporting lower diversity floras, during the Oligocene and earliest Miocene, followed by more perhumid climates from 20 Ma onward (Figure 9.14).

The drier Oligocene and earliest Miocene also corresponds with the time of radiation of the Dipterocarpaceae in SE Asia, following their dispersal from the Indian Plate, as evidenced from their pollen (Muller, 1981), wood record and biogeography (Ashton, 1982; Ashton and Gunatilleke, 1987a) and also the record of the geochemical biomarker bicadinane, which, as noted earlier, has been identified with dipterocarp resin and has been widely reported in petroleum source rocks in SE Asia. As noted in Section 9.4.2, the oldest records for dipterocarp geochemical fossils are from the Middle and Late Eocene of Myanmar. They are subsequently widespread in the Oligocene of most basins in the Sunda region (except intermontane basins), but have not been reported from the Mio-Pliocene of Irian Jaya, where dipterocarps probably immigrated at a late stage. Bearing in mind the Middle Eocene dispersal of dipterocarps into Myanmar, one might have anticipated dispersal as far as Sulawesi prior to the opening of the Makasar Straits, and their significant representation today to the east of Wallace's Line. Dipterocarp pollen becomes common in SE Asian Late Oligocene (30–25 Ma) and earliest Miocene sediments (Figure 9.15), at which time its parent plants are thought to have been important

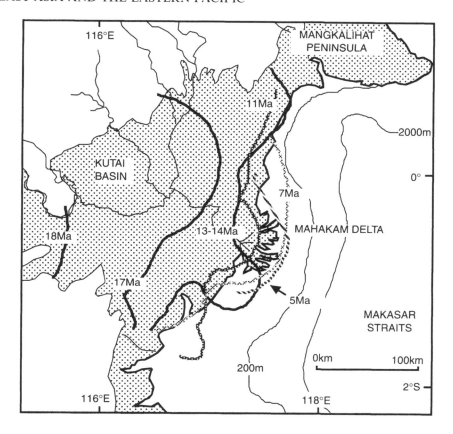

Figure 9.12 Mahakam Delta, E Kalimantan, showing positions and ages of main delta lobes during the Miocene and Pliocene. The shaded area reflects the extent of Tertiary sediments in the Kutai Basin (van der Weerd and Armin, 1992). Reproduced with permission of American Association of Petroleum Geologists.

elements of strongly monsoonal vegetation, with dipterocarps radiating into everwet rain forests after 20 Ma (cf. Ashton, 1982). The main time of radiation of Dipterocarpaceae in SE Asia would therefore have taken place after the opening of the Makasar Straits, and formation of Wallace's Line.

## 9.6.1 Mid-Tertiary, Oligocene to Earliest Miocene, Predominantly Subhumid or Monsoonal Climate Vegetation

Evidence for Oligocene perhumid lowland climates in the Sunda region is very restricted,

being limited to Central Sumatra, where coals are preserved in the Sawahlunto Formation of the Ombilin Basin. The age of these coals is based on the occurrence of spores of the aquatic fern *Ceratopteris* (Parkeriaceae), generally thought to be restricted to Oligocene and younger sediments, but with records of this spore type from the Late Eocene of South America (Graham, 1985; Gonzalez, personal communication, 1984), Africa (Kedves, 1971; Morley unpublished) and India (Kar, 1982; Handique, 1993), a Late Eocene age for this coal should also be considered, especially since the coals also yield the iguanurinoid palm pollen type *Palmaepollenites kutchensis* (Bartram and Nugrahaningsih, 1990). If this is the

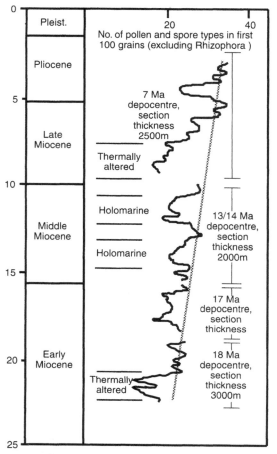

Figure 9.13 Palynomorph assemblage diversity through Miocene of Mahakam Delta, E Kalimantan. The diversity curve is based on the analysis of two 3000 m well sections and two seismic lines (from Carter and Morley, 1996) from the 18, 17, 13–14, 11 and 7 Ma delta lobes shown in Figure 9.12. Low diversity estimates for some intervals are due to analysis of samples (a) from holomarine sediments and (b) from sediments from the base of well sections or seismic lines which have been subject to thermal alteration as a result of deep burial. Diversities are based on number of pollen types recorded in a count of 100 grains, excluding Rhizophoraceae.

case, evidence for perhumid lowland Oligocene climates is restricted to N Myanmar and Assam in India (Chapter 8).

Determination of former occurrences of vegetation indicative of subhumid and mon-

soonal climates in SE Asia, in the pre-Miocene, poses special problems which may be summarised as follows. Firstly, there is a great deal known today about moist SE Asian vegetation types, but, until recently, relatively little was known about dry ones. This is partly due to the fact that huge areas of monsoon forests in, for instance, Java, Thailand and Vietnam have long been destroyed, and partly because Myanmar, Vietnam and Cambodia have until recently been largely inaccessible for study. Secondly, virtually all pollen rain studies in SE Asia have been undertaken in moist climate settings; knowledge of pollen production in dry climate settings is minimal. Thirdly, as mentioned in Chapter 3, and so clearly evident in Australia (Martin, 1978), rich microfloras are prolifically preserved in moist climate facies, whereas dry climates are not conducive to the widespread preservation of organic matter, except in particularly restricted depositional settings. Fourthly, due to the tendency for dry climates to coincide with periods of low sea level, wet and dry climate sediments are rarely juxtaposed, except in deep marine facies which are little studied, and often poor in pollen; low sea level facies are also often poor in microfossils and difficult to date. Fifthly, pollen of grasses, which is invariably used as the main indicator of dry conditions in the Neogene, may be rare in pre-Miocene sections as a result of their low diversification at this time. Due to all these problems, Muller (1972) suggested that climates in Sarawak were perhumid throughout the Oligocene to Pliocene.

The extent of subhumid, or monsoonal vegetation in the SE Asian region is shown by the pollen record from the thick lacustrine and fluviatile Oligocene to earliest Miocene sediments of the Java Sea, Malay Basin, Natuna Sea, Gulf of Thailand, Sumatra and Vietnam. Some of the features of this succession for the Malay and Natuna basins have previously been brought to attention by Morley and Flenley (1987) and Morley (1991). The main features of the palynological succession for these successions are summarised in Figure 9.16.

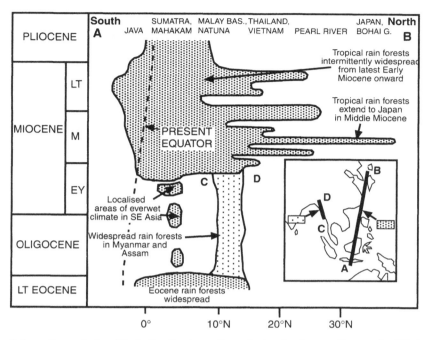

Figure 9.14 Schematic and simplified distribution of tropical rain forest climates in SE Asia during the Tertiary. Note that Eocene climates were moist, whereas in the Sunda region Oligocene climates were dry or seasonal, and opportunities for tropical rain forests were limited, possibly to localised areas with orographic rainfall. Rain forest climates did occur during the Oligocene in Assam and Myanmar. The greatest northward extension of rain forests occurred in the earliest Middle Miocene. Position of palaeoequator according to Smith et al. (1994).

Early Oligocene records are known from the West Natuna Basin and offshore Vietnam, although sometimes these sediments are attributed to the Late Eocene, usually in the absence of evidence (e.g. Ginger et al., 1993). These sediments are mainly lacustrine in origin, and their pollen and spore content reflects the character of fringing freshwater swamp communities, and suggests a vegetation dominated by *Barringtonia* and plants producing *Brownlowia* type and aff. *Lagerstroemia* pollen (*Florschuetzia trilobata* vars) together with common pteridophytes. Gramineae pollen is also a common constituent of these assemblages, suggesting either savanna vegetation, or grass-dominated freshwater swamps. The abundance of *Barringtonia* pollen is reminiscent of the 'forêt inondée' (seasonal swamp forest) of the Tonle Sap in Cambodia (Section 2.4.2), within which *Bar-*

*ringtonia* is a dominant component, together with *Lagerstroemia* (Dy Phon, 1981), and suggests that these lakes were bordered by a fringe of such swamp forest. As noted previously, the common occurrence of *Brownlowia* type pollen together with *Florschuetzia trilobata* in this setting should not be taken to indicate brackish conditions, but emphasises the likelihood that many mangrove taxa probably adapted to tidal habitats through first becoming adapted to seasonally inundated freshwater swamp settings.

A similar scenario is provided by palynomorph records from the Pematang Formation in Sumatra (Pribatini, 1993 and unpublished). Thin coals, presumably reflecting organic accumulation in ephemeral oxbow lakes, are characterised by the presence of Gramineae pollen, schizaeaceous spores (*Cicatricosisporites*

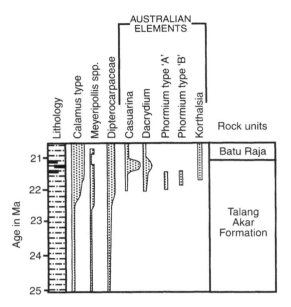

Figure 9.15   Some distinctive pollen types from the Early Miocene of the Java Sea, showing abundance of dipterocarp pollen, immigrants from Australia and the representation of *Meyeripollis*.

*dorogensis*) and smooth fern spores, with pollen of rattans, suggesting low, fern-dominated, grassy marsh communities with Schizaeaceae, or perhaps open savanna occurring beyond the swamps. This succession also yields regular pollen of *Barringtonia* and *Alchornea* (Euphorbiaceae), and also the palm *Oncosperma*, whose Early Oligocene appearance is consistent with dispersal from India, as its closest relatives occur today in the Seychelles and Mascarenes (Dransfield, 1987).

The Late Oligocene of the West Java, Malay and West Natuna basins is characterised by alternations of lacustrine shales and fluvial sand-prone facies. The fluvial-dominated intervals are characterised by pollen indicative of low diversity freshwater marsh and swamp communities. Very shallow ponds and lakes may be reflected by high percentages of spores of the rooted aquatic fern *Ceratopteris*, whereas swamp thickets are reflected by maxima of calamoid pollen and fern spores.

Earliest Miocene palynomorph assemblages from the Malay and Natuna basins are thought to reflect drier climates than those of the Late Oligocene (Figure 9.16), due to the common occurrence of pollen of Gramineae, and the low representation of fern spores, rarity of pollen characteristic of peat swamps, and generally low assemblage diversity. The most noteworthy feature of this period, especially for the section coinciding with the upper part of the Barat Formation in the Natuna Sea, its lateral equivalent, the Trengganu Shale, in the Malay Basin, and also stratigraphically equivalent sediments in the West Java Sea (Figure 9.15), is the common occurrence of small tricolpate pollen, comparable to that of the dipterocarps *Shorea* or *Hopea*. The very widespread nature of this event suggests that low diversity dipterocarp monsoon forests must have been extremely widespread at this time. This association disappears after about 20 Ma, following a rapid and widespread increase in sea levels, and coinciding with a change to an everwet climate.

A further, very characteristic feature of Oligocene and earliest Miocene palynomorph assemblages from sediments from north of the palaeoequator, is the presence of conifer pollen of Laurasian affinity, including *Abies*, *Picea*, *Tsuga*, and possibly *Keeteleria*, together with the temperate angiosperms *Alnus* (Betulaceae) and *Pterocarya* (Juglandaceae) (Figure 9.17), first brought to attention by Muller (1966). They form a common element in a broad belt from N Borneo, through the Natuna and Malay basins, to Indochina, where they may comprise up to half of the total pollen recorded, with additional temperate angiosperms, such as *Betula* (Betulaceae), *Carya* and *Juglans* (Juglandaceae) becoming common in Indochina (Figure 9.18), where they may be as common as the gymnosperms. The abundance and subsequent demise of Laurasian montane vegetation in Borneo was previously explained by Muller (1972) by the former presence of extensive, moist montane vegetation on high mountains, which were later

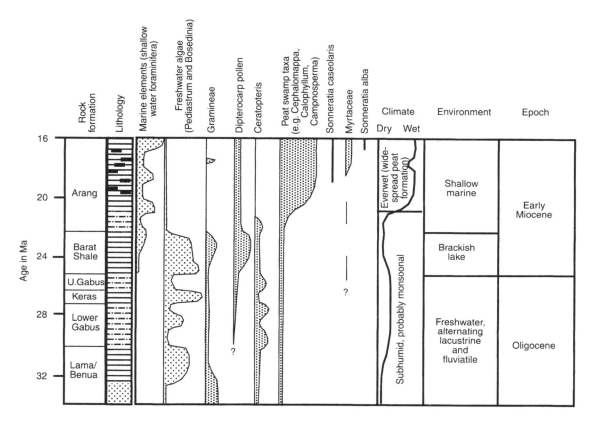

Figure 9.16    Distinctive features of the Oligocene and Early Miocene palynological record for the W Natuna Basin. This pattern is closely mirrored in the adjacent Malay Basin, and broadly similar climatic signatures are suggested by the palynological records in the Java Sea and Sumatra.

subject to erosion, whereas Stein (1978) suggested that its decline was more likely due to competition with other taxa. These assemblages are probably better explained in terms of a combination of drier, at least in the lowlands, and cooler climates at this time, rather than the erosion of previous upland regions, since geological evidence suggests mountain building after, rather than during or before this period (Hall, Pers. comm).

The common occurrence of temperate conifers such as *Abies*, *Picea* and *Tsuga* at this time probably relates to cooler climatic conditions in the low latitudes, possibly with freezing temperatures occurring on some tropical mountains after the terminal Eocene cooling event.

Montane vegetation would have been altitudinally depressed in a manner possibly analogous to the depression of montane vegetation belts during the Quaternary. Such a scenario is wholly consistent with the distribution of dipterocarp pollen records from this time (Figure 9.19), and also with evidence from Thai intermontane basins for the widespread occurrence of oak forests at latitudes now characterised by tropical vegetation (Watanasak, 1988, 1990).

The abundant occurrence of *Pinus* pollen in Oligocene and earliest Miocene sediments in SE Asia requires a different explanation. This pollen is more likely to have been derived from dry conifer forests occurring at low altitudes, as

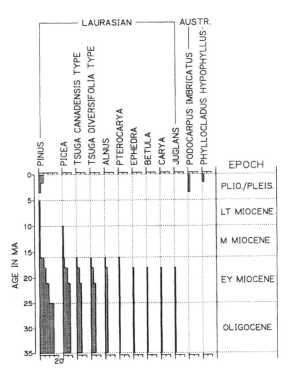

Figure 9.17 Stratigraphic distribution of temperate taxa in the South China Sea region. The diagram brings together records from NW Borneo to offshore Vietnam. The taxa need not all occur in one location. Horizontal axis percentage total miospores. Reproduced by permission of Bakhuys Publishers.

is currently the case in Thailand and the W Philippines, and not from a montane source (Morley, 1991).

Laurasian conifer pollen has never been recorded in significant levels of abundance south of the palaeoequator,[1] although *Alnus* pollen occurs regularly in the earliest Miocene of Java (Figure 9.18). The latter may be due to long-distance transportation (cf. Muller, 1959), but, equally, may indicate the presence of *Alnus* without conifers at lower elevations, reflecting the present situation in S Myanmar, where *Alnus* is frequent at above 1200 m altitude, above the level of monsoon forests, but below the zone of Laurasian conifers (Dudley-Stamp, 1925).

## 9.6.2   Early Miocene to Pliocene, Predominantly Perhumid Climate Vegetation

The former distribution of perhumid vegetation is provided by the pollen record of diverse rain forests and heath forests. The most complete evidence, however, is forthcoming from the history of pollen of peat swamp forests, and of the occurrence of coals, which comprise the compressed remains of the oligotrophic peats. Coals are extensively preserved in many sedimentary basins in the Sunda region, especially from the latter part of the Early Miocene (about 20 Ma) onwards.

### Peat swamp vegetation

The earliest extensive laterally continuous coals in the Sunda region occur in the Early Miocene Talang Akar Formation in the Java Sea and S Sumatra. These are mostly characterised by calamioid pollen, often with *Pandanus*, suggesting a swamp thicket vegetation. Sometimes they contain common pollen of *Dacrydium* and *Casuarina* (Figures 9.7e and 9.15), which suggest that the vegetation of some of the peats from which the coals were formed may have been similar to that of *kerapah* or watershed peats (Morley, in press), rather than zoned coastal peats. Within coals dating from the latter part of the Early Miocene, calamioid pollen ceases to be common, and pollen of present-day typical peat swamp taxa, such as *Durio*, *Cephalomappa* (Euphorbiaceae) and *Calophyllum* (Guttiferae) take over, sometimes with *Casuarina* in association, suggesting that, at this time, peat swamps took on a more modern aspect.

The vegetation of Middle Miocene peat swamps from SE Kalimantan can be inferred from palynological analyses of a 20-m-thick coal by Demchuck and Moore (1993). Allowing for compression, such a thick coal would represent probably more than 100 m of peat accumulation, and for such peats there are no modern analogues. Much of the section contained pollen of typical peat swamp taxa, but in relatively low diversity. Mangrove and back-

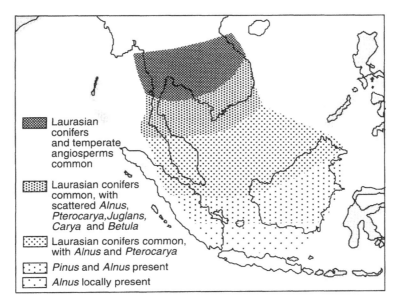

Figure 9.18  Areal distribution of Laurasian montane elements in the Early Miocene of SE Asia (Morley, 1998). Reproduced by permission of Bakhuys Publishers.

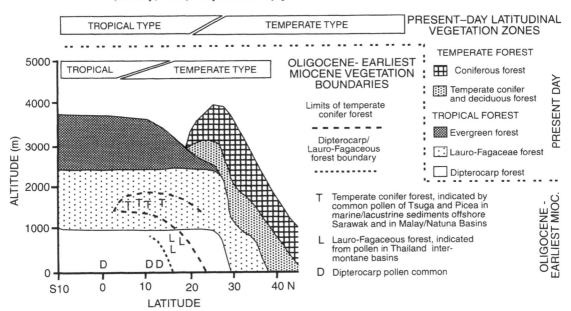

Figure 9.19  Altitudinal and latidudinal representation of forest zones in SE and E Asia (ref. Fig 2.33), compared to the latitudinal positions of some important Late Oligocene to earliest Miocene palynomorph records. 'D' = Dipterocarp-rich assemblages in the earliest Miocene of the Java Sea, Natuna Basin and Malay Basin; 'L' = Lauro-Fagaceous forest, indicated by palynological records of Watanasak (1988); T = assemblages rich in temperate angiosperms from Brunei/Sarawak, Natuna Basin and Thai Basin. These assemblages suggest that Late Oligocene/earliest Miocene climates were substantially cooler than present-day climates in SE Asia.

mangrove pollen was common at some horizons, suggesting that the peat accumulated
partly under brackish conditions, whereas
elsewhere *Dacrydium* and *Casuarina* pollen
were locally common, again suggesting a vegetation comparable to *kerapah* or watershed
peats. Detailed study of closely spaced samples
would be needed before it would be possible to
recognise any form of succession which might
allow comparison with that seen in modern peat
swamps.

Such detailed analyses have been performed
on a thin (1 m thick) Middle Miocene[2] coal
from Brunei by Anderson and Muller (1975),
who estimated that their sample spacing was
sufficiently close to differentiate individual tree
generations (Figure 9.20). They emphasised the
similarity with assemblages from a Holocene
peat from the same area, and suggested that the
diverse peat swamp flora of the Sunda region
had evolved little since the Middle Miocene, but
this must be viewed as an oversimplification,
since the Berakas coal provides evidence for the
first phasic community of peat swamp forest
only, and there is a strong possibility that
Phasic Communities 2 to 6 became established
after this time.

Thick and laterally extensive coals of earliest
Middle Miocene age from Brunei contain
abundant pollen of Rhizophoraceae, suggesting
formation wholly under brackish-water conditions (Figure 9.21). The only modern settings
where mangroves form peats is on carbonates in
the Caribbean; none are known from SE Asia
(Morley, in press). These peats formed at a time
of maximum Miocene global sea levels and
temperatures, and it is suggested that conditions
somewhat warmer than today are necessary for
the formation of mangrove peats.

So far, no studies of low latitude Tertiary coals
have demonstrated the occurrence of a temporal
succession comparable to that seen in the zoned
peat swamps of Sarawak, or even the more
simple succession seen in S Kalimantan (Morley,
1981a), Sumatra and Peninsular Malaysia. With
respect to Sarawak peat swamps, it is important
to note that several of the phasic communities

reported are due wholly to the representation of
*Shorea albida*, which does not occur in the peat
swamps of S or W Kalimantan, Sumatra or West
Malaysia (Anderson, 1976). Its limited geographical distribution, but aggressive behaviour,
suggests that *S. albida* may be, geologically
speaking, a rather young species, and that the
complex ecological succession seen in Sarawak
would also be very young.

### Freshwater swamp forests and streamside communities

The presence of freshwater swamp forests may
be reflected in the occurrence of pollen of
swamp forest taxa, but in the absence of coal
accumulations. Such palynomorph associations
generally also include common *Ilex* pollen, and
are particularly well represented in the Middle
and Late Miocene of Mahakam Delta, and
Miocene sediments in the Malay Basin. Streamside communities are reflected from the Middle
Miocene onward by pollen of *Pometia* (Sapindaceae), *Canthium* (Rubiaceae), and *Pandanus*
in association with Myrtaceae.

### Heath forests (kerangas)

Muller (1972) suggested that former occurrences
of heath forests can be identified by pollen
spectra of *Casuarina*, *Dacrydium* and spores of
the fern ally *Lycopodium cernuum* (Lycopodia-
ceae). In addition to the vegetation of heath
forests, *Casuarina* pollen is abundantly produced by beach vegetation and, as noted above,
by sclerophyllous savanna from Java, and
*Lycopodium cernuum* spores are generally
associated with Gramineae pollen maxima,
suggesting a source from savanna or herbaceous
swamp vegetation. It is believed, however, that
*Dacrydium* pollen is a good indicator of heath
forests, especially where there is impeded
drainage, with or without peat formation.
Maxima of *Dacrydium* pollen, perhaps associated with that of *Casuarina*, occur at distinct
intervals at different times through the Neogene,

199

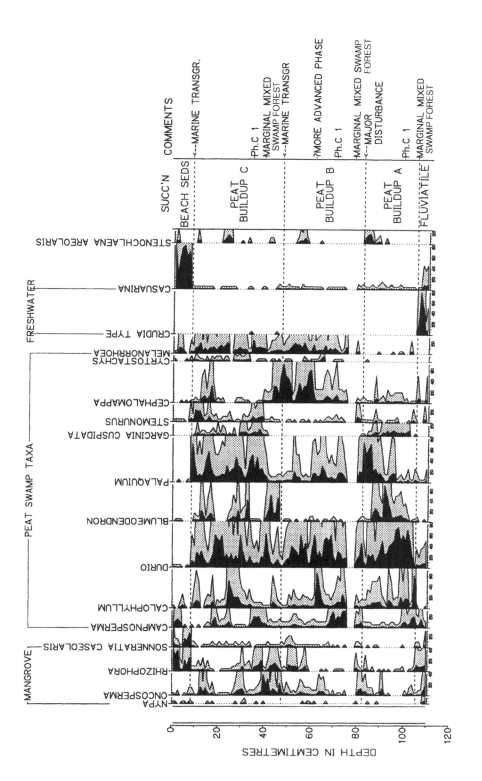

Figure 9.20   Summary of palynological succession through a Middle Miocene coal from Berakas, Brunei. Stipple = ×5 exaggeration (from Anderson and Muller, 1975); interpretation from Morley, (in press).

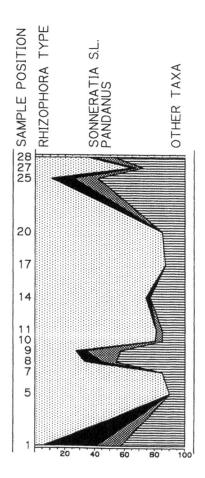

Figure 9.21  Summary of palynological succession through a 5 m thick Middle Miocene coal and carbonaceous shale from Subok, Belait Formation, Brunei, dominated by mangrove pollen (Morley, in press).

possibly relating to the present-day widespread representation of heath forests from Sarawak to Indochina (Whitmore, 1975).

### Dry climate phases

Climates were not uniformly moist during the Mio-Pliocene. Shortlived maxima of Gramineae pollen within the Miocene of the Mahakam Delta and Malay Basin suggest that drier climates supporting more open savanna vegetation intermittently replaced the rain forests, possibly during periods of low sea level. Muller (1972) noted such Gramineae maxima, which he attributed to volcanic activity in Brunei and Sarawak, but which, in the discussion which followed his paper, were thought to be better explained by climatic factors. Such Gramineae maxima are more common in Late Miocene and Pliocene sediments than in the latter part of the Early and Middle Miocene. Dry climate, low sea level intervals may also explain the occurrence of the mangrove taxon *Aegialites* (Plumbaginaceae) in the Sarawak region, which is now restricted to seasonally dry localities. The distribution of the mangrove genus *Camptostemon* (Bombacaceae) may also relate to phases of dry climate; within the Late Miocene and Pliocene of Sarawak *Camptostemon* pollen shows successive phases of expansion, coinciding with periods of low sea levels (Chow, 1996). Similar observations have been noted in the Mahakam Delta sediments over the same time period (Morley, unpublished).

There is strong evidence for seasonal climates from the Pliocene of Java, based on the common occurrence of Gramineae pollen (Semah, 1984; Polhaupessy, 1990). Gramineae pollen is particularly abundant in the younger Pliocene where it is associated with abundant charred grass cuticle (Morley et al., 1999; Pribatini and Morley, 1999), which is thought to indicate savanna fires (Morley and Richards, 1993). Gramineae pollen maxima in the Javanese Pliocene are also often characterised by abundant *Casuarina* pollen, and where the two pollen

at least within individual basins, suggesting that there were times when heath forests were particularly widespread. Such maxima occur in the earliest Miocene of Sarawak, as noted by Muller (1972), in the Early Miocene of the Malay Basin, and intermittently within the Middle Miocene of the Mahakam Delta. The most distinctive occurrence, however, is within the Pliocene (5–1.6 Ma) of the Malay and Thai basins, where an abundance peak defines the *Dacrydium* palynological zone of Morley (1978), types occur together they are thought to be derived from an open sclerophyllous savanna, dominated by *Casuarina*. It is possible that the occurrence of *Casuarina* savanna in this area relates to phases of forest destruction as a result of volcanic activity, since *Casuarina junghuhniana* is presently dominant on volcanoes of East Java and Nusa Tenggara, where it forms a fire-climax forest.

The appearance of Gramineae pollen in the Javanese Pliocene closely follows the pattern of Late Neogene desiccation seen on the Australian continent to the south (Chapter 10). It is suggested that the Pliocene expansion of savanna vegetation in Java relates to the northerly drift of the Australian Plate into the southern hemisphere subtropical high pressure zone coupled with Late Neogene global cooling; today, the Javanese monsoon is controlled primarily by the development of high pressure over N Australia.

The thick sediments of the Irawaddy Delta also contain a record of the Late Neogene expansion of savanna and herbaceous vegetation. Gramineae pollen is common in lowstand deposits of latest Middle and Late Miocene age (unpublished data). Latest Middle Miocene palynomorph assemblages from lowstand deposits also contain common charred grass cuticle fragments, indicating that burning of savannas, presumably as a result of lightning strikes, was taking place almost as early in SE Asia as in W Africa (Figure 9.22). Evidence for grasslands is very limited through most of the Pliocene, but subsequently shows a marked increase, together with charred grass cuticle fragments, during the Early Pleistocene, again indicating the expansion of savanna vegetation, which was subject to burning.

### Montane vegetation

From the Early Miocene onward, the representation of pollen of Laurasian conifers and temperate angiosperms undergoes a gradual decline (Figure 9.17), and during the Late Miocene such records are very rare.

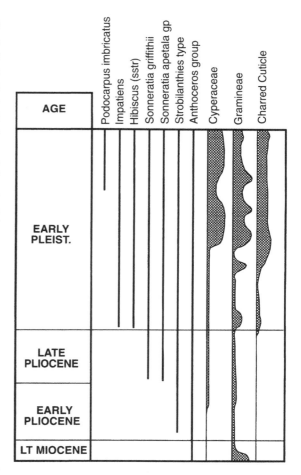

Figure 9.22 Schematic indication of stratigraphic distribution of pollen of herbaceous and some mangrove and montane taxa and grass cuticle from the delta of the Irawaddy River, Myanmar. The diagram shows presence only, except for Gramineae microfossils and Cyperaceae pollen, which are presented according to Figure 4.8.

Montane elements reappear in the record in the Pliocene. The southern conifer *Podocarpus imbricatus* (Figure 9.17) shows a clear immigration into the Sunda region and Indochina in the Early Pliocene, closely followed in the earliest Quaternary at about 1 Ma by *Phyllocladus*. The migration into SE Asia of these taxa clearly relates to the establishment of a dispersal path from Australasia, following Late Tertiary uplift in E Indonesia and the Philippines, and is discussed more fully in Section 9.8. At the same time, there is a distinct return of Laurasian conifers in the latest Pliocene and Quaternary (1.6–0 Ma), and this relates to the alternation of cooler/drier and warmer/wetter equatorial climates with phases of global warming and cooling after 3.0 Ma.

Gondwanan taxa such as *Dacrydium* and bisaccate *Podocarpus* cannot be used as microtherm indicators, since, as noted above, these taxa are common representatives of monsoonal and lowland *kerangas* vegetation (Morley, 1991), and most fossil pollen is more likely to be derived from such lowland sources.

### Migration routes from Asia

An Early Tertiary direct montane connection of the Sunda region with E Asia via the Malay Peninsula and the Kra Isthmus corroborates with van Steenis' (1934a,b, 1936, 1972) proposal for Asian Tertiary migration tracks into Malesia from the north, but most likely predates his tracks. His Sumatra track is based mostly on distributions of tropicalpine herbs which probably dispersed from the Himalayan region to Sumatra and Java after the Late Miocene or Pliocene, because this mountain range was first uplifted during the Middle Miocene (uplift beginning in N Sumatra at about 13 Ma; Cameron et al., 1980; Kirby et al., 1993). His Luzon track, on the other hand, most likely reflects dispersals between the Philippines and Taiwan during times of low Pleistocene sea levels; an older age for migrations is unlikely since these areas came into close juxtaposition only during the Pleistocene, prior to which the Philippines were located much further to the south (Hall, 1995, 1996).

The tectonic history of the microcontinent Palawan also needs to be taken into consideration with regard to the dispersal of Asian taxa into the Sunda region. As pointed out by Rangin et al. (1990) and Hall (1995, 1996), this land mass was rafted from the latitude of S China (22°N) to its present position at 8°N since the Eocene (mostly between 32 Ma and 20

Ma), and could have acted as a 'Noahs' Ark' for E Asian microthermal taxa.

The widespread occurrence of montane forests, with an unbroken montane connection to the north, throughout the Tertiary is thought to have had an important bearing on the present-day diversity of primitive angiosperms in the montane forests of SE Asia. This land connection allowed elements of northern hemisphere megathermal forests to find refuge on a scale unparalleled either in Europe/Africa or in the Americas following deteriorating mid-Tertiary global climates, since in those areas low and mid-latitude rain forest floras were separated by wide seaways through most of the Tertiary (see also Chapter 11). There is no need to invoke SE Asia as their area of origin, as suggested by Takhtajan (1969) and Thorne (1976).

### 9.6.3  Neogene Extension of Rain Forests into East Asia

As noted in Section 9.5, Oligocene megathermal vegetation did not extend further north than about 20°N in the SE Asian region. Beyond this latitude, warm temperate *Taxodium* swamps with rattans were present in the vicinity of South China (Morley, unpublished) giving way to a semi-arid vegetation with common *Ephedra* in the vicinity of the Gulf of Bohai (China Petroleum Industry, 1978) in Early Oligocene times, whereas, in the Late Oligocene, wet conifer forests with common Loranthaceae were prominent in S China, which were succeeded by dry conifer forests in the Early Miocene. Toward the latter part of the Early Miocene, rising global temperatures and sea levels corresponded with a change to predominantly moist forests in Indochina, and tropical and paratropical rain forests once again became established beyond the tropics (Figure 9.14). From this time, Dipterocarpaceae became prominent in Thailand (Watanasak, 1990) (Figure 9.23) and alternating wet and dry climates were characteristic of Vietnam (Dzanh, 1994). During the latest Early

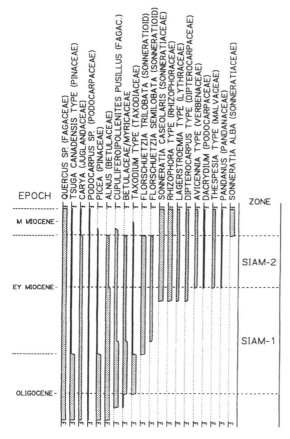

Figure 9.23 Palynological succession from Thailand (Watanasak, 1988). Line thickness reflects approximate abundance. Reproduced with permission of Elsevier Science.

pollen types of tropical aspect comprise only a small proportion of the total palynomorphs, most taxa recorded being characteristic of warm temperate climates.

Subsequent to the Daijima Flora, tropical rain forests probably extended only as far as the Pearl River in S China. The pattern of rain forest development in E Asia, following the Early Miocene change to predominantly wet, equatorial climates in the Sunda region, shows a very close relationship to sea levels, since, for instance, the development of the Daijima Flora in Japan coincides with the phase of highest Miocene sea levels in the Malay and Thai basins.

## 9.7  EAST MALESIA AND THE EASTERN PACIFIC

From the Late Eocene to the end of the Oligocene, the region of New Guinea and most of the islands of E Indonesia to the east of W Sulawesi were submerged, as indicated by the ubiquitous occurrence of carbonate facies during this time (Simanjuntak and Barber, 1996). Land areas would have occurred around the margins of the Philippine Plate, as evidenced from the presence of small sedimentary basins of probable Oligocene age containing terrestrially derived sediments in the Philippines and Halmahera. Palynological study of the Palaeogene sediments from these basins may provide a first indication of the character and diversity of the Early Tertiary Pacific flora; unfortunately, coals studied from the Palaeogene of Halmahera have so far proved barren of pollen. Hall (1996) records the first collision of the Australian and Philippine plates in the latest Oligocene, to the north of New Guinea, where tectonic activity in Irian Jaya at this time resulted in uplift, and deposition of the clastic Sirga Formation. Palynological study of this sequence yielded very low diversity pollen assemblages dominated by *Casuarina* pollen (Morley, unpublished), suggesting a restricted sclerophyllous, perhaps oceanic flora. The main phase of collision and uplift, and colonisation of this

Miocene, rain forests characterised by Sapotaceae and *Dacrydium* extended as far north as the Pearl River in S China, whereas in the earliest Middle Miocene (planktonic foraminiferal zone N8) many tropical taxa extended as far north as Japan (Figures 9.9; 9.24), where the Daijima Flora has been intensively studied for macrofossils (Tanai, 1961) and palynology (Yamanoi et al., 1980; Tsuda et al., 1984). Tropical taxa recorded here by Yamanoi et al. (1980) include several mangroves, such as Rhizophoraceae, *Excoecaria* (Euphorbiaceae), *Sonneratia* (*Florschuetzia claricolpata*), as well as the southern conifer *Dacrydium* (Yamanoi, 1974). However,

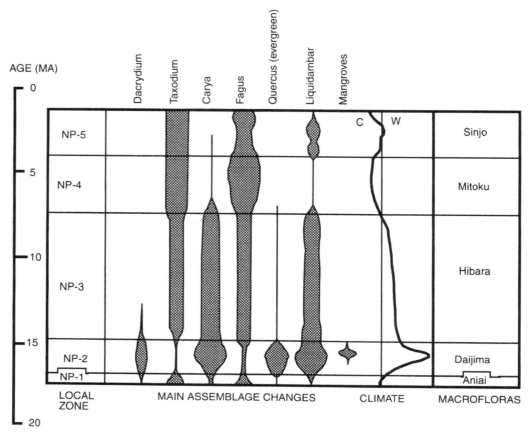

Figure 9.24   Differential representation of macrofossil elements in the Neogene of Japan (Tanai, 1972). Reproduced by permission of Elsevier Science.

region by diverse angiosperms was in the Early Miocene in Papua New Guinea, and Middle Miocene in Irian Jaya.

Some of the features of the Late Neogene flora of New Guinea are illustrated from studies of the thick deltaic sediments of the Fly River Delta by Khan (1974a,b, 1976), which show that Myrtaceae, *Casuarina*, Rubiaceae and Palmae were important components of the vegetation throughout the Late Miocene to Pleistocene, together with mangrove taxa, such as Rhizophoraceae, *Sonneratia* and possibly *Camptostemon* (Bombacaceae)[2] (Figure 9.25). His studies clearly show the dispersal of *Nothofagus* into New Guinea; initially, in the earlier Late Miocene, low frequencies within the oldest samples

examined suggest the initial phase of dispersal, perhaps when mountain ranges were of modest elevation, and the subsequent increase in abundance of this pollen type in the later Late Miocene is thought to relate to the proliferation of *Nothofagus* forests as the New Guinea mountains became more elevated. The subsequent reduction of *Nothofagus* pollen is thought to be a regional feature, and probably relates to diversification of the flora, with the gradual reduction of *Nothofagus* through competition. Khan (1976) also records increased frequencies of Proteaceae pollen in the Quaternary, a feature corroborated by unpublished regional data, suggesting immigration at a relatively late stage in this region, but his Pleistocene records

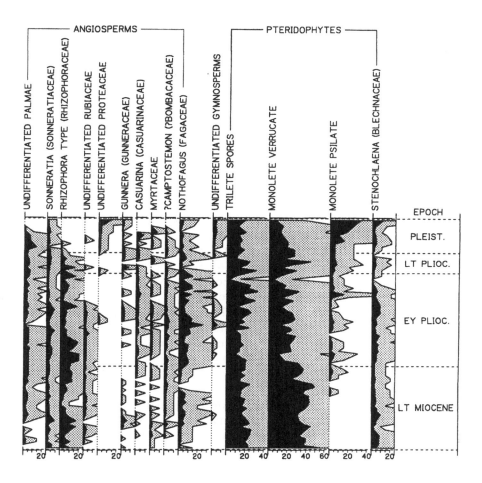

Figure 9.25    Palynological succession through the Late Miocene to Pleistocene of the Fly River Delta, stipple = ×5 exaggeration (from Khan, 1976).

of gymnosperm pollen, such as *Microcachrys* type (*Microcachryidites antarcticus*), *Phyllocladus glaucus* (*Trisaccites macropterus*) and *Araucaria* (*Araucariacites australis*) are thought to be due to reworking from the Mesozoic, since reworking is very common in the Neogene of Papua New Guinea.

Palynomorph assemblages from similar aged coals from the Huon Peninsula (Playford, 1982) differ markedly from those of Khan, and show little of the diversity expected from the East Malesian flora. These assemblages are mainly dominated by fern spores, but contain some

angiosperm grains, such as *Barringtonia*, and can perhaps best be explained in terms of pioneer or shoreline plant communities growing on ephemeral islands.

Much of the speculation which has previously been made with respect to SE Asia being the area of origin of ancient plant lineages relied heavily on the overlap of modern *Nothofagus*, and the northern hemisphere members of the family Fagaceae in New Guinea (van Steenis, 1971; Whitmore, 1981). It is now accepted that *Nothofagus* evolved in Gondwanaland during the Late Cretaceous, and that the overlap of *Nothofagus* and Fagaceae in New Guinea relates wholly to plate collision in this area, and has nothing to do with the origin of these taxa.

### Did Australian microcontinents act as 'Noah's Arks'?

During and after the time of latest Oligocene collision, it is possible that Australian affinity continental fragments, such as Banggai–Sula, Tukang–Besi/Buton, Timor or Ceram may have maintained localised emergent areas which allowed some Australian taxa to be introduced directly into E Indonesia. Possible candidates to be considered are *Eucalyptus deglupta* (Myrtaceae) and other *Eucalyptus* spp. in the Maluku and *Casuarina junghuhniana* in Nusa Tenggara and East Java. However, there is no positive geological evidence to support these suggestions.

### Oceanic floras

Leopold (1969) describes a Miocene pollen association derived from shoreline and coral reef vegetation from Eniwitok in the central Pacific. The assemblage includes pollen comparable to *Thespesia lampas* (Malvaceae), *Sophora* (Leguminosae), *Terminalia* (Combretaceae), *Morinda* and *Randia* (Rubiaceae), and also pollen of *Pisonia* (Nyctaginaceae) which today forms the dominant component of the vegetation cover of many tropical Pacific atolls. It is noteworthy that most of the pollen types recorded from this locality can be compared to modern genera and species.

Palynological studies from New Guinea do little to elucidate the occurrence of diverse Laurasian elements in the present-day East Malesian flora, which Diels (1934), Good (1962) and van Steenis (1979) thought were the result of wholesale dispersal across Wallace's Line. Clarification of the origin of these Laurasian elements comes from consideration of the vegetational history of the geologically complex island of Sulawesi, and the time of origin of the Makasar Straits.

## 9.8  WESTERN SULAWESI, AND DISPERSAL ACROSS WALLACE'S LINE

In the Middle Eocene, the southwest arm of Sulawesi formed part of a low-lying swampy area along the southeastern margin of Kalimantan, which also included most of Java and the Barito area, and an area to the north of Lombok, now to the east of Wallace's Line. This region was then characterised by a 'Laurasian' affinity flora (Morley, 1998) as noted in Section 9.4.2, with characteristic taxa such as *Durio*, *Gonystylus*, Calamoidae, *Ixonanthes*, *Ctenolophon* and Iguanurinae. Although part of the southwestern arm of Sulawesi became submerged from the Late Eocene to Middle Miocene, the presence of a continuous pollen record in clastic sediments close to this area (Lelono, unpublished) indicates that some areas remained emergent, and it is suggested that the Laurasian flora survived on emergent land masses which existed in the region of C or N Sulawesi (Figure 9.26). This flora is believed to have provided the source for many of the 'continental Laurasian' taxa present today to the east of Wallace's Line; such taxa probably dispersed eastward from Sulawesi as land masses of Maluku and New Guinea rose above sea level from about the Middle Miocene onward (Figure 9.27), negating the need to invoke large-scale dispersal across the Makasar Straits, which both biogeographical (Dransfield, 1981, 1987; van Balgooy, 1987) and geological evidence suggests has been a formidable barrier to plants, as well as animals, from the time of its origin in the Late Eocene (Morley, 1998). The latter conclusion was also reached by Truswell et al. (1987), who carefully reviewed Australian palynological data and saw minimal evidence for the invasion of elements from SE Asia at the time of the collision. The observation of Good (1962) that the present-day New Guinea flora is essentially Laurasian need not indicate that this flora dispersed wholly from the continental SE Asian region; the Early Tertiary island arcs of

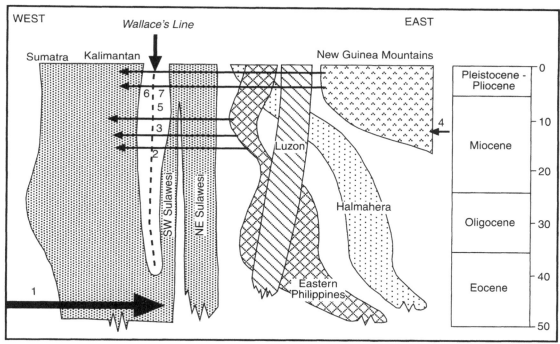

Figure 9.26   Proximity of some Sundanian and East Malesian land masses through time (data source, Hall, 1995). SW Sulawesi and Sunda were joined in the Middle Eocene and shared the same flora; whereas most islands of E Indonesia were not formed until the Middle Miocene. Halmahera and the Philippines have a much older history, and would have borne a flora of tropical aspect throughout the Tertiary. (1) Dispersals from the Indian Plate, *c*. 45 Ma; (2) Myrtaceae, *c*. 17 Ma; (3) *Camptostemon*, *c*. 14 Ma; (4) *Nothofagus*, Middle Miocene; (5) *Stenochlaena milnei*, *c*. 9.5 Ma; (6) *Podocarpus imbricatus*, *c*. 3.5 Ma; (7) *Phyllocladus*, *c*. 1 Ma. Reproduced with permission of Bakhuys Publishers.

the Philippines and Halmahera could also have been a primary source.

### Neogene dispersal events across Wallace's Line

Following the collision of the Australian Plate with Sunda several dispersal events into the Sunda region can be demonstrated by palynology (Figures 9.26; 27). Most involved taxa well adapted to dispersal, and probably took place at periods of low sea level. The nature of such events support the view that Wallace's Line has been an important barrier to plant dispersal.

The first evidence for such dispersal can be seen in the Early Miocene of the West Java Sea, between about 22 and 21 Ma (immediately following the initial collision of the Asian and Australian plates (Hall, 1996)), where there is a

succession of appearances with Australian and New Guinean affinities (Figure 9.15). The appearance of *Casuarina* was closely followed by two types of trichotomosulcate pollen comparable to that of the Australasian genus *Phormium* (Figure 9.7c), formerly within the Liliaceae, but now in its own family. This pollen type has Oligocene and Eocene records in New Zealand (Couper, 1960; Pocknall, 1982) and Australia (Stover and Partridge, 1973). A further appearance is pollen of *Korthalsia* (Palmae) at about the same time. It is noteworthy that, at this time, there were a few dispersals in the reverse direction, from SE Asia to Australia, confirming the presence of a significant dispersal path (Chapter 10). However, it is likely that this dispersal path was a filter, and not a corridor; the pollen record from

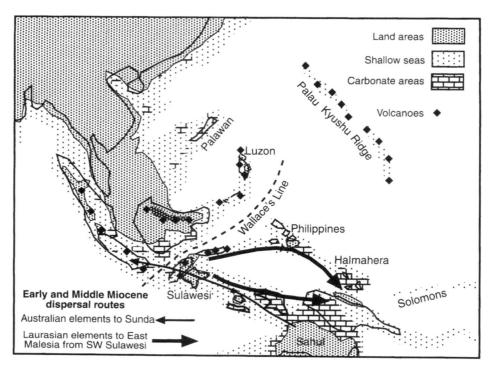

Figure 9.27  Early Miocene palaeogeographical reconstruction for SE Asia by Hall (1998a), showing position of Wallace's Line, and likely dispersal paths for Laurasian taxa from SW Sulawesi into the islands of E Indonesia as they were formed during the Middle Miocene. The dispersal path for Australian taxa into Sunda is also shown. Map base reproduced with permission of Bakhuys Publishers.

Java shows that dipterocarp pollen forms a common and morphologically varied element both below and above the incoming of Australian taxa. If this route was a dispersal corridor, surely we would find dipterocarps in Australia?

The next dispersal event occurred at approximately 17 Ma, and is marked by a distinct increase in abundance of Myrtaceae pollen. This event has been observed, and independently dated, at four widely separated localities: in the Mahakam Delta (Carter and Morley, 1996), Sarawak (Muller, 1972; Morley, unpublished), Natuna Sea (Morley, unpublished) and the Malay Basin (Azmi et al., 1995). Muller (1972) was the first to suggest that this event was due to dispersal from the east, and not to deteriorating soil conditions, as suggested by Martin (1982). It is noteworthy that the 'Australian' Myrtaceae

occurring today in the region of the Sunda Shelf are either taxa characteristic of poor, freely drained, oligotrophic soils (*Baeckea, Leptospermum, Rhodomyrtus*), of landslips and riparian fringes (*Tristaniopsis*), or of coastal regions (*Melaleuca*), suggesting that dispersal was probably confined to coastal taxa. Dispersal is likely to have taken place during a period of low sea level. The occurrence today of several of these taxa in Sundanian upper montane forests testifies to their facility to disperse over considerable distances.

The third event occurred at about 14 Ma, at which time pollen of the mangrove taxon *Camptostemon* (Bombacaceae) first appears in the mid Middle Miocene in Sarawak (Muller, 1972), and somewhat later, at about 10 Ma in the earliest Late Miocene, in the Malay Basin (Azmi et al., 1995). *Camptostemon* subsequently

became much reduced in abundance in Sundaland in the Quaternary, and is now virtually
restricted to New Guinea and the Philippines. A
further dispersal followed at about 9.5 Ma
during, or immediately after, the period of
lowest Neogene sea levels at the beginning of the
Late Miocene, when the East Malesian climbing
fern *Stenochlaena milnei* (or *S. cumingii*) (Figure
9.7g) spread rapidly and widely throughout the
Sunda region, and into Asia (Figures 9.28; 9.29),
with its earliest appearance being independently
dated within the earlier Late Miocene in Java
(Rahardjo et al., 1995), Sarawak and the
Mahakam Delta. This species spread as far
north as the Pearl River in S China, and through
Myanmar to India (Morley, 1991, 1998). *S.
milnei* became extinct in the earliest Pleistocene
throughout the whole region to the west of
Wallace's Line, and today occurs only in the
Philippines and New Guinea.

Further phases of dispersal from the east can
be observed in the record of montane pollen,
the Australasian *Podocarpus imbricatus* dispersing into Borneo and Java in the Early Pliocene,
at about 3.5 Ma, followed close to the Plio-
Pleistocene boundary by *Phyllocladus hypophyl-
lus*, into the Philippines (van der Kaas, 1991b)
and Borneo (Muller, 1966, 1972; Morley, 1978,
1998; Caratini and Tissot, 1987) (Figures 9.9;
9.17). These dispersals occurred immediately
after a shift in the movement of the Sorong
fault zone (Figure 12.1) and are thought to
relate to the uplift of mountains in the S
Philippines (van der Kaas, 1991b). They may be
envisaged as an example of filter dispersal, since
poorly dispersed *Nothofagus*, which followed
the same dispersal path to New Guinea, was
never able to disperse further west. *Podocarpus
imbricatus*, being bird dispersed, subsequently
extended its range as far north as Indochina,
where today it is widely distributed in moist
montane forests, and also occurs in lowland
*kerangas* in Cambodia (P.S. Ashton, personal
communication). Dispersal to Indochina probably occurred in the Quaternary, since its pollen
has been recorded from the Early Pleistocene of
Myanmar (Figure 9.22), and is absent from the

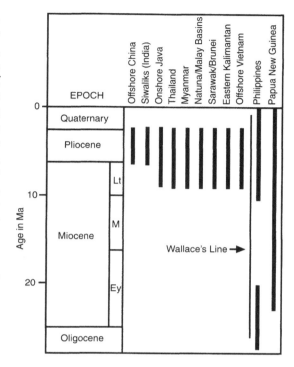

Figure 9.28 Stratigraphic range of *Stenochlaena
milnei/cumingii* spores in SE Asia (Morley, 1998).
Reproduced by permission of Bakhuys Publishers.

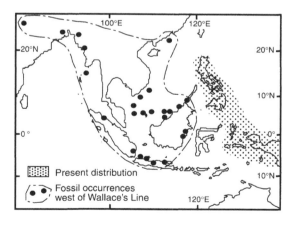

Figure 9.29 Modern distribution of *Stenochlaena
milnei* and *S. cumingii* in the Philippines and Irian Jaya
(shaded) and fossil distribution of *S. milnei/cumingii*
spores west of Wallace's Line (Morley, 1998). Reproduced by permission of Bakhuys Publishers.

Pliocene of the Malay Basin. *Phyllocladus*, however, never extended its range beyond Borneo.

The fossil records for southern hemisphere podocarps particularly clearly reflect the development of the Australian track of van Steenis (1934a,b, 1936), especially since he places the primary dispersal route through the Philippines.

Truswell et al. (1987) list 22 angiosperm taxa which they suggest may have migrated into SE Asia from Australia during the Late Cenozoic, by considering the published palynological record in both areas. Most of their taxa can be dismissed as migrants because: (a) present-day distributions are relict (e.g. *Gunnera* (Gunneraceae), Symplocaceae (widespread across northern mid-latitudes during the early Tertiary)); (b) records of earliest occurrences from SE Asia were previously unpublished (e.g. *Gardenia* (Rubiaceae), Middle Eocene (from Nanggulan, Java); Malvaceae, Early Miocene (from Mekong Basin, Vietnam); Loranthaceae, Late Eocene, becoming widespread in the Oligocene); (c) their pollen has not yet been routinely differentiated, but may well be present (e.g. *Weinmannia*, Cunoniaceae); and (d) they do not occur in Sundaland (*Sphenostemon*, Aquifoliaceae).

## 9.9  QUATERNARY VEGETATION

The history of latest Quaternary vegetation in SE Asia and New Guinea has been fully reviewed by Flenley (1979a,b, 1984), Morley and Flenley (1987) and Stuijts et al. (1988) and is accordingly just summarised here. Data from Sumatra, West Java and New Guinea suggest that climates were markedly cooler prior to the Holocene, resulting in the downward movement of montane rain forest zones (Figure 9.30), with the greatest depression at 18 000 BP. The degree of altitudinal movement at lower altitudes (e.g. Morley, 1982b; Stuijts, 1984) was less than that at higher altitudes, which has generally been attributed to different lapse rates during the last glacial maximum compared to today (Flenley, 1979a,b, 1984), although Flenley (1995) has

recently speculated that the changes in the amount of ultraviolet radiation rather than changes in lapse rates may be the cause of these differences. Walker and Flenley (1980) discussed changes in composition of Late Quaternary montane vegetation and suggested that higher altitude forests did not effectively 'migrate' up and down mountain slopes with changing temperatures, but were freshly created with each climatic amelioration, each time recruiting taxa from lower altitude forests. Such a process would also be consistent with the suggestion that vegetation zonation on tropical mountains is primarily edaphic (P.S. Ashton, personal communication), rather than relating to temperature alone.

The first low latitude estimates of temperature depression at sea level were necessarily conservative, being influenced by palaeotemperature data for 18 000 BP by CLIMAP (1976), but the CLIMAP temperature model is now being strongly contested (Flenley, 1997), and sea level temperatures of the order of 4°C below those of the present day are currently viewed as more probable. In SE Asia, however, loss of lowland rain forest acreage at these times through temperature depression would have been more than compensated by the expansion of rain forests onto the continental shelves.

The palynological analyses mentioned above suggested that there was little evidence for drier climates prior to the Holocene in those areas, although the widespread occurrence of drier climates during 'glacial' periods has been proposed for many years on the basis of plant distributions (van Steenis, 1939, 1961), primates (Brandon-Jones, 1996), vertebrate fossils (Medway, 1972) and geomorphology (Verstappen, 1973, 1975). The first direct evidence for drier Pleistocene climates came from pollen evidence from Middle Pleistocene lake muds from the Kelang Valley in Malaysia, which contain abundant pollen of *Pinus*, Gramineae and Compositae (Morley and Flenley, 1987; Morley, 1998), suggesting a *Pinus* savanna (Figure 9.31). Unfortunately, the outcrop at

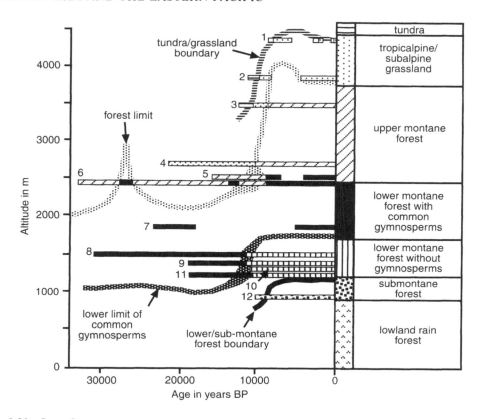

Figure 9.30   Late Quaternary vegetational history of the New Guinea Highlands, Sumatra and West Java, from palynological evidence (modified from Morley and Flenley, 1987). Horizontal numbered lines reflect pollen profiles, plotted at their representative altitudes, their length reflecting the time interval represented, in radiocarbon years. 1 = Summit Pool, Mt Wilhelm, New Guinea; 2 = Brass Tarn, Mt Wilhelm; 3 = Imbuka Swamp, Mt Wilhelm; 4 = Komanimambuno Mire, Wabag area, New Guinea; 5 = Lake Inim, Wabag area; 6 = Sirunki, Mt Hagen, New Guinea; 7 = Draepi Swamp, Mt Hagen; 8 = Danau Di-Atas, Sumatra; 9 = Pea Sim-Sim, Sumatra; 10 = Rawa Sipingan, Sumatra; 11 = Bayongrong, West Java; 12 = Danau Padang, Sumatra.

this tin mine locality was destroyed by dredging shortly after it was exposed. This occurrence demonstrates that open savanna of a type now found only in Thailand extended well into the Malay Peninsula during the Middle Pleistocene, perhaps forming the 'savanna corridor' proposed by Medway (1972) to account for the widespread occurrence of fossils of Asian herbivorous mammals from the Pliocene and Early Pleistocene of Java.

Further evidence for former drier 'glacial' climates is forthcoming from recent studies of deep-sea cores from south of Nusa Tenggara and offshore Halmahera in Indonesia by van der Kaas (1991a) and from Bandung Lake in Java by van der Kaas and Dam (1995). The Lombok Ridge core was strategically collected through deep-marine sediments in which 'glacial' low sea level and 'interglacial' high sea level lithologies were more or less equally represented (Figure 9.32). The 9 m core penetrated sediments deposited during the three last glacials, and the last two interglacial periods. Holocene and interglacial sediments contain abundant fern spores, and intermediate frequencies of Gramineae pollen, whereas glacial

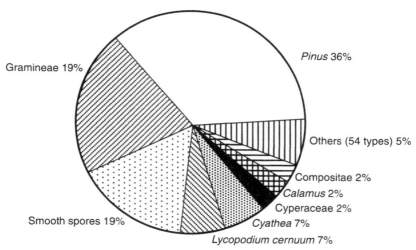

Figure 9.31  Percentage representation of the main palynomorph types from sample 3/15, from a probable mid-Pleistocene site close to Subang Airport, Malay Peninsula (Morley, 1998). Reproduced by permission of Bakhuys Publishers.

periods are characterised by abundant Gramineae and the low representation of spores, clearly indicating drier climates, and corresponding to periods of expansion of savanna vegetation which coincided with glacial periods.

Markedly drier climates in West Java were suggested for the last glacial period in the region of Bandung Lake, where freshwater swamp forests of the last interglacial gave way to grass-dominated swamps. The presence of common *Ulmus lanceifolia* pollen within this section also suggests a much drier climate, such as that currently experienced in East Java. This raises the suggestion that the evidence for a moist 'glacial' from Bayongrong by Stuijts (1984) may reflect a local moist refuge, and that drier climates may have been more the rule. A long palynological record from the Misador Well, in the Mahakam Delta, spanning the entire Quaternary (Caratini and Tissot, 1987), showed a predominance throughout of pollen indicative of wet conditions, such as peat swamp pollen, with only the sporadic occurrence of Gramineae pollen indicative of dry climates. Sequence stratigraphic studies of the Mahakam Delta (Debec and Allen, 1996), however, show that in the area of the current subaerial delta there is a predominance of

highstand (high sea level, 'interglacial') sediments. Lowstand (low sea level, 'glacial') sediments would have been deposited at more distal localities and these would not have been properly sampled by the Misador core. For this reason, the dominance of evidence for wet climates from the Misador section cannot be used as evidence for continually moist conditions in E Kalimantan, but simply the predominance of wet climates during times of high sea level 'interglacial' periods.

### Pleistocene refuges

Although there is clear evidence from SE Asia for the expansion of dry climates during Pleistocene glacial maxima, few attempts have been made to identify Pleistocene refugia. Brandon-Jones (1996) proposed two phases of regional deforestation, coinciding with the last two glacial maxima, to explain present-day primate distributions. The first encompassed virtually all of Sundaland, whereas the second left forested refugia in N Sumatra, NW Borneo and West Java. Such a scenario would clearly be incompatible with present-day plant distributions and Late Quaternary palynological data. The presence of inter-riverain endemism,

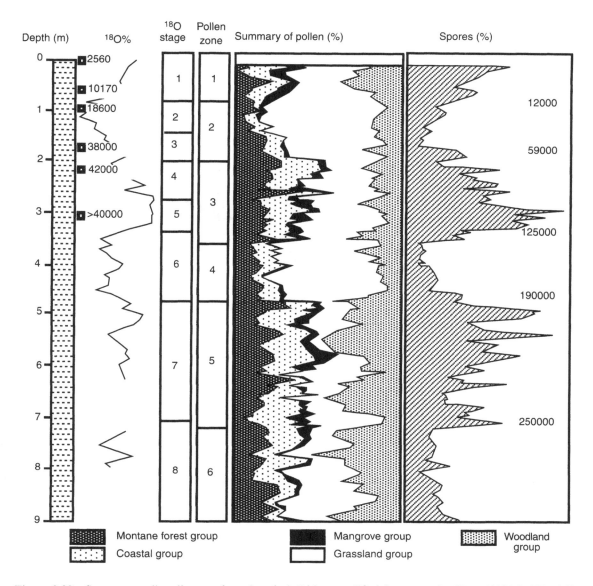

Figure 9.32  Summary pollen diagram from Lombok Ridge, modified from van der Kaas (1991a). 'Glacial' climates, coinciding with oxygen isotope stages 2+3, 6 and 8, are characterised by abundant Gramineae pollen, but low representation of pollen of coastal plants and mangroves, and fern spores, reflecting periods of widespread savanna vegetation. 'Interglacial' climates, coinciding with oxygen isotope stages 4+5 and 7, are characterised by abundant pteridophyte spores, and increased pollen of coastal plants and mangroves, but greatly reduced frequencies of Gramineae pollen, reflecting periods of forest and mangrove swamp expansion during periods of wetter climates. Dates to left of diagram are radiocarbon dates, whereas those to the right refer to oxygen isotope stage boundaries.

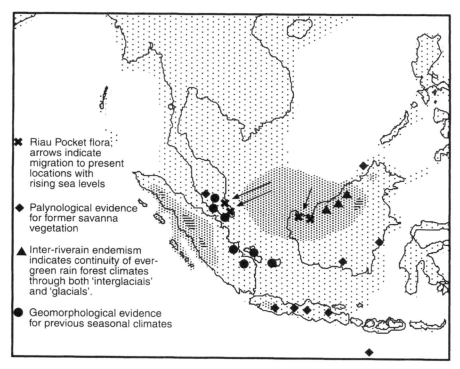

Figure 9.33    Climate map for SE Asia, 18 000 years BP, based on the assumption that evidence for a seasonal climate for an unspecified Quaternary 'glacial' interval can be applied to all glacial intervals, and hence to the last glacial maximum. Based on (a) geomorphological evidence (landforms, laterites, caliche deposits); (b) palynological evidence for savanna; and (c) biogeographical evidence for species-continuity. Arrows indicate presumed dispersal paths with rising sea levels of coastal taxa of the 'Riau Pocket' of Corner (1940). Lined stipple = montane rain forest; dark stipple = lowland rain forest

particularly among dipterocarps, in NW Borneo, coupled with very high species-richness (Ashton, 1972), infers continuity of lowland evergreen rain forests on an evolutionary time scale, and Quaternary studies from Sumatra and westernmost Java suggest moist climates throughout the last glacial maximum. The flora of the 'Riau Pocket' of Corner (1978) also suggests continuity of moist climates in coastal regions from S Malay Peninsula to NW Borneo.

A first approximation to a vegetation map for the last glacial maximum is presented in Figure 9.33, which is based on palynological and geomorphological data as well as the high species diversity and endemism in NW Borneo, relative to SE Borneo and Sumatra. The SE Asian region differs from the other two rain forest

centres in lying close to, or below, present-day sea level, a situation which has continued approximately since the basal Miocene. During periods of low sea level, the exposed land area of SE Asia increase substantially, and it is likely that rain forested areas contracted less here than in other tropical areas. In the SE Asian region, the refuge theory needs to be considered from a different viewpoint, with changing distributions of rain forests being determined not only by climate (although this certainly remains important), but also from the point of view of the successive drowning and re-exposure of the region's continental shelves. Also, the time scale for the creation of refugia needs to be considered not so much on a Quaternary time scale, but over the whole of the Neogene.

Glimpses of the mode of evolution of SE Asian vegetation are forthcoming from consideration of the palynomorph record from Neogene sediments from SE Asian depositional basins, where phases of sea level stillstand are reflected by periods of deposition of fluvial and deltaic sediments, whereas phases of rising sea levels are frequently represented by widespread shallow marine mudstones. Many such sea level oscillations are recorded through the Neogene, and some of these relate to global sea level changes. Palynomorph assemblages generally demonstrate considerable uniformity between successive phases of rising sea levels, but marked assemblage changes coincide with shortlived transgressive marine horizons. Parallel patterns of change can be seen in assemblages derived from mangroves, from freshwater swamps, and also of many indeterminate types which currently cannot be matched with extant taxa. The inference to be drawn from this is that vegetation types on the previously submerged shelves were re-created, with taxa being recruited from those areas remaining vegetated at the time of maximum transgession, with each successive fall in sea level. The Pleistocene Refuge theory has been used to infer that speciation increased during the Quaternary, with the expansion and retraction of rain forest taxa from their Pleistocene refuges. Evidence from Neogene palynomorph assemblages, however, suggests that diversity has increased more or less uniformly through the Neogene (Figure 9.13), and that the successive flooding and recolonisation of the continental shelves may have been as important a factor in speciation as expansion and contraction of rain forests as a result of climatic change.

There is little historical data from the island of New Guinea which might infer the presence of refugia. However, a recent plant collecting programme in the Bird's Neck area of Irian Jaya suggests levels of species-richness in that area are comparable to the richest areas of NW Borneo or even the lower flanks of the Andes in South America (Sands et al., 1998). This observation is particularly noteworthy since, whereas the latter two regions have very long geological

histories, the Bird's Neck area of Irian Jaya became established as a land area only during the Middle Miocene, some 14 Ma ago (Simandjuntuk and Barber, 1996), suggesting that 14 Ma is sufficient time for rain forest floras to attain their highest levels of species-diversity.

## 9.10  MANGROVE ORIGINS AND EVOLUTION

The tropical Far East is noteworthy in having the most floristically diverse mangrove communities (Tomlinson, 1986), the successive appearance through time of pollen of mangrove taxa from the Late Cretaceous onwards being brought to attention by Muller (1964, 1972) and Thanikaimoni (1987) and summarised in Figure 9.34. Although Muller's records clearly demonstrate the stratigraphic ranges of pollen types now produced by mangrove plants, whether all of these were produced by mangroves throughout their history is debatable. Also, the fossil record provides little evidence to suggest that mangrove lineages originated in this area, although there is clear evidence for their diversification. For instance, the oldest records of *Nypa* pollen are from the Maastrichtian of Africa, India and South America, the oldest Rhizophoraceae fossils are fruits of *Ceriops* and *Palaeobruguiera* from the Early Eocene London Clay (Collinson, 1983), and the oldest pollen records are from the Late Eocene of South America (Germeraad et al., 1968) and SE Asia (Morley, in press). The following examples illustrate that the actual history of several mangrove taxa which were previously considered to be of SE Asian origin was quite different to that suggested from present-day biogeography.

### *Rhizophoraceae*

As noted in Section 2.5, Figure 2.16, Rhizophoraceae exhibit their greatest diversity in SE Asian mangroves (*Rhizophora*, *Bruguiera*, *Kandelia* and *Ceriops* with 10 species), compared to

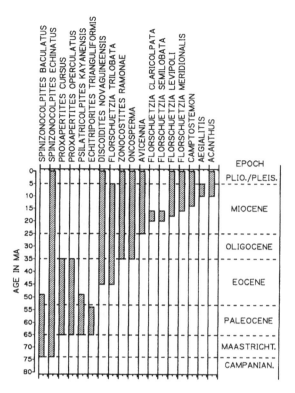

Figure 9.34 Stratigraphic ranges of main pollen types now produced by mangroves (from Thanikaimoni (1987), with modifications).

one genus (*Rhizophora*) with three species each in W Africa and South America. The current distribution of Rhizophoraceae (Figure 9.35), and fossil record for *Rhizophora* type pollen and macrofossils (Figure 9.36), are enigmatic. The W African species of *Rhizophora* are closely related to those from South America, and since *Rhizophora* type pollen is recorded in W Africa only from the basal Miocene, dispersal to W Africa from South America is generally envisaged, where the oldest records are Late Eocene. However, the E African representatives show closest affinities to SE Asia, leading van Steenis (1962b) to conclude that the South American/ W African representatives dispersed across the Pacific, and E African species dispersed across the Indian Ocean from a centre of origin in SE Asia. This scenario assumes their origin in

SE Asia, where the oldest fossils are Late Eocene. Bearing in mind the Early Eocene *Palaeobruguiera* and *Ceriops* fossils from the London Clay, a Tethyan centre of origin for the mangrove representatives of Rhizophoraceae is considered more probable.

### Sonneratia *and its lythraceous precursors*

*Sonneratia* is a genus of five species, confined to mangroves in the eastern tropics and E Africa, and is generally placed in its own family, Sonneratiaceae, which is closely allied to Lythraceae. The pollen record of *Sonneratia* (Figure 9.37) and its precursors and allies is of great interest to students of evolution, since its pollen is commonly recorded through many sedimentary basins in the region and elsewhere (being referred to the form-genus *Florschuetzia*), and all of its extant species can be differentiated on pollen characters (Muller, 1969) and all have a fossil record (Morley, 1991). Also, hybridisation can be recognised in modern populations on the basis of transitional characters between the pollen types (Muller and Hui-Lui, 1966), and similar patterns of variation seen in Early Miocene *Florschuetzia* spp. may be interpretable in a similar manner. Furthermore, as noted above, fossil types are recorded which are clearly derived from ancestral species, and demonstrate that *Sonneratia* evolved from lythraceous ancestors allied to *Lagerstroemia* (Germeraad et al., 1968; Muller, 1978, 1981) and possibly *Duabanga* (Sonneratiaceae). The earliest records of *F. trilobata* and *Lagerstroemia* type pollen occur together in the Middle Eocene of the Nanggulan Formation in Central Java together with transitional forms (Morley, unpublished), possibly reflecting the initial phase of differentiation of this lineage. However, this need not be taken as evidence of the area of *origin* for this taxon, since its pollen has also been recorded in the Late Eocene of Assam (Handique, 1993) and the mid-Tertiary of the Red Sea and Nile Delta (Morley, unpublished). Taking into account sonneratiaceous fossil woods from the Middle Eocene of N Africa (Louvet, 1975; Boureau et

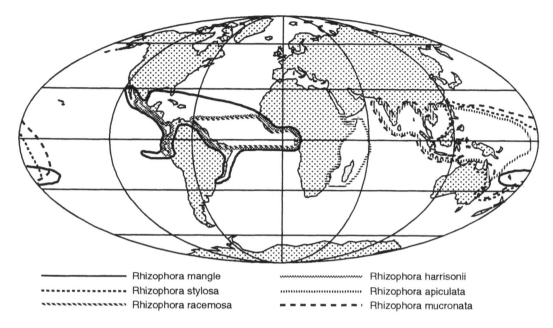

Figure 9.35   Present-day distribution of species of *Rhizophora* (after van Steenis, 1962b in Muller and Caratini, 1977).

al., 1983), and intertrappean fossils from India (Bande, 1992), a Tethyan rather than SE Asian origin for the parent plants of *Florschuetzia trilobata* pollen is most likely (cf. Muller, 1978).

Although *Sonneratia* spp. are currently restricted to brackish, or at least, coastal habitats, this was probably not the case for their immediate precursors. From the Middle Eocene to Early Miocene, *Florschuetzia trilobata* and pollen comparable to *Lagerstroemia* are common in wholly freshwater lacustrine sequences, and even in intermontane basins, such as Ombilin in C Sumatra, and S Thailand, where they clearly had nothing to do with mangroves, although, in other instances, a clear association between *Florschuetzia trilobata* vars and other mangrove pollen can sometimes be demonstrated. It appears probable that in the mid-Tertiary, the precursors to the genus *Sonneratia* grew in both freshwater and brackish environments (possibly involving several species) and it is suggested that it was their adaptation to (probably seasonal) freshwater

swamps which ultimately led to adaptation to the mangrove habitat. It was not until the latter part of the Early and Middle Miocene that obligate mangrove Sonneratiaceae evolved with the appearance of the pollen of *Sonneratia caseolaris* (Figure 9.7h) at about 19 Ma and *S. alba* shortly afterward in the earliest Middle Miocene (or slightly earlier) at 16 Ma. *Sonneratia caseolaris* is currently a species of low salinity mangroves, and the fossil record suggests that this has been the case throughout its history, whereas the later *Sonneratia alba* prefers more saline habitats and is now the most widespread species. The adaptational trend within *Sonneratia* has therefore been to successively greater tolerance of salt, and frequency of inundation.

The remaining three *Sonneratia* species, *S. ovata*, *S. apetala* and *S. griffithii*, occur commonly today in the mangroves of Bangladesh and Myanmar, where they largely replace the previously discussed species (Dudley-Stamp and Lord, 1923). All three species have a fossil record (Morley, 1991). The *S. griffithii*

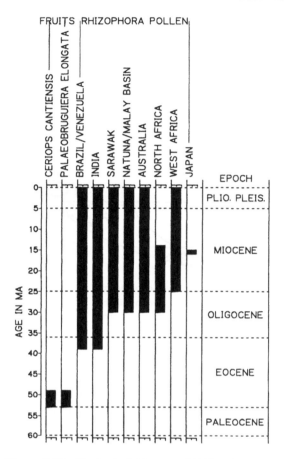

Figure 9.36   Geological history of Rhizophoraceae macrofossils and pollen.

type shows several morphological similarities with *Florschuetzia trilobata*, and it is possible that the precursor of this species was one of the producers of *F. trilobata* (Morley, 1991). Pollen of the *Sonneratia ovata* and *S. apetala* types both appear from the basal Pliocene onwards in the region of the Bay of Bengal (Figure 9.22).

There are many variants within the *Florschuetzia* group, some of which are informally referred to as *F. 'ovalis'* (Morley, unpublished) which are closely allied to *F. trilobata*, and these are currently undescribed, making it difficult for stratigraphic palynologists to consistently name the stratigraphically useful species. They include both colporate and porate specimens, in roughly equal proportions, and are intermediate between Sonneratiaceae and Lythraceae. Their greatest diversity is seen in the Early to Middle Miocene, and may relate to increased floristic diversity, and/or hybridisation at this time. There is a clear trend between morphological diversity and latitude, since they attain their greatest diversity between 10° and 15°N, and show most variation from the Natuna Sea to Vietnam. The full morphological variety within this group needs to be carefully documented in order to further clarify evolutionary history of this remarkable lineage, and at the same time allow improvement in the precision with which *Florschuetzia* pollen can be used for stratigraphic correlation.

A further remarkable episode with respect to the latter group concerns the water chestnut *Trapa* (Trapaceae), which is usually placed in

Figure 9.37   (A) Suggested geological history of sonneratioid and related taxa. Following initial radiation in Tethys, ancestral lythraceoid/sonneratioid freshwater swamp/mangrove plants developed in two separate lineages following dispersal across the Atlantic in the Late Eocene. The Old World lineage underwent extensive diversification in the eastern tropics, particularly in the Early Miocene with the evolution of *Sonneratia*, which later diversified in the region of the Bay of Bengal, but became extinct in the western Tethys with Neogene climatic deterioration. The Neotropical lineage dispersed to W Africa during the Early Miocene, and underwent diversification comparable to that seen in *Sonneratia*, but this lineage became extinct in W Africa at the end of the Middle Miocene, and coastal species became extinct in South America in the Pliocene. This clade is represented in South America today by the lythraceous trees *Lafoensia* and *Diplusodon*.

Only a few of the SE Asian pollen types which reflect this history are described in the literature. A more complete sketch of the extent of variation is illustrated in (B). The *Florschuetzia trilobata* and *F. 'ovalis'* groups show additional substantial variation; several variants within these groups are identical to *Verrutricolporites laevigatus* from W Africa. Similarly, some variants of *F. semilobata* are identical to the *V. rotundiporus* group from W Africa.

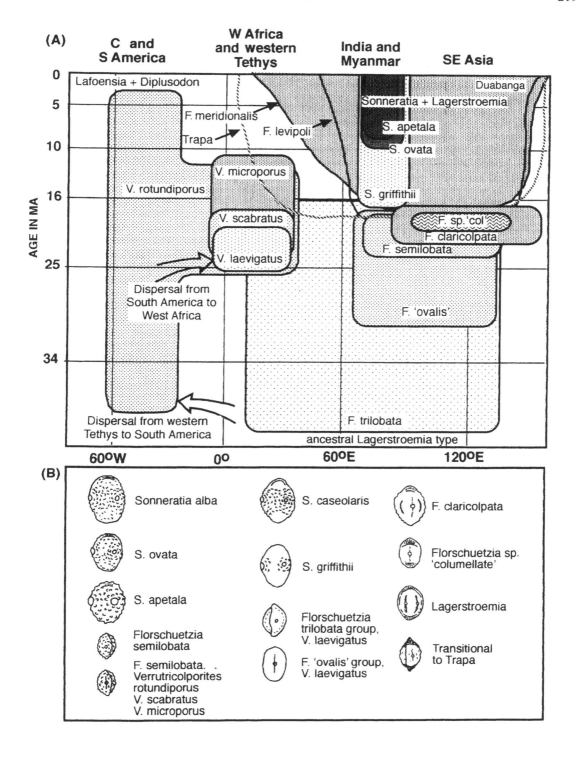

the Lythrales. *Trapa* has an extensive pollen record through the Miocene of China, where it is termed *Sporotrapoides* (e.g. Song et al., 1981), and in the Vietnam region transitional forms can be seen between *Sporotrapoides* and undescribed forms of *Florschuetzia* with strongly thickened, and columellate polar caps, suggesting a common derivation.

The *Florschuetzia* story becomes more complex when the African and South American Tertiary pollen record is taken into consideration, where a group of pollen types similar to those in *Florschuetzia*, but referred to the genus *Verrutricolporites*, has been described by Germeraad et al. (1968) and Legoux (1978). Germeraad et al. (1968) originally attributed these to the lythraceous South American genus *Crenea*, although this affinity was disputed by Graham and Graham (1971). Muller (1981) subsequently confirmed its affinity to the Lythraceae, but accepted that identification with *Crenea* was in doubt. A more plausible explanation is for derivation from an extinct lineage of coastal plants allied to a parent taxon of *Florschuetzia trilobata*, which dispersed to South America from the region of Tethys in the Late Eocene, and to W Africa from South America in the Early Miocene (following the same route as *Rhizophora*). The African *Verrutricolporites* group of pollen exhibit a similar style of temporal variation to that seen in *Florschuetzia* (Figure 7.6) and is described in detail in Chapter 7, and Muller (1981) suggested that similar variation occurred in South America, although this has not yet been properly confirmed by others. The dispersal of this clade to South America in the Early Tertiary, and subsequent extinction of ancestral forms, would also explain the present-day occurrence of other genera in that area which possess a similar pollen type to those in *Sonneratia*, such as *Lafoensia* and *Diplusodon*.

### Other mangroves

The Paleocene occurrence of *Discoidites borneensis* was considered by Muller (1964) to mark the evolutionary appearance of the backmangrove

genus *Brownlowia*. However, this need not be the case for, within the Paleocene, this pollen type is more likely to have been derived from plants growing in lake margin vegetation and, as with *Sonneratia*, the precursors of the mangrove representatives of *Brownlowia* were probably trees of freshwater swamps. The *Brownlowia* pollen type is also produced by several upland genera, such as *Pentace* and *Jarandersonia*, and a mangrove origin for the *Brownlowia* pollen type can only be assumed if it is associated with pollen of other mangroves. It is not until the Middle Eocene that a clear association is seen between *Discoidites* pollen spectra and that of other, more definitive mangroves, or with marine microfossils such as foraminifera. In a similar manner, *Oncosperma*, which has both brackish and upland representatives, is first recorded in SE Asia in the Early Oligocene, in freshwater deposits; the oldest definitely brackish sections bearing this pollen type are Early Miocene.

## 9.11   SUMMARY

The character of latest Cretaceous/earliest Tertiary vegetation in SE Asia remains poorly understood. Current evidence suggests that Palmae were important in the earliest Tertiary, but except for nypoid palms in mangroves, the the taxa present were very different from those of the Palmae Province in Africa and South America and also differed from modern SE Asian genera, and, on the basis of these, and dicotyledonous pollen, the Sunda region is placed in a distinct palaeogeographical subprovince. At this time, montane vegetation was well developed and much more extensive than in other low latitude regions, and New Guinea bore a sclerophyllous vegetation of Australian affinity. There is no evidence for a land connection between Australia and Sunda, as has been variously proposed in the past, nor is there a need for such a connection; most disjunct distributions of taxa which occur in both Australia and SE Asia can be explained by reference to the collision of the Gondwanan Indian Plate with Asia.

Diverse, megathermal vegetation became established through much of the SE Asian region in the Middle and Late Eocene. The high diversity of this vegetation was due in part to the wet climate at this time, but also to wholesale dispersal from the Indian subcontinent, following its collision with Asia in the Middle Eocene.

Laurasian elements to the east of Wallace's Line probably dispersed from SW Sulawesi, which already bore a rich Laurasian flora prior to the formation of the Makasar Straits in the Late Eocene. There is no need to invoke wholesale dispersal of such taxa across Wallace's Line in the Neogene.

It is likely that the Pacific island chains bore distinct tropical floras throughout the Early Tertiary, probably of Laurasian affinity, since southern hemisphere land masses at this time lay far to the south. These floras may also have contributed elements to the present-day East Malesian flora.

Global climatic deterioration at the end of the Eocene, coinciding with tectonic restructuring, resulted in a marked change in the flora and vegetation throughout the region, and a major retraction in range of megathermal rain forests, with many extinctions. Lowland rain forests were largely replaced during the Oligocene and earliest Miocene by seasonal climate (monsoonal) vegetation types, and with cooler climates, montane forests, with frost-tolerant conifers, became common in upland areas. Evergreen rain forests were largely restricted to Myanmar and Assam in India, but refuges may also have been present in Sumatra and probably within upland regions. At this time, much of the region also underwent extensive subsidence, resulting in the markedly reduced representation of high altitude terrain, and reduced niches for montane vegetation.

From the Oligocene to Pleistocene, the flora went through a phase of uninterrupted diversification during which time dipterocarps became an important component of the vegetation.

During the latter part of the Early and Middle Miocene, the widespread expansion of more moist climates resulted in the expansion of rain forests across most of the region. The latitudinal distribution of rain forests at any one time was related closely to sea levels, with their greatest expansion during periods of highest sea levels, at which time global climates were at their warmest, culminating with their greatest expansion as far north as Japan when sea levels were at their highest during the earliest Middle Miocene (about 16 Ma). During periods of low sea levels, there was a corresponding expansion of vegetation adapted to seasonal climates.

Peat swamp floras underwent modernisation during the Middle Miocene. *Kerapah* and watershed peats were probably more widespread during the Miocene than at present, and mangrove peats were widespread during periods of high sea levels and warmer climates. The complex catena seen in present-day basinal peats in Sarawak and Brunei probably became established only after the evolution of *Shorea albida* as a peat swamp tree.

The presence of a continuous land connection between SE Asia and mid-latitude Asia since the earliest Tertiary allowed elements of Early Tertiary northern hemisphere megathermal forests to find refuge in the lower montane forests of SE Asia following mid-Tertiary global climatic deterioration in a manner which has no parallel in other regions. There is no need to invoke SE or E Asia as a major area of radiation of primitive angiosperms simply because they are presently well represented in SE Asian rain forests.

Instances of dispersal from the east, resulting from collision of the Australian and Asian plates at the end of the Oligocene, are recorded at about 22 Ma, and then at 17, 14, 9.5 and 3.5 Ma. Dispersal probably took place at periods of low sea level. Dispersal routes were 'filters' at 22 Ma and 3.5 Ma, whereas other dispersal events are better envisaged as examples of sweepstake (chance) dispersal.

In the Late Miocene, although there were at least two periods with the widespread representation of rain forests, dry climates, coinciding with periods of marked sea level lowstand, were intermittently widespread.

During the Pliocene and Quaternary, following a regional phase of tectonic adjustment, several montane gymnosperms of Australian affinity were able to disperse from New Guinea, via the Philippines into Borneo, with *Podocarpus imbricatus* migrating to Indochina in the Quaternary.

During the Pliocene, moist climates were widespread within Kalimantan, but dry savanna vegetation became extensively established in the region of Java, with the development of the Javanese monsoon climate, which probably related to the northward drift of Australia into the southern hemisphere subtropical high pressure belt coupled with Late Neogene global climate deterioration. Savanna vegetation also became widespread in Myanmar during the Pleistocene.

During the Quaternary, evidence from deep-sea cores clearly emphasises that 'glacial' stages were characterised by dry savannas with abundant Gramineae, whereas 'interglacial' stages corresponded with the expansion of more moist climates and associated vegetation types. Moist climates probably persisted during 'glacial' intervals to the north of Kalimantan, and in W Sumatra and, together with widespread areas of the Sunda Shelf which are currently submerged, probably formed the glacial rain forest 'refuges' in the SE Asian region. Quaternary studies from Sumatra and New Guinea show that much cooler climates prevailed during the last glacial stage.

It is suggested that diversification of the SE Asian flora became accentuated as a result of the successive reformation of lowland vegetation on the continental shelves during periods of low sea level, although the successive expansion and retraction of rain forests as a result of climatic change may have had some effect on speciation. It is likely that diversification resulting from the successive recolonisation of the continental shelves would have taken place over the whole of the Neogene, rather than being most pronounced during the Quaternary, as propounded by the refuge theory.

The SE Asian region is not visualised as the primary centre of radiation of mangroves, which probably originated along the shores of Tethys during the Early Tertiary. The higher diversity of SE Asian mangroves is due largely to their extinction in other tropical regions during the course of the later Tertiary. *Sonneratia* shows a clear diversity increase during the later Tertiary, but the genus may have originated outside the region. During the Early Tertiary, the parent plants of several pollen types presently produced by mangrove plants are thought to have been produced by vegetation growing on freshwater swamps, or may possibly have been facultive mangroves.

## NOTES

1  The records of *Pinus*, *Cathaya*, *Abies*, *Picea* and *Platycarya* from DSDP 262 in the Timor Trench (Zaklinskaya, 1978) are believed to be laboratory contaminants.
2  Muller (1981) suggests that *Malvacearumpollis* sp. of Khan (1974a) may be *Camptostemon* pollen.

# CHAPTER 10

# Australasia

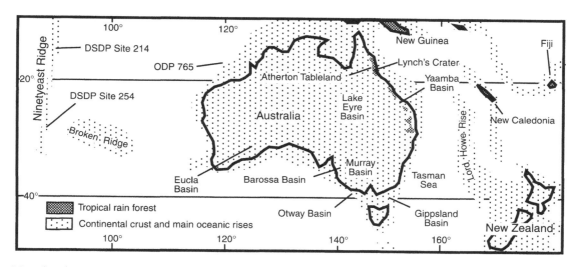

Map showing present-day Australian rain forest distributions (after Richards, 1996), and locations mentioned in the text.

## 10.1  INTRODUCTION

Palaeobotany has turned Australian biogeography upside-down. Only 30 years ago, following the classical views of Hooker (1860), the Australian flora was visualised as having three principal elements: an autochthonous Australian element, characteristic of sclerophyll and woodland, and two allochthonous elements, the Indomalayan, present in the northeastern tropical and subtropical rain forests, invading from the north, via New Guinea, and an Antarctic element in temperate forests and montane areas, invading from the south (Burbridge, 1960). Today, as a result of both palaeobotanical and palynological studies pioneered by Isabel Cookson, our view is reversed; the rain forest element is mostly autochthonous, with a long Tertiary and Late Cretaceous history, with the characteristically Australian sclerophyll element *evolving from rain forest ancestors*. The Antarctic element is also autochthonous, and was also much more widely distributed when the Australian Plate lay south of its present position, firmly attached to Antarctica. Dispersals from the north, from Sunda via New Guinea, have probably been minimal, since plate tectonic reconstructions show that Australia and SE Asia were widely separated until the later part of the Tertiary, although because Early Tertiary and Cretaceous palaeobotanical data for N Australia and neighbouring SE Asia are virtually non-existent, many biogeographers continue to imagine early dispersal routes from the north, but without supporting direct evidence.

Today, the Tertiary vegetational history of Australia and New Zealand is probably better understood than anywhere else (e.g. Smith, 1982; Hill, 1994a), perhaps due to the need to have a historical explanation for the flora of a region which has evolved in greater isolation than any other. Another factor is that the palynological record within the region has been of great value in deciphering the stratigraphic record for the offshore petroleum industry, and this has generated a huge database which has not remained in its entirety in oil company files. It is also noteworthy as an area where nomenclatural problems in palaeobotany are minimal (Hill, 1994b), and where a recent successful attempt has been made to base classification of one of the southern hemisphere's most characteristic genera, *Nothofagus* (Fagaceae), soundly on an equal combination of palaeo- and actuobotanical data (Hill and Read, 1991).

The picture emerging from Australian palaeobotanical studies is a fascinating one, and reflects the evolution of a flora which has been carried northward through several climatic zones as a result of its Tertiary drift from Antarctica, at the same time as global climates have switched from 'greenhouse' to 'icehouse' mode. Any discourse on this region must also attempt to explain why the concentration of primitive angiosperms in Australian rain forests, and in the region surrounding the Coral Sea, is the highest in the world (Barlow and Hyland, 1988), with eight of the fourteen families[1] considered by Takhtajan (1969) as the most primitive, occurring in NE Australia.

This chapter also reviews evidence for tropical rain forests in New Zealand and also the Ninetyeast Ridge in the Indian Ocean, which consisted of a string of oceanic islands during parts of the Tertiary. The history of the development of the New Guinea flora is mainly discussed in Chapter 9, and, since there is no fossil record for those Pacific islands which bear primitive angiosperms, such as New Caledonia

and Fiji, speculations on their history will be deferred until Chapter 13.

## 10.2  TECTONIC SETTING

The Australian Plate lay close to Antarctica throughout the Cretaceous. Rifting along Australia's southern margin began about 110 Ma, and a tongue of oceanic crust, forming the proto-Southern Ocean, extended almost as far east as Tasmania by the Turonian (92–89 Ma) (Stephens, 1989; Wilford and Brown, 1994), although at this time the Australian mainland plus Tasmania and Antarctica remained closely juxtaposed (Figure 10.1a). Between Turonian and end Cretaceous times, sea-floor spreading resulted in the formation of open ocean in the Tasman Sea, isolating New Zealand and New Caledonia from the remainder of Gondwana (Stephens, 1989), and at about the same time, sea-floor spreading between NE Australia and E New Guinea resulted in the formation of the Coral Sea, which reached its present form by the end of the Paleocene (66–54 Ma).

Thus at the beginning of the Tertiary, the Australian mainland still lay in a southerly latitude, between about 60 and 40°S (Figure 10.1b). New Zealand formed part of a more extensive land mass which incorporated the Campbell Plateau (now largely submerged) and New Caledonia (although according to Wilford and Brown (1994), direct evidence for the latter connection is lacking), and was already separated from Australia by the Tasman Sea. As mentioned in Section 9.3, Fiji formed part of the Gondwanan Outer Melanesian Arc, which formed along the collision zone between the Australian and Pacific plates (Figure 9.2). To the south, the timing of separation from Antarctica remains unclear, but was probably during the Early Tertiary.

At about 44 Ma, in the Middle Eocene (49–39 Ma), the spreading rate between Australia and Antarctica increased, and by 38 Ma a deep marine strait had formed between Tasmania and Antarctica (Kennett, 1977, 1980). From

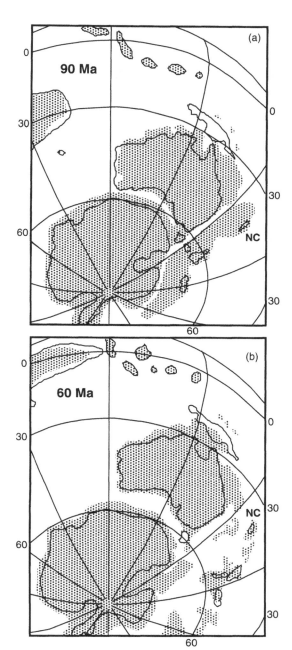

Figure 10.1  Palaeogeographic reconstruction showing land areas (stippled) for (a) 90 Ma (Turonian) and (b) 60 Ma (Paleocene). From Wilford and Brown (1994). Note position of New Caledonia (NC). Reproduced by permission of Cambridge University Press.

this time onward, the Australian Plate drifted northward to its present position, with its leading edge eventually colliding with the Pacific, Philippine and Sunda plates. The result of these collisions was the formation of New Guinea, and the formation of the islands of the Banda Arcs in Indonesia (discussed in detail in Section 9.7). New Zealand, however, which had drifted rapidly northward during the latest Cretaceous and earliest Tertiary, drifted very little from the Eocene onward.

During the early Tertiary, islands also became intermittently established along the Ninetyeast Ridge (see map), a north–south trending seamount chain in the Indian Ocean (now wholly submerged) which formed as the Indian and Australian plates drifted northward from Antarctica.

## 10.3  AUSTRALIAN EARLY TERTIARY (PALAEOCENE TO EOCENE) VEGETATION

Australia was apparently mostly clothed with dense rain forests throughout the Early Tertiary. These included temperate rain forests to the south, characterised by *Nothofagus* and gymnosperms, and rain forests of more tropical aspect to the north, with the boundary being determined on the one hand by climate and on the other by the degree of drift of the Australian Plate (Figure 10.2). The concentration of Early Tertiary palaeobotanical localities in SE Australia ensures an accurate and detailed interpretation, for this area, with data quality, and precision of dating and interpretation decreasing to the north and west of this region. This review relies heavily on the recent comprehensive review by Macphail et al. (1994).

### Paleocene

During the earliest Paleocene, SE Australia was clothed with a low diversity moist, temperate forest, dominated by gymnosperms (mainly Podocarpaceae and Araucariaceae) with

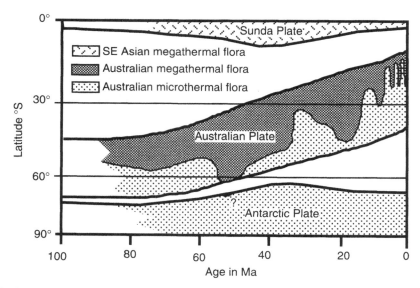

Figure 10.2   North–south latitudinal profile for E Australia through time showing the separation of the Australian and Antarctic plates, the northward drift of the Australian Plate, and the approximate representation of tropical/paratropical and temperate rain forests with deteriorating global climates.

common ferns and fern allies, and with a Gondwanan angiosperm component, increasing in diversity with time, which included Proteaceae and the Madagascan endemic family Didymelaceae (Figure 10.3a). During the latest Paleocene, *Nothofagus* (Figure 10.3b) and Araucariaceae became more common (Figure 10.4), along with ferns and angiosperms at the expense of podocarps as the climate became warmer. Some of the newly appearing angiosperms had megathermal affinities (Figure 10.5), including *Anacolosa* (Olacaceae) (Figure 10.3c), Sapindaceae and Polygalaceae, and many Proteaceae, some of which can be confidently compared to modern genera, such as *Beauprea* (Figure 10.3e), *Gevuina/Hicksbeachia*, *Xylomelum*, *Agastachys* and *Telopea*. Macphail et al. (1994) note that the earlier Paleocene vegetation probably has few modern parallels, whereas the latest Paleocene forests may have been analogous to *Nothofagus*–conifer–broadleaved forests, now widely distributed in New Zealand, the New Guinea mountains and New Caledonia.

Late Paleocene (60–54 Ma) palynological data from the Lake Eyre region indicate that inland regions were characterised by forests in which Cunoniaceae and diverse Proteaceae were dominant, rather than *Nothofagus*, and in which angiosperm diversities were higher. Palynological assemblages include rare megathermal elements, such as *Anacolosa*, together with pollen of primitive angiosperms, such as Trimeniaceae and Winteraceae (Figure 10.3d). Many of the proteaceous pollen types in this area do not occur in more southerly coastal settings until the Early/Middle Eocene, during periods of warmer climate (Wopfner, 1974; Sluiter, 1991; Macphail et al., 1994), which suggests that the differences in palynomorph assemblage between the two regions reflect a latitudinal vegetation gradient, with the Lake Eyre region bearing marginal paratropical rain forests.

### Early Eocene

The Early Eocene (54–49 Ma) in SE Australia is perhaps more remarkable than the London Clay (Section 11.3.2) in that both macrofossil and microfossil data indicate the presence of rich

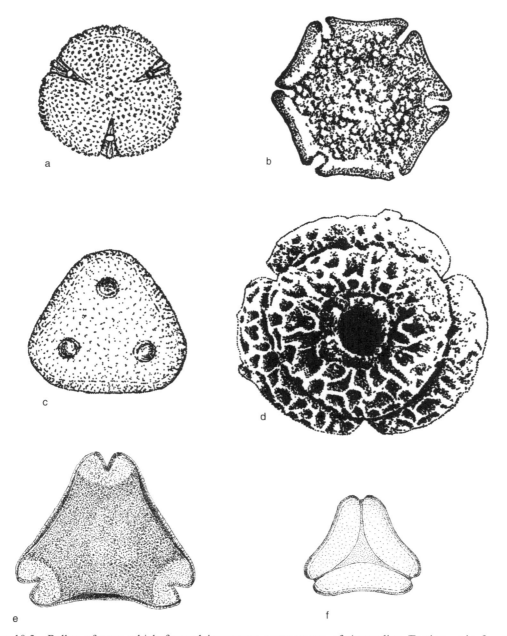

Figure 10.3   Pollen of taxa which formed important components of Australian Tertiary rain forests: (a) *Didymeles*[1] (Didymelaceae) ×3000, this Madagascan endemic was widespread in the Australian Palaeogene; (b) *Nothofagus* (Fagaceae) ×1500, key genus in plant geography, according to van Steenis (1971), but not in the manner that he supposed, evolving in Gondwanaland; (c) *Anacolosa*[1] (Olacaceae) ×2000, originated in Australia; (d) *Drimys*[2] (Winteraceae) ×1800, a primitive angiosperm, widespread throughout the Australian Tertiary, still relict to Australian rain forests; (e) *Beauprea* (Proteaceae) ×1000, formerly widespread from Australia to India, now restricted to New Caledonia; (f) Myrtaceae[1] ×1500, dominant element throughout Tertiary. [1], Erdtman (1952); [2], Walker (1976). Drawn by Harsanti Pribatini.

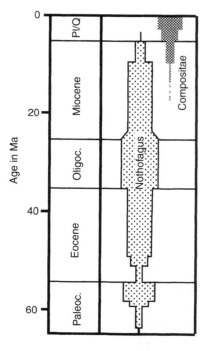

Figure 10.4   Abundance of *Nothofagus* and Compositae pollen through time, Gippsland and Murray Basin (after Macphail, 1996). Reproduced by permission of Australian Geological Survey Organisation.

and diverse paratropical vegetation, with widespread *Nypa* (Palmae) swamps in coastal areas reported at palaeolatitude 58°S in Tasmania (Pole and Macphail, 1996), latitudinally equivalent to N Scotland or Alaska. Perhaps even more remarkably, this vegetation appeared very suddenly, becoming established during a time interval with very tight stratigraphic control over a period of less than 200 000 years (Macphail et al., 1994), following a widespread marine transgression, suggesting extremely rapid climatic change. The mangrove swamps which included *Nypa* also contained the mangrove fern *Acrostichum* (Pteridaceae). The palynological assemblages suggest highly variable inland vegetation with Araucariaceae, *Casuarina* (Casuarinaceae), *Austrobuxus/Dissiliaria* (Euphorbiaceae), various Proteaceae and ferns, including Gleicheniaceae, being prominent, and with numerous megathermal indica-

tors, such as *Anacolosa*, Sapindaceae, *Santalum* (Santalaceae), Sapotaceae, the climbing fern *Lygodium* (Schizaeaceae), and in the latest Early Eocene, *Alangium villosum* type (Alangiaceae) (Martin et al., 1996). Eocene macrofossils of *Casuarina s.l.* are widespread in SE Australia (Christophel, 1980; Hill, 1994b), all referable to the segregate genus *Gymnostoma*, which today is a rain forest rather than sclerophyll tree.

Early Eocene macrofossil localities are well represented in Tasmania (Carpenter et al., 1994), and provide some more detailed glimpses of the southernmost localities with megathermal elements. All localities are dominated by gymnosperms and large-leaved angiosperms, the latter suggesting mean annual temperatures of 16°C (Figure 10.6). In addition to *Nypa*, macrofossils of cycads are also recorded, which include the extant genus *Bowenia*, now confined to E Queensland megathermal rain forests and open forest (Carpenter et al., 1994). Another curiosity is *Eucryphia* (Eucryphiaceae), now restricted to microthermal rain forests in Tasmania, New South Wales and Chile (Hill, 1991). The macrofossil data emphasise that the Early Eocene climate was everwarm and everwet, and the forest has no modern structural or floristic analogue. Floristic elements which have endured the climatic perturbations of the Tertiary have survived either where it is everwet and warm, or everwet with fluctuating day length.

On the mainland, away from the coast, rain forest communities appear to have been more transitional between paratropical and warm temperate, and many taxa were shared with the coastal paratropical forests. Inland lakes were bordered by herbaceous marsh, characterised by Cyperaceae, Gramineae, Restionaceae and Typhaceae/Sparganiaceae (Sluiter, 1991); and the surrounding forests were mostly dominated by Araucariaceae, Cunoniaceae and Myrtaceae, and diverse angiosperms, which included *Anacolosa*, *Bombax* (Bombacaceae), some palms, Didymelaceae, Sapindaceae and Winteraceae.

The very limited representation of temperate forests at this time is clearly indicated by the

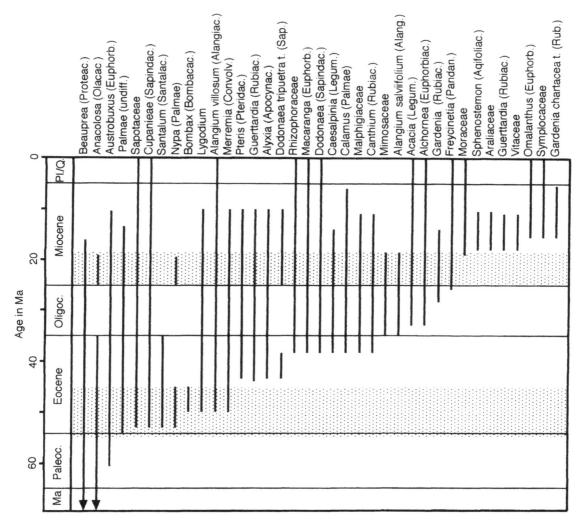

Figure 10.5  Stratigraphic ranges in Australia of pollen of taxa with broadly megathermal affinities; stippled intervals are periods of highest Tertiary temperatures (modified from Table 1 of Martin, 1992). Reproduced by permission of the *Palaeobotanist*.

distribution of *Nothofagus*, which was rare throughout mainland Australia, and was largely confined to Tasmania, where it occurred only in localities in which megathermal angiosperms are absent (Macphail et al., 1994).

There are no records from N Australia, but a glimpse of coeval vegetation at this time is forthcoming from Irian Jaya, from sediments rich in anhydrite beds, which suggest a hot arid climate; palynomorph assemblages from this

locality were described in Chapter 9 (Morley, 1998). In this area, *Casuarina* and Myrtaceae (Figure 10.3f) were dominant, and coastal vegetation included *Acrostichum* and several species of *Nypa*.

### Middle and Late Eocene

During the Middle (49–39 Ma) and Late Eocene (39–36 Ma), Australia remained densely forested

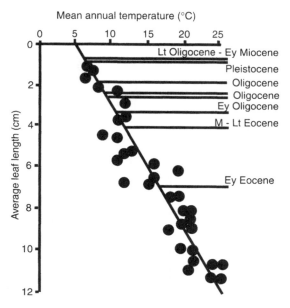

Figure 10.6  Closed circles show the plot of average leaf length (excluding *Casuarina*) versus mean annual temperature for present-day rain forest sites in Tasmania and E Australia (leaves were obtained from forest-floor litter). The horizontal lines show the average leaf length of Tasmanian fossil floras, dated as indicated. Approximate palaeotemperatures for these floras are indicated by their relationship to the average leaf size (regression line) of recent assemblages (from Carpenter et al., 1994). Reproduced by permission of Cambridge University Press.

for virtually all areas for which there is a fossil record. Paratropical rain forests were, however, less widespread, and the abundance and diversity of megathermal elements declined throughout this time interval. The generally cooler temperatures resulted in the disappearance of mangroves from the southeast, although *Nypa* remained further to the north, in S Queensland, at 45°S palaeolatitude (Foster, 1982).

In the southeastern region, the palynomorph assemblages are dominated by *Nothofagus*, but some megathermal elements initially remained, and within the region of the Murray Basin included some taxa which were missing from the warmer Early Eocene, including *Canthium* (Rubiaceae), Caesalpinoidae, Malphigiaceae and the fern *Pteris* (Pteridaceae). The mega-

thermal elements became progressively rarer by Late Eocene time throughout the southeast. Macphail et al. (1994) suggest that, in broad terms, SE Australian Middle to Late Eocene vegetation appears to have been a mosaic of *Nothofagus*-dominated rain forest associations, mesothermal rather than megathermal in character, but with a diversity much higher than present-day *Nothofagus* communities. Greenwood's (1994) reconstruction of Middle Eocene vegetation, on the basis of macrofossil data shows considerable support for this suggestion, with megathermal sclerophyllous and ?semideciduous mesophyll vine forest in mid Australia, and temperate rain forests in the southeast, with the exception of the Murray Basin, where transitional associations are interpreted (Figure 10.7).

The persistence of paratropical vegetation in S Queensland is indicated by the continued presence of megathermal elements, which included *Alangium salvifolium*, *Anacolosa*, *Canthium*, Loranthaceae, *Lygodium*, *Merremia* (Convolvulaceae), *Santalum* and Sapotaceae, together with rattans and Caesalpinoidae within Yaamba Basin sediments (Foster, 1982; Dudgeon, 1983). Palynomorph assemblages here were dominated by *Casuarina* and Araucariaceae with minor *Nothofagus*.

In Western Australia, *Nothofagus*, Proteaceae and *Casuarina* were dominants, and megathermal elements, such as *Austrobuxus/ Dissiliaria*, were locally common. The presence of other megathermal taxa is indicated by the occurrence of pollen of Caesalpinoidae and Malphigiaceae. Also noteworthy here is the New Zealand flax, *Phormium* (Phormiaceae), the pollen of which is recorded at a slightly later time in Java (Section 9.8). The most remarkable feature of Western Australian Middle–Late Eocene palynomorph assemblages, however, within the western part of the Eucla Basin, is an unbelievable diversity of proteaceous pollen (which can be divided into at least 46 different types), suggesting an extremely active period of diversification within this family (Macphail et al., 1994).

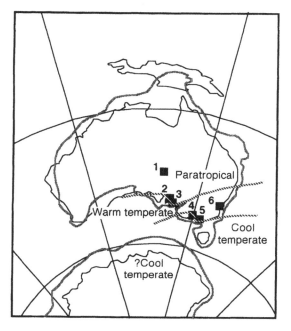

Figure 10.7 Middle Eocene reconstruction of Australia showing palaeocoastline, and climatic zones based on macrofossil data. 1 = ?megathermal sclerophyllous forest or monsoonal megathermal ?deciduous mesophyll vine forest; 2 = mesothermal simple/complex notophyll vine forest; 3 = mesothermal/megathermal complex mesophyll vine forest; 4 = microthermal microphyll fern forest; 5 = mesothermal simple notophyll vine forest; 6 = mesothermal complex notophyll vine forest (after Greenwood, 1994). Reproduced by permission of Cambridge University Press.

## 10.4  AUSTRALIAN MID-TERTIARY (OLIGOCENE TO EARLY MIOCENE) VEGETATION

The earliest Oligocene coincided with one of the most important cooling episodes in the Southern Ocean (Wei, 1991), with glacial climates already becoming established in E Antarctica, and ice reaching sea level at the beginning of the Oligocene (36–25 Ma). At the same time, South America finally became separated from Antarctica, resulting in the opening of the Drake Passage (Kennett, 1980), and this may have encouraged the development of the Westerlies, resulting in increased precipitation in S Aus-

tralia (Kemp, 1978), which at that time lay just to the south of the southern subtropical high pressure zone. Since S Australia experienced a very wet climate, and with the cooler conditions, ombrotrophic peat swamps formed in many areas. The response of vegetation was the expansion of temperate rain forests, with abundant *Nothofagus* in many areas, and a marked reduction in diversity of angiosperm floras and the further demise of megathermal elements, although a few megathermal elements remained in some areas, such as the Murray Basin region, and included *Alangium salvifolium* type, *Austrobuxus/Dissiliaria*, *Canthium* and possible palms; new arrivals included members of Mimosoidae. The widespread peat swamps bore swamp forest in the Murray Basin region, with *Casuarina*, *Lagarostrobos* (Podocarpaceae) or Myrtaceae as dominants, whereas in the Gippsland region, open swamp woodland, with *Lagarostrobus* and *Typha/Sparganium* and some Proteaceae, was widespread.

Outside SE Australia, data are more restricted, but there is a valuable locality in Queensland, near Brisbane (Wood, 1986), with low frequencies of *Nothofagus*. Palynomorph assemblages are dominated mainly by spores, but the presence there of regular Myrtaceae and Proteaceae, together with Mimosoidae, Convolvulaceae, Caesalpinoidae and *Alangium villosum* and *Guettardia* type (Rubiaceae), suggest a vegetation bordering on the megathermal, and possibly with a mildly seasonal climate (Macphail et al., 1994).

Climates remained cool into the Late Oligocene, as evidenced by leaf-size data from Tasmania, with Late Oligocene to Early Miocene leaf assemblages suggesting the same temperatures as the present-day Tasmanian flora (Carpenter et al., 1994). However, there was probably a climatic amelioration in the latest Oligocene and Early Miocene (26–16 Ma), and this resulted in the return of some warmer elements in the region of the Barossa Basin (Alley, unpublished, in Macphail et al., 1994), indicated by the presence of pollen of *Nypa*, *Anacolosa* and Sapotaceae. The abundance of

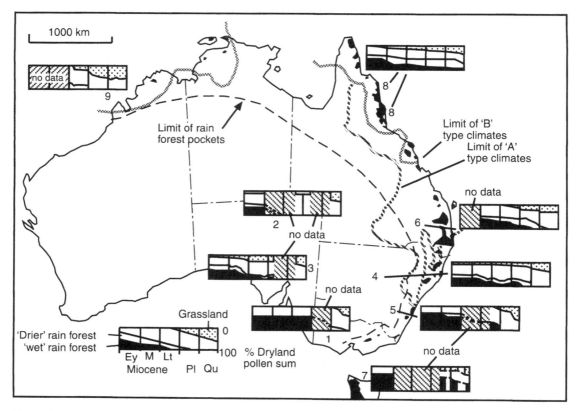

Figure 10.8   The Late Cenozoic pattern of rain forest decline and the expansion of grasslands (from Kershaw et al., 1994), superimposed on current distribution of rain forests (Adam, 1994), and limits of type 'A' and type 'B' (tropical rain forest) climates (from Webb et al., 1984). 1) The Latrobe Valley; 2) Lake Frome Basin; 3) W Murray Basin; 4) E Murray Basin; 5) SE Highlands; 6) N New South Wales; 7) Tasmania; 8) NE Australia; 9) NE Australia. Reproduced by permission of Cambridge University Press.

*Nothofagus* pollen in this sequence suggests, as for the Late Eocene, that vegetation consisted of a mosaic of *Nothofagus*-dominated warm temperate rain forest communities, and was meso-thermal rather than megathermal in character.

## 10.5   THE NEOGENE AND THE DEMISE OF AUSTRALIAN RAIN FORESTS

During the Early Miocene, the central axis of the Australian Plate drifted into the southern subtropical high pressure zone and, with falling global temperatures, Australian rain forests were to face a catastrophic decline. Deciphering

details of this decline, sufficient to permit concrete judgements about causes, has been problematic, mainly because suitable well-dated sedimentary successions bearing palynomorphs or macrofossils are of limited occurrence compared to the mid-Tertiary. Available data have been summarised by Kershaw et al. (1994).

In the Early Miocene, warm temperate rain forests, characterised variously by *Nothofagus*, *Elaeocarpus* (Elaeocarpaceae), Podocarpaceae and Cunoniaceae, were widespread in all areas for which data are available, including NE Queensland, and the W Murray Basin. Their subsequent decline is shown by the reduction in representation of pollen of rain forest elements in palynological profiles, summarised in Figure

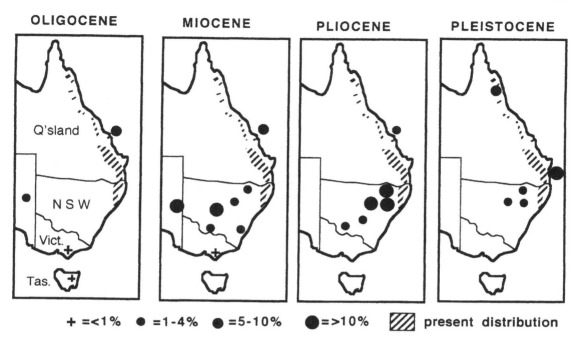

Figure 10.9   Representation of *Araucaria* in pollen samples from E Australia in the Oligocene through Pleistocene (from Kershaw, 1988) in comparison with the present distribution from Webb and Tracey (1967). Reproduced by permission of Kluwer Academic Publishers.

10.8. Initially there was a decline in the Middle Miocene (16–10 Ma) in Queensland, and significantly in the southeast, with further declines in the Middle and Late Miocene (10–5 Ma) in several areas. Some amelioration was likely in the Early Pliocene (5–3.5 Ma) (Martin, 1973), but during the Late Pliocene (3.5–1.6 Ma) rain forest elements became of minor significance through most of Australia. Conversely, indicators of open vegetation, such as Gramineae and Compositae, show some increases in representation in the Middle and Late Miocene, but are mainly characteristic of the Late Pliocene and Quaternary (1.6–0 Ma). 'Dry' rain forests (a term widely used in Australia, e.g. Adam, 1992), dominated by Araucariaceae (Figure 10.9), and sclerophyll vegetation with the xeromorphic segregates *Casuarina* and *Allocasuarina*, rather than *Gymnostoma* (identified on the basis of macrofossils by Hill, 1990), became widespread after the decline of 'wet' rain forests and before the Pliocene expansion of grasslands.

This gross generalisation probably requires modification of detail when any area is examined more closely. For instance, palynological analyses of a piston core from ODP 765 offshore NW Australia (McMinn and Martin, 1993) provide a first glimpse of Late Miocene and Pliocene vegetation from that area (Figure 10.10). The succession is initially overwhelmingly dominated by *Casuarina* pollen, suggesting that sclerophyll vegetation was dominant. However, Restionaceae pollen is frequent in this section. Today, Restionaceae are generally associated with permanent swamp environments, and elsewhere form a common associate of Tertiary rain forest assemblages. The possibility may be raised that small patches of rain forest may have occurred in the northwest, but were palynologically invisible, lacking taxa which were high pollen producers (Kershaw and Hyland, 1975; Kershaw et al., 1994).

There has been some debate as to whether the development of aridity on the Australian

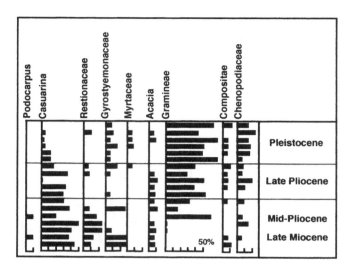

Figure 10.10   Summary of palynological profile from ODP 765, offshore NW Australia (from McMinn and
Martin, 1993). Pollen sum 'total pollen'. Reproduced by permission of Cambridge University Press.

mainland was due to northward drift into the
mid-latitude high pressure zone (Beard, 1977;
Bowler, 1982) or to movement away from
Antarctica (Kemp, 1978). The coincidence of
the main periods of rain forest withdrawal, and
expansion of grasslands with, firstly, the onset
of the Late Miocene, and, secondly, the Late
Pliocene, which are the periods of most
pronounced global temperature fall, suggest
that global temperature decline is as important
as northward drift in causing the decline of
Australian rain forests.

### Mid-Tertiary dispersals from southeast Asia

The classical view that Australian tropical rain
forest elements were invaders from the north,
and the clear evidence for dispersals of taxa into
SE Asia whose centre of origin was clearly
Australian, prompted the search for evidence
(Truswell et al., 1987; Kershaw, 1988). The
conclusion drawn was that there was no invasion of tropical elements as previously supposed. Instead, Truswell et al. (1987) proposed
additional invaders from Australia to SE Asia,
but almost all of these can be disregarded
(Morley, 1998; Section 9.8). In addition to the

lack of continuous land bridges from SE Asia,
the pattern of global climate change, strength-
ening north–south climatic gradients, would
also have inhibited dispersal. The result is that
only a few taxa are currently contenders for
dispersal from SE Asia, and include *Merremia*,
*Pteris*, *Guettardia*, Caesalpinoidae, *Brachypteris*
(Malphigiaceae) some Mimosoidae, and the
fern *Stenochlaena palustris* (Blechnaceae).
These are mostly well-dispersed plants, all
appearing before the main period of climatic
deterioration in the Middle Miocene.

### Survival of primitive angiosperms in Australia

Primitive angiosperms, such as members of
Winteraceae, Chloranthaceae, Trimeniaceae
and Didymelaceae and *Gunnera* (Gunneraceae),
were widespread elements of evergreen rain
forests through the latest Cretaceous and
earliest Tertiary. Some, such as Didymelaceae
and *Ascarina* (Chloranthaceae), died out in the
mid-Tertiary (Macphail et al., 1994; Martin,
1994), but others continued throughout the
remaining Tertiary, as evidenced from their
pollen record. Their survival in Australia relates
to the continuous occurrence throughout the

Neogene of wet, frost-free refuges along the eastern coast of Queensland, maintained by warm and moist onshore trade winds, as Australia drifted north into the subtropical high pressure zone, and climates became too dry inland, and too cool, with frosts, to the south.

## 10.6  AUSTRALIAN RAIN FORESTS IN THE QUATERNARY

Today, only 0.25% of Australia is clothed with rain forest (Adam, 1992), and prior to European settlement, the total area was probably not more than 1%, of which half can reasonably be considered 'tropical'. Living in an interglacial interval, tropical rain forests are at their approximate maximum extent for the Quaternary. During glacial intervals, however, with cooler and drier low latitude climates, one might have expected Australia's tropical rain forests to have shrunk almost to nothing, but the very existence today of diverse rain forests, which in their 0.25% of Australia's land surface include 50% of its biota, demonstrates that these forests must have survived. The extent to which rain forests disappeared from the Atherton Tableland, now bearing the most extensive pocket of tropical rain forests, and the fact that many taxa did not make it through the glacial maxima, is clearly illustrated by the classic pollen diagram from Lynch's Crater (Kershaw, 1974, 1976, 1985), which extends through the penultimate 'glacial' period (Figure 10.11) and, until recently, was the only detailed pollen diagram from a moderately low altitude (650 m), low latitude setting from anywhere in the tropical zone which included the last interglacial.

The Lynch's Crater succession was produced from a 60 m core consisting of peat overlying lake sediments and is believed to span a 190 000 year time interval. The section includes two full glacial/interglacial cycles (including the Holocene), sufficient to provide an approximate analogue for the 20 or so oscillations of the

Quaternary period. Each of the interglacial intervals were characterised by complex notophyll/mesophyll vine forests (following the classification of Webb, 1978) which consist almost wholly of angiosperms, although each had a markedly different association of dominant taxa. Glacial intervals were mostly characterised by araucarian microphyll/mesophyll vine forest, which comprise a mixture of rain forest gymnosperms and angiosperms, and sclerophyll taxa. The latter part of the last glacial interval, however, was wholly dominated by sclerophyll taxa, suggesting that rain forests were completely absent from the region during this period.

It is noteworthy that the expansion of sclerophyll vegetation in the region of Lynch's Crater occurred only during the latter part of the last glacial interval, just after the time of arrival of Man in Australia. At this time, charcoal records show a major increase in many parts of Australia, indicating increased burning, presumably from human activity (Singh and Geissler, 1985). The replacement of araucarian vine forests by sclerophyll vegetation might therefore be due to human activity, which might be responsible for the extinction of several gymnosperm taxa in this area, which occurred at the same time (Kershaw and McGlone, 1995).

The question as to where rain forests found refuge has been raised many times, but, up to now, no palynological sites have been investigated which convincingly demonstrate a refuge. It has been suggested that refuges occurred on damp mountain slopes, or damp valley bottoms kept moist by groundwater (Adam, 1992), where preservational sites are improbable, in areas unaffected by fire. Webb and Tracey (1981) have used plant distribution patterns to map possible refugial areas. The presently submerged continental shelf is also a possibility. Wherever rain forests found refuge, their distribution was clearly more restricted than at present, emphasising the fragility of this ecosystem, which is virtually all we have left of the endless rain forests which once clothed much of Eastern Gondwana.

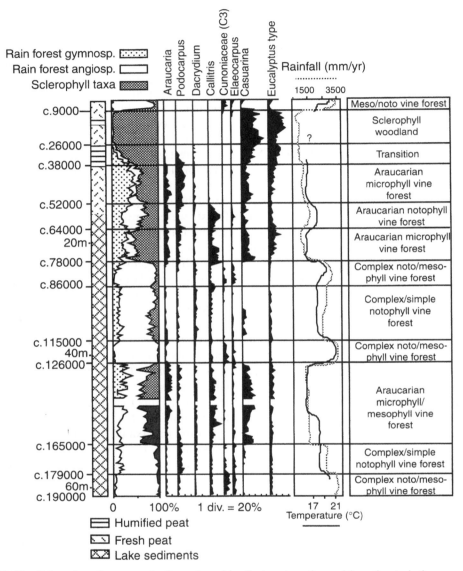

Figure 10.11    Selected pollen records from Lynch's Crater, together with estimated time scale, climatic parameters and inferred vegetation (adapted from Kershaw, 1985). Reproduced by permission of Ecological Society of Australia.

## 10.7   NINETYEAST RIDGE

Early Tertiary sediments from DSDP 214 and 254 have been shown to yield rich palynomorph assemblages (Kemp and Harris, 1975, 1977), clearly indicating that this ridge was vegetated during the Paleocene (site 214) at palaeolatitude 40°S and Oligocene (site 254) at 23°S. The Paleocene flora was wholly of Gondwanan aspect, dominated by Podocarpaceae and *Ascarina* (Chloranthaceae), with abundant palm pollen. Rare pollen types included *Nothofagus*,

*Casuarina* and Proteaceae and it is suggested that these may have blown from the Australian mainland. The Oligocene assemblages were dominated by Myrtaceae with common palm pollen, which included grains of *Nypa*, and abundances of *Casuarina* suggest that it was growing locally rather than wind-blown from Australia. Less common types included Didymelaceae, *Gunnera*, Restionaceae, megathermal elements such as Sapotaceae and Sapindaceae, and rare specimens of Compositae. Kemp and Harris (1975) interpret these floras as the result of long-distance plant dispersal. The wholly Australian (and Madagascan) character of the assemblages, other than *Nypa*, strongly suggests that, even if the islands were wholly oceanic throughout their history, they were more closely associated with the southern land masses, and that continuity to the Indian subcontinent was unlikely.

## 10.8   NEW ZEALAND

There are many similarities between the Tertiary floras and climatic histories of New Zealand and Australia, and also some remarkable differences, especially as revealed from the pollen and spore record.

The Early and Middle Eocene New Zealand climate was very wet and warm, and supported a paratropical rain forest vegetation in the same manner as SE Australia with *Nypa*, *Bombax*, *Anacolosa*, *Austrobuxus/Dissiliaria*, *Santalum*, Sapindaceae and Sapotaceae, and with only low frequencies of *Nothofagus* (Pocknall, 1990). During the Late Eocene, following a transitional period characterised by *Casuarina* and Proteaceae with Palmae and Sapindaceae, paratropical forests were replaced by temperate rain forests dominated by *Nothofagus* (Pocknall, 1989), although subordinate megathermal elements continued throughout the Oligocene and into the Early Miocene. Pocknall (1989) interprets the association of *Nothofagus* and megathermal elements in terms of a vegetation comparable to the lower montane *Nothofagus* forests of New

Guinea and New Caledonia, which he terms 'cool temperate', although 'warm temperate' would be a better term.

The different time of first appearance of palynomorph taxa in New Zealand and Australia provides one of the most convincing demonstrations of the extent of long-distance plant dispersal. Macphail et al. (1994) have compiled data on the earliest appearance of 66 palynomorph taxa common to both regions which are represented diagrammatically in Figure 10.12. Twenty show a first appearance at the same time in both areas, mostly in the Maastrichtian and Paleocene, when dispersal between the two land masses was relatively unhindered. However, of the remaining 46 types, 41 first appear in Australia, and only 5 in New Zealand. This difference emphasises the isolation of New Zealand, relative to the Australian mainland, and the reality of long-distance dispersal, across the Tasman Sea, which was already established at the beginning of the Tertiary and is now over 1000 km in width. Van Steenis (1962a) considered long-distance dispersal across water bodies greater than 500 km in width to be a myth.

It has already been mentioned that northward drift of the Australian Plate accelerated in the Eocene, whereas New Zealand's rate of drift slowed down, with the result that it always lay south of the subtropical high pressure belt, and did not suffer the effects of desiccation which caused such devastation to rain forests in Australia. However, as global temperatures continued to decline through the Neogene, it eventually became too cold for megathermal elements, despite the equable maritime climate, with the result that they virtually all became extinct during the Late Pliocene and Quaternary (Figure 10.13), leaving only a tiny refuge of subtropical forest to the north of Auckland.

## 10.9   SUMMARY

Rain forests are one of the original vegetation types of Australia and New Zealand. Relatively

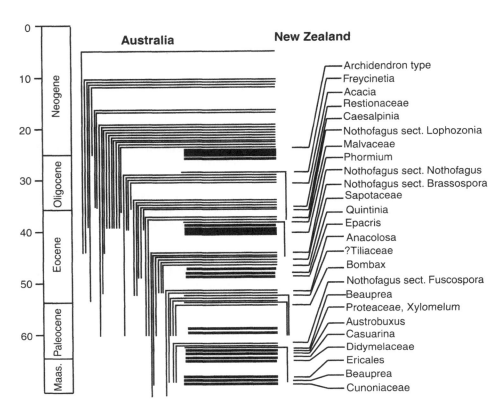

Figure 10.12   The pattern of dispersal of plant taxa into Australia and New Zealand according to their palynological record. The base of vertical lines shows the first appearance in either Australia or New Zealand, and the horizontal line shows the time of dispersal across the Tasman Sea. Thick horizontal lines (sometimes overlapping) indicate simultaneous dispersals to Australia and New Zealand; names of only selected dispersals are given to the right hand side. Constructed from Table 10.3 in Macphail et al. (1994).

few of their elements have dispersed to the region from SE Asia, as proposed by classical biogeography.

A few early, generalised angiosperms may have dispersed to Australia from India via the Kohistan Arc during the mid-Cretaceous (Turonian). The primitive family Chloranthaceae probably dispersed via South America and Antarctica, since it first appeared earlier in Australia (Late Barremian) than India (Aptian). Other primitive angiosperms, such as members of Winteraceae and Gunneraceae, together with ancestral Proteaceae, also dispersed to Australia via South America and Antarctica during the later part of the Cretaceous (Section 5.2.3).

Most of the tropical/warm temperate rain forest elements which did not originate in Australia dispersed from South America via Antarctica during the Paleocene and Early Eocene, especially at the time of the Late Paleocene–Early Eocene thermal maximum. Immigrants at this time included members of Bombacaceae, Cunoniaceae, Myrtaceae, Polygalaceae, Restionaceae and Sapindaceae.

In the Early Eocene, everwet, everwarm climates enabled the proliferation of paratropical vegetation with mangrove swamps extending as far south as palaeolatitude 58°S in Tasmania, where annual variations in day length would have been the same as in Antarctica today. The vegetation growing at this time was very different

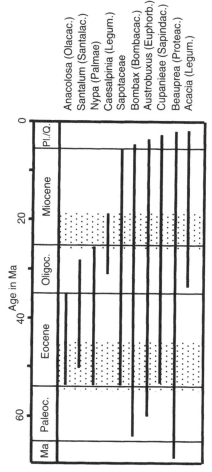

Figure 10.13   Times of disappearance of pollen of megathermal taxa in the New Zealand Tertiary. Stippled intervals are periods of highest Tertiary palaeotemperatures. Data updated from Mildenhall (1980).

from any in existence today; those elements which have survived the perturbations of Tertiary climate change have adapted either to everwet, everwarm tropical climates, or to everwet, strongly seasonal temperate climates.

Australia remained forested through most of the Middle Eocene to Middle Miocene. Paratropical forests were widespread in the Middle Eocene, but diminished in representation through the Late Eocene as the Australian Plate drifted north and global climates cooled. They

were probably only represented in N Australia in the Oligocene, although they became more widespread again in the Early and Middle Miocene.

As a result of the continued northward drift of Australia, coupled with global climatic deterioration, the climate of Australia became much drier in the Middle and Late Miocene and later Pliocene, resulting in the withdrawal of tropical rain forests from all but the east coast region.

During the Late Pliocene and Pleistocene, the extent of rain forests oscillated between glacial and interglacial cycles. During interglacial intervals, their distribution was probably similar to that of today, whereas, during glacial intervals, they are thought to have withdrawn to very localised moist mountain slopes and valley bottoms or to the presently submerged continental shelf.

The rain forests of New Zealand had a similar history to those of Australia up until the Middle Miocene, but New Zealand did not suffer Neogene desiccation in the manner of Australia since it always lay south of the southern mid-latitude high pressure zone. Megathermal elements were of more limited occurrence in New Zealand compared to Australia, and those which did occur there mostly died out in the Pliocene and Early Pleistocene as a result of global cooling.

The survival of primitive angiosperms in the rain forests of Australia is due to the continuous occurrence through the Tertiary of everwet, frost-free refuges along the eastern coast, resulting from the effect of moist and warm onshore trade winds as Australia drifted north into the subtropical high pressure zone.

## NOTE

1  The families which Takhtajan (1969) considered primitive are: Magnoliales: Annonaceae, Canellaceae, Degeneriaceae, Eupatomiaceae, Himantandraceae, Magnoliaceae, Myristicaceae, Winteraceae; Laurales: Amborellaceae, Austrobaileyaceae, Calycanthaceae, Monimiaceae; Trochendrales: Tetracentraceae, Trochendraceae.

# CHAPTER 11

# Northern Hemisphere Megathermal Rain Forests

## 11.1 INTRODUCTION

Occurrences of tropical plant and animal fossils at high latitudes in both Europe and North America, such as *Nypa* fruits in the London Clay, and alligators, monitor lizards and primates in Eocene deposits from Ellesmere Island, at 78°N, have been a puzzle for over a century, and have even been used as evidence for a possible change in the angle of the Earth's axis at the end of the Eocene (Wolfe, 1978).

There is abundant fossil evidence to indicate that, during the Palaeogene, rain forests of tropical aspect spread across much of North America, Europe and beyond. These forests contained diverse megathermal elements, but also many temperate taxa, such as *Carya* and *Juglans*, and some gymnosperms, and to describe their northern geography and the thermophilous character of their component taxa they were termed the 'boreotropical flora' by Wolfe (1975, 1977).

Although very uniform climatic conditions occurred across the northern hemisphere during the Palaeogene, the northern continents provided very different opportunities for megathermal plants while global climates deteriorated during the later Cenozoic, with the result that today a large number of the constituent taxa of the boreotropical flora have found refuge in the rain forests of China and SE Asia, and intermediate numbers occur in refuges in Middle America, especially in the region of Veracruz in Mexico, whereas hardly any have survived in the region of S Europe or N Africa, although tiny refuges may remain in montane forests on isolated Atlantic islands such as the Canaries (Takhtajan, 1969) and the Colchic region of the Black Sea.

This chapter compares the Palaeogene megathermal vegetation of North America, Europe and E Asia, and discusses evidence for suitable dispersal paths between these areas, paying particular emphasis as to whether dispersals mainly took place at higher latitudes, or whether the more southerly Tethyan seaway provided the most important avenue for dispersal, as has been generally supposed. It also addresses the Late Cenozoic demise of megathermal elements in the northern continents, and suggests an explanation as to why such different numbers of their constituent taxa have found refuge in each of the present three rain forested regions.

## 11.2 TECTONIC SETTING AND LAND CONNECTIONS

The North American Plate remained at approximately the same latitude throughout the Tertiary, whereas Europe drifted northward by about 12°. The north–south oriented epicontinental seas which divided North America during the Late Cretaceous, closed in the Paleocene, whereas during the Early Tertiary the European continent was an archipelago of islands. North America and Europe remained in tectonic contact until the Miocene (Parrish, 1987), although it is most likely that, except at very high latitudes, a narrow seaway existed between the two areas, except during the latest Paleocene and Early Eocene, coinciding with the global temperature maximum, at which time a land connection was established at latitudes of 45–50°N across S Greenland. This land bridge was broken during the Early Eocene, after which time there was a major fall in faunal similarity between the two areas (Simpson, 1946; McKenna, 1973). There was a clear continental connection between North America and E Asia for most of the Late Cretaceous and Early Tertiary via Beringia (Tiffney, 1985b; Parrish 1987), although dispersals of megathermal taxa between North America and Asia were inhibited by the very high latitude of this corridor (75°N). Dispersals between Europe and E Asia were limited by the Turgai Straits, which formed a wide barrier throughout the Eocene (Vinogradov, 1967/8), its closure during the Early Oligocene allowing the immigration of Asian mammals into Europe, after which many Eocene mammals of European origin became extinct (*Le Grande Coupure*, Stehlin, 1909; Prothero, 1994). In the Neogene, the area of the Bering Straits continued to be a land bridge during low sea level periods.

There was a land connection between North and South America until the end of the Paleocene, after which the Americas remained quite separate until the uplift of the Isthmus of Panama in the Pliocene. Tethys divided Europe from the African Plate until its closure in the Middle Miocene, although the Iberian Peninsula and N Africa were probably sufficiently close by the Late Eocene to facilitate interplate plant dispersal, yet remaining a barrier to land mammals. The character of land connections between North and South America, and from Europe to Africa, have been outlined more fully in Chapters 6 and 7 respectively.

## 11.3  PALEOCENE/EOCENE

### 11.3.1  North America

Following the annihilation of the North American forests by the end-Cretaceous meteorite

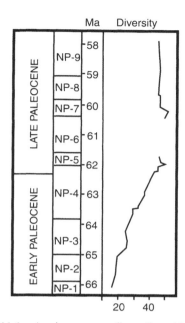

Figure 11.1 Angiosperm pollen diversities during Paleocene of the Gulf Coast. Diversities calculated using the 'range-through' method of Cheetham and Deboo (1963), which assumes that a taxon is present in every sample from its first to last occurrence. The gap reflects an unconformity, and barren sand (Frederiksen, 1994a). Reproduced by permission of Elsevier Science.

impact, which resulted in the extinction of up to 75% of the region's flora (Crane, 1987), recovery was slow; it took 4 Ma before floristic diversity stabilised (Figure 11.1). Vegetational recovery physiognomically resembled that of a modern secondary succession within tropical lowland evergreen rain forest, but over a longer time scale (Figure 11.2; Upchurch and Wolfe, 1987). Early Paleocene temperatures were not dissimilar to those of the latest Cretaceous (Figure 5.27), but increased leaf sizes, and higher percentages of species with drip tips and hairless leaves indicate much wetter conditions (Upchurch and Wolfe, 1987). Wolfe (1985) emphasised that the interpretation of vegetational gradients for the North American Paleocene presented severe difficulties, despite a voluminous literature, since most plant fossils reflect floodplain communities, which were temperature insensitive, and show the

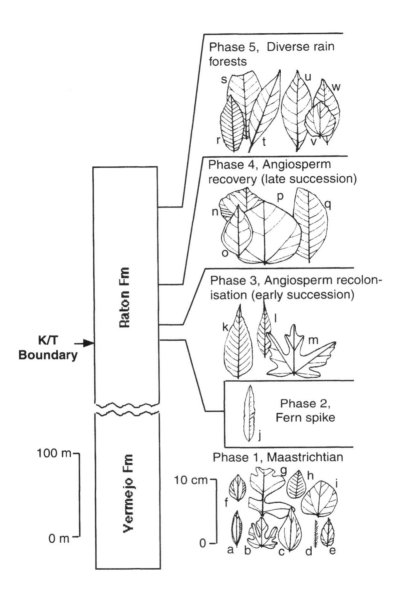

Figure 11.2   Changes in leaf physiognomy from the latest Cretaceous to Early Paleocene in the Raton Basin, New Mexico and Colorado (Wolfe and Upchurch, 1987). Phase 1, high diversity flora indicating warm, subhumid climate (the iridium-rich clay interpreted as the K/T boundary occurs between phases 1 and 2); phase 2, vegetation dominated by a fern; phase 3, angiosperms dominate, but in low diversity and exhibit early successional morphology, and suggest a warm, wet climate; diversity increased during phases 4 and 5, but even in phase 5, 1.5 Ma after the K/T boundary event, diversities were low compared to phase 1. a, f, g, h, l, o, u, Laurales; b, c, m, p, Euphorbiaceae; d, *Geinitzia* (Coniferae); e, Illiciales; i, Menispermaceae; j, *Stenochlaena* (Blechnaceae); k, Celastrales; n, Platanoid; r, Juglandaceae; v, Tiliaceae; q, s, t, w, unnamed. Reproduced by permission of the authors.

same characters in Alaska and Wyoming. Nevertheless, Upchurch and Wolfe (1987) proposed that paratropical rain forests occurred as far north as 48° along the margins of North American epicontinental seas, and tropical rain forest in the Mississippi Embayment (Figure 11.3).

At the beginning of the Early Eocene, coinciding with the global thermal maximum, megathermal vegetation extended to 60°N and beyond (Figure 11.4). A large proportion of the taxa which grew in these forests have been determined on the basis of fruit and, less reliably, leaf fossils. Tropical trees, and vines/lianes were prominent and have been briefly summarised by Chaney (1947) (with some additions by Wolfe, 1977). The most prominent tree family was Lauraceae, represented by many genera, with other trees including members of Anacardiaceae (*Dracontomelon*); Annonaceae (*Cananga*); Burseraceae (*Canarium*); Dilleniaceae (*Dillenia* and *Tetracera*); numerous Euphorbiaceae and Leguminosae; Meliaceae (*Carapa*, *Cedrela*); Myristicaceae (*Knema*, *Myristica*); Olacaceae (*Olax*); Palmae; Rutaceae (*Euodia*, *Luvunga*); and Sabiaceae (*Meliosma*). Lianes were represented by Icacinaceae (*Iodes*, *Miquelia*, *Phytocrene*, *Pyrenacantha*); Menispermaceae (*Anamirta*, *Diploclisia*, *Hypserpa*, *Limacia*, *Pycnarrhena*, *Tinomiscium* and *Tinospora*) and Vitaceae (*Tetrastigma*), and gingers and tree ferns were also common. Other megathermal genera have been recorded from pollen, and include *Anacolosa*, members of Sapotaceae (Taylor, 1989), Sapindaceae, and Bombacaceae/Sterculiaceae/Tiliaceae The latter group exhibits great diversity of morphotypes (e.g. Wingate, 1983; Frederiksen, 1988), indicating a major phase of diversification.

Interpreting Eocene leaf floras and pollen assemblages in terms of vegetation and climate has resulted in widespread debate. On the basis of leaf margin analyses, Upchurch and Wolfe (1987) proposed that paratropical rain forests (with mean annual temperatures over 20°C) grew as far as 60°N along the Pacific coast (or over 70°N according to Wolfe, 1985), with

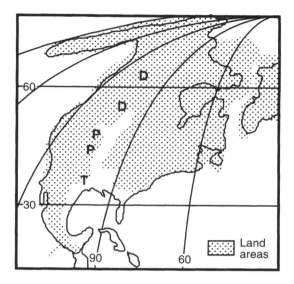

Figure 11.3 Early Paleocene vegetation map for North America, based on physiognomic analyses of leaf floras. Symbols as follows: T = tropical rain forest; P = paratropical rain forest; D = broadleaved deciduous forest, from Upchurch and Wolfe (1987). Plate tectonic reconstruction and palaeocoastlines according to Smith et al. (1994). Reproduced by permission of Cambridge University Press.

tropical rain forests (reflected by mean annual temperatures of over 25°C) extending to 50°, with Wolfe (1985) projecting these estimates across the whole of the northern hemisphere. Others have proposed lower mean annual temperatures, but with essentially frost-free, equable climates, even in the continental interior (Wing and Greenwood, 1993) which allowed palms, cycads and gingers to occur widely up to 55°N (Figure 11.4). Although tropical reptiles and mammals are well known as far north as Ellesmere Island, in Arctic Canada, at 78°N, floras from this area have no frost-intolerant plant taxa (Wing and Greenwood, 1993), and hence cannot be considered as reflecting a tropical climate. The anomalously high latitudes for paratropical rain forests in some parts of W North America may relate to the northern drift of allochthonous terranes, of which Alaska is largely composed (Ben Avraham et al., 1981), and on which several floras

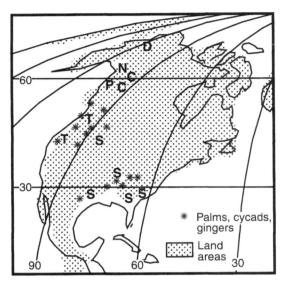

Figure 11.4 Late Middle Eocene vegetation map for North America, based on physiognomic analyses of leaf floras. Symbols as follows: T = tropical rain forest; P = paratropical rain forest; S = tropical semi-deciduous forest; N = notophyllous broadleaved evergreen forest; D = polar broadleaved deciduous forest; C = mixed coniferous forest. From Upchurch and Wolfe (1987), with positions of floras with palms, cycads according to Wing and Greenwood (1993). Plate tectonic reconstruction and palaeo-coastlines according to Smith et al. (1994).

The Middle and Late Eocene were characterised by progressive drying as well as cooling climates. Semi-deciduous and deciduous forests became widespread from the Middle Eocene onward, for example, as indicated by the Green River flora in Wyoming (MacGintie, 1969), and palynological studies from the Gulf Coast also indicate a cooling and drying trend, beginning in the mid-Middle Eocene (Frederiksen, 1991). During the Late Eocene, closed-canopy rain forests were replaced by open woodland, with savanna patches, as interpreted by Retallack (1983) from the character of palaeosols (Figure 11.6).

### 11.3.2 Europe

The European K/T boundary event is difficult to evaluate from the vegetational viewpoint since much of the region was submerged, and records are fragmentary (Knobloch et al., 1993). Following Early Paleocene regression, the latest Paleocene and Eocene have preserved a remarkable record of tropical plant and animal fossils, especially from the London and Paris basins, and in Germany. As with North America, megathermal floristic elements were extensively represented, and have received detailed study. The European story is based primarily on seeds, from S England and Germany, and pollen from the Paris Basin, and provides valuable contrasts with the record from North America.

The latest Paleocene climate was very wet, and in S England, at 40° palaeolatitude north, palm-dominated freshwater swamps became widely established (Collinson and Hooker, 1987), whereas at palaeolatitudes of 50°N Taxodiaceae were dominant on the deltas which now form the oilfields to the east of the Shetlands, implying a major floristic boundary between the two areas. Vegetation within the region of the London and Paris basins must have borne many similarities to tropical rain forest, since it included trees within the megathermal families Burseraceae, Lauraceae, Rutaceae, Sapotaceae

are situated. These typically collided with the North American continent at different times at the latitude of British Columbia, and then slid north to Alaska. Such accretion was largely over by the Early Tertiary, but some may have experienced considerable mid-Tertiary movement (Cowan, 1982; Bruns, 1983).

North American megathermal vegetation underwent two subsequent, well-documented phases of poleward extension and withdrawal (Figure 11.5), one during the Middle Eocene, at about 42 Ma, and one in the Late Eocene, although neither reached so far north as during the Early Eocene. During intervening phases, tropical aspect vegetation withdrew about 15° to the south. The significance of these fluctuations is unclear, since Eocene sea levels exhibit much higher cyclicity (Haq et al., 1988), and Milankovich cycles were of *much* higher resolution.

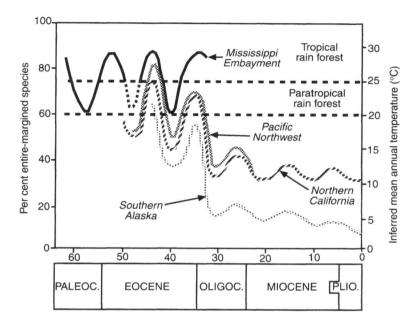

Figure 11.5    Inferred Tertiary palaeotemperature curves estimated from percentages of entire-margined leave in four locations in North America (Wolfe, 1978). Note the sharp drop in palaeotemperatures following the terminal Eocene event, and the oscillating temperatures during the Eocene.

and Theaceae, together with abundant climbers, referable to Icacinaceae, Menispermaceae and Vitaceae (Gruas-Cavagnetto, 1978; Collinson and Hooker, 1987).

As in North America, it was the vegetation of the Early Eocene which contained the greatest representation of tropical elements, especially of seeds from the London Clay initially described by Reid and Chandler (1933) and summarised by Chandler (1964) and Collinson (1983). Tropical trees were best represented, and included members of Anacardiaceae (*Lannea* and *Dracontomelon*, with four extinct genera); diverse Annonaceae; Burseraceae, with four extinct genera; Dilleniaceae (*Hibbertia* and *Tetracera*), Euphorbiaceae; Flacourtiaceae (*Oncoba* and two extinct genera); Lauraceae (*Endiandra*, *Cinnamomum*, *Beilschmeidia*, *Litsea* and extinct forms); extinct members of Lythraceae; Palmae (*Nypa*, ?*Oncosperma*, *Sabal*, ?*Livistona*, *Corypha*, *Serenoa* and many extinct forms); Sabiaceae, with *Meliosma*; and Sapotaceae in two

form-genera. Bombacaceae and *Anacolosa* are represented by pollen (Collinson et al., 1981), and the dipterocarp *Anisoptera* (Figure 4.5) has recently been determined on the basis of the anatomical features of a single twig (Poole, 1993). Seeds of lianes are particularly abundant and include Icacinaceae (*Iodes*, *Natsiatum* and five extinct genera); common representatives of Menispermaceae (attributable to *Parabaena*, *Tinospora*, *Calycocarpum*, *Tinomiscium* and five extinct genera); and Vitaceae (*Tetrastigma*, *Ampelopsis*, *Parthenocissus*, *Vitis* and an extinct genus). Compared to the latest Paleocene, the London Clay Early Eocene vegetation clearly exhibited many more features of closed, megathermal rain forest. Many of the above taxa were shared with boreotropical forests of North America, 24% of fruit and seed genera occurring in both areas at this time (Manchester, 1994).

The Early Eocene of W Europe is perhaps best known for its fossils of *Nypa* (Figure 5.20), which are found together with other mangroves, such

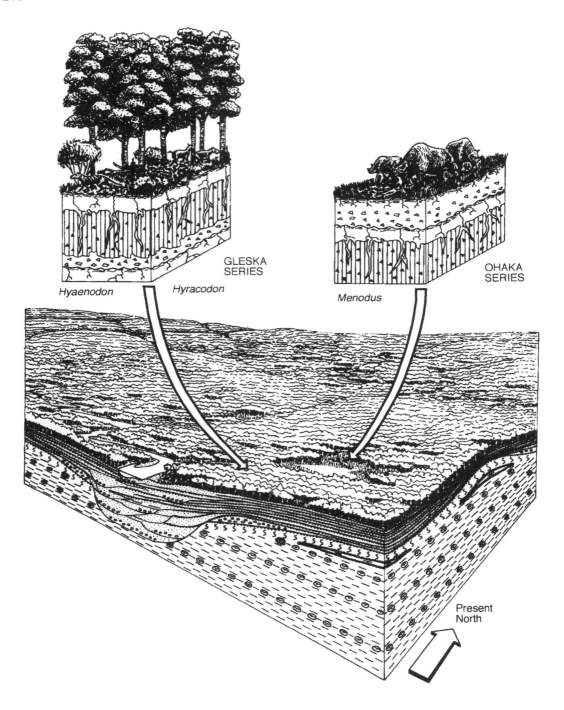

Figure 11.6   Late Eocene landscape for the Big Badlands of South Dakota for the Chadron Formation (Late Eocene age indicated by Prothero, 1994); open woodland with savanna patches (Retallack, 1983).

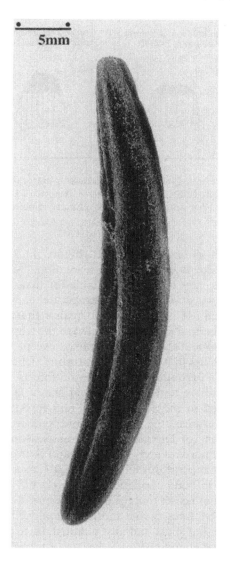

Figure 11.7   Fruit of *Ceriops cantiensis*, from the London Clay. Photo courtesy of M. Collinson.

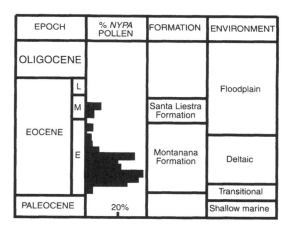

Figure 11.8   *Nypa* pollen frequencies in the Early and Middle Eocene of Spain (Haseldonckx, 1972). The high frequencies of this low pollen producer clearly indicate that *Nypa* was growing abundantly in the local area. Reproduced by permission of Kluwer Academic Publishers.

as *Ceriops* (Figure 11.7) and *Palaeobruguiera* (Rhizophoraceae), *Pelliciera* (Pellicieraceae) and *Acrostichum* (Pteridaceae), together with extinct, supposed mangroves, such as *Wetheriella* and *Palaeowetheriella* (?Euphorbiaceae). *Nypa* has been recorded at many localties across W Europe (Ollivier-Pierre and Caratini, 1984), with notable records from Belgium (Stockmans, 1936) and

Spain (where Haseldonckx (1972) recorded *Nypa* in high frequencies, Figure 11.8) and east to Hungary (Kedves, 1969), and reflect the development of a widespread belt of mangrove swamps bordering the northern coast of Tethys. *Nypa* fruits from different localities show marked size variations, possibly indicating different species, but Collinson (1993) suggested that such variations are taphonomic, and that only a single species was present in the European Eocene. This mangrove element remained, reduced in representation, into the Middle Eocene, and persisted in S Europe until the Bartonian (early Late Eocene) (Cavagnetto and Anadon, 1995).

As with North America, there has been much discussion about the detailed nature of the tropical aspect vegetation of W Europe, and of the London Clay in particular, which in the Early Eocene lay at 41°N. Reid and Chandler (1933) concluded that the London Clay flora compared closely with the present-day vegetation of the Indo-Malayan region and Montford (1970) made a close analogy with multistoreyed evergreen rain forests of Borneo. On the other hand, Chaney (1940) listed the London Clay flora as subtropical, and van Steenis (1962a) considered that the seeds of tropical affinity had been transported from more southerly latitudes by Tethyan marine currents.

Daley (1972) made a critical review of the London Clay climate, physiography and vegetation, and concluded that it did not represent a true tropical rain forest climate, but a climatic type not represented at the present time. The flora includes a significant number of 'temperate' elements which were previously thought to have come from nearby mountains, analogous to those bearing montane vegetation in tropical regions, but there is no geological evidence for such uplands in the vicinity of S England during London Clay times. Some of the supposed 'temperate' taxa which he considered as 'upland' are well known from low altitudes in tropical vegetation: *Engelhardia* has one species which occurs in lowland swamps in Malaysia (Ng, 1972), *Araucaria* grows in rain forests at sea level in New Caledonia (Florin, 1962) and Australia, and is a widespread component of some Australian rain forests (Adam, 1994), and *Pinus* is a widespread lowland tree in the deciduous forests of Indochina and Central America. Collinson and Hooker (1987) suggest that the 'tropicality' of the London Clay flora may have been under- rather than overemphasised during the past, since in present-day paratropical forests temperate affinity taxa often predominate along streamsides (Wolfe, 1979), and may therefore be over-represented in fossil assemblages.

Daley (1972) also emphasised the seasonal fluctuations in insolation for the Eocene London Clay flora and, in this respect, the Eocene climate of W Europe clearly differed from any present-day equatorial climates. However, Collinson (1999) emphasised that large woods from the London Clay lack growth rings, which are also absent from 70% of twigs, and suggests that any seasonality which did exist related to water deficiency and not temperature. Their closest analogue is probably the climates of the Tertiary refuges in Indochina and Mexico, which are equable and wet, but with a short period of low

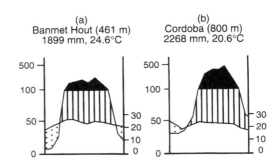

Figure 11.9   Present-day climates in boreotropical refuges in Indochina and Central America (Tiffney, 1985a). For interpretation of climate diagram see Figure 2.1.

rainfall during the winter (Figure 11.9) and increased fluctuations in insolation. Such a climate may have been suitable for taxa which today we would consider 'temperate' as well as 'tropical'. It is important to realise that moist megathermal taxa are restricted to the tropics by *temperature* and not seasonality, except where this results in a substantial moisture deficiency. Even in perhumid equatorial rain forests, many taxa clearly respond to fluctuations of climate, reflected in the phenology of rain forest trees. For instance, the irregular, but synchronised flowering of Dipterocarpaceae in aseasonal SE Asia (approximately every 5 years) is triggered when temperatures fall down to 20°C as a result of the El Niño oscillation (Ashton et al., 1988). This emphasises that the most widespread family of forest trees of the most perhumid climates of the Far East initially adapted to areas of seasonal climate before it became established in the evergreen rain forests of SE Asia (Section 9.6).

### Middle and Late Eocene climatic change

Palynological and macrofossil studies through the Eocene of S England clearly indicate gradually deteriorating climates from the Early Eocene onward, witnessed by the gradual decline of megathermal elements (Collinson et al., 1981), but with occasional warmer excursions (Figure 11.10), especially in the mid-Middle Eocene at

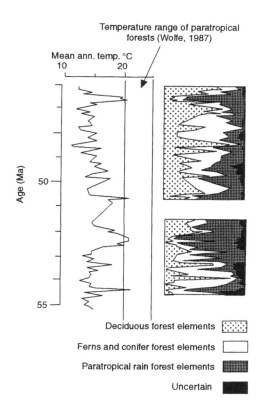

Figure 11.10 Summary of fluctuations of paratropical, deciduous forest, fern/conifer and undifferentiated pollen groups through the Eocene of S England (Hubbard and Boulter, 1983), together with estimates of palaeotemperatures based on multivariate analyses of palynological data.

about 45 Ma (Hubbard and Boulter, 1983). There was a marked temperature decline at the end of the Middle Eocene, and by Late Eocene times in S England, riverine and coastal settings bore warm temperate taxodiaceous swamp, with a rich freshwater swamp flora, and megathermal elements had all but disappeared (Collinson and Hooker, 1987). The palynological succession from the Eocene of the Paris Basin provides a similar story (Figure 11.11), with two warm periods shown by diversity maxima of tropical and subtropical elements, one in the Early

Eocene, and the second in the early Bartonian, also at about 42 Ma (Ollivier-Pierre et al., 1987). There is thus some accord between the palaeoclimatic signatures of Europe and North America up until the early part of the Late Eocene.

Evidence for a sudden cooling at the end of the Eocene in Europe is much less clearcut than in North America. Hochuli (1984) demonstrates that, whereas vegetation changes at this time in NW and SW Europe were minimal, there was a clear change to cooler climates in central Europe, suggesting that the more limited degree of change in the west related to marked oceanic influence at this time.

### 11.3.3 East Asia

Most reconstructions of Tertiary vegetation from China differentiate three floristic regions: the southern, tropical to subtropical region to the south, the middle subtropical region, which occupied a belt between 25 and 35°N, passing inland in a WNW direction, and a more northerly, northern warm temperate to subtropical region (Song Zhichen, 1989). The middle region, coinciding approximately with the subtropical high pressure zone, was characterised by arid climates throughout most of the Palaeogene, whereas during the 'middle' Eocene the northern region bore megathermal vegetation which included palms and other taxa of tropical affinity (Song Zhichen, 1989). Tropical aspect vegetation was predominant in the southern tropical to subtropical zone throughout the Paleogene. Although there were some very broad similarities with the boreotropical floras to the west, it is likely that E Asian Palaeogene floras bore few close relationships to those of other areas, emphasised by palynological studies. For instance, normapolles were more poorly developed, and appeared later than in Europe or North America (Zhao et al., 1981), and also E Asia included many endemic elements (Song Zhichen et al., 1981; Zhao Xun et al., 1992).

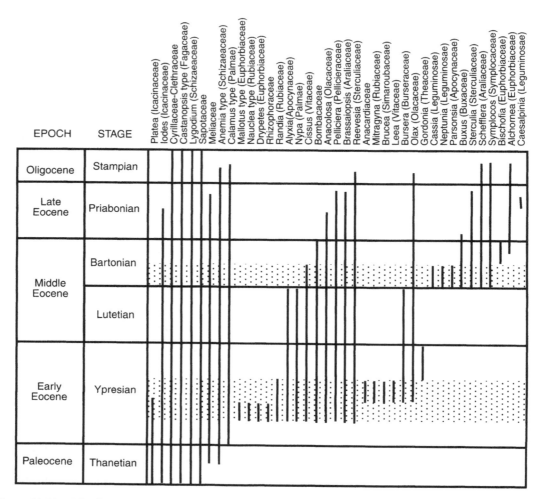

Figure 11.11  Distribution of pollen of tropical/subtropical elements in the Palaeogene of the Paris Basin (simplified from Ollivier-Pierre et al., 1987).

## Dispersals into and between the northern hemisphere rain forest blocks

Early Eocene frost-free and equable climates close to the Arctic Circle are thought to have provided opportunities for interregional dispersal for many megathermal plants, accounting for the close similarities between elements in North America, Europe and E Asia. Tiffney (1985a) reviewed both geological and palaeobotanical evidence for such pathways, and concluded that there is good evidence for a land bridge between Scotland and E North America via S Greenland (the 'Thulean' route) from the Late Paleocene to Early Eocene at a latitude of 45–50°N, and that this was responsible for dispersals of most megathermal elements between the two continents. An additional route (the 'de Geer' route) at about 70°N was open for a longer period of time, but was too far north to act as a significant path for megathermal taxa. He also played down the importance of the Bering land bridge, in view of its far northerly position (75°N). Palynological data documents transatlantic dispersals of wind-pollinated warm temperate taxa at this time, such as *Platycarya* (Wing, 1984; Frederiksen, 1994c) and *Eucommia* (Pocknall, 1987) from Europe to North America, and *Carya* in the reverse direction (Muller, 1981). Evidence for dispersals of megathermal taxa is less clear, but a few examples are Sapotaceae, which probably dispersed to North America in the Early Eocene, and Bombacaceae, which dispersed to Europe in the latest Paleocene.

The shores of Tethys may not have provided such an ideal setting for dispersal of moist megathermal plants between Europe and the Far East at the time of the Late Paleocene/Early Eocene thermal maximum, since at this time the route would have been blocked by a wide epicontinental sea (the Turgai Straits), and also, central Asia was characterised by very dry conditions, reflected by the widespread occurrence of Eocene evaporites, but may have provided a suitable route for dispersal of mangroves. The Turgai Straits eventually became closed at the beginning of the Oligocene, coinciding with *Le Grande Coupure* (Section 11.2), and it is likely that there may have been a (possibly shortlived) dispersal corridor for European megathermal elements along the northern shores of Tethys to the Far East at the end of the Eocene, and possibly during the earliest Oligocene. This corridor would have been in place at the time of the closure of the Turgai Straits, but before global temperatures became too low for megathermal taxa in the northern mid-latitudes, or elevations became too high as a result of uplift of the Tibetan Plateau as a result of the collision of India and Asia.

There were a number of noteworthy dispersals into W Europe during the Eocene, which deserve mention, including *Alangium* (section *Marlea*) in the latest Early Eocene into S England (Collinson et al., 1981), remarkably at precisely the same time as the dispersal of *Alangium* section *Villosum* into Australia (Martin et al., 1996). Caesalpinoidae appeared in France at the same time (Gruas-Cavagnetto and Gruas-Cavagnetto, 1990). Also remarkable was the Middle to Late

Eocene dispersal of African taxa into Spain, at which time N Africa had drifted very close to the Iberian Peninsula. The immigrants included *Mirabilis* (Nyctaginaceae), *Acacia*, *Albizia*, and plants producing *Crudia* type pollen, *Barringtonia* (Lecythidaceae), *Amanoa* and *Alchornea* (Euphorbiaceae) and the SE Asian genus *Bownlowia* (or a close ally) in the family Tiliaceae (Cavagnetto and Anadon, 1995). Eocene pollen records of the South American mangrove *Pelliciera* (Pellicieraceae) might suggest dispersal from equatorial latitudes, where this taxon has been known for many years (e.g. Wymstra, 1968; Graham, 1977), but its first appearance in the European Early Eocene, at the same time as many other mangrove taxa, and its taxonomic affinity to the northern megathermal family Theaceae, suggest that its first appearance in the mangrove swamps of the Tethyan Ocean should be given consideration.

Examples of dispersals from South America are few, despite the presence of a land connection (Hallam, 1994). The Paleocene appearance of *Anacolosa* and *Longapertites* (Palmae) in North America, and Bombacaceae and *Symplocos* in South America, probably reflect such dispersals.

## 11.4 OLIGOCENE TO PLIOCENE

The effect of the earliest Oligocene cooling event was reflected across the northern hemisphere by the expansion of broadleaved microthermal vegetation and the disappearance of megathermal elements from wide areas. Wolfe (1985) suggested that globally Early Oligocene tropical vegetation was restricted to areas equatorward of 15° (compared to 20–25° today). This may have been the case in North America, where the effects of the 'terminal Eocene event' were particularly dramatic, but in Europe the change to cooler climates was more gradual (Collinson et al., 1981), with tropical elements persisting in the region of the Paris Basin until the Early Oligocene (Hochuli, 1984). During the Oligocene and Neogene, northern hemisphere megathermal elements would have found refuge in Central America, which extended to 5° north, but, with increasingly dry climates developing within the subtropical high pressure zone, suitable refuges for moist megathermal taxa would have been limited. In Europe, such refuges would have been even more restricted until the closure of Tethys in the Middle Miocene, and suitable niches would have been further reduced by the uplift of the Alps, inhibiting north–south dispersal, and the development of summer-dry climates in the Mediterranean. Only in the Far East was there a continuous land area, characterised mainly by moist climates extending into the low latitudes (Chapter 9). The region of E Asia and Indochina therefore provided many more opportunities for the survival of elements of northern hemisphere Early Tertiary megathermal floras than either Europe or North America, clearly illustrated by Tiffney (1985b) who has reviewed the present-day distributions of megathermal and mesothermal angiosperm taxa which are recorded from northern hemisphere Eocene floras. Out of a total of 52 genera reviewed, 34 have survived in the summer-wet forests of S China and Indochina, whereas 22 are recorded in Central and South America and only 8 in Africa (Figure 11.9). Similarly, this area has provided a refuge for numerous genera of conifers, such as *Cunninghamia*, *Glyptostrobus* and *Metasequoia*.

Before the Late Miocene and Pliocene periods of global cooling, there was one further phase of warming, accompanied by the expansion of megathermal vegetation into northern latitudes, probably coinciding with the period of high sea levels of the latest Early Miocene to earliest Middle Miocene. This warm period has already been discussed with respect to the Far East, when mangrove swamps with *Rhizophora*, and southern conifers, such as *Dacrydium*, extended as far north as S Japan (Section 9.6.3). This warming event is also reflected by macrofossils, which show subtropical elements in both S and N Japan at this time (e.g. Tanai, 1972). In North America, megathermal elements occurred as far north as New Jersey during the Middle Miocene

(Wolfe, 1985), whereas in C Europe some megathermal taxa became widespread elements of swamp vegetation. A few of these underwent a phase of explosive speciation, such as *Symplocos*, which was represented by more than a dozen species during the latter part of the Early Miocene.

## 11.5  SUMMARY

At the end of the Cretaceous, open-canopied, subhumid megathermal forests, which were widespread across the northern mid-latitudes were destroyed, and following a successional stage which resembled the succession within extant tropical rain forest, but on a much longer time scale, and a widespread change to wetter climates, were replaced by closed-canopy forests. These resembled present-day tropical and paratropical rain forests in many respects, but also included some temperate elements.

As global climates became warmer and equable, toward the end of the Paleocene, these forests extended in range, to typically 60°N, and diversified, and mangroves with *Nypa* became widespread in coastal regions. At the same time, between the Late Paleocene and Early Eocene, the establishment of a land bridge from North America to Europe via S Greenland allowed the fairly free interchange of megathermal floras, with the result that during the time of the Late Paleocene/Early Eocene thermal maximum, megathermal vegetation in these areas shared many of their constituent genera. Dispersal paths via the northerly Bering or by the Turgai Straits were probably less effective as routes for megathermal plants, with the result that the megathermal vegetation of E Asia developed in a greater degree of isolation, although the northern shores of Tethys may have formed a dispersal avenue for coastal plants, such as mangroves.

Following the Late Paleocene/Early Eocene climatic maximum and a phase of cooling after about 49 Ma, tropical and paratropical rain forests in both Europe and North America underwent further periods of expansion during successive warm episodes, but without reaching the very high latitudes of the Early Eocene. These warm intervals appear to have continued into the Late Eocene in W North America, while drier climates developed in E North America, and there was a tendency toward cooler climates in Europe. With the closure of the Thulean land bridge during the Early Eocene, the two areas also began to differentiate floristically.

The terminal Eocene cooling event had a very pronounced effect on megathermal vegetation in North America, which was replaced by deciduous forests over most of the continent, but presumably found refuge at southerly latitudes, in Middle America. The effect of Early Oligocene cooling in Europe was less marked in the west, presumably as a result of oceanic influence, but was pronounced in central areas; however, megathermal elements had all but disappeared from the European mid-latitudes by the mid-Oligocene. At this time, the closure of the Turgai Straits may have provided increased opportunities for dispersal of megathermal elements from Europe to E Asia.

A pronounced warming episode during the Middle Miocene resulted in a further phase of northern expansion of tropical forests in all areas but, with an additional phase of global cooling during the later Middle and Late Miocene and Late Pliocene, areas suitable for the survival of tropical elements became very limited.

With the formation of the Panamanian Isthmus during the Pliocene, some North American megathermal elements were able to find refuge in the warmer, tropical regions of Central and South America, and these are preserved today as the amphi-Pacific element of van Steenis (1962a). In Europe, however, the creation of east–west mountain chains of the Alps, of summer-dry climates in the Mediterranean, and the expansion of Pleistocene glaciers, resulted in the extermination of megathermal elements, which today can be found only on offshore Atlantic islands and the Colchic region to the east of the Black Sea.

In the E and SE Asian region, the presence of a land connection to equatorial latitudes throughout the Tertiary, coupled with the development of moist, monsoonal climates at mid-latitudes during the Early Miocene, resulted in much greater opportunities for the survival of elements of the boreotropical flora in SE Asia than was the case in either the Americas or Europe, and this accounts for the floristic similarity first reported by Reid and Chandler (1933) between the Early Eocene London Clay flora and the present-day floras of the SE Asian region.

# CHAPTER 12

# Interplate Dispersal Paths and Land Bridges

## 12.1  REVIEW OF PALYNOLOGICAL EVIDENCE FOR DISPERSAL PATHS

This chapter summarises evidence for the location and timing of dispersal paths and land bridges which have been followed by megathermal taxa (Figure 12.1). The database consists mainly of angiosperm pollen (and some macrofossil) records, together with a few selected pteridophyte spores and gymnosperms, and uses a total of about 160 taxa which have been positively determined on adjacent plates, and which are generally accepted as being megathermal, or megathermal *pro majore parte*, although instances of dispersals of some microthermal taxa, especially those which reflect the development of tropical montane vegetation, are also included. Herbs, such as Compositae and Acanthaceae are, however, not considered. For each route, suggestions are given as to whether dispersal paths were 'corridors', 'filters' or whether dispersal events were rare 'sweepstake' occurrences.

### South America and Africa

As brought to attention in Chapter 5, land connections between the African and South American Plates were severed at the end of the Albian (96 Ma), until which time there was clearly a dispersal corridor for megathermal plants between the two plates. However, the frequency of plant dispersals across the newly formed ocean after this date suggests that some

form of land connection, or series of islands acting as stepping stones, remained throughout the Late Cretaceous and into the earliest Tertiary, possibly in the region of the Walvis (Figure 12.2) and Sierra Leone ridges. Oligo-Miocene (36–5 Ma) crossings, however, such as the swamp tree *Symphonia globulifera* (Guttiferae) and a climbing fern allied to *Lygodium scandens* (Schizaeaceae), were probably instances of sweepstake dispersal.

The Walvis Ridge may also have acted as a dispersal path for southern hemisphere elements, such as *Casuarina* (Casuarinaceae), which appears in both southern Africa and southernmost South America in the Paleocene.

### Africa and India

Many plant dispersals occurred between the African and Indian plates while India was juxtaposed to Madagascar in the Turonian (92–89 Ma) to early Maastrichtian (74–70 Ma), at which time island chains were likely to have been present between Africa and Madagascar. The dispersal path from Africa to India was a filter, for many African taxa failed to make the crossing.

After the separation of the Indian Plate from Madagascar, there were relatively few dispersal events between Africa and the Indian Plate until the Eocene (54–36 Ma), at which time dispersals were facilitated as India approached Asia. A further phase of dispersal from Africa to India took place during the Late Miocene (10–5 Ma)

255

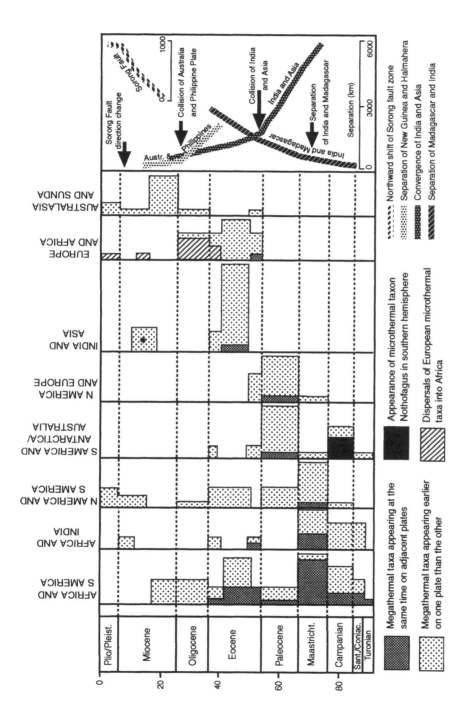

Figure 12.1   Main times of interplate dispersals according to the palynological record (or macrofossil record where asterisked*). Dispersals fall into the following groups: (a) those which relate to the separation of the African, South American, North American and Indian plates in the Late Cretaceous and earliest Tertiary; (b) those relating to the expansion of tropical rain forests to high latitudes during the Late Paleocene/Early Eocene thermal maximum; (c) dispersals relating to the collision of the Indian and Asian plates, and the convergence of Africa and Europe in the Eocene; and (d) dispersals relating to Neogene plate collisions in the Far East and the formation of the Isthmus of Panama. The timings of the main plate collisions, or separations, are indicated to the right; the Sorong Fault extends from New Guinea into the Maluku.

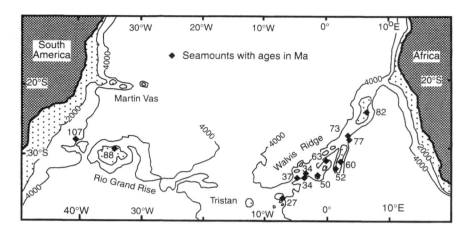

Figure 12.2   The Walvis Ridge, in the S Atlantic, is a seamount lineament which would have formed an island chain between Africa and South America up until the Eocene (McDougal and Douglas, 1988). Published by permission of Elsevier Science.

and Pliocene (5–1.6 Ma) (based on macrofossil records only). This phase of dispersal probably related to the Late Neogene expansion of seasonally dry climates.

### India and Australia

It is possible that, during the Turonian, an island arc along the leading edge of the Indian Plate, between India and Australia, provided a pathway for plant dispersal to Australia, enabling the dispersal of a number of plants producing elaterospores (Gnetales) to New Guinea (Figure 5.22). This route may also have been followed by some angiosperms.

### South America and Antarctica/Australia

Clear dispersal events occurred between South America and Antarctica through to New Zealand and Australia, via the South Sandwich Islands and South Georgia, which would have formed a continuous connection during the Late Cretaceous and Paleocene (Figure 12.3). As noted in Chapter 10, this path was followed by primitive angiosperms, such as winteraceous *Bubbia/Zygogynum* and *Drimys*. It is likely that

the South America–Antarctic connection involved a direct land bridge to facilitate dispersal of taxa such as the microthermal *Nothofagus* (Fagaceae), although due to its near polar position it would strictly have acted as a filter for megathermal plants, since plant taxa sensitive to either cold or varying day length would be excluded except during the warmest episodes. The warmest climates were experienced at the time of the Late Paleocene/Early Eocene thermal maximum. At this time there was a floristic interchange, with South American megathermal/warm elements dispersing to Australia, typified by Myrtaceae and Sapindaceae (Section 10.5), and with the Australian *Casuarina* dispersing in the reverse direction (Section 6.4.1).

### South America and North America

The presence of a dispersal pathway from N to South America between the Campanian (84–74 Ma) and Paleocene (66–54 Ma) is clearly evidenced from faunal distributions, but Hallam (1994) considered that the Antillean island chain, which connected these continents, was a dispersal filter, rather than a corridor, since the number of vertebrate taxa which made the crossing was

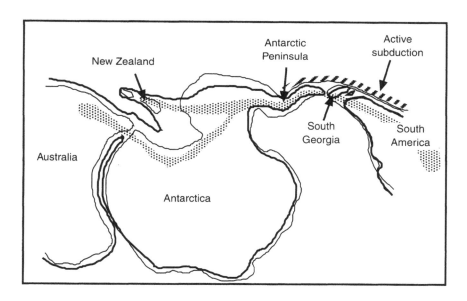

Figure 12.3   Mid-Cretaceous palaeogeography of the Antarctic region, simplified from Woodburne and
Zinsmeister (1984) by Hallam (1994). Reproduced by permission of the Palaeontological Society.

limited. Palynological data supports this view. Firstly, most dispersal events occurred over the same time interval, and, secondly, the number of dispersals were few compared to those making the S Atlantic crossing, which, as noted above, was also a filter.

Only well-dispersed taxa made the crossing during the mid-Tertiary, but with the formation of the Isthmus of Panama in the Pliocene there were numerous noteworthy dispersals into South America from the North, such as *Alnus* and *Quercus*, and possibly megathermal taxa such as *Hedyosmum* (Chloranthaceae) and other amphi-Pacific elements. However, there were few dispersals in the reverse direction, as noted in Chapter 6.

### North America and Europe

Although land bridges existed between North America and Europe during much of the Late Cretaceous and Early Tertiary at very high latitudes, these were mostly too far north for megathermal plants, but could easily have provided pathways for temperate elements.

However, as noted in Chapter 11, a shortlived land connection across S Greenland during the latest Paleocene to Early Eocene would have existed at about 45–50°N at the precise time of the Late Paleocene/Early Eocene thermal maximum, and most likely provided a route for the dispersal of megathermal elements between the two areas for this short time period. The high degree of similarity at the generic level of the macrofloras of Europe and North America during the Early Eocene (Lehmann, 1963; Manchester, 1994) argues strongly for a direct land connection between the two regions.

### India and Asia

By far the most marked instance of angiosperm interplate dispersal during the Tertiary occurred following the collision of the Indian Plate with Asia in the Middle Eocene, as noted in Section 9.4. This collision brought the Indian and S

Table 12.1   Major Tertiary and Cretaceous dispersal paths.

| Dispersal paths | Epoch | Equivalent land bridge (vansteenis) |
| --- | --- | --- |
| 1  Africa – South America | Mid-Cretaceous (C), Late Cretaceous – ?Eocene (F) | Transatlantic |
| 2  Africa – India | Turonian – Maastrichtian (F) | Madagascar – Ceylon |
| 3  South America – Antarctica/ Australia | Santonian – Paleocene (F + C) | Subantarctic |
| 4  North – South America | Campanian – Paleocene (F) | 'Isthmus of Panama' represented by Greater Antillean island arc |
| 5  North America – Europe | Paleocene – Eocene (F + C) | |
| 6  India – Asia | Eocene (C) | |
| 7  ?North America – Asia | Eocene (F) | Bering |
| 8  Europe – Africa | Middle Eocene – Oligocene (F) | |
| 9  Southeast Asia – Australia | Neogene and Quaternary (F) | Malesian |
| 10  North – South America | Pliocene – Quaternary (C) | Isthmus of Panama |

C = corridor; F = filter. Sweepstake dispersal routes omitted.

Asian/Sundanian floras, which lay in the same climatic zone, into direct contact. The Indian flora seems to have been the more aggressive of the two, with wholesale dispersal into the SE Asian region.

### Africa and Europe/Asia

Tethys formed a major barrier for plant dispersal between Europe and Africa throughout the Late Cretaceous and Early Tertiary. However, as noted in Chapter 11, there is clear palynological evidence for dispersals of African megathermal taxa into the Iberian Peninsula during the latest Middle and Late Eocene, at which time the the Iberian Peninsula and N Africa were closely juxtaposed and enjoyed a tropical climate, although they were still separated by the Straits of Gibraltar. A few temperate taxa dispersed to Africa at the same time. There was no big floristic interchange during the Middle Miocene, comparable to migrations of vertebrates, with only a few temperate taxa, such as *Juniperus* (Cupressaceae) and *Alnus* (Betulaceae), possibly making the crossing at this time.

### West and East Asia

This dispersal route has not been assessed in this account, but presumably would have been open

for the dispersal of megathermal plant taxa following the closure of the Turgai Straits at the end of the Eocene. This route most likely became closed as a result of tectonic uplift in S Asia following the collision of the Indian and Asian plates, the mid-Tertiary deterioration of global climates, and development of cold deserts during the Neogene. This route may possibly have been open to dispersal of boreotropical taxa into E Asia during the Oligocene.

### Australia and Sunda

Several instances of dispersal are noted between SE Asia and Australia following the latest Oligocene collision of the Australian Plate with Halmahera (Section 9.8).

A second phase of interplate dispersal began at about 3.5 Ma, as a result of major tectonic readjustments at the time of initiation of the Sorong Fault. This involved the dispersal of montane conifers including *Podocarpus imbricatus* and *Phyllocladus* into the Sunda region.

### Wallace's Line

Whereas the convergence of the Australian and Sunda plates facilitated interplate dispersal, the opening of the Makasar Straits had the opposite effect within the archipelagic area of Wallacea, lying between Borneo and New Guinea. Since the Oligocene, only a few plant taxa appear to have made the crossing, and those are thought to be rare instances of sweepstake dispersal.

### North America and Asia

Dispersals via the Bering land bridge have not been assessed here, but it is unlikely to have formed a pathway for diverse elements of the North American Boreotropical flora except,

perhaps, during the warmest phase of the Late Paleocene/Early Eocene climatic optimum.

## 12.2  DISPERSAL PATHS AND 'LAND BRIDGES'

The major Tertiary and Cretaceous dispersal paths and their relationship to the land bridges of van Steenis (1962a) are summarised in Table 12.1.

# CHAPTER 13

# Synthesis

## 13.1 OVERVIEW OF TROPICAL RAIN FOREST HISTORY

### Areas of angiosperm origin

Although it is considered that angiosperms initially evolved in the tropics (Hickey and Doyle, 1977), and today megathermal groups are virtually confined to the tropics, there is no need to invoke a tropical origin for all moist megathermal angiosperm groups. Geological evidence clearly shows that from the time of origin of angiosperms up until the end of the Eocene (36 Ma), warm, frost-free climates persisted throughout the northern and southern mid-latitudes, and that each of these areas, as well as the equatorial zone, were important centres for the primary radiation of many of the taxonomic groups characteristic of tropical rain forest.

Following the expansion of angiosperms to the mid and higher latitudes, moist megathermal angiosperm lineages developed in three, parallel belts (Figure 13.1), separated by the subtropical high pressure zones, and to some degree by oceanic barriers. The northern belt, which encompassed the moist mid-latitudes of Europe and North America, formed an important centre of origin between the Turonian (92–89 Ma) and Maastrichtian (74–66 Ma), within which many moist megathermal groups initially radiated, such as the families Bombacaceae, Icacinaceae, Menispermaceae, Rutaceae, Sabiaceae, Saurauiaceae, Theaceae and Zingiberaceae. At the same time, the southern belt, centred on S South America and Eastern Gondwanaland, gave rise to Aquifoliaceae, Olacaceae and diverse Proteaceae, together with the microthermal genus

*Nothofagus* (Fagaceae), and became a harbour for Winteraceae and Chloranthaceae, which disappeared from equatorial and northern latitudes after the Albian/Cenomanian (108–92 Ma) (Muller, 1981). The equatorial belt was characterised by ancestral palms, Gunneraceae, Myrtaceae and Sapindaceae during the Santonian/Coniacian (89–84 Ma), when climates were hot and subhumid, with the addition of Annonaceae, Ctenolophonaceae, Leguminosae and Restionaceae in the Campanian (84–74 Ma) and Maastrichtian, following the development of more moist conditions. It is within these three belts that the angiosperm-dominated megathermal forests first appeared, and within which their constituent taxa more or less independently evolved.

### Physiognomy of Late Cretaceous moist megathermal forests

The earliest moist megathermal forests, which developed only after the rise to *dominance* of angiosperms in the Cenomanian (96–92 Ma), may not have been identical to our classic impressions of present-day tropical rain forests, in that they may not have been closed, multistratal communities, but more likely they were single-stratum open forests, and may have been kept open by browsing, generalist herbivores, although it is possible that closed-canopy forests developed locally. These forests included virtually all the physiognomic foliar adaptations in present-day tropical forests (Upchurch and Wolfe, 1987), including trees with entire, serrate and lobed, simple, pinnately and dichotomously compound, cordate, palmate

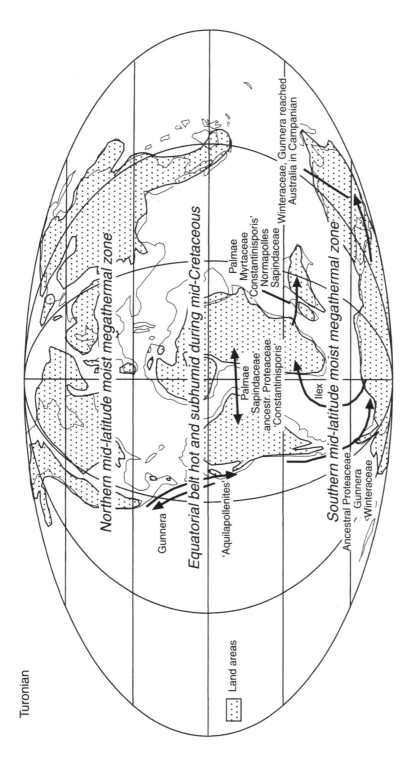

Figure 13.1   The three latitudinal belts within which moist megathermal angiosperm taxa first evolved. Turonian plate tectonic reconstruction with palaeogeography and coastlines according to Smith et al. (1994). Moist megathermal angiosperm-rich forests were widespread in northern and southern mid-latitudes during the earlier part of the Late Cretaceous, but did not develop in equatorial latitudes until the Campanian, prior to which time the equatorial climate was hot and subhumid. Noteworthy dispersals of megathermal taxa are indicated for the Turonian and Santonian/Coniacian, suggested by the palynological record.

and stenophyllous leaves, often with drip tips. However, their low stature is evidenced by the rarity of large angiosperm woods and also by the absence of large seeds, which would enable germination under the shade of a closed rain forest canopy. Perhaps the closest present-day analogues to Late Cretaceous megathermal forests are those of Madagascar, which are distinguished by a lower canopy than that found elsewhere in the tropics (Shuurman and Ravelojaona, 1997). Large angiospermous seeds are first recorded in the latest Cretaceous in equatorial latitudes, and it was probably these forests, in equatorial Africa, with presumed parallels in South America, which first took on the appearance of present-day closed-canopy rain forests.

## Paleocene (66–54 Ma)

Although the Cretaceous/Tertiary boundary meteorite impact had a major effect on both fauna and flora, the elements which appear to have replaced those which were destroyed by the effects of the bolide impact were essentially descended from lineages already present within each respective belt, rather than by immigrants from elsewhere. This was probably for three reasons. Firstly, very high sea levels of the Maastrichtian restricted opportunities for inter-plate dispersal; secondly, earliest Paleocene climates differed little from those of the Maastrichtian, although they were perhaps a little wetter; and, thirdly, since vegetation was probably disrupted globally, no individual flora would have had much competitive advantage.

It was in the Early Paleocene (66–60 Ma) that closed, multistratal, tropical aspect rain forests became widespread in each of the three moist megathermal belts (Figure 13.2). Their expansion probably paralleled the diversification of mammals which, given the opportunity to evolve into the niches left empty by the demise of the dinosaurs, developed fruit and seed eating, arboreal frugivorous habits, and created a vector for seed dispersal of large, closed-canopy trees.

The three latitudinal moist megathermal vegetation belts remained in place throughout the Paleocene, with the result that in each hemisphere, and also within the equatorial zone, the floras of these three belts developed to a large degree independently, although some interchange may have taken place, for instance with respect to the Americas, and possibly in the Far East. Opportunities for dispersal *within* these belts, however, would have been much greater, especially at the time of establishment of a land bridge between Europe and North America via S Greenland, coinciding precisely with the latest Paleocene/Early Eocene thermal maximum. At this time, megathermal forests would have extended to 60°N. Similarly, at this time the southern continents were in connection via Antarctica.

Following Wolfe's (1975) term 'Boreotropical flora', proposed for the Early Tertiary megathermal forests of Europe and North America, the northern hemisphere belt is here termed the 'Boreotropical Province', whereas the term 'Palmae Province' is used for the moist forests of the equatorial belt, a term which was originally proposed by Herngreen and Chlonova (1981) for the palm-rich latest Cretaceous and Paleocene of equatorial Africa and South America. The character of vegetation in SE Asia at this time still remains poorly known, but probably fell within the Palmae Province, but in a modified form. The southern hemisphere belt is here termed the 'Southern Megathermal Province', and equates with the 'Nothofagidites-Proteaceae' province of Zaklinskaya (1977), or the 'Nothofagus' province of Srivastava (1994), but excludes areas in which the microtherm genus Nothofagus became dominant.

During the subsequent 60 Ma, as an effect of the pressures brought about primarily by climatic change, and secondarily as a result of interplate plant dispersals, which took place following plate collisions or following the formation of migration corridors along connecting island arcs, floras of these provinces became variously modified, or replaced, or in

263

Paleocene

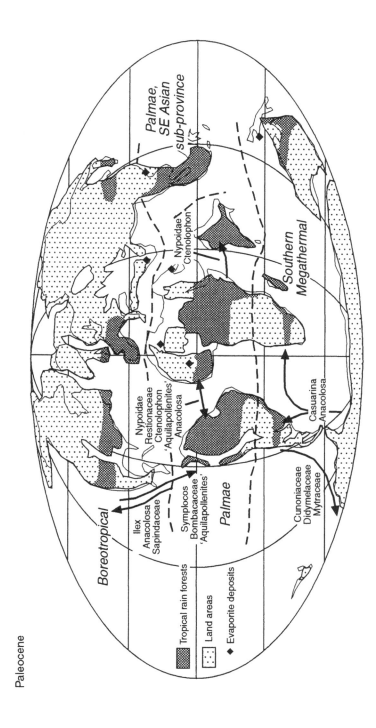

Figure 13.2 Closed-canopy tropical rain forests first became widespread during the Paleocene. Reconstruction based on synthesis of Chapters 6–11, and, in the absence of positive evidence, to the 'greenhouse' climatic scenario presented in Figure 4.12c. Palaeogeography and palaeocoastlines from Smith et al. (1994); occurrences of evaporites from Parrish et al. (1982) with additions; megathermal floristic provinces as suggested in the text. Noteworthy Maastrichtian and earlier Paleocene dispersals of megathermal taxa (prior to the Late Paleocene/Early Eocene thermal maximum) are indicated, as suggested by the palynological record.

some instances persisted as relics in subsequent floral provinces.

### Eocene (54–36 Ma)

Toward the end of the Paleocene, corresponding to the Late Paleocene/Early Eocene thermal maximum, the floras of the Boreotropical and Southern Megathermal Provinces expanded poleward (Figure 13.3), restricting microthermal boreal and southern *Nothofagus* forests to polar and upland regions. Tropical aspect and paratropical rain forests and widespread mangroves became established over much of Europe and North America, and reached very high latitudes along the American West Coast at this time. With a land connection via S Greenland, North American and European megathermal floras were floristically very similar, but those in E Asia developed somewhat in isolation, separated from Europe by the Turgai Straits, and connected to North America only by the very high latitude Bering land bridge. Similarly in the southern hemisphere, megathermal rain forests of the Southern Megathermal Province expanded throughout Australia and much of New Zealand, S South America, southern Africa and Madagascar.

The effect of the Late Paleocene/Early Eocene thermal maximum on equatorial climate and vegetation remains very poorly understood, but major changes took place across the whole of the equatorial belt at this time. Particularly noticeable is the reduced representation of Palmae as the dominant element from South America to India, and their replacement by dicotyledonous angiosperms, several of which produced bizarre pollen types, only to disappear shortly after in the Middle Eocene (49–39 Ma). Several suggestions have been made that the Eocene global temperature gradient was very subdued, and that equatorial temperatures were little different to those at mid-latitudes, but the maintenance of the subtropical high pressure zones, clearly indicated by the global distribution of evaporites (Figure 13.3) argues against this, and the possibility needs to be raised that

equatorial temperatures at the time of the Late Paleocene/Early Eocene thermal maximum were in fact higher than at present, and that the equatorial belt at this time may have included vegetation that has no real present-day analogue. Clearly, a critical evaluation of low latitude Eocene climates is needed in order to construct reliable global climate models for the thermal maximum. At this time, equatorial and mid-latitude rain forest blocks in both South America and Africa were probably connected across the subtropical high pressure zone along eastern coastlines where everwet climates were maintained by moist, onshore trade winds, but North America, Europe and Australia were isolated from equatorial latitudes by oceanic barriers.

Following the Late Paleocene/Early Eocene thermal maximum, boreotropical forests in North America and Europe underwent further periods of expansion during successive warm phases, but without reaching the very high latitudes of the Early Eocene. These warm periods continued into the Late Eocene (39–36 Ma) in North America, whereas in Europe there was a tendency toward cooler climates after the Middle Eocene, during which time megathermal forests became much reduced in extent. In Australia and South America, mid and Late Eocene climatic pertubations have not been recorded, but the concordance of the northward drift of the Australian Plate with deteriorating climates after the Late Paleocene/Early Eocene thermal maximum ensured the widespread occurrence of moist megathermal forests across much of the Australian continent. The precise meaning of the Eocene climatic oscillations recorded in North America and Europe remain unclear. A possible explanation is that they relate to climatic change on the scale of the eustatic sea level curve (Figure 3.6), but that part of the record, preserved in lowstand sediment packages, remains unsampled.

In the Middle and Late Eocene, equatorial floras were characterised by the appearance of many elements of modern aspect in each of the three tropical blocks. By this time, the floras of

Ey Eocene

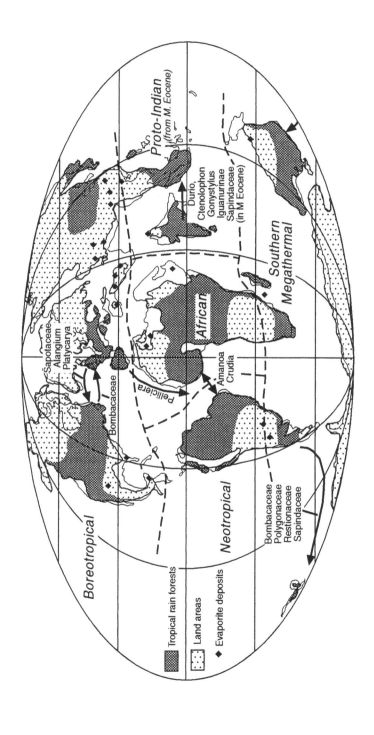

Figure 13.3 Distribution of closed-canopy tropical rain forests during the Late Paleocene/Early Eocene thermal maximum. Reconstruction based on synthesis of Chapters 6–11, and, in the absence of positive evidence, to the 'super greenhouse' climatic scenario presented in Figure 4.12d. Palaeogeography and palaeocoastlines from Smith et al. (1994); occurrences of evaporites from Parrish et al. (1982) with additions; megathermal floristic provinces according to the text. Noteworthy dispersals of megathermal plants relating to the thermal maximum, are indicated, as well as Middle Eocene dispersals into SE Asia, relating to the collision of the Indian and Asian plates, as suggested by the palynological record.

South America and Africa were isolated from each other, and subsequently evolved independently, although each retained many common elements of the Palmae Province, and these now exhibit disjunct African/South American (amphi-Atlantic) biogeographic distributions. Due to their geographic isolation and different evolutionary histories, these areas are referred to different floristic provinces from the Middle Eocene onward. Following Romero (1993), the megathermal vegetation of the South American Middle Eocene and later periods is referred to the 'Neotropical Province', whereas the term 'African Province' is proposed for the African moist megathermal floras for the same period.

As a result of the collision of the Indian Plate with Asia, many elements of its constituent flora, which comprised allochthonous African, Southern Megathermal and endemic groups, dispersed into SE Asia, which at the time lay in the same latitudinal and climatic zone. The Indian flora must have been quite aggressive, for the number of Asian taxa which dispersed into India at this time were few, and there were many extinctions in SE Asia (Section 9.4.2). After this phase of immigration, the flora of the region from India to Sunda exhibited considerable homogeneity, being characterised, for instance, by palms of the subtribe Iguanurinae and *Eugeissona*, and *Ctenolophon*, the parent taxon of the indeterminate *Meyeripollis*, and many others. It is here referred to the 'Proto-Indian Province'.

### The terminal Eocene event (36 Ma)

Moist, megathermal floras underwent great changes at the time of the terminal Eocene cooling event, which brought freezing temperatures to tropical mountain climates in SE Asia. At this time, megathermal elements of the Boreotropical Province virtually disappeared from northern mid-latitudes (Figure 13.4), although remnants persisted locally in S Europe and Middle America, the latter being expressed today as the amphi-Pacific element of

van Steenis (1962a) in Middle and South America and SE Asia. Opportunities for survival in both Europe and Central America were severely hindered because of the absence of dispersal corridors to the African or South American plates. In Europe, the uplift of the Alps, the maintenance of the Mediterranean as an east–west divide, and the barrier of the Sahara severely limited north–south dispersals, with the result that boreotropical megathermal elements virtually became extinct. Due to the close proximity of N Africa and the Iberian Peninsula by the Late Eocene, a few African elements were able to disperse into S Europe, but cooling climates resulted in their rapid disappearance in the mid-Tertiary.

Following the closure of the Turgai Straits in the Late Eocene, many of the European elements of the Boreotropical Province may have been able to disperse into E Asia, if they had not already done so during the Late Paleocene/Early Eocene climatic maximum via the Bering land bridge, and with deteriorating global climates were able to find refuge in the moist mesothermal to megathermal rain forests of China and Indochina, and also in the mountains of S Asia. During cooler periods of the Oligocene (36–25 Ma) and Miocene (25–5 Ma), it was thus only in the moist rain forests of E and SE Asia that diverse elements of the Boreotropical Province could find refuge, in the absence at this time of land bridges either to South America or Africa.

The terminal Eocene cooling event had a similar impact on the forests of the Southern Megathermal Province in S Africa and S South America, with the result that tropical aspect rain forests disappeared in these regions from areas south of the southern subtropical high pressure zone. In Australia, they were pushed northward, but with the continued northern drift of the Australian Plate through the Oligocene, Australia retained tropical aspect rain forests along its eastern coast north of about 35°S.

Within equatorial Africa and South America, the terminal Eocene cooling event resulted in

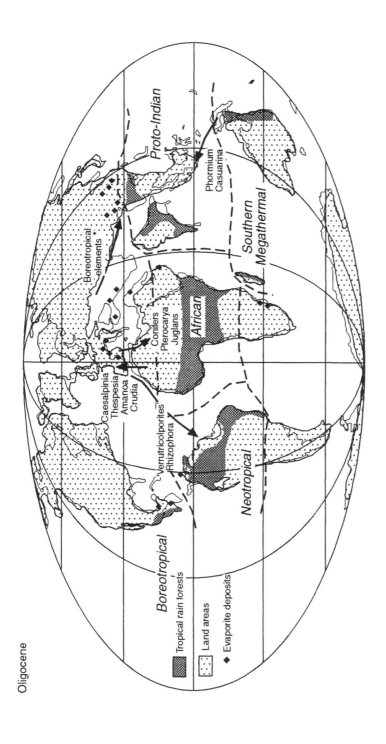

Figure 13.4 Distribution of closed-canopy tropical rain forests during the Oligocene, following the terminal Eocene cooling event. Reconstruction based on synthesis of Chapters 6–11, and, in the absence of positive evidence, to the 'interglacial' climatic scenario presented in Figure 4.12b. Palaeogeography and palaeocoastlines from Smith et al. (1994); occurrences of evaporites from Parrish et al. (1982) with additions; megathermal floristic provinces according to the text. Noteworthy dispersals are indicated for (a) megathermal and microthermal plants which migrated at the time of the Late Eocene convergence of Europe and Africa; (b) boreotropical migrations (*conjectural) relating to the closure of the Turgai Straits; and (c) migrations of megathermal elements in relation to the latest Oligocene collision of the Australian Plate with SE Asia and the Philippine Plate.

Oligocene

numerous extinctions, for instance of the palm *Nypa*. However, there is clear evidence from W Africa and South America for the continuity of moist equatorial climates throughout the Oligocene. It is also noteworthy that the reduced number of extinctions at the end of the Eocene in South America, and the continuity of mauritioid and other palms into the Neogene, which became extinct in Africa at the end of the Eocene, suggests that the effects of this cooling event were perhaps less marked in South America than anywhere else.

On the other hand, the terminal Eocene cooling had a profound effect on the vegetation of the Proto-Indian Province, initially in the region of SE Asia. In this area, the combination of global cooling and a probable change in atmospheric circulation patterns, thought to have been brought about following the formation of the Himalayas, resulted in the replacement of rain forests by monsoonal vegetation across most of the region. Rain forests continued into the Oligocene in NE and S India, but those in the northeast eventually also suffered decline. It was not until the later part of the Early Miocene (about 20 Ma) that tropical lowland evergreen rain forests again became extensive in SE Asia, but these forests were of different composition, with diverse Dipterocarpaceae as their most prominent member. On the basis of marked differences with the flora of the Proto-Indian Province, the latest Early Miocene and later flora of the SE Asian region is referred to the 'Malesian Province', which continues to the present day, although it retained many of the characteristic taxa of the Proto-Indian Province.

The flora of the Malesian Province underwent further modifications following the collision of the Sunda and Australian Plates in the latest Oligocene to earliest Miocene, and the Miocene formation of the islands of New Guinea and E Indonesia, and became enriched, particularly in the mountains, as a result of dispersals from the Australian Plate into the East Malesian floristic province. The Makasar Straits, which opened in the Late Eocene, and

which are followed by Wallace's Line, formed a substantial barrier to dispersal, and so Southern Megathermal elements to the west, although noteworthy, are few. The predominance of elements of the Malesian Province, such as rattans, oaks, some diptertocarps, Sapindaceae, *Gonystylus* (Gonystylaceae), *Ixonanthes* (Ixonanthaceae) etc., in the islands of Eastern Indonesia and New Guinea which formed after the opening of the Makasar Straits, appears incongruous, but is readily explained since a fragment of the Sundanian Eocene flora became stranded on the southwest arm of Sulawesi, to the east of the Makasar Straits, and provided a source for perhaps more aggressive Malesian Province elements to colonise islands to the east, as they rose above sea level, and land connections became available.

### Middle Miocene (16–10 Ma) climatic amelioration

Renewed global warming during the latest Early and earliest Middle Miocene resulted once again in the expansion of moist megathermal forests poleward of the subtropical high pressure zones (Figure 13.5), although this time for only a short period. In the northern hemisphere, mangrove swamps with *Rhizophora* (Rhizophoraceae), and rain forests with *Dacrydium* (Podocarpaceae), extended northward to Japan, *Symplocos* (Symplocaceae) and *Mastixia* (Mastixiaceae) diversified in S and C Europe, and megathermal elements extended along the eastern coast of North America. In South Africa, palm-dominated vegetation became widespread at two separate time intervals, and in Australia the combination of warmer climates and northward drift once again resulted in the development of mangrove swamps with *Nypa* as far south as the Murray Basin in the southeast. Elements of the Malesian Province, such as *Anisoptera*, *Dipterocarpus*, *Hopea* and *Shorea* (Dipterocarpaceae) and *Koompassia* (Leguminosae) spread to the Indian Plate at this time.

269

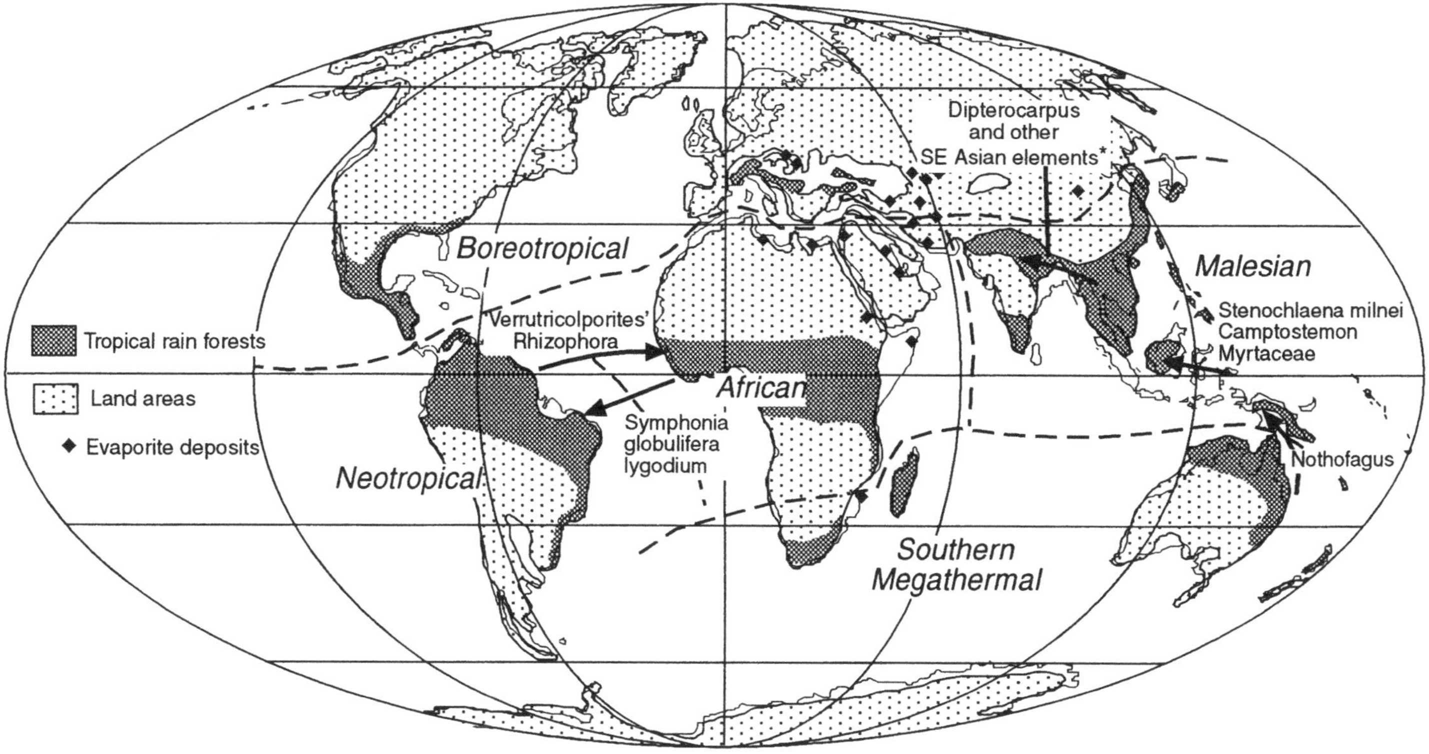

Figure 13.5 Distribution of closed-canopy tropical rain forests during the Middle Miocene, coinciding with the Miocene thermal maximum. Reconstruction based on synthesis of Chapters 6–11, and in the absence of positive evidence, to the 'greenhouse' climatic scenario presented in Figure 4.12c. Palaeogeography and palaeocoastlines from Smith et al. (1994); occurrences of evaporites from Parrish et al. (1982) with additions; megathermal floristic provinces according to the text. Noteworthy Miocene dispersals of megathermal plant taxa marked (*) are based on macrofossil data, otherwise based on the palynological record.

*Neogene global climatic deterioration*

The penultimate stage in the history of rain forests, following global climatic deterioration at the end of the Middle Miocene, and again in the mid-Pliocene, resulted in the withdrawal of moist megathermal vegetation to the tropical zone, accompanied by the expansion of grasslands and deserts throughout much of the lower to mid-latitudes.

The northward drift of the Australian Plate at this time accentuated the effect of Late Neogene desiccation, as it drifted into the southern, subtropical high pressure zone, with the result that elements of the Southern Megathermal Province became restricted to tiny pockets along its east coast, maintained by moist, easterly trade winds; rain forests in Madagascar probably also became restricted to eastern coasts at this time in a similar manner. India also lost much of its moist vegetation, as it continued to drift into the northern subtropical high pressure zone, and monsoonal climates developed with the further uplift of the Himalayas. In New Zealand, with virtually no northward drift after the Eocene, most megathermal elements disappeared after the mid-Pliocene climatic deterioration. The remnants of the Boreotropical Province, which survived into the Miocene in Europe, finally became extinct, whereas in Central America the formation of the Isthmus of Panama in the Pliocene (5–1.6 Ma) created a land bridge to equatorial latitudes which allowed some of the North American elements of the Boreotropical Province to find eventual refuge within the present-day tropical zone as the amphi-Pacific element.

In Africa, Late Neogene climatic pertubations had a particularly deleterious effect, probably because of mid-Tertiary uplift relating to the formation of the East African rift system, resulting in limited opportunities for lowland rain forest taxa to find refuge during periods of drier and cooler climate, and subsequently many more extinctions occurred within the rain forests of equatorial Africa compared to other equatorial regions. These extinctions, coupled with the more limited opportunities for dispersal of moist megathermal elements to the African Plate in the Early Tertiary, account for the depauperate nature of the African rain forest flora, and rarity or absence of many characteristic angiosperm groups present in other equatorial floras. Several taxa which became extinct in Africa during the Neogene may still be found in the rain forests of South America (e.g. aff. *Arapatiella* (Leguminosae), *Pelliceria* (Pellicieriaceae) and *Sicyos* (Cucurbitaceae) and SE Asia (aff. *Sonneratia*, Sonneratiaceae, and *Oncosperma*, Palmae) or both, the *Anacolosa* pollen type occurring in the Madagascan/SE Asian genus *Anacolosa*, and also *Cathedra* and *Ptychopetalum* from South America. Phases of drying and cooling associated with the glacial episodes of the Quaternary (1.6–0 Ma) affected all rain forests in a similar manner; rain forests were successively restricted to often tiny refugia (Figure 13.6), from which they subsequently expanded to approximately their present extent during interglacial, moist and warm intervals. Such refuges were particularly restricted in equatorial Africa and Australia.

The scenario proposed above for the evolution of moist megathermal vegetation over the last 100 million years satisfies many of the questions posed by the present distributions of rain forests and rain forest taxa, and also of fossil data, especially those listed below:

1.  Anomalies in the distribution of primitive angiosperms, used by Takhtajan (1969) to propose that angiosperms evolved in an area between Assam and Fiji, as follows:
    (a) concentration of primitive angiosperms in SE Asia (e.g. Magnoliaceae) and the region of the Coral Sea, such as members of the families Austrobaileyaceae, Chloranthaceae, Degeneriaceae and Winteraceae.
    (b) the occurrence of many instances of bihemispheric family pairs in SE Asia, but their more limited representation elsewhere. For example, Fagaceae, with *Lithocarpus* and *Castanopsis* (northern) overlapping

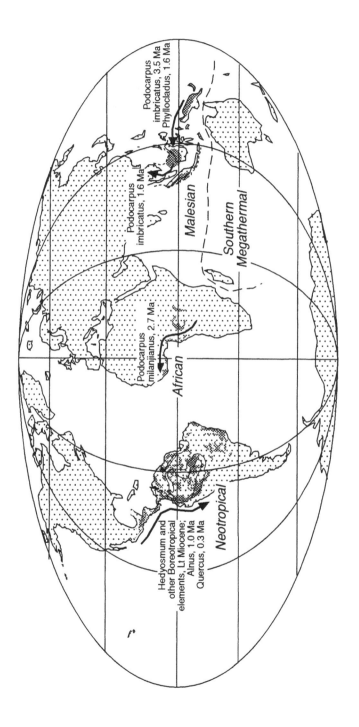

Figure 13.6 Distribution of closed-canopy tropical rain forests during the last glacial maximum, based on the synthesis of Chapters 6–11. Contour lines in South America are postulated 1500 mm and 2000 mm isoyets for the last glacial maximum (Bush, 1994). Also shown are noteworthy instances of Pliocene and Pleistocene dispersals of microthermal taxa into the low latitudes.

with *Nothofagus* (southern); Staphyleaceae (northern) and Cunoniaceae (southern); Saxifragaceae (northern) and Escalloniaceae (southern).

(c) the amphi-Pacific element of van Steenis (1962a), composed of taxa which occur on both Pacific coasts, but are absent from Africa and Europe.

(d) the reduced representation of primitive magnoliales, but occurrence of the most primitive palms in South American rain forests.

(e) the abundance of primitive representatives of families such as Magnoliaceae in SE Asia, which are relics from the Boreotropical Province.

2.  The suggestions of Wolfe (1971) regarding Early Tertiary megathermal rain forests as follows:

(a) the existence of broadleaved, paratropical rain forest at latitudes of 60–61°N, and marginally tropical rain forest at 52°N during part of the Palaeogene.

(b) the occurrence of summer-wet climatic regimes along mid-latitude west coasts during part of the Tertiary.

(c) the development of deserts during the later Neogene.

(d) the apparently contradictory patterns of Palaeogene climatic change in the northern mid-latitudes, depending on latitude.

## 13.2  THE DURIAN THEORY OF CORNER, AND EVOLUTION OF THE RAIN FOREST TREE

Durianology, developed by Corner (1949, 1964), inspired a generation of botanists in rain forest evolutionary studies. The Durian theory, named after the fabled durian (*Durio zibethinus*, Bombacaceae) of the Far East, attempted to explain the evolution of angiosperms through the recognition of associated features of rain forest trees which he considered to be primitive. His model of the primitive

angiosperm tree as a stout, monopodial 'pachycaul' with a dense crown of pinnate leaves and heavy, spiny, dehiscent fruit bearing black seeds in a colourful aril on persistent funicles, was envisaged as the basic model for all angiosperms, and Corner's emphasis of the importance of tree growth and form in evolutionary studies was the first attempt to disentangle the diversity of plant architecture, subsequently built on by Hallé and Oldeman (1970), Oldeman (1974) and Hallé et al. (1978).

The fossil record shows that the principal components of Corner's archetypal angiosperm first appeared at widely differing times. Pinnate leaves evolved early in angiosperm history, in the Albian, their appearance relating to early physiognomic foliar diversification. Stout trunks probably appeared later in the Cretaceous, whereas large fruit show a clear increased representation in the latest Cretaceous and Paleocene, associated with the diversification of mammals, following the extinction of the dinosaurs. The fossil record thus provides little support for durianology as a theory of angiosperm evolution. Can the fossil record throw any light on this diverse association of features which Corner thought to be primitive?

Firstly, colourful arillate fruit with black seeds hanging from funicles (Figure 13.7) forms a central theme to durianology. These characters suggest the early development of bird dispersal, likely to have been of great importance to early angiosperms prior to the earliest Tertiary proliferation of mammals. A further theme of durianology is pachycauly. Large-dimensioned angiosperm wood appeared late in the history of angiosperm evolution, in the latest Cretaceous, coinciding with the appearance of large fruits, at least in W Africa. The rarity of large-dimensioned angiosperm woods at low latitudes prior to this time may reflect the widespread representation of plants with soft, pachycaul stems when lowland climates were aseasonal and subhumid (Section 5.2.2). Corner's association of colourful arillate seeds and pachycauly could be explained if these features were common when low latitude, closed-canopy

Figure 13.7    Fruit of *Sterculia macrophylla*, Corner's archetype 'ancestral' fruit according to his Durian theory.

rain forests first appeared in the latest Cretaceous. Later such plants were probably shaded out with the proliferation of the leptocaul habit with sympodial branching in the Early Tertiary. Relict occurrences of pachycauls with arillate fruit in today's tropical rain forests most likely reflect the morphology of the earliest *low latitude* rain forest plants and their immediate precursors, which grew in areas where rain forests replaced the vegetation of mid-Cretaceous hot, subhumid aseasonal equatorial climates, rather than reflecting the morphology of the earliest angiosperms.

## 13.3    THE OLDEST RAIN FORESTS?

It is generally acknowledged that rain forests are of great age, but how old? Each rain forest block includes some taxa of great antiquity, but it is inappropriate to view an entire block as being as old as its oldest component. If age is considered to reflect the period of time during which the flora of each rain forest block has shown some degree of coherence, without major disruption by changing climate, or replacement by immigrant floras, the island floras surrounding the Coral Sea and Australian and Madagascan rain forests of the southern hemisphere clearly take first place, since the palynological record suggests, at least for those within E Australia, that these forests have probably had an uninterrupted history since the Late Cretaceous.

There are four reasons why the island floras surrounding the Coral Sea, Madagascar and E Australia are the oldest, and contain the greatest number of primitive angiosperms. Firstly, these land areas were located at mid- rather than tropical latitudes in the Cretaceous, and, as suggested in Chapter 5, moist megathermal forests developed at mid-latitudes before their establishment at the equator. Secondly, these forests have each experienced continuity since their inception during the Late Cretaceous, and were at no time seriously threatened by invasions by elements of more aggressive megathermal floras, since these regions have been areas of plate disassembly, rather than collision, restricting opportunities for the dispersal of megathermal elements from elsewhere. Thirdly, the northward Tertiary drift of the Australian Plate, Madagascar and their associated detached continental fragments into warmer climatic zones resulted in these rain forested areas more or less keeping pace with Tertiary global climatic deterioration (Figure 13.8), permitting the survival of their frost-sensitive floras. This was achieved to some degree by the

Australian and Madagascan rain forest floras, which also had to contend with desiccation as a result of drift into the southern hemisphere subtropical high pressure zone, and subsequently, rain forests survived only along eastern coasts, where they received moisture from easterly trade winds. New Zealand, on the other hand, just failed to keep up with deteriorating climates, with the result that much of its former megathermal flora became extinct, probably during the mid-Pliocene climatic deterioration. Fourthly, the isolation of fragments of the flora of the Southern Megathermal Province on oceanic islands, sufficiently small to have had an oceanic climate even when within the southern subtropical high pressure zone, and away from other more aggressive floras, created a setting particularly favourable to the preservation of these ancient forests. New Caledonian rain forests probably most closely reflect the megathermal forests of the Late Cretaceous or earliest Tertiary period, since this continental fragment has been isolated from other possibly aggressive floras since its separation from Australia in the Early Tertiary. Consequently, it is rich in gymnosperms (including over 10% of the world's gymnosperm species) as well as archaic angiosperms, and probably takes first place as the world's oldest rain forest flora.

It was this combination of processes which led to the widespread survival of archaic angiosperm families in these areas, with representatives of Winteraceae, Himantandraceae, Degeneriaceae, Austrobaileyaceae, Amborellaceae and Trimeniaceae being concentrated in NE Australia and on continental fragments surrounding the Coral Sea, which brought Takhtajan (1969) to the conclusion that the 'cradle of the angiosperms' lay in the Far East, 'somewhere between Assam and Fiji'. Taking into account data from fossils and plate tectonics, it is more likely that Takhtajan's premise should be reversed – the most archaic angiosperms have in fact survived in those areas furthest from their place of origin in Western Gondwanaland, and thus bring new life to the old 'age and area' theory of Willis (1922) which proposed that the most primitive

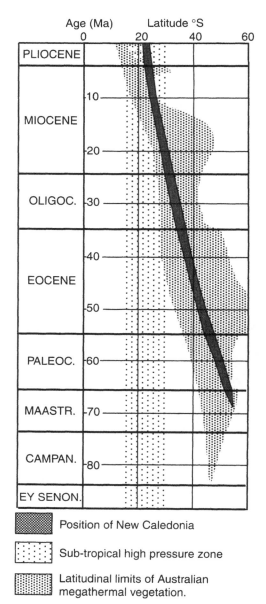

Figure 13.8  Latitudinal position of New Caledonia through the last 70 Ma, superimposed on proposed latitudinal representation of tropical aspect rain forests in E Australia over the same time period.

members of a lineage should occur furthest from their place of origin, having been displaced from their radiation centre by the appearance of subsequent more aggressive lineages.

## 13.4 AGE OF SOUTHEAST ASIAN RAIN FORESTS

The SE Asian region is often credited as bearing the world's oldest flora; even Richards (1996) hypothesised that the occurrence of gymnosperms such as *Dacrydium* in the heath forests of Borneo may reflect the great age of these forests, but this is not the case. The present-day dipterocarp-dominated rain forests of SE Asia developed in the Miocene, and replaced monsoon forests, which were widespread throughout the Sunda region during the Oligocene and earliest Miocene. The present-day richness of the SE Asian rain forest flora is due to the widespread dispersal of megathermal elements into this area, and the mixing of floras of different geographical origin, in a manner not seen elsewhere. Firstly, in the Middle Eocene, the collision of the Indian and Asian plates allowed the mixing of the Indian and SE Asian Eocene floras and, since the Indian Plate carried many elements of the African Cretaceous flora, brought elements of African origin as well as endemic Indian ones. Secondly, the collision of the Australian and Sunda plates at the end of the Oligocene created pathways for the dispersal of Gondwanan elements into SE Asia, such as the southern conifers *Agathis*, *Podocarpus* and *Phyllocladus*. Thirdly, the presence in E Asia of a continuous continental connection across latitudinal climatic zones from the equator to 60°N allowed opportunities for the survival of diverse elements of the northern hemisphere Boreotropical Province in this area in a manner not seen elsewhere either.

## 13.5 DISPERSAL OF MEGATHERMAL PLANTS AND THE ANTIQUITY OF BIOGEOGRAPHICAL PATTERNS

Outside areas of Neogene plate collision such as Wallaceana and the Isthmus of Panama, which are currently areas of active dispersal of megathermal plants, most interplate dispersals took place during the Late Cretaceous and Early Tertiary (Figure 13.9). Dispersal events clearly fall into four groups: firstly, those which relate to the Late Cretaceous to earliest Tertiary separation of the American, African and Indian plates; secondly, those which occurred during the earliest Tertiary, culminating with the latest Paleocene and Early Eocene thermal maximum (which remarkably coincided with the only time in the history of angiosperms at which there were clear dispersal corridors from Europe to North America, between North and South America, and from South America to Australasia, allowing exceptional opportunities for interplate dispersals of megathermal plants on a virtually global basis); thirdly, those which relate to the collision of the Indian and Asian plates in the Middle and Late Eocene; and, fourthly, those relating to the incipient collision of Africa and Europe. Most higher rank biogeographical patterns observed today reflect these relatively ancient phases of dispersal, and, especially with respect to those taxa which came to characterise mid-latitude rain forests, their subsequent range withdrawal to isolated refuges as global climates deteriorated during the Neogene and Quaternary.

## 13.6 DISTRIBUTIONS OF PALMS, OAKS AND DIPTEROCARPS

### Palms

The present-day concentration of the more primitive palm genera in South American rain forests, which is the only region where palms can be important contributors to the forest canopy, can be explained by the Tertiary climatic history of the three tropical provinces. The Palmae are a very ancient group, dating back to the Turonian, and in the latest Cretaceous and Paleocene were dominant elements throughout the equatorial zone. Although they suffered many extinctions as a result of the terminal Cretaceous

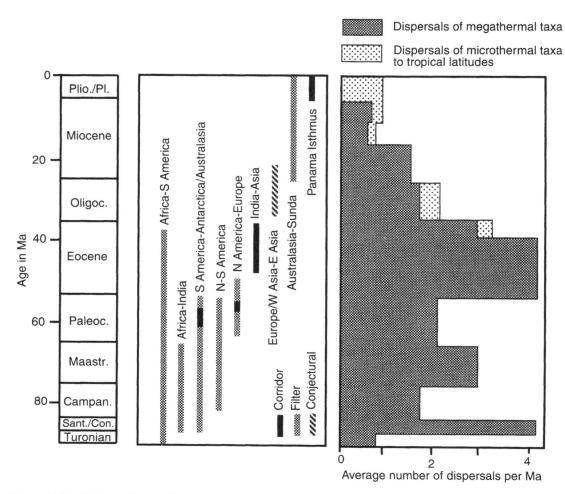

Figure 13.9 Timing of main dispersal routes for megathermal plants over the last 90 Ma, and estimate of rates of dispersal based on palynological records. Left diagram: dispersal corridors in black, filters stippled. Right diagram: dark stipple, megathermal dispersals; light stipple dispersals of temperate taxa into tropical latitudes.

event, there is no evidence to suggest that extinctions at this time are reflected in present-day biogeographical patterns. They subsequently suffered a marked reduction in contribution to equatorial vegetation at the time of the Late Paleocene/Early Eocene thermal maximum, but probably retained much of their diversity into the Eocene. The terminal Eocene event, however, was detrimental to the Palmae in many areas, not only in the northern and southern mid-latitudes, but also in equatorial regions. However, it appears to have resulted in fewer extinctions in South America than in either Africa or SE Asia. For instance, numerous mauritioid palms suffered extinction at this time in Africa, but continued in South America, and whereas the parent plant of the nypoid *Proxapertites operculatus* and *P. cursus* must have suffered extinction in Africa and SE Asia, *P. operculatus* continued in South America well into the Neogene. Also, with the widespread change to a monsoonal climate in the Sunda region at the beginning of the Oligocene, many palms became much less well represented in that area, with the disappearance of many iguanurinoid forms, which were particularly common in the SE Asian Middle Eocene. However, palms continued to be well represented in E India, which retained an everwet climate, both in northern and southern areas, well into the Oligocene.

The very low diversity of palms in the African continent, compared to the other two tropical regions, is a result of the much greater Neogene desiccation experienced in Africa compared with either SE Asia or South America and reduced representation of low altitude refuges, with clear extinction episodes in the Early Miocene at the end of the Middle Miocene and mid-Pliocene.

## *Oaks*

The concentration of species of oaks in SE Asian rain forests, coupled with the occurrence of the southern beech *Nothofagus* together with *Lithocarpus* and *Castanopsis* in New Guinea, has led many to consider the Far East as the area of origin of the Fagaceae. This idea was strengthened with the discovery in the 1960s of a new genus of Fagaceae, *Trigonobalanus*, intermediate between *Nothofagus* and *Fagus*, in the lower montane rain forests of Mount Kinabalu in Borneo (van Steenis, 1971). The juxtaposition of so many genera of Fagaceae in the Far East has nothing to do with their area of origin; *Nothofagus* dispersed into the New Guinea mountains from Australia as they formed during the Middle Miocene, only about 14 Ma ago. Although there is no conclusive Tertiary fossil pollen record for *Lithocarpus* or *Castanopsis* in the tropical Far East (since their pollen is of a rather generalised type), it is likely that these genera either dispersed to New Guinea from SW Sulawesi during the Neogene along with other Laurasian taxa, or dispersed across Wallace's Line at about the same time. *Trigonobalanus*, on the other hand, was subsequently demonstrated

to be an amphi-Pacific genus, being recorded as far afield as Thailand and the Andean forests of Colombia, and with macrofossils from the Early Tertiary of Europe and North America (van der Hammen and Cleef, 1983). *Trigonobalanus* was thus a genus of the Early Tertiary Boreotropical Province which became relict to the montane rain forests of SE Asia following the extinction of megathermal taxa in the northern hemisphere mid-latitudes as a result of Neogene global cooling. It also found refuge in N South America following the creation of the Isthmus of Panama during the Pliocene.

Leaf anatomical studies of Fagaceae suggest that *Nothofagus* and *Fagus* are not as closely related as previously supposed, and that they evolved together with Betulaceae from a common Fagalean ancestor (Jones, 1986). This initial radiation must have taken place during the mid-Cretaceous, presumably in Western Gondwanaland, since *Nothofagus* pollen (which is very distinctive) is reported from the Santonian (88–84 Ma) of the Antarctic Peninsula and is thought to have radiated from this area (Hill, 1994b).

Oaks, beeches and chestnuts are known as fossils only from the northern hemisphere from the Eocene onward, from which time macrofossils display considerable diversity, suggesting a somewhat earlier (possibly Paleocene) origin (Jones, 1986). Their common ancestor was probably in South America, rather than Africa as suggested by Raven and Axelrod (1974), in view of the fossil record of *Nothofagus* alluded to above, and since there was a Late Cretaceous/Paleocene land connection between North and South America, but the African continent was somewhat isolated from other areas at this time.

Fagaceae *sensu strictu* and *Nothofagus* have therefore been essentially isolated to their respective hemispheres since their initial radiation. It is only during the Neogene that plate collisions in the Far East have created dispersal pathways which have enabled oaks and southern beeches to occur together on the same land masses.

*Dipterocarps*

Although dipterocarps today show their greatest diversity in Far Eastern rain forests, they did not originate in that area, but in either South America or Africa, prior to the final severance of dispersal opportunities between the two continents, probably at some time during the Late Cretaceous. The recent discovery of the most primitive dipterocarp *Pakaraimaea* in South America (Ashton and McGuire, 1977) may point to a New World origin for the family, although of course this genus may be relict. Even the subfamily Dipterocarpoideae originated within the West, since its most primitive representatives are in rain forest outliers in the Seychelles (*Vateriopsis*) and Sri Lanka, and there are well-authenticated records of *Dipterocarpus* from the E African Tertiary (Ashton and Gunatilleke, 1987a). Dipterocarpaceae were clearly extensively represented in the monsoon forests of the Sunda region during the Late Oligocene and Early Miocene, and thus were already in place across the SE Asian region at the time of widespread expansion of evergreen rain forests in the later part of the Early Miocene. It is probably only since this period that dipterocarps have become a major component of the SE Asian rain forests. Their origin in more seasonal climates is revealed by their flowering pattern; irregular, 4–5 yearly flowering within the ever-wet tropics is triggered by sudden cool spells resulting from the El Nino oscillation, whereas annual flowering occurs in areas of seasonal climate (Ashton et al., 1988; Section 9.6).

Many palaeobotanical interpretations rely on the 'nearest living relative' approach, which assumes that the ecology of today's taxa did not differ substantially from their ancestors. The dipterocarps clearly provide an example of the palaeobotanist's nightmare taxon, evolving in a moist rain forest environment, to account for the occurrence of relict species in South America, the Seychelles and Sri Lanka, adapting to monsoonal climates in the mid-Tertiary, and then exhibiting explosive radiation in the moist, evergreen forests of SE Asia in the Neogene.

## 13.7 THE DISTRIBUTION OF MANGROVES

Fossil evidence argues strongly against the Far East as the centre for the radiation of mangroves, although today they are richest there. Most evidence points to the shores of Tethys as the main area of origin of many groups of mangrove plants, including Rhizophoraceae, with earliest records from the Early Eocene London Clay, the ancestors of Sonneratiaceae (which produced the pollen types *Florschuetzia trilobata* and *Verritricolporites*) and possibly also the South American relict *Pelliciera rhizophorae* (Pellicieriaceae). Even *Brownlowia* (Tiliaceae) is likely to fall within this group, with a pollen record now from the Eocene of S Europe. *Nypa* is clearly relict to SE Asia, and enjoyed a pantropical distribution up until the end of the Eocene, and the palm *Oncosperma* was formerly much more widely distributed, with macrofossil records from the London Clay, and pollen records in India and possibly also in West Africa until the end of the Middle Miocene. However, there is clear fossil evidence to suggest that SE Asia is the area of origin for *Acanthus* (Acanthaceae) and radiation of *Sonneratia* (Sonneratiaceae).

## 13.8 SURVIVAL OF RAIN FORESTS DURING QUATERNARY GLACIAL MAXIMA

The 'Pleistocene Refuge Theory' explains many of the plant and animal distributions seen in African rain forests, which were reduced to a fraction of their present distribution as dry climate vegetation expanded during glacial maxima. However, up until now few historical data have been produced to support the theory in South America, where a great deal of work has been done on present-day biogeographical distributions plus interpretations of contemporaneous geoscientific evidence (soils, landforms and river patterns). Recent palynological studies of Quaternary cores suggest some drying during the last glacial maximum, but not so pronounced as in Africa. Some of the South American refuges, especially those proposed in the central part of the Amazon Basin, are simply artefacts of differential collecting. Of the remainder, those which occur along the lower flanks of the Andes, and contain the world's most species-rich rain forests, most probably relate to continued orographic rain over a very long time period, through both 'glacial' and 'interglacial' periods.

In SE Asia, the application of the refuge theory has not been widely discussed, because of the archipelagic nature of the region, but it has long been recognised that drier climates were more widespread during glacial periods, and that Quaternary climatic changes have left their mark on many present-day plant distributions. The presence of widespread inter-riverain endemism in NW Borneo, where SE Asia's most species-rich forests occur, brought to attention by Ashton (1972), is also best explained in terms of continued moist conditions over a very long time period. It is noteworthy that the richest centres of endemism and species-richness in both South America and SE Asia are most likely the result of long-term *continuity* of moist climates within the equatorial zone. This makes earlier suggestions that species-richness in tropical rain forests was a reflection of long-term stability more understandable, and suggestions that areas of highest species-richness are not areas of maximum stability, but of maximum disturbance (e.g. Bush, 1994), require critical re-examination.

Extreme species-richness comparable to that of NW Borneo and the lower flanks of the Andes in South America has been recently reported from the Bird's Neck area of Irian Jaya (Sands et al., 1998). This region became established as a land area during the Middle Miocene, some 14 Ma ago, and suggests that 14 Ma is sufficient time for rain forest floras to speciate to their highest levels in areas of continuously moist climate.

Palynological data from low latitude 'glacial' sites unanimously argue for greater temperature depressions at equatorial latitudes than were suggested by the CLIMAP (1976) study, which has long been used to infer lesser reductions of temperature at sea level than has been proven at high altitudes. In both South America and Africa, lowland rain forests were pushed to the lowest altitudes, and at mid-elevations lower montane forest taxa grew together with lowland rain forest elements in plant associations which have no modern analogue.

The three regions show major differences in the representation of upland and lowland terrain, which need to be taken into account when considering the distribution of tropical rain forests at the last glacial maximum. Africa clearly experienced the driest climates at this time, but also, with easily the lowest representation of low altitude terrain (Figure 7.1) and minimal representation of continental shelves, provided by far the fewest opportunities for rain forests to find refuge. In SE Asia, dry climates clearly affected large areas, but the huge land areas which would have become available when sea levels were more than 100 m below their present levels would have significantly compensated for the expansion of drier climates. In South America, on the other hand, the expansion of dry climates was probably much less marked than in Africa, and diverse rain forest floras found refuge by migrating to the river basin floors; however, as for Africa, little new terrain became available with lower sea levels, due to the steep continental slope.

An aspect of the Pleistocene Refuge Theory which clearly needs revision is the suggestion that successive isolation of populations through the *Quaternary* acted as a 'species pump', triggering speciation by restricting gene flow between refugia. It is likely that speciation has taken place over a much longer time period, with different forcing mechanisms (e.g. from orogeny and the formation of giant rivers) inhibiting dispersal. Palynological data from the SE Asian Neogene also demonstrates that the diversity of the SE Asian flora became accentuated as a result of the successive re-formation of lowland vegetation on the continental shelves during periods of low sea level. Diversification of tropical rain forest floras has continued through a major part of the Tertiary, as a result of their successive expansion and retraction and fragmentation by physical barriers, and is not exclusively a Quaternary phenomenon.

# CHAPTER 14

# The Future of Rain Forests?

The evolution and diversification of tropical rain forests has been dependent on, and proceeded parallel with, a succession of geological and climatic events, controlled by internal stresses beneath the Earth's crust, and by astronomical processes, in parallel with evolutionary pressures for plants to reproduce and colonise all available land space. These events have occurred in a time sequence which cannot be repeated. The result is that today, each geographically separated rain forest area contains its own association of species, descended from ancestors which became established perhaps over 70 million years ago, and subsequently became modified, and diversified, so as to occupy all the available niches within each region.

Tropical rain forests contain more than half of the Earth's biological diversity, yet form only under a relatively narrow range of climatic conditions: more or less permanently moist and frost-free, which during our present interglacial happen to coincide with the tropical zone (Figure 1.2). In the past, during cooler, glacial periods, they were much more restricted, being confined to refuges, mainly in the equatorial zone (Figure 14.1), whereas during periods of warmer 'greenhouse' global climates, they were able to expand poleward beyond the subhumid subtropical high pressure zones (which have been a permanent feature of Earth's climate) into the mid-latitudes wherever permanently moist and frost-free conditions could be maintained. However, during the hottest periods of Earth's history, the rapidly changing character of the palynomorph record in equatorial regions suggests that tropical rain forests may

have occurred in a modified form in the equatorial zone at that time, or were replaced by vegetation with no modern analogue.

In a world governed by the same controls as over the last 800 000 years, future tropical rain forests would maintain a distribution initially similar to that of today, eventually gradually diminishing in range until the combined effects of changes in the Earth's tilt and orbital variations around the sun heralded the onset of the next ice age, with full glacial conditions being reached some 25 000 years from now (Imbrie and Imbrie, 1979), at which time tropical rain forests would once again become restricted to refuges in the equatorial zone.

However, the geological record provides evidence for past changes in the distribution of rain forests which are the result of fundamental changes in the Earth's climate system, or to astronomical causes, neither of which can be predicted by reference to astronomical events. Such changes have caused tropical rain forests to go through a number of major crises since their first appearance more than 75 million years ago, but affecting rain forests differently in different areas. Firstly, following the terminal Cretaceous meteorite impact, tropical rain forests were extensively affected across the globe, suffering severe diversity loss, but probably with most destruction in the Americas. Secondly, the terminal Eocene cooling resulted in the virtual disappearance of rain forests poleward of the subtropical high pressure zones, and in the major retraction of rain forests in SE Asia. The third major crisis occurred during the Late Neogene, particularly during the period of expansion of polar ice caps

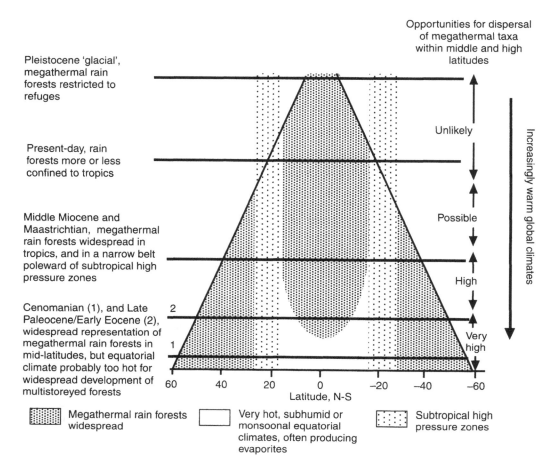

Figure 14.1   Latitudinal distribution of tropical rain forests during different global climate scenarios. The question as to whether tropical rain forests occurred at equatorial latitudes during global thermal maxima, or were replaced at these times by vegetation without modern analogue, remains open to debate.

in the northern hemisphere, and was especially destructive with respect to the rain forests in Africa, where the combined effect of global cooling and Late Tertiary uplift resulted in fewer localities for rain forest taxa to find refuge during periods of drier climate, compared to other tropical areas.

The present-day species-richness displayed by rain forests is strongly related to the number and timing of these crises. Within the three main centres of tropical rain forest development, greatest richness has been found in Amazonian forests, which survived the ravages

of the terminal Eocene cooling event more successfully than their counterparts in SE Asia, and the lowest diversities are seen in equatorial Africa, its moist megathermal flora suffering most from the effects of cooler and drier climates since the Late Miocene.

Tropical rain forests are now going through a crisis more severe, and more destructive, than any other of the past 70 million years which were brought about solely by natural processes. This crisis is affecting all rain forests, whether they are the world's oldest, in New Caledonia, richest in endemics, in New Guinea or Madagascar, or

Figure 14.2   Rain forest destruction in Borneo. (Courtesy of A. McRobb, Media resources, Royal Botanic
Gardens, Kew.)

the most diverse, in Amazonia and SE Asia. This new crisis has no obvious historical parallel; it has come about solely as a result of the expansion of the population of a single mammalian species – Man (Figure 14.2).

Man must already take responsibility for the destruction of temperate forests across much of the middle latitudes. For instance, most of the forests of the United Kingdom were destroyed following the immigration of Neolithic settlers about 6000 years ago (Figure 14.3), so that by the Norman conquest only 15% of the land area remained forested (Rackham, 1986). Similar patterns of deforestation can be demonstrated elsewhere in Europe and the Far East, and, with the arrival of European settlers in North America, New Zealand and Australia, massive

forest destruction took place in these areas in a fraction of the time taken in Europe.

With the inexorable growth of land-hungry populations, and the insatiable demand from developed countries for timber and other forest products, tropical rain forests have become one of the last great forest frontiers to be rolled back by the human species (Whitmore, 1998). With the advent of modern hauling machinary and the chain-saw, this is being achieved at a much faster rate than the destruction of temperate forests (Figure 14.3). In Guatemala, half of the rain forests have been destroyed in 23 years, and in the Malay Peninsula 40% deforestation took place in 40 years. Massive deforestation is taking place in the Amazon, Nigeria and Sumatra and elsewhere. Most predictions of rates of forest

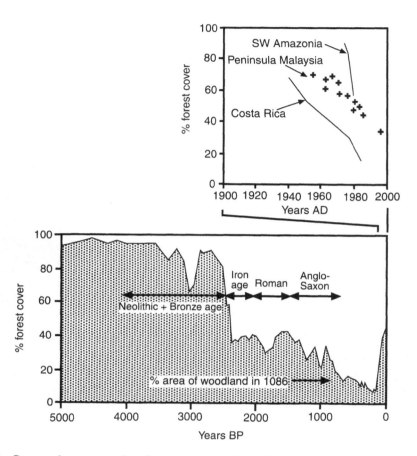

Figure 14.3 Present-day rates of deforestation in Costa Rica, Peninsular Malaysia and Rondonia, Amazonia (from Whitmore, 1998) compared to European deforestation rates by Neolithic and later farmers, as suggested by the ratio of arboreal to non-arboreal pollen from Diss Mere, Norfolk, UK (data from Peglar et al. (1989), placed in linear time scale). The increase of arboreal pollen during the last 150 years reflects widespread tree planting during the 19th century.

destruction over the last few decades have been exceeded (Richards, 1996), and Sayer and Whitmore (1991) believed that the rate of forest destruction was still accelerating in 1990. The prediction of Paul Richards in 1952, that *the whole of the tropical rain forest may disappear in the lifetime of those now living, except for a few inaccessible areas and small forest reserves* is now close to fulfilment.

The consequences of the destruction of tropical rain forest across the tropics are profound, and their destruction far more sinister than deforestation in the mid-latitudes. A major

difference is in loss of biodiversity. Rackham (1986) estimated that during the process of deforestation over 4000 years in the British Isles, only 15 species of flowering plants (all herbs) and ferns, or about 1% of the British native flora, have become extinct. Temperate floras are better adapted to change than tropical ones. They have to endure long winters with climates hostile to plant growth, and with fluctuating glacial and interglacial climates only species able to make successive migrations of thousands of kilometres with the march of Quaternary global climate change have been able to contribute to such floras. The severity of climate is closely linked to biodiversity, with the result that the diversity of their tropical counterparts is up to an order of magnitude greater. This increased diversity is reflected in less dense populations, and smaller geographical ranges of many species. With large-scale deforestation of tropical rain forests, thinly distributed species are reduced to unsustainable population levels, and local endemics are entirely eradicated. With deforestation now occurring on a global scale, and the remaining forests covering an area which is only a fraction of the levels of a century ago, a major proportion of the Earth's plant and animal species is actively in the process of becoming extinct. Estimates of such diversity losses, however, are few, though reasoned calculation suggests a loss of about 13 600 species were the Amazon rain forests to be reduced to half of their original extent by the end of the century (Whitmore, 1998).

A clear understanding of the historical events which were responsible for the occurrence of rain forest refugia is crucial in order to plan a long-term strategy for rain forest conservation. The preservation of rain forest fragments in parks may provide a short-term answer to biodiversity maintenance, but with future inevitable climatic changes, either through global warming or as a result of changes in the Earth's orbit, many such fragments may subsequently prove to be in areas unsuitable for maintaining rain forests and suffer diversity loss despite the best management efforts. The realisation that the the most floristically diverse refugia may in fact occur in areas which have experienced *long-term climatic continuity* provides a crucial key as to the choice of conservation areas. The most obvious of such refugia are on the lower flanks of the Andes, in NW Borneo and possibly the Bird's Neck area of Irian Jaya, but there are most likely to be many more. Every effort should be made to maximise our understanding of those areas which have the greatest species concentrations, and also to greatly expand our database of geological evidence detailing the history of such areas in

order to help confirm their importance for conservation of biodiversity on a long-term basis.

On a geological time scale, a substantial loss of tropical rain forest biodiversity will significantly deflect the future course of evolution, since rain forests form the primary gene pool for the flowering plants. Most temperate plant taxa have evolved from less specialised megathermal ancestors, now confined to tropical rain forests (Bews, 1927; Takhtajan, 1969), and with the loss of these forests, the gene pool for future evolution will have been destroyed.

The loss of tropical rain forests will also have major economic consequences, since they form the only source of a wide range of plant and animal products and tropical hardwoods, and also of many chemical compounds, which have been developed in plants as protection against attack by herbivores. Their disappearance might also have a major effect on local and global climate, and may affect global carbon dioxide levels, contributing to global warming. Tropical rain forests are uniquely rich communities of plants and animals, which include many of the most beautiful and bizarre forms of life. They have an important intrinsic value and must be preserved for the wonder and inspiration of future generations.

The rates of tropical forest destruction which have taken place over the last century have no geological parallel, at least over the last 66 million years. Only the terminal Cretaceous bolide impact, which, as noted in Section 5.3, caused the extinction of 38% of the genera of marine animals and the dinosaurs and innumerable plant species on land, could in any way be considered comparable with the present catastrophic deforestation process taking place across the tropical zone. The fossil record (Section 11.3) demonstrates that the biodiversity loss at that time took many millions of years to replace, and that diversity levels stabilised only after four million years, yet remained well below the levels of the end Cretaceous until the Late Paleocene/Early Eocene thermal maximum, some 10 Ma later. Natural selection ensures that the primary aim of most species, whether plant or animal, is to secure the future proliferation of their species. Man is currently doing the reverse, playing a game with the Earth's ecosystem and living beyond its resources, solely to satisfy short-term human greed, and creating a scenario which has its nearest parallel in a cataclysmic event caused by a major meteorite impact. Can we afford to destroy our own children's heritage in this manner, and leave them with a barren planet? If we do choose to take this route, what would be the long-term consequences? Provided there are no humans around, rain forests will come back, perhaps in another four million years or so, and hopefully, a new form of intelligent life may evolve at the same time which will show a more responsible attitude to the natural resources of this planet than that shown by *Homo sapiens*.

# Appendix – Form-taxon names for fossil pollen referred to in the text

Throughout the text, reference is made to extant plant taxa wherever this is feasible, since the non-palaeobotanist/palynologist will certainly find such names more informative than form-taxon names used for fossils. In most instances, fossils have been described as form-taxa, and this Appendix lists those form-taxa, together with the extant species, genus or higher taxon from which the fossils are thought to have been derived.

The word 'type' after a taxon name indicates that the fossil may also have been derived from closely related taxa, but the named taxon is chosen as representative. For instance, spores referred to the form-species *Stenochlaenidites papuanus* are found in *Stenochlaena milnei*, and also *S. cumingii*, but not other species of *Stenochlaena*, and hence are referred to as '*Stenochlaena milnei* type'. Similarly, pollen referred to the form-genus *Liquidambarpollenites* may have been derived from the genera *Liquidambar* or *Altingia*, and is hence referred to as '*Liquidambar* type' pollen. Records of fossil wood (W) and leaves (L) mentioned from tropical latitudes, and their affinities are also listed. The classification follows Takhtajan (1969). Nomenclature follows Mabberley (1987) for extant plant genera, and Muller (1981) for fossil pollen, with updates for the Australasian region according to Hill (1994).

**Note**: Some names (indicated) are applicable in a restricted geographical area only. Fossil pollen referred to in the text but not on this list remain undescribed as form-taxa.

| PLANT TAXON | FORM-TAXON | PLANT TAXON | FORM-TAXON |
|---|---|---|---|
| **ANTHOCERALES** | | Blechnaceae | |
| | | *Stenochlaena milnei* type | *Stenochlaenidites papuanus* |
| Anthoceraceae | | | |
| *Phaecoceros* | *Anthocerisporis* spp. | *Stenochlaena palustris* | *Verrucatosporites usmensis* |
| | | Family unknown | *Apiculatisporites ferox* |
| **PTERIDOPHYTA** | | | *Cheilanthoidspora monoleta* |
| Gleicheniaceae | | | *Dandotiaspora* |
| *Gleichenia* | *Gleicheniidites* | | *Matonisporites equiexinus* |
| Schizaeaceae | | | *Stereisporites assamensis* |
| Genus indet. | *Appendicisporites tricornitatus* | | |
| | *Cicatricosisporites* | **GYMNOSPERMAE** | |
| ?*Anaemia* | *Cicatricosisporites dorogensis* | Araucariaceae | |
| | | *Araucaria* | *Araucariacites* |
| *Lygodium scandens* type | *Crassoretitriletes vanraadshooveni* | | *Araucariacites australis* |
| | | Cheirolepidaceae | |
| *Schizaea* | *Cicatricosisporites eocenicus* | Genus indet. | *Classopollis* |
| | | | *Exesipollenites tumulus* |
| Parkeriaceae | | Cycadaceae | |
| *Ceratopteris* | *Magnastriatites howardi* | Genus indet. | *Cycadopites* |
| | *Magnastriatites grandiosus* | Pinaceae | |
| | | Genus indet. | *Alisporites* (outside Africa/South America) |
| Pteridaceae | | | *Alisporites similis* |
| ?Genus indet. | *Distaverrosporites margaritatus* | | *Callialasporites* |
| | | | *Rugubivesiculites reductus* |
| *Pteris* | *Polypodiaceoisporites retirugulatus* | *Abies* | *Abiespollenites* |

| PLANT TAXON | FORM-TAXON | PLANT TAXON | FORM-TAXON |
|---|---|---|---|
| *Picea* | *Piceapollenites* | Myristicaceae | |
| *Pinus* | *Pinuspollenites* | Genus indet. | *Myristicoxylon princeps* (W) |
| | *Pinuspollenites* cf. *spherisaccus* | *Pycnanthus* | *Echimonocolpites minutus* |
| *Tsuga canadensis* type | *Zonalapollenites igniculus* | Winteraceae | |
| *Tsuga diversifolia* type | *Zonalapollenites spinulosus* | | *Walkeripollis gabonensis* |
| Podocarpaceae | | | *Afropollis* |
| *Dacrydium* | *Lygistepollenites florini* | | *Afropollis jardinus* |
| *Lagarostrobos* | *Phyllocladites mawsonii* | | *Afropollis operculatus* |
| *Phyllocladus hypophyllus* | *Phyllocladites palaeogenicus* (Borneo) | | *Afropollis zonatus* |
| | | *Drimys* | *Gephyropollenites* |
| *Phyllocladus glaucus* | *Trisaccites macropterus* | *Pseudowintera* type | *Pseudowinterapollis wahooensis* |
| *Podocarpus* | *Alisporites* (Africa/South America Cretaceous) | | |
| | *Podocarpidites* (outside North America/Europe) | **Laurales** | |
| (*Dacrycarpus*) | *Dacrycarpidites australiensis* | Monimiaceae | |
| | | Genus indet. | *Xymaloxylon zeltenense* (W) |
| *Microcachrys* | *Microcachrydites antarcticus* | *Atherosperma* | *Atherospermoxylon aegypticum* (W) |
| Taxodiaceae | | Trimeniaceae | |
| *Taxodium* | *Inaperturopollenites hiatus* | *Trimenia* | *Periporopollenties fragilis* |
| | *Inaperturopollenites scabratus* | Chloranthaceae | |
| Family unknown | *Dicheiropollis etruscus* | *Ascarina* | *Clavatipollenites* |
| | *Ginkgocycadopites nitidus* | | *Clavatipollenites* cf. *tenellis* |
| | *Vitreisporites pallidus* | | *Tucanopollis crisopolenisis* |
| | | Lauraceae | |
| | | *Cinamommum* | *Inaperturopollenites palaeogenicus* |
| **ANTHOPHYTES** | | | *Inaperturopollenites spicatus* |
| Unclassified | *Eucommiadites* | | |
| | | **Illiciales** | |
| **GNETALES** | | Family indet. | *Retitricolpites gigantoreticulatus* |
| Genus indet. | *Elaterocolpites castelaini* | | |
| | *Elateropollenites* | **Didymelales** | |
| | *Elateropollenites africaensis* | Didymelaceae | |
| | *Elaterosporites* | Genus indet. | *Hexaporotricolpites* |
| | *Galeacornea* | | *Hexaporotricolpites emelianovi* |
| *Ephedra* | *Ephedripites* | | *Hexaporotricolpites lamelliferus* |
| | *Ephedripites jansonii* | | *Hexaporotricolpites mulleri* |
| | *Ephedripites multicostatus* | | *Hexaporotricolpites potoniae* |
| | *Ephedripites ovalis* | | |
| | | *Didymeles* | *Schizocolpus marlinensis* |
| **DICOTYLEDONS** | | | |
| | | **Hamamelidales** | |
| **Magnoliales** | | Hamamelidaceae | |
| Annonaceae | | *Liquidambar* type | *Liquidambarpollenites* |
| | *Madanomadhiasulcites maximus* | | |
| *Annona* | *Inaperturopollenites reticulatus* | | |
| *Malmea* type | *Foveomorphomonocolpites humbertoides* | | |

| PLANT TAXON | FORM-TAXON | PLANT TAXON | FORM-TAXON |
|---|---|---|---|

**Urticales**

Ulmaceae
  ?*Celtis*  — *Triorites minutipori*
  *Ulmus*  — *Verrutriporites lunduensis*
  — *Ulmipollenites*

**Casuarinales**

Casuarinaceae
  *Casuarina*  — *Triorites (Haloragacidites) cainozoicus*

**Fagales**

Fagaceae
  *Castanea* type  — *Cupuliferoipollenites pusillus*
  *Nothofagus*  — *Nothofagidites*
  *Quercus*  — *Tricolpopollenites asper* group

**Betulales**

Betulaceae
  *Alnus*  — *Alnipollenites verus*
  *Betula*  — *Trivestibulopollenites betuloides*

**Myricales**

Myricaceae
  *Myrica*  — *Triatriopollenites* (in part)

**Juglandales**

Juglandaceae
  *Carya*  — *Caryapollenites*
  *Engelhardia*  — *Triatriopollenites engelhardioides*
  — *Momipites quietus* group
  — *Momipites* sect. *coryloides* group
  *Juglans*  — *Multiporopollenites maculosus*
  *Platycarya*  — *Platycaryapollenites*
  *Pterocarya*  — *Polyatriopollenites stellatus*

**Caryophyllales**

  Family undiff.  — *Cretacaeiporites*
  — *Cretacaeiporites polygonalis*
  — *Cretacaeiporites scabratus*

Chenopodiaceae/Amaranthaceae
  Genus undiff.  — *Chenopodipollis*
  — *Periporopollenites*
  — *Polyporina*

Nyctaginaceae
  *Mirabilis*  — *Magnaperiporites*

**Plumbaginales**

Plumbaginaceae
  *Aegialitis*  — *Warkallipollenites*

**Theales**

Caryocaraceae
  *Caryocar*  — *Retisyncolporites angularis*

Dipterocarpaceae
  *Anisoptera*  — *Anisopteroxylon ramunculiformis* (W)
  *Dipterocarpus*  — *Dipterocarpophyllum* (L)
  — *Dipterocarpoxylon africanum* (W)
  — *Dipterocarpuspollenites retipilatus*

Gonystylaceae
  *Gonystylus*  — *Cryptoporopollenites cryptus*

Guttiferae (Clusiaceae)
  *Keilmeyera*  — *Keilmeyerapollenites eocenicus*
  *Pentadesma butryacea* type  — *Psilastephanocolporites boureaui*
  *Symphonia*  — *Pachydermites diederixi*
Hypericaceae
  Genus indet.  — *Harunganoxylon vismoides* (W)

Pellicieriaceae
  *Pelliciera rhizophorae*  — *Psilatricolporites crassus*
Theaceae
  *Gordonia*  — *Tricolporopollenites srivastavai*
  — ?*Verrutricolporites irregularis*
  — ?*Verrutricolporites magnotectatus*
  — ?*Verrutricolporites theacoides*

**Curcurbitales**

Cucurbitaceae
  *Sicyos*  — *Hexacolpites echinatus*

**Ericales**

Eriaceae/Epacridaceae
  Genus undiff.  — *Ericipites*
Cyrillaceae/Clethraceae
  Genus undiff.  — *Cyrillaceaepollenites megaexactus*
  *Clethra* type  — *Triporopollenites andersonii*

| PLANT TAXON | FORM-TAXON |
|---|---|
| **Ebenales** | |
| Sapotaceae | |
| Genus undiff. | *Sapotaceoidaepollenites* |
| | *Sapotaceoidaepollenites robustus* |
| *Butryospermum* type | *Psilastephanocolporites perforatus* |
| aff *Chrysophyllum* | *Belskipollis elegans* |
| Symplocaceae | |
| *Symplocos* | *Symplocospollenites* |
| | *Symplocospollenites austellus* |
| | *Triporopollenites andersonii* |
| | *Triporopollenites scabroporatus* |
| | *Porocolpopollenites vestibulum* |
| **Malvales** | |
| Bombacaceae | |
| *Bombax* type | *Bombacacidites* |
| | *Bombacacidites annae* |
| | *Bombacacidites baculatus* |
| | *Bombacacidites bellus* |
| | *Bombacacidites brevis* |
| | *Bombacacidites ciriloensis* |
| | *Bombacacidites foveoreticulatus* |
| | *Bombacacidites soleaformis* |
| *Camptostemon* | *Malvacearumpollis papuensis* (New Guinea) |
| *Catostemma* | *Jandufouria seamrogiformis* |
| Durioneae, Genus indet. | *Lakiapollis matanomadhensis* |
| *Durio* type | *Lakiapollis ovatus* |
| *Rhodognaphalon* | *Echitriporites kwaense* |
| Malvaceae | |
| *Thespesia populnea* type | *Echiperiporites estelae* |
| Tiliaceae | |
| *Brownlowia* type | *Discoidites borneensis* |
| | *Discoidites novaguineensis* |
| Sterculiaceae | |
| *Reevesia* | *Reevesiapollis* |
| **Euphorbiales** | |
| Buxaceae | |
| *Buxus* | *Buxapollis* |
| Euphorbiaceae | |
| ?Genus indet. | *Palaeowetherella* |
| *Alchornea* | *Psilatricolporites operculatus* |

| PLANT TAXON | FORM-TAXON |
|---|---|
| *Amanoa* | *Retitricolporites irregularis* |
| *Austrobuxus* type | *Malvacipollis* spp. (Australia) |
| *Klaineanthus* type | *Crototricolpites densus* |
| *Macaranga* type | *Tricolporopollenites endobalteus* (Australasia) |
| **Rosales** | |
| Rosaceae | |
| *Parinari* | *Psilatricolporites undulatus* |
| **Saxifragales** | |
| Cunoniaceae | |
| *Gilbeea* type | *Concolpites leptos* (Australia) |
| Escalloniaceae | |
| *Quintinia* | *Quintiniapollis psilatispora* |
| **Fabales** | |
| Leguminosae (Mimosaceae, Caesalpinoideae, Fabaceae) | |
| Genus indet. | *Praedapollis flexibilis* |
| | *Spirosyncolpites bruni* |
| *Acacia* | *Polyadopollenites myriosporites* |
| | *Polyadopollenites vancampoi* |
| *Adenanthera* type | *Adenantherites simplex* |
| *Amblygonocarpus* | *Amblygonocarpidites areolatus* |
| *Arapatiella* | *Praedapollis africanus* |
| *Bauhinia* type | *Striatricolporites cephalus* |
| *Brachystegia* | *Peregrinipollis nigericus* |
| *Caesalpinia* type | *Margocolporites vanwijhei* |
| | *Caesalpiniaepollenites eocenicus* (Europe) |
| *Calpocalyx ngoumiensis* | *Adenantherites intermedius* |
| *Crudia* type | *Striatricolpites catatumbus* |
| | *Striatricolporites bellus* |
| *Detarium microphyllum* | *Detariophyllum coquinense* (L) |
| | *Detarioxylon aegypticum* (W) |
| *Dinizia?* | *Triporotetradites gemmatus* |
| *Entandrophragma* | *Entandrophragmoxylon candollei* (W) |
| | *Entandrophragmoxylon magnieri* (W) |
| *Fillaeopsis* | *Fillaeopsidites reticulatus* |

| PLANT TAXON | FORM-TAXON | PLANT TAXON | FORM-TAXON |
|---|---|---|---|
| *Leucaena* | *Foveotricolporites gonzalezii* | | *Verrutricolporites rotundiporus* |
| *Mimosa* | *Quadraplanus* | | *Verrutricolporites scabratus* |
| *Parkia* | *Parkiidites microreticulatus* | | *Sonneratioxylon aubrevillei* (W) |
| *Pentaclethra macrophylla* | *Brevicolporites guinetii* | Trapaceae | |
| *Pterocarpus erinaceus* | *Pterocarpophyllum erinacoides* (L) | *Trapa* | *Sporotrapoidites* |
| *Sindora* | *Sindorapollis* (South America) | *Trapa* (ancestral) | *Florschuetzia* sp. (columellate) |
| *Sindora* cf. *kleineana* | *Loranthcites nataliae* (Africa) | | |
| | | **Hippurales** | |
| | | Gunneraceae | |
| **Myrtales** | | *Gunnera* | *Tricolpites reticulatus* |
| Combretaceae | | **Rutales** | |
| Genus undiff. | *Heterocolpites* | Burseraceae | |
| *Anogeissus* | *Combretoxylon bussoni* (W) | *Bursera* | *Brosipollis striatobrosus* |
| | | Meliaceae | |
| *Anogeissus leiocarpus* | *Combretoxylon primigenium* (W) | Genus undiff. | *Meliapollis quadrangularis* |
| | | *Entandrophragma* | *Entandrophragmoxylon candolei* |
| Melastomataceae | | | *Entandrophragmoxylon magnieri* |
| Genus undiff. | *Heterocolpites* | *Trichila* | *Psilastephanocolporites grandis* |
| Lecythidaceae | | | |
| *Barringtonia* | *Marginipollis concinnus* (India, SE Asia) | **Sapindales** | |
| | *Barringtonioxylon* (W) | Sapindaceae | |
| *Petersianthus* | *Marginipollis concinnus* (Africa) | Genus indet. | *Cupanieidites reticularis* |
| | | | *Cupanieidites acuminatus* |
| Lythraceae | | | *Syncolporites* sp. 148 of Jardine and Magloire (1965) |
| *Cuphea* | *Striasyncolpites zwardii* | | |
| *?Lagerstroemia* | *Verrutricolporites* | *Pometia* | *Drasipollenites cryptus* |
| Myrtaceae | | *Mischocarpus* type | *Cupanieidites flaccidiformis* |
| Genus undiff. | *Myrtaceidites psilatus* | | |
| | *Myrtaceidites lisamae* | **Geraniales** | |
| | *Myrtaceidites* spp. | Balsaminaceae | |
| | | *Impatiens* | *Impatiensidites brevicolpus* |
| Onagraceae | | Ctenolophonaceae | |
| *Jussieua* | *Corsinipollenites* | *Ctenolophon* | *Ctenolophonidites* |
| Rhizophoraceae | | | *Ctenolophonidites costatus* |
| ?Genus indet. | *Flacourtioxylon gifaense* (W) | | *Ctenolophonidites ertdmanii* |
| | *Palaeobruguiera elongata* | | *Ctenolophonidites keralensis* |
| *Rhizophora* type (SE Asia) | *Zonocostites ramonae* | | *Ctenolophonidites lisamae* |
| *Rhizophora* (elsewhere) | | | *Ctenolophonidites neyveliensis* |
| Sonneratiaceae | | | *Ctenolophonidites saadii* |
| *Sonneratia alba* | *Florschuetzia meridionalis* | | *Ctenolophonidites septacolpites* |
| *Sonneratia* aff. *alba* | *Florschuetzia claricolpata* | | *Ctenolophonidites stellatus* |
| *Sonneratia caseolaris* | *Florschuetzia levipoli* | | |
| *Sonneratia* (ancestral) | *Florschuetzia semilobata* | | |
| | *Florschuetzia trilobata* | | |
| | *Florschuetzia 'ovalis'* | | |
| | *Verrutricolporites laevigatus* | | |
| | *Verrutricolporites microporus* | | |

| PLANT TAXON | FORM-TAXON |
|---|---|
| | *Polybrevicolpites cephalus* |
| | *Polycolpites* spp. (India) |
| | *Polycolpites barmerensis* |
| | *Polycolpites flavatus* |
| | *Polycolpites granulatus* |
| | *Polycolpites septatus* |
| | *Pseudonothofagacidites cerebrus* |
| | *Pseudonothofagacidites kutchensis* |
| | *Retistephanocolpites* spp. |
| | *Retistephanocolpites septacolpites* |
| | *Stephanocolpites* spp. (India) |
| *Ctenolophon engleri* | *Ctenolophonidites costatus* |
| *Ctenolophon parvifolius* | *Retistephanocolpites williamsi* |
| Ixonanthaceae | |
| *Ixonanthes* | *Spinulitriporites spinosus* |
| Olacaceae | |
| *Anacolosa* | *Anacolosidites* cf. *luteoides* |
| | *Anacolosidites* |
| *Olax* | *Olaxipollis matthesi* |
| Malphigiaceae | |
| *Brachypteris* | *Perisyncolporites pokornyi* |

**Polygalales**

Polygalaceae
  *Polygala* — *Polygalacidites clarus*

**Cornales**

Alangiaceae
  *Alangium*
  Sect. *Conostigma* — *Lanagiopollis* (part)
  — *Pellicieroipollenites langenheimei* (India)
  *Alangium ebenaceum* type — *Lanagiopollis nanggulanensis*
  *Alangium havilandii* type — *Lanagiopollis emarginatus*
  Sect. *Marlea* — *Lanagiopollis* (part)
  — *Lanagiopollis eocenicus*
  *Alangium rotundifolium* type — *Alangiopollis barghoornianus*
  Sect. *Alangium*
  *Alangium salvifolium* type — *Clavastephanocolporites blysus*
  Sect. *Rhytidandra*
  *Alangium villosum* — *Clavastephanocolporites meleosus*

**Celastrales**

Aquifoliaceae
  *Ilex* — *Gemmatricolpites pergemmatus*

| PLANT TAXON | FORM-TAXON |
|---|---|
| | *Ilexpollenites chmurae* (Africa, Late Cretaceous) |
| | *Ilexpollenites* |
| Hippocrataceae | |
| *Campylostemon* | *Triporotetradites campylostemoniodes* |
| *Hippocratea* | *Polyadopollenites macroreticulatus* |
| Icacinaceae | |
| *Iodes* | *Echiperiporites icacinoides* (Africa) |
| | *Compositoipollenites rhizophorae* (Europe) |
| *Platea* | *Favitricolpites baculoferum* (part) |

**Santales**

Family indet. — *Aquilapollenites*
— *Aquilapollenites wilfordi*
Loranthaceae
  Genus undiff. — *Gothanipollis*
Santalaceae
  *Santalum* — *Santalacidites cainozoicus*
Balanophoraceae
  *Balanophora* type — *Balanopollis minutus*

**Proteales**

Proteaceae
  Genus indet. — *Triorites africaensis*
  — *Proteacidites* cf *helicoides*
  *Beauprea* — aff. *Beaupreadites matsuokae*
  — *Beaupreadites*
  *Gevuina* type — *Propylipollis reticuloscabratus*
  *?Grevillea* — *Triangulorites bellus*
  *Telopea* — *Triporopollenites ambuguus*
  *?Xylomelum* — *Propylipollis annularis*

**Gentianales**

Apocynaceae
  *Alstonia* — *Psilodiporites wolfendeni*
  *Landolphia* — *Brevicolporites molinae*
  *Rauwolfia* — *Margocolporites rauvolfii*
Periplocaceae
  *Taccazea* — *Polyporotetradites laevigatus*
Rubiaceae
  Genus indet. — *Retibrevitricolporites ibadanensis*
  — *Retibrevitricolporites obodoensis*

| PLANT TAXON | FORM-TAXON |
|---|---|
| | *Retibrevitricolporites protrudens* |
| *Canthium* | *Canthiumidites reticulatus* |
| *Gardenia* | *Triporotetradites letouzeyi* |
| *Guerttardia* | *Guerttardiidites* |
| *Macrosphyra* | *Triporotetradites hookenii* |
| *Mitragyna* | *Retitricolporites annulatus* |
| *Morelia* | *Retitricolporites boltenhageni* |
| *Oligodon* | *Triporotetradites* sp |

**Polemoniales**

| | |
|---|---|
| Convolvulaceae | |
| Genus indet. | *Calystegiapollis* |
| *Merremia* | *Perfotricolpites digitatus* |

**Scrophulariales**

| | |
|---|---|
| Acanthaceae | |
| *Isoglossa* type | *Nummulipollenites neogenicus* |
| *Justicia* type | *Multiareolites formosus* |
| | *Multiareolites vespiformis* |
| *Strobilanthes* | *Strobilanthidites* |
| *Tricanthera* type | *Multimarginites vanderhammeni* |

**Campanulales**

| | |
|---|---|
| Goodeniaceae | |
| *Scaevola* | *Poluspissusites digitatus* |

**Asterales**

| | |
|---|---|
| Compositae | |
| *Artemesia* type | *Echitricolporites mcneillyi* |
| Liguliflorae | *Echitricolporites spinosus* |
| Tubiflorae | *Fenestrites spinosus* |

**MONOCOTYLEDONS**

**Liliales**

| | |
|---|---|
| Family indet. | *Liliacidites* |
| Phormiaceae | |
| *Phormium* | *Luninidites phormioides* |

**Zingiberales**

| | |
|---|---|
| Musaceae | |
| *Musa* | *Musocaulon* (W) |

**Cyperales**

| | |
|---|---|
| Cyperaceae | |
| *Carex* type | *Cyperaceaepollis* |

| PLANT TAXON | FORM-TAXON |
|---|---|
| **Restionales** | |
| Restionaceae | |
| Genus undiff. | *Milforfia* |
| | *Restionidites* |
| | *Monoporites punctatus* |
| **Poales** | |
| Gramineae (Poaceae) | |
| Genus undiff. | *Monoporites annulatus* |
| **Arecales** | |
| Palmae (Arecaceae) | |
| Genus indet. | *Arecipites* |
| | *Arecipites crassimuratus* |
| | *Arecipites exilimuratus* |
| | *Couperipollis* |
| | *Couperipollis varispinosus* |
| | *Couperipollis brevispinosus* |
| | *Echimonocolpites major* |
| | *Foveomonocolpites bauchiensis* |
| | *Gemmamonocolpites* spp. (Africa) |
| | *Grimsdalea* |
| | *Grimsdalea polygonalis* |
| | *Monocolpopollenites marginatus* |
| | *Monocolpopollenites sphaeroidites* |
| | *Monocolpopollenites* |
| | *Monocolpites medius* |
| | *Neucouperipollis kutchensis* |
| | *Palmaepollenites* spp. (undiff.) |
| | *Palmaepollenites communis* |
| | *Palmaepollenites eocenicus* |
| | *Psilamonocolpites medius* |
| | *Retimonocolpites* spp. |
| | *Retimonocolpites abeokotaensis* |
| | *Retimonocolpites anabaensis* |
| | *Retimonocolpites irregularis* |
| | *Retimonocolpites noremi* |
| | *Retimonocolpites obaensis* |
| | *Retimonocolpites pleuribaculatus* |
| | *Retimonocolpites yemojoensis* |
| Subfamily Nypoidae | |
| Genus indet. | *Proxapertites operculatus* |
| | *Proxapertites cursus* |

| PLANT TAXON | FORM-TAXON |
| --- | --- |
| *Nypa* | *Spinizonocolpites echinatus* |
| | *Spinizonocolpites baculatus* |
| Subtribe Iguanurinae | *Palmaepollenites kutchensis* |
| Other subfamilies | |
| *Calamus* type | *Dicolpopollis malesianus* |
| | *Dicolpopollis elegans* |
| *?Daemononops* | *Diporoconia* |
| *Eugeissona* | *Quillonipollenites* |
| *?Eugeissona* (ancestral) | *Longapertites* spp. |
| | *Longapertites andriesii* |
| | *Longapertites vaneendenbergii* |
| | *Longapertites proxapertitoides* |
| *Iriartea* | *Racemonocolpites* spp. (South America) |
| | *Racemonocolpites racematus* |
| | *Clavamonocolpites* |
| *?Lepidocaryum* | *Echimonocolpites rarispinosus* |
| *Mauritia* | *Mauritiidites fransiscoi* (South America) |
| *?Mauritia* | *Mauritiidites crassibaculites* |
| | *Mauritiidites lehmanii* |
| | *Mauritiidites crassiexinus* |
| *Metroxylon* | *Dicolpopollis metroxylonoides* (excl. Australia) |
| *Oncosperma* | *Racemonocolpites hammenii* |
| *?Oncosperma* | *Racemonocolpites hians* |

**Pandanales**

Pandanaceae
| | |
| --- | --- |
| *Pandanus* | *Pandanidites* spp. (in Old World only) |
| *Freycinetia* | *Lateropora glabra* |

**Cyclanthales**

Cyclanthaceae
| | |
| --- | --- |
| Genus indet. | *Cyclanthodendron* (W) |

**Order/Family indeterminate**

*Andreisporis*
*Buttinia andreevii*
*Auriculopollenites echinatus*
*Auriculiidites*
*Cheilanthoidospora enigmatica*

| PLANT TAXON | FORM-TAXON |
| --- | --- |
| | *Cheilanthoidospora monoleta* |
| | *Cinctiporipollis mulleri* |
| | *Compositaipollenites dilatatus* |
| | *Constantinisporis* |
| | *Crassitriaperites* |
| | *Crassitricolporites* |
| | *Cristaecolpites* |
| | *Cristaeturites* |
| | *Dactylopollis magnificus* |
| | *Dipterocarpacearumpolle- nites* |
| | *Doualidites laevigatus* |
| | *Droseridites senonicus* |
| | *Echistephanoporites obscurus* |
| | *Echitriporites* |
| | *Echitriporites longispinosus* |
| | *Echitriporites trianguliformis* |
| | *Kurzipites* |
| | *Meyeripollis* |
| | *Periretipollis spinosus* |
| | *Periretisyncolpites* |
| | *Psilatricolpites acuticostatus* |
| | *Psilatricolporites prolatus* |
| | *Psilatricolporites kayanensis* |
| | *Retidiporites magdalensis* |
| | *Retitricolpites peroblatus* |
| | *Retitricolpites sarawakensis* |
| | *Retitricolpites vulgaris* |
| | *Retitricolporites* spp. |
| | *Retitricolporites semistriatus* |
| | *Retitriporites aspidipori* |
| | *Retitriporites variabilis* |
| | *Stellatopollis* |
| | *Striamonocolpites rectostriatus* |
| | *Striamonocolpites undatostriatus* |
| | *Striatopollis* |
| | *Striatricolporites conspicuus* |
| | *Striaticolporites minor* |
| | *Syndemicolpites* |
| | *Tricolpites* |
| | *Triorites festatus* |
| | *Triorites tenuiexinus* |
| | *Victorisporis* |

# Glossary

## BOTANICAL

**Allopatry** Where related species have different non-overlapping geographical areas of occurrence.

**Anemophily** With pollen (or seeds) dispersed by wind.

**Aril** A fleshy, coloured covering of the seed, typified by mace in the nutmeg, and the flesh of the durian.

**Basal area** The cross-sectional area of a tree trunk, or trees within a block of forest, usually measured at breast height. Basal area is proportional to timber volume, and is a useful measurement in both forestry and ecology as an index of the contribution of tree species to vegetation.

**Catena** A gradual succession of vegetation (or soil types) over an area, usually due to variation in drainage.

**Cauliflory** Bearing flowers on the trunk of trees.

**Diaspore** Collective term for spores and seeds dispersed from a plant.

**Disjunct** Taxa which occur in two or more widely separated areas.

**Diversity** The number of species in a community or region.

**Ecotone** A narrow, and generally sharply defined, transition between two plant communities.

**Endemic** Relating to a species which is confined to a particular geographical region.

**Eutrophic** Rich in nutrients.

**Formation** (with respect to vegetation) A vegetation type recognised by a particular combination of structural and physiognomic characters, regardless of its flora.

**Funicle** The stalk of an ovule or seed by which it is attached to the placenta.

**Jungle** Popular term often used inaccurately as a synonym for tropical rain forest. The word 'jungle' comes from the Hindi word 'jangal', which refers to the dense, impenetrable forest and scrub around settlements.

**'k' selection** Of the reproductive strategy of species characteristic of stable environments.

**Leptocaul** A tree with a thin primary stem and slender construction, generally many branched and with intermediate-sized or small leaves, typified by the willow.

**Megaphyll** Very large leaves, over 25 cm long.

**Megathermal** Relating to plant taxa which are wholly frost-intolerant, and hence restricted to the frost-free tropics.

**Mesophyll** Large leaves within the range of 12.5 to 25 cm in length, characteristic of most tree species within tropical rain forests.

**Mesotherm** Relating to plant taxa with mild frost tolerance, intermediate between megatherm and microtherm, particularly characteristic of warm temperate climates.

**Microphyll** Small leaves within the size range 2.5 to 7.5 cm.

**Microthermal** Relating to plants which are tolerant of frosts, and hence are widespread in temperate regions and in tropicalpine vegetation.

**Monopodial** Relating to a tree crown with a single leading stem with lateral branches, often resulting in tall, symmetrical crowns, typified by a Christmas tree.

**Nannophyll** Very small leaves, less than 2.5 cm in length.

**Notophyll** Intermediate-sized leaves within the size range 7.5 to 12.5 cm.

**Oligotrophic** Poor in nutrients.

**Pachycaul** A plant with a thick primary stem, and massive construction, without branching, generally with large leaves, typified by many palms.

**Palaeotropical** Relating to the Old World tropics.

**Pantropical**   Throughout the tropics.

**'r' selection**   Of the reproductive strategy of species characteristic of unstable environments, reproducing quickly with abundant progeny.

**Ramiflory**   Bearing flowers on the main branches of trees.

**Rheophyte**   A plant adapted to fast-moving streams, typically with very slender leaves.

**Sclerophyll**   A tough leathery leaf, in the humid tropics characteristic of heath forest.

**Sympatry**   The situation in which related species occur together within the same geographical area.

**Sympodial**   Relating to a tree crown with several main leading stems, often resulting in irregular, broad crowns.

**Synusia**   A life form community, such as big woody climbers, or epiphytes.

**Vessel**   A part of the xylem consisting of a tube-like series of cells which conduct water and mineral salts and provide mechanical support, found in most woody angiosperms, but absent in gymnosperms.

**Xeromorphic**   Relating to a plant with morphological and anatomical characters which appear adapted to withstand drought.

**Xylem**   Wood. Vascular tissue which provides mechanical support and conducts water and mineral salts through the plant.

**Zoophily**   With pollen (or seed) dispersal via animal vectors.


## ASTRONOMICAL/GEOLOGICAL

**Caliche**   Deposits, often in nodular form, of concretionary calcium carbonate, formed within soil as a result of evaporation of mineral-rich water under a strongly seasonal or arid climate.

**Clastic**   Relating to sediments consisting of fragments of broken rock (clasts) which are the result of erosion, and subsequently transported and deposited at a different site. Clastic rocks include mudrocks, siltstones, sandstones and conglomerates.

**Continental shelf**   That part of a continent which is covered by shallow seas during times of globally high sea levels.

**Continental shelf break**   The seaward boundary of the continental shelf.

**Distal deposition**   Deposition occurring toward the seaward margin of a sedimentary basin.

**Eccentricity**   Cyclical change of the elliptical orbit of the Earth around the Sun as a result of the combined effect of the gravitational pull of the planets on the Earth. Over cycles of about 100 000 years, the Earth's orbit around the Sun varies from virtually circular to an elliptic orbit with an eccentricity of about 6%.

**Eustacy**   The process of changing sea levels caused primarily by the incorporation into, or removal of ice from polar ice caps, as a result of changing climate.

**Fluviomarine**   Relating to sedimentation within deltas where rivers discharge into the sea.

**Formation**   (with respect to rocks) Fundamental unit of lithostratigraphic classification. A rock formation is a mappable succession of rocks which can be differentiated from adjacent rocks on the basis of readily observable lithological features.

**Greenhouse mode**   Relating to periods during which the Earth's atmosphere is enriched in greenhouse gases, such as carbon dioxide, and during which ice caps are poorly developed or absent from polar regions.

**Highstand systems tract**   Stratigraphically highest package of sediments within a sequence, deposited following a phase of relative sea level rise; generally deposited on the continental shelf.

**Icehouse mode**   Relating to periods during which the Earth's atmosphere is poor in greenhouse gasses, such as carbon dioxide, and during which ice caps develop in polar regions.

**Lowstand systems tract**   Stratigraphically lowest package of sediments within a sequence, deposited following a pronounced phase of sea level fall; generally deposited on the continental slope.

**Ombrogenous**   Maintained wholly by rainfall.

**Paralic**   Relating to deposition in a coastal setting which is predominantly fluvial to brackish, but with intermittent marine incursions.

**Podsol**   A soil characterised by an acid A horizon, and an iron- or humus-rich B horizon, sometimes in the form of a compact pan.

**Precession**   The cyclical shift of the equinoxes along the Earth's elliptic orbit as a result of the combined effect of the wobble of the Earth's axis and other astronomical movements. The precession of the equinoxes completes a full cycle every 22 000 years. Today, the Earth is furthest from the Sun at the time of the summer solstice, whereas 11 000 years ago, the Earth was furthest from the Sun during the winter solstice.

**Proximal deposition** Deposition occurring toward the landward margin of a sedimentary basin.

**Sequence** A conformable succession of genetically related sediments bounded by unconformities or their correlative conformities, deposited during a single cycle of relative sea level fall, followed by rising sea levels. A sequence is composed of three distinct sediment packages with different geometries, termed systems tracts, with the lowstand systems tract being formed when sea levels were at their lowest, following a relative sea level fall. The transgressive systems tract is formed during the subsequent phase of sea level rise, and the highstand systems tract is formed during the highest phase of sea levels.

**Subduction** The process of destruction of oceanic crust where one lithospheric plate is overridden by another.

**Systems tract** A lithological subdivision of a sequence, of which the detailed geometry depends on whether relative sea levels were low, rising or high within a single sea level cycle of fall and rise.

**Tilt** The angle of inclination of the Earth's axis relative to its plane of orbit is currently 23.5°. Axial tilt varies through time between 21.8° and 24.4° with a cyclicity of 41 000 years.

**Transgressive systems tract** The middle package of sediments within a sequence deposited during a phase of relative sea level rise, deposited predominantly on the continental shelf.

**Unconformity** A surface separating younger from older sediments along which there is evidence of erosion or subaerial exposure.

# PALYNOLOGICAL/PALAEOBOTANICAL

**Bisaccate** Of gymnosperm pollen with two separate air sacs developed within the pollen wall, characteristic of many Coniferae (e.g. *Abies*, *Cedrus*, *Picea*, *Pinus*) and Podocarpaceae, such as *Podocarpus* and *Dacrydium*.

**Colpus** Longitudinal furrow in pollen wall, associated with germination. Plural colpi.

**Crassaperturate** Of pollen in which the inner layer of the exine is greatly thickened around the apertures, particularly characteristic of many pollen types of uncertain affinity from the latest Cretaceous.

**Diorate** Of pollen with two subequatorial pores on each colpus, characteristic of the monotypic Madagascan family Didymelaceae, as well as certain Late Cretaceous and Early Tertiary fossil pollen types from Africa, South America and Australasia.

**Elater** Elongated threads derived from the spore wall in *Equisetum*, with parallels in a mid-Cretaceous group of pollen of Gnetalean affinity, which are termed elaterospores, such as *Galeacornea* and *Elateropollenites*.

**Exine** Outer, generally resilient, layer of pollen grain wall which may become fossilised. The inner part of the wall, termed intine, is not resilient and does not fossilise.

**Macrofossil** A fossil which requires observation in hand specimen using a lens.

**Microfossil** Fossil requiring microscope study, not visible to the naked eye in rocks in the field.

**Monad** A single pollen grain.

**Monosulcate** Pollen grains with a single, distal sulcus, or germination furrow, particularly characteristic in the monocotyledons (especially palms), and in primitive angiosperms, and also found in the earliest recorded angiosperm pollen, from the Early Cretaceous.

**Nannofossil** Very small planktonic plants which bear calcite plates, such as coccolithophores.

**Normapolles** Prominent group of Late Cretaceous to Eocene triporate pollen, mainly characteristic of the region from E North America to W Russia but also occurring elsewhere. They often have complex apertures, possibly from plants in part ancestral to Juglandales.

**Periporate** Angiosperm pollen with pores equally distributed over the whole exine surface, typical of Amaranthaceae, Chenopodiaceae, Caryophyllaceae, Malvaceae, *Plantago* (Plantaginaceae), Polygonaceae, many Theaceae, the genera *Altingia* and *Liquidambar* (Hamamellidaceae), as well as Late Cretaceous pollen of uncertain affinity attributed to the form-genus *Cretacaeiporites*.

**Polyad** A cluster of four or more pollen tetrads, fused into a single unit, as in many Leguminosae (e.g. *Acacia*, *Albizia* and *Parkia*).

**Pore** Generally circular thinning of exine in pollen grain, associated with germination.

**Porotrichotomosulcate** Pollen grain with three sub-equatorial pores positioned radially on the distal face of a pollen grain. This configuration occurs in the W African palm *Sclerosperma*, and several Late Cretaceous and Early Tertiary pollen types from Africa and India of uncertain taxonomic position.

**Syncolpate** Of pollen in which meridional colpi join at poles, as in Myrtaceae, many Sapindaceae, *Barringtonia* (Lecythidaceae) and many Loranthaceae.

**Tetrad** Symmetrical group of four pollen grains or spores resulting from the meiotic division of one mother cell. Typical of certain families and genera, such as Ericaceae, Epacridaceae, *Mimosa*

(Leguminosae), Typhaceae, many Annonaceae, *Lophopetalum* (Celastraceae), *Gardenia* (Rubiaceae), *Drimys* (Winteraceae) and *Selaginella* (Selaginellaceae).

**Trichotomosulcate** Of monosulcate pollen in which the sulcus is three-rayed, present in many palms, and the small family Phormiaceae, allied to Liliaceae.

**Tricolpate** Of pollen with three, meridionally arranged colpi, characteristic of many dicotyledonous angiosperms.

**Trisaccate** Of gymnosperm pollen with three separate air sacs developed within the pollen wall, characteristic of certain Podocarpaceae, such as the genus *Podocarpus* section *Dacrycarpus* (sometimes given generic status).

# References

Aarssen, B.G.K. van, Cox, H.C., Hoogendoorn, P. and de Leeuw, J.W. 1990. A cadinane bipolymer present in fossil and extant dammar resins as a source for cadinanes and bicadinanes in crude oils from Southeast Asia. *Geochimica et Cosmochimica Acta* 54, 3021–31.

Aarssen, B.G.K. van, Hessels, J.K.C., Abbink, O.A. and de Leeuw, J.W. 1992. The occurrence of polycyclic sesqui-, tri- and oligoterpenoids derived from a resinous polymeric cadinane in crude oils from Southeast Asia. *Geochimica et Cosmochimica Acta* 56, 1231–46.

Aarssen, B.G.K. van, de Leeuw, J.W., Collinson, M., Boon, J.J. and Goth, K. 1994. Occurrence of polycadinene in fossil and recent resins. *Geochimica et Cosmochimica Acta* 58, 223–9.

Absy, M.L., Cleef, A.M., Martin, L., Servant, M., Siffedine, A., da Silva, M., Soubies, F., Sugiuo, K., Turcq, B. and van der Hammen, T. 1991. Mise en évidense de quatre phases d'ouverture de la foret dense dans le sud-est de l'Amazonie au cours des 60000 dernièrs années. Premiere comparison avec d'autres regions tropicales. *Comptes Rendus de l'Academie des Sciences* (Paris) Series 2, 312, 673–8.

Adam, P. 1994. *Australian rainforests.* Oxford Biogeography Series 6, Clarendon Press, Oxford, 308 pp.

Adams, C.G., Lee, D.E. and Rosen, B.R. 1990. Conflicting isotopic and biotic evidence for tropical sea-surface temperatures during the Tertiary. *Palaeogeography, Palaeoclimatology, Palaeoecology* 77, 289–313.

Adegoke, O.S., Jan du Chene, R.E., Agumanu, A.K. and Ajayi, P.O. 1978. Palynology and age of the Kerri-Kerri Formation, Nigeria. *Revista Espanola de Micropalaeontologia* 10, 276–83.

Alexander, P.O. 1981. Age and duration of Deccan volcanism: K–Ar evidence. In: Subbarao, K.U. and Sukheswala, K. (eds), *Deccan volcanism and related basalt provinces in other parts of the world.* Memoirs Geological Society of India 3, pp. 244–50.

Alvarez, L.W., Alvarez, W., Asaro, F. and Michel, H.V. 1980. Extraterrestrial cause for Cretaceous–Tertiary extinction. *Science* 208, 1095–1108.

Ambwani, K., Bande, M.B. and Prakash, U. 1981. Pollen grains of *Ctenolophonidites* from the Neyveli Lignites of South India. *The Palaeobotanist* 27, 100–6.

Anderson, J.A.R. 1963. The flora of the peat swamp forests of Sarawak and Brunei, including a catalogue of all recorded species of flowering plants, ferns and fern allies. *Gardens Bulletin, Singapore* 20, 131–238.

Anderson, J.A.R. 1964. The structure and development of the peat swamps of Sarawak and Brunei. *Journal of Tropical Geography* 18, 7–16.

Anderson, J.A.R. 1976. Observations on the ecology of five peat swamp forests in Sumatra and Kalimantan. In: *Peat and podzolic soils and their potential for agriculture in Indonesia.* Bulletin Soil Research Institute, Bogor, pp. 45–55.

Anderson, J.A.R. 1983. The tropical peat swamps of western Malesia. In: Gore, A.J.P. (ed.), *Ecosystems of the world, Part B: Mires, swamp, bog, fen and moor.* Elsevier, Amsterdam, pp. 181–99.

Anderson, J.A.R. and Muller, J. 1975. Palynological study of a Holocene peat and a Miocene coal deposit from N.W. Borneo. *Review of Palaeobotany and Palynology* 19, 291–351.

Andrade Marin, L. 1945. *Cuadro Sinoptico de Climatological Equatoriana.* Quito, Ecuador.

Andrews, C.W. 1906. *A descriptive catalogue of the Tertiary Vertebrata of the Fayum, Egypt.* British Museum (Natural History), London.

Andrews, P. and Van Couvering, J.A.H. 1975. Palaeoenvironments in the East African Miocene. In: Szalay (ed.), *Approaches to primate paleobiology.* Contributions to Primate Biology 5, pp. 62–103.

Andriessen, P.A.M., Helmens, K.F., van der Hammen, T., Hoogheimstra, H. and Riezebos, P.A. 1993. Absolute chronology of the Pliocene–Quaternary sediment sequence of the Bogotá area, Colombia. *Quaternary Science Reviews* 12, 483–501.

Arber, E.A.N. and Parkin, J. 1907. On the origin of angiosperms. *Journal of the Linnean Society, Botany* 38, 29–80.

Archangelsky, S. 1973. Palinologia del Paleoceno de

Chubut. *Revista de la Asociacion Paleontologica Argentina* 1973, 339–99.

Ashton, P.S. 1972. The Quaternary geomorphological history of Western Malesia and lowland forest phytogeography. In: Ashton, P. and Ashton, M. (eds), *The Quaternary era in Malesia*. Transactions of the 2nd Aberdeen–Hull Symposium on Malesian Ecology, University of Hull Department of Geography Miscellaneous Series No 13, pp. 35–49.

Ashton, P.S. 1982. Dipterocarpaceae. *Flora Malesiana* 9, 283–5.

Ashton, P.S. and Gunatilleke, C.V.S. 1987a. New light on the plant geography of Ceylon 1. Historical plant geography. *Journal of Biogeography* 14, 249–85.

Ashton, P.S. and Gunatilleke, C.V.S. 1987b. New light on the plant geography of Ceylon 2. The ecological biogeography of the lowland endemic tree flora. *Journal of Biogeography* 17, 295–327.

Ashton, P.S. and McGuire, B. 1977. Pakaraimoideae, Dipterocarpaceae of the Western Hemisphere 2. Systematic, geographic and phyletic considerations. *Taxon* 27, 343–60.

Ashton, P.S., Givnish, T.J. and Appanah, S. 1988. Staggered flowering in the Dipterocarpaceae: new insights into floral induction and the evolution of mast fruiting in the aseasonal tropics. *The American Naturalist* 132, 44–66.

Audley-Charles, M.G. 1987. Dispersal of Gondwanaland: relevance to evolution of the angiosperms. In: Whitmore, T.C. (ed.), *Biogeographical evolution of the Malay Archipelago*. Oxford Monographs on Biogeography 4, Oxford Scientific Publications, pp. 5–25.

Awad, M.Z. 1994. Stratigraphic, palynological and palaeoecological studies in the east-central Sudan (Khartoum and Kosti basins) Late Jurassic–Mid Tertiary. *Berliner Geowissenschaftlische Abhandlungen* 161.

Awad, M.Z. and Brier, F.A. 1993. Oligo-Miocene to Quaternary palaeoenvironment in Gezira area, Central Sudan. In: Thorweihe, U. and Schandelmeier, H. (eds), *Geoscientific research in northeast Africa*. A.A. Balkema, Rotterdam, pp. 465–70.

Awasthi, N. 1992. Changing patterns of vegetation succession through Siwalik succession. *Palaeobotanist* 40, 312–27.

Axelrod, D.I. 1959. Poleward migration of early angiosperm flora. *Science* 130, 203–7.

Axelrod, D.I. 1970. Mesozoic palaeogeography and early angiosperm history. *Botanical Review* 36, 277–319.

Axelrod, D.I. and Raven, P.H. 1978. Late Cretaceous and Tertiary vegetation history of Africa. In:

Werger, M.A. (ed.), *Biogeography and Ecology of Southern Africa*, W. Junk, The Hague, pp. 79–130.

Azmi, M.Y., Awalludin, H., Bahari, M.N. and Morley, R.J. 1995. Integrated biostratigraphic zonation for the Malay Basin. *Proceedings of the AAPG Convention, Kuala Lumpur, Malaysia*, August 1995 (abstract).

Bailey, I.W. and Sinnot, W.E. 1916. The climatic distribution of certain types of angiosperm leaves. *American Journal of Botany* 3, 24–39.

Baker, B.H. and Wohlenburg, J. 1971. Structure and evolution of the Kenya Rift Valley. *Nature* 229, 538–42.

Baker, B.H., Mohr, P.A. and Williams, L.A.J. 1972. Geology of the eastern rift system of Africa. *Geological Society of America Special Paper* 136.

Baksi, S.K. 1962. Palynological investigation of Simsang River Tertiaries, South Shillong Front, Assam. *Bulletin of the Geological, Mining and Metallurgical Society of India* 26, 1–21.

Baksi, S.K. 1972. On the palynological biostratigraphy of the Bengal Basin. *Seminar on Palaeopalynology and Indian Stratigraphy*, Calcutta, pp. 188–205.

Baksi, S.K. and Deb, U. 1976. On new occurrence of *Aquilapollenites* from eastern India. *Pollen et Spores* 18, 399–406.

Baksi, S.K. and Deb, U. 1981. Palynology of the upper Cretaceous of the Bengal Basin, India. *Review of Palaeobotany and Palynology* 31, 335–65.

Balgooy, M.M.J. van 1987. A plant geographical analysis of Sulawesi. In: Whitmore, T.C. (ed.), *Biogeographical evolution of the Malay Archipelago*. Oxford Monographs on Biogeography 4, pp. 94–102.

Bancroft, H. 1935. Some fossil dicotyledonous woods from Mount Elgon, East Africa. *American Journal of Botany* 22, 164–82.

Bande, M.B. 1992. The Palaeogene vegetation of Peninsular India (megafossil evidences). *Palaeobotanist* 40, 275–84.

Bande, M.B. and Prakash, U. 1986. The Tertiary Flora of Southeast Asia with remarks on its palaeoenvironment and phytogeography of the Indo-Malayan Region. *Review of Palaeobotany and Palynology* 49, 203–33.

Bande, M.B., Mehrotra, R.C. and Prakash, U. 1986. Occurrence of Australian element in the Deccan Intertrappean flora of India. *Palaeobotanist* 35, 1–12.

Barker, P., Dalziel, I.A.W. et al. 1976. Evolution of the southwestern Atlantic Ocean basin: results of Leg 36, Deep Sea Drilling Project. *Initial Reports of the Deep Sea Drilling Project* 36, 993–1014.

Barlow, B.A. and Hyland, B.P.M. 1988. The origins

of the flora of Australia's wet tropics. *Proceedings of the Ecological Society of Australia* 15, 1–17.

Barron, E.J. and Washington, W.M. 1982. Cretaceous climate: a comparison of atmospheric simulations with the geologic record. *Palaeoclimatology, Palaeogeography, Palaeoecology* 40, 103–33.

Barron, E.J. and Washington, W.M. 1985. Warm Cretaceous climates: high atmospheric $CO_2$ as a plausible mechanism. In: Sundquist, B.T. and Broeker, W.S. (eds), *The carbon cycle and atmospheric $CO_2$: natural variations, Archaean to the present.* American Geophysical Union, pp. 546–53.

Barton, J. 1988. A palynological investigation of Eocene sediments from the Nanggulan Formation, Central Java. Unpublished MSc thesis, University of Hull, 101 pp.

Bartram, K. and Nugrahaningsih, L. 1990. A palynological study of the Sawahlunto Formation, Ombilin Basin, West Sumatra. *Scientific Contribution* Special Issue, pp. 123–35.

Beard, J.S. 1944. Climax vegetation in tropical America. *Ecology* 25, 127–58.

Beard, J.S. 1977. Tertiary evolution of the Australian Flora in the light of latitudinal movements of the continent. *Journal of Biogeography* 4, 111–18.

Beccari, O. 1904. *Wanderings in the great forests of Borneo.* Reprinted 1986 with introduction by Earl of Cranbrook. Oxford University Press, 424 pp.

Belsky, C.Y. and Boltenhagen E. 1963. Sporomorphes de position taxonomique incertaine du crétacé superiéur de Gabon. *Grana Palynologica* 4, 262–9.

Belsky, C.Y., Boltenhagen E. and Potonié, R. 1965. Sporae dispersae der Oberen Kreide von Gabun. *Aequatoriales Afrika. Paläeont. Z.* 39, 72–83.

Ben Avraham, Z., Nur, A., Jones, D. and Cox, A. 1981. Continental accretion; from oceanic plateaus to allochthonous terranes. *Science* 213, 47–54.

Berggren, W.A., Kent, D.V., Swisher III, C.C. and Aubrey, M.-P. 1995. A revised Cenozoic geochronology and chronostratigraphy. *Society of Economic Palaeontologists and Mineralogists Special Publication* 54, 129–212.

Berry, E.W. 1938. Tertiary flora from the Rio Pichileufu, Argentina. *Geological Society of America, Special Paper* 12, 149 pp.

Bews, J.W. 1927. Studies in the ecological evolution of the angiosperms. *New Phytologist* 26, 1–21.

Birks, H.J.B. and Line, J.M. 1990. The use of rarefaction analysis for estimating palynological richness from Quaternary pollen-analytical data. *The Holocene* 2, 1–10.

Blow, W.H. 1979. *The Cainozoic Globigerinida: a study of the morphology, taxonomy, evolutionary relationships and stratigraphical distribution of some Globigerinida (mainly Globigerinacea)*, 3 vols. E.J. Brill, Leiden, 1413 pp.

Boltenhagen, E. 1975. Pollen périporé du Crétacé supérieur du Gabon. *Revue de Micropalaeontologie* 17, 164–70.

Boltenhagen, E. 1976. Pollen et spores Sénoniens du Gabon. *Cahiers du Micropalaeontologie* 3, 3–21.

Bonnefille, R. 1984. Cenozoic vegetation and environments of early hominids in east Africa. In: Whyte, R.O. (ed.), *The evolution of the East Asian environment.* University of Hong Kong, Centre of Asian Studies 2, pp. 579–612.

Bonnefille, R. and Riollet, G. 1988. The Kashiru Pollen Sequence (Burundi). Palaeoclimatic implications for the Last 40,000 yr B.P. in Tropical Africa. *Quaternary Research* 30, 19–35.

Bouillienne, R. 1930. Un voyage botanique dans le vas-Amazone. In: Boullienne, R., Ledoux, P., Brien, P. and Navez, A. (eds), *Une mission biologique au Brésil (Aôut 1922–Mai 1923), à la mémoire de Jean Massart.* Imprimerie Medicine et Science, Brussels, pp. 1–185.

Boureau, E., Cheboldaeff-Salard, M., Koeniguer, J.-C. and Louvet, P. 1983. Evolution des flores et de la végétation en Afrique, au nord de l'Equateur. *Bothalia* 14, 355–67.

Bowler, J.M. 1982. Aridity in the Late Tertiary and Quaternary of Australia. In: Barker, W.R. and Greenslade, P.J.M. (eds), *Evolution of the flora and fauna of arid Australia.* Peacock Publications, Frewille, pp. 35–45.

Brandon-Jones, D. 1996. The Asian Colobinae (Mammalia: Cercopithecidae) as indicators of Quaternary climatic change. *Biological Journal of the Linnean Society* 59, 327–50.

Bransden, P.J.E. and Matthews, S.J. 1992. Structural and stratigraphic evolution of the East Java Sea, Indonesia. *Proceedings of the 21st Indonesian Petroleum Association Convention*, Jakarta, 1992, pp. 417–54.

Brenac, P. 1988. Evolution de la végétation et du climat dans l'Ouest Cameroun entre 25000 et 11000 ans BP. Actes Xeme Symposium Association Palynologiques Langues Français. *Travaux de la Section des Sciences et Techniques de l'Institut Français de Pondichéry* 25, pp. 91–103.

Brenan, J.M.P. 1978. Some aspects of the phytogeography of tropical Africa. *Annals of the Missouri Botanical Garden* 65, 437–78.

Brenner, G.J. 1968. Middle Cretaceous spores and pollen from Northeastern Peru. *Pollen et Spores* 10, 341–83.

Brenner, G.J. 1976. Middle Cretaceous floral provinces and early migration of angiosperms. In: Beck, C.B. (ed.), *Origin and early evolution of angiosperms*. Columbia University Press, New York, pp. 23–47.

Brenner, G.J. 1984. Late Hauterivian angiosperm pollen from the Helez Formation, Israel. *Sixth International Palynological Conference, Calgary, Abstracts*, 1984, p. 15.

Brett-Surman, M.K. 1979. Phylogeny and palaeobiogeography of hadrosaurian dinosaurs. *Nature* 277, 560–2.

Brunig, E.F. 1968. Der Heidewald von Sarawak und Brunei (The heath forests of Sarawak and Brunei). I Standort und vegetation (Site and vegetation) II. Artenbeschreibung und Anhange (Species descriptions and Appendices). *Mitt. Bundesforschungsanst. Forst. u. Holzwirtsch*, Reinbeck (Hamburg) Band 1 and 2, 68.

Brunig, E.F. 1974. *Ecological studies in Kerangas forests of Sarawak and Brunei*. Borneo Literature Bureau for Sarawak Forest Department, Kuching, 250 pp.

Brunig, E.F. 1990. Oligotrophic forested wetlands in Borneo. In: Lugo, A.E., Brinson, M. and Brown, S. (eds), *Ecosystems of the World, Vol. 15, Forested Wetlands*. Elsevier, Amsterdam, pp. 299–344.

Bruns, T.R. 1983. Model for the origin of the Yakatar block, an accreting terrane in the northern Gulf of Alaska. *Geology* 11, 718–21.

Buffetaut, E., Suteethorn, V., Martin, V., Chaimanee, Y. and Tong-Buffetaut, H. 1993. Biostratigraphy of the Mesozoic Khorat Group of Thailand: the contribution of vertebrate palaeontology. In: Thanasuthipitak, T. (ed.), *Biostratigraphy of mainland Southeast Asia: facies and palaeontology*. Chiang Mai University, Thailand, pp. 51–62.

Burbridge, N.T. 1960. The phytogeography of the Australian region. *Australian Journal of Botany* 8, 75–212.

Burger, D. 1991. Early Cretaceous angiosperms from Queensland, Australia. *Review of Palaeobotany and Palynology* 65, 153–63.

Burke, K. and Wilson, J.T. 1972. Is the African Plate stationary? *Nature* 239, 387–9.

Bush, M.B. 1994. Amazonian speciation: a necessarily complex model. *Journal of Biogeography* 21, 5–17.

Bush, M.B., Colinvaux, P.A., Wiemann, M.C., Piperno, D.R. and Liu, K.-B. 1990. Late Pleistocene temperature depression and vegetation change in Ecuadorian Amazonia. *Quaternary Research* 34, 330–45.

Caccavari, M.A. 1996. Analysis of the South American fossil pollen record of Mimosoideae (Legumuminosae). *Review of Palaeobotany and Palynology* 94, 123–35.

Cameron, N.R., Clarke, M.C.G., Aldiss, D.T.,

Aspden, J.A. and Djundin, A. 1980. The geological evolution of Northern Sumatra. *Proceedings of the 9th Indonesian Petroleum Association*, 1980, pp. 150–86.

Caratini, C. and Tissot, C. 1987. Le Sondage Misedor, Etudes palynologique. *Etudes Géographie Tropicale CNRS* 3, 49 pp.

Caratini, C., Tissot, C., Kar, R.K., Venkatachala B.S. and Sar, R. 1991. Paleocene palynoflora of Senegal from Walalane borehole, Senegal. *Palaeoecology of Africa* 22, 123–33.

Carpenter, R.J., Hill, R.S. and Jordan, G.J. 1994. Cenozoic vegetation in Tasmania: macrofossil evidence. In: Hill, R.S. (ed.), *History of Australian vegetation, Cretaceous to Recent*. Cambridge University Press, pp. 276–98.

Carter, I.S. and Morley, R.J. 1996. Utilising outcrop and palaeontological data to determine detailed sequence stratigraphy of the Early Miocene sediments of the Kutai Basin, East Kalimantan. *Proceedings of the International Symposium on Sequence Stratigraphy in Southeast Asia*. IPA Jakarta, May 1995, pp. 245–64.

Cavagnetto, C. and Anadon, P. 1995. Preliminary palynological data on floristic and climatic changes during the Middle Eocene–Early Oligocene of the eastern Ebro Basin, northeast Spain. *Review of Palaeobotany and Palynology* 92, 281–305.

Chandler, M.E.J. 1957. The Oligocene flora of the Bovey Tracey lake basin, Devonshire. *Bulletin of the British Museum (Natural History) Geology* 3, 71–123.

Chandler, M.E.J. 1973. Some Upper Cretaceous and Eocene fruits from Egypt. *Bulletin British Museum (Natural History) Geology* 2, 147–87.

Chandler, M.E.J. 1961. *The Lower Tertiary floras of southern England. I. Paleocene Floras. London Clay Flora* (Supplement). Text and Atlas. British Museum (Natural History) London, 354 pp.

Chandler, M.E.J. 1964. *The Lower Tertiary floras of southern England; A summary and survey of findings in the light of recent botanical observations*. British Museum (Natural History), London, 151 pp.

Chaney, R.W. 1940. Tertiary forests and continental history. *Bulletin of the Geological Society of America* 51, 469–88.

Chaney, R.W. 1947. Tertiary centers and migration routes. *Ecological Monographs* 17, 139–48.

Cheetham, A.H. and Deboo, P.B. 1963. A numerical index for biostratigraphic zonation in the mid-Tertiary of the eastern Gulf. *Gulf Coast Association Geological Society Transactions* 13, 139–47.

Chen, Y.Y. 1978. *Jurassic and Cretaceous palynostratigraphy of a Madagascar well*. Unpublished PhD thesis, University of Arizona, 264 pp.

Chesters, K.I.M. 1955. Some plant remains from the Upper Cretaceous and Tertiary of West Africa. *Annals and Magazine of Natural History* 12, 498–504.

Chesters, K.I.M. 1957. The Miocene flora of Rusinga Island, Lake Victoria, Kenya. *Palaeontographica* 101, 30–67.

Chiarugi, A. 1933. Legni fossili della Somalia Italiana. *Palaeontogr. Italia* 32, Supplement 1, 97–167.

China Petroleum Industry Oil Exploration Research Centre, 1978. Early Tertiary spores and pollen grains from the coastal region of Bohai. *Journal of Nanking Geology and Palaeontology Research Centre Bulletin* 1978.

Chmura, C.A. 1973. Upper Cretaceous (Campanian–Maastrichtian) angiosperm pollen from the western San Joaquim Valley, California, USA. *Palaeontographica* B 141, 89–171.

Chow, Y.C. 1996. Application of climatic biosignals to stratigraphic studies offshore Sabah/Sarawak, Malaysia. *Proceedings of the 9th International Palynological Congress*, Houston Texas, June 1996, Abstracts, p. 25.

Christen, H.V. 1973. Climatic classification and land-use of the humid parts of Colombia with particular consideration of Forestry. Unpublished manuscript, Hamburg (in Brunig, 1990).

Christophel, D.C. 1980. Occurrence of *Casuarina* megafossils in the Tertiary of southeastern Australia. *Australian Journal of Botany* 28, 249–59.

Clayton, W.D. 1958. A tropical moor forest in Nigeria. *Journal West African Science Association* 4, 1–3.

Cleef, A.M. and Hoogheimstra, H. 1984. Present vegetation of the area of the High Plain of Bogotá. In: Hoogheimstra, H. (ed.), *Vegetational and climatic record of the High Plain of Bogotá: a continuous record for the last 3.5 million years*. Dissertationes Botanicae Band 79, J. Cramer, pp. 42–66.

CLIMAP, 1976. The surface of the ice-age Earth. *Science* 191, 1131–44.

Coetzee, J.A. 1978. Climatic and biological changes in south-western Africa during the late Cainozoic. *Palaeoecology of Africa* 10, 13–29.

Coetzee, J.A. 1981. A palynological record of very primitive angiosperms in Tertiary deposits of the south-western Cape Province, South Africa. *South African Journal of Science* 77, 341–3.

Coetzee, J.A. 1993. African flora since the terminal Jurassic. In: Goldblatt, P. (ed.), *Biological relationships between Africa and South America*. Yale University Press, pp. 37–59.

Coetzee, J.A. and Muller, J. 1984. The phytogeographic significance of some extinct Gondwana pollen types from the Tertiary of the southwestern Cape (South Africa). *Annals of the Missouri Botanical Garden* 71, 1088–99.

Coetzee, J.A. and Praglowski, J. 1984. Pollen evidence for the occurrence of *Casuarina* and *Myrica* in the Tertiary of South Africa. *Grana* 23, 23–41.

Colinvaux, P.A., De Oliviera, P.E., Moreno, J.E., Miller, M.C. and Bush, M.B. 1996. A long pollen record from lowland Amazonia: forest and cooling in glacial times. *Science* 274, 85–8.

Collinson, M.E. 1983. *Fossil plants of the London Clay*. Palaeontological Association Field Guides to Fossils, No. 1, Palaeontological Association, London, 121 pp.

Collinson, M.E. 1993. Taphonomy and fruiting biology of Recent and fossil *Nypa*. *Special Papers in Palaeontology* 49, 165–80.

Collinson, M.E. 1999. Cainozoic evolution of modern plant communities and vegetation. In: Culver, S. and Rawson, P.F. (eds), *Biotic response to global change: the last 145 million years*. Natural History Museum, London (in press).

Collinson, M.E. and Hooker, J.J. 1987. Vegetational and mammalian faunal changes in the early Tertiary of southern England. In: Friis, E.M., Chaloner, W.G. and Crane, P.R. (eds), *The origins of angiosperms and their biological consequences*. Cambridge University Press, Cambridge, pp. 259–304.

Collinson, M.E., Fowler, K. and Boulter, M.C. 1981. Floristic changes indicate a cooling climate in the Eocene of southern England. *Nature* 291, 315–17.

Collinson, M.E., Boulter, M.C. and Holmes, P.L. 1993. Magnoliophyta ('Angiospermae'). In: Benton, M.J. (ed.), *The fossil record*. Chapman & Hall, London, pp. 809–41.

Corner, E.J.H. 1940. *Wayside trees of Malaya*. Government Printer, Singapore.

Corner, E.J.H. 1949. The durian theory and the origin of the modern tree. *Annals of Botany*, New Series 13, 367–414.

Corner, E.J.H. 1964. *The life of plants*. Wiedenfeld & Nicholson, London, 325 pp.

Corner, E.J.H. 1978. *The freshwater swamp-forest of South Johore and Singapore*. Gardens Bulletin Supplement 1, 266 pp.

Couper, R.A. 1953. Upper Mesozoic and Cainozoic spores and pollen grains from New Zealand. *New Zealand Geological Survey Palaeontological Bulletin* 32, 1–87.

Couper, R.A. 1960. New Zealand Mesozoic and Cainozoic plant microfossils. *New Zealand Geological Survey – Palaeontological Bulletin, New*

*Zealand Department of Scientific and Industrial Research* 32, 1–82.

Courtillot, V., Ferand, G., Maluski, H. and Vandamme, D. 1988. Deccan flood basalts and the Cretaceous/Tertiary boundary? *Nature* 333, 843–5.

Couvering, J.A.H. Van and Couvering, J.A. Van 1975. Geological setting and faunal analysis of East African Early Miocene. In: Isaac, L.G. (ed.), *Perspectives in human evolution III*.

Cowan, D.S. 1982. Geological evidence for post-40 My BP large-scale northwest displacement of a large part of southeastern Alaska. *Geology* 10, 309–13.

Craddock, C. 1982. Antarctica and Gondwanaland. In: Craddock, C. (ed.), *Antarctic geoscience*. University of Wisconsin Press, Madison, pp. 3–13.

Crane, P.R. 1987. Vegetational consequences of the angiosperm diversification. In: Friis, E.M., Chaloner, W.G. and Crane, P.R. (eds), *The origins of angiosperms and their biological consequences*. Cambridge University Press, Cambridge, pp. 107–44.

Crane, P.R. and Lidgard, S. 1990. Angiosperm radiation and patterns of Cretaceous palynological diversity. In: Taylor, P.D. and Larwood, G.P. (eds), *Major Evolutionary Radiations*. Systematics Association Special Volume 42, pp. 377–407.

Crane, P.R., Friis, E.M. and Pedersen, K.R. 1995. The origin and early diversification of angiosperms. *Nature* 374, 27–34.

Cranwell, L.M. 1959. Fossil pollen from Seymour Island. *Nature* 184, 1782–5.

Creber, G.T. and Chaloner, W.G. 1985. Tree growth in the Mesozoic and early Tertiary and the reconstruction of palaeoclimates. *Palaeogeography, Palaeoclimatology, Palaeoecology* 52, 35–60.

Crepet, W.L. and Friis, E.M. 1987. The evolution of insect pollination in angiosperms. In: Friis, E.M., Chaloner, W.G. and Crane, P.R. (eds), *The origins of angiosperms and their biological consequences*. Cambridge University Press, Cambridge, pp. 181–201.

Curiale, J.A., Kyi, P., Collins, I.D., Din, A., Nyein, K., Nyunt, M. and Stuart, C.J. 1994. The central Myanmar (Burma) oil family – composition and implications for source. *Organic Geochemistry* 22, 237–55.

Daley, B. 1972. Some problems concerning the Early Tertiary climate of Southern Britain. *Palaeogeography, Palaeoclimatology, Palaeoecology* 11, 177–90.

Daly, M.C., Hooper, B.G.D. and Smith, D.G., 1987. Tertiary plate tectonics and basin evolution in Indonesia. *Proceedings of the 16th Indonesian Petroleum Association*, pp. 399–428.

Dalziel, I.W.D. and Eliott, D.H. 1973. The Scotian Arc and Antarctic margin. In: Nairn, A.E.M. and Stehli, F.G. (eds), *The ocean basins and margins*, Vol. 1, The South Atlantic. Plenum Press, New York, pp. 171–246.

Darwin, C. 1859. *On the origin of species by means of natural selection, or the preservation of favoured races in the struggle for life*. John Murray, London.

Davis, T.A.W. and Richards, P.W. 1933–34. The vegetation of Moraballi Creek, British Guiana: an ecological study of a limited area of tropical rain forest. Parts I and II. *Journal of Ecology* 21, 350–84, 22, 106–55.

De Lima, M.R. 1980. Palinologia da formação Santana (Cretáceo do Nordeste do Brasil). III. Descripcao sistemática dos polens da turma plicates (subturma costates). *Ameghiniana* 17, 15–47.

Deb, U., Baksi, S.K. and Ghosh, A.K. 1973. On the age of the Neyveli Lignite – a palynological approach. *Quarterly Journal of the Mineralogical and Metallalogical Society of India* 45, 23–8.

Debec, P. and Allen, G.P. 1996. Late Quaternary glacio-eustatic sequences and stratal patterns in the Mahakam Delta. In: *Proceedings of the International Symposium on Sequence Stratigraphy in Southeast Asia*. IPA Jakarta, May 1995, pp. 381–2.

Demchuck, T. and Moore, T.A. 1993. Palynofloral and organic characteristics of a Miocene bog-forest, Kalimantan, Indonesia. *Organic Geochemistry* 20, 119–34.

Dettmann. M.E. 1994. Cretaceous vegetation: the microfossil record. In: Hill, R.S. (ed.), *History of Australian vegetation, Cretaceous to Recent*. Cambridge University Press, Cambridge, pp. 143–170.

Dettmann, M.E. 1997. Structure and floristics of Cretaceous vegetation of southern Gondwana: implications for angiosperm biogeography. *Palaeobotanist* 41, 224–33.

Dettmann, M.E. and Jarzen, D.M. 1990. The Antarctic/Australian Rift Valley: Late Cretaceous cradle of northeastern Australasian relics? *Review of Palaeobotany and Palynology* 65, 131–44.

Dewey, J.F., Cande, S. and Pitman III, W.C. 1989. Tectonic evolution of the India/Eurasia collision zone. *Eclogae Geologicae Helvetiae* 82, 717–34.

Diels, L. 1934. Die Flora Australiens und Wegner's Verschiebungstheorie. *Sitzungsberichte der Preussischen Akademie der Wissenschaften zu Berlin* 33, 533–45.

Doyle, J.A. 1969. Cretaceous angiosperm pollen of the Atlantic Coastal Plain, and its evolutionary significance. *Journal of the Arnold Arboretum* 50, 1–35.

Doyle, J.A. 1977. Patterns of evolution in early angiosperms. In: Hallam, A. (ed.), *Patterns of evolution as illustrated by the fossil record*. Elsevier, Amsterdam, pp. 501–46.

Doyle, J.A. 1978. Origin of angiosperms. *Annual Review of Ecology and Systematics* 4, 365–93.

Doyle, J.A. and Donaghue, M.J. 1986. Seed plant phylogeny and the origin of angiosperms: an experimental cladistic approach. *Botanical Review* 52, 321–431.

Doyle, J.A. and Donaghue, M.J. 1987. The origin of angiosperms: a cladistic approach. In: Friis, E.M., Chaloner, W.G. and Crane, P.R. (eds), *The origins of angiosperms and their biological consequences*. Cambridge University Press, Cambridge, pp. 17–49.

Doyle, J.A. and Hickey, L.J. 1976. Pollen and leaves from the Mid-Cretaceous Potomac Group and their bearing on early angiosperm evolution. In: Beck, C.B. (ed.), *Evolution of angiosperms*. Columbia University Press, New York, pp. 139–206.

Doyle, J.A. and Hotton, C.L. 1991. Diversification of early angiosperm pollen in a cladistic context. In: Blackmore, S. and Barnes, S.H. (eds), *Pollen and Spores*. Systematics Association Special Volume 44, pp. 169–95.

Doyle, J.A., Biens, P., Doerenkamp, A. and Jardine, S. 1977. Angiosperm pollen from the pre-Albian Cretaceous of equatorial Africa. *Bulletin des Centres de Recherches Exploration–Production Elf-Aquitaine* 1, 451–73.

Doyle, J.A., Jardine, S. and Doerenkamp, A. 1982. *Afropollis*, a new genus of early angiosperm pollen, with notes on the Cretaceous palynostrati-graphy and palaeoenvironments of northern Gondwana. *Bulletin des Centres de Recherches Exploration–Production Elf-Aquitaine* 6, 39–117.

Doyle, J.A., Hotton, C.L. and Ward, J. 1990. Early Cretaceous tetrads, zonosulculate pollen, and Winteraceae. 1: Taxonomy, morphology and ultrastructure. *American Journal of Botany* 77, 1544–67.

Dransfield, J. 1981. Palms and Wallace's Line. In: Whitmore, T.C. (ed.), *Wallace's Line and plate tectonics*. Oxford Monographs in Biogeography 1, Oxford Scientific Publications, pp. 43–56.

Dransfield J. 1987. Bicentric distributions in Malesia as exemplified by palms. In: Whitmore, T.C. (ed.), *Biogeographical evolution of the Malay Archipe-lago*. Oxford Monographs on Biogeography 4, Oxford Scientific Publications, pp. 60–72.

Drumm, A., Heggemann, H. and Helmcke, D. 1993. Contribution to the sedimentology and petrogra-phy of the non-marine Mesozoic sediments in northern Thailand (Phrae and Nan Provinces). In:

Thanasuthipitak, T. (ed.), *Biostratigraphy of mainland Southeast Asia: facies and palaeontology*. Chiang Mai University, Thailand, pp. 299–318.

Dudgeon, M.J. 1983. Eocene pollen of probable Proteaceous affinity from the Yaamba Basin, Central Queensland. *Memoirs of the Association of Australian Palaeontologists* 1, 339–62.

Dudley-Stamp, L. 1925. *The vegetation of Burma*. University of Rangoon Research Monograph 1, 65 pp.

Dudley-Stamp, L. and Lord, L. 1923. The ecology of part of the Riverine Tract of Burma. *Journal of Ecology* 6, 128–59.

Duncan, R.A. and Pyle, D.G. 1988. Rapid eruption of Deccan flood basalts at the Cretaceous/Tertiary boundary. *Nature* 333, 841–2.

Duperon-Laudoueneix, M. 1991. Importance of fossil woods (conifers and angiosperms) discov-ered in continental Mesozoic sediments of north-ern Equatorial Africa. *Journal of African Earth Sciences* 12, 391–6.

Dupont, L.M. and Weinelt, M. 1996. Vegetation history of the savanna corridor between the Guinean and the Congolian rain forest during the last 150,000 years. *Vegetation, History and Archaeobotany* 5, 273–92.

Duzen, P. 1907. Uber die Tertiare Flora des Seymour Insel. *Wiss. Ergebn. Nordsk. Schwed. Sudpolar-exped.* 1901–1903, 3, 1–27.

Dy Phon, P. 1981. Contribution á l'etude de la vegetation du Camboge. PhD thesis, Universite de Paris-Sud, Centre d'Orsay, 252 pp.

Dzanh, T. 1994. Successional development of Neogene fauna and flora, with main Neogene events in Vietnam. In: *Pacific Neogene events in time and space* 246, 57–64.

Ediger, V.S., Bati, Z. and Alisan, C. 1990. Palaeopalynology and palaeoecology of *Calamus*-like disulcate pollen grains. *Review of Palaeobo-tany and Palynology* 62, 97–105.

Eldredge, N. and Gould, N.J. 1972. Punctuated equilibria: an alternative to phyletic gradualism. In: Schopf, T.J. (ed.), *Models in palaeobiology*. Freeman, Cooper, San Fransisco, pp. 82–115.

Ellenberg, H. 1959. Typen tropischer Urwälder in Peru. *Schweitz. Zeitschr. Forstwirtsch.* 110, 167–87.

Endert, F.H. 1920. Die woudboomflora van Palem-bang. *Tectona* 13, 113–60.

Erdtman, G. 1952. *Pollen morphology and plant taxonomy – Angiosperms*. Almqvist and Wiksell, Stockholm, 539 pp.

Erdtman, G. 1972. *Pollen and spore morphology/plant taxonomy (an introduction to palynology II)*. Hafner Publishing Co, New York, 127 pp.

Erdtman, G., Praglowski, J. and Nilsson, S. 1963. *An*

*introduction to a Scandinavian pollen flora.* Almqvist and Wiksell, Stockholm, 89 pp.

Evrard, C. 1968. Recherches écologiques sur le peuplement forestier des sols hydromorphes de la Cuvette centrale congolaise. *Publ. Institute Agronomy Congo Belge (INEAC)*, Ser. Science 110.

Ewel, J. 1980. Tropical succession. *Biotropica* 12 (Supplement), 1–95.

Faegri, K. 1966. Some problems of representativity in pollen analysis. *The Palaeobotanist* 15, 135–40.

Fanshawe, D.B. 1952. The vegetation of British Guyana. A preliminary review. *Imperial Forestry Institute, Oxford University*, Institute Paper 29.

Ferguson, I.K. 1987. A preliminary survey of the pollen exine stratification in Caesalpinoideae. In: Stirton, C.H. (ed.), *Advances in legume systematics* 3, pp. 355–85.

Flenley, J.R. 1973. The use of modern pollen rain samples in the study of the vegetational history of tropical regions. In: Birks, H.J.B. and West, R.G. (eds), *Quaternary Plant Ecology*. Blackwell Scientific Publications, London, pp. 131–41.

Flenley, J.R. 1979a. *The equatorial rain forest: a geological history*. Butterworths, London, 162 pp.

Flenley, J.R. 1979b. The Late Quaternary vegetational history of the equatorial mountains. *Progress in Physical Geography* 3, 487–509.

Flenley, J.R. 1984. Late Quaternary changes of vegetation and climate in the Malesian mountains. *Erdwissenschaftliche Forschung* 18, 261–7.

Flenley, J.R. 1992. UV-B insolation and the altitudinal forest limit. In: Furley, P.A., Proctor, J. and Ratter, J.A. (eds), *Nature and dynamics of forest–savanna boundaries*. Chapman & Hall, London, pp. 273–82.

Flenley, J.R. 1996. Evidence for Late Quaternary climatic change on Easter Island. *IX IPC Meeting, Houston, Texas, USA*, June 23–8, 1996. p. 44 (abstract).

Florin, R. 1962. *The distribution of Conifer and Taxad taxa in time and space*. Acta Horti Bergiani. Band 20, 312 pp.

Flynn, L.J., Pileam, D., Jacobs, L.L., Barry, J.C., Behrensmeyer, A.K. and Kappelman, J.W. 1990. The Siwaliks of Pakistan: time and faunas in a Miocene terrestrial setting. *Journal of Geology* 98, 589–604.

Foster, C.B. 1982. Illustrations of Early Tertiary plant microfossils from the Yaamba Basin, Queensland. *Queensland Department of Mines* Publication 381, 33 pp.

Fournier, G.R. 1981. Method of analysis of Tertiary basins using the computer. *VI International Palynological Conference, Lucknow* 1976–7. 3, 349–65.

Fournier, G.R. 1982. Palynostratigraphic analysis of cores from site 493. *Deep Sea Drilling Project Leg 66*, 661–70.

Frederiksen, N.O. 1988. Sporomorph biostratigraphy, floral changes and palaeoclimatology, Eocene and earliest Oligocene of the eastern Gulf coast. *US Geological Survey Professional Paper* 1448, 68 pp.

Frederiksen, N.O. 1991. Pulses of Middle Eocene to earliest Oligocene climatic deterioration in southern California and the Gulf Coast. *Palaios* 6, 654–71.

Frederiksen, N.O. 1994a. Paleocene floral diversities and turnover events in eastern North America and their relation to diversity models. *Review of Palaeobotany and Palynology* 82, 225–38.

Frederiksen, N.O. 1994b. Middle and Late Paleocene angiosperm pollen from Pakistan. *Palynology* 18, 91–197.

Frederiksen, N.O. 1994c. Differing floral histories in southeastern North America and western Europe: Influence of palaeogeography. *Historical Biology*.

Frederiksen, N.O. and Christopher, R.A. 1978. Taxonomy and biostratigraphy of the Late Cretaceous and Palaeogene triatriate pollen from South Carolina. *Palynology* 2, 113–45.

Frederiksen, N.O., Wiggins, V.D., Ferguson, I.K., Dransfield, J. and Ager, C.M. 1985. Distribution, palaeoecology, palaeoclimatology and botanical affinity of the Eocene pollen genus *Diporoconia* n. gen. *Palynology* 9, 37–60.

Friis, E.M. 1983. Upper Cretaceous (Senonian) floral structures of juglandalean affinity containing normapolles pollen. *Review of Palaeobotany and Palynology* 39, 161–83.

Friis, E.M., Chaloner, W.G. and Crane, P.R. 1987. Introduction to angiosperms. In: Friis, E.M., Chaloner, W.G. and Crane, P.R. (eds), *The origins of angiosperms and their biological consequences*. Cambridge University Press, Cambridge, pp. 1–15.

Friis, E.M., Crane, P.R. and Pedersen, K.R. 1991. Stamen diversity and in situ pollen of Cretaceous angiosperms. In: Blackmore, S. and Barnes, S.H. (eds), *Pollen and spores*. Systematics Association Special Volume 44, pp. 197–224.

Friis, E.M., Pedersen, K.R. and Crane, P.R. 1994. *Plant Systematics and Evolution* 8 (supplement), pp. 31–49.

Fuchs, H.P. 1970. Ecological and palynological notes on *Pelliciera rhizophorae*. *Acta Botanica, Neerlandica* 19, 884–94.

Gentry, A.H. 1988a. Tree species richness of upper Amazonian forests. *Proceedings National Academy of Science USA* 85, 156–9.

Gentry, A.H. 1988b. Changes in plant community diversity and floristic composition on environmental and geographical gradients. *Annals of the Missouri Botanic Garden* 75, 1–34.

Germeraad, J.H., Hopping, C.A. and Muller, J. 1968. Palynology of Tertiary sediments from tropical areas. *Review of Palaeobotany and Palynology* 6, 189–348.

Ghazali, G.E.B. El 1993. A study on the pollen flora of Sudan. *Review of Palaeobotany and Palynology* 76, 99–345.

Gill, E.D. 1964. Rocks contiguous with basaltic curiass of western Victoria. *Proceedings Royal Society Victoria*, NS, 77, 331–55.

Ginger, D.C., Ardjakusamah, W.O., Hedley, R.J. and Pothecary, J. 1993. Inversion history of the West Natuna Basin: examples from the Cumi-Cumi PSC. *Proceedings of the 22nd Annual Convention, Indonesian Petroleum Association*, pp. 635–58.

Givnish, T. 1979. On the adaptive significance of leaf form. In: Solbrig, O.T., Jain, S., Johnson, G.B. and Raven, P. (eds), *Plant population biology*. Columbia University Press, New York, pp. 375–407.

Gobbett, D.J. and Hutchinson, C.S. 1973. *Geology of the Malay Peninsula*. Wiley-Interscience, New York.

Gonzalez Guzman, A.E. 1967. *A palynological study of the Los Cuervos and Mirador Formations, Lower and Middle Eocene, Tibu area, Colombia*. E.J. Brill, Leiden, 68 pp + 30 plates.

Good, R. 1953. *The geography of the flowering plants* (2nd edition), Longman, 452 pp.

Good, R. 1962. On the geographical relationships of the angiosperm flora of New Guinea. *Bulletin of the British Museum (Natural History), Botany* 12, 205–26.

Gore, A.J.P. 1983. *Ecosystems of the World, Part B: Mires, swamp, bog, fen and moor*. Elsevier, Amsterdam.

Graham, A. 1976. Studies in Neotropical paleobotany. 2. The Miocene communities of Veracruz, Mexico. *Annals of the Missouri Botanical Garden* 63, 787–842.

Graham, A. 1977. New Records of *Pelliceria* (Theaceae/Pelliceriaceae) in the Tertiary of the Caribbean, *Biotropica* 9, 48–52.

Graham, A. 1979. *Mortoniodendron* (Tiliaceae) and *Sphaeropteris/Trichipteris* (Cyatheaceae) in Cenozoic deposits of the Gulf–Caribbean region. *Annals of the Missouri Botanical Garden* 66, 572–6.

Graham, A. 1985. Studies in Neotropical paleobotany 4. The Eocene communities of Panama. *Annals of the Missouri Botanical Garden* 72, 504–34.

Graham, A. 1987a. Tropical American Tertiary floras and paleoenvironments: Mexico, Costa Rica, and Panama. *American Journal of Botany* 74, 1519–31.

Graham, A. 1987b. Miocene communities and paleoenvironments of southern Costa Rica. *American Journal of Botany* 74, 1501–18.

Graham, A. 1988a. Studies in Neotropical paleobotany 6. The Lower Miocene communities of Panama – The Cucaracha Formation. *Annals of the Missouri Botanical Garden* 75, 1467–79.

Graham, A. 1988b. Studies in Neotropical paleobotany. 5. The Lower Miocene communities of Panama – The Culebra Formation. *Annals of the Missouri Botanical Garden* 75, 1440–66.

Graham, A. 1989a. Late Tertiary paleoaltitudes and vegetational zonation in Mexico and Central America. *Acta Botanica Neerlandica* 38, 417–24.

Graham, A. 1989b. Studies in Neotropical paleobotany 7. The Lower Miocene communities of Panama – The la Boca Formation. *Annals of the Missouri Botanical Garden* 76, 50–66.

Graham, A. 1991a. Studies in neotropical paleobotany 8. The Pliocene communities of Panama – introduction and ferns, gymnosperms, angiosperms (monocots). *Annals of the Missouri Botanical Garden* 78, 190–200.

Graham, A. 1991b. Studies on Neotropical paleobotany 9. The Pliocene communities of Panama – angiosperms (dicots). *Annals of the Missouri Botanical Garden* 78, 201–23.

Graham, A. 1991c. Studies in Neotropical paleobotany 10. The Pliocene communities of Panama – composition, numerical representations, and paleocommunity paleoenvironmental reconstructions. *Annals of the Missouri Botanical Garden* 78, 465–75.

Graham, A. 1992. Utilisation of the Isthmian land bridge during the Cenozoic – palaeobotanical evidence for timing, and the selective influence of altitude and climate. *Review of Palaeobotany and Palynology* 72, 119–28.

Graham, A. and Barker, G. 1981. Palynology and tribal classification of the Caesalpinioideae. In: Polhill, R.M. and Raven, P.H. (eds), *Advances in legume systematics* 1, pp. 801–832.

Graham, A. and Graham, S.A. 1971. The geological history of the Lythraceae. *Brittonia* 23, 335–46.

Gregor, H.J. 1978. The Miocene fruit- and seed-floras of the Oberpfalz brown-coal. I Findings from the sandy interbeds. *Palaeontographica* Abt B 167, 8–103.

Greenwood, D.R. 1994. Palaeobotanical evidence for Tertiary climates. In: Hill, R.S. (ed.), *History of Australian vegetation, Cretaceous to Recent*. Cambridge University Press, Cambridge, pp. 44–59.

Gruas-Cavagnetto, C. 1978. Etude palynologique de l'Eocene du Bassin Anlo-Parisien. *Memoires*

*Societie Geologique France*, Nouv. Ser. 56, Mem. 131, 1–64.

Gruas-Cavagnetto, S.S. and Gruas-Cavagnetto, C. 1990. *Caesalpiniaceaepollenites* (Caesalpinioideae, Legumineuse), une nouvelle forme de genre dans l'Eocène inférieur du Bassin de Paris. Position systématique et phylogenetique. *Review of Palaeobotany and Palynology* 66, 13–24.

Grubb, P.J. 1974. Factors controlling the distribution of forest types on tropical mountains – new facts and a new perspective. In: Flenley, J.R. (ed.), *Altitudinal zonation of forest in Malesia.* University of Hull Dept Geography Miscellaneous Series 16, pp. 13–46.

Grubb, P.J., Lloyd, J.R., Pennington, T.D. and Whitmore, T.C. 1963. A comparison of montane and lowland rain forest in Equador I. The forest structure, physiognomy and floristics. *Journal of Ecology* 51, 567–601.

Guiraud, R. and Maurin, J.C. 1991. Le rifting en Afrique au Crétacé Inférieur synthese structurale, mise en èvidence de deux etapes dans la genese des bassins, relations avec les ouvertures oceaniques peri-africaines. *Bulletin de la Societe Geologique de France* 162, 811–23.

Guleria, J.S. 1992. Neogene vegetation of peninsular India. *Palaeobotanist* 40, 285–331.

Haberle, S.G. and Piperno, D. 1996. Evidences of last glacial vegetation change in the Amazon Basin from phytolith and pollen analysis of deep-sea Amazon Fan sediments (ODP Leg 155). *IX IPC Meeting, Houston, Texas, USA*, June 23–28, 1996, p. 57 (abstract).

Haffer, J. 1969. Speciation in Amazonian birds. *Science* 165, 131–7.

Haffer, J. 1987. Biogeography and Quaternary history in tropical America. In: Whitmore, T.C. and Prance, G.T (eds), *Biogeography and Quaternary history in tropical America.* Clarendon Press, Oxford, pp. 1–18.

Haile, N.S. 1981. Palaeomagnetic evidence and the geotectonic history and palaeogeography of Eastern Indonesia. In: Barber, A.J. and Wiryusujono, S. (eds), *The Geology and Tectonics of Eastern Indonesia.* Geological Research and Development Centre, Bandung, Special Publication 2, pp. 81–7.

Hall, R. 1995. Plate tectonic reconstructions of the Indonesian region. *Proceedings 24th Annual Convention, Indonesian Petroleum Association*, pp. 71–84.

Hall, R. 1996. Reconstructing Cenozoic SE Asia. In: Hall, R. and Blundell, D.J. (eds), *Tectonic evolution of Southeast Asia.* Geological Society Special Publication 106, pp. 152–84.

Hall, R. 1998. The plate tectonics of Cenozoic SE Asia and the distribution of land and sea. In: Hall, R. and Holloway, J. (eds), *Biogeography and geological evolution in SE Asia.* Bukhuys Publishers, Amsterdam, pp. 99–124.

Hallam, A. 1985. A review of Mesozoic climates. *Journal of the Geological Society of London* 142, 433–45.

Hallam, A. 1992. *Phanerozoic sea level changes.* Columbia University Press, New York, 265 pp.

Hallam, A. 1994. *An outline of Phanerozoic biogeography.* Oxford University Press, 246 pp.

Hallé, F. and Oldeman, R.A.A. 1970. *Essai sur l'architecture de la dynamique de croissance des arbres tropicaux.* Masson, Paris.

Hallé, F., Oldeman, R.A.A. and Tomlinson, B.P. 1978. *Tropical trees and forests. An architectural analysis.* Springer-Verlag, Berlin.

Ham, R.W.J.M. van der 1980. New observations on the pollen of *Ctenolophon* Oliver (Ctenolophonaceae), with remarks on the evolutionary history of the genus. *Review of Palaeobotany and Palynology* 59, 153–60.

Ham, R.W.J.M. van der, 1989. *Nephelieae pollen (Sapindaceae): form, function and evolution.* Rijksherbarium/Hortus Botanicus, Leiden, 255 pp.

Hamilton, A.C. 1976. Significance of patterns of distribution shown by forest plants and animals in tropical Africa for the reconstructions of Upper Pleistocene palaeoenvironments: a review. *Palaeoecology of Africa* 9, 63–97.

Hamilton, A.C. 1982. *Environmental history of East Africa. A study of the Quaternary.* Academic Press, London.

Hammen, T. van der, 1954. El desarollo de la flora Colombiana en los períodos geológicos I. Maestrichtiano hasta Terciario más Inferior. *Boletin Geologico* 2, 49–106.

Hammen, T. van der, 1957. Climatic periodicity and evolution of South American Maestrichtian and Tertiary floras. *Boletin Geologico* 5, 49–91.

Hammen, T. van der, 1961. Late Cretaceous and Tertiary stratigraphy and tectogenesis of the Colombian Andes. *Geologie et Mijnbouw* 40, 181–88.

Hammen, T. van der, 1963. A palynological study on the Quaternary of British Guiana. *Leidse Geologishe Mededelingen* 29, 125–80.

Hammen, T. van der, 1964. Paläoklima, Stratigraphie und Evolution. *Geologishen Rundschau.* Ferdinand enke Verlag Stuttgart, 54, pp. 428–41.

Hammen, T. van der, 1974. The Pleistocene changes of vegetation and climate in tropical South America. *Journal of Biogeography* 1, 3–26.

Hammen, T. van der and Absy, L. 1994. Amazonia during the last glacial. *Palaeogeography, Palaeoclimatology, Palaeoecology* 109, 247–61.

Hammen, T. van der and Cleef, A.M. 1983. *Trigonobalanus* and the tropical amphi-Pacific element in the North Andean forest. *Journal of Biogeography* 10, 437–40.

Hammen, T. van der and Garcia de Mutis, C. 1965. The Paleocene pollen flora of Colombia. *Leidse Geologische Mededelingen* 35, 105–16.

Hammen, T. van der and Gonzalez, E. 1960. Upper Pleistocene and Holocene climate and vegetation of the 'Sabana de Bogotá' (Colombia, South America) *Leidse Geologische Mededelingen* 25, 261–315.

Hammen, T. van der and Gonzalez, E. 1964. A pollen diagram from the Quaternary of the Sabana de Bogotá (Colombia) and its significance for the geology of the northern Andes. *Geologie en Mijnbouw* 43, 113–17.

Hammen, T. van der and Wymstra, T.H. 1964. A palynological study on the Tertiary and Upper Cretaceous of British Guiana. *Leidse Geologische Mededelingen* 30, 183–241.

Hammen, T. van der, Werner, J.H. and van Dommelen, H. 1973. Palynological record of the upheaval of the northern Andes: a study of the Pliocene and Lower Quaternary of the Colombian Eastern Cordillera and the early evolution of its high-Andean biota. *Review of Palynology and Palaeobotany* 16, 1–122.

Handique, G.K. 1993. Stratigraphy, depositional environment and hydrocarbon potential of Upper Assam Basin, India. *Symposium on Biostratigraphy of Mainland Southeast Asia: Facies and Palaeontology*, Chiang Mai, Thailand, vol. 1, pp. 151–69.

Haq, B.U. 1991. Sequence stratigraphy, sea-level change, and significance for the deep sea. *Special Publication of the International Association of Sedimentologists* 12, 3–40.

Haq, B.U., Hardenbol, J., Vail, P.R. and Baum, G.R. 1988. Mesozoic and Cenozoic chronostratigraphy and eustatic cycles. In: Wilgus, C.K., Hastings, B.S., Posamentier, H. and Van Wagoner, J. (eds), *Sea level change: an integrated approach*. Society of Economic Palaeontologists and Mineralogists Special Publication 42, pp. 71–108.

Harland, W.B., Armstrong, R.L., Cox, A.V., Craig, E.L., Smith, A.G. and Smith, D.G. 1990. *A geological time scale 1989*. Cambridge University Press, 263 pp.

Harley, M.M. 1991. Pollen morphology of the Sapotaceae. *Kew Bulletin* 46, 379–491.

Harley, M.M. 1996a. Pollen morphology of recent palms and the fossil record: some comparisons. *Ninth International Palynological Congress, Program and Abstracts*, Houston, p. 61.

Harley, M.M. 1996b. Palm pollen and the fossil record. PhD thesis, University of East London, 2 vols.

Harley, M.M. and Morley, R.J. 1995. Ultrastructural studies of some fossil and extant palm pollen, and the reconstruction of the biogeographical history of the subtribes Iguanurinae and Calaminae. *Review of Palaeobotany and Palynology* 85, 153–82.

Harris, P.M., Frost, S.H., Seiglie, G.A. and Schneidermann, N. 1984. Regional unconformities and depositional cycles, Cretaceous of the Arabian Peninsula. In: Schlee, J.S. (ed.), *Inter-regional unconformities and hydrocarbon accumulation*. American Association of Petroleum Geologists, Memoir 36, pp. 7–35.

Harrison, C.G.A., Brass, G.W., Salzman, E., Sloan, J., Southam, J. and Whitman, J.M. 1981. Sea level variations, global sedimentation rates and the hypsographic curve. *Earth and Planetary Science Letters* 54, 1–16.

Haseldonckx, P. 1972. The presence of *Nypa* palms in Europe: A solved problem. *Geologie en Mijnbouw* 5, 645–50.

Hastenrath, S. 1985. *Climate and circulation of the tropics*. Reidel, Dordrecht.

Herngreen, G.F.W. 1972. Some new pollen grains from the Upper Senonian of Brazil. *Pollen et Spores* 14, 97–112.

Herngreen, G.F.W. 1974. Middle Cretaceous palynomorphs from northeastern Brazil. *Sciences Geologiques Bulletin* 27, 101–16.

Herngreen, G.F.W. and Chlonova, A.F. 1981. Cretaceous microfloral provinces. *Pollen et Spores* 23, 441–555.

Herngreen, G.F.W. and Duenas-Jimenez, H. 1990. Dating of the Cretaceous Une Formation, Colombia, and the relationship with the Albian–Cenomanian African–South American microfloral province. *Review of Palaeobotany and Palynology* 66, 345–59.

Herngreen, G.F.W., Kedves, M., Rovnina, L.V. and Smirnova, S.B. 1996. Cretaceous palynological provinces: a review. In: Jansonius, J. and McGregor, D.C. (eds), *Palynology: principles and applications*. American Association of Stratigraphic Palynologists Foundation 3, pp. 1157–88.

Heywood, V.H. 1978. *Flowering plants of the world*. Oxford University Press, 336 pp.

Hickey, L.J. and Doyle, J.A. 1977. Early Cretaceous fossil evidence for angiosperm evolution. *The Botanical Review* 43, 1–183.

Hildebrand, A.R., Penfield, G.T., King, D.A., Pilkington, M., Camargo, Z.A., Jacobsen, S.B. and Boynton, W.V. 1991. Chicxulub Crater: a possible Cretaceous/Tertiary boundary impact crater on the Yucatan Peninsula, Mexico. *Geology* 19, 867–71.

Hill, R.S. 1990. Evolution of the modern high latitude southern hemisphere flora: evidence from the Australian macrofossil record. In: Douglas, J.G. and Christophel, D.C. (eds), *Proceedings, Third IOP Conference*, A–Z Printers, Melbourne, pp. 31–42.

Hill, R.S. 1991. Leaves of *Eucryphia* (Eucryphiaceae) from Tertiary sediments in south-eastern Australia. *Australian Systematic Botany* 4, 481–97.

Hill, R.S. 1994a. *History of Australian vegetation, Cretaceous to Recent*. Cambridge University Press, Cambridge, 433 pp.

Hill, R.S. 1994b. The history of selected Australian taxa. In: Hill, R.S. (ed.), *History of Australian vegetation, Cretaceous to Recent*. Cambridge University Press, pp. 390–419.

Hill, R.S. and Read, J. 1991. A revised infrageneric classification of *Nothofagus* (Fagaceae). *Botanical Journal of the Linnean Society* 105, 37–72.

Hill, R.S. and Scriven, L.J. 1995. The angiosperm-dominated woody vegetation of Antarctica: a review. *Review of Palaeobotany and Palynology* 86, 175–98.

Hochuli, P.A. 1979. Ursprung und Verbreitung der Restionaceen. *Vierteljahrschr. Naturforsch. Ges. Zurich* 124, 109–31.

Hochuli, P.A. 1984. Correlation of middle and late Tertiary sporomorph assemblages. *Palaeobiologie Continentale, Montpellier* 2, 301–14.

Holdridge, L.R. 1947. Determination of world plant distributions from simple climatic data. *Science* 105, 367–8.

Hoogheimstra, H. 1984. *Vegetational and climatic history of the High Plain of Bogotá, Colombia: A continuous record of the last 3.5 million years.* Dissertationes Botanicae Band 79, J Cramer, 368 pp.

Hoogheimstra, H. 1995. Environmental and palaeoclimatic evolution in Late Pliocene–Quaternary Colombia. In: Vbra, E.S., Denton, G.H., Partridge, T.C. and Burcke, L.H. (eds), *Paleoclimate and evolution, with emphasis on human origins.* Yale University Press, New Haven and London, pp. 249–61.

Hoogheimstra, H. and Agwu, C.O.C. 1988. Changes in the vegetation and trade winds in Equatorial Northwest Africa 140,000–70,000 yr BP as deduced from two marine pollen records. *Palaeogeography, Palaeoclimatology, Palaeoecology* 66, 173–213.

Hoogheimstra, H. and Ran, E.T.H. 1994. Late Pliocene–Pleistocene high resolution pollen sequence of Colombia: an overview of climatic change. *Quaternary International* 21, 63–80.

Hooker, J.D. 1860. Introductory essay. *Botany of the Antarctic voyage of H.M. Discovery Ships 'Erebus' and 'Terror' in the years 1830–1843.* III. Flora Tasmaniae. Reeve, London.

Hoorn, C., Guerraro, J., Sarmentier, G.A. and Lorente, M.A. 1995. Andean tectonics as a cause for changing drainage patterns in Miocene northern South America. *Geology* 23, 237–40.

Hopkins, B. 1974. *Forest ecology* (2nd edition). Heinemann Educational Books, Kingswood, Surrey.

Hopping, C.A. 1967. Palynology and the oil industry. *Review of Palaeobotany and Palynology* 6, 23–48.

Horrell, M.A. 1990. Energy balance constraints on $^{18}$O based paleo-sea surface temperature estimates. *Paleoceanography* 5, 339–48.

Hubbard, R.N.L.B. and Boulter, M.C. 1983. Reconstruction of Palaeogene climate from palynological evidence. *Nature* 301, 147–50.

Hudson, J.D. and Anderson, T.F. 1989. Ocean temperatures and isotopic compositions through time. *Transactions Royal Society of Edinburgh, Earth Sciences* 80, 183–92.

Hughes N.F. 1976. *Palaeobiology of angiosperm origins*. Cambridge University Press, 242 pp.

Hughes, N.F. 1994. *The enigma of angiosperm origins*. Cambridge Paleobiology Series 1, 303 pp.

Hughes, N.F. and McDougall, B. 1987. Records of angiospermid pollen entry into the English Early Cretaceous succession. *Review of Palaeobotany and Palynology* 50, 255–72.

Hutchins, L.W. 1947. The bases for temperature zonation in geographical distribution. *Ecological Monographs* 17, 325–35.

Hutchison, C.S. 1989. *Geological evolution of South-East Asia*. Clarendon Press, Oxford.

IEDS (Copesake, P. et al.) 1995. Sequence stratigraphy of the Upper Jurassic–mid Cretaceous of the Indus Basin, Pakistan, and the Rajastan area of India. In: *Proceedings International Symposium on Sequence Stratigraphy*, Indonesian Petroleum Association, Jakarta, pp. 477–81 (and wall poster).

Imbrie, J. and Imbrie, K.P. 1979. *Ice ages, solving the mystery*. Macmillan Press, London and Basingstoke, 224 pp.

Imbrie, J., Hays, J.D., Martinson, D.G., McIntyre, A., Mix, A.C., Morley, J.J., Pisias, N.G., Prell, W.L. and Shackleton, N.J. 1984. The orbital theory of Pleistocene climate: support from a revised chronology of the marine $^{18}$O record. In: Berger, A. et al. (eds), *Milankovich and climate* 1. Reidel, Dordrecht, pp. 269–305.

Jaeger, J.J., Courtillot, B. and Taponnier, P. 1989. Palaeontological view of the age of the Deccan

Traps, and the Cretaceous/Tertiary boundary, and the India–Asia collision. *Geology* 17, 316–19.

Jardiné, S. and Magloire, L. 1965. Palynologie et stratigraphie du crétacé des bassins du Senegal et de côte d'Ivoire. *Mém. Bur, Rech. Géol. Min.* 32, 187–245.

Jardiné, S., Doerenkamp, A. and Legoux O. 1967. Le genre *Hexaporotricolpites* Boltenhagen 1967 morphologie, systématique, stratigraphie et extension géographique. *Quatrieme Colloque Africain de micropaleontologie*, pp. 175–90.

Jardiné, S., Keiser, G. and Reyre, Y. 1974. L'individualisation progressive du continent africain vue à travers les données palynologiques de l'ère secondaire. *Bull. Sci. Géol. Strasbourg* 27, 69–85.

Jones, J.H. 1986. Evolution of Fagaceae: the implication of foliar features. *Annals of the Missouri Botanical Garden* 73, 228–75.

Junk, W.J. 1970. Investigations on the ecology and production-biology of the 'Floating Meadows', Part 1, the floating vegetation and its ecology. *Amazonia* 2, 449–95.

Junk, W.J. 1989. Flood tolerance and tree distribution in the central Amazonian floodplain. In: Holm-Neilsen, L., Balslev, H. and Nelson, I. (eds), *Tropical forests: botanical dynamics, speciation and diversity*. Academic Press, London, pp. 47–64.

Kaas, W.A. van der, 1983. A palynological-palaeoecological study of the lower Tertiary Coal-Bed sequence from el Cerrejon (Colombia). *Geologia Norandina* 8, 33–48.

Kaas, W.A. van der, 1991a. Palynology of eastern Indonesian marine piston-cores: A Late Quaternary vegetational and climatic history for Australasia. *Palaeogeography, Palaeoclimatology, Palaeoecology* 85, 239–302.

Kaas, W.A. van der, 1991b. Palynological aspects of site 767 in the Celebes Sea. *Proceedings of the Ocean Drilling Program, Scientific Results* 124, 369–74.

Kaas, W.A. van der and Dam, M.A.C. 1995. A 135,000–year record of vegetational and climatic change from the Bandung area, West-Java, Indonesia. *Palaeogeography, Palaeoclimatology, Palaeoecology* 117, 55–72.

Kar, R.K. 1982. On the original homeland of *Ceratopteris* Brong. and its palaeogeographical province. *Geophytology* 12, 340–1.

Kar, R.K. 1985. The fossil floras of Kachchh – IV, Tertiary palynostratigraphy. *Palaeobotanist* 34, 1–279.

Katz, B.J. 1991. Controls on lacustrine source rock development: a model for Indonesia. *Indonesian Petroleum Association 20th Annual Convention*, Jakarta, pp. 587–620.

Keay, R.W.J. 1959. *An outline of Nigerian vegetation* (3rd edition). Government Printer, Nigeria.

Kedves, M. 1968. Etudes palynologiques des couches du Tertiare inférieur de la région Parisienne. *Pollen et Spores* 10, 315–34.

Kedves, M. 1969. *Palynological studies on Hungarian Early Tertiary deposits*. Akademiai kiacto Budapest, 84 pp. + 22 plates.

Kedves, M. 1971. Presence de types sporomorphs importants dans les sédiments préquaternaires Egyptiens. *Acta Botanica Academiae Scientarum Hungaricae* 17, 371–8.

Kedves, M. 1986. Etudes palynologiques sur les sédiments préquaternaires de l'Egypt, Eocene. *Revista Espanola de Micropalaeontologia* 18, 5–26.

Kemp, E.M. 1978. Tertiary climatic evolution and vegetation history in the southeast Indian Ocean region. *Palaeogeography, Palaeoclimatology, Palaeoecology* 24, 169–208.

Kemp, E.M. and Harris, W.K. 1975. The vegetation of Tertiary islands on the Ninetyeast Ridge. *Nature* 258, 303–7.

Kemp, E.M. and Harris, W.K. 1977. The palynology of Early Tertiary sediments, Ninetyeast Ridge, Indian Ocean. *Palaeontological Association of London, Special Paper in Palaeontology*, 19, 69 pp.

Kennett, J.P. 1977. Cenozoic evolution of Antarctic glaciation, the circum-polar Antarctic Ocean, and their impact on global paleoceanography. *Journal of Geophysical Research* 82, 3843–60.

Kennett, J.P. 1980. Palaeoceanographic and biogeographic evolution of the Southern Ocean during the Cenozoic, and Cenozoic microfossil datums. *Palaeogeography, Palaeoclimatology, Palaeoecology* 31, 123–52.

Kershaw, A.P. 1974. A long continuous pollen sequence from northeastern Queensland. *Nature* 251, 222–3.

Kershaw, A.P. 1976. A Late Pleistocene and Holocene pollen diagram from Lynch's Crater, Northeastern Queensland, Australia. *New Phytologist* 77, 469–98.

Kershaw, A.P. 1985. An extended late Quaternary vegetation record from northeastern Queensland and its implications for the seasonal tropics of Australia. *Proceedings of the Ecological Society of Australia* 13, 179–89.

Kershaw, A.P. 1988. Australasia. In: Huntley, B. and Webb, T. (eds), *Vegetation history*. Kluwer Academic, Dordrecht, pp. 127–306.

Kershaw, A.P. and Hyland, B.P.M. 1975. Pollen transfer and periodicity in a rain forest situation. *Review of Palaeobotany and Palynology* 19, 129–38.

Kershaw, A.P. and McGlone, M.S. 1995. The Quaternary history of the southern conifers. In:

Enright, N.J. and Hill, N.S. (eds), *Ecology of the southern conifers*. Melbourne University Press, pp. 31–63.

Kershaw, A.P., Martin, H.A. and McEwen-Mason, J.R.C. 1994. The Neogene: a period of transition. In: Hill, R.S. (ed.), *History of Australian vegetation, Cretaceous to Recent*. Cambridge University Press, pp. 299–327.

Khan, A.H. 1974a. Palynology of Tertiary sediments from Papua New Guinea I. New form-genera and species from Upper Tertiary sediments. *Australian Journal of Botany* 24, 753–81.

Khan, A.H. 1974b. Palynology of Tertiary sediments from Papua New Guinea II. Gymnosperm pollen from Upper Tertiary sediments. *Australian Journal of Botany* 24, 783–91.

Khan, A.H. 1976. Palynology of Neogene sediments from Papua (New Guinea) stratigraphic boundaries. *Pollen et Spores* 16, 265–84.

King, L.C. 1962. *The geomorphology of the Earth: a study and synthesis of world scenery*. Hafner, New York.

Kirby, G.A.K., Morley, R.J., Humphreys, B., Matchette-Downes, C.J., Sarginson, M.J., Lott, G.K., Nicholson, R.A., Yulihanto, B., Widiastuti, R., Karmajaya, Sundoro, Fitris, F., Sofyan, S. and Sri Wijaya, 1993. A revaluation of the regional geology and hydrocarbon prospectivity of the onshore Central North Sumatra Basin. *Proceedings 22nd Convention, Indonesian Petroleum Association, Jakarta*, pp. 234–64.

Knaap, W.A. 1972. A montane pollen species from the Upper Tertiary of the Niger Delta. *Journal of the Mining, Geological and Metallurgical Society of Nigeria* 6, pp. 23–9.

Knobloch, E. and Mai, D.H. 1986. Monographie der Fruchteund Samen in der Kreide von Mitteleuropa. *Rozpravy Ustredniho Ustavu Geologickeho Praha* 47, 1–219.

Knobloch, E. and Mai, D.H. 1991. Evolution of the Middle and Upper Cretaceous floras in Central and Western Europe. *Jahrb. Geol. Bundesant. Wien* 134, 257–70.

Knobloch, E., Kvacek, Z., Buzek, C., Mai, D.H. and Batten, D.J. 1993. Evolutionary significance of floristic changes in the Northern Hemisphere during the Late Cretaceous and Palaeogene, with particular reference to Central Europe. *Review of Palaeobotany and Palynology* 78, 41–54.

Koesoemadinata, R.P. and Matasak, T. 1981. Stratigraphy and sedimentation, Ombilin Basin, Central Sumatra, Indonesia. *Proceedings of the 10th Indonesian Petroleum Association Convention, Jakarta*, pp. 217–49.

Krutzsch, W. 1966. Die sporenstratigraphische Gliederung des älteren Tertiär im nördlischen Mitteleuropa (Paleozan-Mitteloligozan). *Abh. Centr. Geol. Inst.* 8, 112–49.

Krutzsch, W. 1970. Die stratigraphische werwertbaren Sporen- und Pollenformen des Mitteleuropaischen Alttertiärs. *Jahrb. Geol. Bot.* 3, 309–79.

Kubitzki, K. 1989 The ecogeographical differentiation of Amazonian inundation forests. *Pl. Syst. Evolution.*

Kumar, M. 1996. Palynostratigraphy and palaeoecology of Early Eocene palynoflora of Rajpardi lignite, Bharuch District, Gujarat. *Palaeobotanist* 43, 110–21.

Kuyl, O.S., Muller, J. and Waterbolk, H.T. 1955. The application of palynology to oil geology, with special reference to Western Venezuela. *Geologie en Mijnbouw* 17, 49–75.

Lakhanpal, R.N. and Guleria, J.S. 1986. Fossil leaves of *Dipterocarpus* from the Lower Siwalik beds near Jawalumukhi, Himachal Pradesh. *Palaeobotanist* 35, 258–62.

Lawal, O. and Moullade M. 1986. Palynological biostratigraphy of Cretaceous sediments in the Upper Benue Basin, N.E. Nigeria. *Revue de Micropalaeontologie* 29, 61–83.

Legoux, O. 1978. Quelques espèces de pollen caractéristiques du Neogene du Nigeria. *Bulletin Centre Recherche Exploration–Production Elf-Aquitaine* 2, 265–317.

Lehmann, U. 1963. Sur Palaographie des Nordatlantiks im Tertiare. *Mitt. Geol. Palaeontol. Inst. University of Hamburg* 42, 57–69.

Lei Zhou, Kyte, F.T. and Bohar, B.P. 1991. Cretaceous/Tertiary boundary at DSDP site 596, South Pacific. *Geology* 19, 604–97.

Leidelmeyer, P. 1966. The Paleocene and Lower Eocene pollen flora of Guyana. *Leidse Geologische Mededelingen* 38, 49–70.

Leopold, E.B. 1969. Miocene pollen and spore flora from Eniwetok Atoll, Marshall Islands. *US Geological Survey Professional Paper* 260, pp. 1133–85.

Leroy, S. and Dupont, L. 1994. Development of vegetation and continental aridity in northwestern Africa during the Late Pliocene: the pollen record of ODP Site 658. *Palaeogeography, Palaeoclimatology, Palaeoecology* 109, 295–316.

Lezine, A.M. and Vergnaud-Grazzini, C. 1993. Evidence of forest extension in West Africa since 2200 BP: a pollen record from eastern tropical Atlantic. *Quaternary Science Reviews* 12, 203–20.

Lidgard, S. and Crane, P.R. 1990. Angiosperm diversification and Cretaceous floristic trends: a comparison of palynofloras and leaf macrofloras. *Palaeobiology* 16, 77–93.

Lobreau-Callen, D. and Caratini, C. 1973. Pollens

des 'Celastraceae' a l'Oligocène en Gironde (France). *Bull. Soc. Linn. Bordeau* 3, 227–31.

Longman, K.A. and Jenik, J. 1974. *Tropical forest and its environment* (2nd edition). Longman, 347 pp.

Louvet, P. 1968. Sur deux Meliacées fossiles nouvelles du Tinrhert (Algerie). *Mem. Sect. Sci. CTHS* 2, 92–111.

Louvet, P. 1971. Sur l'évolution des flores tertiare de l'Afrique nord-equatoriale. PhD thesis, CNRS Paris, 497 pp.

Louvet, P. 1975. Sur deux espèces fossiles nouvelles du Lutetien supérieur de Libye. *Actes 95e Congr. Nat. Soc. Sav. Reims 1970*. Paris Sci. 3, 43–58.

Mabberley, D.J. 1977. The origin of the Afroalpine pachycaul flora and its implications. In: Mabberley, D.J. and Chang Kiaw Lan (eds), *Tropical Botany, Gardens Bull. Singapore* 29, pp. 41–55.

Mabberley, D.J. 1987. *The plant book. A portable dictionary of the higher plants*. Cambridge University Press, 706 pp.

Mabberley, D.J. 1992. *Tropical rain forest ecology*. Blackie, Glasgow, 300 pp.

McDougal, I. and Douglas, R.A. 1988. Age progressive volcanism in the Tasmanitid seamounts. *Earth and Planetary Science Letters* 89, 207–20.

McElhinny, M.W., Haile. N.S. and Crawford, A.S. 1974. Palaeomagnetic evidence shows Malaya was not part of Gondwana. *Nature* 252, 641–5.

MacGintie, H.D. 1969. *The Eocene Green River Flora of northwestern Colorado and northeastern Utah*. Publications of the Geological Society, University of California 83, 203 pp.

McKenna, M.C. 1973. Sweepstakes, filters, corridors, Noah's Arks, and beached Viking funeral ships in palaeogeography. In: Tarling, D.H. and Runcorn, S.K. (eds), *Implications of continental drift to the earth sciences*. Academic Press, London, pp. 293–308.

McMinn, A. and Martin, H.A. 1993. Late Cainozoic pollen history of Site 765, Eastern Indian Ocean. *Scientific Reports of the Ocean Drilling Programme*, Leg 123.

Macphail, M.K. 1996. *Palynostratigraphy of the Murray Basin, inland southeastern Australia*. Australian Geological Survey, Record 57, 38 pp.

Macphail, M.K., Alley, N.F., Truswell, E.M. and Sluiter, R.K. 1994. Early Tertiary vegetation: evidence from spores and pollen. In: Hill. R.S. (ed.), *History of Australian vegetation, Cretaceous to Recent*. Cambridge University Press, pp. 262–75.

Mai, D.H. 1970. Subtropische Elemente im europäischen Tertiare. *Palaeontol. Abh. Abt. Palaobot.* 3, 441–503.

Maley, J. 1987. Fragmentation de la forêt dense humide africaine et extension des biotypes montagnards au Quaternaire récent: nouvelles données polliniques et chronologiques. Implications paléoclimatiques et biogéographiques. *Palaeoecology of Africa* 18, 307–44.

Maley, J. 1989. Late Quaternary climatic changes in the African rain forest: forest refugia and the major role of sea surface temperature variations. In: Leinen, M. and Sarnthein, M. (eds), *Palaeoclimatology and palaeometeorology: modern and past patterns of global atmospheric transport*. Kluwer Academic Publishers, Leiden, pp. 585–616.

Maley, J. 1991. The African rain forest vegetation and palaeoenvironments during the Late Quaternary. *Climatic Change* 19, 79–98.

Maley, J. 1996. The African rain forest – main characteristics of changes in vegetation and climate from the Upper Cretaceous to the Quaternary. In: Alexander, I.J., Swaine, M.D. and Watling, R. (eds), *Essays on the ecology of the Guinea–Congo rain forest*. Proceedings of the Royal Society of Edinburgh, 104b, pp. 31–73.

Maley, J. and Livingstone, D.A. 1983. Extension d'une élément montagnard dans le sud du Ghana (Afrique de l'Ouest) au Pléistocène supérieur et a l'Holocène inférieur: premieres données palynologiques. *Comptes Rendus de l'Academie des Sciences, Paris 2*, 296, 1287–92.

Maley, J., Caballe, G. and Sita, P. 1990. Etude d'un peuplement residuel à basse altitude *de Podocarpus latifolius* sur le flanc Congolaise du Massif du Chaillu. Implications palaeoclimatiques et biogeographiques. Etude de la pluie pollinique actuelle. In: Lanfranchi, R. and Schwartz, D. (eds), *Paysages Quaternaire de l'Afrique central Atlantique*, ORSTROM, Paris, pp. 336–52.

Manchester, S.R. 1994. Fruits and seeds of the Middle Eocene Nut Beds Flora, Clarno Formation, Oregon. *Palaeontographica Americana* 58, 205 pp.

Marcellari, C.E. 1988. Cretaceous palaeogeography and depositional cycles of western South America. *Journal of South American Geology* 1, 373–418.

Marshall, L.G. 1980. Marsupial palaeobiogeography. In: Jacobs, L.L. (ed.), *Essays in honor of Edwin Harris Colbert*. Museum of North Arizona Press, Flagstaff, pp. 345–86.

Martin, H.A. 1973. Upper Tertiary palynology in southern New South Wales. *Special Publications of the Geological Society of Australia* 4, 35–54.

Martin, H.A. 1977. The history of *Ilex* (Aquifoliaceae) with special reference to Australia: evidence from pollen. *Australian Journal of Botany* 25, 655–73.

Martin, H.A. 1978. Evolution of the Australian flora and vegetation through the Tertiary: evidence from pollen. *Alcheringa* 2, 181–202.

Martin, H.A. 1982. Changing Cenozoic barriers and the Australian palaeobotanical record. *Annals of the Missouri Botanical Garden* 69, 625–67.

Martin, H.A. 1992. The Tertiary of southeastern Australia: was it tropical? *Palaeobotanist* 39, 270–80.

Martin, H.A. 1994. Tertiary phytogeography: palynological evidence. In: Hill, R.S. (ed.), *History of Australian vegetation, Cretaceous to Recent*. Cambridge University Press, pp. 104–42.

Martin, H.A., Macphail, M.K. and Partridge, A.D. 1996. Tertiary *Alangium* (Alangiaceae) in eastern Australia: evidence from pollen. *Review of Palaeobotany and Palynology* 94, 111–22.

Martin, W., Alfons Gierl and Heinz Saedler, 1989. Molecular evidence for pre-Cretaceous angiosperm origins. *Nature* 339, 46–8.

Martini, E. 1971. Standard Tertiary and Quaternary calcareous nannoplankton zonation. *Proceedings 2nd Plankton Conference, Rome*, 1969, pp. 739–85.

Martinson, D.C., Pisias, N.G., Hays, J.D., Imbrie, J., Moore, T.C. and Shackleton, N.J. 1987. Age dating and the orbital theory of the Ice Ages: development of a high resolution 0–300 000-year geochronology. *Quaternary Research* 27, 1–29.

Mathur, Y.K. 1984. Cenozoic palynofossils, vegetation, ecology and climate of the north and northwestern subhimalayan region, India. In: Whyte, R.O. (ed.), *The evolution of the East Asian environment*. Vol. II, Centre of Asian Studies, University of Hong Kong, pp. 433–551.

Mayr, E. and O'Hara, R.J. 1986. The biogeographic evidence supporting the Pleistocene refuge hypothesis. *Evolution* 40, 55–67.

Medus, J. 1976. Palynologie de sédiments tertiares du Sénégal meridional. *Pollen et Spores* 16, 545–608.

Medus, J., Popoff, M., Fourtanier, E. and Sowunmi, M.A. 1988. Sedimentology, pollen, spores and diatoms of a 148m deep Miocene drill hole from Oku Lake, East Central Nigeria. *Palaeogeography, Palaeoclimatology, Palaeoecology* 68, 79–94.

Medway, Lord, 1972. The Quaternary mammals of Malesia: a review. In: Ashton, P. and Ashton, M. (eds), *The Quaternary era in Malesia*, Transactions 2nd Aberdeen–Hull Symposium on Malesian Ecology, University of Hull Department of Geography Miscellaneous Series 13, pp. 63–98.

Mehrota, R.C. and Awasthi, N. 1995. Status of gymnosperms in the Indian Tertiary flora. *Palaeobotanist* 43, 83–88.

Menke, B. 1976. Pliozäne unt ältesquaternaire Sporen- und Pollenflora von Schleswig-Holstein. *Geol. Jarb.* A 32, 3–197.

Meon, H. 1990. Palynologic studies of the Cretaceous–Tertiary boundary interval at El Kef outcrop, northwestern Tunisia: palaeogeographic implications. *Review of Palaeobotany and Palynology* 65, 85–94.

Merton, F. 1962. A visit to the Tasek Bera. *Malaya Nature Journal* 16, 103–10.

Metcalfe, I. 1988. Origin and assembly of Southeast Asian continental terranes. In: Audley-Charles, M.G. and Hallam, A. (eds), *Gondwana and Tethys*. Geological Society of London Special Publication 37, pp. 101–18.

Metcalfe, I. 1996. Pre-Cretaceous evolution of SE Asian terranes. In: Hall, R. and Blundell, D. (eds), *Tectonic evolution of SE Asia*. Geological Society Special Publication 106, pp. 97–122.

Mildenhall, D.C. 1980. New Zealand Late Cretaceous and Cenozoic plant biogeography: A contribution. *Palaeogeography, Palaeoclimatology, Palaeoecology* 31, 197–233.

Miller, K.G., Fairbanks, R.G. and Mountain, G.S. 1987. Tertiary oxygen isotope synthesis, sea level history and continental margin erosion. *Paleoceanography* 2, 1–19.

Misra, B.K., Singh, A. and Ramanujam, C.G.K. 1996. Trilatiporate pollen from Indian Palaeogene and Neogene sequences: evolution, migration and continental drift. *Review of Palaeobotany and Palynology* 91, 331–52.

Monteillet, J. and Lappartient, J.-R. 1981. Fruites et graines du Crétacé supérieur des Carrieres de Paki (Senegal). *Review of Palaeobotany and Palynology* 34, 331–44.

Montford, H.M. 1970. The terrestrial environment during Upper Cretaceous and Tertiary times. *Proceedings of the Geological Association* 81, 181–204.

Moore, P.D., Webb, J.A. and Collinson, M.E. 1991. *Pollen analysis* (2nd edition). Blackwell Scientific Publications, Oxford, 216 pp.

Moreau, R.E. 1963. The distribution of tropical African birds as an indicator of past climatic changes. In: Howell, F.C. and Bourliere, F. (eds), *African ecology and human evolution*. Aldine Press, Chicago, pp. 28–42.

Moreau, R.E. 1966. *The bird faunas of Africa and its islands*. Academic Press, London.

Morgan, R. 1978. Albian to Senonian palynology of site 364, Angola Basin. *Initial Reports of the Deep Sea Drilling Project* 40, 915–51.

Mori, S.A. 1989. Diversity of Lecythidaceae in the Guianas. In: Holm-Nielsen, L.B., Nielsen, I.C. and Balslev, H. (eds), *Tropical forests*. Academic Press, London, pp. 319–332.

Morley, R.J. 1976. Vegetation change in West Malesia during the Late Quaternary Period: a palynological study of selected lowland and lower montane sites. PhD thesis, University of Hull, 506 pp.

Morley, R.J. 1978. Palynology of Tertiary and Quaternary sediments in southeast Asia. *Proceedings of the 6th Annual Convention, Indonesian Petroleum Association*, May 1977, pp. 255–76.

Morley, R.J. 1981a. Development and vegetation dynamics of a lowland ombrogenous swamp in Kalimantan Tengah, Indonesia. *Journal of Biogeography* 8, 383–404.

Morley, R.J. 1981b. Palaeoecology of Tasek Bera, a lowland swamp in Pahang, West Malaysia. *Singapore Journal of Tropical Geography* 2, 50–6.

Morley, R.J. 1982a. The origin and history of Tasek Bera. In: Furtado, J.I. and Lim, R.P. (eds), *The ecology of a tropical freshwater swamp, the Tasek Bera, with special reference to biological production*. Ecologicae Monographicae, The Hague, 411 pp.

Morley, R.J. 1982b. A palaeoecological interpretation of a 10000 year pollen record from Danau Padang, Central Sumatra, Indonesia. *Journal of Biogeography* 9, 151–90.

Morley, R.J. 1982c. Fossil pollen attributable to *Alangium* Lamarck (Alangiaceae) from the Tertiary of Malesia. *Review of Palaeobotany and Palynology* 36, 65–94.

Morley, R.J. 1986. New approaches to stratigraphic and palaeoenvironmental modelling in Neogene deltaics with emphasis on the Niger Delta. *Proceedings 3rd Annual Conference Nigerian Association of Petroleum Explorationists*, 2, pp. 29–30.

Morley, R.J. 1991. Tertiary stratigraphic palynology in South-East Asia; current status and new directions. *Proceedings of the Geological Society of Malaysia* 28, 1–36.

Morley, R.J. 1996. Biostratigraphic characterisation of systems tracts in Tertiary sedimentary basins. *Indonesian Petroleum Association, Proceedings of International Symposium on Sequence Stratigraphy in SE Asia*. May 1995, pp. 49–70.

Morley, R.J. 1998. Palynological evidence for Tertiary plant dispersals in the SE Asia region in relation to plate tectonics and climate. In: Hall, R. and Holloway J. (eds), *Biogeography and geological evolution of SE Asia*. Bakhuys Publishers, Leiden, pp. 177–200.

Morley, R.J. in press. Tertiary ecological history of Southeast Asian peat mires. In: Moore, T. et al. (eds), *Advances in Sedimentology*, Elsevier.

Morley, R.J. and Flenley, J.R. 1987. Late Cainozoic vegetational and environmental changes in the Malay Archipelago. In: Whitmore, T.C. (ed.), *Biogeographical evolution of the Malay Archipe-*

*lago*. Oxford Monographs on Biogeography 4, Oxford Scientific Publications, pp. 50–9.

Morley, R.J. and Richards, K. 1993. Gramineae cuticle: a key indicator of late Cenozoic climatic change in the Niger Delta. *Review of Palaeobotany and Palynology* 77, 119–27.

Morley, R.J. and Rosen, R. 1996. High resolution biostratigraphic zonation and palaeoclimatic record for the Offshore Niger Delta. *Proceedings of the IXth IPC Meeting, Houston, Texas USA*, June 1996, pp. 111–12 (abstract).

Morley, R.J., Eko Budi Lelono, Lucila Nugrahaningsih and Nur Hasjim, 1999. LEMIGAS Tertiary palynology project: aims, progress and preliminary results from the Middle Eocene to Pliocene of Sumatra and Java. *GRDC Palaeontology Series* (in press).

Mouret, C., Heggemenn, H., Gouadain, J. and Krisadasima, S. 1993. Geological history of the siliclastic Mesozoic strata of the Khorat Group in the Phu Phan range area, northeastern Thailand. In: Thanasuthipitak, T. (ed.), *Biostratigraphy of mainland Southeast Asia: facies and palaeontology*. Chiang Mai University, Thailand, pp. 23–50.

Muller, H. 1966. Palynological investigations of Cretaceous sediments in northeastern Brazil. *Proceedings of the 2nd West African Micropalaeontological Colloquium*, Ibadan, pp. 123–36.

Muller, J. 1959. Palynology of Recent Orinoco Delta and shelf sediments: reports of the Orinoco Shelf Expedition; Volume 5. *Micropaleontology* 5, 1–32.

Muller, J. 1963. Palynological study of Holocene peat in Sarawak. *Symposium on Ecological Research in Humid Tropics Vegetation*, Kuching, Sarawak, pp. 147–56.

Muller, J. 1964. A palynological contribution to the history of mangrove vegetation in Borneo. In: Cranwell, L.M. (ed.), *Ancient Pacific floras – The pollen story*. Pacific Science Congress Series, University of Hawaii Press, Honolulu, pp. 33–42.

Muller, J. 1966. Montane pollen from the Tertiary of N.W. Borneo. *Blumea* 14, 231–5.

Muller, J. 1968. Palynology of the Pedawan and Plateau Sandstone Formations (Cretaceous – Eocene) in Sarawak. *Micropalaeontology* 14, 1–37.

Muller, J. 1969. A palynological study of the genus *Sonneratia* (Sonneratiaceae). *Pollen et Spores* 11, 223–98.

Muller, J. 1970. Palynological evidence on early differentiation of angiosperms. *Biological Reviews of the Cambridge Philosophical Society* 45, 417–50.

Muller, J. 1972. Palynological evidence for change in geomorphology, climate and vegetation in the Mio-Pliocene of Malesia. In: Ashton, P.S. and Ashton, M. (eds), *The Quaternary Era in Malesia.*

Geography Department, University of Hull, Miscellaneous Series 13, pp. 6–34.

Muller, J. 1974. A comparison of Southeast Asian with European fossil angiosperm pollen floras. *Symposium on Origin and Phytogeography of Angiosperms*, pp. 49–56.

Muller, J. 1978. New observations on pollen morphology and fossil distribution of genus *Sonneratia* (Sonneratiaceae). *Review of Palaeobotany and Palynology* 26, 277–300.

Muller, J. 1979. Reflections on fossil palm pollen. *Proceedings IVth Palynological Conference, Lucknow* I, pp. 568–79.

Muller, J. 1981. Fossil pollen records of extant angiosperms. *The Botanical Review* 47, 1–142.

Muller, J. and Caratini, C. 1977. Pollen of *Rhizophora* (Rhizophoraceae) as a guide fossil. *Pollen et Spores* 19, 361–89.

Muller, J. and Hui-Lui, S.Y. 1966. Hybrids and chromasomes in the genus *Sonneratia* (Sonneratiaceae). *Blumea* 14, 337–43.

Muller, J., De di Giacomo, E. and Van Erve, A.W. 1987. A palynological zonation for the Cretaceous, Tertiary and Quaternary of northern South America. *American Association of Stratigraphic Palynologists*, Contributions Series 16, 7–76.

Nandi, B. 1984. Palynostratigraphy of the Gumaghat Formation, Meghalaya, India, with special reference to the significance of the normpolles group. In: *Evolutionary botany and biostratigraphy*, A.K. Ghosh Commemorative volume. Today and Tomorrow's Printers, New Delhi, pp. 521–40.

Nandi, B. 1991. Palynostratigraphy of Upper Cretaceous sediments, Meghalaya, northeastern India. *Review of Palaeobotany and Palynology* 65, 119–29.

Nelson, B.W., Ferriera, C.A.C., da Silva, M.F. and Kawasaki, M.L. 1990. Endemism centres, refugia and botanical collecting density in Brazilian Amazonia. *Nature* 345, 714–16.

Ng, F.S.P. 1972. Juglandaceae. In: Whitmore, T.C. (ed.), *Tree flora of Malaya*, I, Longman, Kuala Lumpur and London, pp. 233–6.

Ng, F.S.P. 1977. Gregarious flowering of dipterocarps in Kepong, 1976. *Malay Forester* 40, 126–37.

Nicklas, K.J., Tiffney, B.H. and Knoll, A. 1980. Apparent changes in the diversity of fossil plants. *Evolutionary Biology* 12, 1–89.

Nilsson, S. and Robyns, A. 1986. Bombacaceae Kunth. *World Pollen and Spore Flora* 14, 59 pp.

Ohsawa, M. 1990. An interpretation of latitudinal patterns of forest limits in South and East Asian mountains. *Journal of Ecology* 78, 326–39.

Ohsawa, M. 1991. Structural comparison of tropical montane rain forests along latitudinal and altitudinal gradients in south and east Asia. *Vegetatio* 97, 1–10.

Ohsawa, M. 1993. Latitudinal pattern of mountain vegetation zonation in southern and eastern Asia. *Journal of Vegetation Science* 4, 13–18.

O'Keefe, J.D. and Ahrens, T.J. 1989. Impact production of $CO_2$ by the Cretaceous/Tertiary extinction bolide and the resultant heating of the Earth. *Nature* 338, 247–9.

Oldeman, R.A.A. 1974. L'architecture de la forêt Guyanaise. *Mem. ORSTOM* 73.

Ollivier-Pierre, M.-F. 1979. Etude palynologique (spores et pollen) de gisements Paléogènes du Massif Armorican. Thesis, Rennes University, 232 pp.

Ollivier-Pierre, M.-F. and Caratini, C. 1984. Les paleomangroves eocenes en Europe occidentale. Valeur du pollen de *Nypa* pour les reconstructions paléogéographique. *Reunion Annuelle des Sciences de la Terre* 10, p. 420.

Ollivier-Pierre, M.-F., Gruas-Cavagnetto, C., Roche, E. and Schuler, M. 1987. Elements de flore de type tropical et variations climatiques au Paléogène dans quelques bassins d'Europe Nord-Occidentale. *Mem. trav. E.P.H.E. Inst. Montpellier* 17, 173–205.

Orlando, H.A. 1963. La flora fosil en las inmediaciones de la Peninsula Ardley, Isla 25 de Mayo, Islas Shetland del sur. *Contribucion 79, Instituto Antarctico Argentino*, Buenos Aires.

Paijmans, K. 1987. Wooded swamps in New Guinea. In: Lugo, A.E., Brinson, M. and Brown, S. (eds), *Ecosystems of the world, Vol. 15, Forested wetlands*. Elsevier, Amsterdam, pp. 335–55.

Parrish, J.T. 1987. Global palaeogeography and palaeoclimate of the Late Cretaceous and Early Tertiary. In: Friis, E.M., Chaloner, W.G. and Crane, P.R. (eds), *The origins of angiosperms and their biological consequences*. Cambridge University Press, pp. 51–73.

Parrish, J.T. and Barron, E.J. 1986. *Paleoclimates and economic geology*. Society of Economic Palaeontologists and Mineralogists Short Course no. 18, 162 pp.

Parrish, J.T., Ziegler, A.M. and Scotese, C.R. 1982. Rainfall patterns and the distribution of coals and evaporites in the Mesozoic and Cenozoic. *Palaeogeography, Palaeoclimatology, Palaeoecology* 40, 67–101.

Patriat, P. and Achache, J. 1984. India–Asia collision chronology has implications for crustal shortening and driving mechanism of plates. *Nature* 311, 615–21.

Peglar, S.M., Fritz, S.C. and Birks, H.J.B. 1989. Vegetation and land-use history at Diss, Norfolk, UK. *Journal of Ecology* 77, 203–22.

Perthuisot, J.-P. 1980. Sites et processus de la formation d'evaporites dans la nature actuelle. *Bulletin des Centres de Recherche Exploration–Production Elf Aquitaine* 4, pp. 207–33.

Pettersen, S. 1958. *Introduction to meteorology.* McGraw-Hill, New York, 327 pp.

Pillbeam, D. 1982. New hominoid skull material from the Miocene of Pakistan. *Nature* 295, 232–4.

Pindall, J.L., Cande, S.C., Pitman, W.C., Rowley, D.B., Dewey, J.F., LaBrecque, J. and Haxby, W. 1988. A plate-kinematic framework for models of Caribbean evolution. *Tectonophysics* 155, 121–38.

Pitman III, W.C., Cande, S., LaBrecque, J. and Pindall, J. 1993. Fragmentation of Gondwana: the separation of Africa from South America. In: Goldblatt, P. (ed.), *Biological relationships between Africa and South America.* Yale University Press, New Haven, pp. 15–33.

Playford, G. 1982. Neogene palynomorphs from the Huon Peninsula, Papua New Guinea. *Palynology* 6, 29–54.

Pocknall, D.T. 1982. Palynology of the Late Oligocene Pomahaka Estuarine Bed sediments, Waikoikoi, Southland, New Zealand. *New Zealand Journal of Botany* 20, 7–15.

Pocknall, D.T. 1987. Palynomorph biozones for the Fort Union and Wasatch Formations (upper Paleocene – lower Eocene) Powder River Basin, Wyoming and Montana. *Palynology* 11, 23–35.

Pocknall, D.T. 1989. Late Eocene to Early Miocene vegetation and climate history of New Zealand. *Journal of the Royal Society of New Zealand* 19, 1–18.

Pocknall, D.T. 1990. Palynological evidence for the Early to Middle Eocene vegetation and climate history of New Zealand. *Review of Palaeobotany and Palynology* 65, 57–9.

Polak, E. 1933. Uber torf und Moor in Niederlandisch Indien. *Proc. K. Ned. akad. Wet.* 30, 1–84.

Polak, E. 1949. De Rawa Lakbok, een eutroof laagveen op Java. *Meded. Alg. proefstn. Landb. Buitenzorg* 85, 1–60.

Pole, M.S. and Mcphail, M.K. 1996. Eocene *Nypa* from Regatta Point, Tasmania. *Review of Palaeobotany and Palynology* 92, 55–67.

Polhaupessy, A.A. 1990. Late Cenozoic palynological studies on Java. PhD thesis, Hull University, 339 pp.

Poole, I.M. 1993. A dipterocarpaceous twig from the Eocene London Clay Formation of southern England. *Special Papers in Palaeontology* 49, 155–63.

Poore, M.E.D. 1968. Studies in Malaysian rain forest 1. The forest on Triassic sediments in Jenka forest reserve. *Journal of Ecology* 56, 143–96.

Potonie, R. 1960. Sporologie der eozanen Kohle von Kalewa in Burma. *Senckenberbiana Lethaea* 41, 451–81.

Poumot, C. 1987. Palynological evidence for eustatic events in the tropical Neogene. *Bulletin Centres Recheche Exploration–Production Elf-Aquitaine* 13, 347–53.

Prance, G.T. 1979. Notes on the vegetation of Amazonia III. The terminology of Amazonian forest types subject to inundation. *Brittonia* 31, 26–38.

Prance, G.T. 1987. Biogeography of Neotropical plants. In: Whitmore, T.C. and Prance, G.T. (eds), *Biogeography and Quaternary history in Tropical America.* Clarendon Press, Oxford, pp. 46–55.

Pribatini, H. 1993. Geologi dan analysis geokimia dalam explorasi penhahuluan mineral logam dasar daerah Tanjung Balit Kecamatan Pangkalan kotabaru Kabupaten Limapuluhkoto Propinsi Sumatera Barat. Unpublished Drs thesis, Trisakti University, Jakarta, Indonesia, 74 pp.

Pribatini, H. and Morley, R.J. 1999. Palynology of the Kaliglagah and Kalibiuk Formations, near Bumiayu, Central Java. In: Darman, H. and Sidi, F.H. (eds), *Tectonics and sedimentation of Indonesia.* Indonesian Sedimentologists Forum, Special Publication 1, p. 53.

Prothero, D.R. 1994. *The Eocene–Oligocene transition. Paradise lost.* Columbia University Press, New York, 291 pp.

Quade, J., Cerling, T.E. and Bowman, J.R. 1989. Development of Asian monsoon revealed by marked ecological shift during the latest Miocene in northern Pakistan. *Nature* 342, 163–6.

Racey, A., Goodall, J.G.S., Love, M.A., Polachan, S. and Jones, P.D. 1994. New age data for the Mesozoic Khorat Group of Northeast Thailand. *Proceedings International Symposium on Stratigraphic Correlation of Southeast Asia*, Bangkok, November 1994, pp. 245–52.

Rackham, O. 1986. *The history of the countryside.* J.M. Dent, London, 445 pp.

Rage, J.C. 1988. Gondwana, Tethys and terrestrial vertebrates during the Mesozoic and Cenozoic. In: Audley-Charles, M.G. and Hallam, A. (eds), *Gondwana and Tethys.* Oxford University Press, pp. 255–73.

Rahardjo, A.T., Polhaupessy, T.T., Sugeng Wiyono, Nugrahaningsih, H. and Eko Budi Lelono, 1994. Zonasi Polen Tersier Pulau Jawa. *Makalah Ikatan Ahli Geologi Indonesia*, December 1994, pp. 77–84.

Ramanujam, C.G.K. 1966. Palynology of the Miocene lignite from south Arcot district, Madras, India. *Pollen et Spores* 8, 149–203.

Ramanujam, C.G.K. 1982. Tertiary palynology and palynostratigraphy of southern India. *Palaeontological Society of India, Special Publication* 1, 57–64.

Rangin, C., Jolivet, L. and Pubellier, M. 1990. A simple model for the tectonic evolution of Southeast Asia and Indonesia region for the past 43 m.y. *Bulletin of the Society of Geologists, France* 8, 889–905.

Rao, M.R. 1995. Palynostratigraphic zonation and correlation of the Eocene–Early Miocene sequence in Alleppy district, Kerala, India. *Review of Palaeobotany and Palynology* 86, 325–48.

Rasmussen, D.T., Bown, T.M. and Simons, E.L. 1992. The Eocene–Oligocene transition in continental Africa. In: Prothero, D.R. and Berggren, W.A. (eds), *Eocene–Oligocene climatic and biotic evolution*. Princeton University Press, Princeton, NJ, pp. 548–66.

Raup, D.M. and Sekopski, Jr, J.J. 1984. Periodicity of extinctions in the geological past. *Proceedings of the National Academy of Sciences* 81, 801–5.

Raven, P.H. and Axelrod, D.I. 1974. Angiosperm biogeography and past continental movements. *Annals of the Missouri Botanical Garden* 61, 539–673.

Regali, M.S.P. 1989. *Tucanopollis*, un genero novo das angiospermas primitivas. *Bolletim de Geosciencias da Petrobras* 3, 395–402.

Regali, M.S., Uesugui, N. and Santos, A.S. 1975. Palinologiá dos sedimentos meso-cenozoicas do Brazil. *Bol. Tec. Petrobras* 17, 177–91.

Reid, E.M. and Chandler, M.E.J. 1933. *The flora of the London Clay*. British Museum (Natural History) London, 561 pp.

Reilley, J.O. and Page, S.E. 1997. *Biodiversity and sustainability of tropical peatlands*. Samara Publishing Ltd, Cardigan, UK, 369 pp.

Reilley, J.O., Sieffermann, R.G. and Page, S.E. 1992. The origin, development, present status and importance of the lowland peat swamp forests of Borneo. *Suo* 43, 241–4.

Reimann, K.U. and Thaung, Aye, 1981. Results of palynostratigraphical investigations of the Tertiary sequence in the Chidwin Basin/Northwestern Burma. *IVth International Palynological Conference, Lucknow* (1976–77) 3, pp. 380–95.

Reitsma, T. 1969. Pollen morphology of the Alangiaceae. *Review of Palaeobotany and Palynology* 10, 249–332.

Retallack, G.J. 1983. Late Eocene and Oligocene palaeosols from Badlands National Park, South Dakota. *Geological Society of America Special Paper* 193.

Retallack, G.J. 1992a. Comment on the paleoenvironment of *Kenyapithecus* at Fort Ternan. *Journal of Human Evolution* 23, 363–9.

Retallack, G.J. 1992b. Middle Miocene fossil plants from Fort Ternan (Kenya) and evolution of African grasslands. *Paleobiology* 18, 383–400.

Retallack, G. and Dilcher, D.L. 1981. A coastal hypothesis for the dispersal and rise to dominance of flowering plants. In: Niklas, K.J. (ed.), *Palaeobotany, Palaeoecology and Evolution*, vol. 2, Praeger, New York, pp. 27–77.

Retallack, G.J., Dugas, D.P. and Bestland, E.A. 1990. Fossil soils and grasses of a Middle Miocene East African grassland. *Science* 247, 1325–8.

Revilla, J.D. 1988. Aspectos floristicos e ecologicos da floresta inundavel (*Varzea*) do Rio Solimoes Amazonas, Brasil. PhD thesis, INPA/FUA Manaus.

Reyment, R.A. 1965. *Aspects of the geology of Nigeria*. University Press, Ibadan, 145 pp.

Richards, P.W. 1952. *The tropical rain forest*. Cambridge University Press, 450 pp.

Richards, P.W. 1973. Africa, the 'Odd man out'. In: Meggers, B.J., Ayensu, E.S. and Duckworth, W.D. (eds), *Tropical forest ecosystems of Africa and South America: a comparative review*. Smithsonian Institution Press, Washington DC, chapter 3.

Richards, P.W. 1996. *The tropical rain forest* (2nd edition). Cambridge University Press, 575 pp.

Robbins, R.G. 1961. The vegetation of New Guinea. *Australian Territories* 1.6, Government Printer, Canberra.

Robbins, R.G. and Wyatt-Smith, J. 1964. Dry-land forest formations and forest types in the Malay Peninsula. *Malayan Forester* 27, 188–217.

Robinson, P.L. 1973. Climatology and continental drift. In: Tarling, D.H. and Runcorn, S.K. (eds), *Implications of continental drift to the Earth Sciences*. Academic Press, London, pp. 449–76.

Robinson, E. 1976. *Report on peat in Jamaica*. Ministry of Mining and National Resources, Jamaica, 30 pp.

Robinson, E. 1978. Possible use of tropical peats as fuel: an example from Jamaica. *Geologie en Mijnbouw* 57, 297–300.

Roche, E. 1973. Etude des sporomorphes du Landénian de Belgique et de quelques gisements du Sparnacian Français. *Serv. Geol. Belg., Mem. Expl. Cartes Geol. Miner. Belgique* 13, 138 pp.

Roche, E. and Schuler, M. 1976. Analyse palynologique (spores et pollen) de divers gisements du Tongrien de Belgique. Interprétation palaeoécologique et stratigraphique. *Serv. Geol. Belg. Prof. Paper* 11, 57 pp.

Romero, E.J. 1986. Palaeogene phytogeography and climatology of South America. *Annals of the Missouri Botanical Garden* 73, 449–61.

Romero, E.J. 1993. South American paleofloras. In: Goldblatt, P. (ed.), *Biological relationships between*

*Africa and South America*. Yale University Press, New Haven, pp. 62–85.

Romero, E.J. and Hickey, J. 1976. A fossil leaf of Akaniaceae from Paleocene beds in Argentina. *Bulletin of the Torrey Botanical Club* 103, 126–31.

Rowley, D.B. 1996. Age of initiation of collision between India and Asia: a review of stratigraphic data. *Earth and Planetary Science Letters* 145, 1–13.

Royen, P. van, 1963. Sertulum Papuanum 7. Notes on the vegetation of South New Guinea. *Nova Guinea Bot.* 13, 195–241.

Sah, S.C.D. and Dutta, S.K. 1966. Palynostratigraphy of the Tertiary sedimentary formations of Assam: 2. Stratigraphic significance of spores and pollen in the Tertiary succession of Assam. *Palaeobotanist* 16, 177–95.

Sahni, A. and Bajpai, S. 1991. Eurasiatic elements in the Upper Cretaceous nonmarine biotas of peninsular India. *Cretaceous Research* 12, 177–83.

Sahni, A., Kumar, K., Hartenberger, J.-L., Jaeger, J.-J., Rage, J.-C., Sudre, J. and Vianey-Liaud, M. 1982. Microvertebres nouveaux des Trapps du Deccan (Inde): mise en evidence d'une voie du communication terrestre probable entre la Laurasie et l'Indee a la limite Cretace–Tertiare. *Bulletin Societe Geologie France* 7(24), 1093–99.

Salami, M.B. 1991. Palynomorph taxa from the 'Lower Coal Measures' deposits (?Campanian–Maastrichtian) of Anambra Trough, Southeastern Nigeria. *Journal of African Earth Sciences* 11, 135–50.

Salard-Chebaldaeff, M. 1976. Mise en evidence de l'Oligocene dans le bassin sedimentiare cotier du Cameroun, d'apres les donnees palynologiques. *Comptes Rendu Acadamie Science (Paris)* D 282, 41–43.

Salard-Chebaldaeff, M. 1979. Palynologie maestrichtienne et tertiare du Cameroun. Etude qualitative et repartition verticale des principales espèces. *Review of Palaeobotany and Palynology* 28, 365–88.

Salard-Chebaldaeff, M. 1981. Palynologie maestrichtienne et tertiare du Cameroun. Results botanique. *Review of Palaeobotany and Palynology* 32, 401–39.

Salard-Chebaldaeff, M. 1990. Intertropical African palynostratigraphy from Cretaceous to Late Quaternary times. *Journal of African Earth Sciences* 11, 1–24.

Sands, M.J.S., Johns, R.J., Coode, M.J.E. and Marsden, J. 1998. Flora of North East Vogelkop. *Fourth International Flora Malesiana Symposium*, Abstracts, p. 32.

Sarthein, M. and Fenner, J. 1988. Global wind-induced change of deep-sea sediment budgets, new

ocean production and $CO_2$ reservoirs ca. 3.3–2.35 Ma BP. *Philosophical Transactions of the Royal Society, London* 318, 487–504.

Saxena, R.K. 1992. Neyveli lignites and associated sediments – their palynology, palaeoecology, correlation and age. *Palaeobotanist* 40, 345–53.

Sayer, J.A. and Whitmore, T.C. 1991. Tropical moist forests: destruction and species extinction. *Biological Conservation* 55, 199–213.

Schimper, A.F.W. 1903. Plant-geography upon a physiological basis. (transl. Fisher, E.W., Eds Groom, P. and Balfour, I.B.), Oxford University Press, 839 pp.

Schmalz, R.F. 1969. Deep-water evaporite deposition: a genetic model. *American Association of Petroleum Geologists Bulletin* 53, 798–823.

Schmid, M. 1974. Vegetation du Viet-Nam Le Massif Sud-Annamitique et les Regions Limitrophes. *Memoires Orstom, Paris* 74, 112 pp.

Scholl, D.W. 1968. Mangrove swamps: geology and sedimentology. In: Fairbridge, P.W. (ed.), *The encyclopedia of geomorphology*. Reinhold, New York, pp. 683–96.

Scholtz, A. 1985. The palynology of the upper lacustrine sediments of the Arnot Pipe, Banke, Namaqueland. *Annals of the South African Museum* 95, 1–109.

Schrank, E. 1994. Palynology of the Yessomma Formation in Northern Somalia: a study of pollen, spores and associated phytoplankton from the Late Cretaceous Palmae province. *Palaeontographica Abt.* B, 231, 63–112.

Scotsese, C.R. and Summerhayes, C.P. 1986. Computer model of palaeoclimate predicts coastal upwelling in the Mesozoic and Cenozoic. *Geobyte*, pp. 28–42.

Semah, A-M. 1984. Remarks on the pollen analysis of the Sambungmacan section (Central Java). *Modern Quaternary Research in Southeast Asia* 8, 29–34.

Seward, A.C. 1935. *Leaves of dicotyledones from the Nubian sandstones of Egypt*. Geological survey, Egypt.

Shackleton, N. and Boersma, A. 1983. The climate of the Eocene ocean. *Journal of the Geological Society* 138, 153–7.

Shackleton, N.J., Berger, A. and Peltier, W.R. 1990. An alternative astronomical calibration of the lower Pleistocene timescale based on ODP site 677. *Transactions of the Royal Society of Edinburgh: Earth Sciences* 81, 251–61.

Shamsuddin, J. and Morley, R.J. 1995. Palynology of the Tembeling Group, Malay Peninsula. *Proceedings International Symposium on Stratigraphic Correlation in Southeast Asia*, 15–20 November, Bangkok, Thailand, p. 208.

Shuurman, D. and Ravelojaona, N. 1997. *Madagascar*. Globetrotter Travel Guide, New Holland Publishers, London, 128 pp.

Siddhanta, B.K. 1986. The age of the Neyveli Lignite with reference to stratigraphy and palynology. *Indian Minerals* 40, 61–82.

Simpson, G.G. 1946. Tertiary land bridges. *Transactions of the New York Academy of Sciences* 8, 255–8.

Simanjuntak, T.O. and Barber, A.J. 1996. Contrasting tectonic styles in the Neogene orogenic belts of Indonesia. In: Hall, R. and Blundell, D. (eds), *Tectonic evolution of Southeast Asia*. Geological Society Special Publication 106, pp. 185–201.

Singh, A. and Misra, B.K. 1991a. New colporate pollen taxa from Neyveli Lignite, south India. *Review of Palaeobotany and Palynology* 67, 205–15.

Singh, A. and Misra, B.K. 1991b. Revision of some Tertiary pollen genera and species. *Review of Palaeobotany and Palynology* 67, 217–27.

Singh, G. and Geissler, E.A. 1985. Late Cainozoic history of vegetation, fire, lake levels and climate at Lake George, New South Wales, Australia. *Philosophical Transactions of the Royal Society of London* 311, 379–447.

Singh, H.P., Rao, M.R. and Saxena, R.K. 1986. Palynology of the Barail (Oligocene) and Surma (Lower Miocene) sediments exposed along Sonapur–Badarpur Road section, Jainta Hills (Meghalaya) and Cachar (Assam). Part VII. Discussion. *Palaeobotanist* 35, 331–41.

Situmorang, B. 1982. The formation and evolution of the Makassar Basin, Indonesia. PhD thesis, University of London, 313 pp.

Sluiter, I.R.K. 1991. Early Tertiary vegetation and climates, Lake Eyre region, northeastern South Australia. *Geological Society of Australia, Special Publication* 18, 99–118.

Smith, A.C. 1970. The Pacific as a key to flowering plant history. *University of Hawaii, Harold L. Lyon Arboretum Lecture* 1.

Smith, A.G., Briden, J.C. and Drewry, G.E. 1973. Phanerozoic world maps. In: Hughes, N.F. (ed.), *Organisms and continents through time*. Special Papers in Palaeontology 12, pp. 1–42.

Smith, A.G. and Briden, J.C. 1979. *Mesozoic and Cenozoic palaeocontinental maps*. Cambridge University Press, 63 pp.

Smith, A.G., Smith, D.G. and Funnell, B.M. 1994. *Atlas of Mesozoic and Cenozoic coastlines*. Cambridge University Press, 99 pp.

Smith, J.M.B. 1982. *A history of Australasian vegetation*. McGraw-Hill, Sydney, 168 pp.

Sole de Porta, N. 1971. Algunos géneros nuevos de polen procedentes de la Formación Guaduas (Maastrichtiense–Paleoceno) de Colombia. *Studia Geologica Salamanca* 2, pp. 133–143.

Sommer, A. Attempt at an assessment of the world's tropical moist forests. *Unasylva* 28, 5–25.

Song Zhichen, 1989. General aspects of the floristic regions on Late Cretaceous and Early Tertiary of China. *Acta Palynologica* 1, 1–8.

Song Zhichen, Zheng Yahui, Liu Jinling, Ye Pingyi, Wang Cong Feng and Zhou Shan Fu, 1981. *Cretaceous–Tertiary palynological assemblages from Jiangsu*. Geological Publishing House, Peking, China, 268 pp.

Sowunmi, M.A. 1991. Late Quaternary environments in equatorial Africa: palynological evidence (Lake Mobutu Sese Seko). *Palaeoecology of Africa* 22, 213–38.

Spackman, W., Dolsen, C.P. and Riegel, W. 1966. Phytogenic organic sediments and sedimentary environments in the Everglades–Mangrove complex. Part 1. Evidence of a transgressing sea and its effects on environments of the Shark River area of Southwestern Florida. *Palaeontographica* Abt B, 117, 135–52.

Srivastava, S.K. 1987/88. *Ctenolophon* and *Sclerosperma* palaeogeography and Senonian Indian plate position. *Journal of Palynology* 23–24, 239–53.

Srivastava, S.K. 1983. Cretaceous geophytoprovinces and palaeogeography of the Indian Plate based on palynological data. In: Maheswari, H.K. (ed.), *Cretaceous of India*, Indian Association of Palynostratigraphy, Lucknow, pp. 141–57.

Srivastava, S.K. 1994. Evolution of Cretaceous phytogeoprovinces, continents and climates. *Review of Palaeobotany and Palynology* 82, 197–244.

Stebbins, G.L. 1974. *Flowering plants: Evolution above the species level*. Belknap Press, Cambridge, MA.

Steenis, C.G.G.J. van, 1934a. On the origin of the Malaysian mountain flora, Part 1 *Bulletin du Jardin Botanique de Buitenzorg* III, 13, 135–262.

Steenis, C.G.G.J. van, 1934b. On the origin of the Malaysian mountain flora, Part 2. *Bulletin du Jardin Botanique de Buitenzorg* III, 13, 289–417.

Steenis, C.G.G.J. van, 1936. On the origin of the Malaysian mountain flora, Part 3, Analysis of floristic relationships (1st instalment). *Bulletin du Jardin Botanique de Buitenzorg* III, 14, 36–72.

Steenis C.G.G.J. van, 1939. The native country of sandalwood and teak. *Handel 8e Nederlandische. Indien. Natuurwet. Congress Soerabaja* 1938, pp. 408–9.

Steenis C.G.G.J. van, 1957. Outline of vegetation types in Indonesia and some adjacent regions.

*Proceedings of the Eighth Pacific Science Congress* (Manila), 4, pp. 61–97.

Steenis, C.G.G.J. van, 1961. Introduction: The pathway for drought plants from Asia to Australia. *Reinwartia* 5, 420–9.

Steenis, C.G.G.J. van, 1962a. The land-bridge theory in botany. *Blumea*, 11, 235–372.

Steenis, C.G.G.J. van, 1962b. The distribution of mangrove plant genera and its significance for palaeogeography. *Proc. Koninkl. Nederland Akad. Wetensch., Amsterdam*, Series C, 65, pp. 164–9.

Steenis, C.G.G.J. van, 1963. Transpacific floristic affinities particularly in the tropical zone. In: Gressitt, J.K. (ed.), *Pacific Basin Biogeography*. Bishop Museum Press, Hawaii, pp. 219–31.

Steenis, C.G.G.J. van, 1971. *Nothofagus*, key genus of plant geography, in time and space, living and fossil ecology and phylogeny. *Blumea* 19, 65–98.

Steenis, C.G.G.J. van, 1972. *The mountain Flora of Java*. E.J. Brill, Leiden, 90 pp.

Steenis, C.G.G.J. van, 1979. Plant geography of East Malesia. *Botanical Journal of the Linnean Society* 79, 97–178.

Steenis, C.G.G.J. van, 1981. *Rheophytes of the world*. Sijthoff and Noordhoff, Rijn, The Netherlands.

Steenis, C.G.G.J. van and Schippers-Lammertse, 1965. Concise plant-geography of Java. In: Backer, C.A. and Bakhuizen van den Brink (eds), *Flora of Java* 2. Noordhoff, Groningen, preface, pp. 1–72.

Stehlin, H.G. 1909. Remarques sur les faunules de mammiferes des couches eocenes et oligocenes du Bassin de Paris. *Bulletin Societee Geologique de France* 9, 488–520.

Stein, N. 1978. *Coniferen im Westlischen Malayischen Archipelago*. Junk, The Hague.

Stephens, G.R. 1989. The nature and timing of biotic links between New Zealand and Antarctica in Mesozoic and early Cenozoic times. In: Crame, J.A. (ed.), *Origins and evolution of the Antarctic biota*. Geological Society of London Special Publication 47, pp. 141–66.

Stockmans, F. 1936. Vegetaux Eocenes des environs de Bruxelles. *Memoires de Musee Royal d'Histoire Naturelle de Belgique* 76, 56 pp.

Stover, L.E. and Partridge, A.D. 1973. Tertiary and Late Cretaceous spores and pollen from the Gippsland Basin, Australia. *Proceedings of the Royal Society of Victoria* 85, 237–86.

Stuijts, I. 1984. Palynological study of Situ Bayon-grong, West Java. *Modern Quaternary Research in Southeast Asia* 8, 17–28.

Stuijts, I., Newsome, J.C. and Flenley, J.R. 1988. Evidence of Late Quaternary vegetation change in the Sumatran and Javan highlands. *Review of Palaeobotany and Palynology* 55, 207–16.

Suc, J.P. 1976. Quelques taxons-guides dans l'étude paléoclimatique du Pliocene et du Pleistocene inférieur du Langedoc (France). *Revue de Micropaléontol* 18, 246–55.

Suszczynski, E.F. 1984. The peat resources of Brazil. *Proceedings of the 7th International Peat Congress*, pp. 468–92.

Takahashi, K. 1982. Miospores from the Eocene Nanggulan Formation in the Yogyakarta region, Central Java. *Trans. Proc. Palaeont. Soc. Japan*, N.S., 126, 303–26.

Takhtajan, A. 1969. *Flowering plants, origin and dispersal* (transl. C. Jeffrey). Oliver & Boyd, Edinburgh/Smithsonian Institution, Washington, 300 pp.

Takhtajan, A. 1987. Flowering plant origin and dispersal: cradle of the angiosperms revisited. In: Whitmore, T.C. (ed.), *Biogeographical evolution of the Malay Archipelago*. Oxford Monographs on Biogeography 4, Oxford Scientific Publications, pp. 26–31.

Tanai, T. 1961. Neogene floral change in Japan. *Journal of the Faculty of Science, Hokkaido University* 10, 119–398.

Tanai, T. 1972. Tertiary history of vegetation in Japan. In: Graham, A. (ed.), *Floristics and paleofloristics of Asia and eastern North America*. Elsevier, Amsterdam, pp. 235–55.

Tarponnier, P., Peltzer, G., LeDain, A., Armijo, R. and Cobbold, P. 1982. Propagating extrusion tectonics in Asia; new insights with simple experiments with plasticine. *Geology* 10, 611–16.

Tarponnier, P., Peltzer, G. and Armijo, R. 1986. On the mechanics of the collision between India and Asia. In: Coward, M.P. and Ries, A.C. (eds), *Collision Tectonics*. Geological Society Special Publication 19, pp. 115–57.

Taylor, D.W. 1989. Selected palynomorphs from the Middle Eocene Clairborne Formation, Tenn., (USA). *Review of Palaeobotany and Palynology* 58, 111–28.

Taylor, D.W. 1990. Palaeobiogeographic relationships of angiosperms from the Cretaceous and Early Tertiary of the North American area. *The Botanical Review* 56, 279–516.

Thanikaimoni, G. 1987. *Mangrove palynology*. Institut Francais de Pondicherry 24, 100 pp.

Thanikaimoni, G., Caratini, C., Venkatachala, B.S., Ramanujam, C.G.K. and Kar, R.K. 1983. *Selected Tertiary angiosperm pollens from India and their relationship with African Tertiary pollens*. Institute Francais de Pondicherry 19, 99 pp. + 72 plates.

Thewissen, J.G.M. 1990. Comments and Reply on 'Paleontological view of the ages of the Deccan Traps, the Cretaceous/Tertiary boundary, and the India–Asia collision'. *Geology* 18, 185–8.

Thom, B.G. 1967. Mangrove ecology and deltaic geomorphology: Tabasco, Mexico. *Journal of Ecology* 55, 301–43.

Thomas, B.A., and Spicer, R.A. 1986. *The evolution and palaeobiology of land plants.* Croom Helm, London, 309 pp.

Thomson, K. and Hamilton, A.C. 1983. Peatlands and swamps of the African continent. In: Gore, A.J.P. (ed.), *Ecosystems of the World, Part B: Mires, swamp, bog, fen and moor.* Elsevier, Amsterdam, pp. 331–73.

Thorne, R.F. 1963. Biotic distribution patterns in the tropical Pacific. In: Gressitt, J.L. (ed.), *Pacific basin biogeography.* Bishop Museum Press, Honolulu, pp. 311–54.

Thorne, R.F. 1968. Synopsis of a putatively phylogenetic classification of the flowering plants. *Aliso* 6, 57–66.

Thorne R.F. 1976. When and where might the tropical angiospermous flora have originated? In: Mabberley, D.J. and Chang Kiaw Lan (eds), *Tropical botany.* Gardens Bull. Singapore 29, pp. 183–189.

Tiedermann, R. 1991. Acht Millionen Jahre Klimageschichte von Nordwest Afrika und Palao-Ozeanographie des angrenzenden Atlantiks: Hochauflosende Zeitreihen von ODP-Sites 658–661. PhD dissertation, Keil University.

Tiffney, B.H. 1985a. Perspectives on the origin of the floristic similarity between eastern Asia and eastern North America. *Journal of the Arnold Arboretum* 66, 73–94.

Tiffney, B.H. 1985b. The Eocene North Atlantic land bridge: its importance in Tertiary and modern phytogeography of the northern hemisphere. *Journal of the Arnold Arboretum* 66, 243–73.

Tomblin, J.F. 1975. The Lesser Antilles and Aves Ridge. In: Nairn, A.E.M. and Stehli, F.G. (eds), *The ocean basin margins, Vol 3, The Gulf of Mexico and Caribbean.* Plenum Press, New York, pp. 467–500.

Tomlinson, P.B. 1986. *The botany of mangroves.* Cambridge University Press, 419 pp.

Traverse, A. 1955. Palynological analysis of the Brandon Lignite of Vermont. *US Department of the Interior Bureau of Mines, Report of Investigations* 5151, 107 pp.

Treloar, P.J. and Coward, M.P. 1991. Indian Plate motion and shape: constraints on the geometry of the Himalayan orogen. *Tectonophysics* 191, 189–98.

Treloar, P.J., Res, D.C., Guise, P.J., Coward, M.P., Searle, M.P., Petterson, M.G., Windley, R.F., Jan, M.Q. and Luff, I.W. 1989. K–Ar and Ar–Ar geochronology of the Himalayan collision in northwest Pakistan: constraints on the timing of collision, deformation, metamorphism and uplift. *Tectonics* 8, 881–809.

Truswell, E.M., Kershaw, A.P. and Sluiter, A.R. 1987. The Australian–south east Asian connection: evidence from the palaeobotanical record. In: Whitmore, T.C. (ed.), *Biogeographical evolution of the Malay Archipelago.* Oxford Monographs on Biogeography 4, Oxford Scientific Publications, pp. 32–49.

Tschudy, R.H. 1973. Stratigraphic distribution of significant Eocene palynomorphs of the Mississippi Embayment. *US Geological Survey Professional Paper* 743, 24 pp.

Tschudy, R.H., Pillmore, C.L., Orth, C.J., Gilmore, J.S. and Knight, J.D. 1984. Disruption of the terrestrial plant ecosystem at the Cretaceous–Tertiary boundary, western interior. *Science* 225, 1030–2.

Tsuda, K., Itoigawa, J. and Yamanoi, T. 1984. On the Middle Miocene palaeoenvironment of Japan with special reference to the ancient mangrove swamps. In: Whyte, R.O. (ed.), *The evolution of the East Asian environment.* Vol II, Centre of Asian Studies, University of Hong Kong, pp. 388–96.

Uhl, N.W. and Dransfield, J. 1987. *Genera Palmarum. A classification of palms based on the work of H.E. Moore Jr.* L.H. Bailey and the International Palm Society. Allen Press, Kansas.

Upchurch, G.R. 1984a. Cuticular evolution in Early Cretaceous angiosperms from the Potomac Group of Virginia and Maryland. *Annals of the Missouri Botanical Garden* 71, 522–50.

Upchurch, G.R. 1984b. Cuticular anatomy of angiosperm leaves from the Lower Cretaceous Potomac Group. I. Zone I leaves. *American Journal of Botany,* 71, 192–202.

Upchurch, G.R. and Dilcher, D.L. 1984. A magnoliid leaf flora from the mid-Cretaceous Dakota Formation of Nebraska. *American Journal of Botany* 71, 119 (abstract).

Upchurch, G.R. and Wolfe, J.A. 1987. Mid-Cretaceous to Early Tertiary vegetation and climate: evidence from fossil leaves and woods. In: Friis, E.M., Chaloner, W.G. and Crane, P.H. (eds), *The origins of angiosperms and their biological consequences.* Cambridge University Press, pp. 75–105.

Vail, P.R. and Wornardt W.W. 1990. Well log-seismic sequence stratigraphy: an integrated tool for the 90's. *GCSSEPM Foundation 11th Annual Conference.* December 1990, pp. 379–88.

Vail, P.R., Mitchum, Jr, R.M. and Thomspon III, S. 1977. Global cycles of relative changes of sea level. *American Association of Petroleum Geologists Memoir* 26, 83–98.

Vakhrameev, V.A. 1981. Pollen of *Classopollis*: Indicator of Jurassic and Cretaceous climates. *Palaeobotanist* 28–29, 301–7.

Vakhrameev, V.A. 1991. *Jurassic and Cretaceous floras and climates of the Earth*. Cambridge University Press, 318 pp.

Valencia, R., Balslev, H. and Paz Y Mino, C.G. 1994. High tree alpha-diversity in amazonian Equador. *Biodiversity and Conservation* 3, 21–28.

Venkatachala, B.S. 1973. Palynological evidence on the age of the Cuddalore Sandstone. *Geophytology* 3, 145–9.

Venkatachala, B.S. 1974. Palynological zonation of the Mesozoic and Tertiary subsurface sediments in the Cauvery Basin. In: Surange, K.R. et al. (eds), *Aspects and appraisal of Indian Palaeobotany*. Birbal Sahni Institute of Palaeobotany, Lucknow, India, pp. 476–94.

Ventatachala, B.S., Saxena, B.K., Singh, H.P., Tripathi, S.K.M., Kumar, M., Sarkar, S., Mandal, J., Rao, M.R., Singh, R.S., Mandaokar, B.D. and Ambwani, K. 1996. Indian Tertiary angiosperm pollen: a critical assessment. *Palaeobotanist* 42, 106–38.

Verstappen, H.Th. 1973. *A geomorphological reconnaissance of Sumatra and adjacent islands*. Wolters-Noordhoff Publishing, Groningen, 182 pp.

Verstappen, H.Th. 1975. The effect of Quaternary tectonics and climates on erosion and sedimentation in Sumatra. *Proceedings of the 4th Indonesian Petroleum Association Annual Convention*, Jakarta, pp. 1–5.

Vinogradov, A.P. 1967/8. Atlas on the lithological-palaeogeographical maps of the USSR, III. Triassic, Jurassic, Cretaceous. *Min. Geol. Akad. Science, Moscow*, 71 plates.

Walker, D. and Flenley, J.R. 1980. Late Quaternary vegetational history of the Enga Province of upland New Guinea. *Philosophical Transactions of the Royal Society of London* B, 286, 265–344.

Walker, J.W. 1976. Evolutionary significance of the exine in the pollen of primitive angiosperms. In: Ferguson, I.K. and Muller, J. (eds), *The evolutionary significance of the exine*. Academic Press, London, pp. 1112–37.

Walker, J.W. and Walker, A.G. 1979. Comparative pollen morphology of the American Myristicaceous genera *Compsoneura* and *Virola*. *Annals of the Missouri Botanic Gardens* 66, 731–55.

Walker, J.W. and Walker, A.G. 1984. Ultrastructure of lower Cretaceous angiosperm pollen and the origin and early evolution of flowering plants. *Annals of the Missouri Botanical Garden* 71, 464–521.

Walker, J.W., Brenner, G.J. and Walker, A.G. 1983. Winteraceous pollen in the Lower Cretaceous of Israel: early evidence of a magnolialian angiosperm family. *Science* 22, 1273–5.

Wang, Chi-Wu, 1961. *The forests of China*. Havard University Maria Moors Cabot Foundation Publication 5, 313 pp.

Watanasak, M. 1988. Palaeoecological reconstruction of Nong Ya Plong Tertiary Basin (Central Thailand). *Journal of Ecology (Thailand)* 15, 61–70.

Watanasak, M., 1990. Mid Tertiary palynostratigraphy of Thailand. *Journal of SE Asian Earth Science* 4, 203–18.

Watson, J.G. 1928. The mangrove swamps of the Malay Peninsula. *Malayan Forest Records* 6, 274 pp.

Webb, L.J. 1968. Environmental relationships of the structural types of Australian rain forest vegetation. *Ecology* 49, 296–311.

Webb, L.J. 1978. A general classification of Australian rainforests. *Australian Plants* 9, 349–63.

Webb, L.J. and Tracey, J.G. 1967. An ecological guide to planting new areas and site potential for hoop pine. *Australian Forester* 31, 224–39.

Webb, L.J., and Tracey, J.G. 1981. Australian rainforests: patterns and change. In: Keast, A. (ed.), *Ecological biogeography of Australia*. Junk, The Hague, pp. 605–94.

Webb, L.J., Tracey, J.G. and Williams, W.T. 1984. A floristic framework of Australian rainforests. *Australian Journal of Ecology* 9, 169–98.

Weerd, A.A. van der and Armin, R.A. 1992. Origin and evolution of the Tertiary hydrocarbon-bearing basins in Kalimantan (Borneo), Indonesia. *American Association of Petroleum Geologists Bulletin* 76, 1788–803.

Wei, W. 1991. Evidence for an earliest Oligocene abrupt cooling in the surface waters of the Southern Ocean. *Geology* 19, 780–3.

Wettstein, R.R. von, 1907. *Handbuch der systematischen botanik* (2nd edition). Franz Deuticke, Leipzig.

White, F. 1979. The Guineo–Congolean region and its relationship to other phytochoria. *Bulletin de Jardin Botanique National de Belgique* 49, 11–55.

White, F. 1981, 1983. *Vegetation map of Africa with descriptive memoir* (map, 1981, memoir, 1983). UNESCO, Paris.

Whitmore, T.C. 1973. A new tree flora of Malaya. *Proceedings Precongress Conference Bogor, of the Pacific Science Association*, 1971.

Whitmore, T.C. 1975. *Tropical rain forests of the Far East*. Clarendon Press, Oxford, 282 pp.

Whitmore, T.C. 1981. *Wallace's Line and plate tectonics*. Clarendon Press, Oxford, 90 pp.

Whitmore, T.C. 1984. A new vegetation map of Malesia at scale 1:5 million, with commentary by

T.C. Whitmore. *Journal of Biogeography* 11, 461–71.

Whitmore, T.C. 1987. Introduction. In: Whitmore, T.C. (ed.), *Biogeographical evolution of the Malay Archipelago*. Oxford Monographs on Biogeography 4, Oxford Scientific Publications, pp. 1–4.

Whitmore, T.C. 1998. *An introduction to tropical rain forests* (2nd edition). Clarendon Press, Oxford.

Whitmore, T.C. and Prance, G.T. 1987. *Biogeography and Quaternary history in tropical America*. Clarendon Press, Oxford.

Whitmore, T.C., Peralta, R. and Brown, K. 1986. Total species count in a Costa Rican tropical forest. *Journal of Tropical Ecology* 1, 375–8.

Wilford, G.E. and Brown, P.J. 1994. Maps of Late Mesozoic–Cenozoic Gondwana break-up: some palaeogeographical implications. In: Hill, R.S. (ed.), *History of Australian Vegetation, Cretaceous to Recent*. Cambridge University Press, pp. 5–13.

Wilgus, C.K., Hastings, B.S., Kendall, C.G.St C., Posamentier, W.H., Ross, C.A. and van Wagoner, J.C. 1988. Sea-level changes: an integrated approach. *Society of Economic Palaeontologists and Mineralogists Special Publication* 42, 407 pp.

Williams, J.G., Harden, G.J. and McDonald, W.J.F. 1984. *Trees and shrubs of rainforests of New South Wales and southern Queensland*. Botany Department, University of New England, Armidale.

Willis, J.C. 1922. *Age and area*. Cambridge University Press.

Wing, S.L. 1984. A new basis for recognising the Paleocene/Eocene boundary in Western Interior North America. *Science* 226, 439–41.

Wing, S.L. and Greenwood, D.R. 1993. Fossils and fossil climate: the case for equable continental interiors in the Eocene. *Philosophical Transactions of the Royal Society of London* 341, 343–52.

Wing, S.L. and Tiffney, B.H. 1987. Interactions of angiosperms and herbivorous tetrapods through time. In: Friis, E.M., Chaloner, W.G. and Crane, P.H. (eds), *The origins of angiosperms and their biological consequences*. Cambridge University Press, pp. 203–24.

Wingate, F.H. 1983. Palynology and age of the Elko Formation (Eocene) near Elko, Nevada. *Palynology* 7, 92–132.

Wolfe, J.A. 1971. Tertiary climatic fluctuations and methods of analysis of Tertiary floras. *Palaeogeography, Palaeoclimatology, Palaeoecology* 9, 27–57.

Wolfe, J.A. 1975. Some aspects of plant geography of the northern hemisphere during the Late Cretaceous and Tertiary. *Annals of the Missouri Botanical Garden* 62, 264–79.

Wolfe, J.A. 1977. Palaeogene floras from the Gulf of

Alaska region. *US Geological Survey Professional Paper* 997, 208 pp.

Wolfe, J.A. 1978. A palaeobotanical interpretation of Tertiary climates in the Northern Hemisphere. *American Scientist* 66, 694–703.

Wolfe, J.A. 1979. Temperature parameters of humid to mesic forests of eastern Asia and relation to forests of other regions of northern hemisphere and Australasia. *US Geological Survey Professional Paper* 1106.

Wolfe, J.A. 1985. Distributions of major vegetation types during the Tertiary. In: Sundquist, E.T. and Broekner, W.S. (eds), *The carbon cycle and atmospheric $CO_2$: natural variations, Archean to present*. American Geophysical Union Monographs 32, pp. 357–76.

Wolfe, J.A. 1990. Palaeobotanical evidence for a marked temperature increase following the Cretaceous/Tertiary boundary. *Nature* 343, 153–6.

Wolfe, J.A. 1991. Palaeobotanical evidence for a June 'impact winter' at the Cretaceous/Tertiary boundary. *Nature* 352, 420–3.

Wolfe, J.A. and Upchurch, G.R. 1987. Leaf assemblages across the Cretaceous–Tertiary boundary in the Raton Basin, New Mexico and Colorado. *Proceedings of the National Academy of Science USA* 84, 5096–6100.

Wood, G.R. 1986. Late Oligocene to Early Miocene palynomorphs from GSQ Sandy Cape 1-3R. *Geological Survey of Queensland Publication* 387, 27 pp.

Woodburne, M.O. and Zinsmeister, W.J. 1984. The first land mammal from Antarctica and its biogeographic implications. *Journal of Palaeontology* 58, 913–48.

Woodroffe, C.D. and Grindrod, J. 1991. Mangrove biogeography: the role of Quaternary environmental and sea-level change. *Journal of Biogeography* 18, 479–92.

Wopfner, H., Callen, R. and Harris, W.K. 1974. The lower Tertiary Eyre Formation of the southwestern Great Artesian Basin. *Journal of the Geological Society of Australia* 1, 17–51.

Wulff, E.V. 1943. *An introduction to historical plant geography*. Chronica Botanica, Waltham, MA.

Wymstra, T.A. 1968. The identity of *Psilatricolporites* and *Pelliciera*. *Acta Botanica Neerlandica*, 17, 114–16.

Wymstra, T.A. 1969. Palynology of the Alliance Well. *Geologie en Mijnbouw* 48, 125–33.

Wymstra, T.A. 1971. *The palynology of the Guiana coastal plain*. Drukkeridj de Kempenaer, Oegstgeest, 62 pp.

Wyatt-Smith, J. 1959. Peat swamp forests in Malaya. *Malayan Forester* 23, 5–32.

Yamanoi, T. 1974. Note on the first fossil record of

genus *Dacrydium* from the Japanese Tertiary. *Journal of the Geological Society of Japan* 80, 421–3.

Yamanoi, T., Tsuda, K., Itoigawa, J., Okamoto, K. and Tacuchi, K. 1980. On the mangrove community discovered from the Middle Miocene Formations in Southwest Japan. *Journal of the Geological Society of Japan* 86, 635–8.

Zaklinskaya, E.D. 1977. Angiosperms on the basis of palynological data. In: Vakhrameev, V.A. (ed.), *Floral evolution at the Mesozoic–Cenozoic boundary*. Geol. Inst. Akad. Nauk. SSR, Moscow, pp. 66–119.

Zaklinskaya, E.D. 1978. Palynological information from Late Pliocene–Pleistocene deposits recovered by Deep-Sea Drilling in the region of the island of Timor. *Review of Palaeobotany and Palynology* 26, 227–41.

Zhao Xun, Witham, A.G., Price, S.P. and Broet-Menzies, C. 1992. The Cenozoic basins of the northern margins of the South China Sea. *Cambridge Arctic Shelf Programme, China Report no. 3. China Series*. pp. 75–81.

Zhao Yingniang, Sun Xiuyu, Wang Daning and Zhousheng, 1981. The distribution of normapolles in northwestern China. *Review of Palaeobotany and Palynology* 35, 325–36.

Zinderen Bakker, E.M. van, 1975. The origin and palaeoenvironment of the Namib Desert biome. *Journal of Biogeography* 2, 65–73.

Zonenshayn, L.P. and Khain, V.V. 1990. Eocene–Miocene plate tectonic history of Melanesia. *International Geology Review*, 1990. pp. 17–29. (From: Izvestiya AN USSR, Seriya Geologicheskaya 6.)

# Species Index

A = Algae; F = Forminifers; M = Mammals; N = Nannofossils

# Subject Index

Lightning Source UK Ltd.
Milton Keynes UK
UKOW07n2215260416

273014UK00001B/12/P

9 780471 983262